# HISTORY OF
# THE LABOR MOVEMENT
# IN THE UNITED STATES

— v. 7 —

## VOLUME VII: Labor and World War I,

### 1914-1918

## BY PHILIP S. FONER

**INTERNATIONAL PUBLISHERS,** New York

© 1987 by International Publishers Co., Inc.
First edition, 1987
All rights reserved.
Manufactured in the United States of America

LIBRARY OF CONGRESS CATALOGING-IN-PUBLICATION DATA
(Revised for vol. 7)

Foner, Philip Sheldon, 1910-
    History of the labor movement in the United States . . .

    "Reference notes": v. 1, p. 525-559; v. 2, p. 440-474; v. 3, p.
439-470; v. 4, p. 559-596; v. 5, p. 265-283; v. 6, p. 232-245;
    Contents: v. 1. From colonial times to the founding of the American
federation of labor. v. 2. From the founding of the American federation of
labor to the emergence of American imperialism. [etc.] v. 7. Labor and
World War I, 1914-1918.
    1. Trade-unions—United      States—History.  2. Labor      and
laboring classes—United States—History.  I.  Title.
HD6508.F57              331.88'0973              47-19381
ISBN 0-7178-0638-3 (v. 7)
ISBN 0-7178-0627-8 (pbk. : v. 7)

HISTORY OF THE LABOR MOVEMENT

IN THE UNITED STATES

VOLUME VII

# CONTENTS

# PREFACE

This is the seventh volume of my *History of the Labor Movement in the United States,* a series which represents the first multivolume effort to encompass labor history since the publications by John R. Commons and Associates in 1918 and 1932, and certainly the first ever by a single scholar. The sixth volume of the series covered the years 1915-1916, and brought the story of the labor movement to the eve of America's entrance into World War I.

Volume 7 begins with the position of the Socialist Party of America and organized labor, especially the American Federation of Labor (AFL), the Industrial Workers of the World (IWW), and the Railroad Brotherhoods toward the outbreak of World War I in Europe in August, 1914. It carries the story to America's entrance into the war in April, 1917, the experiences of organized labor and the Socialist Party during the war, and ends with the situation of the labor movement at the end of the war in November, 1918. Special attention, as in previous volumes, has been paid to the experiences of Black and women workers.

It was my original intention to include a discussion of the position of the labor and Socialist movements toward U. S. imperialism and militarism from the turn of the century through the Mexican Crisis of 1916. However, lack of space for its full treatment in this volume made this plan impractical. This material is being published as an independent volume by the Marxist Educational Press, Minneapolis.

As in the case of the previous volumes, this work could not have been completed without the generous assistance of numerous libraries and historical societies. I am again indebted to Dorothy Swanson and her staff at the Tamiment Institute, Elmer Bobst Library, New York University, for kind assistance and cooperation. I also again wish to thank the staff of the State Historical Society of Wisconsin for assistance in the use of the Archives of the American Federation of Labor. I also wish to thank the staffs of the Library of Congress, National Archives, New York Public Library, U. S. Department of Labor, Arthur and Elizabeth Schlesinger Library on the History of Women in America, Radcliffe College; Bancroft Library,

University of California; and the libraries of New York University, Duke University, Columbia University, University of Wisconsin, Catholic University of America, Cornell University, University of Virginia, Swarthmore College, Temple University, Haverford College, University of Pennsylvania; University of Maine, Orono; University of Chicago, Washington University, St. Louis; University of Washington, Seattle; Northwestern University, University of California, Berkeley; University of New Mexico, University of Arizona, Arizona State University, Claremont Graduate School, Wayne State University, University of Oklahoma. I also wish to thank the members of the library staff of the Langston Hughes Memorial Library, Lincoln University, Pennsylvania for assistance in obtaining materials through interlibrary loan from libraries, historical societies, and other institutions. Finally, I wish to thank my brother Henry Foner, who read the entire manuscript, helped prepare it for publication, and made valuable suggestions.

Philip S. Foner
Professor Emeritus of History
Lincoln University, Pennsylvania

# CHAPTER 1

## The Socialist Party and World War I: From Outbreak to U.S. Entrance

### WHAT KIND OF WAR?

In her prize-winning book, *The Guns of August,* Barbara Tuchman recounts how Europe's heads of state were astonished to discover that they were unable to stop the war momentum once the troop trains had begun rushing toward the frontier. At war's end, one of those responsible for the initial mobilization wondered of his counterpart on the other side, "How did it all happen?" His former enemy replied equally perplexed, "Ah, if only one knew."[1]

But there has never been a truly "accidental" war in history—least of all the First World War. For a generation, the great powers of Europe had scrambled for markets and raw materials, for control of trade routes and strategic bases, for railroad and mining franchises in the "backward" areas of the world, and for domination of peoples and the wealth of their lands. By 1914, most of the available world had been gobbled up, and as their rivalries grew more intense, the powers embarked on unprecedented programs of militarization and naval construction in preparation for the showdown.

On June 28, 1914, the Crown Prince of the Austro-Hungarian empire was assassinated in Sarajevo, Serbia. Austria-Hungary mobilized its forces and presented ultimatums, and Russia mobilized to thwart her rival for domination of the Balkan peninsula. On July 28, Austria declared war on Serbia; a chain of alliances was set in motion, and by August 4, 1914, all the great powers in Europe were at war. That same day, President Wilson issued his official proclamation of neutrality.

In the war, which ended on November 11, 1918, some 10 million soldiers were killed, an estimated 20 million more were maimed, crippled, burned, and wounded; 13 million civilians perished, 5 million were made war orphans, and there were 10 million war refugees. When the carnage was over, President Woodrow Wilson, in a rare flash of candor, told the truth. Wilson had been reelected in 1916 on the slogan, "He kept us out of war," and had in April 1917 taken the United States into the war on the slogan that Americans should be fighting "to make the world safe for democracy." But in 1919, touring the country to arouse support for the League of Nations project, he blurted out this revelation at the St. Louis Coliseum on September 5th: "Is there any man here or woman—let me say is there any child—who does not know that the seed of war in the modern world is industrial and commercial rivalry?" Then he said explicitly, referring to the war just ended: "This was a commercial and industrial war. It was not a political war."[2]

"This was a commercial and industrial war." For uttering this truth before and during the war as part of the fight for peace, thousands of Americans had been arrested and imprisoned as subversive, as foreign agents, and as unpatriotic. Among them were many of the leaders and members of the Socialist Party of America.

## THE EUROPEAN SOCIALISTS CAPITULATE

During the hectic weeks of international negotiation preceding the outbreak of war, American Socialists expressed the belief that the workers of any one country would refuse to take up arms against their comrades in other nations. Since the war had been brewing from the beginning of the century, its character had been analyzed and predicted at several international Socialist congresses. There, it had been foretold that the big powers would come into conflict over the division of colonial areas and the reshuffling of spheres of economic influence and penetration. As far back as 1907, such a congress in Stuttgart had resolved that if the war did come, "the Socialists shall take measures to bring about its early termination and strive with all their power to use the economic and political crisis created by the war to arouse the masses politically and hasten the overthrow of capitalist rule." This policy was reaffirmed unanimously in 1912 at a conference in Basel and was supposed to guide all participating Socialist parties, including that of the United States.[3]

However, with the exception of those in Italy and Russia, the various Socialist parties of the warring countries ignored the resolutions adopted at previous congresses and yielded to the pressure of their ruling classes and to the propagandistic description of their war aims. The Socialist leaders declared a truce in the class war and gave support to the bourgeois governments. Where before they had recognized predatory empires at home,

they now saw only homelands and fatherlands to be defended. Each justified the support of its own ruling class in the war by invoking the necessity
of defending its country against invaders. The vaunted Social Democratic
Party in Germany, the largest, most influential, and regarded generally as
the most "advanced" in Europe, capitulated most supinely. Of the 110
Socialist members in the Reichstag, only Karl Liebknecht voted against
the war and the war budget. In each belligerent country, only minorities of
the Socialist leadership adhered to the Socialist position; of these, the largest and most influential were the Bolsheviks in Russia.[4]

## THE REACTION OF AMERICAN SOCIALISTS

Some U.S. Socialists, like Eugene V. Debs, condemned the war Socialists in Europe as traitors to the working class, but more common was the
tendency to excuse the majority Socialists in Germany and the Allied
Powers for their support of the war. Thus, the Socialist Party's National
Executive Committee declared: "We do not presume to pass judgment
upon the conduct of our brother parties in Europe. We realize that they are
the victims of the present vicious industrial, political and military system
and that they did the best they could under the circumstances." When a
member of the NEC from the state of Washington introduced a motion to
condemn the conduct of the war Socialists as "unsocialistic and as a
betrayal of the working class cause and of civilization," the motion died
for lack of a second.[5]

Not content to merely apologize for the European war Socialists, some
actually saw a positive good in their support of the bourgeois governments. The New York *Call* viewed it as "by no means an insignificant
thing that the bourgeois government of France, in the time of its deadliest
peril, recognized the Socialists as among the strongest, clearest-headed
men in the nation, and implored them to accept the portfolios [in the gov-
ernment]. Under such conditions it became practically impossible to
refuse the service asked." After the war, the *Call* assured its readers, the
French Socialists would be able to go before the country and "point out
without possibility of denial that they did their part in striving against German military despotism." Unless they did this, they would be regarded by
their countrymen as "traitors who stood by while the country perished
under the heel of iron despotism and put forth no effort to avert it."[6]

This attitude infuriated the left-wing Socialists,* who regarded it as akin

---

*For an analysis of the right, center, and left Socialists, *see* Philip S. Foner, *History of the
Labor Movement in the United States* 3 (New York, 1964): 360-77.

to "suggestions that the class struggle, that impregnable fortress of the revolutionary workers, be dropped as obsolete, because, presumably it is unpopular in the drawing rooms of the ultra-respectable middle class." Karl Liebknecht argued, in voting against war credits, that the war had been instigated by imperialist rivalries and was not for the defense of Germany.[7]*

Pointing to his argument, the left-wing Socialists insisted that it was farcical to claim that defense of the fatherland justified Socialist participation in capitalist war governments, since the workers had no government to support. Their interests were international, not national, and their governments were simply the political organs of the bourgeoisie to facilitate exploitation of the workers. Why, therefore, should they fight one another? The net effect of Socialist participation in capitalist wars was that the workers "murder one another in time of war that they may all be robbed in time of peace." To the workers, the left wing said:

> You have no country. Every national flag in the world today means protection for the employing class, who appropriate the things produced by the worker. It has no message for those who toil. . . . There is only one flag worth fighting for and that is the red flag, which means universal brotherhood of the workers of the world in their fight to abolish the profit system.[8]

## SOCIALISTS ON THE CAUSE OF THE WAR

Two main schools of opinion emerged in the Socialist Party of America on the cause of the war. The majority view regarded it as a manifestation of the capitalist quest for markets. The other school regarded the war essentially as a tactic of capitalist governments to crush the rising working-class movement. A third group combined both opinions. Debs, espousing the first thesis, saw the war as the outcome of fifty years of commercial competition among the capitalist nations. The ruling class in each nation had the same goal: "To extend the domination of their exploitation, to increase their capacity for robbery, and to multiply their ill-gotten riches." John Reed advanced the same thesis, calling the war a "clash of traders" that resulted from Germany's search for colonial markets that had been monopolized by England and France. On the other hand, Robert Hunter, who favored the second thesis, doubted that the capitalists of Germany, France, Russia and England "had any quarrel among

---

*Already well-known in the United States because of a national tour he had made in 1910, Karl Liebknecht was also famous for his opposition to Prussian militarism and to reformism in the Socialist Party. (*See* Philip S. Foner, *Karl Liebknecht and the United States* [Chicago, 1978], pp. 3-25.)

themselves that necessitated the war." Instead, he saw the conflict as the one way in which the European capitalists could save their system—"to induce the working class to cut its own throat."[9]

William English Walling probably spoke for the majority of Socialists when he wrote: "The Socialist diagnosis of the causes of modern wars may be . . . summed up in one sentence: The basic cause is capitalism, the contributory causes are imperialism, militarism, social unrest, international grudges, and pseudo-patriotism." However, the *International Socialist Review* did not accept the idea that imperialism was only a "contributory" cause, but featured an article that insisted "the real cause, the originator of the war, is not one state alone, but every one that maintains an imperialistic policy—Germany, England, France, Austria, Russia, Belgium, Japan—every one and all together, they are the originators of the war." While other nations were also drawn into the war, these "are insignificant compared to the great imperialist nations. . . ." "All the states of Europe have been preparing for the contest for years. They all want to satisfy their greed; they are all equally guilty."[10]*

## "AMERICA MUST END THE WAR"

Early in August 1914, the Socialist Party established the Committee on Immediate Action to handle matters pertaining to the war. Its first proclamation extended "fraternal sympathy" to the workers in Europe and urged the United States to open immediate negotiations for a speedy termination of the conflict. It then hinted that if the belligerents were in any way reluctant to comply, the United States should cut off their food supplies, thus

*In his pamphlet, *Imperialism: The Highest Stage of Capitalism,* written in 1916 and published in Russia in Petrograd in 1917, Lenin wrote: ". . . we must give a definition of imperialism that will include the following five essential features:

"1. The concentration of production and capital, developed to such a high stage that it has created monopolies which play a decisive role in economic life.

"2. The merging of bank capital with industrial capital and the creation, on the basis of this 'finance capital' of a financial oligarchy.

"3. The export of capital, as distinguished from the export of commodities, becomes of particularly great importance.

"4. International monopoly combines of capitalists are formed which divide up the world.

"5. The territorial division of the world by the greatest capitalist powers is completed."

Lenin's definition of imperialism then followed:

"Imperialism is capitalism in that stage of development in which the domination of monopolies and finance capital has taken shape; in which the export of capital has acquired pronounced importance; in which the division of the world by the international trusts has begun, and in which the partition of all the territory of the earth by the greatest capitalist countries has been completed."

(V.I. Lenin, *Imperialism: The Highest Stage of Capitalism,* [New York, 1933], p. 81.)

forcing them to the conference table. The proposal had varying purposes. Although President Wilson appeared to be opposed to American involvement in the European war, he was also cooperating with the capitalists of this country in their rush to supply the Allied nations. This action was not only unneutral but was bound to drag the United States into the war on the side of the Allied Powers. It was also causing prices to rise in the United States. One aim of the embargo, then, would be to keep down the cost of food in the USA. Another would be to slow down and possibly halt completely the war in Europe. Raising the slogan, "Starve the War and Feed America," the *American Socialist*, the party's official organ, editorialized:

> America can stop the war.
> War in Europe can continue only if fed by America.
> To feed that war, the workers of America must starve.
> While the war lords of Europe are leading the workers to slaughter the money and food lords of America seek to profit by that slaughter by increasing the cost of food.
> To curb the war in Europe and to curb the monopolists in this country, also to keep the nation from being drawn into the conflict, two things must be done: (1) We must starve the war by cutting off supplies; (2) We must feed our own people by seizing all sources of supplies.
> We must stop the shipping of all supplies into the war zone.
> Not a penny for loans, not an ounce of food should leave these shores to prolong this terrible shedding of blood.[11]

In the name of the Committee on Immediate Action, the Socialist Party's executive secretary, Walter Lanfersiek, called upon the American people to protest the high cost of living, which he blamed on "unscrupulous capitalists, using the European war as a pretext." Lanfersiek demanded that the government seize packing plants, cold storage houses, grain elevators, and flour mills—in short, "seize the sources of food supplies, the sources of credit, the railroads, and all the means of transportation and communication to break the grip of trusts and speculators." He insisted that through government control of these industries, "the exportation of food to Europe can be prevented. The rulers of Europe, unable to secure foods for their armies, will be forced to call off their soldiers." Finally, the Socialist Party's executive secretary demanded "that the exportation of money and of munitions of war to the European nations be prohibited."[12]

These demands were picked up by the Women's National Committee of the Socialist Party, which launched an antiwar petition to be circulated among American women and to be presented to both the President and

Congress. The petition urged a ban on the export of loans, munitions, and food to the warring countries of Europe. It also called for government action against speculators "who are robbing the people, multitudes of whom are already in dire need." It called upon the government "to establish Supply Depots in the strategic industrial and agricultural centers of the nation for the purpose of maintaining a just market for the producers and for the purchase of food products and for the sale of this necessity of life direct to the people."[13]

On February 27, 1915, the petition, bearing 100,000 signatures, was presented to Congress and referred to the House Committee on Interstate and Foreign Commerce. There it was buried.[14]

## THE SOCIALIST PARTY ANTI-WAR MANIFESTO

Meanwhile, the Party's National Executive Committee had been working on a tentative peace program which came to be known as the "Socialist Party Anti-War Manifesto." Published in the *American Socialist* in late December 1914, the "Manifesto" was a lengthy restatement of the belief that the causes of war lay in the inherent conflicting tendencies of the capitalist system:

> Capitalism, inevitably leading to commercial rivalry and imperialism and functioning through the modern state with its vast armaments, secret diplomacies, and undemocratic governments, logically leads to war.

The document did acknowledge that wars could be caused on occasion because "reactionary ruling classes" wished to crush progressive political movements by creating false patriotic excitement, and thus sidetracking the real class issues. "Every war, furthermore," it went on, "is used by the capitalists in order to destroy the organized forces in the labor movement." The implication was that there was no conflict of interest between the workers of various countries engaged in the war. Indeed, this section of the Manifesto concluded by exhorting the Socialist and labor press of the world to unite in this time of crisis to proclaim internationalism and peace.[15]

The peace program that followed stated that at the end of the war the terms of peace must be such as to protect nations from future wars and preserve the identity of smaller nations. These ends could best be served by establishing the principles of no indemnities and no arbitrary transfer of territories, and by setting up both an international police force for the settlement of disputes and a congress representing all nations. This latter body would be vested with both legislative and administrative powers and would pursue the goals of disarmament and the neutralization of the seas.

In internal politics, Socialists were to seek an extension of democracy in both the political and industrial arenas. To this end, the "Manifesto" called for a popular referendum before there could be any declaration of war, the institution of universal suffrage, and the socialization of all natural resources.

The program was somewhat vague on the question of immediate action but optimistic about the prospects of reviving the Second International, especially if all Socialists would strive to have their countries adopt the program as a course of action. Finally, it called for the unity of all peace forces. This latter plea was particularly weak, because in pursuing its aim of genuine neutrality the document not only refrained from discussing the relative guilt of the belligerents, but it was also silent about the causes of the war. It simply contented itself with a blanket denunciation of the war—in fact, of all wars—and thus was more of a pacifist than a Socialist declaration.[16]

## HOW TO KEEP OUT OF THE WAR?

Overshadowing every other problem was the emerging danger of U.S. involvement in the European war. Allan L. Benson* warned that the "war spirit if unchecked would bring the world war to the United States." Chester M. Wright, editor of the New York *Call*, warned that U.S. involvement could take place at any moment: "Some unforeseen violation of neutrality, some American citizen caught in the European whirl, some diplomatic *faux pas* of the command of capital—and might not America be swept into the world flame?"[17]

But how to keep out of the war? It soon became clear that it would be difficult to win widespread support for the proposal for an embargo on shipments of all merchandise, including food and munitions, from the United States to the belligerents. An economic depression was in full swing, and it was estimated that by the winter months of 1914-1915, the total number of unemployed reached as much as four million, possibly higher.** In addition, several million were working part-time.[18] It was becoming clear that supplying the markets created by the European war

*Born in Plainwell, Michigan in 1871, Benson was a newspaperman who had worked with the *Salt Lake Tribune*, had been assistant managing editor of the *Detroit Journal*, and managing editor of the Washington (D.C.) *Times*. He lived in Yonkers, New York at the time of his nomination, working mainly as a pamphleteer and magazine writer. See p.18.

**For a detailed discussion of the economic depression of 1913-15, *see* Philip S. Foner, *History of the Labor Movement in the United States* 4 (New York, 1965):435-61.

would soon restore prosperity and reduce unemployment. By April 1915, the depression did begin to lift as war orders caused mills and factories to rehire workers, and as farmers frantically increased the production of food supplies for Europe. Thus, an embargo would halt this economic revival and return the country to a national economic depression. Even Socialist workers and farmers, much as they insisted on American neutrality and opposed American involvement in the European war, began to be concerned about the effect of an embargo on their own status.[19]

The Socialist proposal to prevent the sale of munitions to belligerents also met with a cool response from the Wilson administration.[20] Indeed, the only Socialist proposal acceptable to the administration was the call to prevent loans to belligerent governments. Secretary of State William Jennings Bryan urged that the U.S. government refuse to approve such loans, declaring that "money is the worst of all contrabands." On August 15, 1914, he wrote to J. P. Morgan, who wished to finance a French loan: "There is no reason why loans should not be made to the governments of neutral nations, but in the judgment of this government, loans by American bankers to any foreign nation which is at war are inconsistent with the spirit of neutrality."[21] But, as we shall see, powerful economic forces in the United States began almost at once to undermine this policy, and within the year they forced its abandonment.

Benson was convinced that the solution lay in a war referendum. Believing that wars are caused by capitalist nations competing for markets, Benson proposed removing from governments the power to declare war and placing the decision in the hands of the voters. He suggested the following constitutional amendment:

> The military forces of the United States shall not be used against any other people except by direct affirmative vote of a majority of all the citizens of the United States more than 18 years of age. The word "citizens" shall be construed to include women as well as men, but the reservation to the people of the sole right to declare offensive war shall not be construed as any limitation upon the duty of Congress and the President, hereby imposed, to resist invasion, or upon American warships to defend themselves if attacked.
>
> War shall be proposed only by a majority vote of both houses of Congress, by the legislature of more than half of the states, or by petition of 30 per cent of the population more than 18 years of age. War having been proposed, a general election to determine the question shall be called to take place not less than 60 days or more than six months from the date of the proposal.

Benson's amendment did not withhold from Congress or the President the power to respond to an attack by a foreign aggressor, but they could do so only in the event of an actual invasion. Mere unfriendly acts were not enough; if the government wanted to respond to these with military force, it must seek the voters' approval.

To make the parlor patriots and barroom generals think twice, Benson added a codicil to his amendment, enjoining the President, in the event of war, to call up first those who had voted in favor of it. And he singled out for special attention the war hawks of the press, the podium, and the halls of Congress:

> Every writer, public speaker, and public official who shall advocate war shall, forthwith upon such advocacy, notify the President thereof, conviction of failure to do so being punishable by imprisonment for not less than five years nor more than ten. In the event of war following such advocacy within five years, such persons shall be required to go to the front as common soldiers and remain in the thick of the fight until the end of the war, unless sooner killed or incapacitated by wounds. If wounded, such persons, upon recovery, shall be sent back to the front if the war be still in progress.[22]

Opponents of the Benson plan criticized it for ignoring the power of the capitalist press to persuade the people to vote for war and for overlooking the possibility that the President might maneuver the nation into a position in which war would be the only alternative. Furthermore, they argued, Benson's plan directed popular attention away from the fundamental cause of war, namely, capitalism, and turned it instead to trivial constitutional safeguards, which were not really safeguards at all.[23]*

## LEFT-WING PROPOSALS

Resolutions introduced by left-wing Socialists to influence their party's National Executive Committee in drafting its program reflected how far in advance they were on the war issue. One resolution, submitted by Charles E. Ruthenberg of Cleveland, proposed that all Socialists pledge not to fight in any except class wars. This put in resolution form the sentiment expressed by Debs when he said: "I am opposed to every war but one; I am for that war with heart and soul, and that is the worldwide war of the social revolution. In that war I am prepared to fight in any way the ruling

---

*On April 30, 1916, the Republican Senator from Wisconsin, Robert M. LaFollette, introduced his own version of the war referendum in the Senate. LaFollette's bill called for the director of the Bureau of the Census to distribute ballots "whenever the President shall sever diplomatic relations with any foreign Government." The ballot would read: "Shall the United States declare war against the Government of----(name of country) with which Government the President has severed diplomatic relations?" (Philip S. Foner, "Putting War To a Vote," *The Nation*, January 29, 1983, p. 108.)

class may make it necessary even to the barricades." This, Debs argued, was where the Socialist Party "ought to stand, on the question of war."[24]* But while a number of locals [including Locals Tacoma and Everett of Washington] supported Debs' position, it failed to gain sufficient support. Nor did a general strike to oppose a declaration of war, a plan advocated by a number of left-wing Socialists, enjoy any greater support.[25]

With all of the left-wing proposals rejected, it is not surprising that the Socialist Party's official peace program expressed in the December 1914 Manifesto remained the party position on the war. But events would soon force a change.

## THE *LUSITANIA* SINKS

On May 7, 1915, the Cunard liner *Lusitania* was sunk by one torpedo fired by a German submarine off the coast of Ireland. When it went down, 1,198 people died, including 124 American men, women, and children. The destruction of the *Lusitania* had far-reaching consequences. It unleased an intense campaign in the United States for war with Germany, and began the real undermining of the "neutrality policy" of the Wilson administration. It led to the resignation of William Jennings Bryan, who refused to take responsibility for Wilson's stiff note of protest to Germany, and it established Bryan's former subordinate, Robert Lansing, in the post of Secretary of State. Lansing says frankly in his memoirs that after the *Lusitania* there was always in his mind the "conviction that we would ultimately become the ally of Britain."[26]**

## THE SOCIALIST PARTY PEACE PROGRAM

On May 9, 1915, two days after the *Lusitania* sinking, members of the Socialist Party's National Committee assembled in Chicago. Hillquit, who was reelected national chairman, announced solemnly to the assembled

*Debs issued this statement in part because of the accusation by some Socialists that he "harbored pacifist illusions." (Frederick C. Griffin, *Six Who Protested: Radical Opposition to the First World War* [Port Washington, N.Y., 1977], pp. 27-28.)

**The sinking of the *Lusitania* is one of the most controversial sea tragedies in history, as illustrated by the 1973 study by Colin Simpson, a British journalist, *The Sinking of the Lusitania*, and by the 1975 book, *The Lusitania Disaster: An Episode in Modern Warfare and Diplomacy* by Thomas A. Bailey. Simpson concludes that the *Lusitania* was really an armed cruiser which was destroyed not by one torpedo but by the tremendous explosion of the secret munitions on board disguised as cheese, and even raises the suspicion that the British, led by Winston Churchill, plotted the destruction of the *Lusitania* as a means of bringing the United States into the war. All of this is denied by Bailey, who asserts that there were no high explosives or munitions on the vessel. However, he does acknowledge that there were 4,200 cases of rifle cartridges aboard, located about 150 feet from the exploding torpedo.

delegates that he knew of no meeting of the Socialist Party that had "ever had such great problems to deal with." He expressed the hope that some policy could be outlined at the session that would "unite all the anti-war elements of (the) party and give it a leading place in the anti-war movement of the nation."[27]

After three days of discussion, the statement on the war that emerged from the subcommittee was adopted by the National Committee, leading the *American Socialist* to announce that the Socialist Party at last had a program on the war.[28]

The program had two parts. The first section was called the "Anti-War Manifesto of the Socialist Party of America" and was essentially a restatement of the subcommittee's "Manifesto" of the previous December, which, it will be recalled, had related the causes of the war to the capitalist system and had urged the laboring forces of the world to overthrow the system so that there could be a permanent peace. The second section was in the form of an open letter to the people of the United States, entitled "A Demand For Peace." It warned that the "insidious propaganda of American Militarism" was working on behalf of the "armament ring . . . to stimulate a war sentiment, which to it means business and profits." It continued:

> In this grave hour of national crisis the Socialist Party of the United States raises its voice in solemn and emphatic protest against this dangerous and criminal agitation, and proclaims its undying opposition to militarism and war. No disaster, however appalling, no crime, however revolting, justifies the slaughter of nations and the devastation of countries.

Referring to the sinking of the *Lusitania*, the program appealed to the people who had been so recently disturbed by the news to resist the upsurge in demands for "strong armaments and military preparations." It warned that they would "inevitably and irresistibly lead to war, as the tragic example of the nations of Europe has conclusively demonstrated." Terrible though the destruction of the *Lusitania* was, it should serve to bring "more closely home to us the fiendish savagery of warfare, and should inspire us with stronger determination than ever to maintain peace and civilization at any cost." The appeal concluded:

> We call upon the people of the United States to profit by the lesson of our unfortunate brothers on the other side of the Atlantic Ocean, and to throttle all efforts to draw this country into the dangerous paths of international quarrels, imperialism, militarism and war.
> We call particularly upon the workers of America to oppose war and all agi-

tation for war by the exercise of all the power in their command, for it is their class who pays the awful cost of warfare without receiving any of its rewards. It is the workers who primarily furnish the soldiers on the battlefield and give their limbs and lives in the senseless quarrels of their masters.

Let us proclaim in tones of unmistakable determination: "Not a worker's arm shall be lifted for the slaying of a fellow worker of another country nor turned for the production of man-killing implements or war supplies!" Down with war! Forward to international peace and the world-wide solidarity of all workers.[29]

## THE DEBATE ON PREPAREDNESS

Soon after the outbreak of the war in Europe, advocates of "preparedness" in the United States, led by Theodore Roosevelt, Elihu Root, Henry Cabot Lodge, and General Leonard Wood, began urging the U.S. to rapidly enlarge its military and naval forces in order to strengthen its defense against possible attack. Formed to exert pressure for military preparedness, the National Security League was organized at a meeting of business leaders and corporation lawyers in December 1914.* At its founding meeting, the tone was clearly alarmist, with speakers picturing "an invasion of this country in which a landing was made easily, the army was routed, and cities were destroyed."[30]

At first these scare predictions were not taken seriously, and even President Wilson in a message of December 1914 disparaged the need for any increase in armaments. But as the National Security League's propaganda intensified and its membership grew by "leaps and bounds" with new branches "springing up everywhere from the Atlantic to the Pacific,"[31] and as the administration drew ever closer to support for the Allied cause, Wilson became a convert to "preparedness." On November 4, 1915, the President reversed himself and came out for an increase in military expenditures. Wilson formally presented the administration's defense program to the country in an address before the Manhattan Club in New York City and urged its adoption. The plan called for the construction of ten battleships, six battle cruisers, ten cruisers, fifty destroyers, one hundred submarines, and lesser craft, at a cost of 500 million dollars. He also not only proposed substantial increases in the regular army, but virtually called for the scrapping of the National Guard as the first line of defense

---

*On December 6, S. Stanwood Menken, a N.Y. corporation lawyer who was the founder of the National Security League, announced the names of 84 representatives of industrial, commercial and financial interests who were active in the movement. (*New York Times*, Dec. 7, 1914.)

and its replacement by a national reserve force, the Continental Army, of 400,000 men. Congress then proceeded to debate the President's proposals.[32]

The National Security League, the Navy League, and other organizations favoring increased military expenditures were dominated by leading business interests. They rallied at once to support Wilson's program. But the Socialist Party immediately announced its opposition to the Wilson policy. Anti-preparedness Socialists insisted that preparedness was designed only to defend capitalist interests. The *Milwaukee Leader* argued that it was "primarily a program to defend the present conquerors and exploiters of the country against any attempt on the part of their subjects to revolt and recover the wealth that has been taken from them." Benson, too, exclaimed: ". . . the American capitalists want a big army to intimidate and, if necessary, attack American workers who object to working for a base living."[33]

John Reed went still further, maintaining that Wall Street was behind the militaristic propaganda not only to make immediate profits from the sale of arms and munitions but also for imperialist ventures of its own: "Wall Street is getting ready to launch the United States upon a gigantic adventure in world imperialism for the benefit of the big financial speculators. And in order to do this Wall Street must have a great army and navy to protect its foreign investments."[34]

"Behind the active agitation for defense," said Helen Keller, the well-known sightless and mute Socialist,* at the Labor Forum in New York City, "you will find J. P. Morgan & Co., and the capitalists who have invested their money in shrapnel plants, and others that turn out implements of murder. They want armaments because they beget war, for these capitalists want to develop new markets for their hideous traffic." On another occasion she declared: "Congress is not preparing to defend the people of the United States. It is planning to protect the capital of American speculators and investors in Mexico, South America, China and the Philippine Islands." She urged the "Appeal Army," the hundreds of men and some women who convinced over half a million people to read the *Appeal to Reason* each week:**

*For a study of Helen Keller as a Socialist, see Philip S. Foner, *Helen Keller: Her Socialist Years* (New York, 1967).

**For a study of the 500-strong "Appeal Army," see James R. Green, "The Salesman-Soldiers of the 'Appeal Army,'" in Bruce M. Stavis, ed., *Socialism and the Cities* (Port Washington, N.Y., 1975), pp. 15-21.

Strike against preparedness and gas bombs and all other tools of murder. Strike against preparedness that means death and misery to millions of human beings. Be not dumb, obedient slaves in an army of destruction. Be heroes in an army of construction.[35]

The chief preparedness argument—that it was necessary for defense against invasion—was met by anti-preparedness Socialists with the contention that because of its geographic location, the United States did not need a big army and navy for defense. In his famous Carnegie Hall debate with Representative August Gardner, one of the leading advocates of preparedness, Morris Hillquit insisted that "the argument of modern American militarism . . . is based on a colossal fallacy. The United States is not in danger of war. It has never been safer from hostile attack than it is at this period." There were two reasons, Hillquit argued, "why no European or Asiatic power will attempt an invasion of the United States: first, they cannot do it, and second they would gain nothing by it, since it would require too great an army and fleet to cross the ocean, force a landing, and hold territory."[36] Other anti-preparedness Socialists added a third reason: the war in Europe would leave the belligerents too exhausted for any adventure across three thousand miles of water. "I believe that we are in less danger of invasion than we have been at any other time in 100 years," Allan Benson insisted. "I believe that this danger, never great, will become less as the European belligerents proceed towards exhaustion."[37]

Nationally, the Socialist Party outlined its position in a brief statement: "Pending complete disarmament, it [the Socialist Party] declares for the abolition of the manufacture of arms and munitions for private profit, and the prohibition of exportation of arms, war equipment and supplies from one country to another. It stands against an increase in existing armaments under any circumstances, against all appropriations for military and naval purposes." The statement concluded with the ringing cry: "We proclaim NOT ONE DOLLAR FOR MILITARISM AND MURDER!"[38]

The statement had scarcely been made public when newspapers reported that Charles Edward Russell had shocked a Socialist audience in Philadelphia by telling them that he disagreed with it and that he favored President Wilson's preparedness program. "German barbarism," he insisted, posed a threat to the democratic nations, including the United States, and it was necessary for this country to arm to defend itself against such a threat.[39]

Russell was by no means the only Socialist to take this position. On January 8, 1916, W. J. Ghent expressed himself as opposed to the party's anti-preparedness commitment, arguing that whatever danger existed that preparedness might drag the United States into war was less menacing than the prospect of a German victory in the European war, since there was nothing in the world worse than the "racial and national fanaticism" of "the vast majority of persons of German blood." Ghent described German militarism as "the most evil force in the world," and added that he wanted to see it "uprooted and destroyed." Hence, for him, loyalty to the mandates of the Socialist Party was "treason to humanity."[40*]

The temper of the Socialist rank-and-file on the issue of preparedness is indicated by the overwhelming approval, in a referendum, of an amendment to the party constitution adding Article II Section 7 which read: "Any member of the Socialist Party, elected to an office, who shall in any way vote to appropriate moneys for military and naval purposes or war, shall be expelled from the party." The vote on the amendment was 11,041 for and 762 against.[41]

Many Socialists went even further. They urged the expulsion from the party of those who expressed themselves in favor of preparedness, especially after Russell came out in favor of a bigger army and navy. Party sections in Indianapolis, Rockford (Ill.), and Washington state, among others, passed resolutions demanding that Russell's name be withdrawn from the list of Socialist speakers. Despite rank-and-file pressure, the pro-preparedness Socialists remained in the party. From his home in Indiana, Debs made a strong appeal for Russell's retention, saying that although he disagreed with his opinions, he admired the man "for having the courage of his convictions."[**] Debs was heeded on this issue.[42***]

*While pro-preparedness Socialists were generally right-wing Socialists, and in the main, left-wing Socialists opposed preparedness, a dissident voice in the left-wing ranks was that of Henry L. Slobodin, a frequent contributor to the *International Socialist Review*, who was also an outspoken proponent of preparedness and a strong advocate of military training. (Henry L. Slobodin, "Socialism and Preparedness," *International Socialist Review* 16 [January 1916]: 428-30.)

**When Upton Sinclair circulated a statement supporting Wilson's preparedness campaign, Debs refused to join in condemning him. Instead, he wrote to Sinclair urging him to reconsider, and reminded him that the "workers have no country to fight for. It belongs to the capitalists and the plutocrats. Let them worry over its defense." (Eugene V. Debs to Upton Sinclair, June 12, 1916, Upton Sinclair Papers, Lilly Library, Indiana University.)

***A move was made to recall Victor Berger from his position on the National Executive Committee because of his opposition to the Socialist Party's stand on preparedness and his use of the Mexican "threat" in 1916 as a justification for increased defense expenditures by the United States. However, with the support of Hillquit, Berger managed to have the referendum on recall defeated. (New York *Call*, July 27, Aug. 15, 1916; Victor Berger to Joseph Gelbart, June 20, 1916, Berger to "Comrade," July 3, 1916, Victor Berger Papers, Milwaukee Historical Society.)

For years Berger had believed that Socialists were not in a position to prevent increased

# THE ELECTION OF 1916

The Socialist Party platform in the 1916 presidential election affirmed the party's "attitude of unalterable opposition to war" and recommended that the President be prevented from placing the nation in a position "which leaves no escape from war." It urged that Congress be given the power to determine policy and conduct diplomatic negotiations, and that the people be empowered to change Congressional policy by referendum. It also demanded that "no war shall be declared or waged by the United States without a referendum vote of the entire people, except for the purpose of repelling invasion." Further, to eliminate the danger of war, the platform called for the United States "to abandon the policy of imperialism which is forcing the conquest of Mexico," to nullify forthwith the Monroe Doctrine, and to grant immediate independence to the Philippine Islands.

The platform pledged the party's opposition to both appropriations for war and militarism, and called for the repeal of laws that provided for increased funds for the armed forces. "The working class," it said, "must recognize the cry of preparedness against foreign invasion as a mere cloak, for the sinister purpose of imperialism abroad, and industrial tyranny at home. The class struggle, like capitalism, is international. The proletariat of the world has but one enemy, the capitalist class, whether at home or abroad. We must refuse to put into the hands of the enemy an armed force even under the guise of a 'democratic' army, as the workers of Australia and Switzerland have done." The peace plank in the platform read:

> The government of the United States shall call a congress of all neutral nations to mediate between the belligerent powers in an effort to establish an immediate and lasting peace without indemnities, or forcible annexations of territory, and based on a binding and enforceable International treaty, which shall provide for concerted disarmament on land and at sea and for an International Congress to adjust all disputes between nations, and which shall guarantee freedom and equal rights to all oppressed nations and races.[43]

armaments, but should use their energy to see that weapons were manufactured under conditions most favorable to the interests of labor. Toward the end of 1915, he began pressing for government owned and operated munition factories. He was also a firm advocate of the Swiss system of arming the people. "Every citizen," he recommended, "should devote one year—between 19 and 20—to the service of the nation," and every school should be equipped with the means by which the students would learn to operate a machine gun. "This will be preparedness by the entire nation, militant and prepared, not by a capitalist class." (*Milwaukee Leader*, May 6, Aug. 14, 1915; Victor Berger to E. C. Sticke, January 30, 1916, Victor Berger Papers, Milwaukee Historical Society.)

Owing to the party's serious financial situation, there had been growing pressure for it to dispense with the cost of a presidential convention in 1916, and instead to nominate a standard bearer by a vote of bona fide party members.[44] Debs, though in poor health, was still a strong favorite in most sections of the country, but in November 1915 he declined to be a candidate, explaining that "there are thousands of comrades who are at least as well qualified as I am for the nomination."[45]

All three of the candidates who received enough support from the locals to get their names on the referendum paper ballot—Allan Benson, Arthur Le Sueur, and James H. Maurer—were staunch opponents of preparedness, as were the two vice-presidential nominees, George E. Kirkpatrick and Kate Richards O'Hare.[*] When Benson and Kirkpatrick were selected, the New York *Call* cried: "THREE CHEERS FOR BENSON AND KIRKPATRICK! ON TO THE WAR ON WAR!"[46][**]

A number of signs pointed to promising prospects for the Socialist Party in the presidential election. While Socialists in Ohio cities had suffered some reversals in the 1915 elections, the party did see Dr. George Lunn returned to office as mayor of Schenectady. In April 1916, the Socialists recaptured the mayoralty of Milwaukee with their candidate, Daniel Hoan. Particularly heartening was the pending demise of the Progressive Party, which has suffered a great decline in the fall election of 1914.[47][***] Socialists believed that their party would now be able, without difficulty, to come forward as the workingmen's alternative to the Democratic Party. As one Socialist commentator wrote: ". . . the field is left for the Socialist Party to stand and fight for the cause of the poor and oppressed."[48]

Leaflets and broadsides supporting the Socialist presidential campaign were widely distributed. The New York local issued thousands of copies of "War and Militarism Versus Labor and Progress." addressed to "Work-

---

[*]Kirkpatrick was the author of the very popular *War—What For?*, the leading anti-war publication of the Socialist Party, while O'Hare's writings and speeches, after the war erupted in Europe in the summer of 1914, concentrated on opposing America's entrance into the war. In "To the Mothers and Maids of America," published in the *Rip-Saw* of August 1915, O'Hare stressed the particular cost of war to the women, and urged them to write to President Wilson demanding that the United States remain out of the war. (See Philip S. Foner and Sally Miller, *Kate Richards O'Hare: Selected Writings and Speeches*, Baton Rouge, La. 1982, pp. 121-75.)

[**]The vote was 16,639 for Benson, 12,265 for Maurer, and 3,495 for Le Sueur. The vice-presidential vote was 20,597 for Kirkpatrick and 11,118 for O'Hare. (*American Socialist*, March 18, 1916.)

[***]For the founding and early history of the Progressive Party, see Philip S. Foner, *History of the Labor Movement in the United States* 5 (New York, 1980): 107-08, 111-15.

ingmen and Citizens." Asking "What Armies and Navies Are For?" the broadside answered: "We Socialists have good authority for saying as we do that militarism (politely called 'preparedness') exists for the material interest of the capitalist class." The rest of the broadside was devoted to proving this assertion. One section was entitled "The Only Real War Danger." and went:

> Months ago, when the campaign for "preparedness" began, when some of the capitalist spokesmen were clamoring about the "German Danger" and others about the "Japanese Peril," we Socialists said that these were false pretenses. If the armed forces of this nation are called into action, we said, it will not be to repel European or Asiatic invaders: it will be either to attack one of the Latin American republics, or to break a strike of workingmen here in the United States.
>
> One part of our prediction has come true; It is to invade Mexico that our militia is now being called out. . . .

The broadside concluded:

> Fellow workingmen, fellow citizens, it is high time for you to choose. On which side do you stand—for Peace or for War?" for Labor or for Capital?" for Industrial Democracy or for Financial Oligarchy? with the Trade Unions or with the Manufacturers' Associations? with the Socialist Party, or with the twin parties of Organized Wealth?
>
> You will soon find that there is no middle ground.[49]

As we have seen in a previous volume [6: pp. 222-31], the vast majority of the trade unions supported Wilson. The *American Socialist* gloomily published a poll of labor leaders conducted by the *Literary Digest* which revealed that 332 were for Wilson, 47 for Benson, and 43 for Charles Evans Hughes, the Republican candidate. Even the official Socialist Party organ conceded that for most workers, the eight-hour day and other domestic issues loomed more important than preparedness, and that Wilson's slogan, "He Kept Us Out of War," appeared to settle the war issue as far as they were concerned.[50]

A special effort was made to debunk the "He Kept Us Out of War" argument. Anyone who really believed that "Wilson, Hughes, or any other man can keep us out of war is nothing more than the ordinary fool who is the ordinary prey of the capitalist politician, who catches him through his political superstitions."[51] Not even a vote for Benson could achieve that goal, the Socialists admitted, but at least a Socialist who voted for Benson knew "that Socialism, when fully realized, can keep us out of war, while capitalism is always just as likely as not to plunge us into it.

The only anti-war party and the only anti-militarist candidates are Benson and Kirkpatrick on the Socialist party ticket."[52]

But as the likelihood grew of a very close presidential vote, an increasing number of Socialists became concerned over whether Wilson or Hughes would win. A number of Socialists believed in Wilson's peaceful intents, and many more were impressed with his domestic policy. On October 20, Walling told the New York *World* that he believed that 99 percent of the Socialists wished to see Wilson elected, and that possibly as many as 200,000 would shift from the Socialist candidate to the Democrat.[53]

In a well-publicized letter to the National Executive Committee, left-winger John Reed announced he was going to vote for Wilson as "considerably the lesser of the two evils." With tortured logic, Reed argued that he did not believe in "anything lasting coming out of purely political action," and then declared that he was going to vote for Wilson because he did not want the United States "to become hell for the next four years."[54] Even the openly revolutionary *International Socialist Review* supported Wilson and printed an unsigned editorial attacking the *Milwaukee Leader* for its criticism of the president. The editorial charged: "To sow suspicions of militarism against a president who has kept the working class of America out of war during a hair-trigger period is a species of treachery to the working class that does no good."[55]

In the final month of the campaign, a group of seventeen Socialist intellectuals, including Harry W. Laidler, Jessie Hughes, Harry Overstreet, Walter Rauschenbush, and J. Phelps Stokes, sought to stem the abandonment of Benson and the desertion to Wilson in the ranks of the party members. A sizeable Socialist vote, they argued, would act as a pacemaker to the party in power, for with the Bull Moose dead, the Socialist Party was the principal "minority pacemaker." Basically, they went on, there was no choice between the major parties that could be decided "other than by a flip of the coin," and three million votes for the Socialist would "convince even the divine-right transportation barons that the recognition of labor as a national factor, is a matter of practical politics."[56]*

It did little good. The Socialists could make little headway against Wilson's record and the slogan, "He Kept Us Out of War." Benson's official vote was only 585,113, which was less than two-thirds of the vote for

*The reference was to the battle between the Railroad Brotherhoods and the managers of the railroads over the demand for the eight-hour day for operating railroad workers. (*See* Foner, 6: pp. 143-88.)

Debs in 1912. While Debs had won 5.9 percent of the total presidential vote, Benson garnered only 3.2 percent. Whereas in 1912 some 26 states gave more than 5 percent of their presidential vote for Debs, there were only nine states in this category in 1916.[57]

At the congressional and state government levels, the election was not so catastrophic. Although the goal of seating ten Congressmen was clearly impossible, the party did manage to re-elect Meyer London in New York's 12th Congressional District and almost succeeded in electing Hillquit in the 20th District. In the state assemblies, the total elected was 25, which included an increase of four members in Wisconsin and one in New York, and the election of a sole representative to each of the lower houses of Vermont and Rhode Island. The Socialists also succeeded in electing a mayor in one more large city when Thomas H. Van Lear became mayor of Minneapolis.[58]

## ANALYSIS OF ELECTION RESULTS

The fact that the party held its own in these elections could not disguise the evidence that at the national level its political impact was significantly weaker than in 1912. The party's official explanation of the election results was presented by Adolph Germer, the national secretary. He gave three reasons for the decline in the Socialist vote. In the first place, general apathy had prevailed in party circles "for the last three or four years," and the party was slow to recover. In addition, the "conflicting elements" over the question of militarism and war had hurt the image of the party. Finally, the passage of the Adamson Act granting the eight-hour day to railroad workers and the slogan "He Kept Us Out of War" had been instrumental in "befuddling the workers." In short, Socialists had deserted the party in part because it was not functioning effectively and also because the Democratic Party, under the specific circumstances of 1916, seemed too alluring.[59]

Speaking for the left wing, Henry Slobodin declared that to blame the war and the Wilson administration for the failure of the Socialist Party had "the double merit of saving hard thinking and diverting the inquirer's attention from causes which are in his control to conditions utterly beyond his control."[60] For the left-wingers, the poor election results in 1916 seemed to prove what they had been charging since 1908—that rigid reliance solely on political action and reformist policies carried with it no guarantee of growth in the Socialist vote. Hence a group called the Socialist Propaganda League, which had emerged from an ideological struggle between reformers and left-wingers within the Massachusetts Socialist

Party, called for a new dedication to the principles of industrial unionism, "internationalism," and "mass action." Immediately after the election, the Boston group announced that it was planning to make a nationwide appeal through the *Internationalist*, a newspaper it had just founded. The *International Socialist Review* immediately endorsed this appeal and added that the election results had demonstrated that workers must be prepared to use their collective industrial strength against the employers, as well as their political power.[61]*

The first issue of the *Internationalist* was published in Boston on January 6, 1917. It appeared just as the danger of American involvement in the European war became critical, and in confronting this renewed danger, the Socialist Party had to push the election results into the background and concentrate on a campaign to prevent American entrance into the war.

## U.S. BREAKS RELATIONS WITH GERMANY

In the winter of 1917, relations between the United States and Germany suddenly took a turn for the worse. The previous spring, the U.S. government had issued a virtual ultimatum to Berlin, warning that any further sinkings of belligerent and neutral merchant vessels without adequate provisions being made for the crews and passengers would result in a rupture of diplomatic relations between the two countries. Unenthusiastically, and with conditions attached, the German government had pledged to observe cruiser rules of warfare.[62]

Then, on January 31, 1917, Germany notified the State Department that it intended to launch unrestricted submarine warfare in the European war zone. On February 3, President Wilson announced to Congress that the German declaration had caused the United States to sever diplomatic relations with Imperial Germany.[63]

"It was the German submarine warfare and nothing else that forced him [Wilson] to lead America into war," wrote historian Charles Seymour in 1934.[64] But historians have demonstrated that the Wilson administration displayed totally different attitudes toward Great Britain and Germany during the various controversies that arose with those two countries. They have shown how the pro-Ally bias and interventionist tendencies of Lansing, House, and Page distorted U.S. neutrality and influenced Wilson to

*According to David A. Shannon, Benson's poor showing was a reflection of the fact that the party had become weaker since 1912. With the expulsion of the pro-IWW Socialists in 1912 and 1913, with the loss of prestige suffered by the European Socialists' failure to prevent the war and their support of their governments in the war, and with the loss of supporters to the progressivism of Wilson, the party membership rolls were about 35,000 names fewer than they had been in 1912. *The Socialist Party of America*, (Chicago, 1967), p. 92.

surrender his country's legal rights to the Allies, while making unprecedented demands on Germany for the protection of British ships, all leading to a declaration of war. Meanwhile, trade between the United States and the Allied countries increased enormously. The increase from 1914 to 1915 was 141 percent, and by 1916 the increase over 1914 was 289 percent. In his book, *Propaganda For War*, H. C. Peterson summed it up in these words: "In the last analysis, the American government was forced to join the Allies in 1917, because it had previously surrendered to them all its material, diplomatic and moral support."[65]

In 1934, the same year that Charles Seymour insisted that only German submarine warfare had brought the United States into the war, a special Senate committee began an investigation to discover whether financial power, notably the Morgan interests, had been a force in bringing the United States into war. The committee, chaired by Senator Gerald P. Nye of North Dakota, published a series of revealing letters. It concluded that U.S. bankers had first compelled the government to authorize large loans to France and Great Britain, and then when those countries faced defeat, the bankers forced the U.S. into war to protect their investments.

As we have seen, during Bryan's year as Secretary of State, the U.S. government refused to approve private loans to belligerents. The first efforts to modify this policy came from the house of J. P. Morgan, which asked permission to extend credits to foreign governments in order to facilitate purchases in the United States. The Morgan company maintained that this was purely a bookkeeping arrangement, very different from the sale of belligerent bonds in the open market. On October 23, 1914, Wilson accepted this distinction, and the firm of Morgan was authorized to open credits of this character for belligerent governments, particularly the French.[66]

In May, 1915, following the sinking of the *Lusitania*, as we have seen, Robert Lansing replaced Bryan as Secretary of State. In August, Great Britain began cancelling many foreign contracts for the purchase of U.S. grain, pleading lack of funds to finance the purchase. On August 21, Secretary of the Treasury McAdoo warned Wilson that it was imperative that Great Britain be permitted to float a loan of $500,000,000 at once. He reminded the President that "the high prices for food products (purchased by Great Britain) have brought great prosperity to the farmers, while the purchases of war munitions have stimulated industry and have set factories going to full capacity. . . . Great prosperity is coming. It is, in large measure, already here. It will be tremendously increased if we can extend reasonable credit to our customers. To maintain our prosperity, we must finance it."[67]

Secretary of State Lansing supported McAdoo's plea. "If the European countries cannot find the means to pay for the excess of goods sold them over those purchased from them," he warned Wilson, "they will have to stop buying and our present export trade will shrink proportionately. The result would be restriction of output, industrial depression, idle capital, idle labor, numerous failures, financial demoralization, and general unrest and suffering among the laboring classes. . . . Can we afford to let a declaration as to our conception of the 'true spirit of neutrality,' made in the early days of the war, stand in the way of our national interests which seem to be seriously threatened?"[68] Pressing home his point, Lansing wrote to Wilson on September 6, 1915: "I believe that Secretary McAdoo is convinced, and I agree with him, that there is only one means of avoiding this situation which would so seriously affect economic conditions in this country, and that is the floatation of large bond issues by the belligerent governments. Our financial institutions have the money to loan and wish to do so."[69]

Two days later, Wilson gave his consent, and shortly thereafter the House of Morgan floated a loan of $500 million on behalf of the British and French governments.[70]

Thus, even before Germany resorted to unrestricted submarine warfare, pressure from the financial community, supported by their spokespersons in the Cabinet, had pushed the Wilson administration into close economic alliance with the Allied Powers. Bryan had warned that "money is the worst of all contrabands," and the events during the opening months of 1917 were to prove him correct.

## REACTION OF THE SOCIALIST PARTY

On February 9, 1917, the National Executive Committee published an anti-war proclamation that was distributed widely as a leaflet and published in the special anti-war issue of the *American Socialist* on February 17, 1917.* Entitled "Down With War! Long Live Peace!" the anti-war proclamation noted at the outset: "The workers of the United States have

---

*The issue contained a reprint of an advertisement that appeared in the Chicago *Tribune* of February 5, signed by Amos R. E. Pinchot, Randolph S. Bourne, Max Eastman, Paul U. Kellogg, and Winthrop D. Lane, on behalf of the American Union Against Militarism, urging the American people to petition the President and Congressmen "to keep this country from an ignominious eleventh hour participation in a struggle for mastery which is not her own." It also contained articles such as "Do You Want War?" by Adolph Germer, "War" by George R. Kirkpatrick, and "Break is Serious" by Morris Hillquit, who emphasized that the break in diplomatic relations with Germany was unjustified, and that "We are being forced into hostilities on the most frivolous pretext imaginable." (*American Socialist*, Feb. 17, 1917.)

no desire and no reason to shed their blood." It then observed: "By a mere executive decree, the President of our country has broken off diplomatic relations with the German empire, and placed the profile of the United States in imminent danger of being actively drawn into the mad war of Europe." After recounting the horrors created all over Europe by the war, it declared that "suddenly, with little notice or warning, without the sanction or consent of the people and without consultation with the people's chosen representatives in Congress, we are practically ordered to join in the mad dance of death and destruction. . . ." The Socialist Party entered "a solemn protest against this wanton attempt to draw us into the European conflict." Granted that the "policy of unrestricted and indiscriminate submarine warfare recently announced by the German Government" was "most ruthless and inhuman," but so was war "as a whole and so are all methods applied by both sides." In any case:

> The German submarine warfare does not threaten our national integrity or independence, not even our national dignity and honor. It was not aimed primarily at the United States and would not affect the American people. It would strike only those parasitic classes that have been making huge profits by manufacturing instruments of death or taking away our food and selling it at exorbitant prices to the fighting armies of Europe.

But the workers of the United States had "no reason and no desire to shed their blood for the protection and furtherance of the unholy profits of their masters," and in this they had the full support of the Socialist Party. The anti-war proclamation closed with a stirring appeal:

> WORKERS OF AMERICA, AWAKE!
> The hour is grave, the danger is imminent, silence would be fatal.
> Gather the Masses in Meetings and Demonstrations! Speak in unmistakable tones!
> Let your voice of vehement and determined protest resound from one end of the country to the other.
> Send telegrams or letters to President Wilson, to the United States Senators and Congressmen. Demand that American citizens and American ships be forbidden to enter the war zone, except at their own risk. Insist that the nation shall not be plunged into war for the benefit of plundering capitalists. . . .[71]

In Cleveland, Charles E. Ruthenberg responded immediately to the appeal to "gather the masses in meetings and demonstrations" by calling a series of anti-war rallies. At the third rally, Ruthenberg shared the platform with Debs, who told the cheering audience: "There is absolutely no reason, no excuse for plunging this country into the European hell of slaughter. To do this would be nothing less than a monstrous crime against the American people."[72]

In New York, the Socialist Suffrage Committee announced that Socialist women "organized for work for Socialism and the winning of woman suffrage, have thrown all our forces unreservedly into the war against war." Praising the Socialist women, national secretary Adolph Germer urged the membership to "Keep Up The War On War!" "Comrades," he wrote, "we have every reason for congratulating ourselves for so far keeping this nation out of the European War. It is largely due to our efforts that Congress has not declared war."[73]

## PROPOSALS FOR A GENERAL STRIKE

But what if the party were unable to check the inexorable drift toward war? On February 4, 1917, James H. Maurer, president of the Pennsylvania Federation of Labor, answered this question at the Socialist Literary Society in New York with the statement that he favored a nationwide strike in opposition to any declaration of war.[74] A month later Debs told a New York audience, overflowing into the streets outside Cooper Union, that all the workers of the country must strike in case of war. With his old fiery spirit, Debs declared that he would "rather be backed up against a granite wall and shot as a traitor than go to war for Wall Street."[75]

Karl Liebknecht—who had been expelled from the Social-Democratic Party, stripped of his Reichstag seat, and sentenced to four years in prison for opposing Germany in the war—embodied, Debs insisted, the "true position and infallible test of international socialism" for all Socialists.* Debs was ready to do everything possible to end the war should the United States become involved, even if this should require a general strike.[76]

But such talk met with opposition in leading Socialist circles. In an interview in the *New York Times Magazine* section on February 11, 1917, Hillquit declared that in the event of war, the Socialist Party would not hinder the government through strikes or by a fight against conscription.

---

*As a member of the Reichstag, Liebknecht could not be arrested. He was therefore conscripted into the army in an effort to silence him. But there, too, Liebknecht continued his fight against the war. On May 1, 1916, while he was on leave in Berlin, he addressed a tremendous anti-war May Day demonstration in the great public square in front of the Kaiser's palace. In full uniform, Liebknecht called upon the German people to stop the war. "Our enemies," he cried, "are not the English, French, or Russian workers, but the great German capitalists and their executive committee, the government." This time he was promptly arrested, and after being dishonorably discharged from the army, given a two-and-one-half year prison sentence. Because he continued to denounce the war and militarism during his appeal to a higher court, the sentence was increased to four years. (Heinz Wohlgemuth, *Karl Liebknecht: Eine Biographie* [Berlin, 1973], pp. 235-354.)

Hillquit had an opportunity to demonstrate that he meant what he said. At a meeting of the New York County Socialist Party on March 4, he vigorously opposed a resolution pledging New York Socialists "to encourage strikes and resist recruiting in the event of war with Germany." Hillquit asserted that "we should be asses to tell members of Local New York that they must risk death and imprisonment rather than join the army." As a consequence of Hillquit's opposition, the resolution was defeated. In its place, a compromise measure was adopted which, though it pledged Socialist opposition to the war, omitted any encouragement of strikes.[77]

Socialist Congressman Meyer London also publicly opposed the idea of a strike against war. In an interview in the *New York Tribune*, London stated that if the United States entered the war, American Socialists would follow the lead of the European Socialists and support their government. Any talk of a general strike was "pure fantasy."[78]

But this did not kill the idea of a strike or other forms of "direct action" in the event the United States become involved in the war. At a large gathering in Minneapolis, the Minnesota Socialist Party adopted resolutions which urged all workers to "refuse to fight in case of war." At a mass anti-war meeting in Cleveland, under the leadership of Ruthenberg, a resolution of the Ohio Socialists was adopted affirming in part: "We refuse to be led forth to slash, stick, shoot, kill other workingmen, for our hearts are not full of hatred, we are not obsessed with vile passions, we are not patriotically insane."[79]

## THE FEBRUARY REVOLUTION IN RUSSIA

On March 12, 1917, the world-shaking Russian Revolution began, and three days later the Czar abdicated. The February Revolution in Russia (March 9-14, 1917, by the Western calendar) aroused widespread rejoicing in the United States. The forces favoring participation in World War I were, of course, pleased by the news from Russia that the Czar had abdicated and that a provisional government under Prince George E. Lvov, a liberal nobleman, had assumed power, with Alexander Kerensky, soon to become Minister of War and Premier of the provisional government, as Minister of Justice. The February revolution had solved a dilemma for them. The U.S. war propaganda machine, beating the drums for a "war for democracy," could not be convincing so long as the Czar of all the Russias was one of the Allies. Now the blood of revolution seemed to have purged Russia of past sins.[80]

Socialists, of course, were thrilled by the news from Russia, and none more so than the Jewish Socialists from eastern Europe who expressed their joy at the overthrow of the hated Czarism with overflow meetings and dancing in the streets.[81] While the Russian Revolution strengthened pro-Ally sentiment in Socialist circles in the United States, including some Jewish Socialists, it also stimulated greater interest in "direct action" to prevent the government of the United States from leading the people into war. As most Americans concentrated their attention on the provisional government in Russia, many Socialists watched the Petrograd Soviet of Workers' and Soldiers' Deputies, which had begun to function as a sort of dual government, issuing its own proclamations. When, on March 27, the Soviet advised the workers of all countries to take matters into their own hands and put an end to the war, men like Hillquit and London were horrified, but many U.S. Socialists were excited.[82]

The wave of strikes in the warring countries in the spring of 1917 further strengthened the forces in the Socialist Party favoring "direct action." In France, Italy, and Great Britain, the strike movement became increasingly prominent. In Great Britain, during the first quarter of 1917, the network of organizations of shop stewards spread all over the country. Simultaneously with this, there were massive successful wage struggles. In Germany, too, the strike movement began to build up. The reduction of the bread ration and the drafting of Richard Müller, the trade union secretary of the war opposition, were the immediate causes of the strike. The shortage of coal, clothing, and food was an additional cause, as well as, in every country, war weariness.[83]

## THE POSITION OF PRO-ALLY SOCIALISTS

But while many in the Socialist membership were moving toward a direct battle against the United States government as the likelihood of war came closer each day, Socialists like John Spargo, Phelps Stokes, Walling, Upton Sinclair, Ghent, and Russell shifted even closer to outright support of the Wilson administration's pro-war policies. (This process was hastened, of course, by the fact that that dubious "democrat," the Czar of Russia, was no longer one of the Allies.) The March 1917 edition of the *Socialist Party Bulletin* carried a statement signed by a number of prominent Socialists labelled "Democratic Defense: A Practical Program for Socialism." The statement ruled out disarmament as "impossible," and urged Socialists to abandon fighting all military expenditure and work instead to ensure that there was a "democratization of the military service." Indeed, "to refuse under any circumstances to vote for military supplies, as has been required by a recent party decree, is to be sentimental rather than scientific, Tolstoian rather than Marxian." Although the statement did not specifically call for support of the Allied Powers, it implied as much by asserting "that the proper aim of Socialist world-politics at the present time is an alliance of the politically advanced nations for the defense of the democratic principle thruout the world."[84]

A statement similar in many respects to the one in the *Party Bulletin*, signed by nearly all the same signatories, was published in the New York *Call* toward the end of March, asserting: "The present opposition of the Socialist Party to national defense is contrary to the interests of democracy and contrary to the hitherto accepted views of the International Socialist Movement." In an editorial two days later, the *Call* invited Socialists to express their opinions on the issues raised by this statement.[85]

It soon became clear that, despite their positions of prominence in the Socialist movement, these dissenting intellectuals did not have even a significant minority of the party membership on their side. The *Call* was flooded with letters attacking the authors of the statement unmercifully. The gist of the criticism was summed up by one correspondent who called the dissenters a group of "bourgeois-minded fellows who cannot be trusted." On March 31, the *Call* estimated that its mail was opposed to the dissenters by a ratio of forty to one.[86]

## CALL FOR EMERGENCY NATIONAL CONVENTION

"What would be our stand in case of war?" the Chicago North Side Finnish Socialist Branch asked the National Executive Committee early in March 1917.[87] The committee was confronted with a host of similar questions when it met at its monthly meeting in Chicago on March 10, 1917. A proclamation issued by the committee appealed to the workers and to "all liberty-loving citizens of the United States" to protest the impending entrance of the nation into the war. But the committee also felt it was necessary to decide what the party policy toward the war should be once this nation became a belligerent. Hence, it decided to call an emergency party convention. It was to be a meeting of 200 delegates from all over the country, selected by the state organizations in whatever manner they saw fit. The states themselves were to finance their own delegates. After several efforts to obtain an available hall elsewhere had failed, the city chosen was St. Louis.[88]

The plan for an emergency convention was quickly approved by the National Committee with only token opposition, and a "Call," signed by Berger, Hillquit, Anna A. Maley, John Spargo, and John M. Work of the NEC, and Adolph Germer, national secretary, was published in the Socialist press. Party members were informed that the special convention would be held on April 7; that it was "not a regular proceeding under our constitution. It is an emergency measure necessitated by the sudden gravity of the situation which confronts the country, the working class and the Socialist movement." Since the executive committee really had no constitutional power to call such a meeting, the call expressed confidence that the decision "will meet the hearty support of the vast majority of the party membership." It went on to explain:

> The time is short. The danger is imminent. Delay may be fatal. If war should break out, our party must present greater fidelity to principle, greater unity of purpose and greater solidarity of action than ever.
>
> Only a full and representative convention, followed by a speedy vote of the whole membership, can lay down an authoritative, uniform and effective Socialist course of action against war and during war. Only the determined and concerted effort of the whole membership will conserve and strengthen our movement in this most critical period of our history.
>
> To work, comrades! Elect your full quota of delegates without delay, contribute the funds to defray the necessary expenses. The war agitation of our ruling classes must be met by us with redoubled energy. War, if it comes, must not find us unprepared.[89]

## U.S DECLARES WAR

On March 20, 1917, President Wilson opened the Cabinet session with the statement that he "· · · did not see from a practical point of view what else could be done to safeguard American vessels more than had already been done unless we declared war or declared that a state of war existed . . . and that the power to do this lay with Congress."[90] He therefore asked whether Congress should be called to an earlier special session, and what course should be recommended to it. In the discussion that followed, Secretary of State Lansing stated that "in my opinion an actual state of war existed today between this country and Germany. . . ." Yet to go to war "solely because *American ships* had been sunk and Americans killed" would cause debate, so he urged that emphasis be placed on larger reasons for war: the democratic struggle against German militarism and autocracy, a struggle made more acceptable by the recent revolution.[91] All the other members of the Cabinet agreed that a declaration of war was necessary, and urged it upon the President.

On March 21, President Wilson called a special session of Congress for April 2. In a last desperate effort to halt the headlong dash for war, the Socialist Party's Emergency Committee on March 30 urged Wilson to oppose a declaration of war, to warn all citizens to avoid the war zones and to submit the question of war to a referendum by the people. "You Will Pay in Blood and Suffering " Ruthenberg warned in a leaflet on April 1, of which 50,000 copies were handed out to Clevelanders that Sunday morning. The leaflet continued in Ruthenberg's words:

> If we make war against Germany it will be to protect the "property rights" and commercial interests of the capitalist class of this country. . . . It is the workers who will pay the cost of war in blood and suffering. The capitalists will make more profits. . . .
> Make your voice heard for peace. Join us in upholding the principles of peace and fraternity.[92]

On April 2, 1917, Wilson delivered his war message to Congress in which he stated that neutrality was no longer desirable, and termed the "recent course" of Germany "nothing less than war" against the United States. He asked Congress to declare war on Germany "for the ultimate peace of the world and for the liberation of the people. . . . The world must be made safe for democracy." Brushing aside a last plea from Senator LaFollette to let the people vote on the question, Congress passed a joint resolution on April 6 declaring war on the German Empire.[93]

On April 7, 192 delegates crowded into the Banquet Hall of the Planters' Hotel in St. Louis to attend the National Emergency Convention of the Socialist Party of America. They found awaiting them a message from Local Cleveland, written by Ruthenberg:

> We are being tested by fire. Let us set an example of fidelity to our principles, and send our Comrades the world over the inspiring message that at least one section of the International working class has kept faith in the hour of trial.[94]

## THE ST. LOUIS CONVENTION

The main question facing the delegates on April 7, 1917 was whether they should abandon their anti-war principles now that the United States Congress had declared war. A. M. Simons, Benson, and Spargo actually hoped that the convention would follow them into the Allied camp and endorse the war, a war which Simons described as "the last great war to abolish all the trumpery of war."[95] A number of delegates feared that the convention might adopt either a lukewarm anti-war declaration or none at all. In fact, Ruthenberg, while he did not completely share this fear, tried to strengthen the anti-war forces in St. Louis by attempting to enlist Debs, probably the most influential anti-war voice in the party. But Debs refused to attend. Ruthenberg and a group of delegates then drove in two cars 150 miles to Terre Haute to make a personal appeal to Debs to change his mind, but they failed. Debs insisted that his opposition to the war was sufficiently well known by the delegates and that his presence was unnecessary.[96]

He turned out to be right. A majority of the 193 delegates from 44 states, assembled at the Planters' Hotel, soon made it clear that they were in no mood to follow the lead of the pro-war Socialists. They were bitterly opposed to the war and prepared to endorse any program of active opposition to it. Hillquit made this clear in the convention's keynote speech:

> We, the Socialist party of the United States, are today the only permanently organized force that has still retained a clear vision, an unclouded mind, in the general din of confusion and passion and unreason, and it devolves upon us to continue our opposition to this criminal war even now after it has been declared.

The stenographic report of the proceedings noted that this declaration was followed by "Applause and cries of Good!"[97]

The responsibility for formulating the party position on the war was given to a special committee on war and militarism that was instructed to hold hearings and receive all proposals. The committee was chaired by Kate Richards O'Hare of St. Louis, who had spent most of her time during the past months opposing the war.* The fourteen other members were Hillquit, Algernon Lee, and Louis Boudin of New York City; Dan Hogan, a Socialist newspaper publisher of Huntington, Arkansas; Ruthenberg and Frank Midney of Ohio; Victor Berger of Milwaukee; Kate Sadler of Washington state; Patrick Quinlan of New Jersey; Job Harriman of California; Spargo of Vermont and New York City; Maynard Shipley of Maryland; George Spiess of Connecticut; and Walter P. Dillon of New Mexico.[98]

Ruthenberg was chosen secretary of the committee, and was placed on the subcommittee to draft resolutions, along with Lee and Hillquit. The committee spent the better part of a week hearing proposals for its report.

---

*On the eve of the convention, O'Hare published the article, "My Country," in *Social Revolution*, in which she rejected patriotism and nationalism in favor of internationalism. She urged Americans to learn a lesson from the experience of the "ten million dead men who rot on the battlefields of Europe," men who had made the mistake of being "nationalists 'first' and Socialists, labor unionists and Christians 'second.'" She vowed: "If need be, I will give my life and the life of my mate, to serve my class, BUT NEVER WITH MY CONSENT WILL THEY BE GIVEN TO ADD TO THE PROFITS AND PROTECT THE STOLEN WEALTH OF THE BANKERS, FOOD SPECULATORS AND AMMUNITION MAKERS." (Kate Richards O'Hare, "My Country," *Social Revolution*, April, 1917, p. 5; reprinted in Philip S. Foner and Sally Miller, eds., *Kate Richards O'Hare: Selected Writings and Speeches*, Baton Rouge, La., 1982, pp. 163-65.

There were three reports to the delegates: a majority report and two minority reports.* The majority report, drafted by Hillquit, Lee, and Ruthenberg, began:

> The Socialist Party of the United States in the present grave crisis reaffirms its allegiance to the principle of internationalism and working class solidarity the world over, and proclaims its unalterable opposition to the war just declared by the government of the United States. . . .

It continued with statements of opposition to class rule and "sham national patriotism," and urged workers to "refuse to support their governments" in war. After analyzing the causes of the war, the report set forth three theses:

> We brand the declaration of war by our government as a crime against the people of the United States and against the nations of the world.
>
> In all modern history there has been no war more unjustifiable than the war in which we are about to engage.
>
> No greater dishonor has ever been forced upon a people than that which the capitalist class is forcing upon this nation against its will.

The report concluded with a call for "an even more vigorous prosecution of the class struggle during wartime" and pledged Socialists to a seven-point program for action. The points included "continuous active and public opposition to the war, through demonstrations, mass petitions, and all other means within our power; unyielding opposition to all proposed legislation for military or industrial conscription;" opposition to "any attempt to raise money for the payment of war expenses by taxing the necessaries of life or issuing bonds which will put the burden upon future generations;" "vigorous resistance to all reactionary measures, such as censorship of press and mails, restriction of the right of free speech, assemblage and organization, or compulsory arbitration and limitation of the right of stike;" "extension of the campaign of education among the workers to organize them into strong, class-conscious and closely unified political and industrial organizations, to enable them, by concerted and harmonious mass action, to shorten this war and establish lasting peace;" "the socialization of the great industries concerned with

*Ruthenberg also presented his own proposal in the form of a "Manifesto Against War," which he had written, and which had already been adopted by Local Cleveland. The Manifesto explained that the war was the result solely of American capitalists' greed for profits, and called upon the workers "to use their organized industrial power to stop this war, by declaring a general strike and thus save the people from the horrors which have engulfed Europe." (*Socialist News*, April 7, 1917.) This call for a general strike was rejected by the War and Militarism Committee and omitted from its recommendations.

the production, transportation, storage and the marketing of food and other necessaries of life;" and "the socialization of all agricultural land which is now held out of use for monopolistic or speculative profit." Finally:

> These measures are presented as means of protecting the workers against the evil results of the present war. The danger of recurrence of war will exist as long as the capitalistic system of industry remains in existence. The end of war will come with the establishment of socialized industry and industrial democracy the world over. The Socialist Party calls upon all workers to join it in its struggle to reach its goal, and thus bring into the world a new society in which peace, fraternity and human brotherhood will be the dominant ideals.[99]

The majority report failed to include in its seven-point program for action a call for a general strike recommended by Ruthenberg, the key Left spokesperson at the convention. But it was mainly Ruthenberg's influence that made the report much more radical than Hillquit, Berger and others of the center and right had envisaged. Before the convention met, Hillquit had predicted that the delegates would not support the war, but would, once it was declared, decide only to urge an early cessation of hostilities.[100] Through the *Milwaukee Leader*, Berger had urged a similar course of action. Believing that Socialists could do nothing to stop the war, he suggested that they work for an early peace and spend the duration of the war urging internal reforms such as widespread nationalization, and ensuring that civil liberties were preserved.[101]

Even though Hillquit read the majority report to the convention, it was clear that he had been pressured by the left into accepting it. In later years, he characterized the report as "extraordinarily aggressive, defiant, and provocative." Had it been adopted under more normal circumstances, he asserted, "it would have been couched in more moderate and less irritating language."[102]

The majority report was signed by eleven members of the War and Militarism Committee: Hillquit, Lee, Berger, Midney, Hogan, Quinlan, O'Hare, Ruthenberg, Shipley, Harrison, and Spiess. Committee members Boudin, Sadler, and Dillon signed a minority anti-war report drawn up by Boudin, while Spargo, the fifteenth member of the committee, issued his own pro-war report.[103]

After going into the causes of the war and warning of a permanent military establishment, Boudin's report concluded "that we must oppose this war with all the powers of our command." But when it came to spelling out a program of action, Boudin's suggestions differed very little from those set forth in the majority report. In fact, most Socialists regarded Boudin's report as unnecessary.[104]

Spargo's report, representing the interventionists, called for support of the war. He set out to prove that this position was not contrary to Socialist principles of internationalism, and his proof consisted of the statement that Socialists were not pacifists, and therefore could fight in just wars, of which this was one. Spargo did not claim that the U.S. entrance into the war was wholly due to a determination to fight for democracy, and he conceded that the war was in the interests of American capitalists. But he pressed the view that regardless of capitalist motives, it was a fact that on one side were ranged the greatest autocracies of the world, while on the other side (especially since the revolution in Russia) were the most progressive and democratic nations in the world. It should be clear to any objective observer that the victory of the Allies would promote freedom and democracy. Therefore, Spargo concluded, now that the war was an accomplished fact, "for the reasons stated we hold that it is our Socialist duty to make whatever sacrifices may be necessary to enable our nation and its Allies to win the war as speedily as possible."[105]

The majority report was adopted overwhelmingly by the convention. It received 140 votes; Boudin's minority anti-war report, 31 votes, and Spargo's pro-war report, five votes.[106]

Thus, the Emergency National Convention of the Socialist Party proclaimed the party's "unalterable opposition to the war just declared by the government of the United States." The American Socialists had not followed the road taken by the vast majority of their comrades overseas, but had maintained their anti-war position even after their government had declared war. Although he had hoped that his proposal for a general strike would be adopted and made part of the majority report, Ruthenberg had only words of praise for the final document. As he informed the members of Local Cleveland:

> "No compromise" was the keynote of the Emergency National Convention of the party at St. Louis.
>
> The declaration in regard to war and militarism is a clear-cut statement of Socialist principles. In adopting it, the Convention wrote one of the finest pages of the history of the working-class movement, for it placed the party on record as opposing the government and refusing to recede the slightest from its previous position after war had been declared. . . .[107]

## DEPARTURE OF PRO-WAR SOCIALISTS

Not all anti-war Socialists were as enthusiastic as Ruthenberg. The New

York *Call* gloomily predicted that the radical tone of the majority report would cause "dissension and disharmony in the party to grow."[108] It did not take long before this prediction was realized. Even before the majority report was adopted, Charles Edward Russell wrote to J. Phelps Stokes proposing that all Socialists who believed in an "Americanized" party should resign in a body if the convention "takes any disloyal action."[109] When the report was adopted, resignations *en masse* did not occur, but from the middle of May 1917, when it was becoming clear that the majority report was going to win a vote of confidence from the membership, the pro-war Socialists began withdrawing one by one from the Socialist Party. Spargo, Russell, Simons, Gaylord, Benson, and others left. A number had held important posts. Spargo was on the National Executive Committee at the time war was declared, Stokes had been president of the Intercollegiate Socialist Society, and Benson, as we have seen, had been the party's presidential candidate in 1916.[110]

Although the departing Socialists each proclaimed his or her disillusionment with the party as they left, they expressed agreement on the following points: (1) The Socialist Party was now "un-American" and pro-German," and had demonstrated treasonable sympathy for Germany; (2) Some party leaders, especially Hillquit and Berger, were openly pro-German; (3) The party no longer represented the best interests of the working class; (4) Men who were both Socialists and patriots could no longer remain in the party, and (5) A new nonpartisan organization should be created which would devote itself to working for true principles of "socialism and industrial democracy."[111]*

The pro-war Socialists were in a minority, however, and they were repudiated by those who remained in the party for, as Debs put it, "attempting to do for the United States just what the cowardly and traitorous German Socialists did for Germany... The patriots who rush to arms, when the cry of danger to the fatherland is raised by the aristocrats and plutocrats who own it, are not socialists," Debs thundered. "They belong to the ruling class as its willing hirelings and the sooner every mother's son of them is out of the movement, the better it will be for the movement."[112]

Apart from Simons, Stokes, and Russell, most of the departing Socialists had delayed their break with the party, hoping that the membership

*Actually, the pro-war Socialists had already begun preliminary work for the establishment of a new organization to be called the Social Democratic League of America. (Kenneth E. Henrickson, Jr., "The Pro-War Socialists, the Social Democratic League and the Ill-Fated Drive for Industrial Democracy in America, 1917-1920," *Labor History* 11 [Summer 1970]: 310.

would reject the majority report when it was submitted to them in a referendum. Spargo, for example, in sending Simons a copy of his minority report, added: "I am quite certain that in the party itself a very large number of people hold most of the views that I have set forth."[113]

In Chicago on July 7, 1917, it was announced that the majority report had been ratified by the party membership by a vote of 21,699 to 2,752.[114] Although a few members now resigned, the vast majority remained in the party, and continued, even with the possibility of imprisonment, to voice their objections to the war.

## WEAKNESSES OF THE SOCIALIST PARTY'S ANTI-WAR STAND

Despite its principled stand in refusing to support the U.S. government in an imperialist war, the Socialist Party's anti-war position was weakened from the outset by at least two important tendencies. One was the refusal of the party to organize or cooperate with non-Socialists against the war. There were, to be sure, Socialist voices raised for such cooperation. Meyer London suggested that the party "get all the labor elements together in an efficient committee, call in delegates of the other organizations that are working for peace—the suffragists, the anti-armament groups, the churches—don't leave one out, and thus organized, a protest against the United States entering any offensive war will be felt in Washington."[115] Paul H. Douglas, executive member of the Intercollegiate Socialist Society, told a Society convention that "the Socialists, while emphasizing the radical difference between the peace movement and that of the bourgeois peace advocates, should cooperate temporarily with the anti-war forces."[116]

Some resolutions were introduced in the Socialist locals, the National Executive Committee and the National Committee endorsing cooperation, and some steps were taken in that direction.* In mid-August, 1914, the executive committee of Local New York invited labor groups to a conference to deal with problems raised by the war. Local New York assured the invited unions: "The Labor Conference will not be under the control of the Socialist Party, but free to act as it deems fit."[117]

The National Committee of the Socialist Party followed suit and adopted a motion by Arthur Le Sueur in September 1914, urging that the Committee on Immediate Action and the National Committee "bring about

---

*Two Socialists, Carl D. Thompson and John C. Kennedy, were on the executive committee of the Emergency Federation of Peace Forces in Chicago. (*American Socialist*, Feb. 13, 1915.)

complete cooperation on the part of labor and labor organizations to call a delegate convention of all labor organizations and for delegates from conventions of unemployed and unorganized labor, for the purpose of formulating a program to cover the concerted activities of labor in reference to: (1) Unemployment; (2) Government by gunmen; (3) Program of labor in case of war."

Opponents of the proposal held it to be futile. Berger said that it would fail because the American Federation of Labor would turn it down and the Railroad Brotherhoods and the IWW were unimportant. Hillquit said it "would meet with little response," and Gaylord called it "impractical and useless."

Without enthusiasm and without any campaign to publicize the idea behind the proposal, letters were sent to various labor organizations and the Socialist Party sat back and waited. Then in December 1914, the National Committee was advised by the National Executive Committee that "no further action looking toward such action be taken at this time" because the national secretary had received "replies . . . almost uniformly of a negative or indifferent character."[118] Thus ended the one and only Socialist Party effort to mobilize organized labor in the United States against the war.

Later, the subcommittee on disarmament and international peace recommended to the NEC that the "Socialist party cooperate in and take aggressive action looking to the federation of all peace forces that will agree to work for the principal elements of our party." But the recommendation got nowhere, its opponents arguing that unless peace advocates were also prepared to support the abolition of capitalism, they were not fit to cooperate with.[119] "What we are asking," the New York *Call* said frankly in an editorial "is that Socialist principles and ideas shall dominate in concerted action for peace, and they cannot coincide with the demand." Until this dilemma was resolved, it concluded, "we cannot perhaps do better than continue with the regular Socialist propaganda."[120]

Another tendency that weakened the Socialist Party's anti-war position was defeatism. Since war was inevitable under capitalism, a number of anti-war Socialists argued there was little point to devoting attention to preventing the entrance of the United States into the war. Moreover, they claimed the Socialist Party simply did not have much power to influence the government. Hillquit, for example, emphasized that "the Socialists are in a minority and do not possess the measure of political power required for effective prevention of the war."[121] E. F. Atwood, Secretary of the South Dakota Socialist Party, wrote: "Why should our efforts be wasted in attempting to curb capitalism at war? We have not the power. War is the legitimate fruit of capitalism. What is the use of cutting off the branches one at a time?"[122] The *Milwaukee Leader* was convinced that American entrance into the European war was "inevitable," and that not even "the voting majority of this country will be able to stop it."[123]

Workers looking for a way to stop the war, or at least to keep the U.S. out of it, found too many groups in the Socialist Party who had no hope of success. "We Socialists do not control events," the *Call* explained to such workers. The best thing was for the workers to understand this truth—that "we simply may not be able to stem the tide of militarism dragging the United States into the war."[124]

Left-wingers challenged the defeatism being expressed in party journals. John Macy wrote that regardless of the obstacles, Socialists must vigorously combat the drive to get the United States into the war. He insisted that "no determined minority relaxes effort even though that effort will meet immediate defeat."[125] Left-wingers at the New York state convention in 1916 pushed through a resolution declaring that "while we consider militarism and war as normal accompaniments of capitalism, we do not accept the fatalistic idea that it is futile to combat war and militarism while capitalism still exists."[126] Local Cleveland, under the leadership of Ruthenberg, rejected the "fatalistic idea," and carried on a persistent and consistent campaign against the war drive.[127]

Fortunately, it was this approach and not the defeatism of the *Milwaukee Leader* and the New York *Call* that prevailed at the emergency convention in St. Louis and in the declaration against the war overwhelmingly adopted by the delegates. While it was not without weaknesses,* the St. Louis majority report was, in the words of one student, "the most eloquent monument to American Socialism."[128]

---

*Louis Fraina was critical of the majority report for not stressing sufficiently the role of American imperialism in bringing the United States into the war. America did not enter the war just because profits were threatened by the renewal of submarine war, although that was a factor, Fraina maintained. It entered to "use the opportunity of war to prepare the necessary national psychology and armed forces for the greater clash of imperialism that is coming." (*Class Struggle*, May-June, 1917, pp. 22-23.)

Later, Anthony Bimba criticized the majority report for failing to call upon European workers "to fight for peace by waging a merciless struggle against their own bourgeoisie. . . ." (*History of the American Working Class* [New York, 1927], p. 258.)

# CHAPTER 2

# Organized Labor and World War I,
# 1914-1915

## THE CAUSE OF WORLD WAR I

The first reaction of organized labor in the United States when the war exploded in Europe in August 1914 was to call it a European squabble that should be widely condemned. As far as labor was concerned, the cause of the war was easy to determine. Perhaps for the first and last time, the Industrial Workers of the World, the AFL unions, the Railroad Brotherhoods, and even the surviving locals of the Knights of Labor agreed in their assessment of blame for the conflict. The IWW declared that "the responsibility of the war rests upon the shoulders of European capitalists." The Coast Seamen saw the cause of the war in "the capitalistic system which is based on organized violence, on the shameful exploitation of all nations." The Locomotive Firemen also located the roots of the war in "business capitalism": "Merchants of one country are being beaten by those of another country and their respective governments proceed to settle the matter by war." The Knights of Labor declared that the war broke out in order that "monopolistic commercialism shall be supreme under some one flag, upholding some one ruler above the rest of the world." "The present war," the Railway Conductors maintained, "is for markets . . . imperial and commercial supremacy." "Greed . . . the desire for more money at any cost," was the reason given by the United Mine Workers, and the Western Federation of Miners declared: "In the final analysis, capitalism is the breeder of war."[1] In discussing the war in his annual report to the Missouri State Federation of Labor, President Reuben Wood voiced the prevalent view in labor circles:

Let us not forget, that this world war is nothing else, but a capitalist business war between the ruling classes of Europe, and the tremendously powerful war machines operated by modern militarism are simply the police power of those ruling classes in the several war countries.[2]

Just as American Socialists found ready excuses for the failure of European Socialists to oppose their governments in the war, so U.S. labor excused international labor's failure to stop the war. "The war came so quickly," declared the Cigar Makers, "that practically no one except the kings and potentates had any chance to take a decided stand against it." The Carpenters charged that "the workers were forced into the struggle." "The trade unions were swept into the conflagration," the Shoe Workers claimed. "It was a matter beyond their control." The Molders believed that the peace policies of international labor were still valid, and had failed only because "they were put to the test too soon and before they had time to take such firm roots as to make them sufficiently strong to stand the strain."[3]

## LABOR FOR STRICT NEUTRALITY

With capitalism identified as the cause of the war, with international labor considered as having been forced into the conflict, U.S. labor immediately raised the cry that the war was of no concern to the United States, that the American nation must be neutral in thought as well as in action! However, while maintaining a position of neutrality in deed, many workers developed partisanship in opinion and sympathy. As might be expected, German-American trade unionists, while opposed to the war, were sympathetic to their native land. The guiding principle that determined the sympathy of most Jewish workers was their deep hatred of Russian czarism. Similarly, large numbers of Irish-American workers expressed their hatred of British oppression of Ireland by being "pro-German."[4]

But the vast majority of trade unions urged a policy of strict neutrality. "For the sake of ultimate peace, for the preservation of what civilization we can claim," warned the United Mine Workers, "America must remain neutral." The Locomotive Firemen proclaimed that "the United States is essentially a non-military nation and in the present crisis is and must be neutral in every sense." "It's the duty of every trade unionist," warned the Molders, "to curb his sentiments at this time, to place a bridle upon his tongue so that it shall give no offense." The Western Federation of Miners called upon the government to begin immediately "putting up bars against loans or furnishing supplies of any character to the nations involved."[5]

But what if the United States faced the danger of being drawn into the conflict? A number of unions suggested radical means of meeting the problem. "If labor unites to use the powers already in its hands," the Stove Mounters suggested, "there will never be a war." Others were more specific. In the event of American involvement, the United Mine Workers threatened to call "a general strike, thereby stopping all industry and transportation." The IWW was positive that this was the only way to prevent U.S. involvement, and urged that "arrangements must be made for the general strike."[6]

Most unions, however, were satisfied that there were more moderate ways to prevent U.S. involvement. "Show war in all its true horror," the Western Federation of Miners suggested, "and there would be no stampede to get into the conflict." The same theme was stressed in a number of trade union journals.[7]

On August 6, 1914, the Central Federated Union (CFU) of Greater New York vigorously denounced the war. The resolution, asserting that it spoke for 600,000 workers, including German-American, Irish-American, Jewish-American and Italian-American working class groups, declared that the CFU

> . . . deprecates this war, which will result in the killing and maiming of millions of innocent people and the destruction of their industries. The continuation of the strife will be reflected in the United States, for, while certain of our productions might be used to supplant those of Europe, this very fact will tend to increased prices here of general commodities and add to the present strained economic conditions of our people.

The CFU called upon "the American Federation of Labor throughout this country to express sympathy with our brothers of the countries affected," and to make certain that the United States would not be drawn into "this butchery and blood-letting."[8]

## GOMPERS BEGINS TO VACILLATE

Although the AFL was not scheduled to meet until November in annual convention, President Gompers did not wait to express his views on the war. When the conflict broke out Gompers immediately denounced the war as "unnatural, unjustified and unholy," and "undesirable from every viewpoint."[9] The war, he charged, had but one aim: to divert attention from domestic problems and to demoralize organized labor so that it could no longer be a threat to the entrenched dynasties. In a letter of August 6, 1914, he wrote: "I will gladly go to any length and associate myself with any movement to bring to an end the present European struggle and which will make for permanent international peace and the democratization of the institutions of the world, and abolish international war for all time to come."[10] Gompers asked the Typographers, who were holding their convention in mid-August, to "protest against this frightful and unjustifiable European war. . . . No international trade union can afford to meet without declaring itself on this brutal, unnecessary war."[11]

Gompers' initial reaction toward the war gave way all too soon. This should not have come as a surprise. Since its inception, there had been distinct limitations to Gompers' pacifism. An example of this is the address he delivered at the First National Arbitration and Peace Congress in New York City on April 12, 1907. The eighth session of the Congress was entitled, "Organized Labor in Relation to the Peace Movement," and Gompers made the principal speech.* He warned: "Nor will the workers longer consent to permit ourselves to be utilized as the fighting force to be murdered and mowed down to conquer the markets of barbarians." But having made his bow to radicalism, Gompers retreated quickly. Turning to disarmament, he cautioned that "to disarm when the world is an armed camp outside would mean for that country to be wiped off the face of the map." To the astonishment of many in the audience, Gompers then offered a defense of war. Labor had to fight for its rights sometimes, he said, and nations had to do the same.[12]

Another example of the limitations of Gompers' pacifism could be seen just before the outbreak of World War 1, when the Carnegie Endowment for International Peace arranged with Gompers to publish a compilation of his antiwar utterances. While the manuscript was at the printer, war broke out in Europe. Gompers rushed to the printer to get "that damn fool stuff" he had written, and stopped its publication.[13]

In contrast to most trade unionists, Gompers acknowledged no economic forces involved in World War I and never once mentioned imperialism. He regarded aristocracy as basically responsible for the war and placed the main blame on the Kaiser. He played down the fact that the Czar of Russia was in the Allied camp, and he made it clear that when he

*The other labor speakers were Terence V. Powderly, former Grand Master Workman of the Knights of Labor, Leonore O'Reilly of the Women's Trade Union League, and James J. Murphy, president of the New York Typographical Union. Powderly echoed Gompers, noting that "the organized working man" wanted peace, but not "Peace at a sacrifice of honor." Leonore O'Reilly made the best speech of the session. Among other things she pointed out that one year of war, based on the statistics revealed during the Russo-Japanese War, cost $730,000,000. All this for "destruction." There was a movement for industrial education of children, but this had to compete with money used to wage war. The way to assure the success of the education movement was "to do away with war." (*Proceedings of the National Arbitration and Peace Congress* [New York, 1907], pp. 232, 234.)

spoke of autocratic power by irresponsible monarchies, he meant Germany and Austria.[14]

As early as Labor Day, September 7, 1914, while condemning the war as one of "aggrandizement and conquest," Gompers saw some positive aspects emerging from the conflict—international labor solidarity, international law, a system of arbitration, and a code of international morality as a standard for the maintenance of peace. At about the same time, as he later confessed in his autobiography, he decided that he was no longer a pacifist: "Intellectual appreciation of peace," Gompers wrote in the *American Federationist*, "does not automatically prevent war." He blamed his retreat from pacifism on the disillusionment that swept over him at the failure of international labor to stop the war.[15]

From the outset of the war, Gompers urged the United States to pursue a policy of strict neutrality. But his secretary, Florence Thorne, who knew Gompers better than anyone else, defined his attitude toward neutrality as similar to that of the U.S. government:

> He was quite oblivious to Great Britain's invasion of our freedom on the high seas but . . . [he] recounted vividly damages to our shipping and losses of lives by German submarines. He seemed personally committed to aid Great Britain. . . .

## THE 1914 AFL CONVENTION

On the eve of the 34th annual AFL convention, held in Philadelphia in November, 1914, Ralph M. Easley, executive secretary of the National Civic Federation, wrote to Gompers expressing his "hope that the American Federation of Labor will make clear to the public the difference between its anti-war standpoint and that of the Socialist Party."* Specifically, Easley hoped that the AFL would repudiate "the campaign being made by the Socialist Party to 'Starve the War and Feed America,'" and Benson's proposal "that no war should be engaged in until after the people had voted upon it."[17]

Gompers assured Easley he had nothing to worry about, and that these issues would be properly taken care of by the AFL convention. On Benson's proposal, he commented: "I wonder how they would have carried out in Germany, France, and England their program for a people's vote in declaring war." As for the Socialist Party's campaign, Gompers was confident that it would not get very far. The United States was becoming a huge

---

*On the activities of the National Civic Federation and its role in shaping class collaboration ideology in the labor movement, *see* Philip S. Foner, *History of the Labor Movement in the United States* 3 (New York, 1964): 61-110.

supplier of goods, including military supplies, for the Allies, and this was the key to recovery from the depression that had set in early in 1914 and then been aggravated by the war's disruption of normal channels of trade. As the recovery grew with the increased sale of war materials to the Allies, the majority of workers, happy to find employment in expanding war production, would reject the campaign to "Starve the War and Feed America."[18]

As Gompers had predicted, the 1914 AFL convention took no stand in favor of either of the proposals that had so concerned Easley. But it did adopt two resolutions relating to the war. The delegates unanimously adopted a proposal calling upon the trade unions to use their economic and political power on behalf of peace, and authorized the Executive Council "to call a meeting of the representatives of organized labor of the different nations to meet at the time and place of the peace conference," and take such action as would lay the foundations "for a more lasting peace." At the same time, the delegates sought to eliminate the economic advantages to be derived from war by unanimously resolving "that all patent rights for arms, munitions and other equipment to be used for war purposes should be acquired by the Government; all such equipment should be manufactured in Government establishments."[19]

But Gompers was able to put across his idea that the war had been started by the Central Powers. Andrew Furuseth, president of the Sailors' Union of the Pacific, proposed that since no government or people could be blamed for the war, the people should "judge none of those who are engaged in this war but to tender to them our profound sympathy." But, pressured by Gompers, who was a member, the union's international relations committee voted nonconcurrence.[20*]

Despite this evidence of his bias in favor of the Allied Powers, the resolutions adopted by the AFL convention caused the San Francisco *Bulletin* to declare with a burst of confidence that "if the AFL stands fast against war, and against policies which lead to war, the peace of the United States will be as safe as men can make it. Without the consent of the 2,000,000 members of the AFL, the United States can never make war."[21] Although Gompers succeeded in preventing a condemnation of *all* the nations engaged in the war, the *Bulletin* did not seem to understand which way the wind was blowing.

---

*Simeon Larson sees the rejection of Furuseth's proposal as evidence that the "AFL opted for a continuation of the war." (*Labor and Foreign Policy: Gompers, the AFL, and the First World War, 1914-1918* [Rutherford, N.J., 1975], p.27.)

## THE 1914 IWW CONVENTION

In the fall of 1914, the IWW convention approved a resolution which, in substance, denounced patriotism and charged the European working class with ignorance for its willingness to continue the war. The Wobblies blamed the Social Democratic movements, such as that in Germany, for instilling "a spirit of patriotism within political boundary lines."

In contrast, "the industrial movement will wipe out all boundaries and establish an international relationship between all races engaged in industry." The resolution specifically stated that IWW members "will refuse to fight for any purpose except the realization of industrial freedom."[22*]

In one respect, the two labor conventions in the fall of 1914 were similar. Neither the AFL nor the IWW called for any concrete immediate step to retard the pro-war forces in the United States. Gompers told reporters he "emphatically, uncompromisingly opposed any scheme to enlarge the United States army and navy," but he said nothing at the convention on the subject, nor did the delegates take any stand on it other than to call for government ownership of the manufacture of armaments. The IWW took a fatalistic attitude that the United States was bound to enter the European conflict, and that there was not much the Wobblies or any other section of the American working class could do to prevent it. As the IWW eastern organ, *Solidarity*, predicted in the fall of 1914, sooner or later the "economic laws of the system" were "bound to plunge America into war." Thus, while it voiced opposition to the war, the IWW did nothing concrete to organize workers in opposition to American intervention. Instead, it took the position that the workers should concentrate their attention on preparing for the class struggle that was certain to erupt following the war's end.[23]

## LABOR'S PEACE ACTIVITIES IN 1915

"This year, 1915, is going to generate a greater hatred of war than has ever been known," the official organ of the Plumbers' Union predicted. The journal of the Locomotive Firemen agreed, and urged: "Let us join . . . one organization after the other in a protest against this inhuman system that makes war."[24]

On February 26, 1915 the New York Central Federated Union responded. Charging that "certain elements" were seeking to plunge the

---

*The Canadian IWW announced that only "suckers" supported the war effort, and the Vancouver and Edmonton locals expelled members who enlisted. (Ross McCormack, *Reformers, Rebels and Revolutionaries: The Western Canadian Radical Movement 1899-1919* [Toronto, 1977], pp. 119-20.)

United States into war, the CFU called on labor throughout the country "to oppose in every way any and all attempts to inveigle the United States into the European conflict."[25] The CFU instructed its secretary to proceed with a peace meeting to be held at the Cooper Union auditorium on April 15, 1915, under the joint auspices of the Federation and a number of peace societies.

The meeting was an overflow affair with hundreds in the streets outside waiting to hear the speakers. The meeting issued a call for an embargo on shipments to the European belligerents, and to make this a reality it endorsed a resolution "for a general strike among those industries employed in the production of ammunition and food supplies destined for any of the belligerents." Reporting this stand, the New York *Call* deemed it "a revolutionary act."[26]

The next day, the CFU adopted a motion urging President Wilson to convene an international peace congress of neutral nations and suggested that Congress devise measures to curtail the export of food and war materials to belligerents.[27]

As hysteria swept the nation in the wake of the sinking of the *Lusitania* on May 7, 1915, the trade unions accelerated their activity on behalf of peace. A few unions remained silent, even though they believed that there was a danger of involvement in the war growing out of the *Lusitania* episode. They placed "complete faith in Woodrow Wilson," and expressed a willingness to accept his advice.[28] Not so, however, with the New York CFU. At its regular meeting on May 28, 1915, Joseph D. Cannon of the Western Federation of Miners suggested that the CFU lay the foundation "for a powerful protest by organized labor from the Atlantic to the Pacific against embroiling this country in the European war." While it was laudable to send a labor delegation to Europe to urge the workers there to bring about peace, as the AFL convention had proposed, "it was more necessary that the workers of this country unite their forces so that the United States will not be plunged into the slaughter."

> For the war is not one for the protection of the workers, but one of aggrandizement for the financial interests. The workers have nothing to gain, while war would still further enrich the bankers and manufacturers of armaments. . . . The workers will be sent to the trenches to do the fighting, they will carry all the burdens of war, and it will be the toilers who must come back and pay off this huge debt, while the moneyed interests stay home and accumulate profits. . . . The organized workers should say that they do not want to fight and that they will repudiate a war debt. Then let us see if the bankers, the mine owners, the railroad presidents will go out and do the fighting.[29]

Following this militant antiwar address, the CFU appealed to all international and central labor organizations throughout the country to arouse their members on behalf of peace so that the United States would not be drawn into the war. Other groups were urged to act in concert with the CFU in a series of peace meetings.[30]

On May 27, 1915, a day before the CFU issued this appeal, eight AFL internationals based in Indianapolis met at the headquarters of the United Mine Workers—United Mine Workers, International Typographical Union, Stone Cutters, Bricklayers, Carpenters, Book Binders, Structural Iron Workers, and Barbers. They voiced their opposition to war in general and called on the government to do everything possible to keep the country out of the European conflict. At the conclusion, the conference urged Gompers to call a meeting of all labor organizations if the United States should reach the point of becoming involved in the war.[31] In his study of the AFL and the First World War, Simeon Larson considers the conference as "of the utmost importance. All the attending trade unions were affiliated with the AFL and represented approximately 900,000 members. Its views were broad-based and thus reflective of wide sections of the labor movement. Furthermore, Gompers could not dismiss lightly the opinions of some of the most powerful trade union leaders. He was reluctant to attack the conference openly."[32]

But he could ignore the conference's request to call a meeting of all labor organizations as the threat of U.S. involvement mounted. He also ignored similar requests from the Maintenance of Way Employees' Union, the Commercial Telegraphers, the Chicago Federation of Labor, and the Pennsylvania State Federation of Labor.[33]

Meanwhile, early in June 1915, Secretary of State William Jennings Bryan resigned, fearing that President Wilson's policy was increasing the danger of war. The New York CFU invited Bryan to address the first of the peace rallies called for in the resolution adopted on May 28. Invited to share the platform with Bryan were Samuel Gompers; Congressmen Frank Buchanan and Meyer London; Joseph Holland, president of the Locomotive Firemen and Enginemen; and leaders of the various clothing unions. "The object of the meeting," Ernest Bohm, CFU corresponding secretary, informed Gompers, "is to propagate peace, and to protest against the attempt to embroil the United States into the European killing, blood letting and maiming." The meeting was to be held at Carnegie Hall on June 19, 1915.[34]

In a statement to the press, Bohm noted that the members of the CFU's

Peace Committee "feel that the peace sentiment is sweeping through the labor movement with rapid and certain strides." The presence of Gompers at the "monster peace convention at Carnegie Hall would strengthen the sentiment of organized labor on the question of peace."[35]

All of the others invited to participate accepted the invitation, but Gompers refused. "You know," he reminded Bohm, "that as far back as my young manhood I have always stood for peace: have had an abhorrence of war, with all the brutality which it entailed." But "there are some things more abhorrent than war—that is to be robbed of the birthright of justice, safety and character." If these "birthrights" should be endangered, "if despite our reserve and self-control, we shall be dragged into it whether we like it or not, there will be one position for us to take, and that is, to be true to ourselves, true to our fellows, true to the highest ideals of humanity for which our movement stands."[36]

Gompers made sure that the press received copies of the letter and he also sent one to President Wilson. The President expressed his appreciation for Gompers' stand, and encouraged his "opposition to labor's involvement with any peace organization."[37]

Despite Gompers' dampening effect on the affair, the Central Federated Union proceeded with its preparations. It was vigorously supported by the United Hebrew Trades, the International Ladies' Garment Workers' Union, and a number of other unions. Gompers called the labor support for the meeting a "small and unimportant faction of the movement," and Timothy Healy, president of the Stationary Firemen and an executive of the National Civic Federation, dismissed labor's support for the meeting as being limited to "Socialists or Germans [who] do not constitute an important part of labor."[38]

Carnegie Hall was packed when Bryan arose to speak. Noting that this was the first address he was delivering since he left the Cabinet, Bryan said it was logical that he should be addressing a meeting organized by the labor movement. "No portion of our community is more deeply interested in the prevention of war than that element known as the labor element." Nor was this surprising, for it was the "labor element" that "not only created the nation's wealth in time of peace, but who also fight the nation's battles in time of war. The families of the laboring men, too, suffer more from war than the families of the rich, for the soldier who is buried in an unknown grave seldom leaves an estate to safeguard his widow and his children; and it must be remembered that on the average, he leaves more children than the rich man." Bryan continued:

It is natural, therefore, that a peace movement should begin with the laboring men, and it is to be expected that organized rather than unorganized labor will take the lead, because organized labor has its machinery for propaganda already existing and in operation. It is natural, also, that labor should favor the Government ownership and operation of the manufacturing plants upon which the nation must rely for its weapons of defense and for the ammunition required. This reform would not only contribute to the Government's independence, but it would rid the country of the menace of a sordid private interest which sails under false flags, and, professing a superior patriotism, preaches the gospel of "preparedness for war" because it sees in this policy the prospect of securing rich Government contracts.

Bryan urged the labor movement "to combat the forces of militarism" and carry on a vast educational program for peace so that the danger of American involvement in the European war would become only "a remote possibility."[39]

Congressman Frank Buchanan of Illinois, who had taken the lead a year earlier in organizing Labor's National Peace Council, called for an embargo on the shipment of arms to the belligerents in Europe. "I believe that to pray for peace on the one hand and to send ammunition to Europe on the other is the height of hypocrisy," he insisted. "Those who want war are the armament ring who make a profit of $200 a ton on steel used for weapons and the capitalist press who back the armament makers. It is that bunch of financial and commercial pirates who will plunge us into war and it's our part to join to prevent it." Buchanan urged the convoking of Congress to lay an embargo on arms.

Joseph Cannon of the Western Federation of Miners voiced the opinion that most of the people of the United States "would be satisfied to have a war if the armies would be raised among the bankers, business men, and editors who wanted war." He was followed by Socialist Congressman Meyer London, Ernest Bohm, and Joseph P. Holland of the International Brotherhood of Firemen, after which resolutions were adopted. One recommended that the government take over and manufacture all armaments. Another resolution favored an immediate extra session of Congress to curb the power of "such criminal conspiracies as the Steel Trust, and other thieving monopolies such as the Oil Trust, Railroad and Money Trusts" which were "behind the campaign to drag the United States into the European war."[40]

## LABOR'S NATIONAL PEACE COUNCIL

The rally at Carnegie Hall proved to be the last important activity by the

New York CFU in 1915. Its subsequent activities were to be channeled through Labor's National Peace Council. As previously indicated, the council's chief organizer was Frank Buchanan, who had been a bridge builder and structural iron worker in Chicago and had served as business agent of the Bridge and Structural Iron Workers' Union. Thereafter, he was elected president of the International Structural Iron Workers' Union in 1901, and ten years later he was elected a Democratic member of Congress. A labor Congressman, Buchanan still retained his membership in the Chicago Structural Iron Workers' Union and associated mainly with union men.[41]

Late in 1914, Buchanan interested a number of Chicago trade unionists in establishing a Labor Peace Council in that city with the aim of organizing labor opposition to U.S. intervention in the European war. To establish the movement on a national basis, Buchanan called a meeting in St. Louis on May 28, 1915. The meeting was attended by Congressmen Fowler of Illinois and Gill of Missouri; Henry B. Martin, national secretary-treasurer of the American Anti-Trust League; and H. B. Perham, president of the Order of Railroad Telegraphers. "The subject for discussion was peace or war for the United States," Perham informed Gompers, adding:

> In view of the fact the the the interests seem to be working assiduously toward the end that the United States shall become involved in the European war, it was suggested that organized labor should hold a meeting at Washington in the near future for the purpose of strengthening the hands of the President of the United States, give our moral assistance in keeping this country free from war, and setting a good example for the working people of all countries by giving expression to humanitarian thoughts that may receive the endorsement of all right thinking people.[42]

Shortly after this meeting, Labor's Peace Council of Chicago issued a call to all "labor organizations that have placed themselves on record favoring peace at home and abroad" to send delegates to a "peace conference of labor . . . in Washington, June 22, 1915, for the purpose of considering the best method of procedure to insure the attainment of organized labor's high ideals and peace sentiments."[43]

A day before the Washington meeting was scheduled to begin, Buchanan talked to Gompers by telephone in an effort to win his support, and urged him to participate in the name of the American Federation of Labor. After the conversation, Gompers dictated a memorandum of his reply to Buchanan. "The whole thing," it stated, "is being engineered by the agents of the German and Austrian governments, our people made fools of, and our movement placed in a questionable position. Hillquit is the agent of the German Government." Gompers warned Buchanan that the movement he was launching could bring "serious consequences not only to the country but to our movement."[44]

Despite this advice, Buchanan refused to call off the Washington meeting. Chicago, New York City, East Orange, N.J., and Washington, D.C. were represented by delegates at the Labor Peace Congress when it opened at the St. James' Hotel on June 22, 1915. Chicago's delegates represented Labor's Peace Council, those from New York City (including Brooklyn and New Jersey) represented the Central Federated Union, and the Washington D.C. delegates represented their Central Labor Union. They had assembled,

> . . . to crystalize [in labor's name] the prevailing sentiment for peace, voiced by the organized toilers of America . . . into practical action that will not only effectually circumvent the hellish designs of the dollar crazed interests, that for the sake of financial gain, are striving to force the United States into the vortex of war's crimson flood of human gore, but will also serve as the long prayed for excuse, that Europe's organized workers have been straining their ears to hear from American shores, and that will enable them to demand, in the name of common humanity, a cessation of hostilities. . . .

The American Federation of Labor and most of its state federations and city central labor councils had adopted "strong resolutions . . . condemning war,* and, in forceful language, voicing a most strenuous protest against the insidious efforts being made to embroil the United States of America in the European conflict." But, in spite of this antiwar position, these organizations were "so overburdened with work dealing with various problems of direct and vital interest to their membership," they could not "find time to devote to the detailed labor essential to properly arousing

---

*There are many such resolutions of state federations of labor and city central labor councils in the AFL Archives in the State Historical Society of Wisconsin. A number of city centrals adopted a resolution originally framed by the Cleveland Federation of Labor and sent to them for their "consideration." The resolution began: "Whereas, The great war of Europe has been waged for a period of more than half a year without an issue having been reached, and, with little advantage on either side, has developed into a siege that staggers mankind as it contemplates the wanton waste of human lives, the destruction of property and the calamitous visitation of unparalleled suffering and starvation and every form of misery upon vast multitudes of people." The resolution then urged all labor groups to support the bill introduced into Congress by Senator Robert M. LaFollette which empowered the President to call a conference of neutral nations that would seek "to re-establish peace." (Cleveland Federation of Labor to All Central Bodies in United States, Cleveland, Feb. 24, 1915, AFL Archives, State Historical Society of Wisconsin.)

the conscience of labor, and urge it to make its presence felt in the preservation of American neutrality and the inauguration of peace universal." Hence, it devolved upon labor's representatives at the Peace Congress "to prove the courage of their convictions by establishment of a national institution having for its sole aim and object the carrying into effect, through practical action, of the essence of Labor's oft-reiterated declaration of peace both at home and abroad. . . ."

The new organization would be known as Labor's National Peace Council, "having for its purpose the establishment and maintenance of peace universal by all honorable means."

Labor's National Peace Council was led by an imposing list of trade union leaders: president, Frank Buchanan; vice-presidents Milton Snelling, vice-president of the Steam Operating Engineers; William Kramer, secretary-treasurer of the Blacksmiths; Rudolph Modest, treasurer of the Meat Cutters; Jacob C. Taylor, vice-president of the Cigar Makers' Union; and Louis Strauke of the Commercial Artists. C.P. Straube of the Chicago Federation of Labor was the secretary, and Ernest Bohm of the Central Federated Union of Greater New York, the treasurer.[45]

The council advocated "the elimination of existing private monopoly in the manufacture of the instrumentalities of war through the substitution of governmental ownership and control," the prohibition of the sale and exportation of arms and ammunition to belligerents, and strict American neutrality. The council also called upon all international labor organizations to unite in the interest of peace and to urge speedy cessation of hostilities, "so as to permit the re-establishment of reason and judgment, thereby ending a barbarous conflict that threatens civilization and checks all hope of human progress."

Frank Buchanan wrote to President Wilson asking for an audience so that a committee of the peace council could acquaint him "with the character of the various resolutions adopted by Labor's National Peace Council." When the council was informed that the President could not be seen, "because of preparation for a long delayed vacation," Buchanan informed the press "that the President was accessible to rich men, but would not see representatives of the laboring classes."[46]*

After the peace congress, Buchanan sent a letter to trade union and progres-

*The committee did visit the Secretary of the Navy and acquainted him with the aims and objects of the organization, "and the Council's desire to honestly co-operate with all true champions of Peace, rather than to take action that would jeopardize or embarrass any venture looking to the preservation of peace at home and the establishment of peace abroad." (Typewritten report of Labor's Peace Council, Washington, D.C., June 22, 1915, AFL Archives, Washington, D.C.)

sive organizations and journals all over the country. He asked: "Will the working people of this country in face of the horrible object lesson being taught them in Europe's war-cursed zone, show the unity of action and solidarity necessary to prevent this country from becoming involved in a similar terrible slaughter, especially when there is nothing to be gained and everything to be lost by engaging in such questionable action?" As for himself, he could see "absolutely nothing" to be gained by becoming involved in the war other than "the slaughtering of the toilers by the tens and thousands, together with the piling up of a war debt of several billion dollars which would bear heavily upon the backs of the wealth producers of this country since they would have to pay for it." Buchanan was not for "peace at any price," but he was definitely "opposed to war unless it is to prevent invasion of this country, or to fight for the rights of men, for democracy against autocracy." He could see none of these issues in the European war. What he could see was that the "war munitions trust" and the Wall Street bankers were engaged in fostering "a military spirit which leads to war."

Only organized action could prevent these forces from dragging the United States into the European war. And labor was the most logical organization to carry out such action:

> Labor being the one element in human society in an efficient state of organization and in full sympathy with the preservation of peace at home and the establishment of peace abroad, was appealed to for assistance in the establishment of an institution dedicated to the attainment of Universal Peace.

The appeal was not in vain. A force for peace had come into existence that could not be ignored. Now was the time for every worker to declare himself "for peace or war." Now was the time to organize local branches of Labor's National Peace Council, "in not only the large metropolitan centers, but in every city, town and village that can muster a sufficient number of peace advocates to establish a local council."[47]

Buchanan was jubilant over the results of his appeal. In a private letter in July 1915 he claimed a million members, and added that "everything now indicates that public sentiment as well as the hundreds of government officials have been powerfully influenced by the work of the Labor Peace Council." He even ventured the opinion that "the United States would have been involved in war before this time had it not been for the work of the Labor Peace Council."[48]*

*Despite his enthusiasm, Buchanan resigned as president of Labor's National Peace Council in August 1915, and was replaced by Jacob C. Taylor. Buchanan's successor was the fourth vice-president and a leader in the Cigar Makers' Union.

# GOMPERS AND THE "MUNITION STRIKES"

While there was no real basis for such sweeping assertions, it does appear that Labor's National Peace Council was making headway in a number of industrial regions.* Gompers was alarmed by reports of the council's "success," and began a campaign to apply pressure on all Federation members to sever their affiliations.[49] He accused the council of being pro-German and of doing the Kaiser's work by influencing longshoremen and seamen not to transport supplies to the Allies, and by stirring up and financing strikes in munitions plants.

As we have seen in a previous volume,** the "munitions strikes" of 1915, under the leadership of the International Association of Machinists and the International Association of Structural Iron Workers, converted Bridgeport, Connecticut from a ten-hour center to the eight-hour day. From Bridgeport, the strikes spread through New England as men and women munitions workers went out for the eight-hour day. In the summer of 1915, the strikes swept across the whole Northeast, establishing the eight-hour day in plant after plant.[50]

As the eight-hour movement swept the munitions plants, the headlines in the commercial press shrieked: "German Influence Behind Munition Strikes!"[51] The fact that John A. Johnson, international president of the Ironworkers and a leader of the strike in Bridgeport, was a member of the executive board of Labor's National Peace Council gave the press an opportunity to link the strikes with the labor peace movement. The *New York Times* reminded its readers that "Congressman Frank Buchanan, president of Labor's Peace Council, had appealed in the name of the Council to President Wilson to stop the exportation of arms to the Allies."*** What better way to accomplish this objective than by the "munition strikes"?[52]

Gompers added his voice to this chorus and was widely quoted as saying that "officers of international unions had received money to pull off strikes in Bridgeport and elsewhere for ammunition factories." Gompers denied that these were his exact words. What he said was "that authentic

---

*An attempt was made to unite with the National Grange and form a farmer-labor anti-war group, but the Grange backed out at the last minute. (*New York Times*, June 24, 1915.)

**See Foner, *History of the Labor Movement*, 6 (1982): 194-200.

***The *Times* also pointed out that Buchanan "is ex-president of the Structural Ironworkers, now in prison for participation in the dynamiting of the *Los Angeles Times* building." (*New York Times*, July 17, 1915. For the McNamara case, *see* Foner, *History of the Labor Movement 5. [1980]: 7-31.)*

information had come to me that efforts had been made to corrupt men for the purpose of having strikes inaugurated," and that the "corrupting influence has been conducted by agents of a foreign government."[53*]

Gompers did not spell out just who these "agents" were, but he implied that they were labor officials who were determined to enforce an embargo on the export of war supplies "in the mistaken belief that this was necessary to maintain the strict neutrality which alone could prevent American involvement in the war."[54] The statement aroused widespread anger in Bridgeport's labor circles. J. J. Kepler, vice-president of the International Association of Machinists and a leader in the strike movement, called a press conference and informed reporters:

> I do not want the public to get the impression that we are warring on the munition plants because we are the evangelists of any peace propaganda. That is rot as much as the German charge. We view the manufacture of arms just as we would the manufacture of any other product. . . . The manufacturers are profiting by the war in Europe; why should we not get something?[55]

Kepler informed reporters that he had written Gompers, enclosing his statement that "money was being used to force American strikes. I called on him to come here and prove something or shut up." Gompers, he noted, was trying to do for the employers what they "couldn't get away with." Asked if Gompers could play a role in settling the strike, Kepler shot back: "The best thing Mr. Gompers can settle is his own rash statements."[56]

At a meeting of the New York Central Federated Union, Gompers was sharply attacked by a number of delegates for having attributed "German influence" to strikes that were caused by "long hours of work, rents driven up and the fact that the cost of living had climbed." The CFU members also took offense at the implications that Labor's National Peace Council, of which the Federation was an important member, had "fostered strikes in plants making ammunition as a way of preventing American involvement in the European war." When a few delegates sought to defend Gompers on the ground that the "capitalist press" had distorted what he had said, they were reminded that while AFL secretary-treasurer Frank Morrison had tried to modify Gompers' charges, the AFL president had

---

*The "authentic information" came from Andrew Furuseth of the Sailors' Union of the Pacific. Furuseth related "that the Seamen and Longshoremen of NY and Vicinity were approached by agents from the German Government to inaugurate strikes among the men and that large financial inducements were offered." (Statement issued by Gompers, July 14-15, 1915, Gompers Papers, AFL Archives, State Historical Society of Wisconsin.)

never repudiated what had appeared in the press.*

The Central Federated Union then sent a letter to Gompers inquiring whether he had been correctly quoted as having stated that "officers of international unions had received money to pull off strikes in Bridgeport and elsewhere in ammunition factories." In his reply, Gompers declared that he had not actually included munition strikes in his original statement, but had referred only to seamen and longshoremen who were being paid not to load and move ships for European ports; that "the corrupting influence was being conducted by agents of a foreign Government, and that I had no doubt the same agencies and influences were at work elsewhere with the same purpose in view." The CFU rejected the reply as unsatisfactory doubletalk.[57]**

At this point, Gompers sought the aid of Ralph M. Easley of the National Civic Federation to substantiate his charges. Easley set up an investigating unit and requested funds from Henry P. Davidson of J.P. Morgan Company, who raised $25,000 by assessing $2,500 each from manufacturers who were making supplies for the Allies.[58] Actually, Gompers did not need evidence provided by the NCF-Morgan-sponsored investigation to convince himself. As his biographer points out: "Every strike among the seamen, longshoremen and munitions workers he believed or suspected to be the work of the Kaiser's agents, every peace meeting a secret plot to commit the United States to pro-German policies."[59]

## THE FRIENDS OF PEACE

While the investigation of the "munition strikes" was under way, Gompers launched an attack on another peace group, the Friends of Peace, which had been organized by German-Americans, Irish-Americans and a

---

*Morrison would not deny that "German influence might be behind the strikes in Bridgeport," but he stated that the "real trouble was a demand on the part of labor for better hours and more pay." (Foner 6: 195.)

**In a letter to the AFL Convention, International Association of Machinists Vermilion Lodge Number 473 expressed itself as being "thoroughly disgusted with the Policies of President Gompers" in attempting "to discredit the honest efforts which are being put forth in the Munition manufacturing plants by the I.A. of M. to secure shorter hours, better working conditions and a larger share of the profits. He asserts he has evidence to show that German interests are behind this movement. We have no such evidence but for that we care not. We are satisfied that the I.A. of M. has been making great gains in the past year in organization, shortening the hours, increasing wages and securing better working conditions. These gains have been made possible mainly through the demand from the European nations for munitions of war." (Frank Schafer, President, to the Officers and Delegates of the A.F. of L. Convention, Danville, Ill., Nov. 9, 1915, AFL Archives, State Historical Society of Wisconsin.)

scattering of non-ethnic pacifists opposed to U.S. entry into the war. The Friends of Peace called a National Peace Convention in Chicago for Labor Day, 1915.* The call stated that the convention was being organized because of the belief "in the existence of a preconceived plot to involve the United States in the European war." The object of the convention was "to urge the early convening of Congress for the purpose of considering an embargo on the exportation of war supplies. . . ." In a special letter to trade unions urging their leaders to sign the call and endorse the meeting, Frank MacDonald of the Western Federation of Miners and chairman of the Friends of Peace labor committee, wrote:

> In the terrible crisis facing this country it is the solemn duty of every American to work for peace. The working class gets from war only the dividends of death. We therefore call upon you, as a representative of the organized working class to use your best effort to make successful the convention to be held in Chicago on Labor Day by the Friends of Peace. . . .[60]

The list of union officials who signed the call, all of whom were affiliated with the AFL, was characterized as "impressive." They included Homer D. Call, president, New York State Federation of Labor; John Golden, president, United Textile Workers; Charles Dodd, president, Piano, Organ and Musical Instrument Workers' Union; Ernest Slattery, general organizer, Horseshoers' International Union; and John Sullivan, vice-president, United Brewery Workers.[61]

On June 10, 1915, the British ambassador in Washington wrote to the Foreign Office pointing in alarm to evidence that the peace movement was growing among American trade unionists and the call for an embargo on war supplies was winning wide labor support. He had faith, however, in Samuel Gompers, and urged that "means . . . be taken to bring home to him how fatal the action of the Labor Unions may be."[62] "Gompers," notes Simeon Larson, "was not to disappoint the Allies. Faced with

---

*The *New York Times* labeled the Friends of Peace "a German-American organization," listing as proposed speakers at the Chicago convention those who had obvious German-American names. It later conceded that William Jennings Bryan, Jane Addams, and four U.S. Senators were also scheduled to address the convention. (*New York Times*, July 19, 23, 1915.)

The letterhead of the Friends of Peace listed the following organizations as being represented: American Truth Society, American Independence Union, American Humanity League, American Women of German Descent, American Fair Play Society, Continental League, German-American Alliance of Greater New York, German Catholic Federation of New York, United Irish-American Societies, United Austrian & Hungarian-American Societies, Upholsterers' International Union, "and other American Societies."

increasing peace sentiment in unions, he used the full power at his command to retrieve many of the labor men caught in the pacifist net."[63] When these men wrote to Gompers asking whether they should endorse the call for the National Peace Convention in Chicago or participate in the gathering, he warned them "not to allow themselves to become the tools of German and Socialist propaganda." He charged that the Friends of Peace had "by insidious and false representation attempted to corrupt financially a large number of representatives among the union members of the United States."[64] He made the same point in responding to John Brisbe Walker, chairman of the National Committee of the Friends of Peace, who had urged him to give the Chicago meeting his "most earnest support." Gompers maintained that "paid emissaries of your 'Friends of Peace' have gone from city to city and by insidious and false representations attempted to financially corrupt a large number of representatives and men among the union workers of the United States. Unfortunately," he continued, "a number of workers have been cajoled into the belief that by attending your meeting they enlist themselves as friends of peace." Gompers concluded that he would do what he could to enlighten them as to the real purposes behind "your movement and your meeting, which is not peace, but . . . to place the people of the United States in a false position before the world, to play into the hands of one side of the waring [sic] nations as against the other."[65]

Gompers applied pressure upon union leaders who had endorsed the Chicago meeting to withdraw their approval. This brought the desired result. John Golden, president of the United Textile Workers, wrote to the Friends of Peace's Labor Committee that Gompers had convinced him that "this so-called Peace Movement is NOT all that the name implies." He gave notice "of my resignation from the Committee to take effect immediately, and that my name be stricken off any official letter heads of the Friends of Peace Association."[66] Homer D. Call, also resigned. Gompers had convinced him that "the movement is not in the best interests of either peace or the labor movement of this country."[67]

Apart from one or two union leaders associated with Labor's National Peace Council, no trade unionists spoke at the Chicago convention. Increasingly under attack as pro-German, the Friends of Peace had all but disappeared by the end of 1915.[68]

## THE COLLAPSE OF LABOR'S NATIONAL PEACE COUNCIL

On the heels of the demise of the Friends of Peace came the collapse of Labor's National Peace Council.

Early in September 1915, a grand jury in the Southern District of New York began investigating charges involving the violation of neutrality laws by Franz von Rintelen, a captain in the German navy, and officers of Labor's National Peace Council. For three months, the grand jury heard testimony presented by Secret Service agents, read letters of Labor's National Peace Council obtained by these agents, and heard testimony by men presently or formerly associated with the Peace Council. According to the records of the grand jury investigation in the National Archives, Franz von Rintelen, chief of German naval intelligence in the United States, and David Lamar, known as "the Wolf of Wall Street," had worked out the plan for the formation of Labor's National Peace Council with the aim of preventing the shipment of arms and other supplies to the Allies. Lamar had won over Frank Buchanan, who was known as "labor's chief champion on the floor of Congress." They had then brought in Henry B. Martin, former leader of the Knights of Labor and secretary of the Anti-Trust League. Buchanan and Martin formed the Chicago Labor Peace Council and arranged for the Peace Congress in Washington, D.C. where the National Council was organized. "Most of the delegates came in good faith," Secret Service agents testified, "convinced that they were serving a good cause", and with no idea that the meeting had been instigated by "agents of the Kaiser."[69]

Several other witnesses before the grand jury made the point that they had come in good faith. Ernest Bohm of the Central Federated Union of Greater New York and treasurer of Labor's National Peace Council until he resigned in the fall of 1915, testified that he and most of the other delegates had gone to Washington in order "to express labor's determination to keep the United States out of the European war. I repeat the object of our being there was to keep this country out of war." James J. McCracken, who represented the Hoisting and Portable Engineers Local Union No. 324 of Detroit, told the grand jury:

> . . . as far as I know the aims and the objects of the convention were legitimate in agitating universal sentiment to prevent American entrance into the war in Europe, thereby creating a universal appeal to the President of the United States by the people to bring about universal peace. That was the purpose as far as I and nearly all of the delegates understood it.[70]

Investigators for the Department of Justice testified that Labor's National Peace Council was not responsible for the "munition strikes" of 1915, but that it did help "materially" once the strikes began.[71] But other evidence presented revealed that Buchanan's reason for resigning as council president in August 1915 was his opposition to a resolution passed on August 1, 1915 to levy an assessment on each member "to use in defraying the support of any workman who may become involved in any strike or lockout for the purpose of paralyzing the private arms and munitions traffic in this country."[72]

On December 28, 1915, the grand jury indicted von Rintelen and seven men associated with Labor's National Peace Council: Congressman Frank Buchanan, former Council president; Jacob C. Taylor, his successor as president; H. Robert Fowler, former Illinois Congressman; Frank S. Monnett, ex-Attorney General of Ohio; David Lamar; Henry B. Martin, Council secretary and officer of the Anti-Trust League; and Herman Schutters, another officer of the Anti-Trust League. The eight defendants were indicted under the provisions of the Sherman Anti-Trust Act for "conspiring to prevent the manufacture and shipment of arms, ammunition, airplanes, automobiles, railway supplies, and other articles needed in modern warfare, from this country to Great Britain, France, and the nations allied with them." The grand jury charged that the defendants had conspired to instigate strikes in munitions factories and, at points where such material was being shipped, by bribing labor officials and by supplying workers with reading matter calculated to induce them to quit their jobs.[73*]

On May 20, 1917, over a month after the United States entered the war, and after a trial of twenty-three days in the Federal District Court of New York, von Rintelen, Lamar and Martin were found guilty and each sentenced to one year in federal penitentiary. Four of the men indicted were found not guilty. They were Frank Buchanan (defeated for re-election to Congress in 1916); H. Robert Fowler, Jacob C. Taylor, and Herman Schutters. Frank S. Monnett was originally one of the eight defendants, but the indictment against him had been dismissed.[74]

Long before the trial of the eight defendants had begun, Labor's National Peace Council had disappeared. All of the labor men associated with the movement had hurriedly resigned immediately after the grand jury handed down its indictment.[75]

In September 1917, Buchanan said of Labor's National Peace Council:

There may have been German agents in Labor's National Peace Council, just

---

*The point about the "reading matter" appears to have been based on a letter written on stationery of Labor's National Peace Council by a council representative who had met with munition workers. "I talked to them," he wrote, and gave them our literature and the intelligent ones were heartily in accord with the movement." (C. J. Cundiff to H. Martin, Ilinon, N.Y., Aug. 8, 1915, in records of *U.S. v. Rintelen, Buchanan et al.*, Criminal Case, U.S. District Court for the Southern District of New York, National Archives.)

as there are crooks in the trade union movement and in all organizations who would use the organization for their purposes. No true, substantial American, however, would permit himself to be used by agents from outside the United States or by interests other than American interests. The trade unionists who joined Labor's National Peace Council and worked for it, did so because they sincerely believed that the policy of opposing the shipment to Europe of munitions of war and the policy calling for Government manufacture of munitions, deserved the support of the entire labor movement as the best and surest way to keep the United States out of the war in Europe. The men who prosecuted me in New York on the charge of conspiracy to foment strikes and obstruct commerce produced false evidence, but were unable to obtain a conviction.[76]

## THE 1915 AFL CONVENTION

The prosecutors had, however, succeeded in stigmatizing labor's activities for peace with the label of "German espionage," and this partially vindicated Gompers' charge that many of labor's peace advocates were wittingly or unwittingly "tools of the Kaiser." The commercial press predicted that with the debacle of Labor's National Peace Council, few trade unionists would be willing to continue to work for peace.[77]

At first glance it appeared that this conclusion was justified. Thus, at the 1915 AFL convention in San Francisco, the delegates adopted a resolution recommended by the Committee on International Relations, of which Gompers was a member, which upheld the right of the United States to ship munitions to belligerents, and explained "it was impossible to distinguish munitions of war and the ordinary articles of commerce." The committee's report called attention to the efforts made by some groups to "use the workingmen of our country to further the interests of some foreign country. . . . Foreign agencies have been trying to reach corruptly some of the organizations of the workers," the report said, "but they have not succeeded."[78]

At one point in the convention, however, a resolution was introduced that called for the elimination of militarist propaganda from the public schools. It included the provision: "that we [the Convention] call upon the workers to desist from affiliating with any branch of the military forces." A heated debate followed which covered seven-and-a-half pages of fine type in the Convention proceedings. It would have continued much longer had not the late hour necessitated the evacuation of the convention hall.

The arguments of those who favored the motion may be paraphrased as follows:

> The AFL has had a long anti-militarist history. It has contended for many years that large armaments helped to provoke wars. Has not this contention been verified by recent European events? It is Morgan, Rockefeller, and men of their kind who are most active in the preparedness campaign. These are the men who derive the greatest profit from wars. They will not go to the trenches; they will let the workers do that. They desire the United States to be prepared so that they may plunge it into war when it will be profitable to do so.
>
> America cannot seriously have fears of invasion. Even the victorious European nations will be in a very weak economic and military condition at the end of the war. How will they be able to come 3,000 miles to attack the United States?
>
> American labor should not be fooled into demanding vengeance for the sinking of the *Lusitania*. It should not forget that it has suffered just as fearful crimes at home for which no restitution has been made. One has only to recall Ludlow and Michigan. Should not redress be demanded first for those murdered by our own military forces?[79]

At one point in the debate, Samuel Gompers left his chair as presiding officer and addressed the delegates. He stated that he had been a pacifist all his life. "I looked forward to the time . . . that if we could not prevent war in any other way the workers would refuse to go to war. I lived under that impression for about forty years of my life." However, when he saw the workers of England, Russia, Austria, Germany, and France supporting their own governments in war, he became disillusioned, and he had to revise his "judgement on questions of international peace and war." He urged the delegates to follow him in the switch from pacifism, and defeat the proposed resolution.[80]

The delegates did vote down the resolution. But the debate at the 1915 AFL convention was the prologue to a much wider discussion in hundreds of labor groups over the issue of military preparedness.

# CHAPTER 3

# Organized Labor and Preparedness

When Congress assembled in December 1915, President Wilson made patriotism and preparedness the keynotes of his annual message. He called for passage of what was to become the National Defense Act of 1916, which provided for the expansion of the regular army, a greatly augmented National Guard, and the creation of a new reserve Continental Army of 400,000 men.[1]

In the speeches he delivered travelling from New York City to St. Louis between January 22 and February 3, 1916, Wilson called for endorsement of his preparedness program. Without military power, he declared, it would not be possible to defend the national honor. Preparedness, he maintained, was not a partisan issue, but a national necessity.[2]

## GOMPERS ENDORSES PREPAREDNESS

Wilson immediately received the support of Samuel Gompers, who became the leading labor supporter of preparedness. Gompers presented a comprehensive statement of his views at the meeting of the National Civic Federation in Washington in January, 1916, and his speech was reprinted as a government document.

After asserting that most of the American people accepted the need for a preparedness program, Gompers went on to develop the theme that such a program must not only include armaments, but must also encompass such vital services as health and education (including physical training), so that the people would be imbued with a spirit of loyalty to their country and a willingness to sacrifice for its protection. Such a spirit, he insisted, could not exist unless the people were assured of equal opportunities and justice for all. To ensure this, it was necessary to recognize the importance of the organizations of workers, not only in determining individual policies but also in directing the political and military agencies that would control the preparedness program.

In a series of editorials that appeared in the *American Federationist* at about the same time, Gompers advanced his views on physical training. "War is a test of physical fitness and of the organization of material resources," he argued, (sounding very much like Theodore Roosevelt) "and the nation that has failed in these can pay dearly. . . ." He also interpreted American history in the light of the nation's preparedness: "Life on the frontier developed virile manhood. . . . But the frontier has vanished. Some definite policy must be devised for physical training. . . ."[3]

As one solution, Gompers advocated recruiting workers for military training in summer camps along the lines of the "Plattsburgh idea," in which the U.S. Army and members of the business community jointly set up summer training camps in 1915 and 1916 in various parts of the country, modeled on the camp in upstate New York. The "Plattsburgh idea" emphasized the training of future U.S. Army officers and was geared to preparing the American people for the "inexorable facts of war" and the total mobilization of the nation for the "inevitable entrance of the United States into the European war."

Although in theory the camps were open to everyone, in practice they were dominated by members of the country's upper classes. This was true not only because the recruits had to have six weeks free time in the summer and paid their own expenses, but also because of the educational and social requirements which were quite consciously set up to exclude all but successful businessmen.[4]

Most trade unionists viewed the "Plattsburgh idea," with its emphasis on total national mobilization, as a threat to the labor movement and as vastly increasing the danger of U.S. involvement in the war.[5] But none of this concerned Gompers. In a letter to General Leonard Wood, who was in charge of the camps, he noted that he saw only one thing wrong with the program—the camps were available only to the well-to-do instead of being "open to all." Since trade unionists "are unable to pay their own expenses and give their services without compensation," Gompers called upon the government to pay for their training. This would not only provide the armed forces with a "group of men that has more practice and ability in organizing and disciplining men" than any other, but it would remove "one of the great difficulties in the way of securing the participation of working men in preparedness."[6]

Once he had publicly announced his support for preparedness, Gompers had to answer his critics. He assured them that if they had interpreted his statements to mean that he favored "militarism and [an] ill-advised effort to rush into war," they had "totally misunderstood" his position. "In fact," he wrote, "preparedness means just the opposite." In his view, "preparedness is not a narrow purpose that deals only with war and militarism. . . . Preparedness has to do with physical development, intellectual training and education that are preparatory for all activities of civilian life." Preparedness, in short, led to "freedom" whereas militarism resulted in "repression."[7]

But many trade unionists were not deceived. The San Francisco *Labor Clarion* declared:

> The people have acquired a certain rudimentary education; they have a knowledge, if not a very extensive one, about the social forces that make for war. The people know by this time who pays the bills in all wars, be they victorious or losing, and they also know who it is who gathers the benefits of these wars. They are getting too wise, and, to use a popular expression, would not any longer "fall" for an open advocacy of war. So a new name for the old thing had to be invented, and that new name is "Preparedness." However, to paraphrase Shakespeare, a sewer by any other name would smell just as bad.
>
> There is no doubt that this preparedness humbug is the cloak and mantle for militarism, and all efforts of Samuel Gompers and other champions of preparedness to sell it to the working class by hiding its real purpose, will fail.[8]

Actually, Gompers' support of preparedness did influence a number of unions to rally behind Wilson's program. Some unions even shifted positions to line up behind the AFL president.*

## LABOR ADVOCATES OF PREPAREDNESS

A segment of organized labor did advocate preparedness. A major reason emphasized by these unions was the danger that an unprepared America would be at the mercy of whichever side won the war. "What will be the situation if Germany emerges from the conflict as master of Europe," the Metal Polishers asked, "or if Germany is crushed and England and Japan rule the roost? . . . ." "To rely on raw troops to meet such legions, is sheer madness," added the Plumbers. "For the United States to remain unprepared," the Shoe Workers warned, "is to invite European militarists to endanger our liberties."[9]

*Prior to Gompers' public support of preparedness, the Cigar Makers took the position that opposition to preparedness was subversive only to "the plutocrats . . . [and] profit mongers in war materials." But once Gompers publicly championed preparedness, they changed their tune and called preparedness "preordained and inevitable." The only problem still to be resolved was for labor to "have some voice in the kind, quality, and quantity it [should] be." (*Cigar Makers' Official Journal*, 39 [Dec., 1915]: 2; 40 [Feb. 1916]: 2; Simeon Larson, "The American Federation of Labor and the Preparedness Campaign," *Historian* 37 [Nov. 1974]: 79.)

Another argument advanced by the labor advocates of preparedness was that war was inevitable, that there was no choice but for the United States to prepare. "There have been wars since Adam and there will be wars to come," declared the Metal Polishers. "We should be prepared for emergencies." The Molders warned that "so long as we have nations still contending for things as of old, so long must we be up and prepared." Neither union mentioned that their members stood to gain economically from an increase in shipbuilding and cannon making.[10]

Finally, labor advocates of preparedness pointed to German submarine warfare as an insult to the United States that might require a military response. "We want peace," declared the Metal Polishers, "but we don't want peace at any price." "We want peace," echoed Arthur B. Garretson, president of the Order of Railway Conductors, "but we must be able to maintain our rights and insure the safety of our citizens on the high seas. We must prepare."[11] That Great Britain was stopping ships, blockading the seas, and searching mail was never mentioned.

## LABOR OPPOSITION TO PREPAREDNESS

Military journals went to great pains to reprint Gompers' statements in favor of preparedness and editorials in the labor press that supported an increase in the armed forces. But these reprints were usually accompanied by the regretful comment that unfortunately the "majority of component parts of the American Federation of Labor are unwilling to follow the patriotic leadership of Mr. Gompers and continue to oppose preparedness." Included in this "majority" were "the unions with the largest membership, many State Federations of Labor and city central labor unions, all of whom are especially outspoken in their opposition to preparedness."[12]

This picture of labor's opposition to preparedness was corroborated from other sources. In its issue of April 8, 1916, the *Literary Digest* featured a report entitled "Labor's Dread of Preparedness." The trade unions throughout the country were reported to be taking a referendum vote on preparedness, and the article presented some of the results. By an overwhelming majority—4,432 to 565—about one-half the local unions affiliated with the Cleveland Federation of Labor voted "to condemn the militaristic schemes that the statesmen at Washington are endeavoring to foist upon this country." Similar polls taken in Spokane, Washington and Allentown, Pennsylvania revealed that an overwhelming majority of trade unionists opposed preparedness as a measure designed to involve the country in the European war.[13]

In June 1916, the *New Republic* conducted its own survey of the attitude in labor circles toward preparedness. It reported that the majority view-point ranged between "cold indifference and opposition to the mobiliza-tion of the United States war strength."[14] An eastern state labor leader took an unofficial poll of the state federations of labor and central labor unions throughout the country. The results indicated practically unanimous oppo-sition to any plan to significantly enlarge the standing army or increase army or navy expenditures.[15]

These revelations did not surprise James Lord, president of the AFL Mine Department. He had found in his travels through the country that preparedness propaganda left the average workingman "cold and sullen." "There is something fundamental in all these military schemes," Lord concluded, "for which he [the worker] cannot stand."[16]

## LABOR'S ANTI-PREPAREDNESS ARGUMENTS

Labor opponents of preparedness stressed several reasons for their opposition. Foremost was the conviction that preparedness led to war. "Preparedness," warned John P. White, president of the United Mine Workers, "did not prevent the war in Europe and everything seems to indi-cate that preparedness makes for war."[17] The Machinists warned that "a country which carries a large standing army and navy is like a school boy with a chip on his shoulder, always courting trouble. . . . If the masters of the country want preparedness let them go to war, but let the working class prepare their unions so that they will not be led into slaughter as their brothers in Europe have been.[18] The Musicians declared that "preparing for war to insure peace is about as logical as to saturate wood in oil to protect against fire; preparing for war means war."[19] The Teamsters also emphasized that preparedness led to war and called on labor to "express itself at every meeting held or at every assembly against any attempt on the part of our government to involve this country in the conflict."[20] The Pressmen endorsed the proposal, noting: "Organized labor cannot be true to its principles unless it voices its total opposition to any plan to increase the nation's armed forces. To this end it should voice its opposition to pre-paredness in meetings, petitions, and demonstrations."[21]

Other labor anti-preparedness arguments emphasized that preparedness was an excuse to militarize the United States, to increase profits, to expand U.S. investments abroad, and to crush labor. The Railroad Main-tenance Employees noted that the "military system is used at the slightest provocation to club and shoot the toilers into submission," and the larger army and navy that would emerge from the preparedness campaign "will be used against labor at home and for the protection of overseas investments abroad."[22] "Is it not a coincidence," asked the Locomotive Firemen, "that certain gentlemen prominently identified with the preparedness campaign are also connected with large industrial concerns that would profit hugely from preparedness?"[23]

The Fur Workers warned that it was the "working class against whom the military forces called for by President Wilson will be used." "Big business wants a huge army and navy," declared the Firemen, "because they are now planning a campaign of world conquest." The Switchmen charged that "preparedness fairly reeks with the smell of private profit," while the Illinois State Federation of Labor denounced preparedness advocates as "profit-seeking war traffickers."[24]

The Pressmen doubted if any preparedness advocates would be willing to volunteer their personal services in case of war because "most of them are interested in the building of battleships or the manufacture of arms, ammunition and other war supplies." To this, James H. Maurer, president of the Pennsylvania State Federation of Labor, added that one of the reasons the munitions manufacturers wanted to see preparedness adopted was that they "are not selling for cash but on credit," and they feared that the European purchasers would refuse to pay their bills after the war ended. "Then a big army and navy would be a good thing. . . . They would like to send our workingmen across as collectors for them!"

"Just why is big business behind the preparedness campaign?" asked the official organ of the Railway Carmen. "The answer is easy," it declared, and went on to charge big business with desiring intervention throughout the world. Big business wanted cheap labor, cheap raw materials, and surplus profits, and it would do anything to get them.

> Foreign invasion is a myth.
> The real question is this:
> Do you prefer to take your chances with an imaginary European enemy who is sure to be economically exhausted and sickened of militarism?
> Or do you prefer to give your assent while this democracy is conquered from within by Act of Congress?
> For if there's any difference between U.S. Steel, or Standard Oil and the worst military ruling class in Europe, the advantage is all with the latter, as far as democracy, liberty and the rights of man are concerned. Remember Youngstown, Bayonne, and Colorado.*

*For the bloody strikes Youngstown and Bayonne, see Philip S. Foner, *History of the Labor Movement in the United States 6* (New York, 1982): 25-64. For the bitter battle in Colorado, see 5 (New York, 1980): 196-213.

The editorial concluded with a quotation from Rear Admiral Chadwick: "Navies and armies are insurance for the wealth of the leisure class of a nation, invested abroad."[25]

"Remember Youngstown, Bayonne, and Colorado!" The memories of industrial battles of the past were constantly revived in the labor press "as a reminder to the workingman of the dangers of an America rearmed." When officers of the California National Guard sought permission to address San Francisco unions on preparedness, the secretary of the labor council told them "not to waste their time; union men had not forgotten the role of the National Guardsmen in the Ludlow massacre."[26*]

The anti-preparedness forces in the labor movement questioned the validity of the argument that preparedness was needed because the United States would be susceptible to attack by one of the belligerent nations after the war. The United Mine Workers pointed out that these countries would need "at least a generation to recover their strength." Since Mexico was wracked by revolution and Canada was a peaceful neighbor, it asked, "why this talk of monster armies?" "Do you prefer to take your chances with an imaginary European enemy who is due to be economically exhausted and sickened of militarism," queried the Firemen, "or else to give your assent [to preparedness] while this democracy is conquered within?" The Pressmen observed: "How silly this hue and cry about preparation . . . it will take Europe fifty years to recover from the war . . . why should we fear attack?"[27]

A number of unions took the word "preparedness" and gave it a different meaning than military usage. The California State Federation of Labor urged:

> The preparedness slogan of organized workers should be "Education, Organization, and Federation." This is the only war cry that will win the workers' battles. It is the only kind of "preparedness" propaganda from which the workers may expect substantial or worthwhile returns.[28]

The Central Federated Union of New York endorsed a resolution demanding, not a bigger and stronger army and navy, but "a bigger and stronger labor movement." It went on "to urge each labor union to prepare its members for a period of increased activity in a determined effort for better economic conditions and the uplift of trade unions."[29] The Milwaukee Federated Trades Council informed the Security League:

*For the Ludlow massacre, see Foner, ibid., pp. 204-08; 212-13.

We are for preparedness of a workday that will not exhaust the worker's vitality and a wage that will enable him to rear his family in comfort, without depriving his children of their childhood heritage.

We would prepare our nation's defenses by keeping its children from being stunted in mine and mill and factory. We would prepare it by making industry less hazardous than war.[30]

In the midst of the preparedness debate, the IWW took its stand, declaring: "We condemn all wars, and, for the prevention of such, we proclaim the anti-militaristic propaganda in times of peace . . . and, in time of war, the General Strike in all industry."[31] The "anti-militaristic propaganda" was based on a single argument, namely, that only the trusts and monopoly capitalists stood to gain by preparedness:

A larger army and navy is wanted by the capitalist class for two purposes: First, to protect the foreign markets that they are gobbling up while the workers of Europe are busy slaughtering each other at the command of their masters who are so busy directing this catastrophe that they cannot attend to "trade"; second, to suppress the rising and threatening revolution of the wage-slaves who are becoming desperate because of frequent "layoffs," starvation wages and the uncertainty of securing enough of the necessaries of life on which to exist.

Preparedness, in short, is a blinding of the real issue. The real issue is to establish an army and navy sufficiently large or strong enough to protect the merchant vessels of the United States in the furthering and enlarging of the foreign market.

In any event, to the Wobblies the preparedness issue was purely a capitalist problem: "'National defense' does not concern the working class as they have no country to defend."[32] Or as Elizabeth Gurley Flynn put it: "Let those who own the country, who are howling for and profit by preparedness, fight to defend their property."[33]

The *Industrial Union News*, official organ of the Detroit IWW*, also took the position that:

National defense does not concern the working class as they have no country to defend. . . . The country is owned by the master class. . . . Let the masters defend their country themselves. . . . Those who voluntarily enlist in the services of the master class . . . are known as soldiers and sailors. . . . A soldier or sailor from the ranks of labor is a traitor to his class. . . .[34]

*From 1908 until 1915 there were two Industrial Workers of the World—one in Detroit and one in Chicago. The Detroiters were Daniel De Leon and a group of his followers who had been expelled from the original IWW at the fourth annual convention in 1908. (*See* Philip S. Foner, *History of the Labor Movement in the United States 4* [New York, 1965]: 108-12).

# THE PREPAREDNESS DAY PARADES

In the spring and summer of 1916, pro-preparedness forces, led by business groups, planned a nationwide series of parades to pressure Congress to pass a series of bills to increase the size of the army and navy. Preparedness parades were staged in every large city and many smaller ones. Despite appeals to their patriotism and the urgings of Gompers, organized labor, in the main, refused to take part in any of the Preparedness Day parades.

A labor historian has pointed out that "the country's strongest union center, Chicago, witnessed the largest Preparedness Day parade."[35] This parade was held on June 3, 1916, and the *International Socialist Review* (whose account influenced the historian) was so impressed by the outpouring of workers that, though its sentiments were anti-preparedness, it expressed admiration:

> Never before has working class power been massed anywhere in the United States since the Civil War as on this day. . . . Though the occasion was a Preparedness Day Parade, engineered and dominated by the economic masters of Chicago, it was a good and proper time for every live working class fellow to look at the marching platoons passing by hour after hour and gazing on miles and miles of workingmen moving elbow to elbow, then say to himself:
>
> "Here's power! This is a human Niagara. If we can only harness this up to a solidarity of action. . . ."[36]

Strangely, the *International Socialist Review*, itself published in Chicago, failed to point out several truly significant facts about the parade in that city. One was that the Chicago Federation of Labor opposed the parade and urged all trade unionists not to participate. The Federation noted that organized labor "has found, at Ludlow alone, military oppression to be a greater menace and evil than any possible foreign invasion." Since the proponents of preparedness in Congress had refused "to forbid the use of the army in labor disputes," the Federation concluded that "the intention becomes clear to use the army against American workers." Under the present economic system, the Federation warned, a great army and navy "would be a powerful instrument for the conversion of the country into a commercial oligarchy."[37]*

---

*The Chicago Federation of Labor also passed a resolution opposing a trip to Washington by a delegation of 200 Illinois business men to show Congress that the "people back home" were in favor of preparedness. The Federation informed Congress that organized labor's opposition to preparedness expressed "the true wishes of the people." (*The Public* 19 [April 26, 1916]: 394.)

The second fact about the parade not mentioned in the *International Socialist Review* was that unorganized workers were "being compelled to march without their wishes being consulted."[38] In a statement signed by officials of the Carpenters and Joiners, Painters and Decorators, Brewery, Machinists, Electrical, Structural Iron, and Civil Service Workers' unions, Chicago employers were accused of threatening workers who were not union members with loss of jobs if they did not sign a pledge to march in the parade.[39] This charge was supported by *The Public*, a liberal, single-tax Chicago weekly, which published a letter sent to all employers in the Chicago area by the president of the Illinois Manufacturers' Association, the organization heading the business group planning the Preparedness Day parade. The letter asked the employer "to inquire of each of your employees whether or not he or she will march," and "to promptly fill out the enclosed card giving the details as to the number of men and women you can furnish, thereby helping the Illinois Manufacturers' Association, with other organizations in Chicago, to make the parade a big success."

"In short," *The Public* concluded, "most workers will be compelled to march or face the loss of their jobs. To avert this real danger, not the imaginary one (of foreign invasion), they will help swell the parade. And the preparationist press, with little regard for the facts, will report the affair as a spontaneous and voluntary movement."[40]

Unfortunately, so did the anti-preparedness *International Socialist Review*. The *Review*, however, published the fact that as the marchers passed the Lake View Building, they saw a sign in front of the building, hung by Captain Horace B. Wild, a Spanish-American war veteran and a member of the U.S. Army Aeronautical Reserves. The sign read: "Five million farmers and a half million mine workers are against what you and Wall Street are marching for."[41]

Wild was arrested and booked on the charge of "disorderly conduct." The following day the Chicago *Tribune* carried the story of Wild's arrest under the headline, "Treason!" Two weeks earlier, it had used the same heading over its report of the action taken by the Chicago Federation of Labor that urged all trade unionists not to participate.[42]

Despite appeals to their patriotism and the risk of being accused of "Treason," organized labor refused to take part in any of the Preparedness Day parades. The Minneapolis Trades and Labor Assembly and the Building Trades Council, which included practically all of organized labor in the city, labeled the preparedness campaign the work of a "few millionaires who arm the country," and whose private armies "at every opportunity have murdered and slain the workers." They jointly called upon their affiliated unions not to participate in Preparedness Day parades.[43] The Industrial Council of Kansas City, Missouri declared itself "unalterably opposed" to the preparedness parade and requested that no Kansas City labor organization participate. In a similar vein, the St. Louis Central Trades voted 133 to 42 against participating in a preparedness parade.[44]

In New York City, the Central Federated Trades came out against the preparedness parade and urged all affiliated unions not to participate. Moreover, some sixty unions who had joined together to form the Anti-Militarist Labor Conference gave the answer to the Preparedness Day parade with a counter-parade.[45*]

In the Northwest, the Central Labor Council of Seattle declared that "various interests in this community, and more especially the press, are seeking to stampede our citizens on the question of preparedness and are endeavoring to divert our attention from the greater enemies of the workers inside our borders to our lesser enemies in foreign lands. . . ." The council, therefore, called upon

> all trade unionists and truly patriotic citizens to refrain from parading or participation of any kind in demonstrations which can have no other result than to thwart the cool, calm and deliberate judgment which is so necessary to the proper solution of this question.[46]

## THE SAN FRANCISCO PARADE

Nowhere did a Preparedness Day parade arouse so much controversy as in the San Francisco Bay area. Sponsored by the Chamber of Commerce and supported by the leading industries in the area, it was opposed by AFL, IWW, and Socialist Party organizations as a scheme to weaken American neutrality, drag the United States into the European war, and furnish more troops to suppress strikes.[47] In an effort to win over San Francisco trade unionists, the Chamber of Commerce and the Pacific Coast Defense League declared their opposition "to using militia for strike duty," and obtained a promise from a number of Western governors,

*A major aim of the counter-parade was to demand the defeat in the state legislature of "The Bloody Five," bills proposed by Governor C. S. Whitman for compulsory army service. Among other things, "The Bloody Five" would enroll all men of military age in the militia, and require all unemployed boys between 16 and 19 years of age to attend summer military schools. The Anti-Militarist Labor Conference, the Central Federated Union of New York, and the American Union Against Militarism joined forces to oppose the legislation, distributing literature which urged all citizens, and especially workers, to "Arouse . . . before the military shackles have so tightened about you, that to object to them means a court-martial and a firing squad." But, without even a single hearing, the state legislature passed the proposed bills into law. (New York *Call*, July 18, 28, Sept. 12, Oct. 29, 1916.)

including Hiram Johnson of California, that they would not so use it. But organized labor in San Francisco stood firm in opposition to the Preparedness Day parade.[48]

One reason that the trade unions remained unconvinced was that the parade was identified with the latest of many open-shop drives sponsored by the San Francisco Chamber of Commerce. In the midst of the first unified coast-wide waterfront strike—which began on June 1, 1916, when approximately 10,000 longshoremen walked out in all major Pacific ports—the San Francisco Chamber of Commerce's Board of Directors threw down a challenge not only to the longshoremen, but to the entire local labor movement. In its publication, *Law and Order in San Francisco: A Beginning*, the Chamber proclaimed that it favored "the open shop and insists upon the right to employ union men or non-union men in whole or in part, as the parties involved may elect . . ."[49] On July 10, twelve days before the Chamber of Commerce-sponsored Preparedness Day parade, the Chamber held a special meeting to which employers throughout the city were invited. To the two thousand businessmen who responded, Frederick J. Koster, Chamber president, declared that the time had come to stamp out "that disease permeating this community, of which the waterfront situation is at present the most outstanding manifestation."[50]

Out of the meeting, which was also addressed by executives of the Bank of California, the Southern Pacific Railroad, and California's largest canning corporation, emerged the Law and Order Committee, which was to spearhead the open-shop drive. When Chamber of Commerce President Koster asked for money to support the Law and Order Committee's open-shop campaign, the business community quickly pledged $500,000.[51]

These developments intensified organized labor's opposition to the Preparedness Day parade. Added to the fact that the Chamber of Commerce and the Pacific Coast Defense League (a strong anti-union employer unit in the Chamber) were the sponsors of the parade and in charge of the preparations, the announcement that Thornwell Mullally, second-in-command of the United Railroads and a long-time open-shop advocate was to be the grand marshal, served to increase opposition in trade union circles. As Robert Knight points out: "The parade thus became a symbol of the cleavage between San Francisco's business leadership and organized labor. . . ."[52]

Central labor councils on both sides of the bay voted resolutions attacking the planned parade. Conservative and Socialist union leaders buried their differences and formed a United Committee which sent out circulars to union members appealing: "Do not march . . . do not let your employers coerce you. . . ." This was a reference to notices appearing in all stores, places of business, and factories reading: "Continued Peace Through Preparedness. Join the March of the Patriots—Join, March and Show Your Colors." Reports from workers poured into the Central Labor Council that "and keep your jobs!" was added verbally.

On Thursday, July 20, the United Committee held a "peace demonstration" at Dreamland Rink. A capacity crowd of more than 5,000 poured into the Rink, and a second overflow meeting was held outside. The San Francisco *Bulletin* reported that "the great gathering developed into one of the most remarkable crusades against the war spirit that has occurred anywhere."[54]

The two meetings heard speakers denounce the Preparedness Day parade, militarism, the United Railroads, other public utility corporations, the Chamber of Commerce, and the Law and Order Committee. Paul Scharenberg, secretary of the California State Federation of Labor, told the huge audiences:

> I am proud of the fact that labor in America refuses to be stampeded toward militarism in any form.
>
> I am even more proud in the knowledge that organized labor in San Francisco will not participate in any parade led by Thornwall Mullally, the notorious enemy of labor and the successful disrupter of a local union.
>
> This great republic may have foes abroad, but some of its most deadly enemies are to be found right at home. They are the industrial vampires who undermine the nation's vitality by cruel, merciless exploitation of labor. Starvation wages and long, enervating hours of toil are imposed upon millions of American toilers, of whom one-third are poverty-stricken all the year round. So deplorable are conditions in the big industrial centers that nearly 20 per cent of the nation's school children are constantly underfed and undernourished, and the babies of the poor die three times as fast as those of the rich. Yet they have the nerve to ask organized labor to take part in military preparedness parades designed to intimidate some unknown foreign foe when the known foes of the nation, who live among us, are brazenly taking the lead in those demonstrations.
>
> Let us prepare against poverty, disease, industrial accidents, unemployment and exploitation.[55]

On Friday night, July 21, the eve of the parade, the labor council adopted a resolution which had just been passed by the San Francisco Building Trades Council:

> Whereas . . . because united labor is opposed to the fostering of the war

spirit by "preparedness parades," an attempt may be made by the enemies of labor to cause a violent disturbance during . . . the parade and charge that disturbance to labor. . . .

Therefore, be it resolved: That in order to forestall any possible frame-up of this character . . . we hereby caution all union men and women . . . to be especially careful and make no other protest than their silent non-participation. . . .[56]

The rather unusual resolution had been introduced because various groups in the business community had been receiving anonymous letters threatening violent reprisals if the parade were held.[57] Fearing that a huge frame-up of militant trade unionists was in the making, the Central Labor Council and the Building Trades Council had taken precautions to warn San Francisco workers to be on their guard.

It was soon to become clear just how justified these warnings were. On Saturday, July 22, 1916, at 1:30 p.m., the Preparedness Day parade got under way. As a result of the boycott of the parade by virtually the entire labor movement of San Francisco, instead of the expected 100,000 marchers, only 22,000 actually took part, mostly "non-union workers." In general, there was an observable lack of enthusiasm among the participants.

The paraders took an hour to march about a mile from the starting point at the Embarcadero, San Francisco's waterfront. A few minutes after 2 p.m., an explosion rocked the intersection of Market and Steuart Streets, one block up from the Embarcadero. A bomb had gone off in the midst of a dense crowd of paraders and bystanders and left eight dead and forty wounded, scattered along the pavement.[58]

The tragic event was followed by one of the most infamous, calculated miscarriages of justice in U.S. history—the frame-up of Tom Mooney and Warren Billings.

# CHAPTER 4

# The Mooney-Billings Frame-up

## PRELUDE TO A FRAME-UP

A series of strange events followed the bomb explosion on July 22, 1916. At 2:46 p.m., the sidewalks and the walls at the scene of the crime were cleaned up by the police and fire departments, thus erasing all marks that would indicate the direction of the explosive forces. This helped the prosecution to frame its theories of the crime.

At 3:30 that same afternoon, District Attorney Charles A. Fickert, who had the backing of the United Railways, arrived at the scene with Frederick Colburn, manager of the San Francisco Clearing House and secretary of the San Francisco Bankers' Association. Colburn used a sledge hammer to enlarge the holes both in the sidewalk and the walls, thereby further altering the physical effects of the explosion.[1]

As a result of the actions taken so soon after the explosion, reliable evidence which might have connected the crime with its perpetrators was destroyed. This early pattern of deliberate frame-up (which some scholars, refusing to confront the real facts, have called just plain stupidity)[2] continued. At 9:30 on the evening of the explosion, District Attorney Fickert assigned Martin Swanson, a former Pinkerton and since then a private utilities detective, to the bomb case as a special investigator.[3]*

The frame-up also operated on another front. Immediately after the bomb explosion, Frederick J. Koster, president of the Chamber of Commerce, announced dramatically: "This outrage is another expression of the disease our Law and Order Committee has started out to combat." Posting a $5,000 reward for the apprehension of the murderers, the Law and Order Committee unhesitatingly linked organized labor to the crime,

*Although he was actually in charge of the bomb investigation, Swanson's name never appeared in the press.

charging that recent strikes in San Francisco had "logically terminated in the damnable outrage on Saturday."[4]

The frame-up was thrown together rapidly. By July 26, a mere five days after the explosion, five people had been arrested without warrants: Thomas J. Mooney and his wife Rena, Warren K. Billings, Israel Weinberg, and Edward D. Nolan.[5]

## TOM MOONEY: MILITANT TRADE UNIONIST

When Chamber of Commerce president Koster spoke at the meeting that gave birth to the San Francisco Law and Order Committee of "that disease permeating the community," one of the most "infectious" elements he had in mind was a militant local trade union leader named Thomas J. Mooney.

Tom Mooney was the eldest son of his Irish-born mother, Mary. His American-born father, Bernard Mooney, was a coal miner and one of the first organizers for the Knights of Labor. Tom Mooney became a self-educated militant trade unionist and Socialist—an advocate of industrial unionism and of the class struggle. He was also an uncompromising proponent for a change in the conservative labor leadership, an attitude that did little to endear him to most San Francisco union leaders. He joined the Socialist Party when he was twenty-five, and gained some national attention as a speaker and fund-raiser while traveling through the country with the "Red Special," the campaign train of Eugene V. Debs in the presidential election of 1908.[6*]

While Mooney held membership in the AFL Molders' Union, he was also active for several months in the IWW, but resigned. In 1909, he settled in San Francisco, mainly to woo and marry Rena Hermann, a local music teacher and Socialist with whom he had fallen in love. Elected a delegate in 1912 to the International Molders' Union convention as a representative of the San Francisco local, Mooney fought for "a militant industrial union" that would unite not only skilled molders but all foundry workers. Although his proposal failed, it brought praise from William Z. Foster.[7]

Soon after his return from the 1912 molders' convention, Mooney volunteered to help the shoe workers in a strike against the San Francisco

---

*"Mooney," Debs wrote after the election, "is one of the most active workers in the labor movement. He is absolutely honest and trustworthy and is filled with energy and ambition to better the class. Comrade Mooney is worthy of any position he may wish to hold in the labor movement and I cheerfully commend him to the Comrades and Friends as one of the best types of the Awakened American Proletariat." (*International Socialist Review* 10 [May, 1910]: 1052.)

firm of Frank & Hyman. There he met Warren K. Billings for the first time. The twenty year-old shoe worker had just arrived from the east, and when offered a job in a struck plant, had refused it. "I'm no strike-breaker," he said. The remark was overheard and carried to Mooney, then leading the strike against the shoe manufacturers. He asked to meet Billings, and hired him as an aide.[8]

Between 1912 and 1913, Mooney worked to build the Syndicalist League of North America, founded by William Z. Foster to organize the militants, including Wobblies, to work inside the AFL for a progressive trade union program.* Within six months, Mooney had chartered four locals among San Francisco iron workers.[9] Together with Billings, Mooney also tried to help the electrical linemen on strike against the Pacific Gas and Electric Company. Billings was arrested in September 1913 on charges of transporting dynamite in a public conveyance, convicted and sentenced to a two-year prison term. He always maintained that the explosives were planted by agents for the utility, and that he was not guilty.[10]

Mooney was arrested three months later on a charge of illegal possession of explosives, but after two trials had ended in hung juries, he won an acquittal.[11] In the eyes of San Francisco's open-shop employers, Mooney was a "disease" that had to be eradicated. This feeling was strengthened by his activity as secretary of the International Workers' Defense League, formed in 1912. Mooney worked indefatigably in defense of Richard "Blackie" Ford and Herman D. Suhr, IWW leaders framed on a murder charge in the Wheatland strike, and on behalf of Joe Hill, the IWW songwriter, also framed on a murder charge in Utah and awaiting execution.[12]**

It is not difficult to understand why Frank P. Walsh, who studied the career of Tom Mooney very carefully, observed that "Mooney . . . through ten years of anti-employer activities had become a *persona non grata* to industrial and civic authorities alike."[13] (He might have added "and to conservative trade unionists as well.") Mooney had made himself a hated figure among shoe, public utilities, and iron molding employers. In the spring of 1916, he was to add the powerful United Railroads to the list.

The 2,000 carmen of the United Railroads had organized a union in 1901, but the company resisted and sought to destroy it by refusing to

*See Foner,4: 427-30 for the Syndicalist League.

**See Foner, *ibid.*,: 263-76 for the case of Ford and Suhr. For the case of Joe Hill, *see* Philip S. Foner, *The Case of Joe Hill*, New York, 1965.
Despite world-wide protests, Joe Hill was executed in 1915.

negotiate. In the end, an agreement was reached that strikers would be rehired and that no discrimination would be practiced by the company. But in 1907, Patrick Calhoun, a bitter anti-unionist, became president of the United Railroads, and he launched a campaign to eliminate the union. On May 1, 1907, after negotiations between the United Railroads and the union broke down, a strike was called. Although the San Francisco and California labor movements supported the strike, the union lost and was eliminated by the company.

Mooney pleaded with the San Francisco Labor Council to unionize the city's main streetcar system. He was especially persistent during the San Francisco World's Fair in 1915, arguing that the employers would not dare risk a strike while the world was watching the Bay City. But Mooney was opposed by the conservative labor leaders who said that a streetcar strike was out of the question because it would disrupt the World's Fair. To this, Mooney replied: "The British miners laid down their tools during a world war. But you're afraid to strike during a World's Fair."[14]

In 1916, Mooney himself undertook the task of organizing the streetcar men of the United Railways. He did so with credentials as an organizer furnished by president W. D. Mahon of the Amalgamated Association of Street Railway Employees, who also asked the San Francisco Labor Council to give Mooney "every assistance and encouragement. . . ." But the council leaders, who had no great love for the militant Mooney, were annoyed by the fact that he had failed to ask their permission to call a walkout—the usual practice followed by the unions of the city.[15]

Nevertheless, Mooney went ahead, assisted by Rena, and by Billings, who had been paroled after serving a little over a year and had been working as a bookkeeper. Despite his well-planned efforts,* Mooney's attempt to organize the carmen of United Railways failed, but he refused to give up. Meanwhile, the business interests of the city were eager, as one report put it, "to neutralize him."[16] Martin Swanson, the former Pinkerton operative and head of the newly organized Public Utilities Protective Bureau, a private detective agency that worked closely with the United Railroads, had Mooney under "constant surveillance," waiting for an opportunity to frame him.[17]

Mooney was regarded as increasingly dangerous by San Francisco busi-

*There are hundreds of cards of individual streetcar men with typed notations in the Thomas J. Mooney Papers, Bancroft Library, University of California, Berkeley. Notations included "Scabbed" and the date, "Doubtful," and "Good." This evidence of how carefully Mooney worked casts doubt on the conclusion of some labor historians that he was a good agitator but a poor organizer.

ness interests because, in addition to his militant union activities, he was a bitter opponent of militarism and preparedness. In the April 1916 issue of *Blast*, an anarchist paper published in San Francisco and edited by Alexander Berkman, Mooney denounced former San Francisco Labor Council president Andrew J. Gallagher for supporting preparedness. He also vigorously attacked the attempt of the Pacific Coast Defense League to establish military training in the public schools in the high grammar grades.[18]

## THE FRAME-UP

In view of the foregoing, it is not difficult to understand why District Attorney Charles Fickert jumped at the chance to prosecute Mooney, the enemy of the United Railways, nor why Detective Swanson, who had been retained by local capitalists interested in public utilities, helped pin the bomb explosion on the "troublesome" Mooney, his wife Rena, his young associate Billings, and two of his friends—Israel Weinberg, a militant jitney driver, and Edward Nolan, a minor union official. Once Mooney, his wife, and his friends were apprehended, no attempt was made to search for alternative explanations for the outrage. Fifteen years later, a Federal fact-finding group, the Wickersham Commission, concluded after a thorough study of the bombing case:

> There was never any scientific attempt made either by the police or the prosecution to discover the perpetrators of the crime. The investigation was in reality turned over to a private detective who used his position to cause the arrest of the defendants. The police investigation was reduced to a hunt for evidence to convict the arrested defendants.[19]

The San Francisco police and the district attorney, aided by a private investigator whose employers had long wanted to "get" Mooney and Billings, proceeded to formulate a theory, based on no real evidence, in order to railroad these men to their death. To do this, they concealed from the grand jury evidence that proved the innocence of Mooney and his wife. On July 31, the day before the grand jury met, Wade Hamilton, a local engineer, turned over to District Attorney Fickert's chief assistant, Edward Cunha, photographs he had taken on the roof adjoining that of the Eilers Building on the afternoon of the parade. The photographs showed Mooney and his wife on the edge of the Eilers roof at the precise time (as revealed by a clock) when they were alleged to have been placing the suitcase containing the bomb against the wall at Steuart and Market Streets, more than a mile away. But Fickert refused to disclose this vital piece of information to the grand jury.[20] Thus, the district attorney's office deliberately suppressed photographs that would have destroyed its case against Tom Mooney—their main target.

The police and the district attorney wanted a speedy conviction, and the grand jury obliged. Mooney, Rena, Billings, Weinberg, and Nolan were indicted for conspiracy among themselves and persons unknown to commit the act that had resulted in the deaths of ten people and the wounding of many more.[21]

The San Francisco press stirred public sentiment against the defendants by publishing, without any investigation, statements issued by the district attorney's office. To make matters worse, liberals, trade unionists, and even radicals in the Bay Area accepted as fact that Mooney and Billings were guilty. Even the libertarian Fremont Older, editor of the San Francisco *Bulletin*, refused to lift a finger for the defendants and swallowed whole the charges issued by Fickert. He expressed the general feeling of the Establishment toward Mooney when he said: "Let the son-of-a-bitch hang."[22]

In this situation, Alexander Berkman revived the International Workers' Defense League for the support of the five indicted labor figures. He contacted the gifted cartoonist and journalist Robert Minor in Los Angeles (Minor was staying at the home of Upton Sinclair), and asked him to take up the case of the defendants. Minor accepted,* quickly familiarized himself with the facts in the case, and wrote to Frank P. Walsh, the nationally famed attorney and former chairman of the U. S. Commission on Industrial Relations, presenting his evaluation of the frame-up. He was convinced that Mooney had been singled out only because he had tried unsuccessfully to call out the United Railways workers; that Rena was being victimized for having supported her husband while he was organizing the workers; that Weinberg was involved in the case because he had been in sympathy with Mooney's organizing activities, Nolan because he had been chief of the pickets in a recent machinists' strike, and Billings because of a previous conviction for carrying a suitcase with dynamite.[23]

---

*A native of Texas who left school at fourteen and became a migratory worker and a Wobbly, Robert Minor developed into one of the great American cartoonists. By 1911, when he turned twenty-seven, Minor, as the chief cartoonist on the St. Louis *Post Dispatch*, was the highest paid cartoonist in the United States. But when the New York *World*, for which he then worked, began to support preparedness in 1915, Minor, already a Socialist, left a lucrative post to work as a cartoonist and journalist for the New York *Call* and the *Masses*. His savagely satirical anti-war, anti-imperialist, pro-labor cartoons became famous. "The last underpinning of respect for the 'democratic' social organization was knocked out of me by the Mooney case," he wrote later. (*Daily Worker*, Jan. 8, 1939). For a study of Robert Minor, including his contributions as a Communist Party leader, *see* Joseph North, *Robert Minor*, New York, 1956.

## THE PRE-TRIAL DEFENSE APPEAL

Signing as treasurer of the International Workers' Defense League, Minor issued the first of scores of appeals for funds to unions across the country. He recounted the events leading up to the Preparedness Day parade, pointing out that "organized labor was . . . completely through with the affair before the day of the march," but that some individuals, "fired by the wild propaganda for military violence, sent hundreds of warnings through the mails saying they would blow up the parade with a bomb." Organized labor, Minor wrote, had discovered this, and the trade unions had "requested their followers to avoid any chance for such a thing to be laid at their door, by abstaining from all activity and treating the parade with silent contempt." This was done, but nevertheless a bomb did explode. "Immediately the Chamber of Commerce, through its tools in public office, swooped down on its most hated enemies in organized labor's ranks." After explaining why the five defendants were selected to be framed, Minor noted: "Five conspicuous enemies of the employers were thus caught and apparently doomed. . . . The prisoners are in the hands of men who consider labor unionism in itself a crime. They are now proving this by making peaceful picketing a prison offense."*

"We are not defending bomb throwers, but innocent men," Minor's appeal concluded. "They will be executed practically without a trial if we don't get the money to defend them."[24] Unfortunately, there was little response.

## BILLINGS SENTENCED

The trial of Warren K. Billings began in September 1916. There were two main witnesses for the prosecution: Estelle Smith and John McDonald. Smith testified that she had seen Billings with the suitcase containing the bomb and saw him place it against the wall. Later, the witness, described in the press as a "demure, young dental assistant," was proved to be a prostitute and a chronic liar, and to have been involved in a previous murder case. She recanted her testimony in installments and then recanted her recantations.

*This is a reference to the fact that shortly after the bombing, the Law and Order Committee began circulating an initiative petition to place an anti-picketing ordinance on the November ballot. Full-page ads were run in all papers charging that picketing was "an instrument of violence. It is un-American. It hurts a city by bad advertisement, leads to crime, and does labor no good." On November 7, 1916, the most heavily unionized city in the United States "voted in landslide proportions to make picketing a crime." (Curt Gentry, *Frame-up: The Incredible Case of Tom Mooney and Warren Billings*, [New York, 1967], p.172.)

John McDonald, a watchman and itinerant waiter, pointed his finger at Billings and said: "That's one of the men I saw with the suitcase." Later he was proved to be a narcotics addict. He signed a full confession, admitting to having been coached in perjury by Fickert, Swanson, and others.[25]

Thus, District Attorney Fickert knowingly put together a case against Billings based entirely on false testimony. Moreover, such was the atmosphere of hysteria that the defense made no impression, while the testimony of the witnesses who perjured themselves was believed.

In his summation at the Billings trial, Fickert asked that "this cowardly hyena, this contemptible criminal" be found guilty of first degree murder. Billings was convicted of second degree murder, and because of an earlier felony conviction, was sentenced to life imprisonment at Folsom Prison. Billings believed that the request of the prosecution for a sentence of life imprisonment was intended to pressure him to confess and name Mooney as his co-conspirator, in return for clemency.[26]

## CALIFORNIA LABOR'S INDIFFERENCE

In a letter to the San Francisco Labor Council on October 1, 1916, Billings insisted he had been convicted on perjured testimony and pleaded for support for the other defendants and for his own appeal of the verdict and sentence.[27] The letter was turned over to the California State Federation of Labor, meeting in convention, and to it was added a resolution adopted by District No. 689 of the International Association of Machinists, Nolan's union. The resolution called for the full support of organized labor on the ground that all five defendants were being prosecuted because of their activities in "past labor wars in and about San Francisco, such as the Pacific General and Electrical Strike, and an attempted strike on the United Railroad." Therefore, the petition concluded, this was a labor case and should be treated as such.[28]

The resolutions committee of the California State Federation of Labor challenged the resolution's thesis, stating "that no one at this time is attempting to connect labor with the bomb outrage, and although statements were made in San Francisco . . . that the outrage was the culmination of a series of crimes by organized labor, so well was our position defined and our policies defended and explained that attacks on us along that line have ceased."[29]

The report of the resolutions committee produced a long debate on the convention floor. Hugo Ernst, later to become the president of the Hotel and Restaurant Union, and at the time a representative of the San Francisco waiters, led the fight against the report. It was defended by Mike

Case of the San Francisco Teamsters, Thomas Tracy of the Printers, and Paul Scharrenberg, secretary of the state federation. The report of the resolutions committee was overwhelmingly adopted, 38,196 to 4,226. Thus, the California labor leaders had made their position clear—the Mooney-Billings frame-up was not a labor case.

Perhaps the most difficult blow was the refusal of Local 164 of the International Molders' Union of North America, of which Tom Mooney was a member, to endorse the appeal of Mooney and his wife for funds to aid them in their forthcoming trials. A "Tom Mooney Molders' Defense Committee" had sent this appeal to locals of the International, but failure to obtain the approval of Local 164 had resulted in a "comparatively small response."

On October 23, 1916, the Tom Mooney Molders' Defense Committee distributed a second appeal, this time signed by Mooney himself. Mooney made his position on the bomb explosion crystal clear. "Ten innocent people were killed and thirty more seriously injured," he wrote. "It was the most cowardly and heinous crime ever committed in this country, and if Billings did it, or anyone else who did it, they should be hanged, and not sentenced to life imprisonment"(as was Billings). After describing the perjured testimony in the Billings trial, Mooney informed the Molders' local union:

> My trial is set for October 30th,* and the powers of the vultures represented in the Chamber of Commerce, the United Railroads and the Pacific Gas and Electric Co. are out to "get me." I have been a member of the I.M.U. of N.A. in good standing for fourteen years, and I and my co-defendants are in jail today because of our activities in the labor movement. The five accused are some of the most aggressive fighters in labor's cause, and that is the reason we have been victimized.[30]

Mooney's new appeal produced no better response. "This is not a labor case," the San Francisco *Labor Clarion* explained in reporting the trade unions' lack of interest in the Mooney-Billings frame-up.[31]**

*The trial was postponed to January 1917.

**Mooney believed that a major reason for the failure of a response to the appeals was that "Brother J. E. Dillon, in addition to being Financial Secretary of Local 164, is an assistant in District Attorney Fickert's office, as Bond and Warrant Clerk. . . . Brother Michael Roche, Treasurer of Local 164, was an Assistant District Attorney under Fickert for a few years until he was promoted in politics. Brother R. W. Burton, Business Agent of Local 164, along with Brothers Dillon and Roche, helped to elect Fickert." This situation continued to make it "impossible" to obtain Local 164's endorsement of the appeal for funds. (Tom Mooney to Dear Sirs and Brothers, San Francisco, Oct. 23, 1916; copy in Papers of Mother Mary Harris Jones, Department of Archives and Manuscripts, Catholic University of America Library.)

# THE LABOR MOVEMENT BEGINS TO RESPOND

Fortunately, the labor movement outside of California was less indifferent. Immediately after the sentence was imposed upon Billings, the International Workers' Defense League put the trade unions throughout the nation on notice that "Not since the Haymarket Tragedy of 1886 has a more deadly blow been struck at the labor movement, and never has justice been so brazenly outraged as by the conviction and sentence of life imprisonment passed upon Warren K. Billings." The sentence, the appeal continued, was a victory for the open-shop employers, but only temporarily:

> We are determined (and we believe every unionite in America is with us) to repeal this verdict, and save the others from the legal lynching mapped out for them by the "Law and Order" employers. These, our brothers, must be rescued from the gallows and we must have funds to do it. . . .
>
> San Francisco is but the first battlefield of a national attack on organized labor. We must win the fight! Hold mass meetings, collect funds and do everything you possibly can—do it now! Funds should be rushed immediately to Robert Minor, Treasurer, 210 Russ Building, San Francisco, Cal.[32]

The appeal received a stimulus when the *Literary Digest* of October 14, 1916 featured a resumé of the events in the case. Mooney himself felt that anyone reading the piece would clearly see the nature of the frame-up, since it presented "both sides of the bomb cases," and he recommended it be distributed to trade unions.[33]

Whatever the reason, not long after Billings' sentence, the labor movement in the midwest and east began to respond. In Chicago, a meeting organized with the assistance of Lucy Robins heard "Big Bill" Haywood, William Z. Foster, James Larkin, and Alexander Berkman urge the launching of a campaign to defend Mooney and the others.* After this, the Chicago Mooney Defense Committee was formally organized.[34] In New York City, the United Hebrew Trades, unions of the fur workers, ladies and men's clothing workers and other unions jointly called a mass meeting in Carnegie Hall to protest "California's big business conspiracy." On

---

*When the Hebrew Institute learned that Berkman was to be one of the speakers, it withdrew its offer of a hall, refusing to let its facilities be used by an anarchist, especially one who had spent fourteen years in prison for attempting to assassinate Henry Clay Frick of Carnegie Steel during the Homestead strike of 1892. The meeting was held in a hall above an Irish saloon on North Clark Street after James Larkin convinced the owners that Mooney was being persecuted because he was Irish. (Chicago *Tribune*, Nov. 28, 29, 1916.)

For the Haymarket Affair, *see* Philip S. Foner, *History of the Labor Movement in the United States 2* (New York, 1955): 105-14; for the Homestead strike, *see ibid.*, pp. 206-18.

December 2, 1916, a mammoth crowd heard Frank P. Walsh, Max Eastman, editor of the socialist monthly *Masses*, Max Pine, secretary of the United Hebrew Trades, Arturo Giovannitti, poet and IWW leader, and Emma Goldman and Alexander Berkman, anarchists active in the defense movement. Writing in the *Masses*, John Reed noted that over a thousand dollars was raised at the meeting, and commented: "His Honor the District Attorney doesn't yet realize that the Labor Movement of the United States is past the stage where its champions can be slaughtered with impunity."[35]

Not only were Mooney defense committees established in many cities, but a National Defense Council was organized to aid the accused. Working with Mooney, Robert Minor published the first pamphlet in the case: *The Frame-Up System; Story of the San Francisco Bomb*. By the time Mooney's trial started, contributions to the defense were averaging $3,500 per month.[36] Still Mooney felt that much more had to be done. Addressing "Mother Jones, Any Where in the United States," on December 28, 1916, Mooney thanked her for her aid,* which "was in itself great encouragement to me and my co-defendants," but complained that the case had not received the publicity it deserved in the labor movement. He urged: "Make an effort in every locality to get the different labor papers to take up the news of our trials and the case in general. Get all of the Central Labor Bodies to endorse our fight."[37]

## MOONEY SENTENCED TO DEATH

Mooney was brought to trial on January 3, 1917, after his case had been totally prejudiced by a hostile press. The defendant did not hold out much hope that he would receive either a fair trial or a fair verdict. "I have just been informed," he wrote to Mother Jones on December 28, 1916, "that the Court has ordered drawn 200 names from the Regular Jury panel box, which contains the full list of names that are thrown into it each year by the different judges. This is not much of an improvement over the Billings selection, and the ones drawn are no better than those that convicted Billings. They are tools of the Police, Prosecutors, and the Judges, and ready and willing tools of the corporations against Labor Men, on trial for their activities in the labor movement."[38]

Mooney had hoped to persuade Frank P. Walsh to take on his case as defense attorney. Walsh had met Mooney and had been impressed by his

---

*For Mother Jones' work in the Mooney defense campaign, *see* Philip S. Foner, *Mother Jones Speaks*, New York, 1983, pp. 301, 613-23. Mooney addressed Mother Jones "Any Where in the United States," because the 76-year-old militant was constantly on the move organizing workers, especially miners.

sincerity and devotion to the working class, and was convinced that he was innocent of the crime. However, he told Mooney that he could not undertake the defense, because he had committed himself to campaign actively for President Wilson's re-election and this would absorb the greatest portion of his time during the fall of 1916. Also, he had neglected his law practice during the two years he had spent as chairman of the Commission on Industrial Relations, and he felt it necessary to stay with his current clients.[39]

Although unable or unwilling to take on Mooney's legal defense in the courts, Walsh was influential in obtaining the services of the highly paid and well-known W. Bourke Cochran. The famous New York lawyer agreed to serve as Mooney's counsel after reading the Billings transcript given to him by Alexander Berkman, following which he declared he had never seen "so gross and monstrous a travesty of justice." Cochran was so moved by the extent of the conspiracy against Mooney that he offered to take the case without fee.[40]

The defense had been tipped off by an anonymous letter from a policeman about the prosecution's possession of the photographs that had been taken during the Preparedness Day parade by Wade Hamilton. The pictures, it will be recalled, showed the Mooneys and others on the roof of the Eilers Building, and they included the clock of a nearby building. Although the pictures of the clock were deliberately kept fuzzy by the prosecution to obscure the exact time, the defense was able to prove that Mooney and his wife had been on the roof of the Eilers Building at 1:58, 2:01, and 2:04 of the afternoon of the parade, rather than at the scene of the bomb explosion.[41]

But the frame-up continued in the face of this evidence. John McDonald had testified during the Billings trial that Mooney was at Steuart and Market Streets, a mile and a quarter away, at two o'clock, but he readily changed his testimony at Mooney's trial to accommodate the clock evidence. He stated now that he had seen Mooney at twenty minutes to two.

But it was the prosecution's surprise witness, Frank Oxman, the "honest cattleman" from Oregon, whose testimony was instrumental in sending Mooney to a San Quentin death cell. Oxman positively identified Mooney as one of the men whom he had seen depositing the suitcase at the place of the explosion. The "honest cattleman" was later found to be both a perjurer and a suborner of perjury![42]

Mooney was convicted of first degree murder. On February 24, 1917, he was sentenced to be hanged. The motion for a new trial was overruled by Judge Franklin A. Griffin, who refused to allow Mooney to make a statement. Condemned to be hung on May 17, 1917, he did make his statement to the American people in a release issued by the International Workers' Defense. In it, Mooney declared that if he had been able to speak to the jury, he would have asked them if they had reached their verdict on the basis of the testimony of McDonald and Oxman, even though "each contradicted the other." He would have shouted out to the jury that his death and that of all of the other defendants "cannot hinder nor give pause to the movement to which it has been our lot to give whatever we may have had of energy and devotion. I wanted to laugh at the fatuous blindness of those who hope to smother the cry for justice within prison walls or strangle it with the hangman's noose." Mooney concluded:

> I am under sentence of death. Whatever may be the legal equivocation, the crime of which I have actually been convicted is not that of having thrown a bomb into a throng of innocent people, which included my wife's brother-in-law, to whom we are both tenderly attached, but that of having striven with what strength I had for the alleviation of the industrial wrongs that labor has suffered and the establishment of the rights which naturally belong to labor. I do not believe—I cannot believe—that because I have thus adhered to the duty and exercised the simple privilege of a human being, I must meet death on the gallows. The fury engendered by industrial strife may defeat justice in a given locality, but so deeply imbedded in the hearts of the people is the desire of justice that it must inevitably find expression in a court of review. In that faith I am content.[43]

## CALIFORNIA LABOR ACTS

After the sentencing and the refusal by Judge Griffin to grant a new trial, Cochran wrote to Mooney assuring him that he was confident "that the appalling judicial crime committed against you will never be allowed to reach the consummation which induced the perpetrators to plan it." To prevent it, he wrote, it was necessary to convince the American people, and especially the labor movement, "that we are in the presence of another Dreyfus case, the only difference being that the object of the French perversion of legal procedure to the perpetration of the very crimes which courts are organized to prevent, was exclusion (by force and threats of force) of Jews from the Army; while the object of your prosecution for a crime repugnant to every element of your nature is to drive laborers from organizing, by killing of a man who has had the temerity to form unions for their own protection."[44]

There was mounting evidence that the labor movement was beginning to understand this, and for the first time labor on the west coast became involved. On February 12, 1917, the Central Labor Council of Alameda County adopted resolutions denouncing the verdicts in the Billings and Mooney trials as part of a conspiracy of the San Francisco Chamber of Commerce "to disrupt the organization of labor on the coast and make it impossible for working people to band themselves together for the purpose of self-protection and better conditions." The convictions of Billings and Mooney were nothing less than "an attempt to disrupt labor on the coast, thereby threatening the life, liberty and purposes of the entire labor movement of this continent."[45]

At the same time, the San Francisco Labor Council affirmed its "belief in the innocence of Thomas J. Mooney and his co-defendants, and pledge them our aid in their efforts to secure justice." Copies of the resolutions were forwarded to the labor and daily press, but not a single San Francisco commercial paper published the resolutions adopted by either the Alameda County or the San Francisco Central Labor Councils.[46]

In a report written by George P. West, "after a field investigation," the Committee on Industrial Relations declared that organized labor understood that Mooney and Billings were victims of a frame-up which was part of "a campaign to crush trade unionism in the Pacific Coast metropolis." Convinced that the two men in jail were not guilty, "organized labor has lined up solidly to fight the case to a finish."[47]

The "finish," as we shall see in detail in our subsequent volumes, was a long, long time in coming. In those volumes, we will deal with the struggle to free Mooney and Billings as it developed over the years until final victory was achieved in 1939. Here we will concern ourselves with the campaign to save Mooney's life.

## SAVING MOONEY

Although he knew he faced overwhelming odds, Mooney continued to fight for his life from his jail cell. He knew that if he was to deny Fickert and the Law and Order Committee the pleasure of hanging him, he would need more than the legal process. Public pressure had to be mobilized.

The first real impact of such pressure occurred not in the United States but abroad. As Mooney sat on death row, Russian workers in Petrograd, led by V. I. Lenin, took up the campaign and gave it international dimensions, as they paraded outside the United States Embassy, chanting "Muni!" "Muni!" U.S. Ambassador David R. Francis was mystified until he was informed that they were protesting the conviction of Tom Mooney in California, nine thousand miles away.

Through Ambassador Francis, President Wilson learned of the protests.

At the same time newspapers and magazines in the United States began publishing reports from correspondents in Russia about the Mooney agitation in that country.* And the press reported, too, that the agitation was spreading to Rome, Paris, London, and other European cities.[48]

In the United States, a movement for a general strike to achieve the release from prison of Mooney and Billings swept the ranks of organized labor during the spring of 1917. Joining in the movement was the Seattle Union Card and Label League, composed of the wives of trade unionists. They prepared to join the trade unions of Seattle in response to a call from the Central Labor Union for a general strike on May 1, 1917 in the event that Mooney and Billings were not "unconditionally released" by then and the charges against the other defendants dropped. Edith Love, president of the league, explained:

> Perhaps no one has ever before heard of housewives going on strike, and we sincerely hope we will be saved the necessity of such action in the "frame-up" case. But I voice the sentiments of all the members when I state that no work will be done in the homes of League members on that day if the conditions are not met with. We believe that no union man would expect his wife to do otherwise.[49]

Gompers, however, opposed the general strike demand. He realized that such a strike might be dangerous to the effort to mobilize labor support for the Allies, and he now considered this labor's first priority. The opposition of the AFL leadership caused cancellation of the plans for a general strike.[50]

But Gompers did join in putting pressure on President Wilson, the State Department, and other federal agencies for some action to save Mooney's life, pointing out that Mooney was regarded in the United States and Europe as a martyr to "capitalistic interests and designs."[51] The pressure built to such an extent that on May 11, 1917, six days before Mooney's scheduled execution, President Wilson sent a telegram to California governor William D. Stephens urging him "in view of certain international aspects which the case has assumed," to commute Mooney's sentence, "or at least suspending its execution until the charges of perjury lodged

---

*The New York *Call* observed that it took a demonstration led by "Nikolai Lenine *(sic)*, a Russian radical" to call attention of the U.S. government to the impending execution of an innocent American labor leader. The *New Republic* observed: "Is it not a remarkable commentary upon the attitude of the American press toward labor that one of the most important and dramatic events in the history of organized labor in America should have come to the attention of American newspaper readers through a mass meeting in Nevsky Prospect." (New York *Call*, April 2, 1917; *New Republic*, April 9, 1917, p. 14.)

For a different view of events in Russia, *see* Gentry, *op. cit., p.216.*

against the witnesses in the case are judicially probed to the bottom." Stephens wired the President the same day that Mooney's sentence was "stayed indefinitely, by appeal pending in the state supreme court." Mooney's appeal in the courts automatically suspended the date of execution.[52]

Wilson's reference to "the charges of perjury" applied to all the key witnesses against Mooney. Almost immediately after Mooney's conviction, evidence came to light that was sufficient to establish misconduct on the part of the prosecution and its witnesses. In April 1917, Andrew Furuseth of the Sailors' Union of the Pacific visited Fremont Older of the San Francisco *Bulletin*. He told Older he had seen letters written by F. C. Oxman to his friend, Ed Rigall, a disreputable character who was urged to come west from Grayville, Illinois in order to corroborate Oxman's testimony in a big case. Oxman promised Rigall that, in addition to having a pleasant trip to California, he would be well paid for committing perjury, as he himself could personally testify.

After Older had checked this information and was convinced that Oxman had admitted writing the frame-up letters, he published the correspondence in his newspaper and began to devote himself to the Mooney defense. In the face of this new evidence, Judge Griffin, who had presided at Mooney's trial, appealed to Attorney General Webb of California for a new trial. Immediately, the Chamber of Commerce of San Francisco inserted full page advertisements in the press, denouncing Older and urging all good citizens to stand by the prosecution.[53]

After months of deliberation, on September 11 the Supreme Court of California refused to intercede, insisting that it was bound by the official record in the case and therefore could not admit new evidence. Oxman was tried, and, as anticipated, acquitted of the charge of perjury on September 21, 1917.[54]

After the Supreme Court of California had rejected Mooney's appeal, a new date for Mooney's execution was set. New pressure from the United States and Europe was exerted upon President Wilson to intercede again. The President appointed a Mediation Commission, composed of representatives of both labor and management, to look into the case while it was studying the causes of labor unrest. The commission's legal representative was a young Harvard law professor named Felix Frankfurter.

The commission was appalled by its findings, and in its unanimous report, written by Frankfurter, recommended that President Wilson "use his good offices to invoke action by the governor of California and the cooperation of its prosecuting officers to the end that a new trial may be had for Mooney whereby guilt or innocence may be put to the test of unquestionable justice. This result can easily be accomplished by postponing the execution of the sentence of Mooney to wait the outcome of a new trial under one of the untried indictments against him."[55]

On January 22, 1918, again noting that the "case has assumed international importance," President Wilson asked Governor Stephens "to postpone the execution of the sentence of Mooney until he can be tried upon one of the other indictments against him in order to give full weight and consideration to the important changes which I understand have taken place in the evidence against him." This time Governor Stephens did not even bother to reply.[56] Later, however, faced with the prospect of 500 AFL-sponsored mass meetings scheduled for July 28, 1918, the second anniversary of Mooney's arrest, Stephens announced that he had granted a postponement of Mooney's execution until December 13th.[57]

After further intercessions from the White House urging that Mooney's sentence be commuted, stressing that this would have a "heartfelt effect upon certain international affairs," and after a second federal investigation (known as the Densmore Report) turned up further serious irregularities in Fickert's conduct of the case, Governor Stephens complied with President Wilson's request. On the evening of November 28, 1918—Thanksgiving Day—angrily conceding that "the propaganda in his [Mooney's] behalf . . . had been so effective as to become world-wide," Stephens announced that he had commuted Thomas J. Mooney's sentence to life imprisonment.[58]

"I demand a new and a fair trial or my unconditional liberty through a pardon," wrote Mooney angrily to Governor Stephens. "If I were guilty of the crime for which I have been unjustly convicted, hanging would be too good for me. Then why commute my sentence to life?"[59]

## THE FRAME-UP CONTINUES

Although President Wilson, the President's Mediation Commission, the labor movement in the United States and abroad, and Mooney himself asked for a retrial, Governor Stephens refused to yield to these requests. Five successive governors of California also refused to either act on the requests or to pardon Mooney.

Tom Mooney's life had been saved, but, yielding again and again to the open-shop employers, official California kept Mooney (and Billings) behind bars for more than two decades. Despite the complete destruction of the credibility of the prosecution witnesses, despite the transparent emptiness of the case against Mooney, despite the strong condemnation of the proceedings in the Mooney case by President Herbert Hoover's

National Commission on Law Observance and Enforcement, better known as the Wickersham Commission, the governors refused to act.[60] The state of California would not release a man it viewed as a dangerous radical, "a symbol of the militant working class." It took twenty-three years to free a man who had been convicted on clearly perjured evidence in a hysterical atmosphere that made a farce of due process.*

*It was Culbert L. Olsen, California's first New Deal governor, who pardoned Mooney in January, 1939. Even then, Billings, whose sentence was only commuted in 1939, did not receive a full pardon until 1961.

# CHAPTER 5

# Labor's Road to War

## KEEP OUT OF WAR!

On February 3, 1917, it will be recalled, President Wilson broke off
diplomatic relations with Germany. "The response from labor," one
scholar points out, "was not all that Gompers desired. Trade union opposition to a war with the Central Powers was widespread."[1] How "widespread" soon became clear. "Fight against war because it means the end
of democracy," demanded the United Mine Workers.[2] The Cigar Makers
declared that "labor is opposed to being drawn into the struggle," and
advised President Wilson "to use every honorable means . . . to keep us
out of this mad struggle."[3] The Pattern Makers advised the nation to
"remain cool and continue to advocate peace."[4] The Carpenters reminded
Wilson that "the labor movement has stood constantly and persistently for
peace," and demanded that the President "keep out of war."[5]

President Walter Carter of the Locomotive Firemen went so far as to
inform Columbia University's Academy of Political Science that "labor
would rather suffer untold wrongs than to engage in war. . . ."[6] The
Switchmen called on the working class to "let Congress and President
Wilson know that it was against war." "Unless the workers of this country
are war-mad," the union urged, "let them cry against such contemplated
slaughter in such manner that Congress and President Wilson will heed
it."[7] With one or two minor exceptions, the entire labor movement
demanded peace and opposed involvement in the war.[8]

On February 11, 1917, the *Minneapolis Tribune* reported that trade
unions and pacifist groups were jointly flooding the President with "thousands of telegrams and letters to influence the United States government
against entering the war against Germany." Although this was an exagger-
ation, it is true that in their zeal to avoid war, trade unions were beginning

to work more closely than before with pacifist groups. This was particularly true in the case of the newly-organized American Union Against Militarism, headed by Rabbi Stephen S. Wise, Lillian Wald, Oswald Garrison Villard, and Rev. John Haynes Holmes. A number of unions urged their members to join with the American Union to defeat the "campaign to militarize this peace loving republic." Even the Western Federation of Miners, which only a short time earlier had ridiculed the efforts of middle-class pacifists, now charged the press with attempting to misrepresent pacifists "as merely mollycoddles, clever talkers and do-nothings."[9]

Increasingly, trade unions began to support an anti-war proposal identified with the Socialist Party—that war should be declared only if a referendum vote of all the American people sanctioned such a course of action. A "Keep Out of War Committee" to support the demand for a war referendum was organized in New York City by the United Hebrew Trades, the International Ladies' Garment Workers' Union, the Amalgamated Clothing Workers' Union, and the International Fur Workers' Union.[10] Joining with the committee in support of the referendum proposal were the Industrial Council of Kansas City, the St. Louis Central Trades Council, the Chicago Federation of Labor, the Trades Assembly of Joplin (Missouri), the Fargo (North Dakota) Trades and Labor Assembly, the unions of painters, cigar makers, bakers, and the Sailors' Union of the Pacific.[11]

The last-named union also organized a campaign of letters and telegrams to Wilson to remind him that he was re-elected on the platform "He Kept Us Out of War," and the workers had supported him for this reason and had "no reason . . . to shed their blood for the protection and furtherance of the unholy profits of their masters. . . ."[12] The idea became the theme of a mass meeting, chaired by Edward Cassidy of the International Typographical Union. It was held at Carnegie Hall, sponsored by the Keep Out of the War Committee.[13]

On February 10, 1917, three thousand men and women packed a hall in Minneapolis at a meeting sponsored by a committee of trade unions. They adopted a resolution that stated:

> We desire to respectfully recall the fact that in the election of November, the citizens of this country strongly favored our keeping out of the war in Europe, and the administration then elected was committed to a policy of peace. To now abandon that policy and plunge us into war, we hold, is to make a solemn mockery of the great American principle of the consent of the governed.[14]

On February 4, 1917, the day after the United States broke off diplomatic relations with Germany, Gompers, with the approval of President Wilson, cabled Karl Legien, leader of the German trade unions in Berlin, asking if he could "prevail upon German government to avoid break with United States and thereby prevent universal conflict?"* Legien cabled that German labor was "opposed to extension of conflict," that the resumption of submarine warfare was provoked by the Allies' rejection of "Germany's sincere offer of immediate peace negotiations" and by the "continuation of cruel starvation war on our women, children, and aged." The reply continued:

> No intervention with Government on my part has any chance of success unless America prevails upon England to discontinue starvation war as being contrary to law of nations. I appeal to American labour not to allow themselves to be made catspaws of the war monger[s] by sailing war zone and thus contribute extending conflict. International labour must unflinchingly work for immediate peace.[15]

Gompers reported that his colleagues of the Executive Council "have formally and officially endorsed my action in sending the cablegram, and that in addition from many quarters in the ranks of labor and of the public generally there has been hearty commendation of the spirit which prompted the sending of the cablegram and the purposes it hoped to achieve."[16] What he did not report, however, was that along with approval of his cable to Legien, he received letters and telegrams from trade unions, city labor councils, and state federations of labor urging him to take immediate steps, in the name of the American Federation of Labor, to prevail upon the President and Congress to keep the country out of war with Germany. A number of letters urged that he act to insure that Congress "not plunge us into war without some sort of referendum to the people."[17]

In evaluating organized labor's reaction to the mounting war crisis, the *New Republic*, which was friendly to Wilson's policies, pointed to the position adopted by the Central Federated Union of New York as "typical of the feeling of union men and women." That body had praised Gompers for his cablegram to Legien but had unanimously called upon President Wilson "to resist the selfish and sinister influences that would plunge our country into the world cauldron of murder." The CFU also urged Gompers to inform Wilson that it was the belief of American workers that the honor of the United States and its international rights could be upheld and maintained without making war upon Germany, and that our Government shall,

---

*President Wilson's assistant secretary called Gompers and told him that the President had read the cable, "that he not only approves it but thinks it is a splendid service and the President is very gratified." (Gompers to Executive Council, American Federation of Labor, "Personal and Confidential," Feb. 4, 1917, AFL Archives, State Historical Society of Wisconsin.)

before engaging in war against any of the present belligerent nations or against any other nation, refer such question for decision to the people of the United States, in a popular election.[18]

## GOMPERS MOVES TOWARD WAR

Nothing was further from Gompers' thoughts than to carry out the mission suggested by the Central Federated Union, even though it was evident that it reflected "the feeling of union men and women." On the contrary, on February 10, 1917, in a letter to Champ Clark, Speaker of the House of Representatives, Gompers noted that there need be no apprehension entertained by the Government that in the event of American participation in the war "the working people will fail in the performance of duty and . . . give service for integrity and ideals of our country."[19]

Ralph M. Easley of the National Civic Federation endorsed Gompers' statement. He assured the nation's business community that "the great labor bodies, such as the American Federation of Labor and the Railroad Brotherhoods, representing three million wage earners, are ready to give their loyal support to the President in any action deemed necessary to maintain the honor of the country." As for Gompers, he should not be judged by his former "pacifist views": "It is evident that the attitude of Mr. Gompers is that of an actively patriotic citizen." If proof were needed, there was the fact that "Mr. Gompers is working night and day in Washington with the Council of National Defense, of which he is a member."[20]

The Council of National Defense was created in accordance with Section 120 of the National Defense Act of June 3, 1916, and Section 2 of the Army Appropriation Act of August 29, 1916. Gompers had called for its creation as early as December 1915, and on October 1, 1916 he was appointed by President Wilson as a member of its Advisory Commission. Soon after, he was chosen to be chairman of its Committee on Labor.[21] In a letter to the AFL Executive Council on February 28, 1917, Gompers pointed out that his position on the Council of National Defense had given him the opportunity to see more clearly than ever before that the United States was bound to enter the war, and he had, as a result, arrived at two conclusions: (1) That American labor, especially organized labor, should let it be known that it would support the government and its policies when war came; and (2) that labor should be prepared with its own program for wartime cooperation; otherwise American trade unionism could suffer a dilution of standards and conditions, with a resultant loss of prestige and importance.[22]

The problem, however, was that organized labor still showed every sign of continuing to be deeply hostile to military preparedness and war. Hence, it was far from certain that when the United States "inevitably" entered the war, the labor movement would rally behind the government. Gompers pledged to the Advisory Commission of the Council of National Defense that he would do everything necessary to convince the labor movement to share his conviction that "War to suppress crime is justifiable." He put it quaintly: he would induce "my boys . . . to follow me."[23]

To carry out this pledge, Gompers called a series of conferences of leaders of organized labor to obtain general agreement regarding their attitudes toward U.S. participation in the war, and the labor problems that would follow its entrance. The aim was not to debate whether or not the United States should enter, but to place the trade union movement on record in favor of such entry. In short, to line the labor movement up for war.

The first such meeting took place on February 27, 1917, with delegates of the metal trades unions of the AFL Railway Employees Department who had gathered in Washington to confer with the railroads regarding wages, standards, and schedules. Gompers asked them to meet with him that evening. "The importance of the conference," he notified the AFL Executive Council, "is manifest by the fact that those present in the conference represented the metal trades—the trades which will be most vitally affected by war."[24] Those "present" were the top officers of the Boiler Makers and Iron Ship Builders, Building Trades Department, International Association of Machinists, Amalgamated Sheet Metal Workers, and International Brotherhood of Blacksmiths, as well as officials of the Metal Trades and Railway Employees Departments.

Gompers told the assembled union leaders that war was imminent and that the labor movement could not wait until it happened before formulating a definite policy and deciding on the role labor must play. It was his firm belief that "the labor movement would lose a great opportunity if it did not make a definite statement as to how far it was willing to go in the movement for preparedness." In England, he went on, the workers had not taken the war seriously when it began, or had been hostile to the war and the government. With no influence in the formulation of policy, British labor had seen the government introduce compulsion both in industry and military service. The workers had had to submit or be regarded "as traitors to their country." Gompers declared that he was "unwilling to contribute to that attitude on the part of the American labor movement," and proposed instead that labor take its place in the war effort, perform its patriotic duty, and at the same time see to it that its rights were protected during the war: "Labor had to choose between casting its lot with the government and 'help guide it right' or withhold its cooperation and be whipped into line."

The union leaders present agreed with Gompers, recommended that "the labor movement must cooperate in the formulation of plans" in the event of war, and suggested that he call a special meeting of the Federation's Executive Council, as well as a conference of all officers of national and international unions and departments of the AFL.[25]

Gompers thereupon issued a call for a special meeting of the Executive Council, and, contingent on its approval, he called upon the national and international unions to meet in Washington in conjunction with the council. He began by stating that he had practically given up hope "that our country may not be drawn into the maelstrom that is rocking the very foundation of world civilization." The sole question that still remained was what part labor should play in "the defense of our Republic."

*"Some plan will be adopted,"* he emphasized. If the labor movement did not make the mistake of remaining aloof, it could participate "in the formulation of national policies." There was no time left for equivocation: *"Now is the time for labor to speak,"*—not on the question of support for the government in war, but on what role "Labor will accept in national defense and in which it will cooperate." He had called a special session of the AFL Executive Council to meet in Washington on March 9, 1917, and he had proposed to the council that it should authorize him "to invite the officers of all international and national unions and of departments to participate in a conference . . . in Washington, D.C., Monday morning, March 12, 1917." He had not yet obtained the votes of the Executive Council authorizing this call, but expected to obtain them within two days. He urged the labor leaders "to lay aside all other duties and engagements," and be prepared to come to Washington when called, ready "to formulate plans that will mean so much for the cause of human welfare and protection, and it may be for the very existence of our Republic."[26]

As Gompers had predicted, the Executive Council authorized the conference.

## "LABOR'S POSITION IN PEACE OR IN WAR"

Meeting on March 9, the Executive Council began deliberation of a declaration, prepared by Gompers, defining the position organized labor should take in the war that appeared inevitable. The meeting was held in secret. No notes as to the discussion were ever released. Not a hint appeared of the widespread opposition in labor circles to involvement in the war. The Executive Council would define not what labor's attitude was, but what Gompers and his colleagues felt it should be.[27]

On March 11, the Executive Council concluded its work. The following morning, its declaration, "American Labor's Position in Peace or in War," was presented to the 148 labor representatives who had gathered in Washington in response to Gompers' call. These delegates represented seventy-nine affiliated organizations, five unaffiliated organizations, and five departments of the AFL.[28]

Starting with the statement that "we speak for millions of Americans," the declaration held that labor's approval of peace or war was now immaterial; the danger was at hand. It pointed out that in previous wars the labor movement had taken no part in directing the activities of conflict and had, if anything, suffered at the hand of military necessity. Thus, the workers had arrived at the conclusion that the war was of no concern to them. But the time was at hand to avoid a repetition of the established pattern. Labor must have a role in determining policies of national defense. Labor standards won by hard fighting must not be tossed aside under the guise of expediency. The trade unions must serve as a connecting link between worker and employer, worker and the government, worker and the war.

The war in Europe was characterized as a life-and-death struggle between the forces of democracy and autocracy. No direct sympathies were expressed as to the side labor favored, but it was not difficult to detect the tilt toward the Allies. What was important was the declaration's conclusion: "Should our country be drawn into the maelstrom of the European conflict, we offer our services . . . to defend, safeguard and preserve the Republic of the United States."[29]

## THE "BLANK CHECK"

The AFL Executive Council, under the sponsorship of Samuel Gompers, had given President Wilson a "blank check" of approval in case of American involvement, and in return asked only for the right to have some control over labor policies.

This was not, however, the first such "blank check" Wilson had received from the AFL. During the crisis following the assassination of Mexican President Madero and the seizure of power by Huerta, who had plotted the murder, but before Wilson intervened militarily and ordered the occupation of Vera Cruz, the 1913 AFL convention, at Gompers' suggestion, had removed from a resolution the clause condemning the demand on the part of "American and foreign corporations, and certain jingo newspapers, to force intervention by the United States government in Mexico." Gompers had even declared that it would be a mistake for the AFL to "resolve under any and all circumstances to denounce intervention. . . ." The Central Federated Union of New York City was more specific. After Wilson had ordered the invasion of Mexico and the occupation of Vera Cruz, it handed the President another "blank check" by voting to uphold his stand in any action necessary to "preserve the honor of the American flag and the dignity of the United States."

Thus, in a real sense, the conduct of the AFL in the second Mexican crisis proved to be a curtain raiser for the drama that unfolded in Washington in March 1917, less than a month before the United States entered World War I.

The delegates in Washington devoted exactly one day to discussing the declaration that Gompers and the AFL Executive Council "had placed ready-made before them."[30] Finally, without a dissenting vote, they adopted it "exactly as it had been submitted to them."[31] Thus, when President Wilson appeared before Congress less than a month later, on April 2, and asked for a declaration of war against Germany, "he was already assured of the support of organized labor."[32]

## THE REAL NATURE OF THE WASHINGTON LABOR CONFERENCE

A closer examination of the situation, however, indicates that there is more to this story. For one thing, it has been generally accepted that the conference in Washington was called upon Gompers' initiative, but the *New York Times* reported that "the meeting was held at the suggestion of the Council of National Defense."[33] This was subsequently confirmed by Lawrence Todd, "a labor journalist close to AFL headquarters in Washington, D.C." Gompers actually inquired as to the feasibility of the government's paying the expense of calling so many labor officials to Washington.[34]

All of these factors led Simeon Larson to conclude that the conference was "the result of a collusive arrangement between leaders of the AFL and elements of the Wilson Administration for the specific purposes of stemming the growing tide of opposition to a foreign policy that might involve the United States in the European conflict and, at the same time, solidly aligning labor with any policy pursued by the Administration in Washington."[35] Indeed, Gompers' correspondence reveals how closely he worked with the Wilson Administration in planning and carrying through the Washington conference.[36]

Although Gompers had wanted the conference to be a meeting "truly representative of organized labor in the United States," it was actually far from that. The Socialist Party and the IWW, for obvious reasons, did not attend. Also absent were representatives from such important AFL unions as the United Mine Workers, the International Ladies' Garment Workers' Union, the International Union of Mine, Mill and Smelter Workers, the International Typographical Union, the United Cloth Hat and Cap Makers, the Steam Engineers Union, the Journeymen Barbers' International Union, the United Brotherhood of Papermakers, the International Photo Engravers' Union of North America, the Pulp, Sulphite, and Paper Mill Workers, the Theatrical Stage Employees Alliance, and the Railway Carmen Brotherhood.[37]

Marsden G. Scott, president of the International Typographical Union, refused to attend. In a letter to Gompers, Scott said that he would not serve Gompers' purpose, "having no confidence whatever in your integrity."[38] John P. White, president of the United Mine Workers, wrote that he would not support a move obviously intended to support U.S. entrance into the war:

> I see no humanitarian issues in the present war. I believe that it is distinctly a commercial war. In my broad travels I find little sentiment among the working people in favor of this terrible war. The United Mine Workers of America has gone on record in a very prominent manner against compulsory military training and we believe that the great masses of the people should determine whether or not they should engage in this unjust and uncalled for war. Therefore, recognizing the sentiments of the people that I represent and expressing my own views, personally, I would most respectfully beg to be excused from participating in the matter referred to in your letter.[39]

*Advance*, the official organ of the Amalgamated Clothing Workers of America (which was ostracized by the AFL and not even invited to the conference)* questioned the authority of the conference to speak for organized labor, since the majority of the unions represented at the conference were actually small unions. The labor journal pointed out that the 148 delegates to the conference, who, according to Gompers, spoke "for millions of Americans," represented, at best, their membership only, and were not representative of the labor organizations affiliated with the American Federation of Labor, as Gompers claimed. Then again, "the rank and file were not consulted prior to the meeting and thus the conference spoke

*For the background of the dispute between the AFL leadership and the Amalgamated Clothing Workers, *see* Philip S. Foner, *History of the Labor Movement in the United States* 5 (New York, 1980): 260-64.

without any real authority." Furthermore, since "no officer of a labor organization can commit his constituents to war without their consent, particularly if such constituents are expected to man the guns and stake their lives," the officers who did so "usurped a power that was not theirs." Concluding on this note, *Advance* contended that the "Washington conference could at best act in an advisory capacity."[40]

Even more damaging to the claim that the conference spoke for organized labor was the information furnished by one who had attended the gathering. Daniel J. Tobin, president of the International Brotherhood of Teamsters, Chauffeurs, Stablemen & Helpers of America, wrote to Gompers that after the conference in Washington he would have nothing further to do with any movement sponsored by the AFL president, "because of the fact that things will have to run as you want them to run or they cannot run at all." He continued:

> This was proved to me conclusively when I accepted the invitation to Washington recently to attend a meeting of labor leaders of National and International Unions, to advise and counsel with the members of the Executive Council of the American Federation of Labor, so that we might arrive at a safe conclusion. When I arrived there, on the strength of your invitation, I found you had a program already prepared; cut-and-dried, to be adopted by this gathering of the so-called labor leaders, and that we could not, or would not, be allowed to change one word of that declaration. I endeavored to have an amendment adopted postponing definite action for three or four days, but this was objected to and voted down by nearly every member of the Council, although we were brought there for a definite purpose, and although we had no power from our International or National Unions to act on the proposition submitted.[41]

In an article in the *International Teamster*, the union's official journal, Tobin added some details. He noted that he had asked for a postponement on the vote so that the delegates who were present could ascertain the position of their memberships on the crucial issue of peace or war. This, however, was "voted down by nearly every member of the [Executive] Council," as was Tobin's other proposal to defer voting on the declaration until the following morning. Finally, Tobin revealed, the conference was asked to adopt the declaration "just as it was read," and it was "rammed down the throats" of the 148 delegates who were "not allowed to change a word." Tobin concluded that "there was really no need for calling the representatives of labor to Washington . . . when there was a cut-and-dried program already prepared which might have been mailed to the International Officers. . . ."[42]

Since the proceedings of the conference were secret, Tobin's disclosures were significant in challenging the picture drawn by Gompers of a gathering of labor leaders who spoke freely for organized labor in support of war. What Tobin did not explain or even discuss, however, was why he refrained from voting against the declaration despite his bitterness over the way it was "rammed down the throats" of the delegates. Or why Arnold Miller, president of the International Fur Workers' Union, and Andrew Furuseth, president of the Sailors' Union of the Pacific, who were leaders of unions vigorously opposed to U.S. entrance into the war, did not vote against the declaration.[43*]

After the conference, these men briefly continued their opposition to U.S. participation in the war, but their failure to vote against the declaration indicated that it would not take much for them to reverse their anti-war stand. Simeon Larson argues that they probably acted as they did at Washington out of fear—"fear of exposing their minority position before a hostile public opinion, and of making their union subject to the displeasure and enmity of the government as well as the Gompers' forces that controlled the machinery of the AFL."[44] But such "fear" did not keep Tobin from publicly exposing the authoritarian methods used to force adoption of the declaration. In truth, these union leaders were behaving consistently. They usually talked militantly, but acted conservatively.[45]

Labor's response to the declaration, "American Labor's Position in Peace or in War," was far from enthusiastic. To be sure, *The Tailor*, official organ of the Journeymen's Tailors' Union of America, viewed the declaration as being "like the Ten Commandments," and warned that "a change would only spoil it."[46] But this was a distinctly minority position. More typical was the indignation voiced by the International Association of Machinists of Cleveland, who wrote to Gompers complaining of "the high-handed action of pledging the members of the A.F. of L. to unlimited support in time of war. We demand to know by whom such authority to pledge the workers of the nation to a bloody war in the interest of the steel and ammunition manufacturers was given." Those who drew up and approved the declaration, the Cleveland Machinists declared, were guilty of "endorsing capital, throwing labor to the dogs, and destroying the highest interest of the nation."[47]

*According to the *New York Times*, Furuseth was "among the chief opponents of the declaration," and afterwards characterized it as "a virtual declaration of war." (March 13, 1917.) Furuseth encountered the bitter anger of his membership when he returned to San Francisco for his failure to vote against the declaration. (Hyman Weintraub, *Andrew Furuseth, Emancipator of the Seamen* (Berkeley, Ca., 1959), p. 143.) Similarly, the fur workers angrily denounced Miller for having voted for the declaration. (Philip S. Foner, *The Fur and Leather Workers Union* [Newark, N.J., 1950] p. 50).

Lewis Lorwin concludes that within the trade unions, "the declaration was met with lukewarm endorsement or unorganized opposition." In any case, since "few labor bodies were given an opportunity to express themselves on this declaration . . . the acceptance of the declaration of March 12 by the labor movement was to a large measure passive."[48]

In an editorial, "Patriotic Organized Labor," the *New York Times* reminded its readers that "it was at the suggestion of the Council of National Defense that a conference of the American trade unions, national and international, was held in Washington." It dismissed "the declaration of rights and wrongs and duties, the demands, conditions and guarantees laid down by the conference" as "largely, theoretical," a "sop to the radical elements," and contended that "the common resolve to defend the country is the prime and essential part of the statement."[49] Evidently Gompers agreed. In reporting on the conference to the Council of National Defense, Gompers did not bother to mention the demands for recognition, protection of rights, and equality of sacrifice. He spoke only of the "comprehensive declaration of loyalty" which the gathering had produced, and proudly boasted that the declaration smoothed the way for America's entrance into the war.[50]

Gompers later explained this statement with the observation that the only thing standing in the way of a declaration of war at the time of the conference was that the President and Congress were not sure of the position that would be taken by the masses of the working people, and that labor's declaration giving the administration a "blank check" also gave it the necessary assurance and encouragement it had sought.[51]

It also gave the AFL leaders and the Wilson administration a weapon with which to isolate the anti-war forces in the labor movement, "and cast them in the villainous role of being traitors to the unions and the workers if they continued in their anti-war crusade." And it made it easier for labor leaders to abandon the peace ship.[52]

Despite tremendous pressure to support whatever steps the administration took, many unions were not yet prepared to abandon their opposition to American intervention. Some voiced this in telegrams to Gompers, such as that sent by the Schenectady Trades Assembly notifying him that the central labor union had "unanimously voted tonight (March 29) to request you to use every influence you can bring to bear to prevent declaration of war."[53] Others expressed this opposition in telegrams to Congress. On April 2, the Joint Board of Cloakmakers in New York cabled Speaker of the House Champ Clark, urging him "in the name of humanity and true patriotism, to exercise your influence to deliver this country from the hor-

Workers advised their members to protest to their Congressmen against the nation's participation "in the European capitalistic conflict."[55] In Seattle, the Central Labor Council informed Congress that it had voted unanimously (250-0) on April 4, "to oppose American entry into the war."[56]

## LABOR'S RESPONSE TO THE DECLARATION OF WAR

When Congress declared war on April 6, 1917, not much of this anti-war sentiment was evident at first as pledges of support for the government came from union after union, state federations of labor, and city central labor councils. As expected, the AFL leadership responded eagerly, never veering from the super-patriotic course it had already adopted. The attitude of many unions and labor leaders who had previously opposed entrance into the war changed dramatically as they literally wrapped themselves in the flag. The Central Federated Union of New York City, which had previously taken a position against the war, not only came out in support, but withdrew its endorsement of the Socialist New York *Call*.[57] The Missouri Federation of Labor, which had criticized Gompers' action in calling the conference of international and national unions in Washington, and had opposed the preparedness campaign until the formal declaration of war, now expressed its "unreserved and heartiest approval of the loyal stand taken in this crisis of our nation by the American Federation of Labor, the recognized and unimpeachable representative of organized labor in this country. . . ."[58]

Andrew Furuseth, who had often declared he did "not believe in our entry in the war," now took the position "that it was the duty of seamen to aid to the best of their ability the nation which had given them freedom."[59*] Daniel J. Tobin also reversed himself and backed the war to the hilt. "If

*Furuseth was repeating the position he had taken sixteen years before on the war with Spain. At first he had written strong anti-war editorials in the *Coast Seamen's Journal*. But once the United States declared war against Spain on April 25, 1898, he pledged labor's allegiance to the nation in its war effort. The war might "have been avoided . . . but having got into the war, no matter how or why, we want to win out as speedily as possible and with as little damage as possible. 'How to win' is the only question worth considering now. The answer is, 'by hard fighting.'" Three years later, Furuseth admitted that he had supported the war in the belief that by proving its "patriotism," labor could prevent setbacks during the conflict and even make advances. This was a false concept of patriotism, he conceded, and he should have opposed the war, even after it had started, "because, under all the circumstances of the case, war would result in injury and possibly an irretrievable set-back to the cause of the working-class advancement in the United States." (Philip S. Foner, *History of the Labor Movement in the United States*2 [New York,1955]:414-15.) Clearly, Furuseth had learned nothing from the earlier experience.

we win the war," he now declared, "the working people will be far ahead of where they were before the war." But "if we lose the war . . . it will mean that oppression, persecution and a dominating influence of tyranny will be aimed and directed against the masses" of our country.[60] Sidney Hillman of the Amalgamated Clothing Workers, an early opponent of Gompers' preparedness campaign and one of the most critical of the "Labor Declaration," now advocated full support of the war effort by organized labor, contending that a victory for Germany would mean "a victory for industrial autocracy" and "a heavy defeat for labor."[61]

Labor leaders who reversed themselves rationalized their support of the war in the moralistic terms made familiar by Woodrow Wilson. They were now willing to join the crusade to make the world safe for democracy, although they sometimes added that they wanted it clearly understood that "a world made safe for democracy is synonymous with a world made safe for the laborer."[62] In any case, these assertions of patriotism and pledges of support were voiced without consulting the rank-and-file workers, and without explaining why a war which they had denounced as capitalistic in character and from which workers could not benefit, had suddenly changed.

Two organizations did not reverse their stands after the American declaration of war. The day after the declaration of war, the Socialist Party of America met in emergency convention in St. Louis to determine the party's position on the war and the delegates overwhelmingly adopted the majority report, which reiterated the opposition that the Socialists "had maintained since the outbreak of the war in 1914," branded the declaration of war as "a crime against the people of the United States and against the nations of the world," and recommended a course of action to oppose the war and conscription, because "the country has been violently, needlessly, and criminally involved in war."

Soon after America's entry into the war, "Big Bill" Haywood, general secretary of the IWW, declared that "All class conscious members of the Industrial Workers of the World are conscientiously opposed to spilling the life blood of human beings, not for religious reasons, as are the Quakers and Friendly Societies, but because we believe that the interests and welfare of the working class in all countries are identical." In short, the Wobblies were not pacifists, but believed deeply that working-class interests cut across national lines and that wars, except the class war, benefited only the capitalists while working men and women bore the cost.

But if they were not pacifists, many leaders of the IWW were now anxious to show that they were realists. While the IWW should and would oppose the war, they argued, the Wobblies should not give it top priority. Haywood and many other IWW leaders were anxious that the Wobblies concentrate on organizing the unorganized and not permit themselves to be targeted for imprisonment and other repressions by active opposition to the war. In fact, shortly before the actual declaration of war, the IWW national office held up production of adhesive stickers it had planned to distribute. These asked "Why Be a Soldier?" with the last word printed in dripping red letters. At Haywood's suggestion, printing was also stopped on the pamphlet "The Deadly Parallel." This had consisted of the antiwar statement adopted at the 1916 IWW convention, printed alongside the pledge of support for the war given by the special AFL conference in Washington in March 1917, which gave President Wilson a "blank check."

We shall later discuss the IWW position on and role in World War I, but observe now that the IWW—unlike the AFL—never supported the imperialist war. Twelve days after the United States entered the war, the *Industrial Worker* featured the following anonymous song:

> I love my flag, I do, I do,
> Which floats upon the breeze,
> I also love my arms and legs,
> And neck and nose and knees.
> One little shell might spoil them all
> Or give them such a twist,
> They would be no use to me;
>     I guess I won't enlist.
>
> I love my country, yes, I do,
> I hope her folks do well,
> Without our arms and legs and things,
> I think we'd look like hell,
> Young men with faces half shot off
> And unfit to be kissed.
> I've read in books it spoils their looks,
>     I guess I won't enlist.[63]

The Socialist Party and the IWW did not speak only for their own members. The assertions of patriotism and pledges of support by AFL leaders were often contradicted by the stand taken in their union journals and locals.[64] Although Sidney Hillman reversed himself and supported the war, the Amalgamated Clothing Workers and its official journal, *Advance*, did not. After Congress had declared war and Hillman had voiced his support, the Amalgamated declared: "Today we have the additional duty of protesting against war by our own country, against saddling the yoke of militarism upon the working class at home. . . . Capitalism wants war and war there will be regardless of the will of the people. The people were not consulted in the other countries at war and they have not been in our own."[65] In an appeal, "Workers Are Urged to Protest on May Day Against All Wars," the Amalgamated called on its members and other workers to participate in the approaching May Day parades as part of a workers' protest against the war.[66]

Two weeks after the United States entered the war, the Amalgamated Clothing Workers hailed the Socialist Party's St. Louis Manifesto against the war and all forms of militarism, declaring that since the Socialist Party had "taken a clear and firm stand against international fratricide and the rule of the bayonet, the socialist movement in this country stands vindicated."[67] Speaking of "opposition and indifference to the war," some thirteen months after American entrance, Secretary of Labor William B. Wilson stated that "one of the first things we had to deal with was to change that attitude of mind . . . on the part of the wage workers of the country, first through the great leaders of the trades-union movement, and then to the rank and file."[68]

# CHAPTER 6

# The People's Council and the American Alliance for Labor and Democracy

## ORGANIZING THE PEOPLE'S COUNCIL

Shortly after America's entry into World War I, the Bolsheviks in Russia made public their demands for a peace based on no annexations, no indemnities, and self-determination for all peoples. These dramatic new peace proposals gave U.S. Socialists and pacifists a program around which to advance a campaign for world peace. On May 2, 1917, the Emergency Peace Federation, the American Union Against Militarism, and the Women's Peace Party met to coordinate their programs and to lay plans for a giant peace rally. A number of Socialists, led by Morris Hillquit, joined the planning sessions.[1]

An organizing committee was also established to form a new peace society based on the workingmen's councils of the Bolsheviks in Russia. (Morris Hillquit was chosen chairman and Louis P. Lochner, of the Emergency Peace Federation, secretary.) The American councils, notes Frank Grubbs, Jr., "were to appeal primarily to the working classes and to those who were unconnected with the capitalist class."[2]

On May 10, 1917, Lochner sent Samuel Gompers a telegram announcing that a "strong group representing Labor, Socialism, Peace, Religion, Politics Plans First American Conference for Democracy and Terms of Peace." The meeting was scheduled for New York City's Madison Square Garden on May 30. Those invited were to accept "in principle . . . speedy and universal peace, no indemnities, no forcible annexations," and a number of other demands, including "opposition to conscription," "defense of free speech and press," "opposition to lowering industrial standards," and "heavy taxation of war industries and incomes." Gompers was asked: "May we use your name in call for Conference"? The AFL president replied that same day: "Telegram received. I prefer not to ally myself with the conscious or unconscious agents of the Kaiser in America."[3]

Although Gompers was not listed, the call for the First American Conference for Democracy and Terms of Peace included the names of officials from some of the leading trade unions in the country, particularly those centered in New York City with large memberships in the garment trades. They included Benjamin Schlesinger, president, and Abraham Baroff, secretary of the International Ladies' Garment Workers' Union; Joseph Schlossberg, secretary of the Amalgamated Clothing Workers of America; James H. Maurer, president of the Pennsylvania State Federation of Labor; Max Pine, secretary-treasurer of the United Hebrew Trades of New York; Rose Schneiderman of the Women's Trade Union League and an ILGWU organizer; Alexander Trachtenberg, research director of the ILGWU and editor of the *American Labor Year Book*; and Joseph D. Cannon, organizer for the International Mine, Mill and Smelter Workers' Union. Also endorsing the call were Judge Jacob Panken, Rabbi Judah Magnes of New York's lower east side, and Morris Hillquit of the Socialist Party.[4]

For two days, beginning on the morning of May 30, dozens of pacifist and Socialist speakers addressed four hundred delegates, emphasizing the need for opposing both the war policies of President Wilson and the labor program of Samuel Gompers. The conference then adopted a number of resolutions endorsing the creation of an international organization dedicated to world peace, the preservation and extension of democracy at home, the repeal of conscription laws, the safeguarding of labor standards, and the demand upon the United States government "that it state concretely the terms upon which it is willing to make peace." Finally, the conference established a permanent organization—the People's Council for Democracy and Terms of Peace. The newly formed organization immediately issued a call to a national gathering in Minneapolis during the first week of September.[5]

When the People's Council was formed, it had the firm backing of the ILGWU and the United Hebrew Trades, but its executive board also included such labor leaders as Maurer, J. Mahlon Barnes, president of the International Cigar Maker's Union, and James Bagley, president of the Brooklyn Central Labor Union. Other permanent officers were Lochner as executive secretary, Rebecca Shelly as financial secretary, and Elizabeth Freeman as legislative secretary. Hillquit, Rabbi Magnes, Judge Panken, and the young Presbyterian minister Norman Thomas, were also executive board members.[6]

During the late summer of 1917, the leaders of the People's Council undertook an expansion program into other areas of the country. Maurer went on a nationwide tour, addressing mass meetings of trade unions and calling upon labor "to organize the anti-war movement."[7] Local conferences were held in Philadelphia, Los Angeles, San Francisco, Seattle, Salt Lake City, Chicago, and many smaller cities and towns. Local branches were established in eighteen states extending from New York and Massachusetts in the east to California and Oregon in the west.[8]

To facilitate activities among trade unionists, the People's Council organized a separate unit known as the Workmen's Council of America. It was explained that "it is the failure of the official leadership of the American Federation of Labor to meet the exigencies created by war, and to stand up for the preservation of labor's rights that caused the creation of the Workmen's Council of America."[9]

In New York City, the Workmen's Council included the United Hebrew Trades and about 65 local unions. Among the latter were fur workers, ladies garment workers, painters, jewelry workers, and bakers. By mid-August 1917, it had grown to 284 branches of the People's Council in New York City, including chapters in 93 unions, representing over 900,000 workers.[10]

By this time, the Council was claiming that a new local union of the AFL was joining it each day, and it envisioned a membership of two million by September, made up largely of AFL members.[11] But several months before this, Gompers had already termed the "situation dangerous" and had swung into action to undermine the People's Council.[12]

## FORMATION OF AMERICAN ALLIANCE FOR LABOR AND DEMOCRACY

Gompers did not take the new labor-pacifist movement seriously at first, even though one of the People's Council's objectives was to oust him from the AFL presidency.[13] But others in or close to the AFL were becoming seriously alarmed lest the Socialists take over the leadership of the labor movement, especially in New York City. Chief among these was Robert Maisel, director of the National Labor Publicity Organization, which operated as a clearing house for most labor publications in New York City. Maisel had formerly been associated with the New York *Call*, and even though he resigned from the Socialist newspaper after America's entry into the war (which he fully supported) he maintained contacts with his former Socialist friends and was thus able to obtain inside information about the growing influence of the People's Council. He soon began to supply Gompers with confidential information concerning the Council's organizing work. He was able to convince the AFL president that if nothing was done to counteract them, the Socialists would soon capture the leadership of the Central Federated Union in New York and put that important labor body on record as opposing the war and urging a speedy peace. From there, Maisel predicted, the movement would infiltrate organized labor with propaganda that would cause interference with the war effort.[14]

Now thoroughly alarmed, Gompers made plans to visit New York and personally urge the Central Federated Union to establish an organization of loyal labor forces designed to counter the People's Council and fully support the Wilson wartime program.[15] He was supported in this by the *New York Times*, which attacked the People's Council as a German-financed Socialist plot "for a German peace." At a meeting of the CFU on June 29, Gompers echoed the *Times'* characterization of the People's Council and urged all loyal trade unionists to avoid "such treasonable elements" who, he said, were attempting to destroy the true American labor movement.[16]

Out of the conferences between Gompers and the General Executive Committee of the Central Federated Union emerged the American Alliance for Labor and Democracy, the organization that was to be the AFL's answer to the People's Council. It was originally established in July 1917, to combat the specific situation in New York City.[17] But when John Spargo, the pro-war Socialist, learned of Gompers' action in New York City, he conferred with President Wilson and was told that the President was "distressed and troubled by the conditions in certain parts of the country with respect to the war," and especially by the "very sullen resentment." Spargo promised to approach Gompers and suggest that the pro-war Socialists "link up with picked men from the AFL" to form a national pro-war labor organization. Gompers agreed, and the American Alliance for Labor and Democracy expanded from a local to a national organization. Wilson was delighted and urged Spargo to proceed and not to worry about money for the organization, since he had "a fund that Congress had voted that is to be spent at my discretion."[18]

At this point, Ralph M. Easley of the National Civic Federation suggested to Gompers that he approach George Creel of the Committee on Public Information and request that he "furnish the funds for both the publicity and organization work" of the Alliance. A few months later, Easley informed Vincent Astor that the American Alliance for Labor and Democracy was "financed by the Creel bureau, the money coming out of the President's $100,000,000 fund." The Committee on Public Information

had agreed to pay for rent and salaries, as well as for the Alliance's published propaganda.[19]

The Committee on Public Information had been established by Wilson
on April 13, 1917 for the sole purpose of keeping Americans loyal to the
war effort. The American Alliance would "actually function as a labor
subsidiary of the Administration's propaganda bureau . . . [and] drum up
support for a pro-war policy among workers." In fact, Creel regarded the
American Alliance as "our most important body" and he informed the
League for National Unity that "the Government is behind it to the limit
of its power." Although Gompers was the chairman and Maisel the director, Creel made most of the Alliance's basic decisions, determining which
pamphlets and statements the Alliance should publish.[20]

Although the Alliance operated as organized labor's adjunct to the
Wilson administration's war propaganda machine, the general public was
led to believe that the AALD was an independent, self-sustaining organization. When James H. Maurer addressed an open letter to Gompers,
asking who was financing the Alliance, the AFL president indignantly
refused to answer.[21]

The list of top officers of the American Alliance reflected the cooperation between AFL leaders and pro-war Socialists. On the Advisory
Council were such AFL men as Ernest Bohm and Hugh Frayne, along
with three of the leading pro-war Socialists: John Spargo, Charles Edward
Russell and William English Walling.[22]

In mid-August, Gompers sent a circular to all international and local
AFL unions informing them of the AALD's existence and asking all AFL
branches to establish local AALD chapters. "Minutes count [and] the pro-
German cause gains by every minute of American delay," Gompers
emphasized as he urged the signing up of members in the Alliance.[23]

All prospective members were required to take the following pledge of
loyalty:

> The undersigned hereby affirms that it is the duty of all the people of the
> United States, without regard to class, nationality, politics or religion, faith-
> fully and loyally to support the government of the United States in carrying on
> the present war for justice, freedom and democracy to a triumphant conclusion
> and gives this pledge to uphold every honorable effort for the accomplishment
> of that purpose, and to support the AFL as well as the declaration of organized
> labor's representatives made March 12, 1917, at Washington, D.C. as to
> "Labor's Position in Peace or in War."[24]

Thus, prospective members were not only obliged to pledge their support of the government's war policies, but also to affirm their loyalty to the AFL and its policies.

## ALLIANCE PROPAGANDA

With the Creel Committee on Public Information providing the funds for renting office space in New York City and hiring a staff to carry on its publicity campaign, the Alliance established a weekly news service and published leaflets and pamphlets on such topics as "labor and the war, socialism, bolshevism, government regulation, profiteering, reconstruction and general industrial adjustment." In addition, it began to supply the labor press with "loyalty material." The purpose of all these endeavors was to counter the influence of the People's Council.[25]

Alliance literature emphasized that "this is labor's war . . . the voice of Uncle Sam is calling every worker to show his colors." A widely distributed Alliance publication centered around Gompers' statement opposing the Stockholm Peace Conference, which all anti-war Socialists supported.* "This is no time for the working people of the Allies to gather in a peace conference," Gompers declared, "the action of which might hamper the efficiency of the nation's fighting forces. . . ."[26] The Alliance made no pretense of involving the workers whom it addressed in any decisions concerning peace. All they were asked to do was to support the position of the Wilson administration and that of the AFL leadership, which endorsed it uncritically. By way of contrast, the People's Council did involve the workers and their representatives in deciding policies. "In every city where a local People's Council has been formed," declared the *Locomotive Fireman*, labor has participated and in most cases dominated the Councils."[27]

## TWO NATIONAL CONVENTIONS

Although the People's Council had chapters in most urban centers by late summer of 1917, it encountered great difficulty in finding a place for its first national convention. The meeting was scheduled for September 1 in Minneapolis, but all the halls and auditoriums were closed to it. When the Council tried to hold the convention in a large tent, it discovered that no one would rent the land on which to erect the tent. Nevertheless, the Council officials persisted and issued a call for the convention which asked:

*The People's Council had elected delegates to attend the Stockholm Peace Conference, but the delegates never received passports from the United States government (New York *Call*, Aug. 14, 1917).

Shall we stand with the high-sounding American Alliance for Labor and Democracy and Gompers, or the People's Council for Labor and Democracy of James Maurer? . . . Samuel Gompers, despite his noble duty of earlier days, no longer speaks for American labor. . . . Come to Minneapolis![28]

But Minnesota Governor J. A. Burnquist placed that state totally off limits to the convention on the ground that it "would give aid and comfort to the enemies of the United States."[29] After the People's Council had received rebuffs from several other localities, Chicago Mayor William Hale Thompson extended an invitation to it to meet in his city and under his personal protection. However, Illinois Governor Frank Lowden forbade Thompson to allow the People's Council to convene in Chicago. While Thompson and Lowden were battling, the delegates were able to rent an auditorium in Chicago and begin their deliberations on September 1.[30]

Before the police were able to interrupt the proceedings, the delegates approved a constitution calling on all anti-war radicals to support the Bolshevik peace proposals and build a "social-democracy similar to that of socialist Russia." They also set up a national administrative council consisting of a general committee of fifty, an executive committee of fifteen, and numerous subcommittees based on national districts. The delegates adjourned just before the arrival of three companies of National Guard troops who had been ordered to Chicago by Governor Lowden to close down the convention. By the time the troops reached the auditorium, the delegates had left and had been replaced by the guests attending a Polish wedding.[31]

Directly after the Chicago convention, the People's Council announced that Scott Nearing, the educator and pacifist, had accepted the chairmanship of its Executive Committee. He would make his headquarters in New York City and devote all of his time to the affairs of the Council. Lochner was to continue as executive secretary and the executive committee included Hillquit, Panken, Schlossberg, Shelly, Magnes and Maurer. "The People's Council movement is now upon a strong, permanent basis," declared Maurer confidently. "We represent some 2,500,000 people and our members are being increased daily."[32]

As soon as Gompers learned that the People's Council was planning to hold its first national convention in Minneapolis, he called the national convention of the American Alliance for Labor and Democracy for the same city to begin on September 5, 1917 and continue for three days. This, he declared, would give the Alliance a great opportunity to refute "once for all time" the Council's claims, and demonstrate not only to the working classes of the Allied countries, but "even of the enemy countries," that the Council did not represent the views of the great mass of trade unionists in the United States.

The fact that the Minnesota authorities did not permit the People's Council to hold its convention in Minneapolis did not deter Gompers from scheduling the AALD convention in that city. A call was sent to every central union body and AFL affiliate urging them to participate. J. Phelps Stokes, the millionaire pro-war Socialist, and Frank P. Walsh, the former head of the Commission on Industrial Relations, sought to recruit participants. George Creel himself worked out the details of the Minneapolis meeting with the Alliance leaders. He informed Walsh that he had "explained fully my ideas and wishes with regard to resolution[s]." Thus, the main resolution "should concern itself with the war and declare it a *war of self-defense . . .* and put the Alliance back of the President squarely."[33] Subsidiary resolutions should go on record in favor of free speech and the right of peaceful assembly, urge that the burden of the war be borne by the wealthy, call for a tax on profits, and support government operation of the railroads and all business in which a Federal role was necessary to maintain munitions production. These resolutions, Creel felt, would give the Alliance a program that would appeal even to radicals, while not detracting from the support of the war effort. But even the proposed resolutions were to be limited in their scope. Thus, even though the convention would go on record in favor of free speech, it would not condemn Minnesota's governor for refusing to allow the People's Council to meet in Minneapolis.[34]

After notifying AFL organizers to pay special attention to recruiting labor representatives to attend the AALD convention, Gompers arranged to charter a special train—the "Red, White and Blue Special"—to carry delegates from New York to Minneapolis. Despite the intensive recruitment campaign, only 170 delegates attended. Governor Burnquist, who had earlier driven the People's Council from the city, welcomed the Alliance delegates with great fanfare and a bodyguard of troops.[35]

In his keynote address, Gompers declared that the aim of the Alliance was "to bring together the AFL and pro-war Socialists into a working organization for the immediate purpose of winning the war." To illustrate the administration's support for the Alliance, Gompers read a message from President Wilson endorsing the organization and its crusade against labor disloyalty. In his message, Wilson conceded that "too often military necessities have been an excuse for the destruction of laboriously erected industrial and social standards," but he stressed that fears that this would occur under his administration were groundless. Labor loyalty, he insisted, would be rewarded by the government's full support in gaining for "the toiler a new dignity and new sense of social and economic security."

The pro-war Socialists at the convention bitterly attacked the leaders of the anti-war forces in the Socialist Party as "tools of Germany" and appealed to "all Socialists in the United States, both organized and unorganized . . . to put all their energy and strength, all their ardor and enthusiasm at the disposal of our Government, so that the war may be carried to a rapid and victorious conclusion." "Socialists of America," the appeal concluded, "join your local branches of the American Alliance for Labor and Democracy." And finally, the pro-war Socialists made the demagogic statement that in supporting the Alliance, Socialists would be following in the footsteps of "Karl Liebknecht and Rosa Luxemburg in Germany."[36*]

In adopting a declaration and resolutions, the AALD convention followed Creel's directives. The declaration, which served as the principal resolution, pledged support to the Government of the United States and its Allies until complete military victory was achieved. It attacked those "enemies of the Republic who falsely assuming to speak in the name of labor and democracy, are now ceaselessly striving to obstruct the operations of the government." It concluded with the assertion that the "great war must be fought to a decisive result," and "that until autocracy is defeated, there can be no hope of an honorable peace. . . ."[37] As Creel suggested, resolutions were also passed urging protection of labor's high living standards, conscription of wealth, the end of profiteering, labor representation on all government boards and at the official peace conference, and equal suffrage for both sexes. A number of these demands were stated vaguely, and little was added to spell out a specific program to accomplish them.[38]

"It was a very successful conference," Gompers told the press, emphasizing that the delegates represented the real voice of organized labor.[39] But the facts did not sustain this conclusion. Of the 170 delegates who attended the convention, 89 were trade unionists and 81 were Socialists and social reformers. But most of the trade union delegates were from small federal labor unions or were officials of the AFL itself. Few represented any of the large unions. This led some unions to object to adoption at the convention of resolutions in the name of organized labor. In fact,

---

*Among the signers of the appeal were John Spargo, J. Phelps Stokes, A. M. Simons and W. J. Ghent. (*New York Times*, Sept. 8, 1917).

many trade unionists came to view the convention as Gompers' "personally conducted conference," which was not "competent to speak for the trade union movement."[40]

## THE 1917 AFL CONVENTION

The rivalry between the People's Council and the American Alliance came to a head at the AFL convention in Buffalo in November 1917. The debate came after the unprecedented appearance at the convention of President Wilson. In the course of his address, Wilson voiced his enthusiastic endorsement of Gompers' leadership, "his patriotic courage, his large vision, and his statesmanlike sense of what has to be done."[41] Robert Maisel assured George Creel that the President's emphatic endorsement of Gompers' policies would "kill entirely" any plan to challenge the American Alliance at the convention, but he did predict that "some trouble may turn up."[42] It did.

Gompers' request that the convention give "full endorsement to the patriotic work which has been undertaken by the American Alliance for Labor and Democracy" provoked an acrimonious floor debate. J. Mahlon Barnes of the International Cigar Makers' Union asked if the convention was being asked to endorse such "patriotic acts" as that of Governor Burnquist of Minnesota, who had prevented "the assembling of a peaceful congress of people and hounded them out of his state," or of Governor Lowden of Illinois, who had sent the militia "to break up a peaceable meeting of citizens." Yet both governors had been invited to address the convention of the American Alliance.[43]

Barnes was answered by John H. Walker of the United Mine Workers, a fervent supporter of the American Alliance. Walker insisted that the governors had been justified in their actions because the union men associated with the People's Council had been "paid by the German government for preaching sedition and weakening our government in the war." Walker felt that such men should have been interned and not allowed to return home.[44]

After further discussion, an amendment was introduced stating that the activities of the American Alliance "are of no concern to this body, and that no action be taken on the matter."[45] The amendment was seconded, and after a discussion that indicated the proposal was gaining support, Matthew Woll warned the delegates that a rejection of the Alliance would be a repudiation of the entire AFL leadership, as well as a signal to Germany that American labor was not ready to support the government in the war. He urged the delegates to remember

> that the President of the Federation is also the President of the American
> Alliance for Labor and Democracy, and a refusal to endorse the good work of
> the Alliance means to place the President of the Federation in a most un-
> enviable and embarrassing light and situation before our people and the public
> generally.[46]

The overwhelming vote in support of the AALD—21,602 in favor, 402
opposed and 1,305 not voting—concealed the fact that those who voted
against the Alliance ran the risk of being labelled enemies of both the AFL
leadership and the government of the United States; in short, "agents of
the nation's enemies."[47]

## ALLIANCE PROBLEMS

The Alliance had gained its ends at the AFL convention, but it was
being weakened by a split between its AFL forces and those under the
leadership of John Spargo. The pro-war Socialists attempted to set up their
own party, which they called the National Party. Although this party
proved to be weak and ineffective, its formation occupied much of the
attention and energy of the Alliance leaders and held back the organization's propaganda work.[48] At the same time, the Alliance began to experience serious financial problems. In spite of its endorsement by the AFL
convention, labor support of the Alliance was both reluctant and sporadic.
A January 21, 1918 appeal by Gompers for funds brought a meager
response. By February 1, only $700 had been collected, which was con-
sidered "poor."[49]

As a result, the Alliance became completely dependent on the government for its survival. Precisely at this time, however, George Creel began
to complain about its repeated requests for funds. Eventually Creel
ordered his staff to cease paying most of the Alliance's bills, and the work
of the organization practically came to a standstill. This was especially
true in areas where organized labor had its greatest strength, such as
Illinois, New York, New Jersey, Connecticut, Pennsylvania, and Rhode
Island.[50] In Chicago, the unions simply ignored the Alliance, while on
New York's east side anti-war feeling was so strong among the Jewish
garment workers that the Alliance organized a special Jewish Department
to combat it. However, Maisel complained to Gompers that the department's effectiveness was limited because "Creel does not seem to recognize that money is involved."[51]

# THE HILLQUIT MAYORALTY CAMPAIGN

Internal conflicts and inadequate funds also weakened the work of the People's Council, but two events in the fall of 1917 served to lift the Council's morale and spirits. The first was the New York City mayoralty election of November 1917. Morris Hillquit, leader of the Socialist Party in New York and an opponent of the war, ran for mayor on a peace ticket, and the Socialist Party decided to use the campaign to test anti-war sentiment in New York City. It was joined by the People's Council, which worked for Hillquit's election. Hillquit was also endorsed by the Amalgamated Clothing Workers, the International Ladies' Garment Workers' Union, the International Fur Workers' Union, the Neckwear Workers' Union, and the United Hebrew Trades. The American Alliance for Labor and Democracy, which agreed with the Socialists that the vote would be a test of anti-war sentiment, opposed Hillquit.[52]

The results astounded the nation. Although not elected, Hillquit polled almost five times as many votes as any previous Socialist candidate. He amassed 22 percent of the vote, carrying 12 election districts. He also carried to victory ten assemblymen and seven aldermen on the Socialist ticket. "The Socialist vote," notes Frank L. Grubbs, Jr., "showed that the Alliance and the Administration had not subdued the radicals, despite weeks of intensive loyalty work."[53]

# THE BOLSHEVIK REVOLUTION

At the same time, news came of the successful Bolshevik revolution in Russia. We will deal more fully with the impact of the revolution on American labor and radicalism, but here we note that the news of the October Revolution prompted a determination on the part of the People's Council movement "to pressure Wilson to accept the Bolsheviks as Russia's legitimate rulers" and "force Wilson to foresake his support of this 'Capitalist war.'"[54] On November 13, 1917, the Council's executive committee announced a revised program for peace and industrial democracy, which included the nationalization of all production, adequate compensation to workers for their labor, and the establishment of an international brotherhood to ensure the peace.[55] In Chicago, at a meeting sponsored by the People's Council, William Bross Lloyd cried out to the audience: "The Bolsheviks are calling you, they are working for an immediate armistice. Are you there? Do your part!"[56]

As the Council's peace offensive mounted and its *Bulletin* increased its circulation by 10,000 copies during the first two weeks of November,[57] the

American Alliance struck back. With the financial support of the Committee on Public Information restored, it distributed a series of loyalty pamphlets, some of them written by John R. Commons, the University of Wisconsin economist. The literature emphasized that American workers could gain national support for their aims only by supporting Wilson's war policies.[58]

## THE ALLIANCE USES ECONOMIC PRESSURE

The Alliance did not rely solely on propaganda. It now added economic pressure to its arsenal. An example is the dispute that arose between the Amalgamated Clothing Workers and the small Cloak Makers' Union of the ILGWU. Although president Sidney Hillman of the Amalgamated was not a member of the People's Council, many of the union's leaders and rank-and-file members were active in it, with Hillman's approval.[59] When the Amalgamated received a number of government war contracts, members of the Cloak Makers' Union, which had not received any, were forced out of work. The cloak makers proclaimed their support of the war and asked the Alliance to assist them in obtaining work. They also made it clear that they did not approve of the fact that ILGWU president Benjamin Schlesinger was a member of the People's Council.[60]

Gompers quickly responded by urging Secretary of War Newton D. Baker to compel the Amalgamated to share its contracts with the cloak makers. Not only was this done, but President Wilson also urged Baker to withdraw contracts from any union associated with the People's Council.[61]

Faced with the loss of government contracts, the Amalgamated and ILGWU officials informed the Alliance that they would cease work on behalf of the People's Council. With Wilson's backing, Gompers then turned his pressure on the United Hebrew Trades to support the Alliance's loyalty work on New York's east side. Although the UHT refused to make a definite commitment, the fear that the garment workers, who made up the bulk of its membership, would lose government contracts if they continued to support the People's Council's peace offensive led the organization to cease its participation in the Council's work.[62] Maisel reported jubilantly in February 1918 that the Jewish press in New York City was "more or less friendly to us now; I can say that all of the Jewish papers, with the exception of the socialist ones, are now loyal to the government."[63]*

---

*In the same report Maisel announced that the Alliance had 136 locals in 39 states, that 150 dailies regularly printed Alliance material, and that dozens of magazines accepted its propaganda. By this time, moreover, 1,500,000 propaganda pamphlets had been distributed by the Alliance.

A month later, even some of the "socialist ones" shifted their positions. In March 1918, the German offensive against Russia led to Russia's capitulation and to the Brest-Litovsk Treaty, which Germany forced on the weak Soviet government. The harsh treaty provisions pushed many anti-war unionists who had been reevaluating their attitude toward American participation in the war, over into the administration camp. Thus, the United Hebrew Trades officially reversed its earlier anti-war position. Then, as we shall see, when President Wilson announced his Fourteen Points, even anti-war Socialists began to waver, and finally supported Wilson.[64]

## DECLINE OF THE PEOPLE'S COUNCIL

These developments reduced the need for the Alliance, and it became less important to the administration, especially since the People's Council was declining in strength under the impact of economic pressure, the repressive policies of the Wilson administration, and the movement of leading anti-war Socialists into the pro-war camp. Its main strength had been in New York City, particularly among the Jewish workers, but repression and capitulation had taken its toll. Scott Nearing, who, with Louis P. Lochner, remained with the People's Council to the end, observed: "The People's Council was a casualty of the war. Any organization taking the Council's stand was in for a rough time. Patriotic support of the war was widespread and vigilantism was general."[65]

There was one difficulty that the Alliance could not overcome, and in the end, it was this that rendered much of its activity useless. As Chester Wright, head of the Alliance's Division of Labor Publications, noted, "intolerable working conditions" undermined the work of the Alliance, and he warned that "any attempt to proceed with loyalty work without an adjudication of industrial conditions would be a pure waste of time."[66]

In the following chapters, we will examine to what extent this warning was heeded.

# CHAPTER 7

# Women and Black Workers
# in Wartime Industry

With the declaration of war by the United States against Germany and its allies on April 6, 1917, U.S. industrial life underwent a profound change. There was a tremendous increase in war orders; the military and industrial demands for labor accelerated rapidly at the very time that immigration from Europe had virtually ceased. Thousands of American workers were being conscripted into the army. In order to fill the gap, employers turned to women and Black workers.

## WOMEN FLOCK INTO INDUSTRY

Writing in the *American Labor Legislation Review* shortly after the armistice, Margaret A. Hobbes commented that the conflict's "most essential by-product was the recognition of the woman worker as an essential factor in industry."[1] While it is true that recognition was slow in coming, and women did not immediately replace men to any great extent,[2] this situation soon changed dramatically. In the fall of 1917, the U.S. Employment Service launched a campaign to replace men with women wherever possible.

The first military draft took place on July 20, 1917 and called 1,347,000 men to the colors. Employers tried to fill their places with experienced female workers, and when they were unable to, they turned to recruiting campaigns to mobilize so-called wageless women for war work.

The figures on the number of women employed in various categories of industries from before the first draft to after the second tell the story:[3]

## WOMEN EMPLOYED PER 1,000 WAGE EARNERS

| Industries | Before the First Draft | After the First Draft | After the Second Draft |
|---|---|---|---|
| Iron and steel and their products | 33 | 61 | 95 |
| Chemicals and allied products | 79 | 98 | 142 |
| Automobile bodies and parts | 21 | 44 | 114 |

In addition, the Women's Bureau of the U.S. Department of Labor conducted a survey of 562 plants engaged in work in metal products other than iron and steel. Before the first draft, the plants employed 14,402 women. After the first draft, there were 19,783 women and 113,061 men employed in 518 firms. After the second draft, there were 23,190 women workers and 106,618 men; the number of firms employing women had risen to 558.[4]

Female labor that had previously been a valuable industrial and commercial resource became a national necessity after the second draft. As thousands of men left for training camps and for duty overseas, and as the need for war materials reached staggering proportions, armament manufacturers had to rely increasingly on women workers.

That more women were now working in industry was not so startling as the fact that they were engaged in so many of what were for them untraditional occupations. In June 1917, *World's Work* had predicted that women's war work "will not consist in putting on trousers or an unbecoming uniform and trying to do something that a man can do better." But it soon had to swallow its words. By the winter of 1917-1918, the YWCA reported: "Avenues of work heretofore unthought of for them [women] have opened up. Calls are coming in for positions all along lines previously held by men, be it business manager, elevator operator, or errand boy."[5] Yet this was just the beginning; soon dozens of articles in such magazines as *Living Age*, *Literary Digest*, *New Republic*, *Delineator*, *Scribner's*, and *Atlantic Monthly* were describing girls' and women's labor in, among other places, dirigible factories, machine shops, steel mills, oil refineries, railway repair sheds, and saddleries. Newspapers carried headlines:

GIRL CONDUCTORS OPERATING STREET-CARS

STEELS MILLS WANT WOMEN

WOMEN PRINT LIBERTY BONDS IN U.S. BUREAU OF ENGRAVING.
ALL BUT PRESSWORK DONE BY FEMININE LABOR.

WOMEN MAKE GOOD SHINGLE PACKERS

WOMEN WORKING IN IDAHO MILLS

The last of these headlines was followed by a dispatch from Moscow,
Idaho, that read:

> Women are being employed in considerable numbers in the lumber mills at
> Potlach, in this county, where lumbermen are engaged in getting out airplane
> stock. They wear overalls, do a man's work and receive a man's wages,
> according to the mill men. . . . Employment of the women is declared due to
> shortage of help in preparing the white and yellow pine for airplane use.[6]

By 1918, overall-clad factory women were toting shells, unloading
freight, painting huge steel tanks, breaking up scrap iron, and wielding
pickaxes. On the railroads they were handling baggage, repairing tracks,
operating bridges, and running the engines. In the cities, they wore the
uniforms of elevator operators, streetcar conductors, and postal workers.
Girls and women who had never worked before and those who had previously worked in non-war trades went into aircraft and munitions plants,
shipbuilding yards, and steel mills, and began operating lathes, drill
presses, milling machines, and other machinery and hand tools. In addition, women continued as part of the labor force in their usual jobs in
textile, clothing, food, and others.

By the time the armistice was signed, almost 10 million U.S. women
had entered into gainful employment. At least 3 million were in factories,
and over one million of these were directly concerned with war equipment; while 100,000 operated long-distance and intracity transport;
250,000 worked in textile manufacturing (from tents to uniforms); and at
least 10,000 were forging metal products. Further, female hands were to
play an essential role in providing sufficient food, clothing, and housing to
equip the four million men in service at domestic installations and on overseas battlefields.[7]

## PERFORMANCE OF WOMEN WORKERS

Women performed ably during the war, and industrial commentators
generally stressed their reliability and efficiency as workers. In August
1917, a committee of Detroit plant managers, having investigated the production record and "teachability" of female operatives, concluded: "Far

from looking forward to the substitution of women for men with dismay, the manufacturer has every reason to welcome the opportunity as one of the blessings in disguise which the war has brought."[8] The New York Merchants Association concurred:

> Employers have stated that women substitutes have proved to be superior to the men whose places they have taken in carrying light materials about shops, in picking and sorting materials, in operating automatic machinery, in light assembly, in winding coils, as drill hands, and as inspectors. In factories, they are proving successful as feeders of printing presses, operators of lathes, machinery-oilers and cleaners, time-keepers, checkers and delivery clerks. They have made satisfactory railroad gate-tenders, ticket-sellers, car-washers, and cleaners. Thus, in nearly every industry they have entered, they are giving an excellent account of themselves.[9]

A Women's Bureau investigation of women employed on lathes in place of men revealed that about 83 percent of the firms that compared women's output to men's declared their production to be as good as or better than that of men.[10] The *American Machinist* confirmed this conclusion when it printed the results of a test conducted by a comptometer manufacturer, which showed that the slowest woman operator equaled the best man's daily performance.[11] But what was probably the most profuse praise of women as workers in the war industries came from the president of an Ohio metal goods plant:

> In reference to the occupations in which women have replaced men, the following may give you some idea of the diversity of the work. In the machine department, women became expert and got out much greater production in running turret lathes, punch presses, bench lathes, milling machines, drill presses, grinding machines, and engraving machines, and in addition to the operation of these machines, we taught them to grind their tools, to act as job setters, and to superintend some of the departments. In the inspection department, practically every inspector was a woman. In the assembly departments . . . all were women, and they did better work and got out more production than men, whom we tried on the job at various times without success. We found, too, that we could place as much, if not more, dependence on women in coming to their work and remaining on the job, which accounts for our having the lowest turnover in help in any factory ever heard of, which was less than 4 percent per year. We taught women to inspect tools and check them over according to the drawings after they came from the tool shop, in which department women became expert. In the optical department, most of the employees grinding lenses were women, who were remarkably successful in the work. In the assembling of lenses, we had none but women on the job, and you will find by

inquiring at the Ordnance Department that our lenses and prisms were as fine as any in the world.[12]

When the war broke out, there already existed a seasoned, well-trained army of women workers in manufacturing industries and an even larger female contingent in other wage-earning activities. Before the war, these women had long been in typically female jobs in factory, mill, and office and were accustomed to the discipline imposed by the daily tasks performed in modern industry. Women had also been employed in metal factories long before the war. They had been at work in the core room of foundries and had fed automatic presses in cartridge, hardware, brassware, tin can, and other metal factories. They had operated automatic machines in manufacturing needles, pins, and jewelry, and had used small drills and tended power screwdrivers, working on rifles, pistols, typewriters, and sewing machine parts—all before the war. Years before the war, they had varnished and lacquered, wrapped and packed, and labeled manufactures. Stamping, punching, and drilling—perhaps even cutting and grinding—this had been the extent of their opportunity to serve in the metal factories before the war.[13*]

The war, of course, brought with it a rapid expansion in the number of women engaged in these repetitive occupations, as well as in general unskilled work. But an important new factor in the picture was that the emergency created by the labor shortage cleared the way for women's access to the "master machines" and the "key occupations" in many industries. In the iron and steel and other metal industries, for example, it opened the machine shop and the tool rooms to them and introduced them, in limited numbers, into the steel works and rolling mills. Moreover, the war emergency forced the experiment of teaching women workers to read blueprints, to adjust their machines, to set up and to measure and mark their own work, and to be responsible for its quality and quantity.

## FACTORS IMPEDING WOMEN'S WORK

Having said all that, it is necessary to add that a number of important factors, stemming from the traditional prejudices concerning women's

*Of twelve women welders at the Mt. Clare shops of the Baltimore & Ohio Railroad during the war, eleven had worked at typically female jobs before the war. One had run a power sewing machine, another had worked in a button factory, a third in a cigarette factory, and a fourth in a silk mill. Others had worked variously as timekeeper, telephone operator, cashier, spooler, and spinner in a cotton mill, home dressmaker, and weaver, while two had worked in munition factories. (Florence Clark, Memo on Electric Welder, Mt. Clare shops, Baltimore & Ohio Railroad, Baltimore, 31 October 1918, RG 14 WSS File 66b, National Archives.)

appropriate work roles impeded the full development of those tendencies. Another impeding factor was that although the emerging labor shortage opened up jobs to women as skilled operators on machines, the private and public training institutions of the country had trained an insignificant number of women for these tasks. The plans that did get under way for training women were either inadequate or were started too late to produce many material results before the armistice.[14]

As hundreds of thousands of women entered the industry during the war years, the hostility of men in their trades magnified and expanded. While strong friendships developed between some male and female workers, in many plants male workers openly expressed their antagonism toward the women and refused to help or even to work alongside them. As we shall see, many men in union shops also vented their displeasure by opposing women for union membership.

A serious problem in both union and nonunion shops was the inadequate toilet facilities—a problem compounded by the rudeness of male employees when using the toilets. Another aspect of this problem stemmed from the custom of changing clothes in the factory. Workers changed to old clothes or to uniforms where required, before starting to work. Foremen often deliberately set up inadequate shelters so that the men could watch the women change. One young woman complained that "the brazen fellers stood round and stared, they wanted to see how I put them [the clothes] on." The men often stripped off their clothes where they worked, regardless of the embarrassment of their female co-workers. One woman voiced a common complaint when she stated: "You have to walk through the room with your eyes shut."[15] Men often left doors to toilets open when they used them in order to embarrass the women. All too often, inspectors for the Women's Bureau of the Department of Labor found that women, afraid of exposure to male employees, or because of the inadequate separation between the women's toilets and the men's workrooms, simply avoided using the toilet for the entire eight-hour shift.[16]

Women working on night shifts reported that men harassed them by shouting obscenities at them as they traveled to and from work. At the Philadelphia Navy Yard night shift, the situation became so bad that police and Navy Yard orderlies had to escort women workers home.[17]

Some of the brutality displayed by the men may have been due to thoughtlessness, but it is clear that the entrance of women into factories in large numbers was by and large bitterly resented by the male workers. Some of the hostility stemmed from the charge that "women were not working on an equality with the men" while demanding the same pay, or that they were being given the more desirable jobs that men had been waiting years to secure.* Some of it was rooted in pre-war work experience when women had on occasion been hired at lower wages and used as strikebreakers. Many men feared that large numbers of women would lead to lowering of the existing wage and other labor standards and, eventually, to the discharge of men. It did nothing to reduce antagonism to the presence of women workers when men read that "in one factory 150 men were discharged, not one of whom had been drafted, and women put in their places, giving them from $3 to $4 a week less than . . . the men." Men particularly resented what came to be known in England as the "Sister Susie Menace." "Sister Susie" was the type of woman worker described as "possessed by the peculiarly infantile form of patriotism which prompts her to volunteer her services or underbid the self-supporting and family-supporting man and woman."[18] As in England, there were many employers in the United States ready to oblige the "Sister Susies."

Women's contribution to the nation's industrial productivity during the war was also limited by the difficulties that prejudice created. This was especially true in the training of women.

In some shops, experienced machinists were instructed to train women right at the machines, and in a few, such as the Brown and Sharpe Manufacturing Company of Providence, R.I., employers placed the newly employed women among the men, who were told to instruct them. In some larger factories, so-called vestibule schools—usually set up in corridors or vestibules of the factory—provided special training. Public or private schools also opened a few training courses for women workers.[19]

The vast majority of the new women workers, however, were trained by foremen, many of whom resented the introduction of women into the factory. In not a few instances, foremen made quite clear their belief that women were not mechanically minded and never would be able to match the skill of male mechanics. Foreman would use mechanical terms that

---

*This was listed as the reason for objections by male postal workers to the introduction of women carriers and clerks. They drew up a statement declaring that "they want it thoroughly understood that they are not prejudiced against women because they are women, but they want them to work on exactly the same equality as the men and not to be given the desirable jobs which take years for a post office employee to get. Men, who have become flatfooted and are suffering with varicose veins and the like as a result of carrying mail, have in the past been given easier routes. Since the women have been employed, these routes have been taken away from the men who have acquired them by seniority and given to the women. . . . Post office officials, in an effort not to have women clerks working until midnight, have shifted around some of the men to the "swing shift" from 3 o'clock to midnight, regardless of the fact that these men have spent years in working up to the day work." (*Seattle Union Record*, Aug. 7, 1918).

were unknown to the average new woman worker, and then point to her lack of understanding as proof that women were unable do the work. Foremen also neglected to correct women workers' mistakes so that the women, unaware that their work was unsatisfactory, continued to make the same mistakes. The foremen could then point to the poor work as further proof of the incapability of women to perform well in the industrial workplace.[20]

Here and there were foremen who were able to instruct women beginners successfully and to maintain satisfactory production. But all too often, the deeply ingrained prejudice against women workers came quickly to the surface, impeding both the productivity of the women workers and their contribution to the war effort.[21] The *Ladies' Home Journal* saw one virtue in the situation: too much training would spoil those characteristics of women that endeared them to men, and at least the current practice guaranteed that those "who take to war work like ducks to water" would remain womanly, "cheerful and abounding in gay spirits."[22]

## DISCRIMINATION AGAINST WOMEN WORKERS

Women entering traditionally masculine occupations rarely received the same pay as men for the same work. Some women felt this custom was warranted because men often did heavier work and supported families, but many expressed justifiable anger over the discriminatory job classifications and wage differentials. Most women hired during the war were classified as helpers, even when they performed the same work as men.

A Women's Bureau investigation of the Philadelphia Navy Yard's sail loft disclosed a fairly typical situation. Detailed job descriptions discriminated against women, although there was no evidence of any real difference between male and female jobs. Women were helpers and sewing machine operators, whereas men were sailmakers, upholsterers, mattress makers, machinists, laborers, general helpers, as well as sewing machine operators. Men cut the material for life jackets with electric knives; women stenciled the marks showing where the material was to be sewed and where it was to be quilted, and this work required them to lift metal stencils onto the material. Women also performed gluing, a job considered undesirable. Women held the least desirable job—stuffing life jackets—which was shunned because it required close work with kapok filling, which irritated the ears, nose, and throat. Men stitched the bottoms of life jackets, a task said to be too dirty for women, but the real reason it was reserved for men was that it paid better—its description showed that it was no dirtier than such women's jobs as stenciling and stuffing.

Although the Navy Yard's sail loft foreman assured the government inspectors that men and women received the same rates of pay, there were very real differences. For example, 81 percent of the men but only 52 percent of the women received the maximum pay for sewing machine operators. Again, 91 percent of the men, compared with 84 percent of the women, received the maximum rate for helpers. Only 11 percent of the male sewing machine operators received the minimum rate; as many as 45 percent of the women were paid the minimum. Clear-cut divisions existed in the salaries of men and women performing the same jobs and between the different jobs performed by the sexes in the Navy Yard.[23]

Other war industries also reflected clear distinctions between men and women. Another government installation paid a minimum daily rate for women of $2 to $2.24, but for men the minimum was $3.20—the same as the *maximum* daily rate for women. Investigation by the Women's Bureau revealed that six private firms with government contracts discriminated by sex in the wages they paid for identical work. At Bethlehem Steel Company, women received 20 percent less than men. The Eddystone Mounts Company paid women 33 cents per hour and men 45 cents for the same work. At the Fox Gun Company, women received 26 cents and men 35 cents, and the International Fabrication Company paid women 22 cents and men 25 cents. The Fayette Company justified the variance in wages on the ground that men performed the heavier tasks, yet an investigation by the Women's Bureau found no evidence of a difference.[24]

When the Pennsylvania Railroad controlled Philadelphia's railroad employees under the National Railroad Administration, it made clear distinctions between men's and women's work and pay.* A supervisor at a Philadelphia terminal refused to consider applications from females for the position of assistant locomotive dispatcher, even though women had previously worked on this job. When the Women's Bureau of the Railroad Administration investigated, they found no reason why women could not hold this position except for the supervisor's personal prejudice. The woman who applied had seniority equal to the male applicants' and fitted the job description, yet she was rejected for the position. Six other women were found to be eligible for the job but did not apply for fear of being rejected by the supervisor. There were other instances of discrimination on the Pennsylvania. Women coach cleaners made 22 cents an hour while men made 25 cents. After a raise in September 1918, women received 34

---

*The federal government assumed direct control over the private railroads from 1918 until 1920. The takeover was intended to establish an economically and militarily efficient, rationalized continental rail system.

cents and men 37 cents. The rationale given by the railroad for this situation was that the men carried buckets, cleaned toilets, and put up scaffolds for women when they cleaned outside the train. Yet observation of the jobs found no difference between the tasks performed by men and women. Women worked at jobs traditionally assigned specifically to men.[25]

Early in 1918, an automobile supply company in Chicago whose men earned $20 a week paid female replacements only $12. An airplane factory on Long Island in New York hired women for two-thirds of a man's wages. In the electrical trades, employers customarily paid a woman a boy's salary.[26]

Inequality in wages was only one of the grievances of women workers. Housing for women workers during the war was scandalous. "Whether the state, the city or the employer is going to advance the enterprise of housing war workers," a study of the situation in 1918 insisted, "the federal government ought to adopt a standard of housing for women to which all building projects should conform."[27] No such standard existed.

In paying tribute to the contributions of women workers in the munitions industry, Benedict Crowell, Director of Munitions, declared with enthusiasm, "Fifty percent of the number of employees in our explosive plants were women who braved the dangers connected with this line of work and to which they have been entirely unaccustomed but whose perils were not unknown to them." They were "not unknown" to the employers either; just before the United States entered the war, an explosion destroyed the Canadian Car and Foundry Company plant in Kingsland, New Jersey, killing many workers. But the industrialists still took no precautions against accidents or disease. In 1917, after a survey of conditions in metal plants throughout the country, Alice Hamilton, the nation's leading expert on industrial hygiene, reported that the managers of the arms factories hardly ever screened machines, provided any safeguards against explosions, or protected workers from the ill effects of mercury, lead, and trinitrotoluene (TNT). Lead poisoning presented particular dangers for women, since it could permanently damage their reproductive organs.[28]

The *Ladies' Home Journal* confirmed that the report of the hazards for women in the munitions industry was accurate, but it concluded ruefully, that it was all for the good of the cause: "Women workers must be willing here, as in England, to accept positions which, in ordinary times, they would not even consider, if the war's demands are to be met."[29]

## IMPACT OF THE WAR ON WOMEN WORKERS

Traditional reports have stressed that women workers during World War

I were able, by their contributions to the war effort and by the capability they displayed, to break down the barriers that had previously kept them out of industry and to lay the foundation for more specialized jobs, increased wages, better working conditions, and a more competitive status in the labor market. In sum, they managed to drastically change the existing sex-segregated patterns of work and the prejudices concerning women's appropriate work roles. Thus Mary Van Kleeck wrote that "industry, not feminism, opened the way" for women to enter new areas of the work experience, and that "the war appears to have released the power of women's industrial processes more effectively than all the preaching of economic independence during the past fifty years." And Theresa Wolfson commented: "'Women's sphere' bade fair to become a thing of the past. The old line 'motherhood occupations' gave way to jobs to be done by available help or 'hands.' Industry became quite sexless in ideology as well as reality."[30]

Anyone reading the wartime popular press might easily have concluded that what was occurring in the railroad industry confirmed this view and that a tremendous shift away from women's traditional occupations was occurring. The reports indicated that although there were still women clerks and stenographers, they were also "filling many other positions," acting in large numbers as "passenger agents, station agents, and agents' helpers, car checkers, car accountants, cashiers, core-makers in the foundry, as brass polishers in the finishing rooms, even as yardmasters." In short: "In many departments women are being employed where formerly the work was done exclusively by men. Some of the new employees have had experience, but most are new in railroad work, but are proving efficient."[31] So many women were depicted as working in so many phases of the railroad industry that it came as no surprise when H. F. Anderson, manager of the Missouri, Kansas & Texas Railroad, predicted that if the war lasted three years "many railroads in this country will be operated largely by women."[32]

The number of women employees rose continually until by October 1918, when a total of 101,785 women were engaged in railroad work, this represented a gain of approximately 321 percent over the 1917 employment level of 31,400 women.[33] But most of the women railway workers performed clerical or semi-clerical tasks. Of the 101,785 women employed on October 1, 1918, 72 percent or 73,620 worked as clerks of all kinds—stenographers, typists, comptometer operators, accountants, ticket sellers, and information agents. Only the last two positions were totally new to women.[34] "Generally," Maurine Weiner Greenwald notes in her study of women workers in the railroad industry,* "women performed routine, unskilled, or semi-skilled office work of the variety they had performed before the war. While a few women obtained supervisory positions during the war through apprenticeship in routine office work, women expert in low-level secretarial skills tended to remain in such positions."[35]

The second largest group of women wartime railway workers were the 5,600 women (5 percent of the total) who toiled in the traditional female occupation of cleaning. Women worked as common laborers in stations, offices, coaches, and Pullman cars. During the war, the scope of this occupation widened somewhat to include work on scrap docks and in freight transfer stations and supply departments. As relatively heavy labor, the latter positions paid correspondingly higher wages.[36]

Personal service workers in dining rooms and kitchens as matrons, janitresses, laundresses, and hospital nurses were the third most numerous group of female railway employees. However, only 2.8 percent (2,830) of the railroad women were working in these traditional female roles. Telephone and telegraph operators composed the fourth and fifth most numerous groups of women railway employees, with the former numbering 2,613, or 2.6 percent, and the latter 2,049, or 2.0 percent of women workers. The presence of women in railroad telegraphy did mark an important breakthrough, for it had formerly been an almost exclusively male occupation, but the women in this field represented a very small percentage of the total, and even that, only temporarily.[37]

None of this is intended to mean that women were not to be found in many new railroad positions. There were women turntable operators, packers of journal boxes, and attendants in toolrooms and storerooms. Women worked as level adjusters in signal towers, as checkers in freight houses, as car clerks, as operators of bolt-threading and nut- and car-bearing machines, of turret lathes, of angle-cock grinders, of hammers, and of cranes. Other women became air-brake cleaners, repairers, and testers, in addition to electrical welders, oxyacetylene cutters and welders, and core makers.[38] But the actual number employed in such positions was small. Of the 5,000 women in wartime shop work, 4,500 were common laborers. "These women," it has been pointed out, "had gained access to a new work place, but the type of work they performed there was mostly unskilled."[39]

*This is part of a larger study, *Women, War, and Work: The Impact of World War I on Women Workers in the United States* (Westport, Conn., 1980). The larger work also corrects some of the information and conclusions in the earlier one.

The same was true in the case of the munitions and related industries. In 1910, there were approximately 3,500 women engaged in the munitions industry; by January 1918, there were 100,000. But a survey by the National League for Women's Service, the first systematic effort to determine the capabilities of women workers in all regions of the country, revealed that the vast majority of women were confined to performing the simpler and lighter processes and work of a repetitive, deadening nature. The work requiring skill was reserved mainly for men.[40]

Recent studies have made it clear that despite all hopes to the contrary, World War I not only did not render "woman's sphere" and the "old line motherhood occupations" a "thing of the past," as Mary Von Kleeck and Theresa Wolfson maintained, but actually had the opposite effect, strengthening the previous restrictions on women's work. Maurine Weiner Greenwald argues: "Some changes did occur during the war, but the *nature* of the changes followed lines established long before the second draft call of 1918 increased the number of women workers. The war merely accelerated former trends in women's work, in the composition of the female labor force, and in attitudes toward women as workers."[41]

To satisfy the demands of a USA that was actively pursuing the war, as well as furnishing the Allies with war materials, a substantial proportion of the country's industrial potential had been converted to war production. These industries experienced an enormous increase in turnover as women sought new positions that would enable them to meet the rising cost of living. The turnover was further stimulated by government war contracts, issued on a cost-plus basis, that induced employers to compete for labor and often pirate workers from other plants. Even government departments competed with one another for women workers: ordnance took women from aviation, and shell production took them from powder production.[42]

Recognizing that as a result of the extraordinary demand for labor in war industries, wages there were bound to rise, women flocked to the industrial centers where the government was letting large contracts for war work. Since manufacturers who did not have such contracts could not compete with the wages being paid by those firms that had received cost-plus contracts, women workers in these industries tended to move toward the highest wages, thereby creating more of a labor turnover than an actual increase in the number of women workers. After the government revealed that many thousands of women workers in industries directly or indirectly associated with the war had formerly been employed in dressmaking, a spokesperson for the dressmaking industry complained that its firms were being forced out of existence by these developments:

With so many opportunities open in other industries more directly connected with the war, many of our workers have left the trade for more congenial occupations, or for more pay. To those who have remained it has been necessary from time to time to grant wage increases, though neither the percentage of profit nor any increased volume of business warranted any such action.[43]

Estimates of the number of women who entered manufacturing during the war period range from 1½ million to the War Department estimate of 2½ million. Whatever the figure, as many as 95 percent of these women came from other gainful occupations.[44] Although accurate figures are not available—because of errors made in the 1910 Census, comparison with 1920 has become impossible—a 1944 study drew the tentative conclusion that the net additions to the female labor force during World War I "were probably of minor proportions."[45] More recent studies have confirmed this hypothesis.

A popular fallacy was that women workers were in industry during the war either for patriotic motives or for "pin money." This theory was exploded by investigations that disclosed that at most, 20 percent of the women were independent workers. The remaining 80 percent used their earnings as a necessary part of their family incomes. The primary reason for the entrance of young women into industry was shown to be the "bankrupt condition of the working families."[46]

By the beginning of 1918 the *Seattle Union Record* had just about lost patience with reports by employers of how efficient women workers were proving to be, how absolutely essential their contribution was to the war effort, and how well they had demonstrated that women were capable of doing whatever men workers had done before the war. It observed sharply: "Every trade unionist will be able to read between the lines and see just what kind of hot air these women are being fed up with. If women are satisfactorily filling men's positions in so many cases, they should be receiving just the same wages as the men would be receiving at this time, and it is up to organized labor to see that this is being done."[47]

We shall see to what extent organized labor fulfilled this mission. But let us now turn to the impact of World War I on another section of the U.S. working class—the Black workers.

## BLACK WORKERS ENTER INDUSTRY

In our preceding volume, we discussed the great migration of Black people that got under way in 1915—a migration of hundreds of thousands from the South seeking the job opportunities and freer life available in the

North and West.* With the nation's usual labor force enormously depleted
through the drying up of immigrant labor during the war in Europe, northern industrialists turned eagerly to the southern black men and women as
the major untapped source of common labor remaining in this country.

Direct involvement of the U.S. in the European conflict in April 1917
brought forth a fresh outpouring of black workers from the South seeking
employment in northern war industries. Once in the North, black migrants
entered a variety of industrial occupations, primarily in iron and steel,
auto manufacturing, shipbuilding, and railroads. The labor recruiting
efforts of Chicago's packinghouses and the Illinois Central Railroad,
together with the appeals of the Chicago *Defender*, made that city a mag-
net for penniless sharecroppers from the South. Some moved along to
Detroit, where the pressure of war-time needs forced open the auto plants
to Afro-Americans. In 1914, less than 1,000 black auto workers were
employed in area plants. As a result of the migration, however, 12,000 to
18,000 gained employment in the Detroit auto industry between 1916 and
1918.[48]

At the same time the stockyards, packinghouses, and iron and steel
mills of Chicago provided employment opportunities for the city's 50,000
black newcomers. And in the same period the Pennsylvania, the Reading
and the Baltimore & Ohio railroads, as well as Midvale Steel and several
munitions and shipbuilding firms in Philadelphia, hired the majority of the
40,000 employable black migrants to that city.[49]

Between 1910 and 1920, largely because of the wartime migration in the
second half of the decade, a net increase of 322,000 occurred in the number of southern-born black workers living in the North, exceeding the
aggregate increase of the preceding forty years. Although the increase is
less than the general estimate made at the height of the migration, it is still
an impressive figure. More important is the fact that the booming wartime
labor demands of rail lines, factories, foundries, mines, and packinghouses, at a time when the normal supply of cheap labor was shut off,
opened these industries for the first time to the black worker.[50]

## IMPACT OF THE WAR ON BLACK WOMEN WORKERS

Since not many women held jobs in the iron and steel industry nor in a
number of other basic industries, and those who did were predominantly
white, black women had much less opportunity to move into industrial
work than did black men.[51] Still they were determined to try. The

*See Philip S. Foner, *History of the Labor Movement in the United States* (New York,
1982)6:206-21.

following letter from a barely literate black woman of Biloxi, Mississippi, published in the *Chicago Defender*, spoke for many:

> From a willen workin woman, I hope that you will healp me as I want to get out of this land of sufring I no there is som thing that I can do here there is nothing for me to do I may be able to get in some furm where I dont have to stand on my feet all day I dont no just whah but I hope the Lord will find a place now let me here from you all at once.[52]

In some areas of work, new opportunities did open for black women. For the first time, jobs were available to them in the textile industry, traditionally the largest employer of women, but only of white women. Even in the South the tradition was broken, at least for the time being. The *Norfolk Journal and Guide* carried the following front page headlines in the September 15, 1917 issue:

### MILLS OPEN TO COLORED LABOR
Women Employed in Hosiery Mills of Elizabeth City Due to Scarcity of Labor

Opening of Labor Opportunity Heretofore Closed to Members of the Race.

"The Hosiery Mills of this city that have heretofore employed white help," the story continued, "on account of the scarcity of labor have opened their doors to Negro women and girls, as a result of which 12 young women went to work at Passage Hosiery and about 14 at the Lawrence St. Mill Monday." Northern mills also opened their doors to black women; following the lead of northern industries, which sent labor agents south to recruit black men, textile concerns began to send agents who brought young black women north to work in the mills.[53]

"Negro women are leaving the kitchen and laundry for the workshop and factory," reported William M. Ashby, executive secretary of the New Jersey Welfare League. The new employees filled "places made vacant by the shifting of Hungarian, Italian, and Jewish girls to the munitions plants."[54] A Mrs. L., who worked as an entry clerk in a Chicago mail-order house, replacing a Jewish girl, explained to a Negro investigator that she "used to be a maid in a private family, but she says she wouldn't work in service again" for any money:

> I can save more when I'm in service, for of course you get room and board, but the other things you have to take—no place to entertain your friends but the kitchen, and going in and out of back doors. I hated all that. Then, no matter how early you got through work, you could only go out one night a week—they

almost make you a slave. But now you can do other work in Chicago and don't
have to work in such places.

Miss T.S., twenty-two years old, who had formerly worked as a cook in
Georgia, came north and, after working as a waitress in Chicago, obtained
a job in a box factory. She told the investigator: "I'll never work in nobody's kitchen but my own any more. No, indeed! That's the one thing
that makes me stick to this job.* You do have some time to call your own,
but when you're working in anybody's kitchen, well you're out of luck.
You almost have to eat on the run; you never get any time off, and you
have to work half the night usually."[55]

In spite of this kind of sentiment, the number of black female domestic
servants in the North actually increased in the war years—from 11.5 percent
in 1910 to 18.5 percent in 1920. With native- and foreign-born white domestics moving into factory jobs, wages paid for household employment
increased, making the long hours and constant personal supervision easier to
bear.[56] Nevertheless, it is still true that the Great Migration and the first world
war meant that black women were able, for the first time, to get out of
domestic service—but not in all cities at once. For example, more than 80
percent of the jobs held by black women in Philadelphia before the migration
were in domestic service. Many of these women worked primarily as "day
work" domestics, living in their own homes and going out to work several
times a week. Only white women worked at the higher paying, more regular
"in-service" types of jobs, where they received free room and board at the
homes in which they worked. When white women left domestic service for
factories during the war, these positions in domestic service became available
to black women who had been born in the North. Meanwhile, southern
migrant women replaced them in their former positions as day workers.
Thus, the first positions available to most black women as they entered Philadelphia from the South were still as domestics. Only slowly did they enter a
score of Philadelphia industries.[57]

But black women did move out of domestic service, not only entering
factories but even in some cases obtaining coveted jobs as office workers.
(About five thousand black women worked for the U.S. government during the war years as typists, stenographers, bookkeepers, and filing
clerks.)[58] In 1918 Emma L. Shields, with the cooperation of the Bureau of
Labor Statistics and the Division of Negro Economics, conducted an

---

*Another factor may have been that "blatant discrimination in Chicago barred black women
from many factory jobs which were open to them in other economically diversified cities."
(Maurine Weiner Greenwald, *Women, War, and Work: The Impact of World War I on Women
Workers in the United States* (Westport, Conn., 1980, p. 24.)

investigation for the Women's Bureau of the conditions under which black women worked. One hundred and fifty plants, distributed over the states of New York, Pennsylvania, Ohio, Illinois, Michigan, Indiana, Virginia, West Virginia, and North Carolina were visited. Of the 28,520 workers employed in these plants 11,812 were black women, or more than 40 percent of all the women workers.[59]

More than half the black women surveyed were engaged in the tobacco industry, doing the same tedious work of stemming, stripping, and twisting of tobacco they had been doing for years. But many were in occupations that had been closed to them before, and in a number of instances they were still holding their own. They had acquired confidence in themselves and a "footing," however insecure, in the U.S. economy outside of domestic service. They were employed in metal industries, where they worked at drilling, polishing, punch presses, molding, welding, soldering, and filing parts of automobiles, stoves, hardware, and enamel products. They were employed in the textile industry not only, as in the past, scrubbing floors and cleaning lint and cotton from machines but also as operators. In the large meat-packing plants, black women had taken the place of men in cutting hogs' ears, and were also trimming, sorting, grading, and stamping various portions of the carcasses, separating and cleaning the viscera, and preparing meats for curing and canning. As general laborers, they washed cans or fruit, sorted rags in rag and paper factories, picked nuts, and pressed clothes. In laundries, most of them did the hot and heavy work, but some were doing more skilled work, and black women were also beginning to sort, mark, and hand-iron as well as machine-iron. In the garment industry, some factories employed only black women, and a few were beginning to admit them to any position they were able to fill.

For the first time in U.S. history, black women were found in considerable numbers operating machinery of various kinds. Many of these jobs involved only simple operations or repetitive movement, but some required a degree of skill. And as we have seen, black women were also working as stenographers, typists, clerks, and bookkeepers.[60]

## BLACK WOMEN SUFFER RACISM AND SEXISM

But there was another side to the story. Investigations made it clear that the more highly skilled jobs, when available to women at all, went in practically all instances, to white women. In the stockyards, black women were the ones who had to work on wet, slippery floors in rooms where the air was overpoweringly odorous and where there were marked variations in temperature and humidity. In the peanut industry, theirs was the job of dragging heavy cumbersome bags. In the tobacco industry, black women did the lowest paying and most numbing and monotonous factory work. In the laundries, black women worked at the dampest and least desirable positions. They worked at mangles—a damp, dangerous job—pressing materials between two heated rollers as they stood in puddles of water or on leaky wooden platforms. In the textile factories, they labored for the lowest wages in the mills that made the cheapest types of goods, like middy blouses, overalls, and housedresses.[61]

The fiction that black workers could endure heat better than whites was employed to keep black women in the hottest jobs in candy and glass factories and bakeries. Essentially, black women performed the hot and heavy tasks that were now being refused by white women. Indeed, they were often able to obtain work only after white women had rejected certain jobs. They substituted for white boys in the glass factories, where they opened and closed molds for hot glass and carried the hot glass after it had been blown in ovens. They replaced white men in bakeries—cleaning, greasing, and lifting hot, heavy pots and pans—and at the dangerous work of dyeing furs. Wherever they worked they were assigned to the oldest and most difficult machines, the darkest and worst ventilated sections of the factory, and the smallest and dirtiest of the available rest rooms.[62]

The wage discrimination from which white women generally suffered applied to an even greater degree to black women. In plants where white women were paid the same wages as men if they were able to do the job, black women were paid less. In many factories, black women's pay regularly started at least $1 per week less simply because they were black. Invariably, too, black women replacing white women, even if they worked as well as their predecessors, would receive from $2.50 to $3 less per week—$7 instead of $10, or $10 instead of $12.50. Where piecework provided black women with a chance to increase their wages, employers forced them to accept a lower piece rate than the one for white women.[63]

Not only did black women start nearly all jobs at a lower wage, but, as government investigators found, in many cases where white women received wage increases after a short period, their black co-workers remained at the starting salaries even after months of satisfactory performance. It was estimated that black women, while earning more money during the war years than ever before, still received only 10 to 60 percent of white women's wages even when both did the same kind of work.[64]

Wage discrimination was only part of the picture. Separate facilities were becoming the pattern of industrial life, even outside of the South. During Wilson's administration, the institution of segregated toilets, lunchroom facilities, and working areas in a number of federal departments paved the way for segregated facilities in war plants and arsenals, where sanitary provisions for white women were superior and black women were segregated into the least desirable washrooms, lunchrooms, and lockers.[65] When black women complained about men entering their toilets through their workroom, they were laughed at. In one case, the plant manager refused to open an outside entrance because "colored women would take everything they could lay their hands on—pillow cases, towels, etc."[66]

Bias against black women was apparent in all aspects of the work experience. In general, under the U.S. Railroad Administration, which controlled the railroads, the higher paid railroad jobs traditionally held by men were, as they became open, available only to white women, while the lower-paying menial tasks were the only jobs available for black women. Black women cleaned railroad cars and followed after the trackmen, picking up the debris they left behind. Some were well-paid, receiving salaries up to $95 a month, but they remained in these positions and other menial posts. Even in menial work, there was discrimination. In one terminal of the Pennsylvania Railroad, three black women and one white woman worked as linen counters. The white woman counted only clean laundry in an airy room on the ground floor, while the three black women sorted soiled linen in a dark basement. Even in car cleaning, color lines were established. In the yards of the Long Island Railroad black women were barred from cleaning dining cars and were restricted to coaches.[67]

Employers' racist attitudes toward black women constituted the chief reason for the discrimination suffered by these women. Some employers acknowledged that black women worked satisfactorily but defended their vicious exploitation by insisting that these women needed more training than white workers because they were mentally backward and less habituated to the factory routine. The most common complaint concerned their irregular attendance, although nothing was said about the extra discrimination these women were forced to endure, which made the work anything but attractive.[68]

The employers' attitude toward black women was all too often reinforced by the bigotry of the workers. In one Philadelphia plant, black women were dismissed because the white women refused to stay on the job with them. Employers often argued that a "better class of white women" would simply refuse to work if they hired Blacks. Still, in one small candy factory in Philadelphia, not only were black and white women working side by side, but white women were working under the direction of a black woman supervisor. The manager acknowledged that the white women had objected strenuously, but they had finally agreed when he explained that the black woman was the only one who knew all the processes and that it was necessary to have someone who could teach the others.[69]

Bias against black women did not stop at the workplace. The Chicago YWCA pointed out that many black "girls" were brought up from the South to work in industry "without any preparation having been made to house them or give them amusements or recreations," and that often they had to live in boxcars.[70*]

## RESTRICTED NATURE OF BLACK EMPLOYMENT

The experience of black women was duplicated in the case of black men who entered industry during the war. "Everywhere," wrote Roger Baldwin, "the Negroes had the hardest and most disagreeable jobs."[71] The superintendent of a Kentucky plow factory expressed the southern view: "Negroes do work white men won't do, such as common labor; heavy, hot, and dirty work; pouring crucibles; work in the grinding room; and so on. Negroes are employed because they are cheaper. . . . The negro[sic] does a different grade of work and makes about 10¢ an hour less."[72] A coke foreman in a Pennsylvania steel mill used somewhat similar language: "They are well fitted for this hot work, and we keep them because we appreciate this ability in them. . . . The door machines and the jam cutting are the most undesirable; it is hard to get white men to do this kind of work."[73]

*This situation was not confined to Chicago and was true for black men as well as women. The increase in the number of black workers in many northern cities at the time of World War I coincided with a developing housing shortage, and placed an additional strain on the already overcrowded housing available. According to Emmett Scott, advisor to the Department of Labor on Negro Problems, "Housing facilities (in Philadelphia) being inadequate, temporary structures were quickly built and when these did not suffice, in the case of railroads, ordinary tents and box cars were used to shelter the new laborers." (*Negro Migration During the War*, New York, 1920, pp. 134-35.) A report made in 1919 on the housing situation in Detroit found the following conditions: "Not a single vacant house or tenement in the several Negro sections of this city is available. The majority of Negroes are living under such crowded conditions that three or four families in an apartment is the rule rather than the exception. Seventy-five percent of the Negro homes have so many lodgers that they are really hotels. Stables, garages, and cellars have been converted into homes for Negroes. The poolrooms and gambling clubs are beginning to charge for the privilege of sleeping on pool-room tables overnight." (Quoted in Joyce Shaw Peterson, "Black Automobile Workers in Detroit, 1910-1930," *Journal of Negro History* 54 [Summer, 1979]L 182).

It was rare to find an industrialist who, like Henry Ford, in an effort to maintain influence with the Black community, allowed a few black workers in his plant to be upgraded to skilled positions. The vast majority of black workers in the automobile industry, as in all industry, were confined to the lowest rungs of the industrial ladder. As Joyce Shaw Peterson points out:

> From the beginning, black workers were concentrated in the most unskilled and unpleasant jobs in the auto industry. They were hired into those jobs that had the lowest pay scales, required the greatest physical exertion, had the highest accident rates, and the largest number of health hazards.

Many black auto workers were employed in foundry departments that everybody considered to be the most undesirable places to work because of the noise, heat and filth.[74]

This state of affairs was established early in the war by employers and unions, often with government approval. The railroad lines and the Railroad Brotherhoods had worked out unwritten agreements confining black workers to low level and menial occupations. When the federal government assumed control of the nation's rail network late in December 1917, it simply sanctioned the informal agreements between railroad management and the unions.

The government also took steps to prohibit the hiring and advancing of black workers to positions they had not occupied prior to the war.[75]

In various shipyards around the country, employers and unions, with government sanction, agreed not to give Blacks positions above that of common laborer. Black carpenters, reamers, riveters, pipefitters, and drillers found it impossible to get work in the shipyards, even though men were badly needed in these occupations. Skilled blacks were forced to accept jobs as helpers to white craftsmen or as "fillers" in tasks demanding few or no skills.[76]

Nothing was done during the war by employers, unions, or the federal government to eliminate the racial prejudice that prevented blacks from being hired as skilled workers.[77] A survey published in August 1917 found "Negro graduate engineers and electricians and experienced carpenters, painters and shipbuilders doing the work of porters, elevator men and janitors."[78] A year later, the situation was reported unchanged.[79]

"The overwhelming concentration of black workers in unskilled positions," John D. Finney, Jr. points out in his study of black labor during World War I, "indicates that the demands for services generated by the war provided them with ample opportunity to enter the lower strata of industry but offered very little access to the top levels."[80*]

There is no doubt, however, that the black worker achieved a substantial industrial advance during World War I. Even work in the lowest industrial occupations was an improvement over peonage in agriculture or domestic service. Although increased costs of living often wiped out a good part of the wage gains, it was generally agreed that black workers substantially improved their economic conditions by moving into northern industry and becoming, for the first time, part of the industrial working class of the United States.

---

*During this same period, the number of Negro artisans declined. Between 1910 and 1920, the number of black blacksmiths, forgemen and pressmen, builders and building contractors, millers, pressmen and plate printers, roofers and slaters, sawyers, stonemasons, and bricklayers decreased. In 1920 the total of white apprentices in all skilled trades was put at 144,177. The total of black apprentices was 2,067. (Philip S. Foner, *Organized Labor and the Black Worker, 1619-1981*, [New York, 1982] p. 134).

# CHAPTER 8

# The Government's War Labor Program

The story of the federal government's war labor program, which culminated in the establishment of the War Labor Administration, has been told by a number of authors, some of whom actually participated in the events.* In the following chapters dealing with labor-government relations after the United States entered the war, we will not cover in detail all aspects of this subject, but deal mainly with the factors that led to the emergence of the war labor program and its operation, especially as it affected women and Black workers.

With the entry of the United States into World War I, the federal government obtained extraordinary powers to oversee the operation of the nation's economic system. Within a year after the declaration of war, the government took over the nation's communications network, assumed direct control of most of its railroad lines, completely dominated the shipbuilding industry through the establishment of the Emergency Fleet

*The most detailed analysis of the emergence of the government's war labor program is Leonard Philip Krivy, "American Organized Labor and the World War, 1917-1918: A History of Labor Problems and the Development of a Government War Labor Program," unpublished Ph.D. dissertation, New York University, 1965. Two important studies written immediately after the war are: Gordon S. Watkins, *Labor Problems and Labor Administration in the United States During the World War*, University of Illinois, *Studies in the Social Sciences*, 2 vols., Urbana, Ill., 1919; and William F. Willoughby, *Government Organization in Wartime and After: A Survey of the Federal Civil Agencies Created for the Prosecution of the War*, New York, 1919. *War-Time Strikes and Their Adjustment* by Alexander M. Bing (New York, 1921) is an account by a dollar-a-year businessman who was associated with the Housing and Ordnance Departments of the National War Labor Shipping Board. *The Industrial Code* by Claude S. Watts (New York, 1922) is a book on the National War Labor Board by the Board's secretary.

Corporation, and under the authority of the Food and Fuel Control Act, regulated the production, distribution, and conservation of foodstuffs and fuel supplies across the land.

On July 28, 1917, the War Industries Board was set up to act as a clearing house for the nation's war production needs, with Frank A. Scott as chairperson, and Bernard Baruch as chief of the raw materials section. In 1918, Wilson appointed Baruch as WIB head and greatly expanded the Board's power to conserve resources, advise government purchasing agencies as to prices, make purchases for the Allies, and determine priorities of production and distribution in industry.[1]

In its enormously expanded role as the arbiter of the nation's economy, the federal government had to develop a policy towards the nation's working class. Widespread industrial unrest could seriously hamper the prosecution of the war. Yet industrial unrest was a natural concomitant of the conditions that had characterized the nation's industrial relations throughout its history. Indeed, one study of wartime strikes, made three years after the end of the war, concluded that "the difficulties which industry experienced in meeting the needs of the war . . . were the result of pre-war difficulties rather than new ones created by the war emergency."[2]

## SOME CAUSES OF LABOR DISCONTENT

Prominent among these difficulties were inadequate housing and transportation, unsafe factory conditions, a deterioration of labor's living standards, the speeding up of machines through the spread of "scientific management," high profits that labor considered exorbitant, the use of gunmen and private and state armies to break strikes, the absence of machinery to settle grievances, and the employers' implacable resistance to labor's demands for wage increases, a reduction in working hours, and union recognition.

The entry of the U.S. into the war only aggravated labor's unresolved discontent. The housing problem, for example, was worsened by "an extremely abnormal distribution of the labor supply."[3] Attracted by higher wages, resulting from war work, to places where there were no industries or only minor ones before, or to cities already congested and lacking adequate housing facilities, workers grew increasingly discontented. Many moved from job to job, thereby creating a huge labor turnover and a resulting decrease in labor productivity.[4] In his study, *Industrial Housing Problems*, produced during the war, Lewis H. Allen noted:

In years gone by wages were lost and the cost of labor turnover was hardly considered, for there was always a long line of new men waiting for a job, and because of this excess supply of men over demand, a man was not so ready to throw up his job to seek another. He would put up with poor housing conditions for the sake of having any job at all. But in the present labor situation, with demand far exceeding supply, the worker will no longer be content with the disgraceful housing conditions he has to put up with.[5]

Unsanitary conditions of employment was another cause of wartime labor discontent. This was particularly evident in the oil, lumber, and mining camps of the southwestern and northwestern states, in the shipyards along the Atlantic and Pacific coasts, and in the factories that produced munitions, food, and clothing for the military services, especially in the Northeast. The lumber camps, for example, were often situated in isolated and inaccessible communities. There, the employers generally furnished both lodging and board, and conditions were especially bad. In many of these camps, bunk houses were dangerously overcrowded, were constructed in an unsanitary manner, and often lacked any source of ventilation except the door. Toilet facilities were few, and usually unsanitary as well.[6]

Conditions among the shipyard and garment workers were equally poor. Working with deficient material and in temperatures sometimes as low as 24° below zero, the carpenters at the Hog Island shipbuilding plant complained of inadequate hospital facilities, defective garbage disposal, and spoiled food. Reporting on the causes of labor dissatisfaction at Hog Island, Rear Admiral Bowles stated that "poor food" was one of the chief conditions responsible, and he reported that workers often suffered from a mild form of food poisoning. He also questioned why workers were charged thirty cents for a meal that cost eleven cents. The *Amalgamated Journal*, organ of the Brotherhood of Carpenters and Joiners, had an answer—"War Profiteering."[7]

Especially troublesome for workers was the situation in the manufacture of uniforms for the armed forces. The first large orders of the Quartermaster General for hundreds of thousands of uniforms were given to non-union shops on the ground that they had submitted the lowest bids. These firms, ill-equipped to do the work, subcontracted it, with the result that much of it was done by non-union workers in tenement houses or in small shops under unsafe and unhealthy conditions—despite army prohibitions against giving out work to "sweaters." Speaking for the clothing workers, Sidney Hillman, president of the Amalgamated Clothing Workers, repeatedly pointed to the glaring contradiction between the government's stated foreign policy of waging "a war for democracy," and its domestic actions that encouraged sweatshops. Hillman insisted that army clothing was being manufactured under extremely unsanitary conditions and in places where contagious diseases were rampant. He suggested that soldiers and sailors were being exposed to tuberculosis germs, while the garment workers who produced their uniforms were being driven back to home work, child labor, long hours, and low wages.[8]

Writing in the *Fur Worker* in September 1917, George A. Hall, Secretary of the New York Child Labor Committee, reported "A Return to Sweatshop Labor":

> Both disease and dirt were present in a number of the homes in which our investigators found army goods. In one flat overcoats were piled all around on the bed, in the dark bedroom, and in heaps on the very dirty kitchen floor. A palefaced boy about ten years old helped the wornout mother to finish these uniforms, they earning together $3 to $4 a week. In another tenement, on a pile of army coats on the kitchen floor, was seated a little child dropping grease crumbs, at the same time wiping on the uniforms the filth of the street which had collected on the tiny bare feet. To get away from the stifling heat of the little rooms in one tenement, the woman had taken army pants to finish on the fire escape. The main pile filled the few kitchen chairs. Nearby was a sick baby, while five other children crowded about the visitor. One of these was suffering from a skin disease, with ugly open sores nearly ready to fester.[9]

In effect, within a few weeks after the nation's entry into the war, many of the protective labor safeguards and standards that the clothing workers had secured after years of bitter struggle were threatened with destruction. Indeed, the question of maintaining existing labor safeguards and standards confronted the labor movement from the very moment of the U.S. entry into the war. Employers complained that they were being deprived of millions of workers by military conscription and by the decrease in immigration (which, in normal times, furnished half a million workers per year). In their desire to reduce their labor costs to a minimum while amassing maximum wartime profits, they called for reductions in labor standards. Labor retorted that the problem lay not in a shortage of labor, but rather in a "shortage of wages," and in the existence of intolerable working and living conditions. But although the Wilson administration expressed opposition to the reduction of labor standards and safeguards, attempts to whittle away at labor's gains intensified.[10]

In the United States, as in England, employers attacked the laws limiting the working hours of women, the child labor laws, and almost all other forms of labor legislation, on the ground that the need for maximum industrial production, and the disturbance of the labor supply resulting from the war, necessitated the "repeal of every restriction on the complete utilization of the country's labor power."[11]

The attempt to modify legislatively-enacted labor protection was defeated in New York, but in several states employers were more successful. New Hampshire, Connecticut, Massachusetts, Vermont, Kansas, and California all authorized their governors to suspend labor laws, especially those affecting women and child workers.[12]

No national industrial conscription law was enacted during the war even though many industrialists and government officials advocated a program of labor conscription and the appointment of a "labor dictator" to restrict the movement of labor.[13]* But twelve states enacted compulsory work laws requiring all able-bodied men not in military service to be gainfully employed. In the South, "work-or-fight" ordinances were applied by local planters and employers to nonworking black women—not, however, to white women—and these women were often illegally forced into employment under conditions set only by the employers.[14]

The most important cause of industrial unrest during the war was the contrast between the rewards received by employers and by workers. Profits increased with production, especially since the increase in demand enabled firms in the United States to put higher prices on their products. While profits soared and the cry of "profiteering" was heard everywhere, wages lagged markedly behind the rising cost of living. Millions of workers whose pre-war wages were insufficient to support what was considered a fair standard of life "found their earnings every day more and more inadequate because of the increase in the cost of food, clothing, and shelter." In fact, from the standpoint of real wages, average workers considered themselves "worse off in 1918, than in 1914."[15] The California State Federation of Labor at its nineteenth annual convention adopted a resolution which stated that the "high cost of living has now become the high

*The President of the United States Chamber of Commerce insisted that if workers could not "be induced to work from patriotism they certainly should be commandeered and forced to work." Others argued that unless conscription of labor was enacted, the "United States would go down to defeat in the war and our boasted liberty would amount to nothing." (John Lombardi, *Mobilizing Labor in 1917 and 1918*[Los Angeles, 1942], p.7; Chicago *Tribune*, April 12, 1918; Krivy, *op. cit.*, pp. 57-58.)

In opposing industrial conscription, organized labor was able to demonstrate that there was no general shortage of labor during the war, even though shortages did exist for particular industries and localities, and that if housing and working conditions were improved where a shortage of labor was reported, that problem would also be quickly solved. "Shortage of Labor is a Camouflage for Profiteers," a headline in the *Miners' Magazine* read, and one in the *United Mineworkers' Journal* read: "Labor Shortage Scare Only Where 1914 Living Standards Prevail." *Miners' Magazine* 19 (May 1918): 4; *United Mine Workers' Journal* 28 (November 8, 1917): 7.

cost of half living. . . . The wage earner buys far less in proportion than in the past. The margin between the producer and the consumer has become so great that the consumer can buy only half of what he produces."[16]

The cost of living rose steadily after the outbreak of war in Europe in 1914, until, by the end of 1918, it stood nearly 75 percent higher than at the beginning of the war.[17]* Wages also advanced during the period between 1914 and 1918,** but increased monetary earnings did not necessarily result in an improved standard of living or even increased purchasing power. Advances in real wages "proved largely illusory," and labor as a whole found itself "unable to obtain wage rates high enough to raise living standards."[18] Selig Perlman and Philip Taft conclude: "It is apparent that during the war years, when the cost of living was advancing so rapidly, it was practically impossible for labor to attain a sufficient increase in wage *rates* to finance a higher standard of living. Such increases could be

*Cost of food in New York City in December 1918 showed an 83 percent increase over 1914, while in Baltimore, Boston, Seattle, and Chicago, the increase was 96, 75, 73, and 79 percent respectively. Clothing prices evidenced an even sharper rise. Prices in New York in December 1918 were 31 percent above pre-war levels, while in Chicago clothing sold at 139 percent more than in 1914. While rising costs of fuel, light and housing were less marked than those in food and clothing, they were not insignificant. The cost of fuel in New York City rose 45.1 percent from December 1914 to December 1918; 46 percent in Baltimore; 56.6 percent in Boston, and 51.8 percent in Seattle. Housing rose only 6.6 percent in New York for the same period, but 13.8 percent in Baltimore and 44.3 percent in Seattle. ("War Time Rise in Living Costs," *Literary Digest*, Sept. 14, 1918, p.16; Charles O. Hardy, *Wartime Control of Prices*, Washington, D.C., 1940, p.200; Krivy, *op.cit.*, pp. 57-59.)

**In all trades, taken collectively, weekly wage rates May 15, 1918 increased over May 15, 1917 by 22 percent and over 1914 by 20 percent. But wage increases were uneven. Commenting in 1918 in the study, *Wages and the War*, Hugh S. Hannah and Jett W. Lauck stated: "In some trades there have been wage advances that a little while ago, would have appeared wildly incredible. In others, the advances have been very moderate, little if any greater, than had occurred during a period of equal length in the preceding years of peace."(Cleveland,1918, p.32.) Wages of iron, steel, shipbuilding and munitions workers rose as much as 50 and 100 percent during the war years, and large wage increases were also registered for railroad workers under government control. But wages of workers in nonessential industries showed a much smaller advance. In the shoe industry, a 30 percent increase in annual earnings was recorded between 1917 and 1918, while in newspaper printing and book and job printing, employees' hourly wages showed a rise of only 6.4 and 10 percent respectively. As a result of the cut-off of immigration by the war and the increase in the demand for unskilled labor, the wages of unskilled workers rose rapidly in the years between 1914 and 1918. But unskilled laborers employed in the meat packing industry earned 42.5 percent more than in the preceding year, while unskilled iron and steel workers received 80 to 87 percent more in 1918. Real wages of office help and others whose services were not as much in demand showed a proportional decline. Office help in manufacturing lost 10 percent, and railroad office employees experienced a loss of 14 percent. (Hannah and Lauck, *op.cit.*, pp. 110-19; Paul H. Douglas, *Real Wages in the United States, 1890-1926* [Boston, 1930], pp. 96, 101, 364.)

obtained only by workmen in occupations where there was a serious labor shortage. In general, labor had its hands full pushing wages up fast enough to equal the increases in living costs."[19]

As early as November 1916, the *New York Times* noted that flour was "higher today than at any time since the Civil War," that potatoes had increased in price during the previous month by more than one hundred percent, and that the rising costs of virtually all food items were "astonishing."[20] According to economist Edward C. Kirkland, food prices went up 82 percent in the two and a half years preceding entry of the U.S. into the war.[21]

"Huge Increases in Food Prices Arouse Protest" read the headline in *Advance* on May 11, 1917. The organ of the Amalgamated Clothing Workers reported that the steady rise in the cost of living was causing workers to become increasingly discontented. *Advance* predicted that "present food conditions cannot continue much longer without an explosion that may be a serious menace not only to the United States, but to the success of the great war in which we are now engaged."[22*] In search of higher wages (and to a lesser extent shorter hours and better working conditions), many workers shifted from less profitable forms of employment to war industries, which were offering the highest wages. The resulting labor turnover was unprecedented in American history. Secretary of Labor William B. Wilson reported in August 1918 that it had increased from "an average of 300 percent" in "ordinary times" to "as high as 3,000 percent" in some cities since the U.S. entered the war.[23]

The practice of awarding cost-plus contracts not only opened new opportunities for greater profits and increased the inflationary spiral already in motion, but aggravated the problems of labor turnover. Employers had a great inducement to compete for labor, and the practice of "stealing" workers from other plants became common.[24]

The awarding of government contracts exacerbated the problem of labor turnover in still another way. In the letting of contracts for war work, the government tended to concentrate on firms situated only in areas of the

---

*Such an "explosion" had already occurred. Beginning on February 19, 1917 in the Brownsville section of Brooklyn, New York, food riots involving thousands of women broke out in working class neighborhoods in several cities. The women protested against skyrocketing food prices and hunger. The police were unable to quell the rioters. The *New York Evening Journal* reported on February 21, 1917: "Again and again the women charged upon the police. Uniforms were ripped, faces of the patrolmen scratched and buttons torn from their clothing." Socialist Congressman Meyer London, representing New York City's East Side, introduced a bill calling for the nationalization of the nation's food industry, but it failed to pass. (William Freidburger, "War Prosperity and Hunger: The New York Food Riots of 1917," *Labor History* 25 (Spring 1984): 217-39.)

country where there were labor shortages. On the other hand, those areas with surplus labor received few government contracts. In general, the concentration of war contracts in the eastern section of the nation while the midwest was neglected helped considerably to create acute shortages of both labor and housing. Except for shipping board contracts, one-half of government contracts were granted to firms in New York, Ohio, and Pennsylvania.[25]

Critical of the industrial confusion created by the lack of national planning, *Advance* proposed a remedy as early as July 1917:

> Would not the government be following a wiser course if it called into consultation the representatives of the manufacturers' association and the union which control 85 percent of the industry, made preferential arrangements with them for the execution of government work and made them jointly responsible for the maintenance of uninterrupted production? Why should not the same thing be done in all other industries in operation under collective agreements? And where unions exist but are "not recognized," why should not the government lend its influence to the creation of collective agreements in the interests of industrial peace and efficiency?[26]

The response of most government departments to this argument was typified by the position taken by the Quartermaster Corps, "that the government was not concerned with the advancement of organized labor."[27] But if the war was to be prosecuted successfully, such an attitude was self-defeating. Officials in Washington soon realized that there was a vital need to keep workers content up to a reasonable point, since widespread industrial unrest could seriously hamper the prosecution of the war. Consequently, the government had no choice but to use its influence to deal with the issues of wages, hours, and working conditions—especially in view of the insatiable rush for wartime profits by industrial concerns.

## GOMPERS AND THE COUNCIL OF NATIONAL DEFENSE

Almost a year before it entered the European conflict, the United States had already taken the first official step toward industrial preparedness for war. In accordance with Section 120 of the National Defense Act of June 3, 1916 and Section 2 of the Army Appropriation Act of August 29, 1916 the Council of National Defense was created. In the summer of 1916, President Wilson appointed the top personnel of the Council, consisting of the Secretaries of War, Navy, Interior, Agriculture, Commerce, and Labor. Newton D. Baker, Secretary of War, was elected chairperson of the Council.

The Council of National Defense was charged with "the coordination of the industries and resources for the national security and welfare," and "the creation of relations which will render possible in time of need the immediate concentration and utilization of the resources of the nation." To advise and assist the Council of National Defense, an Advisory Commission was established. On October 11, 1916 President Wilson appointed the commission's seven members, each of whom was named for his "special knowledge of some industry, public utility, or the development of some natural resource."[28]

The Advisory Commission of seven private citizens turned out to be the basic force in the Council of National Defense. It was given the authority to execute what had been decided upon. Samuel Gompers, as chairperson of the Committee on Labor, selected an executive committee of fourteen members, which reflected Gompers' belief that representation should be accorded to all elements concerned "in determining or regulating labor conditions." It included employers, financiers, directors of corporations, and representatives of workers. The last-named category consisted of only four men, all top labor bureaucrats: Warren S. Stone, grand chief of the Brotherhood of Locomotive Engineers; Frank Morrison, secretary of the AFL; James O'Connell, president of the Metal Trades Department of the AFL; and James Lord, president of the AFL's Mining Department. The other members were Ralph M. Easley, Gompers' assistant; Secretary of Labor William B. Wilson, secretary; W. Everitt Macy, president of the National Civic Federation; A. Parker Nevin of the National Association of Manufacturers; Lee M. Frankel of the Metropolitan Life Insurance Company, and Louis B. Schram of the Accident Department of the National Civic Federation.[29]

To assist the executive committee and to deal with specific questions arising between labor and management, eight national committees were established by the Council of National Defense. One was the National Committee on Mediation and Conciliation, which was empowered to urge the parties to a labor dispute to select their own arbitrators in cases where mediation and conciliation failed. National committees were also organized on Wages and Hours, Women in Industry, Welfare Work, Cost of Living and Domestic Economy, Information and Statistics, and Publicity and Press.[30]

"My committee," Gompers informed President Wilson, "consists of about two hundred men and women—representative trade unionists, employers, specialists, publicists, experts in welfare work and other interests." None, however, were Black! In fact, the entire Council of National

Defense was lily-white. Moreover, despite repeated appeals by leaders of the National Women's Trade Union League that he appoint two women to the 75-member National Committee on Mediation and Conciliation, Gompers deferred action. It took many requests from the League, some of them harshly worded, before he would agree to a committee on women in industry. It was chaired by the wealthy J. Borden Harriman, and no trade unionists were appointed to the committee until the League protested. Gompers made sure that the board was kept merely advisory, so that the women still had no actual power. No black person was appointed to any of the national, divisional, or sectional subcommittees of the Committee on Labor.[31]

Not long after these appointments were made public, labor reporters began to point to workers' rising discontent over the absence of trade union representation on committees associated with the letting of war contracts. It was observed that there was no labor representation on the Committees on Supplies, Transportation and Communication or on their subcommittees—the bodies that dealt with every commodity needed for the war—and that they were "made up exclusively of bankers, merchants, and industrialists."[32] Only one production committee, in fact, had a trade union representative on it—the Coal Production Committee—and this was the result of an ultimatum by the United Mine Workers that it would not cooperate with the committee as long as it had no labor representative. On June 15, 1917, after this ultimatum was made public by UMW President John P. White, seven labor men were added to the thirteen employer and government officials already on the committee.[33]

Under growing pressure from its membership, the AFL began to insist that the Council of National Defense grant labor representation "coequal with all other interests, upon all agencies, boards, committees, and commissions entrusted with war work." This was followed up by a visit to the White House. Gompers, accompanied by the president of the Illinois Federation of Labor and the chief officers of the Chicago Federation of Labor, urged Wilson to grant labor direct representation on all committees associated in one way or another with the Council of National Defense. Gradually, labor achieved its goal, and all of the special commissions that were established, except one, had representatives from organized labor. The exception was the Board of Control of Labor Standards in Army Clothing, and the explanation for this was that the dispute between the Amalgamated Clothing Workers and the United Garment Workers over the right to represent the clothing workers had still not been resolved.[34]*

In December 1917, President Wilson seized the railroads and placed them under the management of the United States Railroad Administration. In taking over the railroads, the federal government acquired not only some 240,000 miles of track and the equipment to operate on them, but jurisdiction over wages, hours, and working conditions of two million railroad workers. W. S. Carter, head of the Brotherhood of Locomotive Firemen, was appointed to run the Division of Labor of the Railroad Administration.[35]

Despite the importance of Carter's appointment, it was generally reported in the press that it was the American Federation of Labor and its president, Samuel Gompers, who were regarded by President Wilson as "the official representative of the country's wage earners."[36] Gompers was certainly closer to the President than any other labor leader. A frequent caller at the White House, and more intimate with Wilson "than many of the latter's cabinet members," Gompers was usually consulted by the President before he arrived at any important decision affecting labor. Whenever labor appointments were to be made, "Gompers was always asked to suggest nominees." As chairperson of the Committee on Labor of the Council of National Defense, he had much to say about the personnel of the various departmental boards dealing with working conditions and other labor issues during the war, as well as with various labor missions that were sent abroad. He was also frequently called upon to advise the President in regard to labor of other countries, and in 1918, with the blessing of the administration, Gompers led a labor mission to Europe. Wilson publicly paid high tribute to Gompers for his "patriotic courage, his large vision, and his statesmanlike sense of what has to be done," when he addressed the thirty-seventh annual convention of the American Federation of Labor in Buffalo, New York, on November 12, 1917, the first time in the history of the United States that organized labor was addressed by the head of the nation.** In return for these words, Gompers reaffirmed to President Wilson "the wholehearted support and cooperation of American organized labor."[37]

## THE ISSUE OF COMPULSORY MILITARY SERVICE

The first task Gompers set for organized labor in carrying out this pledge was to accept the principle of compulsory military service and to cooperate fully in the administration of the Selective Service Act of May 18, 1917. At

*For the background of this dispute, see Philip S. Foner, History of the Labor Movement in the United States 6 (New York, 1982): 105-10.

**It was also the first occasion following the declaration of war that Wilson left Washington to deliver a public address.

the March 12, 1917 trade union conference in Washington of labor representatives, discussed at length in Chapter 5, the delegates insisted that military
conscription was "repugnant to the Constitution of the United States and the
genius of our republic." They further contended that the "fullest opportunity
must first be given to voluntary service before so drastic a departure as compulsory service, conscription, shall even be attempted." "Until such a test
shall have been made," they concluded, "there was no good reason for abandoning the principles which were born of the ideals and traditions of the 'spirit
of '76,' [which have] enabled us to establish the ideals and traditions that have
given the republic meaning as a country, free, efficient, capable of meeting
any condition or emergency."[38]

This view was the one part of the statement defining organized labor's
position on war and peace that met with universal approval. The Seattle
Central Labor Council cited it in informing the Congressional representatives of the state of Washington that the majority of organized labor was
opposed to military conscription.[39] The *United Mine Workers' Journal*,
which, like the *Seattle Union Labor Record*, disapproved of the declaration adopted in Washington giving President Wilson a "blank check" to
proceed to declare war, also endorsed that part of the document. "There is
not now nor is there likely to be any *future* contingency that may be anticipated, a need so urgent that we should turn this country into an armed
camp," it declared. If a demand should arise "in this time of general
excitement," for compulsory military service, "we must resist it with all
power we can muster."[40]

With this the dominant attitude of AFL affiliates, the Federation's Executive Council voted by an overwhelming majority to oppose compulsory military service. Gompers was by now a vehement advocate of compulsory
military service, but he was required by the AFL constitution to abide by the
will of the Executive Council. This he pledged to do. In a letter to first vice-
president James Duncan,* he assured him that he would "do nothing by word
or act in advocacy of universal military service . . . until after mature discussion with you and the other associate members of the Council."[41]

In letters and speeches, and in a personal appearance before the House

*Duncan, international president of the Granite Cutters' International Association, refused to
oppose the war but also refused to actively support it. On April 17, 1917 he wrote to Gompers: "We received your second letter with reference to being associated with your subcommittee on National Defense, etc. I have not changed my mind upon the subject. Much as
I love the institutions of our great country, our flag, and everything it represents, there is so
much connected with war and war arrangements so entirely uncongenial to me, and as I feel I
could not participate in the conferences, kindly leave me out of consideration in the makeup
of your committee." (AFL Archives, State Historical Society of Wisconsin.)

Military Affairs Committee, Gompers did campaign against the adoption of compulsory military service. "The organized labor movement has always been fundamentally opposed to compulsion," he told the Military Affairs Committee. "It has maintained that institutions and relations of a free people can and should be based upon the voluntary principle. It now maintains that what has been the directing basic principle in industrial organization and service must be the initial basic principle in the military."[42] At the same time, however, at a joint meeting of the Advisory Commission and the Council of National Defense, Gompers made clear his own support for compulsory military service, but indicated that his organization opposed it. Hence, he recommended that the meeting take no stand on the issue, and it followed his recommendation.[43]

The result was that the press, including the labor press, published two versions of where Gompers stood on the issue. Some labor correspondents accepted the version that Gompers opposed compulsory military service, and sent him telegrams like the following from the Kansas City Labor Council: "Organized labor of Kansas City endorses your stand against conscription and pledges its support to help defeat the vicious and subversive bills before Congress threatening the suspension of our constitutional rights of freedom of speech press and assembly. Keep up the fight against these measures."[44]

Others, however, could not make out just where Gompers stood. The editor of the *Labor Monitor of Imperial Valley*, organ of the Imperial Valley (California) Trades Council, wrote to Gompers:

> . . . enclosing two clippings from Labor papers, one quotes you as being opposed to compulsory service of any sort and the other stating that you favor compulsory military training.
>
> On behalf of a number of my fellow workers here, all of whom are against compulsory military service of any kind, or for that matter any kind of compulsory service, I write to ask if you have been correctly quoted in these articles. . . .
>
> We are hopeful that the article stating that you were in favor of the law to place the workers of the nation in a state of serfdom to the privileged class, has misquoted you, and that you stand as we have always stood for humanity at all times. . . .[45]

The Stenographers, Typewriters, Bookkeepers & Assistants' Union No. 14268 was not interested in what Gompers may or may not have said on compulsory military service. It wanted him to do more immediately to try to prevent passage of legislation by Congress for compulsory service. "We call upon you," they wired, "to start vigorous opposition at once to forestall establishment of Prussianism in America under guise of Democracy. Act at once before too late."[46] But Gompers replied that he had already made his position clear and there was no need for further action.[47]

On May 18, 1917, the Selective Service Act became law, requiring the registration of all men between 21 and 30 years old. As chairperson of the Committee on Labor of the Advisory Commission, Gompers presented to the War Department a request that representatives of organized labor be appointed as members of the five-man District Exemption Boards that had appellate jurisdiction over all exemption cases, and direct jurisdiction on all individual conscription cases. This, Gompers maintained, would assure a more efficient implantation of the Selective Service Act, and would aid the war effort by preventing "men being drafted into military service who are absolutely indispensable to the production of munitions of war and things necessary to maintain the civilian population."[48] The War Department agreed, and by the end of 1917 union representatives sat on nearly all district and local exemption boards. This action was taken with the consent of the AFL Executive Council.[49] Thus, from originally opposing compulsory military service, the AFL Executive Council now offered its cooperation to help implement compulsory service. Gompers had given token support to his pledge to carry out the Executive Council's original opposition to compulsory military service, but by speaking out of both sides of his mouth, he had only confused the labor movement and weakened its opposition to compulsory military service.

## THE ISSUE OF STRIKES

The second task Gompers undertook in his capacity as chairperson of the Committee on Labor was to deal with the question of interruption in industrial production by conflicts between labor and capital. On April 6, 1917, the Council of National Defense released a declaration drafted by the Committee on Labor's executive committee, and approved by the Advisory Commission. The declaration was designed ostensibly to prevent the enactment of legislation repealing labor laws, which had established standards of health and safety. But its opening statements gave an entirely different impression, declaring:

> The defense and safety of the Nation must be the first consideration of citizens. To avoid confusion and to facilitate the preparation for national defense, and give a stable basis upon which the representatives of the government may operate during the war, we recommend:

That the Council of National Defense should issue a statement to employers and employes in our industrial plants and transportation systems, advising that neither employers nor employes shall endeavor to take advantage of the country's necessities to change existing standards. When economic or other emergencies arise requiring changes of standards, the same should be made only after such proposed changes have been investigated and approved by the Council of National Defense.[50]

With almost complete unanimity, the press carried headlines such as the following in the Chicago *Tribune*: "UNIONS PLEDGE LOYALTY TO U.S.: BAR ALL STRIKES." The subheadline read: "Gompers Committee Acts with National Defense Council."* This was followed by the following from the paper's Washington correspondent: "Full and loyal support to the government in war against Germany has been pledged by organized labor of America. . . . No strikes or labor disputes of any kind during the war is the program."[51] Editorially, the *Tribune* was full of praise for the AFL. "American Labor Speaks," was the title of the editorial, as it announced "the pledge of the representatives of the chief labor organization of the country, the American Federation of Labor, that there will be no strikes during the war. . . . This is wisdom and patriotism combined. It puts the nation on an assured ground from which it can fight the war to a successful conclusion, without fear that any class will exploit the commonweal. . . . Americanism is not dead. It is living and will prove itself again to the world."[52]

Gompers was immediately deluged with angry telegrams and letters from trade unions, state federations of labor, and city central labor councils from all over the country. Unions proclaimed in these messages that they

will not support anybody who offers the rights of the workers for a merely imaginary cause and that the union has not authorized anybody to give assurance, which may help to bring about a situation, where the rights of the workers as well as those of the people may be set aside.[53]

"As President of the Tri-City Federation of Labor [Davenport, Iowa, and Rock Island and Moline, Illinois], I was instructed to communicate with you and ascertain if the report of your pledge that workers would not strike during the war was correct," wrote Charles MacGowan, "and if so, what assurance, if any, you have from the administration that food

*The headline and subheadline in the *New York Times* of April 9, 1917 read: "NO WAR STRIKES, LABOR'S PLEDGE." "Gompers Promises Full Support of Government During Hostilities."

speculators will not be permitted to strangle the Nation with their insidious practices. Also what further assurances have you that the employers will not take advantage of the opportunity to lower our standards of life, by increasing hours, reducing wages, and saddling upon the workers inhuman and unbearable conditions."[54]

In fact, Gompers received reports that employers were already using the press report to refuse to meet with strikers or to grant any demands workers were requesting. One employer, Watson Malone & Sons, a dealer in lumber in Philadelphia, informed Gompers that it had received requests for wage increases from the International Longshoremen's Association and the International Brotherhood of Teamsters, Chauffeurs, Stablemen and Helpers, with the threat of strikes if the demands were not granted. The company went on: "We are under the impression that both of these associations are members of the American Federation of Labor. If this is a fact and the report in the papers that you have issued orders there would be no strikes during the period of the war is correct, are they justified in making the above demands?"[55]

Daniel J. Tobin, president of the Teamsters, one of the two unions involved in the Philadelphia dispute, sent an angry letter to Gompers, enclosing a copy of the telegram he had just received from Sioux City, Iowa:

> We have endeavored to get a meeting with the bosses and they ignore us on every occasion. Will not grant an audience of any kind. The boys are very restless. President Gompers' article in the press stating there will be no strikes has made bosses stand pat. What would you advise? Answer by wire, Local 315.

Tobin said he had not seen Gompers' statement, but neither had he seen any denial by the AFL president of the reports in the press. In any event, Tobin wrote, if he had made such a pledge, he had "no right to do so. Before any such action should be taken or a pledge of this kind made, my opinion is, a special convention of the American Federation of Labor should have been held, and before it was held International officers should have been asked to consult with their several unions and get instructions so that when they did attend the special convention of the American Federation of Labor they would be in a position to know the feeling of their membership."

"This particular time," Tobin continued, "is the worst period in the history of our International Union, due principally to the fact that our membership are starving resulting from high prices and low wages." The answer he would send to the local in Sioux City was that "our International Union is going along just as we did before, settling with our employers who are willing to be fair, but determined to fight unfair employers, many of whom we still have with us." To Gompers he declared that "the International I represent will continue to fight and struggle, even to the extent of striking for better conditions, war or no war. . . ."[56]

Of the scores of other telegrams and letters of protest Gompers received, the following is typical: "Employers understand that no strikes can occur and are taking advantage of this recommendation to crucify labor by discharging our members and taking away conditions that we have enjoyed for years. It is unfair to labor that employees should be throttled while employers are free to do as they please. We insist that your committee take such action as may be necessary to counteract this. . . ."[57]

Frank Duffy of the Carpenters and Joiners insisted that his union would have "no part of a no-strike pledge without specific safeguards to protect the carpenters," and that "patriotic manifestations unsupported by definite administrative plans . . . offer no such guarantee." The lack of guarantees also troubled the *Cleveland Citizen*, official organ of the Ohio AFL, which, in criticizing the declaration, expressed the opinion that "to prohibit strikes without pulling the teeth of the trusts that control flour, meat, sugar, coal, and other necessaries of life is nothing short of treason to the masses in this country."[58] C. O. Young, general organizer for the AFL, informed Gompers that he was being called a "traitor" to the working class in many parts of the Southwest. Young said he could understand this rage: "There are many wage increases pending over this entire country at this time, and if the impression is general that there is to be a ban placed upon efforts for betterment of wages and other conditions of labor, it will be a great detriment to organized labor."[59]

Since even conservative trade unionists like Frank Duffy and C. O. Young sharply criticized his stand, Gompers knew that he had to do a lot of explaining, and quickly. He denied that any promises had ever been made by the Committee on Labor, or that he had ever made any statements or ever agreed that there "shall be no strikes of any kind during the war." Insisting that "a strike is not resorted to lightly, but as a last resort," he maintained that "if the workers met with the same spirit of cooperation that they have manifested, strikes may be averted—but they cannot be prohibited." Furthermore, the clause providing for no departure from present standards "in no way precluded the effort to obtain necessary improved conditions." Moreover, although he hoped "patriotic regard will be had by all citizens to the need of a possible maximum of industrial peace everywhere," he did not mean, nor did the statement mean, that labor was willing to forego any attempts to organize non-union shops. On the contrary, the right to organize and to bargain collectively were integral principles in a "war for democracy."[60]

A second or "amplifying statement" was adopted by the executive committee of the Committee on Labor, approved by the Advisory Commission of the Council of National Defense, and made public. It reinterpreted, the phrase "no departure from present standards" to mean "no lowering of present standards." It stated, too, that the Council of National Defense was not averse to having unduly low standards of living raised, even during the war emergency, but it recommended that changes in wages to meet the rising cost of living should be made only after investigation, mediation, or arbitration, and that in no event should there be a stoppage of work until all conciliatory measures had been exhausted. In the precise words of the amplifying declaration:

> No arbitrary changes in wages should be sought at this time by either employers or employees through the process of strikes or lockouts without at least giving the established agencies, including those of the several states and of the Government, and of the Mediation Board in the transportation service and the Division of Conciliation of the Department of Labor in other industries, an opportunity to adjust the difficulties without a stoppage of work occurring.[61]

Clearly, the Council of National Defense had asserted that while labor was justified in seeking to maintain its standard of living, it would not be justified in striking to advance its standards, no matter how much the cost of living increased, until the long and weary process of trying to settle the dispute by all other means had been exhausted.

At the same time, the Council accepted Gompers' interpretation that labor would not forego, during the duration of the war, the right to bargain collectively or the right to organize non-union shops. Reaffirmed, at least in words, this became the labor policy of the Wilson administration.[62]

## THE BAKER-GOMPERS MEMORANDUM

But words and deeds often did not correspond. The letting of contracts for the construction of training camps was put in the hands of Louis B. Wehle, who suggested to Secretary of War Newton D. Baker that the open shop should be permitted in construction work in exchange for an agreement that the adjustment board, established to decide all disputes and representing the army, labor, and the public, could use union scales of hours and wages, modified by changes in the cost of living, as a basis for contract agreements. Baker thought it a very good idea, but doubted that Gompers would go along with the principle of the open shop. But Wehle argued for trying, and took the proposal to Gompers' office.

After a lengthy discussion, Wehle did get Gompers' signature on what became famous as the Baker-Gompers agreement. It provided that the labor aspects of cantonment (barracks) construction would be governed by a commission of three appointed by the Secretary of War and representing the army, labor, and the public, with the labor representative nominated by Gompers. The commission was to use the union scale of wages, hours, and conditions in force in each locality, with consideration for subsequent changes in the cost of living. Standards fixed by the board were to be binding on all parties.

According to Wehle, Gompers agreed orally to the open shop, in exchange for these concessions. But when he asked him to confirm his oral agreement in writing, Gompers wired that the agreement "had reference to union hours and wages; the question of union shop was not included." But the unwritten understanding was accepted by both the employers and the government, and the open shop prevailed.[63]

The Baker-Gompers memorandum of June 19, 1917 was "the prototype" of a number of such agreements, and "the first instance of the federal government's entering into a contract with a labor union or group of unions."[64] To many unionists it was evidence that "Gompers' loyalty program was starting to look suspiciously like a sellout."[65] Gompers again received many complaints from union presidents, in the form of protesting telegrams and letters, particularly from those in the building trades. There was a good deal of bitterness expressed over the fact that Gompers had agreed to the memorandum without the express authorization of the Executive Council or the national convention, and it was clearly called "in direct violation of the AFL constitution, which granted absolute autonomy to the national and international unions making up the Federation."[66]

But, as was becoming more and more the custom, the protesters did not challenge Gompers to the bitter end, lest they be called disloyal, and they ultimately accepted the written and unwritten terms of the Baker-Gompers agreement. Only William Hutchinson of the Carpenters spoke out against the agreement and refused to retreat. Hutchinson charged that the agreement did not guarantee the closed shop in areas where it had been a long-standing tradition, and that as interpreted by the War Department it even violated a fundamental AFL principle. For the War Department was asserting that Gompers had agreed that union workers could work with non-union men, and Gompers did nothing to knock down this assertion.

Hutchinson therefore refused to recognize the agreement or to serve on the adjustment board that represented the army, labor, and the public. But he was the only AFL leader to take such a stand.[67]*

On the question of strikes, Gompers quickly retreated from the position he had taken when he tried to mollify union leaders who accused him of surrendering labor's right to strike. At first he had indignantly denied it, but in a letter to all trade union officers, he practically admitted the charge which he had denied. "No strike ought to be inaugurated," he wrote, "that cannot be justified to the men facing momentary death. A strike during the war is not justified unless principles are involved equally fundamental as those for which fellow citizens have offered their lives—their all."[68] With such a criterion there was hardly a need for a formal no-strike pledge.

But it was one thing to advocate that kind of patriotism and another to convince the workers of its fairness. Even Gompers conceded that the increase in the cost of living was creating such widespread worker discontent that he was receiving protests over his statement about strikes. "Many similar communications," he wrote to Henry Cabot Lodge, "are received at this office, indicating that the reason for this is the distress that exists in this country through the high cost of living, and the necessity for Congressional action to relieve these many people."[69] But there was not a hint that economic action by the workers themselves, which Gompers usually demanded in place of Congressional action, should be considered.

Despite their criticism, the AFL union presidents, in the main, went along with Gompers on the issue of strikes. The United Mine Workers and the Electrical Workers even went beyond it. They argued that the government would protect labor's interests. Hence, the two unions agreed to "lay aside for the time being, and if the experiment is successful, for all time, the weapon of defense—the strike."[70]

## SOME WARTIME STRIKES

But few unions followed their lead. To be sure, during the single month of June 1917, members of the Committee on Labor of the National Committee on Mediation and Conciliation successfully settled industrial disputes that were threatening in Cincinnati, Philadelphia, San Francisco, Omaha, Pittsburgh, and Jackson, Ohio.[71] But more strikes and lockouts

*When Gompers agreed to similar labor adjustment machinery for shipbuilding, including the open shop, Hutchinson was again the only AFL union leader who refused to sign or approve the document. (Louis B. Wehle, *Hidden Threads of History*, New York, 1953, pp.40-45.)

occurred in 1917 than in any preceding year.[72] The figures compiled from reports of the U.S. Bureau of Labor Statistics indicate that during the period between 1914 and 1918 there were a total of 19,915 work stoppages. Of these, 7,414 or approximately 56 percent occurred in the two years in which the nation was at war. Moreover, the largest number of work stoppages occurred in 1917, the first year of the war. During that year, 4,359 work stoppages were recorded, an increase of nearly seven hundred over the preceding year, and more than 3,000 over 1914.[73]

On July 23, 1917 hundreds of Italian workers, men and women, went on strike at several fruit and vegetable canneries in the San Francisco Bay area—the first strike in the history of the industry in California. They struck against low wages and long hours and for recognition of their recently-formed union, the Toilers of America. Headquartered in San Jose, California, the Toilers of America had been granted a charter as a Federal Labor Union by the American Federation of Labor in the Spring of 1917.[74]

By the summer of 1917, the production of canned fruits had become a vital part of the war effort, and the industry was expanding its production to meet the needs of the soldiers in the field. The day after the canning strike began, federal troops from nearby Camp Fremont occupied the canneries at San Jose, prepared to take action to crush the strike. At the same time, volunteer crews of housewives and college students acted to keep the canneries going, while San Jose Rotary Club members, prominent lawyers, and businessmen, organized by the cannery owners, formed "pick-handle brigades" to force the strikers back to work.[75]

In a telegram to President Wilson, the Canners' League of California insisted that the conflict was more than a controversy over wages:

> This is not a strike, but a conspiracy to stop fruit and vegetable packing resulting in the destruction to large quantities of food products necessary for the use of army and navy, our allies and the country at large. Imperative that the National Government take action to control this desperate movement of the enemies of our country which is sweeping over many Western States.[76]

As Elizabeth Reis points out in her study of the strike: "In the cannery executives' nightmare, the 'enemy' was an IWW—German alliance."[3] Actually, there was little evidence that the IWW played any role in the strike. But the cannery owners used the IWW-scare to charge the Italian strikers with lack of patriotism.[77]

However, fear that the IWW might replace the AFL in the leadership of the strike, if it continued, led the cannery owners to agree to proposals by mediators to end the walkout. On July 31, eleven canning companies in and around San Jose accepted the mediators' terms under which the men would have their wages increased from 25 cents to 30 cents an hour, while women's wages would be increased from 16 cents to 17½ cents per hour, and the piece-rate scale was also raised a few cents.* The companies also agreed to reemploy all strikers without discrimination. On this basis the strike ended and the workers returned to the canneries.[78*]

More general strikes took place in the United States after the nation entered World War I than during any period of American history. In September, 1917 a general strike occurred in Springfield, Illinois. It began with a strike by the street car workers for union recognition. On Labor Day, September 3, 1917, the parade was organized to support the street car strikers. When over 1,000 sympathizers, led by Illinois miners, attacked the headquarters of the street railway company to protest its refusal to negotiate with the strikers, members of F Company, North Illinois Infantry, attacked the protesters with bayonets and gun butts. One worker was bayonetted in the arm.[79]

The response of Springfield workers was a general strike. On September 29, 1917, the AFL weekly newsletter reported that 10,000 workers representing all trades, had joined the street car workers in a general strike. The strike ended when the authorities guaranteed that the right of free assemblage would be maintained in Springfield, and the street railway company agreed to meet with representatives of the striking street car workers.[80]

A general strike occurred in Waco, Texas in March, 1918 after the street car workers were locked out by the street railway company. In April, 1918, a general lockout of union workers occurred in Billings, Montana. This event grew out of a general strike in Billings the previous year after the mechanics in the building trades had been locked out by the Billings Employers' Association.[81]

The men and women who quit work in sympathy with the building trade mechanics in 1917 were all members of unions affiliated with the Federated Labor Union, and included icemen, city employees, gasmen, creamery workers, truck drivers, and other trades. The general strike lasted two weeks, and was finally settled when the strikers, including the building

---

*Under the terms of the agreement, the AFL agreed to represent only the male workers while the women would be represented by the Industrial Welfare Commission of California. Elizabeth Reis views this as further evidence of the unwillingness of the AFL to organize women. ("Cannery Row: The AFL, the IWW, and the Bay Area Italian Cannery Workers," *California History*, LXIX [Summer, 1985]: 191.)

trades mechanics, received an increase in wages and regained their former positions.[82]

In April, 1918, the laundry workers of Billings struck for a further increase in wages. Thereupon the Billings branch of the Montana Employers' Association, bent upon forcing the workers of the city to accept the open shop, locked out all of the employees affiliated with the Building Trades Council, "as well as the clerks, cook, and waiters, laundry workers, common laborers and teamsters in the jurisdiction of the Trades and Labor Assembly." The workers responded with a general strike. But this time, although wages were increased when the men returned to work, the employers' association succeeded in establishing the open shop in Billings.[83]

The most important general strike during World War I was that in Kansas City, Missouri. Its origin was a dispute between the laundry workers and their employers over the issues of union recognition and increase in wages. In July, 1917, laundry drivers organized a union, which by December of that year had achieved a membership of 125 men, or 38 percent of the Kansas City drivers. Most of the city's remaining 200 drivers joined the union when laundry employers refused to grant a wage increase in February, 1918.[84]

The organization of laundry drivers encouraged laundresses to seek a wage increase. By mid-February 1918, all of the city's 1800 laundry workers had gone on strike, demanding union recognition, increased wages, and the enforcement of state legislation regulating laundress' hours and conditions of labor.[85]

For five weeks the laundry workers continued their strike, militantly picketing the laundries in Kansas City. But the laundry employers not only refused to meet with a committee of employees, but even to sit down with federal Department of Labor conciliators. After repeated attempts by labor sympathizers among the clergy and prominent citizens failed to force a change in the employers' opposition to trade unions, organized and unorganized workers throughout Kansas City called for a general cessation of work as of March 27, 1918 to support the laundry workers' demands.[86]

On March 27 the city-wide strike in sympathy with the laundry workers began. It involved most segments of the city's working population, including street railway employees.[87]

The general strike began peacefully, but this changed when the Kansas City Railways Company attempted to run the street cars with scab labor. Then rioting broke out, and the city brought in the National Guard to keep the street cars running. On March 30 the Jacks County Grand Jury returned indictments charging twenty men and four women with "unlawful assembly in connection with riots growing out of the general strike in progress here." That same day, the press reported the first death in connection with the general strike. Alonzo A. Millsap, a striking laundry driver, had been shot during a battle with the police protecting scabs at a laundry plant. He died on March 30 at a Kansas City hospital.[88]

At this point the Mayor requested a conference of laundry owners and employees. Because the laundry owners now agreed to grant the workers the right to organize, the laundry workers voted to return to work under conditions prevailing before the strike. A later agreement between the employers and employees increased by one dollar the weekly wages of laundresses.[89]*

The general strike lasted a full week and revealed a high degree of cooperation between men and women workers in Kansas City. The strike is credited with partial responsibility for the creation of the Kansas Industrial Court.[90]

## THE PRESIDENT'S MEDIATION COMMISSION

We will examine below some of the other work stoppages during the war, but we should note here that the industrial unrest was not confined to any one section of the country or to any single industrial group, but rather it characterized almost every industry in every section of the country. The greatest disturbances, however, were those that occurred in the oil fields of California, Louisiana, and Texas; the telephone systems of the Pacific Coast; the sugar refineries in New York and Philadelphia; the copper mines of the Southwest; the iron and steel mills in Pittsburgh; the packinghouses in Chicago, St. Louis, and Omaha; and the various clothing industries in New York, Philadelphia, and Chicago.[91]

By midsummer of 1917 the problem of industrial unrest had become so acute, especially in the western states, that Gompers urged President Wilson to intervene. He recommended that "the moral influence of the United States government should be brought to bear through a Federal investigation of the whole western labor situation."[92] This helped produce a commission that was given the name The President's Mediation Commission. The Commission spent several months visiting the copper

---

*The union, however, made no progress on the issue of enforcement of state statutes concerning women's wages and working conditions. Moreover, the laundry owners later refused to pay the promised wage increases. (Maurine Weiner Greenwald, *Women, War, and Work: The Impact of World War I on Women Workers in the United States*, Westport, Conn., 1980, p.175.)

districts of the Southwest, the oil fields of California, the meatpacking plants of Chicago, the Pacific Northwest timber districts, and other sections where industrial unrest was widespread, with results which we will examine below.[93]

The President's Mediation Commission was dissolved in January 1918, after submitting its recommendations to President Wilson. It attributed disruption of production not to any wilful disloyalty or unAmericanism on the part of labor, but rather to the existence of "uncorrected specific evils and the absence of a healthy spirit between capital and labor." To correct these evils, the commission offered the following recommendations:

1. The elimination to the utmost practical extent of all excessive profit-taking during the period of the war.

2. The establishment of continuous administrative machinery for the orderly disposition of industrial problems and the avoidance of an atmosphere of conflict and the waste coming from work stoppages.

3. The adoption of the basic eight-hour day, except for cases of emergencies in war industries.

4. A unified labor administration to replace the existing centralized administrative system.

5. The surrender by labor of all practices leading to the withdrawal of maximum efficiency.

6. The constructive education of both parties to the industrial conflict in order to guarantee a national solution of disputes and other serious labor problems.[94]*

Of special importance was the Commission's recommendation to Wilson that a more centralized labor administration be organized to cope with industrial problems. The haphazard labor policy of the government, based on the often contradictory tenets of the Council of National Defense, had caused considerable confusion along with a pattern of adjustment agencies with overlapping jurisdiction. It was this confusion that led the Mediation Commission to recommend the creation of an agency to centralize the efforts of the various adjustment boards. The need was urgent, the Commission emphasized. The causes of industrial unrest were general and deep-seated, but the nation's existing labor policy was inadequate to correct the evils that were responsible for this condition. To correct these evils, among other things, priority had to be given to the creation of a centralized control in labor administration with full power to determine and establish the necessary administrative structure.[95]

*As we have noted, at the request of President Wilson the Commission also investigated and issued findings in a separate report relating to the Mooney-Billings case.

# THE NATIONAL WAR LABOR BOARD

Acting upon the Commission's report, Secretary of Labor William B. Wilson, with the support of the President, called together an advisory council in January 1918 to evolve a comprehensive plan that would centralize the machinery of industrial relations. The War Labor Conference Board, as this council became known, was composed of five employer representatives and five labor representatives (nominated by the AFL), with each group selecting one member to represent the public.

As one of its first actions, the War Labor Conference Board adopted the policy that workers may not be denied the right to join trade unions if they so desired. Modeling itself on this policy, on February 21, 1918, the United States Railroad Administration issued General Order No. 8, giving all employees the right to organize into trade unions regardless of their previous status.[96]

In March 1918, the War Labor Conference Board recommended that a National War Labor Board be organized, made up of the same type of membership as its own group, functioning with specific powers and observing definite, stipulated principles. This suggestion was accepted by Wilson, and the National War Labor Board was created on April 9, 1918, by Presidential proclamation.

The membership of the National War Labor Board was to consist of five representatives of employers, five representatives of organized labor, and two representatives of the public. As in the case of the War Labor Conference Board, the five employer and five labor representatives were to be nominated, respectively, by Magnus W. Alexander, executive secretary of the National Industrial Conference Board, and Samuel Gompers, president of the A.F. of L. The two representatives of the public, who were to serve also as joint chairmen of the board, were to be selected one each by the employers and by labor. In addition to the aforementioned members, twelve alternates were to be named to act in the event of the absence of regular members.

At the suggestion of Secretary Wilson, the membership of the National War Labor Board as constituted at the time of its appointment was as follows: (1) co-chairmen and representatives of the public: William Howard Taft and Frank P. Walsh; (2) representatives of employers: L. F. Loree, C. Edwin Michael, Loyall A. Osborne, W. H. Van Dervoort, and B. L. Worden; (3) representatives of labor: Frank J. Hayes. William L. Hutchinson, Thomas Savage, Victor Orlander, and T. A. Rickert. Except for Worden, the employer representative, the composition of the National War Labor

Board was the same as that of the War Labor Conference Board.[97]

The National War Labor Board's code of principles and policies, unanimously adopted by the War Labor Conference Board and sanctioned by President Wilson, set forth, as its main objective to "govern relations between workers and employers in war industries for the duration of the war," and thereby facilitate unhampered war production. The principles guiding the Board in the implementation of its objective were:

1. There should be no strikes or lockouts during the war.

2. The right of workers to organize in trade unions and to bargain collectively through chosen representatives is recognized and affirmed. This right shall not be denied, abridged, or interfered with by the employers in any manner whatsoever. . . .

3. Employers should not discharge workers for membership in trade unions, nor for legitimate trade union activities.

4. The workers, in the exercise of their right to organize, should not use coercive measures of any kind to induce persons to join their organization nor to induce employers to bargain or deal therewith.

Other principles were: (1) Existing conditions were frozen—where a union shop existed, the union standards were to continue; however, union organizing was not to be denied under this ruling; (2) women on men's jobs should get "equal pay for equal work" but not be allotted tasks "disproportionate to their strength"; (3) the basic eight-hour day was to continue where existing law required it, and hours of labor must be adjusted with due regard to health standards; (4) availability of workers was to be filed with the Department of Labor for the purpose of more effective wartime labor mobilization; (5) prevailing local standards must be taken into consideration in adjustments of hours, wages, and conditions of labor; (6) the right of all workers to a living wage, including common laborers, was "hereby declared." In fixing wages, a minimum living wage had to be established that "will insure the subsistence of the worker and his family in health and reasonable comfort."[98]

In a resolution adopted shortly after the creation of the National War Labor Board, the National Association of Manufacturers placed itself on record as being in favor of the Board's code of principles and policies, and recommended to its members that they "cooperate with the said War Labor Board to the end that the aims and purposes for which it was created may be effectuated." Statements of support also came from the National Industrial Conference Board and other employers' associations.[99]

The AFL and the Railroad Brotherhoods also gave the Board their immediate endorsement. The Bakers pictured the Board as ushering in a "new era in the settlement of industrial disputes," while other unions spoke of a "new deal for American labor."[100]* No word of dissent came from Daniel J. Tobin, who, it will be recalled, had written to Gompers that "the International I represent will continue to fight and struggle, even to the extent of striking for better conditions, war or no war. . . ." Tobin and his union, the International Brotherhood of Teamsters, Chauffeurs, Stablemen, & Helpers, joined the other unions in the AFL and the Railroad Brotherhoods in surrendering the right to strike.[101]

The *Literary Digest* reported the formation of the National War Labor Board under the headline "Labor and Capital Bury the Hatchet."[102] The New York *Globe* went into sheer ecstasy, hailing the Board's principles as representing "the Magna Carta of labor." As the *Globe* saw it: "Here is a treaty of peace in itself worth what the war has cost, the realization of the dream of labor since it became self-conscious."[103]**

But IWW and Socialist trade unionists condemned the no-strike pledge as representing a complete departure from fundamental trade union principles. They warned that this close class collaboration in an alliance of labor, capital, and government was creating a situation that might lead to greater numerical strength of the unions in the short run, but in the long run, it would drastically weaken the fundamental power of organized labor. When the trade union officials voluntarily gave up the right to strike, they warned, they were transforming their organizations from independent trade unions to a government department and surrendering the labor movement to the employers.[104]

One other point regarding war labor policy needs emphasis. The cooperation of the AFL with the war effort signalled legitimation of its place in society, but it also exposed those in the labor movement who opposed the war to fierce repression.

---

*Thirty-one years later, labor historian Foster H. Dulles, echoed this contemporary estimate by characterizing the Board as "a reflection of the new governmental attitudes toward labor," foreshadowing those "later to be incorporated in the legislation of the New Deal." (*Labor in America*, [New York, 1949] p. 227.)

**In her study of the National War Labor Board, Valerie Jean Conner argues that while the board had no enforcement powers, its decisions were supported by President Wilson and the general public because it seemed to offer a solution to the problem of industrial unrest plaguing the nation. She also argues that although the board's decisions on the eight-hour day, minimum wage, equal pay for women in some jobs, and collective bargaining, were controversial, the constant fear of federal intervention caused both management and labor to accept them during the war. (*The National War Labor Board: Stability, Social Justice, and the Voluntary State in World War I*, Chapel Hill, N. Car., 1983).

# CHAPTER 9

# The Government and Women and Black Workers

Even before the United States entered World War I, the government had found it necessary to make special provisions for women workers. Some federal agencies established departments for this purpose for the first time. In 1916, the U.S. Employment Service—established originally in 1909 as the Division of Information of the Bureau of Immigration because it functioned as an aid for immigrants seeking employment but integrated into the Department of Labor in 1913—formed a Women's and Girl's Division.[1] A report from Washington after the United States entered the war described an office on the top floor of an old building in which sat a "quiet-voiced woman dressed in black." It continued: "There is nothing spectacular about the office or the woman. Yet that office is of interest to every man and woman in America. Margarette Neal's exact title is Assistant Director General of the United States Employment Service in charge of woman's work." Through her department, "the government offers its employment service to every employer of women, to every organization that is interested in the employment of women."[2]

## THE COMMITTEE ON WOMEN IN INDUSTRY

The defense agencies had established special offices for female employees before America entered the war. Early in 1917, the Council of National Defense set up its Committee on Women in Industry, made up of leaders of the Women's Trade Union League and the Consumers' League, to advise it on means for safeguarding the health and welfare of women workers during the war. This was supplemented once war was declared by the Board of Labor Standards, established by the army to prevent "sweaters" from processing its uniforms. The U.S. Railway Administration set up a women's section to protect female operatives on hazardous jobs; and the Ordnance Department organized a women's branch to supervise the work in the munitions industry.[3]

Despite the proliferation of agencies charged with protecting women workers, problems and grievances multiplied. Improperly organized in a number of cases, inadequately staffed and financed in most cases, and generally lacking the power to enforce their decisions, these agencies demonstrated that much more would have to be accomplished before even the first steps could be taken to meet the needs of women workers.

Although the Women's Committee of the Council of National Defense had issued a set of labor standards, the committee publicly acknowledged that war contractors usually ignored them.[4] Sophonisba Breckenridge, a member of the Women's Committee affiliated with the Council of National Defense, charged in November 1917 that a Philadelphia arsenal employed women on rotating shifts that regularly called for eighteen consecutive hours, in spite of official guidelines calling for an eight hour day; that it did not allow an adequate lunch period or provide eating facilities; and that it required female employees to lift weights in excess of 50 pounds— all in violation of Pennsylvania law and War Department orders. Grace Abbott, another committee member, pointed out that foremen at the Brooklyn Navy Yard continually scheduled women for seven-day work weeks, in violation of state regulations.[5] And Pauline Goldmark, still another committee member (representing the Consumers' League), protested the employment of women by the railroads on section gangs, on freight crews, in shop work, scrap collection, and other heavy jobs at barely the minimum wage.[6]

Practically all of the railroads, electrical firms, and munitions plants, according to a Women's Trade Union League report, still refused to pay their female help more than 60 percent of men's wages, no matter how important their positions were.[7] As we have seen, the situation in the manufacture of uniforms for the armed forces was especially outrageous. Moreover, with the suspension of labor laws in a number of states, especially those affecting women and child workers, labor safeguards and standards rapidly deteriorated soon after the United States entered the war.

Instead of combatting this trend, Gompers and the AFL Executive Council were totally indifferent to what was taking place. Although the leaders of both the Women's Trade Union League and the Consumers' League were anything but indifferent to the trend, they refused to criticize the AFL's stand. But *Advance* (organ of the Amalgamated Clothing Workers) pointed to "the strange spectacle" of the leaders of the AFL unions "assisting the exploiters of labor in their efforts to suspend labor laws for the duration of the war." It was particularly critical of President Gompers, who, it contended, "led all the rest with the suggestion to labor to give up all it had won."[8]

Repeated complaints to government war agencies protesting the failure to maintain labor standards, coupled with predictions of a "labor explosion" unless changes were made, produced results.[9] A special committee appointed to investigate unfavorable labor conditions surrounding the manufacture of military clothing for men recommended in its report, among other things, that all government contracts awarded for the manufacture of army uniforms should contain provisions for an eight-hour day, equal pay for equal work without distinction as to sex or race, no employment of persons under sixteen years of age, and no award of a contract to any firm whose facilities had not been previously inspected and approved.

In accordance with these recommendations, a Board of Control of Labor Standards in Army Clothing was created in August 1917, with Florence Kelley, secretary of the National Consumers' League, as a member.[10] The board was later replaced by a single individual who became the Administrator of Labor Standards in Army Clothing. As a result of the work of both the board and the administrator, a standard contract was instituted in all factories engaged in the production of army uniforms, and machinery was developed for the inspection and supervision of conditions of employment. Many former sweatshops were abolished, and the general level of sanitary and safety conditions in clothing factories was raised considerably while the principle of equal pay for equal work was more widely applied than ever before.[11]

## THE WOMEN'S SERVICE SECTION OF RAILROAD ADMINISTRATION

One of the major problems the Railroad Administration had to face was the scarcity of workers. Unskilled labor had begun to desert the railroads in increasing numbers to go into munitions plants and shipbuilding yards for higher pay. Even the operating crafts, normally more stable in terms of employment turnover, felt the impact as workers went into other occupations. By November 1918, moreover, about 70,000 railway men had joined the armed forces in one capacity or another—about four percent of the total domestic work force.[12]

To alleviate the shortage of labor, particularly among the non-operating crafts, W. S. Carter, director of labor policy under the United States Railroad Administration, created the Women's Service Section of the Division of Labor on August 29, 1918, and placed Pauline Goldmark, secretary of the National Committee on Women in Industry, in charge. The Women's

Service Section recruited women through handbills and newspaper advertisements. By October 1918, as we have seen, the USRA employed
101,785 female employees.[13]

Before the railroads came under federal control, women were paid less
than their male counterparts for the same work, 22 cents per hour for
common labor compared to 28-30 cents per hour for men. When the
USRA and the Women's Section was created in 1918, Carter specified not
only that healthful conditions be provided, but also that equal pay be given
for the same class of work, regardless of sex. Provision was also made to
allow women employees the same right of appeal to the Board of Wages
and Working Conditions.[14]

Nevertheless, wages of railroad workers, especially common laborers,
still lagged behind those in other industries. (The average weekly earnings
in the railroads in 1918 was $26.40, but in iron and steel it was $38.43,
and in the building trades $29.58.[15] After a study of the situation, the Lane
Commission reported on April 30, 1918 that wages on the railroads were
inadequate to maintain the standard of living enjoyed as recently as 1915.
The commission proposed the granting of some $300 million in wage
increases, to be given mostly to those in the lower income brackets. The
Lane Commission report was adopted in the main by the USRA and made
the basis for General Orders No. 27 and 28. Workers whose wages were
less than $46 per month received a raise of $20, or some 43 percent or
more; those receiving $150 per month got a raise of $24.25, or 16 percent. But those receiving a wage of $250 or more per month got no raise at
all.[16]

Not only were wages of women and black workers raised as a result of
General Orders No. 27 and 28 and the subsequent wage decisions of the
Board of Wages and Working Conditions, but standardization of wages in
terms of sex and race developed on the railroads. Blacks received the same
wages as whites; women the same as men. Unfortunately, the aristocracy
of railroad labor—the engineers, firemen, conductors—resented these
developments. The largest pay increases went to the lowest paid classes of
railway labor. The raises were badly needed, but the higher-paid workers,
such as the engineers, were antagonized. They claimed not only that they
were being discriminated against economically in this instance, but that
the traditional wage differential between them and the non-operating
classes was being destroyed. The shopmen also complained that they too
were being discriminated against because their wages were higher. The
Railroad Brotherhoods did all they could to further the resentment,
blaming both women and blacks for the erosion of the traditional wage

differential between the operating and non-operating railroad workers.[17]

Although relatively few women gained access to higher paid railroad positions during the war, as a whole, women benefited from the special labor provisions put into effect by the USRA. Federal control of the railroads brought about extensive changes in working conditions, including the recognition of collective bargaining; enforcement of the eight-hour day, with time-and-a-half pay for overtime; elaborate provisions for promotions, seniority, and grievances; elimination of piecework; standardization of pay scales, and recognition of the equal rights of women and black workers.[18]

## THE WOMEN-IN-INDUSTRY SERVICE

The war emergency also made a reality of what had until then been only a dream of the leaders of the Women's Trade Union League and other social reformers: the creation of an autonomous federal Women's Bureau, an independent women's division in the Department of Labor, with a guarantee of continuous operation and freedom of action. Previous efforts to achieve this goal had failed, even though by the fall of 1916 the Consumers' League had obtained endorsements from at least a hundred labor, civic, and women's organizations and had won over a reluctant Secretary of Labor, William B. Wilson. Unfortunately, the League had not won over the A.F. of L., and in the end this proved to be an insuperable obstacle.[19]

The war emergency, however, pushed all obstacles aside. The chaotic situation created by having several agencies—the defense departments, the Shipping Board, and the transportation administrations—each with its own commissions for the determination of standards, produced such wide variations in the enforcement of regulations that the mountain of workers' grievances kept piling higher and higher. In addition, slow operation of the federal bureaucracy was causing workers to express their discontent in widespread strike activity. By the fall of 1917, strikes were reported to be occurring with such "dangerous frequency" that it was predicted that unless the government did something quickly to ease the workers' grievances, the war effort would be seriously impaired.[20]

As we have seen, to remedy the conditions complained of, to "allay industrial unrest, and to create a real cooperation between labor and capital during the war," President Wilson issued an executive order on January 4, 1918, setting up a central War Labor Administration. In turn this body established a War Policies Board to draw up employment guidelines for all war industries. The Women's Trade Union League leaders demanded that the new body provide a special bureau for women workers equal in size to the entire War Labor Administration. The government, anticipating the extension of the draft to include all men from eighteen to forty-five, did contemplate a new department to protect the increasingly important female labor force. However it refused to accept the WTUL plan, and for several months heated discussions took place between league representatives and government officials.[21]

The difficulty was finally resolved. William B. Wilson, who had been appointed War Labor Administrator to head the new War Labor Board, appointed Agnes Nestor, president of the Chicago Women's Trade Union League, to represent the interests of women workers on his seven-member Advisory Council. Late in June 1918, after meetings with the Advisory Council, Wilson announced an eight-point program under which new service sections of the War Labor Administration would operate. The third point called for "a Woman-in-Industry Service to meet the problems connected with the more rapid introduction of women into industry as a result of war conditions." The purpose of the new organization was set forth:

> . . . to secure information on all matters relating to women in industry and to put such information into useful form, to develop in the industries of the country such policies and methods as would result in the most effective use of women's service in production for the war and at the same time prevent their employment under injurious conditions, to coordinate work for women in other divisions of the Department of Labor, and in industrial service sections of other departments of the federal government, and cooperate with state departments of labor for bringing about unified action by states in national problems relative to women's work.[22]

The Women's Trade Union League greeted the agency, which it had advocated since 1909, with "rejoicing that the doors of opportunity and industrial justice are to be thrown open to women." Actually, the new agency, with a staff of only four and a one-room office in the Labor Department, appeared to more critical observers to be little more than a "glorified information bureau," which would follow the lead set by Gompers in his role on the Council of National Defense, that of being willing to sacrifice the interests of the workers in the name of patriotism. Trade unionists who were critical of Gompers' actions in allowing employers to evade long-established standards and working conditions asked ruefully what guarantee there was that the new women's service would not do likewise.[23]

The fact is that only the appointment of Mary Van Kleeck as its director prevented the Women-in-Industry Service from becoming merely a concil-iatory device for the government. At the time the War Labor Administra-tion was seeking a director, Van Kleeck had been the Ordnance Bureau's supervisor of women's work for six months. She was an experienced administrator, a noted social investigator, and a veteran women's rights activist, and had developed close contacts with the labor movement. In fact, at first she opposed a special women's agency because she felt it would hinder united action between men and women in the labor move-ment. By early 1917, however, she came to favor it as necessary to ensure "special counsel for women in the government, continuous attention to their needs, and the opportunity to blaze new trails in practical research."[24]

In one respect, Van Kleeck's experience in the Ordnance Bureau was destined to put her on a collision course with social reformers. She had learned that protective regulations denying women employment in particu-lar jobs because of physical demands or other factors were not universally approved by many women in war industries. The unusual opportunity to earn relatively high pay in such work weighed heavily in their attitude toward regulations that would have the effect of forbidding their employ-ment. This was especially true of black women, who also suffered from the absence of viable alternatives to the forbidden employment. A young woman employed as a railroad trucker, who had previously been in domestic service, summed up the attitude of many black women when she explained to a field agent the ramifications of a discontinuance order pre-venting her from working:

> All the colored women like the work and want to keep it. We are making more money at this than any work we can get, and we do not have to work as hard as at housework, which requires us to be on duty from six o'clock in the morning until nine or ten at night, with mighty little time off and at very poor wages. . . . What the colored women need is an opportunity to make money. As it is, they have to take what employment they can get, live in old tumble-down houses or resort to streetwalking, and I think a woman ought to think more of her blood than do that. What occupation is open to us where we can make really good wages? We are not employed as clerks, cannot all be school-teachers, and so we cannot see any use in working our parents to death to get educated. Of course, we should like easier work than this if it were opened to us, but this pays well and is no harder than other work open to us. With three dollars a day, we can buy bonds. . . . We can dress decently, and not be tempted to find our living on the streets. . . . Please don't take this work away from us.[25]

Almost immediately after taking up her new position in July 1918, Van

Kleeck persuaded the War Policies Board, on which she held a seat, that it should consider each case separately in determining whether or not to allow women to enter hazardous occupations, rather than arbitrarily classifying jobs as unsuitable for women, as was desired by its chairperson, Felix Frankfurter. A professor at Harvard Law School and head of the War Policies Board, Frankfurter echoed the viewpoint of the WTUL and Consumers' League leaders. The Board's decision, however, forced the government to develop realistic and enforceable guidelines for war work. Accordingly, after innumerable conferences with official agencies, reform groups, trade unions, and employers, the Woman-in-Industry Service formulated a list of standards, including a basic forty-eight hour week, equal pay for equal work, a forty-five minute lunch period, no tenement operations, appropriate sanitary facilities, and safety precautions. The Service and the Policies Board also recommended that employers appoint women supervisors for female operatives and allow the workers a voice in employment policies. In August 1918 the defense departments began to insert these guidelines into war contracts.

Maintaining close liaison with trade union women through frequent conferences, Van Kleeck, her assistant Mary Anderson, a former WTUL organizer, and Helen Brooks Irvin, a black WTUL organizer appointed at Anderson's suggestion to advance equality for black women, continued to agitate to make the protections that had been incorporated into government contracts a reality in the workplaces. The decline in the number of complaints reaching Van Kleeck during the last months of the war indicated that the Service was having some success.[26]

In the fall of 1918, the Service tackled the application of these new standards to two persistent problems: night work and labor in dangerous trades. Under the guidelines, a contractor who wished to employ women at night had to show not only that he required such labor to maintain adequate production but also that he had exhausted a long list of alternative remedies, ranging from the transfer of male workers from nonessential industries, to the extension of plant capacity and more effective management. These stringent requirements, insisted upon by the social reformers, did result in a sharp drop in applications for night work certificates. It is open to question, however, whether or not they pleased the workingwomen, who were thereby deprived of an opportunity to earn higher wages at night.

On the issue of the entrance of women operatives into hazardous jobs, Van Kleeck had at first opposed closing specific jobs to women, believing that a case-by-case procedure should be followed. But the leaders of both the WTUL and the Consumers' League opposed her policy and insisted that these jobs be closed, regardless of whether or not this action resulted in dismissals and, where no alternative work was available, in unemployment. Their stand was fortified by the exposé of abuses in the Niagara Falls chemical industries. After an extensive investigation, a survey team reported in August 1918 that these industries had not significantly reduced the hazards criticized by the Factory Commission in 1912, including poor control of poisonous fumes and inadequate safeguards against injury. Van Kleeck surrendered to the pressure of the social reformers in October 1918, calling on the government to prohibit the employment of women in such industries as abrasive manufacturing and the processing of lead. Her hope was that the restrictions would persuade manufacturers to substitute machinery for manual labor, thus eliminating the hazards for male workers as well. However, the orders were not accompanied by any proposals for alternatives to the women removed from work by the restrictions.[27]

In general, while the Woman-in-Industry Service had a good deal of success in dealing with such issues as working hours, sanitary facilities, and safety precautions, it was much less successful in achieving wage parity. In the hope of ending the age-old custom of paying female workers less than men for the same work, Van Kleeck and her assistants and advisory board had inserted into the guidelines the provision that employers should establish wage scales for all workers in a given occupation, and that the minimum rates should cover the cost of living for families—not merely for the individual man or woman. But the Service soon discovered that employers evaded the guidelines by making slight changes in the tasks when women assumed them, designating them as "new" positions and compensating the female workers at lower rates. Nor did it help matters much when the National War Labor Board—established by President Wilson in April 1918 to serve as a quasi-court to which disputes between employers and employees could be brought for mediation and conciliation—announced a minimum rate for men of 40 to 42 cents an hour while that for women was 30 or 32 cents an hour, despite the fact that its guiding principles had included: "If it shall become necessary to employ women on work ordinarily performed by men, they must be allowed equal pay for equal work." It was difficult for the Woman-in-Industry Service to persuade employers to operate in accordance with the principle of "equal pay for equal work" when the War Labor Board did not make this a requirement.[28]

Despite its short life—only five months elapsed before its establishment and the Armistice—the Woman-in-Industry Service compiled a good record of achievement. The WTUL praised it for having raised standards for women workers, investigated exploitation, and stimulated needed improvements. Only on the wage issue could its work be faulted. Women were "doing their share of our country's work," the Women's Trade Union League declared in October 1918, but they were still being paid according to the "durable custom" of less wages than men for the same work, which was not the league's idea of "a square deal."[29]*

## THE DIVISION OF NEGRO ECONOMICS

A number of the agencies devoted to handling the wartime problems of women workers dealt in a varying degree with the specific problems of black women, but there was no agency like the Woman-in-Industry Service established for black workers. The closest thing to it was the Division of Negro Economics, established by the Department of Labor in May 1918 and headed by George Edmund Haynes. Chairperson of the Social Science Department at Fisk University and the first director of the National League on Urban Conditions among Negroes, Haynes was the author of *The Negro at Work in New York City*, a pioneering study of conditions of blacks in industry.** When the Great Migration of black people to the North began in 1916, Haynes studied the process carefully. In 1917 he produced one of the first significant contributions to the literature when he published for the Home Mission Council, *Negro Newcomers in Detroit*, a study of the industrial and living conditions of black migrants from the South. Haynes, in short, was considered qualified for what one aide to Secretary of Labor William B. Wilson called "probably the most important position ever held by a Negro in the United States."[30]

The agency Haynes headed was assigned the mission to

study, plan and advise in a cooperative spirit and manner with employers of Negro labor, with white workmen, with Negro workers, and with the United States Department of Labor in securing from Negro laborers greater production in industry and agriculture through increasing the morale of Negro workers and through improving their general condition.[31]

*In June 1920, after intensive lobbying by the Women's Trade Union League, Congress passed the Kenyon-Campbell bill, transforming the Woman-in-Industry Service into a Women's Bureau of the Department of Labor, "to formulate standards and policies which shall promote the welfare of wage-earning women, improve their working conditions and advance their opportunities for profitable employment." After more intensive lobbying by the league, Mary Anderson was named to head the Women's Bureau.

**The study was Haynes' doctoral dissertation at Columbia University and was published by Columbia University Press in 1912. While still a student at Columbia University, Haynes was appointed to the Chair of Social Science at Fisk University.

To carry out this mission, the Division of Negro Economics established Advisory Committees, made up of blacks, in states of both the South and North. The Division and its Advisory Committees then launched an extensive campaign to convince black workers of their responsibility in helping win the war, emphasizing how important it was that they give steady and reliable service in order that one hundred percent production be achieved. Public mass meetings, pamphlets, bulletins, posters, and speeches were used to achieve this objective, all stressing that black workers were playing a significant part in the prosecution of the war, and would receive their reward in the form of a more democratic society.[32]

In the area of research, its major undertaking, the Division of Negro Economics gathered useful data relating to black employment in war industries. This was published by the U.S. Department of Labor as *Negroes at Work*. The study revealed the glaring lack of representation of black workmen in the skilled levels of work. Of the 85 occupations analyzed, less than 10 percent had black workers in a skilled capacity, and of these, six involved foundry work, "which was one of the few skills the Negro brought with him in the flight from the South." The overwhelming concentration of black workers in unskilled positions "indicates that the demands for [their] services generated by the war provided . . . ample opportunity to enter the lower strata of industry but offered very little access to the top levels."[33]

But when it came to doing anything to alleviate this situation or other grievances of black workers, the record of the Division of Negro Economics was not impressive. It is true that the agency operated only during the last six months of the war and hardly had a real opportunity to create a basic organizational structure, but it is also true that although it accumulated a good deal of evidence of discrimination against black workers, it did little to remedy the situation. In fact, the experience of the Division of Negro Economics in this respect provides a good picture of the relationship of the United States government to the black worker during the months after April 1917.

The story of black employment on the railroads is a case in point. The demand for wartime labor opened new opportunities of employment for blacks on the railroads. They entered an industry in which their employment by the time of World War I was confined largely to menial jobs such as janitors and Pullman porters. Even in the South where they had been employed as firemen and brakemen at lower wages than their white counterparts, they had been eliminated almost entirely as a result of collusion between the railroad managers and the Railroad Brotherhoods.[34]

When the United States took over the railroads, black workers hoped that the restrictions on the nature of their employment on the railroads would end.[35] Hence they were shocked when C. R. Gray, Director of Operations of the United States Railroad Administration, issued the following directive in answer to an inquiry from one of the Regional Directors:

> Replying to your letter . . . in regard to the employment of Negro firemen and hostlers.
>
> I think it is advisable that instructions be issued to Federal Managers that the employment of Negro firemen, hostlers, switchmen, brakemen, etc.; is not to be extended beyond the practice heretofore existing, and caution them against employing Negroes for this class of service upon any line or in any service where they have not heretofore been engaged, or to take the places of white men.[36]

These instructions became public knowledge within a week, and angry black workers expected that the Division of Negro Economics, in the face of an order that so blatantly discriminated against black railroad workers, would lodge some form of protest with the Director General of the Railroad Administration, or at the very least would inform the Secretary of Labor of its concern over the adoption of such a policy by a government agency. But Haynes' office did nothing.[37]

Fortunately, officials of the NAACP and the National Urban League decided to take action. The Urban League learned of the Railroad Administration's directive while assembled for its annual convention in Columbus, Ohio. League leaders promptly sent a letter to George Foster Peabody, a wealthy white supporter of black Americans, asking him to use his personal influence in Washington to achieve a revocation of the discriminatory order. "We are at a loss to understand," they wrote, "how those in high authority at Washington can satisfy Negroes that they really have been fighting for freedom, when, on returning victorious, these soldiers find themselves confronted with a barrier against advancement solely because they are Negroes." They then warned that to deny rights to blacks after they had learned military organization might bring a "disaster" upon all concerned. "We have ample evidence at our conference here," they continued, "that an unrest is even now developing in the Nation, which needs only knowledge of some such order as this . . . to fan it into a real menace."[38]

The NAACP fired off a telegram to William G. McAdoo, Director-General of the USRA, demanding a full explanation of the order discriminating against the employment of blacks. Like the Urban League, the

NAACP emphasized the blatant hypocrisy of a government which, while fighting for freedom and democracy abroad, sanctioned policies denying opportunity for employment at home strictly on grounds of color—policies that deprived a portion of its citizens of fundamental rights.[39] A copy of this telegram was also dispatched to the White House with an appeal to President Wilson's "high sense of justice" that he give proper consideration to this important matter.[40]

The Armstrong Association of Philadelphia, an organization devoted to studying and aiding in the economic needs of black people, and the American Railroad Employees Association, a group composed solely of black rail workers, registered complaints with McAdoo over the USRA's policy limiting black employment.[41]

In replying to the complaints, Director-General McAdoo threw additional light on the issue. The order, he revealed, stemmed from the employment of black workers on a northern railroad line where they had not been employed before. The appearance of these workers had led the president of the Railroad Brotherhood on the line to instruct his men not to work alongside the newcomers. Confronted with the serious possibility of a union walkout that would halt railroad traffic, Director of Operations Gray had handed down the now controversial order. While McAdoo felt that the order had been "misunderstood"—the real purpose was not discrimination but a desire to avoid a halt in production and conflict between white and black workers—he notified the NAACP and the Urban League that he had directed Gray to recall the letter.[42]

McAdoo's action won him the "grateful thanks" of the two black organizations. But, as John D. Finney, Jr., who has made a detailed study of the episode, points out: "Their praise would have been greatly tempered, however, had they been privy to the policy memorandum upon which McAdoo based his decision . . . to revoke Gray's discriminatory order."[43] This memorandum, by Walter D. Hines, who advised McAdoo on the matter, noted that although it was desirable to remove the "unfortunate effects" of Gray's directive:

> It is also equally desirable to avoid bringing about a lot of unfortunate effects through any possible encouragement to Federal Managers to rush in and employ Negroes and thereby stir up race agitation, which is likely to result not only in tie-ups of railroad operations but also in injury to the Negro situation. I have no doubt that in many instances a Federal Manager has a sort of subconscious desire to employ Negroes who are not members of labor unions, rather than employ white men who are. Any stimulation of this desire is going to cause trouble to the Railroad Administration and also to the Negro.

Therefore, I think any letter of withdrawal must be so worded as not to let the Federal Managers feel that they are now free, and in fact expected to go ahead regardless of understandings with organized labor, and regardless of settled prejudices which cannot safely be ignored and employ Negroes. The letter, therefore, to the Regional Directors has been worded as carefully as possible to meet honestly both sides of the problem. . . .[44]

It is clear from this memorandum that Hines also drafted the letter of withdrawal which was sent out over Gray's signature to the Regional Directors of the USRA at various points across the country. In this letter, Gray declared that his original order was no longer to be considered in effect because it had created the impression that the Railroad Administration wished to erect new barriers in the way of Negro employment. He urged the Regional Directors in handling the matter of Negro employment to be motivated by a sympathetic desire not to add to the difficulties under which blacks already labored. At the same time, however, Gray cautioned his subordinates that it was frequently an "injury" rather than a "service" to blacks to force them into employment where race prejudice would be fostered anew. "The problem needs to be handled with discretion and sympathy," he concluded in his new instructions, "and always with the necessary regard for the requirements established in pre-existing working conditions."[45]

The "pre-existing working conditions" referred to the unwritten agreements worked out between the railroad lines and the Railroad Brotherhoods concerning the type of jobs left open to black railroad workers. They invariably provided for their restriction to the low level and menial occupations in railroad work.[46] "Consequently," Finney concludes, "in advising Regional Directors to deal with problems of Negro employment within the context of such existing arrangements, Gray made the withdrawal of his original order practically meaningless. While going through the motions of repudiating the directive restricting Negroes to certain classes of occupations, he simultaneously sanctioned the informal agreements between railroad management and the unions which embodied equally stringent restrictions. . . . It is obvious that the USRA had no intention whatsoever of removing the basic obstacles to full and equitable employment of colored workers on the nation's rail lines."[47]

It also had no intention of encouraging the rail lines to deal with other than the racist unions. The USRA handled labor relations through national adjustment boards and national bargaining agreements. Adjustment boards settled grievances arising out of existing agreements, and their decisions were binding. Disputes over new terms of employment were made subject to a Board of Wages and Working Conditions.

To set up the adjustment boards, the USRA negotiated only with standard (national) unions. Generally, the local or nonstandard unions were made up of black workers, since they were either denied membership in most standard unions or assigned to segregated locals in the case of AFL railroad unions. Although, as we shall see, there was some growth among independent black unions on the railroads during the war, at the end of the conflict only 30 percent of the non-operating workers, many of them black, were unionized, as compared with 80 percent of the operating employees.[48]

The ineffectual role, or rather the absence of any role, of the Division of Negro Economics in the case of the USRA's restrictive employment policy was, unfortunately, repeated on several other occasions where discrimination existed against black workers in federally controlled or supervised industries. On August 17, 1918, the War Labor Policies Board forwarded a letter to Division Director Haynes from L. A. Gabriel, president of the Key West, Florida, branch of the NAACP, protesting the action of white union carpenters in preventing black carpenters from working on a government project constructing army cantonments. According to Gabriel, the white unionists discriminated against them because the black workers were not union men. But on repeated occasions, he noted, the black carpenters had petitioned the white union for admittance, even asking the unionists to grant them a separate charter if the white workers did not allow black workers into their union. Both of these proposals were turned down. Hence he was bringing the matter to the attention of the government in the hope that it would arrange for the black carpenters to be granted a union charter, or, if this was not feasible, to make some provision that would allow them to work on the government building jobs opening up in the city.[49]

But the director of the Division of Negro Economics, pleading that the supervisor for Florida had only recently been appointed, did nothing. So informed, the War Labor Policies Board filed the matter, and it was soon forgotten.[50]

But even after the machinery for the Division of Negro Economics was in place and functioning, Haynes refused to intervene in cases of employment discrimination brought to his attention. When five black bricklayers were denied employment at the Air Nitrate Corporation in Sheffield, Alabama, because of the opposition of white masons, and the NAACP called upon the Division to intervene, Haynes passed the matter on to the Labor Department's Investigation and Inspection Service for an investigation. But the investigation never took place and discrimination against the black bricklayers continued without interference.[51]

An even more blatant case of discrimination concerned thirty-six black carpenters, all union men, who were dismissed from work at Camp Lee, Petersburg, Virginia, because white carpenters refused to work beside them. In this circumstance the director of the Division of Negro Economics did hold a conference with one of the officials at Camp Lee. But after the conference he merely advised the black carpenters "to continue to be patient," and to hold themselves in readiness in case they were restored to their jobs. They never returned to work.[52]

It was in the shipbuilding industry, a major stronghold of job bias against black workers during the war, that the ineffectiveness of the Department of Negro Economics was most evident. Black carpenters, reamers, riveters, pipe fitters, and drillers found it very difficult to get work in their respective trades in the shipyards, and were usually forced to accept jobs as helpers to white craftsmen or as "fillers" in menial tasks demanding few or no skills.[53] Skilled black shipyard workers were also deprived of the opportunity to learn new trades in spite of the fact that in some lines of work, such as riveting, men were badly needed.[54]

The files of the Emergency Fleet Corporation, a subsidiary of the United States Shipping Board responsible for the production of ships in the nation's shipyards, are replete with the protests of individuals and groups of black workers over the unjust treatment that was their common lot in various shipyards around the country. They also furnish evidence of the unwillingness and/or inability of the federal government, including the Department of Negro Economics, to do anything to redress the grievances. The letters placed a major part of the blame on the racism of the shipyard employers, but they also noted that even in cases where an employer was willing to hire a black skilled worker in the yards, he found it difficult to continue in the face of the hostility of white foremen and white unionists. As one black yard worker put it, "the foreman is the one who makes it so warm for us that we will either quit or he will credit our record so debase[d] that it will make it easy for our discharge."[55] A black worker from the Hog Island complex near Philadelphia commented on the racial prejudice of his immediate supervisor: "We have been subjected to numerous, studied, consistent and persistent discrimination by foremen, instructors in the training school and employment supervisors. Discrimination is rampant."[56]

The bitter irony of supporting a war dedicated to the principles of democracy while having to suffer "most undemocratic limitations on their personal rights" is reflected in scores of letters from black workers in the records of the United States Shipping Board. Thus, a black worker in the

employ of the American International Shipping Corporation of New York
wrote to Charles Schwab, head of the USSB:

> If the power of drafting men to fight across the seas for what you term
> democracy, were invested in you, would you really have the heart to take a man
> that you had refused to give bread to eat? How could you expect us to render an
> honest day's work at hard labor which you try to press upon our shoulders,
> when we are aware of the fact that we are absolutely competent of earning a far
> better living at our trades which you refuse to give us? . . . If, Mr. Schwab, we
> are not fit to have a position as mechanics and officials then I contend that we
> are not good enough to fight for the country.[57]

A black riveter in California sent the following bitter and impassioned
plea to governmental authorities:

> Can you understand what must be the feelings of our people when every day
> men are called from these yards to take up for our country, to give up their life
> on the firing line with hundreds of thousands of Colored troops in France doing
> their bit to make democracy safe for the world? I or any of us may be called
> tomorrow, and how gladly would I give this life of mine if I knew, in giving
> that life to make Democracy safe for the worlds [sic] I was making Democracy
> safe to give to my people. . . .
> We don't ask Social Equality, we only ask an equal chance to take our part in
> the industrial world, to be given the right and opportunity to perform the work,
> which almighty God saw fit to give us the brains and strength to do and for
> which hundreds of years in the most cruel school of slavery qualified and made
> us to do. . . .
> I beg of you take up this matter at once, don't let the word be taken from the
> shipyards of America that . . . discrimination is being made in the matter of
> even Negro labor. What will our boys feel that they have to fight for, what
> hopes have they to look forward to when after the war they return and the work
> is done? We can no longer remain silent to this condition among our people.[58]

But the United States government could and did remain silent. Nor is
there any evidence that the Division of Negro Economics spoke out
against the conditions that caused these black workers to voice their
dissatisfaction.

Neither the government nor the Division of Negro Economics spoke out
in behalf of the interests of black workers as they were affected by racist
policies in the implementation of the "Work-or-Fight" rule promulgated
by the federal government, and the compulsory work legislation this rule
inspired in state and local communities during the last year of the war. On
May 24, 1918 the Provost Marshal of the United States Army, General
Enoch E. Crowder, announced a Work-or-Fight Order, which stipulated

that all able-bodied persons between the draft age limits must be engaged in some necessary employment.[59]

At first this included only males up to thirty-one years of age. Later, it included males up to forty-one years of age. But General Crowder's directive evidently was not sufficient to maintain a labor supply to satisfy the needs of employers who had lost substantial numbers of their workers to the armed forces. As a result, state legislatures in various sections of the country, but especially in the South, where the labor shortage was aggravated by the Great Migration, enacted compulsory work laws that compelled all able-bodied men to work under penalty of law. Georgia, Kentucky, Louisiana, Maryland, and West Virginia were among the southern states that adopted such legislation. In addition to state work laws, cities and small towns passed compulsory labor ordinances. One such ordinance (that in Wrightsville, Georgia) stated that "it shall be unlawful for any person from the ages of sixteen to fifty to reside in or be upon the streets of Wrightsville unless he is actively and assiduously engaged in useful employment fifty hours or more per week." It further provided that each person must carry an employment card signed by his employer showing that he was employed as the law provided.[60]

It is obvious that employers could use an ordinance of this nature to force employees to work for low wages by threatening them with dismissal and confiscation of their employment cards, leaving them to suffer the consequences. Statutes of this type also provided local officials with a convenient tool to prevent strikes, mass emigrations, or any other action that they could charge hindered war production.[61] In fact, Louis F. Post, Assistant Secretary of Labor, announced, following a tour around the country, that he had found that the Work-or-Fight-Order was being used in many places for peonage purposes and that employers were conscripting labor for private use rather than for service for the war effort. This was especially true, he reported, in states where the majority of the workers were black. He cited as an example, but only one of many, a demonstration held by a hundred Ku Klux Klansmen in Montgomery, Alabama, to rid the city of "slackers, immoral women and spies." The Klansmen, in what was the first organized appearance of their society in Montgomery in forty-two years, passed through the city in a car caravan scattering the following warning printed in bold red letters:

> Work, fight, or go. No slackers allowed in Montgomery. We protect good women—bad ones must go. . . . You can't be a slacker in any way and live happily in Montgomery. If there is a German spy in Montgomery County he

will be properly handled. This is a warning and a final notice. Do your duty.[62]

The following day, city officials announced that a dragnet would be thrown over the city to snare work or fight slackers.[63] Post pointed out that on the face of it the warning applied to everybody, but since it was issued by a mob of fully robed Ku Klux Klansmen and the circulars distributed were signed by the Klan, it was commonly understood that the warning was meant to intimidate the black population.[64]

All this did not come as a surprise to the Division of Negro Economics. Even before Post made his findings known to the government, John R. Shillady, executive secretary of the NAACP, wrote to Dr. Haynes informing him of an NAACP report revealing a large number of instances where unfair advantage had been taken of Negroes under administrative orders enacted to insure full wartime employment. He was particularly incensed, as were many other black people, at the reports that in southern towns Work-or-Fight ordinances were applied by local planters and employers to nonworking black women and not to white women.[65]

Shillady urged Haynes to arrange a conference with the Department of Labor, the War Labor Policies Board, and other departments of the government, with representatives of the NAACP, the National Urban League, and Louis F. Post. They would place before the government a mass of evidence concerning mistreatment of black workers in the South and would insist that government action be taken to correct the situation.[66] But when Dr. Haynes brought the matter to the attention of the various departments of the government Shillady had proposed, he was informed that it was beyond the authority of the federal government to interfere in cases where state, county, or local officials initiated legislation of their own affecting black employment.[67] Consequently, the Division of Negro Economics abandoned the whole idea of doing something about the situation facing black workers in the South. The ability of Southern employers to take advantage of the need for unlimited wartime production "to force Negro workers into a condition bordering on peonage went largely unchecked."[68]

Whether it was because Haynes did not want to disturb the amicable relations he enjoyed with white Southern business men and prominent Northern philanthropists,* or because he knew that protests to the

---

*Dr. Haynes was endorsed for the post of Director of the Division of Negro Economics by the Commercial Club of Nashville, the association of the city's leading business and professional men, and by such wealthy white philanthropists as George Foster Peabody and Bruce Payne. (John D. Finney, Jr., "A Study of Negro Labor During and After World War I," unpublished Ph.D. dissertation, Georgetown University, 1957, pp. 154-55.)

government would produce little of consequence, the Division of Negro Economics did nothing to challenge the widespread job bias against black workers on the railroads, in the shipyards, in a variety of government work projects, and in the case of the Work-or-Fight racist practices in the South. Rather it was the NAACP, the National Urban League, and similar organizations that exposed, protested against, and sought to eliminate discriminatory treatment of black workers. This lack of initiative and of concrete efforts on the part of the Division of Negro Economics was part of the general indifference of the United States government to discrimination against black workers during "the war to save the world for democracy."

# CHAPTER 10

# Organized Labor and the Woman Worker

## THE GOVERNMENT REQUESTS UNIONS ADMIT WOMEN

"Another important problem also confronts us, that is the question of women's labor," president John F. Hart informed the locals and members of the Amalgamated Meat Cutters and Butcher Workmen shortly after America's entry into World War I. He revealed that the federal government had requested that national and international unions admit women where contracts included closed or union shops, and where the unions excluded women or blacks as a rule. The Amalgamated, Hart pointed out, had approved the request although it had already opened its ranks to women. The federal government, he explained, was striving to employ as much female labor as possible to meet the war emergency, and women were actually being placed "in positions formerly occupied by men."

Members of the Amalgamated union already knew this from their own experience: "They are entering the ranks of the Butcher Workmen by the thousands. In the sausage departments, in the trimming departments and in the sales departments, the women are doing the work and doing it equally as well as men ever performed, and are unfortunately doing it for a much lower wage." Hart had little doubt that when the war was over and the men returned from the trenches,

> these women will say, "we have demonstrated the fact that we could perform this labor equally as well as you and we now demand that we be continued in these positions, as we stepped into the breach when the necessities of the war called you men away and now we demand that you continue us in our positions." Hence, we will not only be met with a business depression, but a determined effort on the part of women to fill the positions which have, in the past, been filled by men.

## RESPONSE TO THE GOVERNMENT'S REQUEST

According to Hart, there was only one intelligent answer to the problem: to adopt the federal government's proposal for "the organizing of the women workers." It was, of course, up to the various locals to reach their own decision on this vital issue, but, Hart warned:

> Do not flatter yourselves for a moment that you are going to change conditions. The only hope we can see is to insist upon their being organized and receiving the same wage for the same work that the men receive. But we leave that for the locals and the membership to think over, assuring them that it is an important question and one that will greatly affect your future interests.[1]

Many international unions complied with the federal government's request that they open their ranks to women and blacks, and they did it by adopting the following statement: "It is understood that no objection shall be made to the employment of women or colored men if the necessity arises." Sometimes the words "for the duration of the emergency" were added, although usually it was understood that the "necessity" was only for the war period. But many of the unions that did comply did so with tongue in cheek. Although they ostensibly supported the policies devised by the Wilson administration to ensure peak production and industrial peace, their executive officers and boards, in keeping with the principle of local autonomy, left the matter up to the locals.

The local unions, in turn, pursued two different policies. In industries in which women continued to perform work traditionally associated with women and men performed work that was clearly differentiated from that of women, the local unions recruited women members in an effort to extend and strengthen collective bargaining. But in occupations where women were introduced for the first time during the war, some local unions endorsed the "necessity clause" approach and allowed women to join only for the duration of the crisis. In many cases, local unions not only refused to organize women workers but resisted their employment altogether. Their international leadership, in practically every case, defended those local unions that ignored the orders to admit women—even for the duration of the emergency.[2]

## THE AFL AND WOMEN WORKERS

Similar duplicity was revealed in the AFL's approach to women workers after America's entry into the war. The widely publicized Resolution No. 92, adopted at the thirty-eighth annual AFL convention in 1918, read:

WHEREAS, The American Federation of Labor stands for equal pay for equal work, believing that these women should receive the same wages as those received by the men whose places they have taken in order to help the prosecution of this war and the elimination of the hun; and

WHEREAS, We believe that the best interests of the labor movement demand that a strenuous and continuous effort be made to organize these women into the trade union bodies of their respective crafts, be it

RESOLVED, That we call upon the officers and organizers of the affiliated international and national unions to make every effort to bring these women into the organization of their respective crafts to which the men, whose places they have taken, are members.[3]

At the same time the AFL was devoting considerably more energy to protecting males from female competition than to improving the lot of working women and organizing them "into the organizations of the respective crafts." Gompers had made it clear that his main concern about women workers was to protect male workers from female competition. In "Don't Sacrifice Womanhood," published in the *American Federationist* in the summer of 1917 and reprinted widely in the official journals of the city central labor councils, Gompers urged that labor take a firm stand against "laying tasks on women they are not able to bear." He conceded that "at least three civilian workers are necessary to maintain one soldier in the field," and that "there must be definite plans formulated to maintain a continuous supply of workers." But, he went on, this must not include the "hastening of women into employment for which they are not fitted." In fact, there was no need "to force women into industry now" but simply to conduct careful studies to determine when they might be needed. Unfortunately, he warned, a skillful campaign was under way "for rushing women into all kinds of employment," and (horror of horrors!):

In Cleveland between 75 and 100 women are running Bradley hammers in one shop. Women are wiping engines in the running house at Akron, Ohio; many are running engines in the machine shops and doing other laborious work around large manufacturing plants. One woman has been employed by the B & O railroad as a shop hand; she packs journal boxes, which are on the axles of wheels and must be filled with waste and oil. Flag women have appeared on railroads. Women are employed in the foundry trade, in machine shops and munition plants. One lumber yard in Chicago is reported to be employing women to handle lumber.

What, Gompers asked, would become of American motherhood if this trend continued? Certainly, the first requirement of the day was to have all women seeking employment obtain physicians' certificates testifying to their ability to do the type of work previously performed exclusively by men.[4]

Gompers urged each international union "in which there are many women members" to place his "Don't Sacrifice Womanhood" message "in the hands of the secretary of every local union of women wage earners throughout the country" in order to influence them not to abandon their traditional occupations and seek to enter those primarily suited for men.[5]

The October 1917 issue of the *American Federationist* featured an article by Gompers urging that women be brought into factory work slowly with due regard for their fragile nature, and suggesting that a committee be formed to determine the jobs from which they should be excluded. Gompers sent copies of the article to international unions with large women's memberships and urged them to furnish the AFL national office with evidence that, where there was no shortage of available men, employers were using women as a device "to hasten the dilution of skilled labor by unskilled." He conceded that there was a shortage "in a comparatively few instances," especially of "the highest skilled mechanics or others possessing technical knowledge," but he suggested that these positions should be filled "by systematic methods of distributing labor throughout the country" rather than by women trained for the purpose.[6]

In each statement he issued on women workers, Gompers made sure to include the phrase "when they do equal work with men they should receive equal pay." But he also made it clear that he supported that principle as a means of reducing female competition with men: "I believe that that proviso established and maintained would be a sufficient deterrent to any employer to unnecessarily bring women into industry."[7]

"Female Labor Arouses Hostility and Apprehension in Union Ranks," declared *Current Opinion* in April 1918, reporting that a conflict had emerged between the leaders of organized labor and of women's groups. While the AFL and most of its affiliated unions were emphasizing that there was no need for women workers to enter occupations traditionally held by men, leaders of the Women's Trade Union League were stressing that America's entry into the war meant that "women will find new avenues of employment—industries formerly closed to them will open their doors, and they will be drawn from unimportant industries to those essential to our national existence." To the trade unionists this prospect meant the inevitable lowering of wage scales, but League spokespersons rejected this gloomy forecast and argued that the answer lay in unionizing the new women workers and establishing the "same wage scale for women and men." Only in this way, they maintained, could men be sure that when they came back from military service they would not find "that not only have their places been taken, but wages cut."[8]

Gompers rejected the League's arguments. He showed his anger over the refusal of the organization's leaders to accept the AFL's reasoning by coldly dismissing an invitation to address the WTUL wartime convention. At his suggestion the AFL similarly rejected a proposal from women unionists that the Executive Council be expanded to thirteen members, two of whom would be women—a rebuff that was criticized by the Federal Council of Churches. The absence of women on the Executive Council was pointed up when the 1918 AFL convention referred to the Executive Council for implementation of a resolution calling "upon the officers and organizers of the affiliated international and national unions to make every effort to bring these women into the organizations of the respective crafts to which the men, whose places they have taken, are members." The Council confined itself to seeking opinions from the officers of all national and international unions as to the most effective way of achieving the intent of the resolution. The replies satisfied the Executive Council that the unions were doing all that was necessary "to safeguard and protect the rights of women wage workers and maintain standards." It thereupon assured working women that, together with these unions, the AFL Executive Council "will make every effort to give wholehearted support in the endeavor to organize the women workers of America to bring them the full fruition of organized effort that they may be accorded as a right, equal pay for equal work with men."[9]

## THE CONDUCTORETTES VS. THE AMALGAMATED ASSOCIATION

The Executive Council for its part never kept the pledge. However, relations of white women with organized labor on the level of international, national, and local unions varied widely. Developments in the streetcar, railroad, telephone, and other industries illustrate these variations in their wartime relations with organized labor.

> Conspicuous among the occupations which were opened to women at the time of our entry into the war was the work of conductor on street and elevated railways and subways. While women had been employed as ticket agents by various companies for many years, the woman streetcar conductor was a complete innovation, and about her employment in this capacity have centered much discussion and several bitter controversies.

So began a Women's Bureau publication of 1921 entitled "Controversy

Regarding the Right of Women to Work as Conductors." As the reader pursued the subject, however, it became clear that the controversy boiled down to the simple, clear-cut issue:

> between the men on the one hand who wished to maintain the work of street car conductors as strictly men's work, and on the other hand the women who had proved that they could do the work well, and who were not ready to accept their exclusion from an occupation where the pay was good, and the hours and working conditions no more unsatisfactory than in many other occupations considered to come within the sphere of women's activities.[10]

The catalytic agent in the dispute was the Amalgamated Association of Street and Electric Railway Employees of America, affiliated with the AFL.

At the time the United States entered the war, the urban transportation work force was clearly stratified by skill and sexual differentiation. Pay scales reflected this stratification and ostensibly denoted skill level, seniority, and ability. Motorman and conductor were the highest jobs on streetcar or train systems. Below these positions were those of the clerks, track and section men, ticket sellers, cashiers, car barn workers, and car service workers, who cleaned and maintained the equipment. The jobs to which women had been admitted before World War I were those of ticket sellers, cashiers, and car cleaners. The jobs of motorman and conductor were classified as open only to males and were guarded jealously by a collective male egoism that extolled virility and physical stamina.[11]

During the last months of 1917, streetcar managers in the larger urban centers began to explore the possibility of recruiting women workers to fill vacancies on the applicant lists for the car crews, where women had not previously been employed, and to employ women as "extras" to replace motormen and conductors who volunteered or were drafted. Rumors of the impending employment of women brought an immediate protest from the organized workers of the industry, who were almost exclusively male.[12]

Slightly more than half of the workers in urban transportation were organized, and the major collective bargaining agent was the Amalgamated Association of Street and Electric Railway Employees, whose president was William D. Mahon. The only other "organized" workers were those represented by company unions or employee representational plans.

The Amalgamated Association was one of the national trade unions that responded affirmatively to the federal government's request that the unions admit women, and agreed at the national level to admit them as a "necessity." But its executive board adopted a two-faced policy on the issue. In May 1918 it held that "the Association is unalterably opposed to the employment of women in the occupation as either motormen or conductors." The union was hostile not only to the immediate employment of women on the cars, but also to any protective legislation that would modify working conditions so as to open the positions to women workers. Streetcar managers who sought to employ women conductors, said union officials, did so with the express intention of holding down wages in order to maximize profits under the guise of wartime emergency conditions.[13]

Criticized for violating its own commitment to the government, the Amalgamated's executive board in August 1917 recommended that women be hired and accepted by the locals "if it is necessary, during the period of the war." The board also established a number of restrictions to be followed where women were employed during the emergency. Female workers were to enter employment on the same basis as men, except that women were to take their places at the bottom of the "extras" seniority list, giving them the least seniority in the work force.* Women were to receive the same wages as men and enjoy the same working conditions. If they were employed in a closed or union shop, they were to be given apprentice permits, which allowed them to work for ninety days without belonging to the union. The board also ruled that "when women do enter the service, they shall become members of the organization, being entitled to the same protection, benefits and conditions that men are entitled to, coming under the working conditions and provisions of the agreement in the same manner."[14]

But of all the unions that, on the surface, followed the labor policy of the Wilson administration, the Amalgamated Association pursued the most treacherous line. Locals simply disregarded the instructions of the executive board and did so with impunity. Indeed, the executive board defended them. Moreover, the Amalgamated Association even conducted a campaign against women conductors, or conductorettes, as they called themselves, in cities where it did not have collective bargaining agreements. The major argument circulated by the union was that employment of women conductors was part of a concerted employer offensive to break the union where it had collective bargaining agreements, to keep it out where it did not, and to reduce wages across the board while the country was distracted by its involvement with the war. Placing women on the cars marked the beginning of industrial "squalor" on a nationwide scale and was "all part of the plan to oust car men from their

*Four vertical seniority lists were established. A worker moved from the temporary to the permanent "extra" list and then from the temporary to the permanent "regular" seniority list. The conductorettes started at the bottom of the temporary "extra" list. (*Motorman and Conductor*, Sept. 1918, p.31.)

jobs." The Amalgamated openly suggested that unless the employment of conductorettes was checked, workingmen would in due time be completely replaced by women.[15]

"Keep the Girls Off the Cars," a poem in the *Motorman and Conductor* of August 26, 1918, put the arguments in verse form:

> *We wonder where we are drifting, where is the*
> *freedom of the stripes and stars*
> *If for the sake of greed and profit we put*
> *women conductors on the cars.*
> *Woman is God's most tender flower, made to*
> *blossom and to bear*
> *To keep our homes, raise our children, and*
> *our joys and sorrows share.*
> *She was made by God the weaker, like a vine*
> *on man to lean;*
> *She was meant to work like her nature, tender,*
> *sweet and clean;*
> *Now, when the Railway Kings for greed and gain*
> *would cover womanhood with scars*
> *We pray God to protect and keep our women off*
> *the cars.*[16]

In this campaign against conductorettes, the Amalgamated Association received the cooperation of government agencies. James M. Lynch, member of the New York State Industrial Commission, claimed that the employment of female conductors on New York City's streetcars would lead to violence, and asked: "How do you think a man will feel who, unable to find a job, boards a car and is obliged to hand his nickel to a woman? That is the problem in a nutshell. There is dynamite in it."[17]

The Department of Labor cooperated with the Amalgamated Association by complying with its request to send an investigator to study the use of conductorettes on New York City's streetcars. The union then widely publicized the investigator's findings that "the operation of the streetcars is one of the last occupations which women should be hired or forced into."[18] The Labor Department's report admitted that the women conductors in New York City (about 30 percent of the conductors employed by the New York Railway Company and 21.7 percent by the Brooklyn Rapid Transit Company) were receiving the same wages as men, but it charged that the employment of women "is responsible in a small part for the fact that wages of all employees of the operating department have not increased as rapidly as have wages in other industries." (What the "other industries" were was not detailed.) While conceding, too, the "comparative lightness" of the work, the report stressed the long hours and the necessity for the conductorettes to be constantly on their feet.[19]

"There is no more reason why a woman shouldn't stand on her feet than anyone else," a woman conductor who had left "a sedentary place as a dressmaker" told a reporter. "Sitting all the time is not good for you; you don't exercise your muscles. Women don't have exercise enough, and if they had more they would have stronger children." (This last was in reply to the Amalgamated Association's lament that the conductorettes were doomed to produce a string of weak children.)[20] The Amalgamated Association did not, of course, publicize such replies to the report. Nor did the union answer the arguments of the conductorettes that steady work and higher wages, needed to meet the wartime inflation, made conducting attractive. Wages for conductorettes averaged about a third more than those of traditional female jobs.[21]

Since the Labor Department investigation did not result in the dismissal of New York City conductorettes, the union next publicized reports that the women were engaging in "gross immorality" in the car barns at the end of their runs, were frequenting nearby saloons, and were returning to their cars "intoxicated." "Women conductors have been seen in these saloons at all hours of the day and night. Sometimes they have been alone, but on many occasions were accompanied by men." It was not uncommon too, the reports went on, to find "the woman conductor and the motorman embracing during part of the run, letting the car find its own way."[22]

A number of trade unionists who shared the Amalgamated Association's hostility to the entrance of women into male-dominated occupations, called for a grand jury investigation of the immorality charge. To the chagrin of these male supremacists, the grand jury investigation found the women conductors to be "working earnestly and honestly in their new occupations to make a living."[23] This finding also helped answer a common charge that the conductorettes worked not because they had to, but because they wanted "to escape their home routines or earn pocket money for personal luxuries."[24]*

*In December 1918, Department of Labor investigators interviewed thirty-three Detroit women who had left positions as janitresses to become conductors in order to discover the reasons motivating the change. Of the thirty-three, eighteen supported dependent parents, husbands, or children, and made it clear that the higher wages as conductorettes had motivated the change. In another Detroit survey, it was revealed that 120 women conductors supported 154 dependents. (Maurine Weiner Greenwald, *Women, War, and Work: The Impact of World War I on Women Workers in the United States* [Westport, Conn., 1980], p. 155.)

## THE CASE OF THE CLEVELAND CONDUCTORETTES

At the beginning of August 1918, the U.S. Employment Service announced a shortage of 36,000 skilled workers for northern Ohio. The Cleveland Street Railway Company (CSR) hired 190 women conductors at the end of the month, on the basis of an estimated shortage. The company's official explanation was that there were not sufficient male workers to fill the vacancies, and that the war emergency required the hiring of women. The women were given a short period of training and placed on the seniority list as "extras" to fill the car crews as needed.[25]

The employment of the women conductors was immediately challenged by the (male) membership of Local 268 of the Amalgamated Association. The union disputed the company's claim that male workers were unavailable and threatened to strike unless the women were dismissed. However, it agreed to a compromise under which the women would be allowed to continue on the job while the Department of Labor investigated the alleged shortage of male workers in the Cleveland area. Meanwhile, Local 268 not only refused to admit the women conductors into the union but rejected their participation in any discussion to determine their future. It was able to convince the Department of Labor to ignore the women as well.

The Labor Department sent Henry B. Dielmann and Margaret Russanowska to Cleveland to confer with the company and Local 268 to determine the validity of the company's decision to hire women workers. After reviewing the company's hiring records and the records of its employment agencies, the investigators reported that there was no real shortage of male workers. It conceded that the turnover rate of the CSR's work force was high and that the dismissal of the women would cause a lowering of standards, since their replacements would not be of a high caliber. Nevertheless, the report concluded that the labor situation in Cleveland did not warrant the employment of the women. It recommended that they be dismissed and their places filled by male workers.[26]

Originally, the two investigators recommended that the women conductors be retained for the time being, since their release would have crippled an already inadequate transportation system. But three weeks later, on September 21, they reversed themselves and recommended termination of the conductorettes by November 1—a reversal that the *Cleveland News* termed a "minor mystery."[27] "The most logical explanation for the termination order," writes Ronald M. Benson in a study of the Cleveland controversy, "is that the union convinced the Department of Labor that the continued presence of the women on the street cars would lead to a serious disruption of service, possibly a city-wide walkout by the car men."[28]

The report issued by the Department of Labor was immediately challenged by the women themselves. At a mass meeting of all the women workers on the cars, the Association of Women Street Railway Employees was organized and Laura Prince was elected president. A former secretary of the Cleveland Waitresses' Union, Prince had had trade union experience before becoming a conductorette, so her choice as president was logical. An executive committee was chosen to speak for the women and to formulate a strategy to defend their jobs. The association appealed to Secretary of Labor William B. Wilson to prevent their dismissal "on the grounds that they are responding to the Government's call for women to seek employment in essential occupations." The women sought a hearing before the National War Labor Board.[29]

In a detailed statement to the public and the government, the association of women conductors pointed out that shortly after the declaration of war the federal government had requested women to fill jobs in "essential occupations." The 190 women who answered the job notices of the CSR did so for patriotic as well as personal reasons. They were doing their "bit for victory," they said. Secondly, the women blamed both the company and the union for their current plight. It was illegal, they declared, for the company and the union to agree to submit the issue to the arbitration of a government investigatory body, since the women had been excluded from any discussion of their own fate. The company had engaged the women to work and had clearly stipulated that the only grounds for their dismissal were "incompetency, insubordination, or other unsatisfactory service." But the charge brought against them by Local 268 was merely that they were "women"; the company had publicly acknowledged that they were satisfactorily fulfilling their duties. The women also charged that their rights had been violated by the Department of Labor's recommendation for dismissal, especially their "constitutional right to work." The most rankling aspect of the controversy, they insisted, was the refusal of Local 268 to admit them to the union, which would have given them protection against arbitrary dismissal. But the union's approach to their request to join was that they had disregarded the contract between Local 268 and the company, under which no women could be employed, and that they had no right either to the job or to union membership.[30]

Women's groups found another aspect of the controversy in Cleveland irritating. The executive board of the Amalgamated Association boasted publicly that it had complied with the Wilson administration's request that women be organized for the war emergency and covered by the collective bargaining

contracts, and the AFL Executive Council even pointed to the union in justifying its claim that the various national and international unions were making
genuine efforts to organize women workers. But the Amalgamated stood
behind Local 268 in Cleveland from the beginning of the dispute, reserving its
criticism for the women conductors. As they moved to gather support for the
conductorettes, women's groups were quick to point to this duplicity. The
National Women's Trade Union League and local leagues, suffrage clubs,
feminists within and without the labor movement, and men sympathetic to the
women's cause eagerly lent their support to the women's association. The
move to dismiss the Cleveland women workers was seen "as a crisis in the
women's struggle for economic independence—a fight for the right to work,
and their equal opportunity with men."[31]

The entrance of feminists and suffragists into the dispute infuriated the
Amalgamated Association. The union had supported the suffrage amendment[32] and felt that for it to become the target of attacks by feminists was
hardly a fitting reward. It explained, however, that its critics were not
really the sound-minded advocates of women's rights: "This controversy
has been taken advantage of by sensationalists, sentimentalists, anti-
unionists, and low-wage advocates, who have shed oceans of tears over a
'denial of women's rights.'" This "distorted clamor" over women's rights
was the work of the "half-baked equality chanter" and the "inexperienced
social reformer," who, if the truth were known, did not come from the
working class at all.[33]

As the November 1 deadline approached, Local 268 refused to modify its
demand that the women conductors be dismissed. Since it was not clear when
the War Labor Board would reach its final decision, the local stepped up its
pressure for the women's immediate removal, threatening to strike if they
were not dismissed. When the deadline arrived without a decision from the
board, Local 268 delivered an ultimatum to president John J. Stanley of the
CSR: Fire the women or the union will halt the cars. The company delayed
until November 29, when it was temporarily "taken off the hook" by an
interlocutory order issued by the War Labor Board. The order restrained the
company from dismissing the women until a decision was issued. On December 1, the union announced a partial walkout, and on the following day service was interrupted on a limited number of cars. At 5 a.m. on December 3, all
the men employed by the CSR—2,400 motormen and conductors—went out
on strike, halting all service on all the cars.[34]

Later that day the War Labor Board released its findings and recommendations in the case and ordered the streetcar workers back to work.[35] The
board recommended that the company hire no more women for the car

crews and that all the women conductors be dismissed within thirty days. The company was directed to "remove and displace the women that are now in its service as rapidly as possible." The board upheld the company's argument that the women had been hired under the "necessity clause," but stated that since the armistice of November 11, 1918, the emergency had ceased to exist. To moderate the anticipated outcry from the suffrage and women's trade union forces, the board issued an addendum to its ruling the next day, urging company president Stanley to try to find jobs elsewhere in CSR for the women dismissed from the car crews. The kind of jobs were not specified, so that the women were suddenly confronted with the threat of being demoted from ticket takers to cleaning women, or to members of the unemployed.[36]

The National Women's Trade Union League, the feminists, and the conductorettes' association all rejected the War Labor Board's recommendations, which they refused to consider binding. On December 21 the women filed a petition for a new hearing, charging that the board had heard only one major witness—the mayor of Cleveland—and had refused to meet with the women or their representatives. The board's decision, the conductorettes' association argued, affirmed the narrowest anti-female viewpoint in trade union circles, and if not reversed it would threaten all the gains made by women workers during the war. The 1921 report on the conductorettes issued by the Women's Bureau drew special attention to this aspect of the ruling: "It seemed to be a very dangerous precedent to deny to women the right to work in any occupation for no other reason than that their dismissal was demanded by the men, and without giving the women a hearing so that they might present their case."[37]

The board took the petition under advisement, agreed to set a rehearing early in March 1919, and assured the women that they would be permitted to argue their case. The company agreed not to dismiss the women until March 1, despite pressure from Local 268. The conductorettes' association then retained as its counsel Frank P. Walsh, one of the most respected labor lawyers in the country and a former chairman of both the Commission on Industrial Relations and the War Labor Board.[38*] Joining the defense were Margaret Dreier Robins, Ethel M. Smith, Emma Steghagen,

*Walsh's decision to represent the women drew the expected chorus of criticism from male unionists. But John Fitzpatrick, president of the Chicago Federation of Labor and a long-time champion of women workers, expressed his personal support of Walsh and admitted that the women's case had its merits. After all, he conceded, labor's original representatives and alternates on the War Labor Board were all men and could hardly be expected to be sympathetic to the plight of the conductorettes. (John Fitzpatrick to Frank P. Walsh, Dec. 26, 1918, Frank P. Walsh Papers, New York Public Library.)

and Elizabeth Christman of the National Women's Trade Union League; Mary Anderson and Mary Van Kleeck of the Women-in-Industry Service; and Anna Howard Shaw of the National Woman Suffrage Association. The simple principle that drew this formidable defense array together was "that a government that demands universal service from its citizens in time of war should provide universal employment at a living wage for its citizens in time of peace."[39]

The case for the conductorettes, prepared by the women themselves and their feminist supporters, emphasized the issues raised in the months during which the women had struggled to keep their jobs: (1) The conductorettes were efficient and capable workers in their own right, whose abilities were documented by the company's personnel records; (2) the women had tried to join the union, Local 268, which would have given them protection against arbitrary dismissal, but the union had refused to admit them; (3) the work of the conductors was "primarily a clerical job, at which they were seated," and it was therefore not a strenuous or hazardous occupation for women; (4) the real reason for their dismissal was the simple fact that they were women and that the male members of the union were prejudiced against them; (5) there were enough vacancies on the cars of the Cleveland Street Railway to accommodate both the women and the returning veterans, so there was no economic reason for dismissing them; (6) Local 268 had violated the War Labor Board's interlocutory order by striking against the women, so the union was in violation of the board's ruling; and (7) the armistice did not end the jurisdiction of the WLB, for the Labor Department's order to replace the women had been appealed before November 1918, and the board was within its competency in ordering the company to retain the women on the cars.[40]

The War Labor Board issued its second decision in the case on March 17, 1919, reversing its position and overturning the original dismissal order. The sixty-four women who had been fired after March 1 were ordered to be rehired, and their seniority rights and all benefits restored. They were not to be removed for any reason other than "just cause" and then only on an individual basis.

The board based its reversal order on two major considerations. First, the women's case had not been presented when the original order was issued, and therefore they had been denied a fair and impartial hearing. Second, the company had sufficient vacancies to keep the women conductors and still rehire male workers returning from military service. Since the women had accepted the jobs in good faith, every effort should be made to retain them.[41]

The victory, however, proved to be of little consequence. Local 268 simply refused to accept the reinstatement order, and president Stanley of the CSR announced that the War Labor Board's new ruling would not be recognized by the company; the women would not be rehired, and the union's objections to women on the car crews would stand. The company could not afford another strike.[42]

Elizabeth Christman and Ethel Smith of the National Women's Trade Union League pleaded with Frank Walsh to telegraph president Mahon of the Amalgamated Association and to press the national union to demand that the local abide by the decision and urge the rehiring of the women and their admission into the union. Walsh did as requested, but the Amalgamated refused to consider such a proposal. Local 268 stood firm in its determination to strike if the women were rehired, and the company not only would not rehire the women but pledged to employ no women in the future.[43]

## DETROIT PREJUDICE; KANSAS CITY SOLIDARITY

A controversy involving the conductorettes on the Detroit United Railways ended in a small victory for the women. The union agreement with the company permitted the company to accept any person who seemed fit, who would then receive a work permit from the union. If, after ninety days of service, the company found the applicant competent and no reasonable objection existed against his membership, he was admitted to the union.

In accepting the employment of women under the "necessity clause" principle, the Detroit local of the Amalgamated agreed to give conductorettes permit cards. But when, after the ninety-day period, they asked for admission into the union, they were refused. After the Armistice, the union demanded the immediate dismissal of those conductorettes already on the job and refused to give permit cards to fifteen women who had been training and were ready to go on as regular conductors. The conductorettes appealed to the War Labor Board, which found, first, that there was a sufficient supply of male labor available and that therefore the necessity for employing women no longer existed. At the same time, it upheld the plea of the conductorettes that they had been engaged in good faith, had performed their work in a satisfactory manner, had fulfilled all the terms of their contracts, and were being discharged only because a group of men refused to work with them. The union, the board ruled, "must be content with the continued employment of women now with the company" as long as they wished to remain, and must issue permits to the fifteen who were ready to work as conductorettes.

Since the union did not challenge the board's decision, the Detroit conductorettes were able to work as long as they wished, even though the union never did issue the work permits. But as far as the future was concerned, the board's decision and the union's male chauvinism was condoned by the company, effectively closing this field of work to women.[44] Not even the unstinting support that the conductorettes already in the union gave the Amalgamated in its June 1919 strike for better working conditions persuaded the Detroit union to rescind its bar against women's employment and union membership.[45]

Only in Kansas City, Missouri, were the conductorettes really successful, and that was the result of special conditions in that community. A strong tradition of labor cooperation, uniting male and female workers, existed in Kansas City before women were introduced as streetcar conductors. Kansas City unions probably had the friendliest relations with the Women's Trade Union League of all labor groups in the United States. Several years before the U.S. entry into the war, every organization in Kansas City's Central Labor Union had started to pay a regular per capita tax to help support the WTUL. In other ways as well, the male unionists of Kansas City helped the League in organizing women workers and improving their working conditions.[46]

A more immediate influence on the streetcar issue in Kansas City emerged as a result of the laundry workers' struggle for union recognition, increased wages, and the enforcement of state legislation regulating laundresses' hours and conditions of labor. A strike for these demands began in July 1917, and by mid-February 1918 all of the city's 1,800 laundry workers, both drivers and laundresses, had gone out. Near the end of March the laundry owners had still refused to yield, and workers in Kansas City, both organized and unorganized, called for a general work stoppage on March 27.

On that day, the most important general strike of the war period began as nearly all segments of Kansas City's working population, including streetcar employees, went out in a citywide action. The strike lasted a week and ended when the laundry owners agreed to grant the workers the right to organize, and also agreed to continue negotiations on the other demands.[47]

Although the laundry workers did not win any new concessions, the solidarity of labor in Kansas during the laundry workers' strike set a pattern that developed further when women were introduced as streetcar conductors by the Kansas City Railway Company. At first, to be sure, the Kansas City local of the Amalgamated Association threatened to strike if women were employed, but convinced by the Women's Trade Union League and other unions in the city, the Amalgamated local reversed itself and announced that the only useful route for both men and women was through labor solidarity and equal treatment.

The union men welcomed women into the local and insisted that the guaranteed minimum pay of the women be raised to equal the guaranteed wage of the men. When the Kansas City Railways Company refused to accede, the conductorettes, supported by the men conductors, appealed to the War Labor Board. The Board directed that "women employees shall receive equal pay for the same work, and the guaranteed minimum for women shall be increased from $60 to $70 per month, as now obtains in the case of men."

The Board's decision, Valerie J. Conner observes in her study of the National War Labor Board, "reflected the harmony between the sexes by granting absolute wage equality, in uncompromising and direct language which the board had never used before and would not use again." The Board's decision actually reflected the "harmony between the sexes" which had emerged in the Kansas City labor movement as a result of some of the sharpest struggles of the war years.[48]

## HOW OTHER UNIONS REACTED TO WOMEN WORKERS

The story of the conductorettes during World War I reveals that relationships between men and women workers varied, even within one union, from place to place and local to local. Nor was the Amalgamated Association of Street and Electric Railway Employees of America the only organization in which this contrast existed.

To prevent women from being used to undermine the craft, the International Association of Machinists passed a resolution in April 1917 to organize women into their union, permitting them to organize with men or in separate locals as specialists and helpers.* By June 1918 women made up nearly 12,500 of the 229,500 IAM members. But in a number of locals, especially those in railroad machine shops, obstacles were continuously placed in the path of women membership. Some locals did not even allow their male members to work alongside the women, much less permit women to become members.[49]

Machinists Hope Lodge Local 79 of Seattle made history in late November 1917 when it inducted sixteen women working as "specialists in the

*In 1894, when she was accepted as a member of the Kansas City, Kansas, local of the International Machinists' Union, Kate Richards O'Hare became the first woman member of the union.

machinists' trade," and included a clause in its contracts that "women working as union machinists alongside of men will receive equal pay for equal work." This was hailed as the "first instance where the principle was established in the entire history of the machinists' union." It seemed the only controversy that arose over the presence of women members centered on the "clouds of tobacco smoke at union meetings." "It is thought likely," wrote a reporter, "that the women now on an equal footing with men in the union will resign the privileges as members of the so-called weaker sex and will abide by a decision of the majority on the smoke question when it comes up to a probable vote in the near future."[50]

Another contrast appeared in the railroad industry. Female membership in the Brotherhood of Railway Clerks had been negligible in 1910, but as the union expanded during the war, women's membership grew; by 1910, they had reached 35,000, or about 20 percent of the 186,000 organized railway clerks. Some women even became officers of their locals, and a few served on railroad system boards, demonstrating by their contributions that the belief of unionized male railway clerks that women were not fit to hold union positions was totally unfounded.

The Brotherhood of Railway Clerks gave their women members the necessary backing to pursue their grievances courageously through the government bureaucracy, and the necessary expertise to fight their cases. The locals helped women employees obtain redress for discriminatory treatment on the part of the railroad authorities, and J.J. Forrester, the grand president of the Brotherhood, spoke out vigorously against discrimination because of sex. "The most flagrant disregard of governmental orders," Forrester told a press conference, "is in the application of the principle of equal pay for equal work for men and women." He pointed to specific cases on the Pennsylvania, Baltimore & Ohio, Lehigh, and Atlantic Coast lines, and on practically every one of the other major roads. He cited the case of a woman employee on the Atlantic Coast Line who had been in the company's service for seven years and whose ability was highly rated, but who was earning only $84 a month for work for which men with lesser service and experience received $130. When he intervened on her behalf, Forrester reported, he was told by a company official that although she worked as well as any man, "she is a woman, and women never did, and, so far as I am concerned, never will receive the same pay as men."

"Well," Forrester told the press, "the Brotherhood of Railway Clerks is not going to let this attitude prevail." Drawing attention to the phenomenal increase in women members, he conjectured whether it might not soon be time to change the union's name to the "Brotherhood and Sisterhood of Railway Clerks."[51]

On the other hand, the Brotherhood of Railway Carmen showed no interest in organizing women workers, even white women. Throughout the war, the Brotherhood made it clear that it desired only white *male* car cleaners as members.[52]

While there were many unions who followed the lead of the Brotherhood of Railway Carmen, there were not a few others who modeled themselves after the Brotherhood of Railway Clerks. Not long after America's entry into the war, Butchers' and Packing House Employees' Local 186 reported that it was "not entirely masculine in its gender." Not only were women being initiated "into full membership along with the men," but the local was seeking "women workers in the packing houses as members." In order to encourage them to join, "the women were not charged the customary initiation fee and pay only half dues."[53]

The Journeymen Barbers' International Union was the AFL organization claiming jurisdiction over the entire barber industry. It had refused to interfere with a decision of the Seattle local union rejecting the application of women barbers for membership. The Seattle Central Labor Council decided to act. It announced that "women barbers shall not be denied the right to organize and become affiliated at least locally with their unions." Not only did the Central Labor Council vote to grant affiliation to the union of women barbers, awarding it a charter directly from the council, but it furnished the new union with "a union shop card with which to attract the patronage of union men." Heartened by this recognition, the Seattle Lady Barbers' Union launched a campaign to unionize women barbers "100 percent." Within four months, the union's delegates to the Central Labor Council reported that the local had achieved its goal.[54]

## THE TELEPHONE OPERATORS

The enrollment of thousands of telephone operators in the International Brotherhood of Electrical Workers, and the remarkable unity displayed by women and men in the telephone industry, during the war, furnished probably the strongest evidence, after the example of Kansas City, of a developing alliance of the sexes. It certainly marked a complete turnabout in the approach of the Brotherhood to the telephone operators.

Throughout the opening decade of the twentieth century, the IBEW had maintained a policy of indifference or outright hostility toward the operators. In general, the official attitude was that since the operators were usually very young women "inexperienced in the philosophy of trade unions," they would strike at the drop of a hat and involve male Brother-hood members in "almost continuous troubles." Moreover, since the job of telephone operator was viewed "merely as a temporary occupation"—an "expedient to get spending money" until the women could marry—it was subject to a constant turnover, so it was pointless for the Brotherhood to spend time and money on organizing campaigns.

In addition, there was the fact that the number of telephone operators had risen from 19,000 in 1900 to 98,000 in 1920. The male-dominated IBEW feared that an effective unionizing drive would bring in so many women that the operators would become a majority and gain control of the international union. The IBEW executive board may have put it rather obscurely but its meaning was clear when it declared: "We think there can be no rule of ethics or human rights which requires men handling the sting of electricity to submit forever to the rule of telephone operators in their methods and conditions of work. . . ." To meet this threat, the IBEW herded the telephone operators into sublocals of linemen's locals, with lit-tle autonomy. When the women became dissatisfied with "second-class citizenship" and pressed for full recognition of their rights, the IBEW agreed to a compromise. Operators' locals were chartered directly but they paid only half the men's per capita dues; consequently they had only half the voting strength of men's locals at IBEW conventions.[55]

Their power may have been limited compared with the men's, but the operators did begin to organize. In 1912, under the leadership of Julia S. O'Connor, the first permanent local of telephone operators in the country was formed in Boston as a sublocal of a linemen's IBEW local in that city. The following year it won a strike against the New England Telephone Company for a union agreement, and the success in Boston helped achieve rapid unionization among telephone operators in Lynn, Springfield, Wor-cester, New Bedford, Framingham, Fitchburg, Salem, Lowell, Lawrence, Haverhill, and other Massachusetts cities. Before the United States entered World War I, telephone operators were unionizing in Maine, New Hampshire, and Vermont, and as far west as the Rocky Mountain states.[56]

After America's entry into World War I, the "hello girls" really flocked into the Brotherhood's operators' locals. A report from the Pacific Coast in August 1917 read: "In one month of existence as an organization, Tele-phone Operators' Local No.42A has perfected virtually a 100 percent union, only a few of the operators employed by the Pacific Telephone & Telegraph Company remaining outside the union and these few with their applications pending. The union now has a membership of over 900, fol-lowing the initiation last Saturday night of 98 new members."[57]

Telephone Operators Local 42A grew rapidly during the summer of 1917, organizing thousands of operators in the states of Washington, Oregon, and California.[58] In September 1917, the telephone operators presented the Pacific Telephone and Telegraph Company, for the first time in its history, with a list of demands and an ultimatum that promised a walkout unless these demands were granted within a reasonable time. The operators asked for a true eight-hour day (no swing shifts), union recognition and the union shop privilege, no discrimination against union activists, and the following wage scale: (1) new operators to receive not less than $1.50 per day for a period of nine months, after which they were to receive a minimum of $2.50 per day; (2) information, complaint, special, and "B" (or experienced) operators to receive not less than $2.75 per day; (3) all operators to receive 5 cents extra for each additional hour or portions of an hour of work after 6 P.M.; (4) night operators to receive 50 cents more per day than day operators; (5) supervisors to receive not less than $2.95 per day when first put on the floor, with a 10 percent increase every three months until they receive $3.25 per day; (6) clerks, monitors, and telephone operators to receive not less than $3 per day; (7) doubletime for work on Sundays and holidays; (8) operators to be allowed a fifteen-minute relief period in both morning and afternoon, without being compelled to make up the half hour; and (9) any operator with twelve months of service to be entitled to two weeks of vacation with one week pay, while operators with two years of service were to be entitled to two weeks off at full pay.[59]

The company did not bother to respond to the operators' demands and refused even to consider a federal government proposal that it submit the issue to binding arbitration. It was confident that the linemen would not join the strike that was threatened. But it miscalculated; the members of Electrical Workers Local 77 had not had an increase in wages for at least three years, and they were ready to walk out with the operators.[60]

On October 31, 1917, 1,300 operators and linemen in Seattle struck, followed by employees of the Pacific Telephone & Telegraph Company in Tacoma, Aberdeen, and other Washington cities. Within a few days, the strike spread into Oregon and California. All along the Pacific Coast, telephone service was "badly crippled."[61] By mid-November 1917, the telephone strike was beginning to cause a slowdown in war production on the Pacific Coast. Secretary of Labor William B. Wilson appointed a mediation commission to settle the dispute, and within a week the commission presented a five point proposed settlement to President Wilson. It included: (1) a minimum wage of $9 a week for operators in large cities on the Pacific Coast, with an average daily increase of $1.40 for day, evening, and night work; (2) proportional increases for workers in all other cities and towns, with a minimum wage of $8 a week; (3) wage increases for men employees, as of November 1, 1917, to bring their daily wage to $4.25 (they had asked for $5 at the beginning of the strike); (4) arbitration of further increases; (5) establishment of machinery to settle grievances; and (6) reemployment of all strikers without discrimination.[62]

Although some dissatisfaction was expressed over the limited wage increases and the failure to include union recognition, the members of Telephone Operators' Local 42A and Electrical Workers Local 77 voted to return to work under the terms proposed by the federal mediation commission. The strikers, the press acknowledged, "yielded to the apparent patriotic necessity for a prompt settlement."[63]

Within a few weeks, additional wage increases were gained as a result of continued conferences at which top IBEW officials were present, and Lillian Schunke and Hazel Holmes, two of the strikers, represented the linemen.* An important paragraph in the final agreement provided that employees kept waiting for four hours or less before resuming work should receive pay for four hours, and those kept waiting for over eight hours were to receive pay for eight hours. There was also a provision for double time for holidays and Sundays. For the first time, an eight-hour day was instituted for telephone operators in the Pacific Coast industry, with provision for compensation for time over the eight hours spent either waiting or working.

An interesting provision of the agreement read: "All employees at work on primary or election days, and who are entitled to vote in the district they are in, will be allowed two hours standard time with full pay in which to cast their vote. Voting hours to be designated by supervisor in charge."[64] A few years earlier, this provision would have affected only the male workers, but with the adoption of woman suffrage by the Pacific Coast states, the operators too were now able to vote.

Unfortunately, the agreement ending the telephone strike had not included either the principle of the union shop or of union recognition. Gradually, the Pacific Telephone & Telegraph Company weeded out many

---

*The final settlement provided that linemen were to receive $4.75 per day and telephone operators an additional 12½ percent increase across the board. The settlement affected operators in Seattle, San Francisco, Los Angeles, Oakland, Portland, Spokane, Tacoma, and Sacramento. (Seattle *Union Record*, Dec. 8, 15, 1917; Julia O'Connor, "History of the Organized Telephone Operators' Movement," *The Union Telephone Operator*, Jan.-Feb. 1921; clippings are in National Women's Trade Union League Papers, Folder F, Arthur and Elizabeth Schlesinger Library on the History of Women in America, Radcliffe College.)

of the union women and replaced them with non-union operators at lower scales. Within a year all that was left was "a core of union members," described as "girls who have had the courage to stick by their union in the face of all opposition."[65] This "core" was soon to assume leadership of new and even greater struggles of the telephone workers.

With a wartime grant of authority, President Wilson placed the entire telephone and telegraph system of the country under federal control at midnight, July 31, 1918. At that time, the IBEW had about twenty thousand organized telephone workers in its ranks,* but with the combined union strength of the telegraphers added to the telephone workers, the beachhead already established in the telephone industry could now be widened. Union hopes were further raised by the precedents set by the wartime nationalization of the railroads a year earlier. While the railroads were under federal operation, national adjustment boards representing management and the rail unions were established to settle grievances, and in many agreements both union recognition and the principle of equal pay for equal work had been included.[66]

Unfortunately for the hopes of union telephone workers, President Wilson placed the telegraph and telephone services under the administration of Postmaster General Albert Burleson, who was decidedly unsympathetic to union organization. In fact, Burleson had already been condemned by the Employees and the National Association of Letter Carriers. The Washington State Federation of Labor urged Wilson to replace him as administrator with "a progressive man more in line with modern governmental policies." The federation referred specifically to the report that Burleson had informed president James Carlton of Western Union: "If the telegraph and telephone lines are taken over, the employees should not be affiliated with any outside organization."[67]

Burleson stayed on as administrator, but he was compelled to appoint Julia O'Connor to represent "the organized telephone workers of the country" on a committee designated to investigate working conditions in the telephone and telegraph service. O'Connor, a former telephone operator herself, was president of the Boston telephone operators' union. She also headed the telephone operators' department of the International Brotherhood of Electrical Workers, was a member of the National

*Under the charter of the International Brotherhood of Electrical workers, telephone operators as well as linemen were eligible to join. But before 1912 little effort was made to organize them. The Brotherhood viewed telephone operators as "flighty and likely dropouts from the union." In 1912, however, this changed and telephone operators were brought into the union. (Philip S. Foner, *Women and the American Labor Movement: From Colonial Times to the Eve of World War I* [New York, 1979]: 251-54, 469.)

Women's Trade Union League Executive Board, and the labor representative on the Massachusetts Minimum Wage Commission. Women trade unionists were excited about O'Connor's appointment, not only because she was a militant union leader and had worked actively with the Women's Trade Union League to help women wage earners better their working conditions, but also because the Post Office had, under Burleson, been backward in appointing women even to clerical positions.[68]

The IBEW was having its convention at the same time that federal services were placed under federal control. The Brotherhood voted to meet what seemed to be a new and promising situation for telephone workers by establishing an autonomous department for the telephone operators' locals, with Julia O'Connor as president.[69] The IBEW convention also asked the government to raise the wages of all telephone operators a minimum of $1 a day and to institute a six-day week for all female employees of the telephone companies. Meanwhile, through the new telephone operators' department, it prepared to organize to press for these and other demands.[70]

The organizing drive was launched immediately with a campaign to unionize Chicago, with its seven thousand operators. "The telephone girls are organizing into one big union," the labor press reported in September 1918.[71] In appealing to the Chicago workers, the IBEW Telephone Department's circular pointed out that since Boston had gotten the ball rolling— "they organized six years ago and won a strike to prevent the company from destroying the union a year later"—strikes had spread to all of New England; next to the Pacific Coast and the Northwest; then to Norfolk, Virginia; St. Paul, Minnesota; Toledo, Ohio; "and many other cities." Now it was up to Chicago:

> Compare your wages with those of organized girls. Why should a telephone operator be rated lower than a typist or stenographer? Today a girl can walk into a factory and learn to run a punch press right off the reel and she gets more money than you make after you train for weeks and weeks and work for years. . . .
>
> The Bureau of Labor Statistics shows that the cost of living has increased 70 percent—have your wages? It is true that even your wages have been increased a little but are left far below the cost of living. . . . What is supposed to look big to the Chicago operators now was in the pay envelopes of the Boston operators two years ago. . . .[72]*

---

*They could have added that since they were organized in 1912, the Boston women had also won an eight-hour day, two-week vacation, standardized pay scales with automatic increases, and improved grievance procedures. (Greenwald, *Women, War, and Work*, p. 205.)

One of the arguments that was most effective in recruiting thousands of Chicago operators was the promise that the government would yield to the organized power of the operators and force the companies to grant the much-needed wage increases and improvements in working conditions. "You are now government employees," the organizing leaflet had stressed, "and no longer at the mercy of a private corporation. You can expect a square deal if you ask the government for a hearing on the question of your wages and conditions."[73]

But events proved that Burleson had not really changed. He refused to consider the demands for wage increases and dodged the issue of union recognition by insisting that negotiations be conducted through the Wage Commission of the Wire Control Board.* He then refused to allow the board to respond to the operators' demands. Julia O'Connor was forced out of her position as a member of the commission. In her letter of resignation she declared that "to retain membership would amount to a serious betrayal of the rights and interests of my fellow workers." The commission, she said, was consistent in only one respect—its "hostility to the organized telephone and telegraph workers."[74]

It was not until the postwar labor upheaval, when a strike completely tied up telephone service in New England and threatened to spread throughout the country, that the government was forced to act. But the telephone operators had already shown in their organizing drives and strikes that they were not acting alone. The repairmen, male telephone installers, line splicers, and switchboard workers had given them full support, and the IBEW, which had displayed little interest in organizing female telephone operators, had very much changed its attitude. How far it had gone in a new direction was illustrated in the story published in the *Seattle Union Record* of August 31, 1918 under the heading "Electricians Elect Woman":

> Miss Margaret Whitman, member of Electrical Workers Local No. 40, probably has the distinction of being the first woman to hold office in a regular "man's local" union of the International Brotherhood of Electrical Workers. She was installed as financial secretary of Local No. 40 at its meeting Thursday night. The office is a salaried one and carries with it the responsibility of handling all of the union's funds.

---

*To manage the telephone and telegraph wires during the war period, the Post Office Department established a Wire Control Board which consisted of three government officials, and American Telephone and Telegraph President Theodore N. Vail as an advisor.

## CONCLUSION

It is abundantly clear that relationships between men and women workers during the war varied considerably. Where women were welcomed into unions, they accepted the invitation gladly and made important contributions toward advancing the interests of both themselves and of men workers. Together they obtained better working conditions. Where they were confronted by union opposition, women defended their own special interests. Their resistance ranged in form from individual refusal to be intimidated by fellow workers to collective mobilization against hostile unions.

In general, the war gave many women their first contact with highly organized, militant male workers. Too often the opposition of these male workers and their unions led the women to consider trade unionism and sex discrimination as synonymous. But for many, the contact taught them the advantages of trade union protection, and they learned from the association with progressive-minded trade unionists the value of being organized into strong collective bargaining units. By 1920, trade union membership was 8 percent female, and 6.6 percent of all workingwomen were unionized—a five-fold increase in one decade.[75]

# CHAPTER 11

## Organized Labor and the Black Worker

During World War I, the national and local unions of the AFL and the Railroad Brotherhoods grew rapidly, enrolling hundreds of thousands of new members; some even tripled in size. Few of these new members were black workers.

## THE PATH LABOR SHOULD FOLLOW

Many black leaders realized early in the Great Migration that active participation in the trade union movement was vital to the economic future of black workers, particularly if they were to rise above the unskilled level. Forward-looking labor leaders also saw that an explosive situation was developing and that the only way to prevent it from detonating, with disastrous consequences to both black and white workers, was through a change in organized labor's traditional approach to black labor.

The *International Molders' Journal* warned: "So long as the Negroes remain unorganized they will continue to be exploited and used to break down the standard of living of not only their own race, but of all men who are forced to compete with them in the industrial field."[1] The Detroit *Labor News* asserted that the time had come for "the American Labor Movement to face squarely the fact that the Negro is a big factor in our industrial life and that he must be taken into account in the adjustment of our economic differences; never again can the Negro be ignored. Unionism must welcome the Negro to its ranks."[2]

The AFL was slow to respond to the problems arising from the Great Migration. The first official reaction came at its 1916 convention. The Ohio State Federation of Labor and the Cleveland Labor Federation jointly sponsored a resolution calling the delegates' attention to "the emigration of Southern Negroes to Northern labor centers . . . which has occasioned anxiety on the part of the organized labor movement because of the danger such emigration will cause the workers in the northern states." Investigations by the resolution's sponsors had revealed that a great many blacks entering Ohio had been imported by employers for the purpose of replacing union men. The scarcity of immigrant labor indicated that the importation of black workmen was certain to continue, which meant that the black worker would be an important element in the future makeup of the northern labor market. The resolution warned that the shortage of European labor guaranteed that blacks would continue to be "brought north for the purpose of filling the places of union men demanding better conditions." It called upon the Executive Council "to inaugurate a movement looking toward the organization of these men in the Southern states, to the end that they be instructed and educated along the lines of the trade union movement and thereby eliminate this menace to the workers of the Northern states."[3]

The convention adopted the resolution and referred it to the Executive Council, which passed the matter on to Gompers. Some organizers were appointed, but they made no effort to reach black workers in either the South or the North. In the first year of the Migration, some AFL affiliates saw that their self interest required bringing the messages of unionism to black workers in the South, but the AFL did not take the matter seriously.[4]

## THE EAST ST. LOUIS RIOT

The need for the action proposed by the Ohio labor federations was dramatically illustrated even before the next annual AFL convention. Although there was a decrease in the number of lynchings between 1916 and 1917, racial violence flared up in several places, including Houston, Texas; Chester, Pennsylvania; and most notably, East St. Louis, Illinois.[5]

Tension between whites and the black migrants over housing, transportation, and recreational facilities was a factor in the East St. Louis riot, but a more fundamental cause was the competition for jobs and wages. Black workers were imported to work at low wages—though high by southern standards—and the unskilled white workers found their own wage scales threatened in turn. When they organized a labor union affiliated with the AFL and demanded higher wage scales, the employers threatened to replace them with black labor. Due to the prevalent anti-black prejudice, no real effort was made in E. St. Louis to include black workers in the union. The number of black migrants who scabbed was never large. But when an April 1907 union-led strike against the Aluminum Ore Company was defeated, the trade unions turned their fury against the black workers instead of against the employers. In East St. Louis, they launched a campaign not only to prevent organization of the black workers but also to bar further black migration to the city. In order to win the unorganized, low paid white workers to this position, rumors were spread that local manufacturers planned to bring in up to 15,000 more black workers.

In a widely distributed letter issued on May 23, the Central Trades and Labor Union, a federation of AFL craft unions, stated that the "immigration of the Southern Negro into our city for the past eight months has reached the point where drastic action must be taken if we intend to work and live peaceably in this community." At least 10,000 "undesirable Negroes" had entered the city, and were "being used to the detriment of our white citizens by some of the capitalists and a few of the real estate owners." The Central Trades and Labor Union then announced that its delegates would call upon the mayor and the city council demanding action to retard this "growing menace" and also to "devise a way to get rid of a certain portion of those who are already there."[6]

At a meeting of delegates with the mayor and the city council, the city officials were warned that if no official action was taken to halt the black migration, "violence" would be employed to accomplish this objective. After the meeting, groups of whites attacked and beat up six blacks. The black community, fearing mob violence, began to arm in self defense.

On the night of July 1, a police car patrolling the black section of the city was mistaken for a carload of white vigilantes; rifle fire broke out, and two of the policemen in the car were shot dead. When news of the attack spread through the city the next morning, mobs of enraged white residents took to the streets and began shooting, lynching, and burning black men, women, and children wherever they found them. The rioting raged for almost two days until order was finally restored.[7]

The savagery of the East St. Louis race riot was incredible. "It was awful," a black woman worker in East St. Louis wrote. "We lost everything but what we had on and that was very little." At least 50 persons were killed and 240 buildings destroyed; estimates of property damage ran as high as $1,400,000. It was one of the worst anti-Negro riots, in terms of lives lost, of the twentieth century.[8]

Shortly after the riot, the St. Louis *Post-Dispatch* quoted the president of the Central Trades and Labor Union of East St. Louis as saying: "Before the tenseness of this situation is relieved, these employers must convince the laboring whites that they will be given preference over imported blacks in applying for work." He and other labor leaders, including AFL President Gompers, placed the blame for the outbreak squarely on the city's large industrial concerns, which they accused of importing Negroes from the South "to destroy organized labor, break down the standards of labor and create strife within the state."[9] Unless this practice ceased, "similar outbreaks would occur in Pittsburgh, Newark and a few other points, where Southern Negroes have been induced to go in larger numbers than can be absorbed in the industries available to them."[10]

After investigating the excuse offered by the unions for the riot, William English Walling, a socialist journalist who had studied previous anti-black riots, wired President Wilson: "The pretext of labor invasion from the South is invalid."[11] Black commentators agreed that employers were partly responsible for the riot by fostering competition for jobs and then standing back to watch the black and white workers kill each other. But they placed the blame chiefly on the racism of the white trade unions. Special investigators for the National Association for the Advancement of Colored People reported that "by all accounts of eye-witnesses, both white and black, the East St. Louis outrage was deliberately planned and executed."[12] W. E. B. Du Bois, one of the two investigators for the NAACP, concluded that the labor leaders in East St. Louis had not purposely plotted the July riot or assumed direction of the massacre of Negroes; most of the whites who had participated in the riot were unskilled, unorganized workers. But, he pointed out, the trade unions in East St. Louis had excluded Negro workers from their ranks, were "antagonistic" to black people, and had stirred up the white population against the Negroes through racist propaganda. "The result was the East St. Louis riots."[13]

A more recent study endorses this conclusion. Elliott M. Rudwick points out that, although labor leaders played a vital role in stirring up the white population against Negroes through racist propaganda, there is no evidence that they plotted the July riot or assumed direction of it.[14]

Ida Crouch-Hazlett wrote from East St. Louis in the Socialist New York *Call*:

> The trouble in the East St. Louis massacre was that union men were fighting the wrong crowd. They should have been fighting the capitalists instead of their fellow workers. They should organize the blacks. This is where the American Federation of Labor has run against a snag. It has resisted their organization, but the capitalists in their rush for profits are bound to bring them in. In lieu of organization, only force and barbarity are left to the union.[15]

Stung by the criticism, the AFL officially denied that any of its affiliates in East St. Louis were to be blamed for the riot. But there is little doubt that the accusation of black spokespersons that the AFL was unwilling "to get rid of its color caste and industrial Junkerism" caused consternation among the federation's leaders.[16]

# THE AFL AND THE BLACK WORKER

At the 1917 AFL convention, three resolutions were proposed relating to the black labor question. One, submitted by representatives of the black trade unions in Virginia directly affiliated with the AFL, requested that black organizers be sent to establish more local labor unions for black wage earners in industrial communities, in cities in the South, and elsewhere.[17] The second resolution, put forth by a delegate from a black railroad local, called for the appointment of a black organizer for the nearly 15,000 black laborers on the fifteen railroad lines operating in the Southeast. (The delegate who introduced this proposal noted that there were only four black locals in existence on the entire Southeastern rail system.)[18] The third resolution, introduced by a delegate from the San Francisco Labor Council, also called for the organization of black workers, but went on to list a number of offenses perpetrated against them, especially in the South, and noted that since black soldiers were fighting abroad under the slogan of democracy, it was reasonable for democracy to be extended to American blacks at home. The convention was asked to direct the Executive Council to influence the President and Congress "to the end that all of the political, civil and economic disabilities so offensive and destructive to the rights of Negroes as human beings and American citizens be removed."[19]

The convention gave short shrift to the last resolution. Even the delegate who proposed it apologized for the resolution and acknowledged that the charges it contained were offensive to delegates from the South. He had simply introduced the resolution on behalf of the International Negro League out of appreciation of the support rendered his organization by black workers in a recent strike.* The Committee on Resolutions refused to approve the resolution and presented it to the convention with a special disclaimer of responsibility for any of its statements. But not even this satisfied the southern trade unionists. Finally the delegates agreed to

---

*This was not the only occasion in that period when black workers rallied to the support of white labor. In the port of Houston the Negro and white locals of the International Longshoremen's Association had an agreement under which they divided the work equally. In 1914 the Southern Steamship Company offered work to black longshoremen only. Members of the Negro local refused to work unless members of the white local were allowed the same privilege, and they held to this demand for three years. The State Federation of Labor in 1917 adopted a resolution "endorsing the fight that the colored men have made for the white men." But at the 1917 AFL convention the delegates of the State Federation of Labor refused to support a resolution calling for removal of "political, civil and economic disabilities" against blacks. (Ruth Allen, *Chapters in the History of Organized Labor in Texas*[Austin, Texas, 1941], pp. 278-82.)

accept only that part of the resolution that referred to the organization of black workers.[20]

The first two resolutions fared better. They were adopted by the convention and sent to the Executive Council with the recommendation that black organizers be appointed "as soon as possible" if the finances of the federation permitted. The council in turn referred the resolutions to Gompers with the request that he draft a plan for organizing black workers on the southeastern railroads. Gompers did not bother with that request, and it was not until 1922 that the AFL concerned itself with organization of black railworkers in the Southeast.[21]

Despite the fact that the delegates had in effect countenanced discrimination against blacks by rejecting the resolution proposed on behalf of the International Negro League, many black leaders cheered the events at the AFL Convention. The AFL's consent to the further organization of black workers sufficed to produce a banner headline in the New York *Age*, a black weekly: "NEGRO IS NOW RECOGNIZED BY FEDERATION OF LABOR." The story beneath the headline went in part:

> Negro labor has been recognized by the American Federation of Labor and the federation has decided to organize the colored working man. A step to take in southern Negroes in large numbers will at once be inaugurated and the plan is endorsed by white delegates from the Southland. . . . It may easily prove that the Negro will come into the unions more rapidly than has any other race in the country now that his own people are to take the initiative to him.

The *Age* went on to describe the AFL's action as especially significant in view of the resolution brought up at the previous convention by the Ohio trade unionists asking that white organizers be sent among Negroes in the South, principally on the grounds that the exodus of black labor to the North was a menace to the wage standards of white labor. There had been no expression of interest a year earlier, the *Age* noted, in the organization of the Negro for his own good.[22]

The *Age* also published the remarks of Emmett J. Scott on the AFL convention, noting that as a former protegé of Booker T. Washington, Scott would be expected to view organized labor as the enemy of the Negro people. But instead he told the black weekly that the action at the convention was "one of the wisest, most just and generous steps ever taken by the A.F. of L." The resolutions adopted by the convention had thrown down "the bars which had been for years serving as insurmountable barriers to colored wage-earners who wished to enlist in the ranks and enjoy the privileges of organized labor. . . . This splendid action is hailed by Negro toilers throughout our country as portending complete unity of desire on the part of the organized labor movement to welcome what will prove one of its most important constituent elements."[23]*

Many black spokesmen, and a number of white liberals,** took the position that the AFL had decided to strike down the color line. But there were others who were not swept off their feet. Both John R. Shillady, executive secretary of the NAACP, and W. E. B. Du Bois, editor of its official organ, *The Crisis*, questioned the significance of the resolution adopted by the delegates and doubted that the promise to appoint black organizers would be kept.[24] (The fact that four months after the convention not a single black organizer had been appointed lent substance to the skepticism.)[25] In March, 1918, Du Bois wrote in *The Crisis*: "The most recent convention of the A.F. of L. is no proof of any change of heart. Grudgingly, unwillingly, almost insultingly, this Federation yields to us inch by inch the status of half a man, denying and withholding every privilege it dares at all times."[26]

As the author of two comprehensive studies surveying the relationship between organized labor and the black worker since the days of Reconstruction, Du Bois knew whereof he spoke.***

Between the 1917 and 1918 AFL conventions, several meetings were held by a committee representing the National Urban League and a number of high-ranking federation leaders. The two groups met to discuss the initiation of a campaign to organize blacks in various industries and trades, skilled and unskilled, North and South, government as well as civilian employees, and women as well as men. In the discussions, Gompers and other federation officials conceded that there were affiliates that refused to admit blacks, but they repeatedly emphasized the AFL position that working people must unite and organize "irrespective of creed, color, sex, nationality or politics" and that, as Gompers put it:

> We, the A.F. of L., welcome Negro workingmen to the ranks of organized labor. We should like to see more of them join us. The interests of workingmen, white and black, are common. Together we must fight unfair wages,

*At the time he made these remarks, Scott was Special Assistant to Secretary of War Newton D. Baker.

**Oswald Garrison Villard, a leading white liberal and long associated with the movement for black equality, characterized the action of the AFL convention as a "momentous happening to make all of us rejoice who have the welfare of the Negro at heart." ("The Negro and the War," *New World* [January 1918]: 17.)

***These studies were *The Philadelphia Negro* (Philadelphia, 1899), and *The Negro Artisan*, (Atlanta, 1902).

unfair hours, and bad conditions of labor. At times it is difficult for the national organization to control the actions of local unions in difficulties arising within the trades in any particular community, in as much as the National body is made possible by the delegates appointed by the locals; but we can, and will use our influence to break down prejudice on account of race, color, or previous condition of servitude, and hope that you will use your influence to show Negro workingmen the advantages of collective bargaining and the value of affiliation with the A.F. of L. But few people who are not thoroughly acquainted with the rapid growth of the Federation of Labor know of the large numbers of colored people who are already members of our organization. The unpleasant incidents in connection with efforts of colored men to get recognition in trades controlled by the A.F. of L. have been aired and given publicity; and for that reason a general attitude of suspicion has been developed towards union labor on the part of colored working people; but I hope that out of this conference will spring a more cordial feeling of confidence in each other on the part of men who must work for a living.[27]

Gompers concluded his remarks by urging the members of the black delegation to impress on black leaders and workers alike the necessity of joining the organized labor movement.[28]

Gompers and other federation leaders at the conference told the black delegation it was necessary to overcome the influence of black preachers, doctors, and heads of various fraternal societies who, with the encouragement of employers, had influenced black workers not to join unions. The members of the Urban League committee promised to do their part to further the principles of unionism among black workers. Both parties agreed that the black delegation would prepare a suggested program to bring about the full participation of black workers in the organized labor movement, which would be submitted to the AFL Executive Council for approval and then reported to the 1918 convention for action.[29]

The memorandum, drafted by Eugene K. Jones of the Urban League, was submitted to the AFL Executive Council. It was a four-point program designed to bring about the full participation of black workers in the organized labor movement. First, the memorandum required Gompers to draw up a declaration along the lines of his remarks to the conference (quoted above) which would then be submitted to the black press for publication throughout the country as the official expression of the AFL president's views on matters involving the relationship between black and white workers. The memorandum pointedly asked that Gompers' statement contain a clear exposition of the reasons why certain international unions could exclude blacks by constitutional provision and still be affiliated with the AFL. Such an explanation was needed, they contended, to overcome the widespread distrust of unions on the part of black editors and ministers whose cooperation was essential to the successful organization of black workers. The memorandum urged Gompers, moreover, to consider recommending to the internationals which still excluded blacks that they eliminate the color bar from their constitutions.

Second, the memorandum called upon the federation to employ more black organizers to promote the organization of black workers in the industries and occupations where they were then employed or likely to be employed in considerable numbers. Third, the memorandum proposed that the Urban League committee meet with a permanent committee of AFL officials on a quarterly basis throughout the year to check on the results of the cooperative activities of the two bodies and to plan for further extension of their work. Fourth, the memorandum asked that Gompers fulfill a promise made at the meeting with the Urban League committee to have the Executive Council voice an advanced position in its report on the organization of black workers at the Federation's approaching annual convention. It was hoped that the Council's sentiments would be endorsed at the convention and given the widest publicity throughout the country.[30]

During the drafting of the Urban League Committee's memorandum, Shillady of the NAACP made a recommendation which, unfortunately, was not included in the final copy sent to Gompers. Shillady's recommendation urged the members of the Urban League Committee to use what influence they had to prevail upon Gompers to accept blacks working in each industry into the unions already organized in that industry, so that there would not arise separate unions whose sole difference in membership was based upon color.[31]

The significance of this proposal is pointed up by John D. Finney, Jr., who has made the most detailed analysis of the relationship between organized labor and the black worker during World War I:

> The matter of separate organization was a vital one in the consideration of Negro wage-earners for membership in the A.F. of L. For when Gompers and other Federation officials discussed the problems of admitting colored men to A.F. of L. affiliates they were thinking primarily of accepting colored men in terms of separate federal or local unions and not on the basis of admitting them through the international or national unions of the different trades as white workers were accepted. The past two decades had clearly shown, however, that separate organization provided anything but a satisfactory type of membership for the Negro. The A.F. of L.'s continuation of this policy, as Shillady correctly

noted, would only serve to reinforce the growing system of "Jim Crow" union-ism that sealed off the Negro wage-earner from any meaningful role within the Federation. It is unfortunate therefore, that the Negro leaders on the committee negotiating with the A.F. of L. did not incorporate Shillady's suggestion in their proposed scheme to Gompers. By doing so, they could have made it quite clear to him that organization apart from white workers was not an acceptable solution to the question of Negro participation in the organized labor movement.[32]

The Urban League committee's memorandum was submitted by Gom-pers to the AFL's 1918 convention in June. As Gompers had pledged, the convention also received a report on Negro organization from the Execu-tive Council. The Council's statement, however, contained nothing of any significance, nor broke any new paths on the question of black member-ship. It merely noted that at the conferences with the National Urban League committee, the black leaders had agreed to call upon black work-ers to join both the regular and separate "colored" unions of the AFL.[33] Actually, the Urban League committee, while unwilling to include Shilla-dy's proposal in the memorandum and urge the AFL to include black workers in the unions already organized, had said nothing about separate unions for blacks.

The delegates at the 1918 convention referred the memorandum of the Urban League to the Committee on Organization for official consider-ation. That body duly reported its appreciation of the black leaders' recog-nition of the need to organize blacks into unions affiliated with the AFL, and recommended that Gompers and the Executive Council give "special attention" to organizing black workers in the future. Nothing was said to imply that the AFL had not done its duty by black workers in the past, but the report conceded that with the cooperation "of leaders of the [Negro] race much better results can be accomplished." The report was unani-mously approved by the convention.[34]

The Committee on Organization had not said how the black leaders' program would be put into effect, but the Urban League committee was optimistic. It's optimism soon vanished. Urban League secretary Jones kept inquiring of Gompers as to what practical steps were being planned to carry out the recommendations the League committee had forwarded to him. At first he was informed by Gompers' secretary—Gompers was too busy to respond—that the recommendations had been endorsed at the 1918 convention and referred to the Executive Council for action, and he would be advised what further was being done in the matter. Months went by and still Jones heard nothing. Again he inquired, complaining that he had received no information from the Executive Council regarding what steps should be taken to work out the program of action agreed upon at the AFL convention. This time he received no answer at all.[35]

Jones turned next in despair to members of the Urban League committee and raised the possibility of holding another conference with the AFL to exert new pressure upon it to follow through on the tentative program for the organization of black workers endorsed at the 1918 convention. He informed his colleagues that an increasing number of complaints the Urban League had been receiving from black workers citing discrimination by AFL unions had made such a conference a necessity. But by the time committee members replied to Jones' proposal, the war had come to an end and other matters took priority for the time being.[36*]

Thus, by the time World War I ended on November 11, 1918, the AFL had done nothing more than discuss the influx of black workers into industry, pat itself on the back for its past declarations, and admit that more would be accomplished now that black leaders saw the necessity of unionizing black workers in affiliation with the federation. The AFL adopted resolutions without creating effective machinery to put them into operation, and silently but eloquently rebuffed the black spokesperson when he dared to inquire what was being done to implement the resolutions.

## RELATIONS ON THE LOCAL LEVEL

Nor was the record on the local level much better. Throughout the war, evidence of discrimination by white trade unions mounted, even in federally controlled or supervised industries. In Key West, Florida, white union carpenters prevented black carpenters from working on the construction of army cantonments by charging that they were not union men. The fact that they had repeatedly petitioned for admittance or for separate charters and had been rejected carried no weight either with the white trade union or the government. Even black union carpenters were shut out of government work because of the opposition of white unionists. In Petersburg, Virginia, thirty-six black carpenters, all union men, were dismissed from work at Camp Lee because white union carpenters refused to work with them.[37]

*About half of the committee members replied to Jones' proposal, and all of these responded affirmatively. Jones took no action on the matter until June 1919, when the National Urban League, at a meeting of its Executive Board, passed resolution calling for renewal of negotiations with the AFL over the question of organizing black workers (New York *Age*, June 28, 1919.) Jones wrote to Gompers proposing such a meeting, but nothing ever came of these efforts. It is clear, John D. Finney, Jr., concludes, "that Gompers has no interest in convening such talks." ("A Study of Negro Labor During and After World War I," unpublished Ph.D. dissertation, Georgetown University, 1957, p. 297.)

Masses of blacks had migrated to Pittsburgh; indeed, by mid-1917 the steel city's industrial life was said to be "partly dependent upon the Negro labor supply." But the unions, which grew rapidly in the Pittsburgh area during the war, continued, with few exceptions, to bar blacks. One union reported a growth of 100 percent in a single year, but there were no black members. The union president claimed that efforts had been made to organize black workers, but a federal investigator found that prospective members were required to pledge "that I will not introduce for membership into this union anyone but a sober, industrious *white* person." The investigator found that in the entire city of Pittsburgh only two unions admitted blacks to membership. They readily "became good unionists," he observed, "but the sentiment seems to be against their becoming members."[38]

The Amalgamated Association of Iron, Steel and Tin Workers set the pattern of racism for unions in Pittsburgh. Although no one was barred from membership because of race, the Amalgamated Association, since its founding in 1876, had made few attempts to recruit or retain black iron and steel workers, and racial exclusion in practice, if not in theory, continued to prevail. During the Great Migration, thousands of blacks poured into the steel industry, but the Amalgamated Association still displayed only hostility or indifference to efforts of the blacks to enter its ranks. As a result, black steel workers came to view the union as their enemy.[39] Richard R. Wright, Jr., a black sociologist, noted in his study of the relations between black workers and the Amalgamated Association that the vicious cycle of union hostility and black anger against the union gave "the opponents of the labor movement a weapon, destined to become more and more powerful, with which to compass the defeat of those plans for the betterment of the conditions of life and work which are cherished by every laboring man, regardless of race or color."[40]

As we shall see in our next volume, the 1919 steel strike proved these words to be prophetic.

## THE CHICAGO PACKINGHOUSE CAMPAIGN

The record of the war years was somewhat better in Chicago, but even there the traditional racism of the AFL national unions and their members limited the unionization of black workers in the great packinghouse drive.

The stockyards, virtually an open shop for over a decade, had witnessed a phenomenal division of labor on, to use labor historian David Brody's play on words, the "disassembly" line.* Until after the Civil War, some

---

*The classic description of life and labor around the packing yards remains Upton Sinclair, *The Jungle*,[New York, 1906], especially pp. 35-46.

yards had entrusted the entire slaughtering process of an animal to a single worker, but by the early twentieth century scores of separate, repeated activities went into the packing trade. As skills were undermined, the jobs became the domain of one or more of the many ethnic groups who crowded the packinghouse neighborhoods.

By 1909, forty-three percent of the workers in the four major centers were from eastern European countries; over one Chicago worker in ten was female, and by 1918 more than twenty percent of the Chicago packing workers were black. For years, most of them had been considered unorganizable. And yet, in a matter of months, they were organized—the first unionized mass production industry in the United States.[41]

Impetus for meatpacking unionization came from an unlikely alliance. William Z. Foster, by this time an unattached syndicalist working as a railway carman in Chicago, later wrote of the simple origins of the movement. "One day as I was walking to work, and I remember well that it was July 11, 1917, it struck me suddenly that perhaps I could get a campaign started to organize the workers in the great Chicago packinghouses."[42*] That night Foster got the approval of the District Council of his Carmen's union: two nights later the Butcher Workmen, a small craft union in the yards, agreed to the plan. On July 15, the two unions obtained approval from the Chicago Federation of Labor to initiate an organizing drive. Within two weeks the Stockyards Labor Council emerged; it was an experiment in federation embracing butchers, carmen, machinists, electricians, coopers, carpenters, office workers, steam fitters, engineers, firemen and other trades with jurisdiction in the yards. With Foster and fellow syndicalist Jack Johnstone as paid organizers, with black organizers supported by the Illinois Federation of Labor, with volunteers from the Chicago Women's Trade Union League, and with two immigrant organizers, one Polish and one Lithuanian (supported, as it turned out, by the

*As we saw in a previous volume, William Z. Foster, a member of the IWW, became convinced, after a year's study of syndicalism in Europe, that the IWW's policy of dual unionism was wrong. Returning to the United States in 1911, he pointed out that the effects of dual unionism were to isolate the militants from the mass of organized workers and to fortify the control of the bureaucracy in the old unions. Foster proposed that the IWW should abandon dual unionism, adopt the policy of "boring-from-within," as successfully applied by the syndicalists in France and England, and devote itself to building the "militant minority" in the old unions in order to revolutionize those bodies. After a lengthy debate, Foster's program was rejected by the IWW. He left the IWW in February 1912, and began the process of "boring-from-within" the AFL by joining the union of his craft, the Brotherhood of Railway Carmen. (Philip S. Foner, *History of the Labor Movement in the United States* 5 [New York, 1965]: 415-34. *See also* Arthur Zipser, *Working Class Giant: The Life of William Z. Foster* [New York, 1981]: 27-37.)

packers and acting as company spies) the Stockyards Labor Council slowly organized, concentrating on minority and unskilled workers. The eight-hour day and the right to organize were the key organizing points from the earliest days.[43]

By November, workers had flocked to the unions. A national meeting of the packinghouse trades was held on November 11, 1917 in Omaha, and a coherent set of demands was drawn up. After the first Butcher Workmen meeting following the Omaha conference, 1,400 workers signed up. By year's end, according to the President's Mediation Commission, between a quarter and a half of all packinghouse employees had joined unions.[44]

When the "Big Five" packers refused to bargain, members at union meetings voted overwhelmingly to authorize a strike. An informal national federation of stockyards unions took shape, headed by John Fitzpatrick, president of the Chicago Federation of Labor, and with William Z. Foster as secretary. But before any strike plans could mature, the Wilson administration pressed for labor peace to insure uninterrupted meat production to fill war orders. On Christmas Day 1917, the unions, the federated trades, and the Big Five signed a no-strike, no-lockout pledge for the duration of the war.[45]

On January 25, 1918, Secretary of Labor William B. Wilson brought labor and management to an initial accord: no preferential union shop, no grievance committees, and no recognition of unions in return for concessions on employment and shop conditions. President Wilson appointed Federal Judge Samuel B. Altschuler to arbitrate all other issues. With members flocking into the unions, Altschuler held hearings in Chicago from February 11 until March 7, 1918. Having heard Frank P. Walsh, John Fitzpatrick, and rank-and-filers present the union's case thoroughly, and with Fitzpatrick worrying aloud that the unions "will be unable to prevent a walkout if the decision is not announced immediately," Altschuler ruled on March 30. He granted, as Foster later reckoned, "85 percent of the union's demands," including the basic eight-hour day with time and a quarter for overtime, and a twenty-minute paid lunch period. A ten percent wage increase was also handed down; along with recognition of the principle of seniority in employment; banning of discrimination in employment and work assignments because of creed, color, or nationality; the abolition of arbitrary dismissal; and proper facilities for dressing rooms, lunchrooms and washrooms.[46]*

*The award was to affect packing plants in Chicago, Kansas City, Sioux City, St. Joseph, St. Louis, East St. Louis, Denver, Oklahoma City, St. Paul, Omaha, and Fort Worth. (William L. Chenery, "Packinghouse Steps Forward," *Survey* 40 [April 13, 1918]: 35-38.)

At an Easter Sunday meeting of 40,000 workers, Fitzpatrick announced the agreement, and added: "It's a new day, and out in God's sunshine you men and women, black and white, have not only an eight-hour day but you are on an equality."[47]

Unfortunately, it did not turn out that way. By November 1918, the Amalgamated Meat Cutters and Butcher Workmen, the major union in packinghouse, was paying per capita to the AFL for 62,857 members— "over twice the number in January 1918, and ten-fold that of January 1916"[48]— but few of the members were black. From the beginning of the organizing drive by the Stockyards Labor Council, it was necessary to overcome the resistance of black workers to unionization, due to the fear that they would be betrayed once the organizing drive was successful.

The campaign also had to overcome the efforts of black politicians and preachers who were subsidized by the packers to keep black workers from joining the unions, and even from forming a company union for black workers only. "Join the American Unity Packers Union," the black agents of the packers appealed in leaflets they distributed among the black workers. "This union does not believe in strikes. We believe all difficulties between labor and capital can be arbitrated. We believe in race solidarity through which Negroes can work for their salvation without anyone else interfering." As Foster later testified before an investigating commission: "We realized that there were two big problems, the organization of the foreign worker and the organization of the colored worker. . . . But we realized that to accomplish the organization of the colored worker was the real problem. . . . We found that we had a tremendous opposition."

Another major obstacle was encountered in the racist provisions of the constitutions and rituals of the stockyard national unions. Foster argued for the elimination of these barriers to the recruitment of black packinghouse workers, but in vain. The Stockyard Labor Council then appealed to Gompers for a solution, and he proposed that the AFL award federal union charters to all-black locals if no serious objections were raised by the national unions.[49]

Despite their dislike for "Jim Crow" locals and the weakness of the federal union structure,* the Stockyards Labor Council succeeded in recruiting a substantial number of black packinghouse workers—estimates vary between 6,000 and 10,000. J. W. Johnstone, secretary of the council,

---

*Affiliated directly with the AFL, the federal labor unions were the neglected stepchildren of the American labor movement. Without a national union to bargain for them, without funds to sustain them when on strike, and subject to raids by craft unions, the federal labor unions could not protect their members' interests. Their life span was generally brief.

repeatedly emphasized that the "non-union Negro is being brought into the yards by the Packers, he must be brought into the Union." Many were enlisted with the promise that they would be transferred later out of the federal labor unions to the locals of their respective crafts. When the AFL unions refused to permit black workers to transfer, many of them simply dropped out of the federal unions.[50] Despite the gains won in the Altschuler award, black packinghouse workers were unwilling to remain in "Jim Crow" unions. The unwillingness of the Amalgamated Meat Cutters and Butcher Workmen to accept them on the same terms as white workers only strengthened the hands of the employers and their agents, who could thus present black workers with genuine reasons for resisting unionization.

"We know there are unions in the American Federation of Labor that have their feet in the 20th century and their heads in the 16th century," Secretary Johnstone of the Stockyards Labor Council said in apologizing to black workers for the necessity of organizing them in separate unions. But black workers were tired of explanations, which only confirmed their belief that white unionists permitted racist prejudice to stand in the way even of their own interests.[51]

## BLACK WOMEN AND THE UNIONS

The successful recruitment of women workers in packinghouse was a vital factor in the great victory won in the Altschuler award. The Stockyards Labor Council, the Chicago Federation of Labor, and the Chicago Women's Trade Union League had worked effectively together in the organizational drive in which the demand for equal pay for men and women was a strong factor in recruiting women. Black women, however, benefitted little, for while the unions in packinghouse had agreed, as we have seen, to eliminate bars against women during the war emergency, the combined efforts of the Urban League, the Chicago and Illinois Federations of Labor, and the Women's Trade Union League "accomplished little toward persuading unions to lower their color bars." Even the federal labor unions for black packinghouse workers were for men only![52]

This, unfortunately, was the common experience of black women workers during the war. While, as we have seen, the relations of white women with organized labor were subject to fairly wide variations, black women were uniformly excluded from nearly all unions.[53]

"Unions don't mean anything to colored people," said a thirty-year-old black woman doing clerical work in a Chicago mail order establishment, when asked by an investigator what trade unionism meant to her and others like her.[54] This did not mean that black women did not understand the value of trade unionism. A black hospital worker in Chicago told an investigator that she had decided to become a nurse after she saw that nurses in her hospital had a union and realized "just how much they can mean to people. They usually make the employers do the right thing by the people; unless the nurses asked too much, they got what they wanted." She decided to take "nurse training" when she saw "how square" the nurses were with each other, "and how the union made them pull together, regardless of whether or not they liked each other. . . . The unions . . . make you treat the other fellow right regardless how you feel toward her." She knew she would not be able to join the nurses' union because of her color, but she hoped to organize black nurses when she completed her training.[55]

The Women's Trade Union League, which had made very little effort to organize black women before World War I, tried to make up for its past neglect as black women now replaced many white women who moved from the traditional women's trades into the better-paying defense jobs. Articles and editorials in *Life and Labor*, the League's official journal, demanded equal opportunity and equal treatment for black females; they were appointed to various League positions and were granted scholarships to the League's labor school.[56]

Appeals were directed to AFL unions to organize black women, and Mildred Rankin, a black social worker, was appointed to direct a national office of Colored Women Workers. But it all added up to very little. One reason was that the effort to unionize black women was inadequately supported because of financial problems. But the major obstacle was the same as that confronting black men: the racism of the AFL and most of its affiliated unions.

With several "colored organizers," Rankin went to the Berkeley and Portsmouth areas of Virginia to try to organize black women there, most of whom were "cooks, day workers, home laundresses, nurse maids," in the hope of forming them into "Federal unions now until there should be enough locals to form a National." But the rebuffs that black male workers in the area were receiving from the AFL convinced her that the plan would get nowhere, and she abandoned the idea. She also evidently abandoned a WTUL plan to form "a colored Women's Trade Union League." It was "too late" for a segregated movement, she informed Margaret Dreier Robins, president of the National Women's Trade Union League.[57]

## THE WOMEN WAGE-EARNERS' ASSOCIATION

An effort by socially minded middle class black women to organize and protect black workingwomen led to the formation of the Women Wage-Earners' Association, with Jeanette Carter as president, Julia F. Coleman as secretary, and Mary Church Terrell, one of the foremost black women of the twentieth century* as treasurer. The association, centered in the nation's capital, sought to unite black workingwomen, with its "main object . . . to better the working hours and the housing and wage-earning conditions of our women, in all lines of work." Recognizing that it would be difficult to bring such women into existing trade unions, the Association hoped to achieve this goal by lectures that would show them how to help themselves while the organization was seeking to persuade the unions to change their policies.[58]

Supported by the black weekly, the *Norfolk Journal and Guide*, domestic servants, housemaids, waitresses, nurses, and tobacco stemmers jointly formed a branch of the Women Wage-Earners' Association and, six hundred strong, demanded improvement in their conditions and increases in their wages to meet the rising cost of living.[59] Three hundred of them were tobacco stemmers employed by the American Cigar Company, and they demanded an increase in wages from 70 cents to $1.50 per day, and recognition of the Association as their bargaining agent. When the company rejected the demands, the black women struck on September 5, 1917.[60] The *Norfolk Journal and Guide* endorsed the walkout and argued in an editorial:

> In view of the present living conditions, *The Journal and Guide* is of the opinion that there are justice and reason in the demand of the women. We do not believe that under present conditions any adult laborer, man or woman, can subsist upon much less than the factory women are asking. The average woman who works in the factory of the American Cigar Company has to provide every week for house rent, for food, fuel, clothing, insurance, Church dues and incidentals. The items will run about as follows:

|  |  |
|---|---|
| House rent | $1.00 |
| Food | 3.50 |
| Fuel | .75 |
| Clothing | 1.00 |
| Insurance | .25 |
| Church dues | .25 |
| Lodge dues | .25 |
| Incidentals | .25 |
|  | $7.25 |

*Active in work among black women, Ms. Terrell was elected first president of the National Association of Colored Women. At the age of eighty-nine she was still fighting Jim Crow in Washington.

At $1.25 a day, the women would earn $6.87 a week, as the working time at the factory is 5½ days.

Even if a woman is married or has other working members in her family her pro rata of house rent cannot fall below $1.00 per week, nor fuel allowance less that 75¢ with slab wood selling at $8 per cord and coal at $9.50 per ton. . . . So in view of these conditions it appears to us that there are both justice and reason in the demands that the striking tobacco stemmers are making for a living wage.[61]

Simultaneously with the strike of the tobacco stemmers, the domestic servants—including cooks, maids, waitresses, and laundresses—decided jointly to ask for a minimum wage of $1 per day, with some modifications in working time. At the same time, the oyster shuckers, most of them husbands and brothers of the tobacco stemmers, went on strike, demanding an increase in wages. "Labor unrest among the colored people of Norfolk has been literally brought home to every household in the city," cried the *Norfolk Ledger Dispatch,* a white daily. The *Virginian-Pilot*, another white paper, reported more calmly: "Norfolk is experiencing an unusual situation in labor circles." But it added the ominous report, with its portent of impending force and intimidation:

LOCAL POLICE BUSY

C. C. Kizer, chief of the Norfolk police department, is also beginning to take a hand in the labor situation. He has detailed a special squad of plainclothes men for this particular duty. The squad is instructed, too, to prevent "loafing" among the colored men and women. All industrial "slackers" reported by them will find themselves in the position of defendants before the police justice.[62]

The police, the paper added, were also asking for a government investigation of the Women Wage-Earners' Association to determine if it was a device to interfere with the war effort. The enraged *Journal and Guide* editorialized:

The police department was not sent out to round up and arrest as slackers and loafers the three thousand white men who quit work in the navy yard because an increase in pay was denied them. No government sleuths and legal sharps were sent down to pry into the charter provisions of the unions to which the men belong. . . . The women are asking for BREAD, WHY GIVE THEM STONE?[63]

The appeal fell on deaf ears. The strikers were arrested as "slackers," while efforts to obtain support from the white trade unions of the city brought no response. By the first week of November, not only were the strikes broken, but the Norfolk branch of the Women Wage-Earners'

Association had disappeared, to be followed within six months by the disbanding of the entire association.[64]

## OTHER INDEPENDENT BLACK UNIONS

The Women Wage-Earners' Association was one of the independent organizations of black workers formed during the war to provide black wage-earners with some sort of protection in their dealings with their employers and at the same time to help in counteracting the discriminatory policies of the white unions.

Independent black unions had existed before World War I but had enjoyed little success. In 1902, the Colored Locomotive Firemen's Association was formed in Georgia, but it never amounted to more than a small benefit society. The National Association of Afro-American Steam and Gas Engineers and Skilled Laborers, founded in 1903 in Pittsburgh, had three locals in that city, and gained the recognition of the city's central labor body. However, it was unable to achieve much in the way of benefits for its members, and it soon disappeared.[65]

The AFL's indifference to black workers during the war, together with the long-established ban against black members by the Railroad Brotherhoods, gave rise to new independent black labor organizations. Many were local bodies, such as those of the sheet metal workers in South Carolina; the plumbers, lathe operators, and electricians in Chicago; the hod carriers and waiters in Baltimore; the asphalt workers in Milwaukee; the elevator operators in New York; and the Pullman porters in Philadelphia. None of them were notably effective. They included at most only a few hundred workers and met with hostility from white trade unions, which, while unwilling to open their ranks to blacks, would not tolerate the operation of black unions within their jurisdiction. When the latter were forced to strike to win their demands, they rarely received support from white unions.[66]

The one area in which an independent black organization attained some effectiveness during the war was that of those railroad occupations in which black labor predominated. There, unions were organized in protest against the exclusion of blacks by the Railroad Brotherhoods and the railway departments of the AFL. In 1913, black workers in the railway mail service, excluded by the AFL's Railway Mail Association, formed the National Alliance of Postal Employees. Two years later, a broader independent union of black railroad workers—the Railwaymen's International Benevolent and Industrial Association—was established. Its purpose was to organize all black railway workers, regardless of craft or skill, into one big union.

Prior to America's entry into the war, the Association had fewer than a hundred members. But when the federal government took over the railroads and in return for organized labor's support of the war effort gave its backing to organization in the industry, the association grew rapidly. By 1920, at its peak, it claimed 15,000 members in 187 locals, and its president, R. L. Mays, asserted that the organization represented every grade of black worker on the roads. As a result of the Association's protests to the U. S. Railroad Association about discrimination in wages caused by the failure of the USRA to apply General Orders No. 8 and 27, black firemen, trainmen, and switchmen were awarded the same wage rights as whites, and Pullman porters and dining-car employees received wage increases.[67] Under the stimulus of these advances, the Railwaymen's International Benevolent and Industrial Association and a few lesser black unions grew rapidly. But, as will be recalled, the RIBIA, the NAACP, and the National Urban League were unable to force the USRA to open the more skilled jobs on the railroads to blacks.

The establishment of a black federation of labor was attempted in July 1917, when the Colored Employees of America (CEA) was formed in New York City. In a booklet entitled "A Message From the North to Negroes," the new organization appealed to migrants from the South to join its ranks as a way of obtaining information about the best employment opportunities available and as a basis for building unions of black workers. Branches of the CEA were to be established in every city with a black population over 5,000, but the organization seems to have disappeared after the summer of 1917.[68]

## RANDOLPH, OWEN, AND *THE MESSENGER*

Meanwhile, two young black Socialists, A. Philip Randolph and Chandler Owen, had been busy organizing blacks in the hotels and apartment houses in New York City into the United Brotherhood of Elevator and Switchboard Operators. Within three weeks after they began they had recruited 600 of the 10,000 black elevator operators in the city. The group immediately put forth demands for an eight-hour day, weekly pay, and a minimum wage of $13. A strike was planned to attain these goals, but it never materialized. The union grew to 2,000, changed its name to the Elevator Operators and Starters Union, and received a federal charter from the AFL. But it, too, soon disappeared.[69]

Randolph and Owen had been editors of a trade journal published by the Headwaiters and Sidewaiters Society of Greater New York. They were forced to resign because the headwaiter elements in the society objected to their tendency to comment critically on the sidewaiters' poor wages and unfavorable working conditions. Randolph and Owen then established their own journal, *The Messenger*, to promote labor unionism and Socialism among black workers.[70]

*The Messenger*, published monthly in Harlem, viewed the black situation as the "great labor problem of America." Since 99 percent of black people were working people, it advocated that they support the Socialist Party, the only political organization that represented the American working class. In this way, black workers, like white workers, would eventually establish a "co-operative commonwealth" in which the ownership of the means of production would be in the hands of the people. But *The Messenger* did not overlook the possibility of improvements under capitalism. Beginning with its first issue in November 1917, it launched a vigorous campaign to educate black workers on the importance of united labor organization. Noting that capitalism drew no color line in exploiting the working class, it concluded that the workers must, out of self interest, unite on the same basis to end exploitation. The solution was to organize every worker in industry, black and white.[71]

At first Randolph and Owen held out some hope for seeing black workers in the AFL. The 1917 convention of that body was even applauded for having displayed "considerable sanity in adopting a resolution calling for the appointment of Negro delegates to organize locals to affiliate with the A.F. of L., a necessary but belated move."[72] But when negotiations between the leaders of the National Urban League and the AFL ended in 1918 without results, Randolph and Owen had had their fill of the AFL. Neither had expected anything substantial to come out of the negotiations—it was hardly logical, after all, for the Urban League, financed by open-shop millionaires like Rockefeller, Carnegie and Armour, to fight hard for the welfare of black workers—but the cold shoulder given to the black leaders was the last straw.[73]

As *The Messenger* saw it, the AFL was too fossilized to hold out any hope for black workers. Hence, their future lay, rather, with the Industrial Workers of the World. In 1917 the IWW initiated a drive to recruit members in the factories and mills of the East, especially the thousands of new black workers from the South. Their appeals were endorsed by *The Messenger*, which enthusiastically predicted that the IWW, augmented "with a million and a half or two million Negroes," would "fairly rival the American Federation of Labor."[74]

But the IWW never did rival the AFL. While its membership grew at first after the U.S. entered the war, as a result of activities in organizing the unorganized and improving working conditions, the war crisis, as we shall see, gave employers and the government the long-awaited opportunity to destroy the IWW, and the Wobblies' opposition to the war was used as the device to achieve that goal. The result was that black workers had only the AFL to look to for organization into trade unions.

It was anything but an encouraging prospect. "The Negro Worker," a poem published in the Seattle *Union Record* and reprinted in *The Messenger*, viewed the record of the AFL and its affiliates as World War I drew to a close, and observed sadly but correctly:

> *I wonder why*
> *They are so shortsighted,*
> *As not to realize*
> *That every time*
> *They keep ANY WORKER,*
> *Man or Woman,*
> *White or yellow, or black,*
> *OUT of a UNION,*
> *They are forcing a worker*
> *To be a SCAB,*
> *To be used AGAINST THEM?*[75]

# CHAPTER 12

# IWW Organizing During the War: The Lumber Industry

The Industrial Workers of the World (IWW) had existed for twelve years before U.S. entry into World War I. It was founded in Chicago in June 1905 by the leaders of various radical trade unions and political parties, such as the Western Federation of Miners, the United Metal Workers, the Socialist Party of America, and the Socialist Labor Party. The IWW brought together workers who believed in the class struggle and were dissatisfied with the class collaborationist, craft unionist ideology of the American Federation of Labor. It was organized along industrial rather than craft lines and believed in the organization of all workers regardless of skill, sex, color, or race. On this basis, the IWW attracted thousands of unorganized workers.*

## EARLY IWW VICTORIES AND DEFEATS

In its first years, the IWW split several times over ideological issues and personal animosities. One after another, the Socialist Party (1906), the Western Federation of Labor (1907), and the Socialist Labor Party (1908) separated or were separated from the IWW. From 1908 to 1917, the Chicago group led by Vincent St. John was the real IWW, as distinguished from the Detroit group led by Daniel De Leon.

Small numbers of Wobblies were capable of achieving spectacular results, such as the great strike of the textile workers in Lawrence, Massachusetts in 1912. With a local union of only 287 members, the IWW was able to lead 30,000 workers, keep them on strike for several months, and

*Among many studies of the IWW are: Philip S. Foner, *History of the Labor Movement in the United States*, 4, New York, 1965: (The Industrial Workers of the World, 1905-1917); Melvyn Dubofsky, *We Shall Be All: A History of the Industrial Workers of the World*, Chicago, 1969; and *Patrick Renshaw, The Wobblies: The Story of Syndicalism in the United States*, New York, 1968.

win wage increases of up to 25 percent when the mill owners finally surrendered. Its militancy and ability to organize immigrant workers in the industrial centers of the East, migratory workers in the lumber and agricultural camps and fields in the West, and black and white timber workers in the deep South, as well as its spectacular free speech fights, made the IWW an internationally famous organization.

The IWW reached a prewar peak in 1912, the year of the great Lawrence strike and the San Diego free speech fight, with an average membership for the year of between eighteen and nineteen thousand. The 1913 defeat in Paterson, N.J. and the economic depression that followed almost killed the IWW. The 1914 annual convention found practically no activity by the organization, especially in the East, where, apart from the Italian bakers in New York and the black and white longshoremen in Philadelphia, the IWW appeared dead. So poor were the prospects and so desperate the need for finances and members, that the 1914 convention saw Vincent St. John, incumbent secretary-treasurer, decline to run for renomination to the highest post in the IWW.

In this situation, Frank Little, an Indian IWW organizer and member of the General Executive Board, came to the rescue. He suggested during the convention that "some means should be taken for concerted and efficient action in the harvest fields next year." It was proposed that a conference be called of members from various locals bordering the harvest district, and that this body determine ways and means "for harmonious grouping of hitherto spasmodic efforts of harvest organization." A resolution embodying Little's proposal was carried; a few months after the convention, William D. ("Big Bill") Haywood, newly elected secretary-treasurer, announced the establishment of a Bureau of Migratory Workers to plan the conference, coordinate information on jobs, and stimulate the organization of the harvest workers. Out of this planning there emerged in 1915 the Agricultural Workers Organization (AWO No. 400), which pulled the IWW back from the edge of oblivion.

We have described in detail elsewhere the AWO's success in the middle western wheat belt.* We also saw that by 1916 Haywood was urging more and more that soap-boxing and free speech fights be soft-pedalled, while upgrading the IWW's activities as an effective labor organization. "On the eve of America's entry into the First World War," Melvyn Dubofsky notes, "the IWW stood poised to open a new and more successful chapter in its history."[1] As we shall see, in the end the war was to fatally affect the

*Foner, *op. cit.*, 4: 474-85.

outcome of that chapter, but it also opened up new opportunities for effective organizing efforts.

## A NEW LEASE ON LIFE

By late 1916 and early 1917, the Wobblies no longer had much of a base in the East, except among the Philadelphia longshoremen (mostly blacks) and in a few other scattered places. In the grain belt, IWW activity was lagging,* but the overall campaigns in the middle west were a source of both new members and considerable finances, which could be used in attempts to organize other industries. The IWW branched out into the iron and copper mines, the oil fields, and the lumber camps and mills. On September 1, 1917, it had between 90,000 and 105,000 paid-up members. According to the Chicago *Daily Tribune* and the New York *Call*, its income between April 1 and September 1, 1917 totaled $176,297.34. This was divided as follows: initiation fees, $63,647.75; dues, $75,419.75; and income from other sources, $37,729.84. Approximately 32,000 new members were recruited during that five month period.[2]

The increase in IWW income came largely from successful organizing campaigns during the spring and summer of 1917 in the copper mining industry of Montana and Arizona and the lumber industry of the Northwest. These organizing efforts differed from most of the IWW's earlier strikes. They were not spontaneous walkouts, in which the IWW was called in after the workers had gone out, and they did not peter out into free speech fights, which diverted attention, time, and energy from the struggle to raise wages, reduce hours, and improve working conditions. Rather, they represented unified action by groups of workers who joined the Wobblies to present a series of demands to their employers, and fought effectively through the IWW to redress their grievances.

The *New York Times*, in the course of a lengthy survey of IWW activity during the summer of 1917 which attributed the most sinister motives to the Wobblies for their organizing drive, declared on July 13, 1917: "Disturbances fomented admittedly by the IWW and spreading into various branches of industry, carry with them in virtually every instance a demand for higher wages." But the *Times* joined the rest of the press and both employers and government in attributing IWW strikes to the desire of the

---

*One reason was the fact that the Nonpartisan League began to grow rapidly in 1917 in the Dakotas, Minnesota and the whole grain belt. Organized in 1915 by A. C. Townley, it grew sensationally. Although the IWW did not endorse political action or support the political campaigns of the League, many individual IWW members did work with the League and helped organize League branches.

Wobblies to help the Germans; it also charged that they were financed by German gold.* This, in turn, provided the rationale for the use of all types of strikebreaking activities, both legal and extra-legal. "The worker in the United States who goes on strike with the IWW as his leader takes his life and the lives of his family in his hands," wrote John Reed.[3] Employers who feared and hated the IWW could now demand that the government destroy it in the name of patriotism. And even as they did so, they insisted that they were not fighting a legitimate labor organization, but rather "Imperial Wilhelm's Warriors." Anti-labor violence, vigilanteism, and government-sponsored tactics to repress strikes—all of which would have been denounced as brutal by liberals in prewar days—became acceptable means of maintaining war production.

In one respect, however, there was no change. Before the war, the American Federation of Labor leadership had cooperated with employers, vigilantes, and state and local governments in the effort to destroy the IWW. After the United States entered the war, this continued and, if anything, with greater intensity.

Thus, when the IWW began to function more than ever before as an effective labor union in organizing the lumber and mining industries, applying the lessons it had learned from past experiences to improve its tactics and strategy,** the Wobblies had to confront an alliance of big business, government, and the AFL—all of whom took advantage of the wartime hysteria in order to defeat their campaigns and destroy their organization.

## CONDITIONS IN THE LUMBER INDUSTRY

Success in the harvest fields led the IWW to start new efforts to organize the lumber workers. Sponsored and financially supported at first by the Agricultural Workers' Organization, a convention was held on March 4, 1917 in Spokane, Washington. One month before America's entry into the

*According to the *New York Times*, after U.S. entry into the war, a major concentration of the IWW in the East was among the oil tanker crews and longshoremen in Bayonne, N.J., and it attributed a number of strikes on the tankers in that port "which approached the seriousness of a mutiny," to the influence of the Wobblies, who were "working for Germany." (Sept. 8, 1917.)

**However, long-held views of the IWW with regard to such matters as contracts and dues checkoffs were not entirely abandoned. The IWW local in Bisbee, Arizona, composed of copper miners, passed a resolution in July 1917 criticizing contracts and dues checkoff as "detrimental to the workers whenever it has been in operation," and resolved further "to oppose the contract and checkoff system and refuse to support any move to obtain one." (*Arizona Daily Star*, July 6, 1917.)

war, Lumber Workers' Industrial Union No. 500 was launched. The union had 6,000 members at the time of its founding convention, where plans were laid for a strike in the Spokane district with demands for an eight-hour day, $60 a month and board, better living and working conditions, and union recognition.

Reacting to the IWW, the AFL revived its moribund Shingle Weavers' and Timber Workers' Union at a convention in April, and formulated demands for an eight-hour day with ten-hours' wages and better sanitary conditions in the camps. These demands were announced together with the threat of a strike if they were not granted.[4]

Time and conditions were ripe for union organization in the lumber industry. Prices had risen considerably since the war began, but neither wages nor conditions had kept pace. The Portland *Oregonian* reported a 500 percent increase in the price of spruce, while wages had remained almost stationary.[5]

Lumber workers still worked ten hours or more a day and six days a week for $1.50 a day, from which board, a commissary charge, and a fee for the employment agency would be withheld. Even this does not accurately reflect the lumber workers' income, because the logging season averaged less than six months per year. In the camp cookhouses the staples fed to the workers were beans, dried peas, and bread, with occasional treats of salt pork, dried prunes, or apples.

In the evening, in company with thirty to fifty others, the lumberjack would hang his wet pants and sweaty wool socks over the pot-bellied bunkhouse stove and play cribbage by the light of a kerosene lamp, while the air turned blue with tobacco smoke and lack of ventilation. He bedded down early in one of the double-decked bunks that solidly lined the walls. "In one camp investigated in 1917," notes Robert L. Tyler, "eighty men crammed into one crude barrack built to accommodate fewer than half that number. The building had no windows, and the doors at either end furnished the only ventilation. When the men pressed into their bunks for the night, they closed the doors against the cold, stoked up the stoves, and went to sleep 'under groundhog conditions.' In another study of logging camps made during the winter of 1917-1918, the investigators discovered that half the camps had only crude wooden bunks, half had no bathing facilities, and half were infested with bedbugs."[6]

Sickness dogged the crowded bunkhouses. In winter it was colds and grippe. In summer the whole camp grew weak from diarrhea, caused by millions of flies that made unhindered trips from the stables and doorless outhouses to the cookshack. When a man was injured, he might lie in his bunk for days with only the volunteer care of his fellows, though at times he might be allowed a horse to take him to town.

The lumberjack was often cheated or overcharged by the commissary. If he aroused the anger of the foreman, he could be fired without pay and blacklisted as a troublemaker. If he quit, his pay had to wait till the spring log drive came in, at which time the lumber company might honor his request at the sawmill office.[7]

It is hardly surprising that when the IWW agricultural section sent organizers into the woods in 1916, the loggers welcomed them. The traveling delegate carried dues stamps and books with him to sign up the men in the camps, and when the on-the-job delegate was discovered by the boss and run out, he either left an already operating core of Wobblies, or made arrangements to send in another organizer with the next batch of newly hired workers.

A Wobbly organizer recalled that the "time and conditions were favorable" for the IWW campaign. The logging industry was profiting from the war in Europe, but "conditions in the woods were deplorable. The same bunk houses that had sheltered the logger for thirty years were provided for his habitation. The speed-up system was at its height and the employment shark was waging his war on the incomes of the men.* Prohibition had robbed the workers of their sedative,** so they had to face the facts as they were. The field was ripe for the harvest and the (IWW) job delegate was the reaper."[8]

## THE BIG STRIKE OF 1917 BEGINS

Following the formation of the Lumber Workers' Union No. 500, strike activity began in north Idaho, and spread to the Montana spring log drive, through the short-log country of Montana, Idaho and eastern Washington, and thence swiftly into the long-log country west of the Cascades in western Washington, western Oregon and northern California. On June 20, 1917, the organizing committee of Lumber Workers' Industrial Union No. 500 issued the following statement:

*Employment sharks were hiring agencies in Spokane, Missoula, Portland, or Seattle through which the logging companies hired the lumberjacks and with whom they often had agreements to share the fees paid by the workers. Many times, after a day in camp, a lumberjack would be fired because between the boss and the employment agency, his job had been sold again.

**The 18th (Prohibition) Amendment was ratified in 1920, but prior to 1920, many states, including those in the Northwest, had enacted laws forbidding the manufacture, transportation, or sale of beverages for intoxicating purposes.

After careful consideration, it has been decided . . . in pursuance of instructions by the General Convention of Lumber Workers, assembled in Spokane, last March, to call a general strike of all workers in the woods and mills. Now is the time to strike to enforce the demands of the I.W.W. . . . Owing to the comparative scarcity of men and the large amount of orders the lumber companies have on hand, we have an opportunity such as we never had before to shorten hours, raise wages and improve conditions.[9]

For the first time, the lumber companies united and formed the Lumbermen's Protective Association, with a $500,000 fund to fight the union drive. The Association took a hard line in defense of the existing conditions in the industry. A fine of $500 per day was to be levied against any mill or camp operating at less than ten hours, and any companies not members of the Association that reduced working hours were to be cut off from all credit and trade. The association resolved

that the establishment of an 8-hour day in the lumber industry at this time when production in all manufacturing industries must be maintained at the maximum is impossible, and that employers therein pledge themselves unequivocally to maintain a 10-hour day for the purpose of maintaining maximum production by the lumber industry.[10]

The IWW responded by extending its big strike of 1917. On July 13, 1917, the Portland *Oregonian* carried the following report:

A general strike in the logging camps and mills of Hoquiam and the Grays Harbor district to take effect tomorrow morning, was called without warning tonight by the Industrial Workers of the World. The strike is to go into effect at 8 o'clock tomorrow morning.

No demands have been presented by the Industrial Workers as an organization and in the call for the strike no demands are set forth except for an eight-hour day.

Later, the *Oregonian* reported that the Wobblies "wanted a minimum wage of $3.50 a day with free hospital service. They wanted each man in the lumber camps to have a separate bed with linen sheets and pillow slips, and they wanted shower-baths erected in connection with sleeping quarters. They also demanded that the timber operators refuse to hire non-union men." However, the *Industrial Worker*, the official western organ of the IWW, listed the demands as an eight-hour day; no work on Sundays or holidays; $60 a month for lumber workers and $3.50 a day for sawmill hands; satisfactory food in porcelain dishes with no overcrowding at dining tables; sanitary kitchens and sleeping quarters with a maximum of twelve in each bunk house; single spring beds and mattresses with clean and adequate bedding to be furnished free of charge; drying rooms, shower baths, and adequate lighting in the bunk houses; free hospital services; semi-monthly payment by bank check with no discount; no employment of anyone under sixteen around a sawmill; and no discrimination against members of the IWW.[11] The demand relating to payment of wages sought to do away with the practice of paying wages in script, which was discounted when exchanged for regular currency.

The call to strike was an immediate success. "Thousands took out cards [in the IWW]," wrote one observer. "At once the things that could be enjoyed together by the workers seemed the most desirable to have. Better conditions, a dry-house, a bath-house, sheets and pillows, spring beds, everything that made for comfort and cleanliness, and was desired by a man who had but a short time before had given little thought to anything but debauchery and individual advantage." IWW sources asserted that the walkout involved between 40,000 and 50,000 men.[12]

## ANTI-IWW TERROR

For six weeks much of the northwest lumber production remained tied up as employers experimented with laws, police, sheriffs, the National Guard and U.S. Army, attorneys, and federal officials to break the IWW. Idaho, where the big strike of 1917 began, passed criminal syndicalist and anti-sabotage laws that were frankly acknowledged as designed to "protect the business people in the state from the malicious and destructive activities of the IWW." The law literally made strike activity subject to confinement in the state prison for not more than ten years or to a fine of not more than $5 thousand, or both. The Idaho Council of Defense urged Governor Moses Alexander to declare martial law and call in federal troops, and when he refused, former Idaho Governor Frank A. Gooding suggested the formation of citizen groups for "protection of life and property." As a matter of fact, vigilante groups were already operating, rounding up IWW strikers and driving them out of town. Arrested without charge by local sheriffs, scores of strikers were kept in "bull pens." After a few weeks, they were charged with criminal syndicalism.

Wherever the strike spread, Wobblies were arrested, beaten, and deported; but the strike front remained solid. On July 15, the State Supreme Court of Washington issued an injunction against picketing in the Grays Harbor area, but picket lines continued and the mills remained shut. Governor Lister thereupon sent in the National Guard to break the strike, and when that failed, the Army was given the task. IWW strikers were arrested and herded into internment camps and jails; no charges were preferred against the prisoners, and they were denied the right to confer with attorneys.[13]

Wobblies were well versed in how to behave in jail, and they applied the traditional techniques of IWW prisoners. They pounded mess kits against the bars, went on hunger strikes, wound blankets around the bars and bent them out of shape, yelled and sang Wobbly songs, refused to work, and applied other techniques they had learned in the great IWW free-speech fights.[14]*

Although a few mills did open with Army protection, all camps in the area were closed tight under the vigilant watch of roving picket lines, and no logs were available.[15]

The lumber company owners made a distinction between, on the one hand the mills and shipyards—where they recognized, they said, the "legitimate demand of organized and unorganized laborers for higher wages and shorter hours,"—and on the other camps, where the "agitation of the I.W.W. evangelists rather than legitimate grievances was the cause of the strike." They charged that the Wobblies had called the general strike in the lumber industry to hinder the war effort, pointing out that spruce was essential for use in airplanes. "Tools of the Germans," "Injuring the War Effort," "Imperial Wilhelm's Warriors," were headline material in the northwest press and spilled over into other parts of the country and into the *Congressional Record*. Forest fires raged in Montana and Idaho, and although the Wobblies were the most active among the firefighters, the IWW was accused of setting the fires. Sabotage of every type was laid at the door of the Wobblies.[16]

Just two days before the IWW lumber workers went out on strike, the story of the Bisbee deportation had been reported in the press. On August 1, Frank Little, the IWW organizer in the mining fields of Butte, Montana, was lynched by citizen-police and vigilantes.** The press in the northwest reported these events gleefully and recommended that similar steps be taken against the lumber strikers and their leaders. Governor Lister of Washington actually proposed a statewide organization of vigilantes, called the "Patriotic League," with a branch in every county, to deal with the Wobblies in the Bisbee-Little manner.[17]

Despite the terror, the strike front remained solid, and three weeks after

*For a description of IWW jail techniques, *see* Philip S. Foner, *History of the Labor Movement in the United States* 4 (1965): 537-39.

**The Bisbee deportation and the murder of Frank Little are discussed in the next chapter.

the first men had walked off their jobs, the *Oregonian* reported from Grays Harbor:

> Although the strike which is tying up the lumber industry of this section is now nearing the close of the third week, the strikers are firm and no sign of a possible settlement has appeared. Of Gray's Harbor's 25 mills, only eight are in operation. Of her camps only three are running and all four shipyards . . . are closed down. It is estimated that 5,600 men are idle as a result of the strike.[18]

The reference to the closing down of shipyards was a reflection of the fact that strikes proliferated in the northwest shipyards as a result of a secondary boycott of "ten-hour lumber" by the workers in the yards.[19]

## THE EMPLOYERS REFUSE TO SETTLE

On July 30, the first break in the employers' front occurred when five mills in Tacoma agreed to institute an eight-hour day. Crews were quickly enlisted while other mills in the area remained closed. But those plants that did settle found themselves unable to obtain either credit at banks or services from other lumber owners who were members of the employers' association. The move to settle was stopped in its tracks.[20]

The AFL had played little part in the strike. It either encouraged scabbing against the IWW,[21] or stood by and tried to enlist members, then appealed to the owners for recognition as a moderate alternative to the IWW. At the suggestion of Samuel Gompers, the president of the Washington State Federation of Labor served on an investigating committee that warned against "the subversive IWW." Government negotiators brought AFL representatives and employers together in an attempt to work out a compromise or to arbitrate the dispute. The AFL agreed to arbitration, but the employers refused even to present their case, insisting they had nothing to arbitrate since it was impossible to institute an eight-hour day in their industry.[22] A leader of the lumbermen's association, in an interview with Robert Bruere, stated that

> . . . in war—and a strike is war—anything is fair. We have fought the IWW, we would have fought any attempt of the AFL unions to control the workers in the camps. And, of course, we have taken advantage of the general prejudice against them as an unpatriotic organization to beat their strike. But we have been consistently opposed to collective agreements with either the IWW or the AFL, and we are opposed to the recognition of any labor organization.[23]

Melvyn Dubofsky has observed that the employers had as little use for negotiating with the "patriotic" AFL as with the "pro-German" IWW.[24]

On August 12, 1917, the Portland *Oregonian* reported that the governors of the states affected by the strike had investigated the conflict and found the IWW menace to be greatly exaggerated. However, this had no effect on the employers' campaign to break the strike. All they said in response was that they would have nothing to do with an "unlawful and treasonable organization—the Industrial Workers of the World."[25]

They made the same response to a proposal by Secretary of War Newton D. Baker. Noting that the lumber industry was the only major industry in the Northwest that was not on an eight-hour day, Baker requested that it grant the eight-hour day. But the lumbermen turned down the request, even though it would have settled the strike, and continued to claim that the IWW was holding up the war effort by prolonging the strike. In fact, these "patriotic" lumbermen announced that they were prepared to allow their plants to stay closed for the remainder of the year rather than come to any agreement with the IWW, since "it is part of their propaganda that upon returning to work it shall not be with the intention of abiding loyally by the results of the compact, but rather with the view of further disorganization."[26]

This was too much even for Washington's Governor Lister. He personally asked the lumbermen to immediately grant the eight-hour day and higher wages and bring the strike to an end. Lister pointed out:

> While it may be true that the so-called I.W.W. organization has had much to do with strikes in the lumber industry, I cannot agree with you in the proposition that all of the present trouble can be attributed to organizers of the I.W.W., or that no favorable results can be attained by acceding to some of the demands of those who are now on strike. There are thousands of men who would, in my opinion, immediately return to work if the eight-hour day were granted by the employers.
>
> It seems to me that one of the best methods to pursue in bringing about a solution of the I.W.W. problem, to which you refer, is to concede to those employed in the lumber industry the points for which they ask and which in justice ought to be granted, and thus alienate from their leaders, to whom you refer, thousands of followers, who are only followers for the reason they have felt that the only way to obtain concessions was to affiliate with this organizaton.[27]

But the employers made no distinction between "the IWW agitators" and the rank-and-file strikers, and they refused to join the governor in trying to influence the strikers to abandon their Wobbly leaders and return to work by granting them their main demand—the eight-hour day. And as the IWW was quick to point out: "The police were never sent around to club the owners because they wouldn't cooperate with the government."[28]

## INTENSIFICATION OF ANTI-IWW TERROR

The terror launched against the strikers by the police, sheriffs and their deputies, vigilantes, the National Guard, and the U.S. Army was soon to reach a climax. James Rowan, strike leader at the IWW headquarters in Spokane, had issued an ultimatum demanding the immediate release of prisoners of the "class war," and threatening a general strike in all industries "if all I.W.W. prisoners are not released before August twentieth." On August 19, Rowan and twenty-six other Wobbly leaders were arrested; the IWW regional headquarters in Spokane was closed, and martial law was proclaimed in Spokane and its environs. One unheard of feature of this series of events: with Washington state Governor Lister's approval, Idaho Governor Alexander dispatched a company of Idaho national guardsmen to Spokane, and it was the Idaho troops who "took charge" of the IWW headquarters and arrested the members of the organization, including Rowan. Meanwhile, in Idaho, Governor Alexander, yielding to the lumber companies, called for federal troops.[29]

The general strike took place on August 20, but, under the circumstances, it proved to be a failure. This did not, however, end martial law in Spokane or the continuation of arrests of Wobblies and their sympathizers.[30]

On August 28, the Portland *Evening Telegram*, reporting that the strike was still solid, estimated that although the war effort demanded 8 million feet of lumber every month from the Northwest, the Wobblies were holding production down to 2 million feet. The solution, the newspaper declared, was for the federal government to use its full force against the IWW.[31]

On September 5, 1917, the federal government did step in with its full force against the IWW. On that day, warrants were served for the arrest of 100 leaders of the Industrial Workers of the World on the charge of violating the Espionage Act. We will examine this shameful episode in American history below, but here we should note that on September 9 the Portland *Oregonian* gleefully reported:

> With their leaders in jail as military prisoners and their literature confiscated, the I.W.W. at a secret meeting last night decided to call off the strike which has practically tied up the lumber industry of the Northwest. Though Don Sheridan, acting secretary in place of James Rowan, now a Federal prisoner, refused to admit that the strike was called off, members of the organization declare they will go back to work on Monday.

# THE STRIKE ON THE JOB

Eight days later, the *Oregonian* reported (this time less gleefully) that the lumber owners were confronted with a new problem. "I.W.W. DECIDE TO STRIKE ON THE JOB," the headline read. The story continued:

> Following their almost unanimous vote of Saturday to return to work in the mills and lumber camps, hundreds of Seattle and Kings County members of the Industrial Workers of the World turned their faces towards the woods today to carry out a purpose that may be unique in the annals of labor controversies. The men propose to "strike on the job."
>
> When the 6,000-odd Industrial Workers employed in Western Washington started the present trouble on July 16, they demanded an eight-hour day. All efforts to induce the employers to meet the demand have failed thus far. So the I.W.W. now proposes to return to work and put in only eight hours' labor a day. Instructions from their leaders are that they are to go to work at 8 o'clock in the morning and quit at 5 o'clock in the afternoon, with an hour off in the course of the day. Members of the Mill Owners Association, when apprised of the plan, declared it would fail, saying that men could not return to their jobs on any terms of the sort, and that all who sought to work only eight hours a day would be discharged the first day.
>
> "The scheme is wholly impracticable and it will not work," was the statement of E. R. Crammer, chairman of the strike committee of the Mill Owners Association.[32]

The first part of the great strike had come to an end, but a new phase, one that had rarely, if ever, been seen before in any strike, was about to get under way. As one Wobbly strike leader wrote later: "Seeing that we could accomplish nothing by staying off the job any longer, there was a resolution drawn up . . . to the effect that we transfer the strike to the job and that it be left to the workers to do what they saw fit, individually or collectively, to enforce the eight-hour day. So back to the job we went."[33]

The new strike aimed to achieve "the height of inefficiency on the job, while retaining their usual efficiency in the cook house at meal times."[34] This took many different forms. The most familiar was "hoosiering up." The workers would go back into the camps, and they might work their regular ten-hour stretch for a few days. Then, when the foreman had stocked up the camp larder with meals for a long period of lumbering, the strike on the job would begin. Under one plan of action the men would work their usual ten hours but in that time they would make a real effort to be inefficient and get only eight hours of productivity. Under another plan one man would accidentally find the whistle chord after eight hours and pull it. The rest of the crew would then walk off the job.

In either case, the result was usually the firing of the whole crew. But with a meal under their belts, the men would merely walk off to the next camp, and repeat their act, this time carrying the other workers with them. Reporting his conversation with a logger, Robert Bruere revealed another method of striking on the job:

> "When you go into a camp today," a lumberjack said to me, "you'll find a spar tree in the middle of the workings with steel cables running out into the woods to bring the logs down the skidway. Running along the skidway you'll see other cables running from the donkey-engine up to the choker chain; well, every now and then one of those cables snaps. When everything is running right, when the men are satisfied with their working conditions, you'd see a half-dozen men—every man within call—jumping in and splicing that cable. But when you are striking on a job and a cable snaps, you just stand there and play the Hoosier; you don't know anything more about splicing than a yokel, and you wait until the boss finds the man who is paid to do that particular job. Before the job is done a half hour is gone—three quarters of an hour—an hour! Say, it's easy to do eight hours' work on a ten hours' job; all you've got to do is play the Hoosier! Practice conscientious withdrawal of efficiency! Fold your arms and look innocent![35]

The newspapers were full of accounts of sabotage employed by the Wobblies during the strike on the job—soaping rails on grades, which sent the timber crashing into a ravine; letting emery dust or similar material get into the "journal box" on railroad trains and in the mill machines; letting water out of engine boilers while the fire was going; putting soap bars or soap flakes in the water tanks of railroad engines and those used in the mills and camps; sawing trees so that when they hit the ground they split; leaving logs on the shores of streams to rot there or be eaten by worms.[36] But even the infuriated press conceded that no violence was done to working men, and while property was damaged or destroyed, plants and woods were not seriously damaged. The Wobblies confidently informed reporters that they expected to take them over in the near future so they saw no point in destroying them.[37]

The charge that strikers drove spikes into logs so that when they were taken to the sawmills they would cause the giant saws to break was heatedly denied by the IWW. One Wobbly, interviewed by Robert Bruere, said: "What would we be putting spikes in logs for? Would we be aiming to kill our fellow workers at the saw—or anyone else for that matter."[38]

The strike on the job started in September 1917, and did not end until the eight-hour day was won in March 1918. During these weeks, the Wobblies boasted, "the companies were forced to run the commissary department of the strike."[39] Labor turnover, meanwhile, ran as high as 1,000 percent. One employer testified that "often he would start the day with a full crew, and finish with none but a cook and a dishwasher."[40] The truth is that by themselves, the employers could not cope with the strike on the job. Senator William E. Borah of Idaho put it this way:

> . . . the I.W.W. are about as elusive a proposition as you ever ran up against . . . it is almost impossible to deal with them. . . . You cannot destroy the organization. That is an intangible proposition. It is something that you cannot get at. You cannot reach it. You do not know where it is, it is not in writing. It is not in anything else. It is a simple understanding between men, and they act upon it without any evidence or existence whatever.[41]

California immigration official and self-styled expert on the "IWW problem," Carleton Parker called the IWW a "groping bond of fellowship" that was almost impossible to defeat in a strike by the usual strike-breaking methods.[42]

Late in the fall of 1917, the President's Mediation Commission visited the Pacific Northwest. The Commission conducted hearings on the labor conflict in the lumber industry, and it found that it was the refusal of the lumber companies to introduce much-needed reforms, and not the IWW, that was basically responsible for the labor unrest. Its published report challenged the lumber companies' assertions that the strike represented only radicalism, sabotage, and pro-Germanism. Whatever the position of the IWW officially, the Commission found that "membership in the I.W.W. by no means implies belief in or understanding of its philosophy. To a majority it is 'a bond of growing fellowship.'"[43]*

## THE U.S. ARMY BREAKS THE STRIKE

The War Labor Board, as well as other special agencies within the War Department, also tried to end the strike. Carleton Parker, the War Department, and the Washington State Council on National Defense made repeated pleas to the lumber companies to grant the eight-hour day and recognize the AFL unions in order to cut the ground from under the IWW. When the employers proved unreceptive and it became clear that as much as 75 percent of spruce production needed for airplanes, vital for the war

*During the federal trials in 1918 and 1919, the IWW presented the Commission's Report on the lumber strike as evidence in its defense.

effort, was being held up by the strike, and when the imprisonment of IWW leaders by the federal government failed to restore production, the military entered the lumber labor picture fully. Lt. Col. Brize P. Disque was dispatched to the Northwest; the *Oregonian* reported that Disque "has been clothed with all but supreme power, with orders to get out the spruce necessary to the airplane building programme of the Government. . . ."[44]

Colonel Disque immediately called in C. B. Ellis, editor of the *Industrial Worker*, which had been carrying articles on how to carry out the strike on the job and reports of its success.[45] Ellis reported that Disque went to great pains

> to tell me he had the power to arrest every man in the woods. "I'll put 50,000 men in there [the woods]," Disque told me. "Have you got 50,000 loggers?" I asked. "No, but I've got 50,000 Texas fighting men," he replied. "Well, good," I told him, "what do you want to do? Arrest the Wobs? Seven deputies can do that and they'd all go to jail singing." "Well," Disque tells me, "they've got to cut wood. I'll put two men at the front of every tree with guns and then they'll work." "And how are the soldiers going to tell how many strokes a minute a man can make with a saw?" I asked. "It's easy for us to strike on the job—to slow down. Nobody can make the lumberjacks go any faster than they will." Well, Disque, he got real mad and told me he'd arrest the leaders. But he knew as well as I did that that wouldn't work because we taught the men that each of them is his own leader. We didn't need any leaders. I just walked out after that.[46]

Enraged, Disque put soldiers to work in the woods. But the Wobblies, working alongside them, pointed out that the conditions, wages, and hours were as bad for the soldiers as for the lumberjacks, and while the men in uniform could not strike because that would be mutiny, they could slow down. After a soldier crew had been in the woods a few days, that was often the result.[47]

Gompers not only supported Colonel Disque's anti-IWW mission, hoping that the Army would aid AFL organizers, but even sanctioned creation of an Army Spruce Protection Division, a special unit composed of ex-lumberjacks who worked, quite illegally, in the spruce forests in civilian clothes.[48]

## THE 8-HOUR DAY WINS IN LUMBER

By the end of February 1918, with the strike on the job still holding sway in the industry, many camps began instituting the eight-hour day as the only way they could get crews to work regularly. On March 1, Colonel Disque, speaking for the lumber operators, announced the official beginning of the eight-hour day in the lumber industry. A number of newspapers, however, noted that in many areas, it was already an established fact.[49]

But Disque performed a final service for the employers. He broke both IWW and AFL unions with the aid of federal troops, and set up a company union, the Loyal Legion of Loggers and Lumbermen (the "Four L's") in their stead. Army officers toured the camps and mills of Washington and Oregon administering a loyalty pledge* which read:

> I, the undersigned, in consideration of my being a member of the Loyal Legion of Loggers and Lumbermen, do hereby solemnly pledge my efforts during the war to the United States of America, and will support and defend this country against enemies both foreign and domestic.
>
> I further swear, by these presents, to faithfully perform my duty toward this company by directing my best efforts, in every way possible, to the production of logs and lumber for the construction of Army airplanes and ships to be used against our common enemies, that I will stamp out any sedition or acts of hostility against the United States Government which may come within my knowledge, and I will do every act and thing which will in general aid in carrying this war to a successful conclusion.[50]

The Loyal Legion and the AFL engaged in a public debate over which organization should receive credit for the eight-hour day. But there was little doubt expressed by contemporary observers that it was the initiative,

---

*The idea of a "loyalty pledge" from workers began soon after U.S. entry into the war. On May 4, 1917, J. A. Franklin, president of the International Boilermakers, Shipbuilders and Helpers of America, notified Gompers of a complaint received from the San Francisco local regarding "the attempt on the part of private employers to use the present conditions, brought about by the war to their own advantage by having their employees swear allegiance not only to the Government but to private employers." Franklin asked Gompers to respond "as a member of the Advisory Commission of National Defense, as to whether or not private employers are to be permitted by the Governor or encouraged in their attempt to restrict the natural activities of the men in their relations with the employer. . . ." (Gompers Files, AFL Archives, State Historical Society of Wisconsin). There is no record of a reply from Gompers. The oath (included separately in Franklin's letter) read:

"I do solemnly swear that I will bear true faith and allegiance to the United States of America and that I will serve them honestly and faithfully against all their enemies whomsoever and that I will obey the orders of the President of the United States and the orders of the officers appointed over me. I do also solemnly swear that I will serve honestly and faithfully the Union Iron Works Company and will allow no person to cause any loss or damage to a fellow employee or any loss or damage to the property or interests of the Union Iron Works Company. . . ." (J. G. Enright, to J. A. Franklin, San Francisco, Calif., May 3-17, Gompers Files, AFL Archives, State Historical Society of Wisconsin.)

agitation, and methods of the IWW that succeeded in breaking the resistance of the lumber millionaires to the eight-hour day and achieving this
and other improvements for the lumber workers.*

*Benjamin G. Rader credits the strike with the fact that conditions for lumber workers
improved. "In order to attract strikers back to work and prevent future strikes," he writes,
"Montana lumbermen began to improve camp conditions." ("The Montana Lumber Strike of
1917,"*Pacific Historical Review* 36 [May, 1967]:206.) On the other hand, Rober E. Ficken,
argues that the only victors in the strike "were employers," and that the "concessions"
granted the lumber workers were "illusory." Even the eight-hour day was not a great victory,
he insists, and the lumber industry "emerged from the strike with a major triumph." ("The
Wobby Horrors: Pacific Northwest Lumbermen and the Industrial Workers of the World,
1917-1928," *Labor History* 24 [Summer, 1983]:325,340-41.)

# CHAPTER 13

## IWW Organizing During the War: The Mining Industry

On April 11, 1917, Charles H. Watson wrote to Bernard Baruch, care of the Advisory Council of the Council of National Defense, informing him as the "legal representative of producers of upwards of two millions of tons, annually, of iron ore," that he had "dependable information that the Industrial Workers of the World are organizing the miners." He claimed that there was no reason for "contention" between the owners of the copper mines and the workers "in relation to either wages or working conditions,"

> ... but the IWW agitators are sowing seeds of sedition among the ignorant classes of the employes, most of whom are foreigners, and a strike will probably be fomented. . . . Our mines are all underground properties, and to try to keep them open during a general strike uncurbed by military force, would be folly. With Bessemer ore mines closed . . . the production of war materials, as you know, would be seriously impaired in a short time.
>
> The propaganda of the IWW in this locality is against the war. . . . The operators are leaving nothing undone to prevent the strike, but if it comes . . . they fear the consequences in view of the history of the IWW organization.

Baruch, who was chairman of the Committee on Raw Materials, Minerals and Metals of the Advisory Commission, sent the letter to Samuel Gompers, chairman of the Committee on Labor. Gompers, in turn, forwarded the letter to Charles H. Moyer, president of the International Union of Mine, Mill and Smelter Workers. (Formerly the Western Federation of Miners, it had changed its name in 1916.) Gompers added: "It may be possible at this time that the employers are in a bit better frame of mind and will assume a more conciliatory policy toward the constructive trade union work of your International Union and I shall, of course, be very glad to aid in any such effort."

At the same time, Gompers wrote to Baruch informing him that he had turned over the letter relating to the IWW to Moyer. This time he added, "in some of the mining districts a feudalism prevails that has prevented the miners from organizing," and this had created "a condition of affairs that assisted the propaganda of the I.W.W.'s. If you could bring some influence to bear upon the mine operators that would make them adopt a different policy toward the constructive trade union movement, you will render the greatest service in defeating the campaign and purpose of the I.W.W."[1]

The fear of the IWW revealed by this correspondence stemmed from the fact that on November 25, 1916, at the annual IWW convention in Chicago, the Committee on Organization and Constitution had passed a proposal authorizing the expenditure of $2,000 to organize the miners in the West. In January 1917, the IWW Metal Mine Workers Industrial Union No. 800 was established, and late that month IWW organizers left Chicago to organize miners and establish locals of the MMWIU. One of the IWW men was Grover H. Perry, who set out to organize an Arizona chapter in Phoenix.[2]

## THE AFL FAILS ARIZONA MINERS

In 1915 and 1916, Arizona had experienced a bitter four month strike in the Clifton-Morenci district,* and the copper companies, led by Phelps-Dodge, had been forced to recognize a grievance committee of their employees, most of whom were Mexican-Americans.

This victory stimulated other struggles in the Arizona copper mines, which arose out of the widespread discontent among the miners. Early in January 1917, some one thousand Mexican, Indian, and Anglo workers in Ajo, Arizona went out on strike seeking wages higher than the existing $1.50 to $2.20 per day, and asked for organizational assistance from the AFL's International Union of Mine, Mill and Smelter Workers. Their efforts were futile. By January 19, twenty-six miners had been arrested and taken to Tucson to stand trial. To insure that no further resistance would occur, gunmen were imported and sworn in as deputy sheriffs.[3]

The failure of the AFL international to come to the aid of the Ajo miners intensified the rising discontent with that organization. When the Clifton-Morenci strikers ended their walkout in 1916, they had voted to withdraw from the union's predecessor—the Western Federation of Miners—since they viewed it as too conservative. The increasingly conservative policies

*For a discussion of the strike, *see* Philip S. Foner, *History of the Labor Movement in the United States* 6 (New York, 1982): 12-24, and James R. Kluger, *The Clifton-Morenci Strike: Labor Difficulty in Arizona, 1915-16,* (Tucson, 1970).

of President Moyer gave the formerly militant WFM "a bad name for subserviency to company interests."[4] As Haywood later noted:

> . . . the Western Federation of Miners had died with the blade of conservatism plunged into its heart. The name of the organization had changed, and it was called the International Union of Mine, Mill and Smelter Workers. They had become affiliated with the American Federation of Labor. The prestige of the W.F.M. was a thing of the past.[5]

As the Arizona miners became more militant, Moyer became disenchanted with the operation in that state. In February 1917, Moyer revoked the Arizona IUMMSW's charter, stating that "the district's attitudes were too radical and independent."[6]

After this action, miners in Arizona increasingly signed up with IWW Metal Mine Workers Industrial Union No. 800. By May 1917, the Bisbee IUMMSW local was made up entirely of men who had signed the little red cards that were the membership books of the IWW.[7]

IUMMSW officers maintained that the IWW takeover of the Bisbee local was facilitated by detective agencies and company men who posed as followers of the IWW. They also claimed that management had hired informers to pose as IWW advocates. Mine owners, they argued, hoped to promote further division among union men, thereby enabling the companies to get rid of both the IUMMSW and the IWW. Philip Taft, in his study of the Bisbee labor scene at the time, notes that James A. Chapman, who had served as secretary of the IUMMSW local in Bisbee, was on the payroll of a private detective agency and later became active in the IWW. But he also says that many of the members of the Bisbee local of the IUMMSW who "transferred their allegiance were not conversant with I.W.W. principles; they simply believed that Moyer's organization was ineffective." In addition he points out that "Moyer never conceded that there existed, rightly or wrongly, deep distrust of his policies."[8]

It is significant that when J. L. Donnelly, the state leader of the IUMMSW, met Grover Perry in Phoenix in January 1917, he asked the IWW organizer for his support in rebelling against the national IUMMSW and President Moyer. Perry refused. Instead, he set about organizing the state for the IWW Metal Mine Workers Industrial Union No. 800. When members of the IUMMSW transferred their allegiance to the Wobblies, they did so because they believed their union had lost its militancy.[9]

The IWW Union No. 800 held its first statewide convention in Bisbee, Arizona on June 15-17, 1917. A week later, on June 24, the Bisbee branch, at a meeting attended by 400 to 500 members, elected an executive committee that drew up the demands that were to be presented to the copper companies.[10]

In 1917, Bisbee had about 8,000 people. Its chief economic activity was copper mining, and the mines belonged to the Copper Queen Mining Company, the Calumet and Arizona Company, and the Shattuck Arizona Company. The city was dominated by Phelps-Dodge, which owned the Copper Queen, and also owned Bisbee's largest hotel, the hospital, department store, library, newspaper, and other enterprises.[11] As the official biographer of this giant Wall Street corporation noted: "In the Phelps-Dodge scheme of things, there is no place for labor union supremacy or domination."[12] He would have been more accurate had he used the words "there is no place for the existence of labor unionism."

The demands that the IWW local presented to the Bisbee mine companies were: (1) abolition of the physical examination; (2) two men to work on each machine; (3) two men to work in raises; (4) discontinuing of all blasting during shift; (5) abolition of all bonus and construct work; (6) replacement of the sliding scale of wages with a flat daily rate of $6.00 for all men working underground; (7) no discrimination against the members of any organization.[13]

## THE IWW BISBEE STRIKE

Gerald Sherman, mine superintendent of the Copper Queen, tore up the written list of demands, and the other companies refused to answer. On June 26, 1917, the IWW called a strike, and more than 3,000 infuriated miners walked out. The turnout consisted of eighty to ninety percent of the miners in Bisbee.[14]

L. C. Shattuck, general manager of the Shattuck Arizona Company, spoke for all the companies in explaining why he had refused even to answer the demands: ". . . The demands of this I.W.W. organization are unreasonable and are the plans of a nationwide conspiracy by enemies of the United States government to restrict or cut off the copper output required to prosecute the war."[15]

Moyer echoed this sentiment. When the strike was called, the IUM-MSW president was asked if his union considered as scabs those who continued to work. Moyer replied that the union regarded the strikers as German agents, and that the IUMMSW, as an affiliate of the AFL, would adhere to the Federation's policy. Since the strike was not called by an "International Union or any *bona fide* organization of labor," he would not permit IUMMSW locals to cooperate with the IWW, or even to aid the strikers.[16]

For two weeks the strike crippled Bisbee. But even the local press, hostile to the strikers, and Sheriff Harry Wheeler of Cochise County, who arrived in Bisbee on the first day of the strike and set up headquarters, agreed that the strike was peaceful. Nevertheless, Wheeler asked Governor Thomas Campbell to request that President Wilson send troops to Bisbee. The governor submitted the request on his own behalf to the White House, but a War Department investigation concluded that troops were not needed, so the request was denied. Instead, President Wilson appointed the former governor George P. Hunt, who was temporarily out of office,* to serve as special strike mediator, in the hope that he could help the parties reach a settlement.[17]**

Wilson's telegram to Hunt, dated July 2, 1917, read: "I have been much concerned to hear of the possible serious misunderstanding between the miners and the operators in the copper mines and I would deem it a very great public service on your part if you would be generous enough to act as mediator and conciliator. I know how confidently I can appeal to your public spirit." Hunt's statement to the press after accepting the President's invitation indicated that he was going to urge a truce until the war was over:

> As conciliator in this trouble I shall endeavor to get the representatives of the miners and operators together and then appeal to both sides to bring an immediate end to this agitation. We should all be patriotic and put aside all personal wishes until a time when the nation is at peace. I would have a truce declared until the war is over.[18]

But Hunt never had a chance to act on this idea. Apart from the fact that the IWW would not consider ending the strike out of "patriotic" duty,***

---

*Facing a well financed corporation campaign against his re-election because he had sided with the workers in the Clifton-Morenci strike, Hunt was defeated by Thomas Campbell, who won by 30 votes out of 15,000 cast. Hunt contested the result, and Campbell was deposed after serving about half of the two-year term. (Alan V. Johnson, "Governor G. W. P. Hunt and Organized Labor," unpublished M.A. thesis, University of Arizona, 1964, pp. 76-85.)

**President Wilson also appointed Judge John McBride, who had defeated Gompers for the presidency of the AFL in 1895, as a mediator in the Arizona strike zones.

***After John McBride had met with the IWW in an effort to mediate the strike in Globe-Miami, Arizona, he reported that the Wobbly leaders had told him that they would not halt the strike for "one week, one day, one hour or one minute." (*Arizona Republican*, Aug. 3, 1917.)

the copper companies would not even sit down to talk with the mediators. Walter S. Douglas, the new president of Phelps-Dodge, spoke for the mine owners when he said as he was about to leave Globe, Arizona for Bisbee in his private railroad car:

> There will be no compromise because you cannot compromise with a rattlesnake. . . . That goes for both the International Union and the I.W.W. . . . I believe the government will be able to show that there is German influence behind this movement. . . . It is up to the individual communities to drive these agitators out as has been done in other communities in the past.[19]

Douglas, son of Dr. James O. Douglas, the developer of Bisbee's Copper Queen mine and a member of the board of directors of the Phelps-Dodge corporation, had visited Morenci during the Clifton-Morenci strike. He was infuriated by the fact that Governor Hunt was sympathetic to the strikers, had refused to allow strikebreakers from outside to enter the community, and had even ordered the state militia to gather food, fuel, and clothing for the strikers and to aid in other ways "the penniless families in this time of industrial trouble."* Douglas had publicly debated with Hunt in the pages of the *New Republic* on the issues in the strike, defending Phelps-Dodge, and he vowed that never again would the company negotiate with strikers. When in November 1916 he was elected president of the American Mining Congress, it was with the understanding that he would be a national anti-union leader.[20]

## THE JEROME DEPORTATION

When Douglas said that the IWW should be run out of communities, he did not have to wait long before seeing his advice put into practice.

In February 1917, a local of the IWW Metal Mine Workers was established in Jerome, Arizona. When a IUMMSW strike in Jerome ended with nothing gained for the miners, the IWW decided to start a new battle. On July 5, they called a strike, demanding $6 per shift and a six-hour day. The IUMMSW called the demands "ridiculous, unpatriotic and disloyal" and urged the miners to continue working, but both Mexican and Anglo miners responded and struck.

On the morning of July 10, some two hundred and fifty businessmen and a group of IUMMSW members embarked on a systematic "rounding up" of suspected Wobblies. By 9:30 a.m. some one hundred men were marched to jail, where company and IUMMSW officials utilized their

---

*For the unusual role played by Governor Hunt in the strike, *see* Foner, *op. cit.*, 6: pp. 17-24.

respective membership rolls to determine who were actually Wobblies. Those accused of being IWW members, about 67 in all, were quickly deported to Needles, California. With this removal, all labor agitation ceased in Jerome, and wages and working conditions remained as they had been before the strike.[21*]

There was some protest against this act, but when the Globe-Miami district of the IWW telegraphed Governor Campbell, complaining of the brutal treatment of workers at the hands of a lawless mob, the *Arizona Republican* charged that the IWW leadership had "threatened" the governor.[22]

The deportations at Jerome occurred at the same time that Bisbee businessmen and professionals were meeting to plan their own deportations. A Citizens' Protective League, organized in 1916, and a Workers' Loyalty League, made up of some former IUMMSW members, stood ready to be deputized for use against the strikers.[23]

Early in the morning of July 12, 1917, citizens of Bisbee read in the *Bisbee Daily Review* the text of a proclamation signed by Sheriff Wheeler, informing them that he had "formed a Sheriff's posse of 1,200 men in Bisbee and 1,000 men in Douglas, all loyal Americans, for the purpose of arresting on the charges of vagrancy, treason, and of being disturbers of the peace of Cochise County all those strange men who have congregated here from other parts and sections for the purpose of harassing and intimidating all men who desire to pursue their daily toil." The sheriff made clear his opposition to the strikers. "This is no labor trouble—we are sure of that—but a direct attempt to embarrass and injure the government of the United States." He warned all women and children to "keep off the streets today," asked for aid and cooperation, and requested that no shot be fired except in self defense. The proclamation concluded:

> All arrested persons will be treated humanely and their cases examined with justice and care. I hope no resistance will be made, for I desire no bloodshed. However, I am determined if resistance is made, it shall be quickly and effectively overcome.[24]

Those who did not read the proclamation in the *Bisbee Daily Review* could do so on sheets posted on poles, fences, and walls.

---

*Vernon H. Jensen maintains that officials of the Jerome local of the IUMMSW opposed the deportation of the Wobblies and that it was supported only by individual members. But John Lindquist insists that both members and officers participated in the round-up and deportation of the IWW strikers. (Vernon H. Jensen, *Heritage of Conflict*, [Ithaca, N.Y., 1950], p. 401; John H. Lindquist, "The Jerome Deportation of 1917," *Arizona and the West* 11 [Autumn, 1969]: 243-44.)

# THE BISBEE DEPORTATION

At 4:00 a.m. that morning, several hundred armed men on foot and on horseback gathered at various assigned posts in alleyways, behind fences, and in other dark places. They wore white armbands for identification, and were instructed to pick up and arrest every "suspicious looking individual." A list had already been drawn up by officials of the mining companies; the list included not only all strikers, but also storekeepers, contractors, and professional people who were sympathetic to labor. In fact, had ex-Governor Hunt been in Bisbee on that day, he too would have been picked up.[25]

By 6:30 a.m., the deputized vigilantes numbered 2,000. Now they went into action. Men were apprehended in their homes, on the street, in restaurants, and in stores, and asked if they were working or willing to work. If they answered "No" they were seized; if their names were on the prepared list, they were seized without even being asked. One man was eating breakfast when two vigilantes shoved their guns through the door and asked if he sympathized with the strikers. When he said "Yes" he was whisked away. One man slept through the knocks on his front door; four gunmen broke down the door, walked in, and pulled him out of bed. When his wife begged them to allow her husband to dress, she was pushed aside and he was dragged out of the house in his nightgown.[26]

Several men who owned grocery stores were seized and taken away, after which "vigilantes took over the stores, sold their goods, and fought with each other over the sharing of the remaining inventory."[27]

"The move," wrote a U.S. marshal who witnessed the shameful event, "was not made against the I.W.W.'s alone, but against every man who has ever been known to give voice to his opinions openly. Men who did not belong to any organization were picked up as well as members of the A.F. of L."[28] People were picked up at random. Thomas N. English, who was not a member of any organization, reported:

> On the morning of the 12th, about seven o'clock in the morning, somebody knocked on the door and I told them to come in, and there were three men who came in and asked me if I was working, and I said, "No, sir," and they said "Well, come out right away and dress; we want you." And I said, "What is this for?" And they said, "Get in line with the rest of them." That was all the information I could get. There was another man rooming with me by the name of Swanson, and they made him get out at the same time.[29]

Two men were killed during the roundup. The victims were Orson P. McCrae, a member of the Citizens'. Protective League and shift boss at one of the Copper Queen mines, and James Brew, a former employee of the Dean mine. McCrae, who had been deputized by Sheriff Wheeler, was killed when Brew fired through the door of his room upon being ordered to line up outside. He, in turn, was killed by three of McCrae's companions.[30]

By 7:30 a.m., a large group had been lined up under armed guard in the plaza in front of the Bisbee Post Office. Two women, who had seen the men standing in the already blistering hot Arizona sun, brought a tub of water and dippers so the prisoners could drink. "Before a drop passed," writes Philip Taft, "several guards approached the tub, kicked it over and declared: 'The sons of bitches don't get a drink.'"[31]

Ten abreast, posse members and their prisoners began the two mile march to the Warren Ball Park. Sheriff Wheeler rode along in an open Ford touring car owned and chauffeured by Father Mandin, a local Catholic priest who had received the car as a gift from his parishioners.* Wheeler shouted instructions to the vigilantes, along with curses at the prisoners. Mounted on the car alongside Wheeler was a new 7.62mm Martin machinegun with a loaded feed belt in position.[32]

By the time the prisoners reached the ball park they numbered 2,000 and they included three women. Once in the ball park stockade, the prisoners were told that if they severed all ties with the IWW and went back to work, they would be released. During the hours in the ball park, several hundred recanted and were set free. The first to be released were the three women, mainly because the vigilante leaders were told the women would sue Phelps-Dodge for mistreatment if they were not let go. Men who were known to be associated with or sympathetic to the labor movement—and this did not mean only the IWW—were given no opportunity to recant. In any case, hundreds refused to back down and answered all such requests with catcalls, hoots, jeers, profane shouts, and songs.[33]

Just before 11:00 a.m., twenty-three cattle boxcars of the El Paso and Southwestern Railroad arrived, in accordance with a prior arrangement made by Douglas of Phelps-Dodge. The prisoners were forced by the armed guards into the boxcars, many of which had over three inches of manure on the floors.[34] Ten miles east of Douglas the train made its first stop; train crews were exchanged, and water barrels placed on the cars.

*Thomas McGuinness, a real estate operator in Bisbee, noted that "the only clergyman of Bisbee to take the part of the strikers was the Rev. Mr. Brewster, pastor of the Bisbee Episcopal Church. . . . The other clergymen of the city have stood solidly with the mine owners and the YMCA has been used as the assembly place of the armed deputies." (*The Public*, Aug. 24, 1917, p.820.)

During the stop, the train was guarded by 200 armed citizens "while machine guns on two knolls guarded the station."[35] The train then headed for Columbus, New Mexico, 173 miles east of Bisbee and close to the Mexican border. The men were forced to stand for hours in crowded, airless cars in the July heat, the water supply long since exhausted. They stood in cow manure over their shoe tops while weaker prisoners were allowed to sit in the filth.[36]

The train arrived in Columbus at 9:30 p.m. July 12, and went on to Hermanas, New Mexico, twenty miles west of Columbus. It arrived at Hermanas at 3:00 a.m. on Friday, July 13. By this time the deportees had been without water and food for twelve hours.[37] At Hermanas, which would be home for the deportees for the next two days, William Cleary, the well-known Bisbee attorney and long-time defender of labor against Phelps-Dodge, distributed a statement to the press describing what had happened since the early morning of July 12 in Bisbee.

This was very important, since two Phelps-Dodge officials had imposed a censorship on Associated Press dispatches sent from Bisbee. They had read every dispatch and decided what could or could not be sent out by Western Union.[38] The result of Cleary's statement was that newspapers all over the country carried headlines like the one in the *New York Times*: "ARIZONA SHERIFF SHIPS 1,100 I.W.W.s OUT IN CATTLE CARS." In its story, the *Times* conceded that "several prominent citizens of Bisbee and Lowell who openly declare they were in sympathy with the I.W.W. movement were forced into the cars with the vagrants."[39] But no mention was made of the fact that AFL members as well as workers not affiliated with any union, along with owners of grocery stores and restaurants, were also shipped out. However, the *Times* did publish the full text of Cleary's statement which opened:

> There were 1,286 men deported from Bisbee yesterday. With few exceptions they were all underground miners, the others being small business men of the Warren district, which includes Bisbee, Lowell, and Warren. The men were on strike for better conditions, particularly for two men on a machine, which is the custom in most mining districts. The men also asked discontinuance of the physical examination which every man is obliged to submit to before obtaining a job and which has been used as a basis of blacklist. Under its guise, men who are physically able have been refused work because of their political affiliations and principles.
>
> "Another demand was for a six dollar wage per day as a minimum, six dollars today not having any more purchasing power than three dollars and fifty

cents had when miners received that sum, and copper was selling at 14 and 15 cents a pound.*

The strike on the part of the miners was most peaceful. In the neighborhood of ninety per cent of the underground workers were out. There was no physical violence. The police records show far fewer arrests during the time of the strike than during ordinary times.

Cleary then described at length the roundup in Bisbee, explaining how "men were forced at the point of a gun to leave their homes, and in many instances their wives and families," the harrowing details of the march to the baseball park, the long and weary ride in the cattle cars without food and water for most of the deportees, the overcrowding in the cars "making it impossible for all of the men to sit down on the floor at the same time, letting the weaker men sit. When we arrived at Hermanas, we were not allowed the privilege of leaving the train and shots were fired from the roofs of the cars for the purpose of intimidating us." He concluded:

> While many of the men, it is true, are members of what is known as the I.W.W., nevertheless they are law-abiding and peaceful.
>
> Many who have lived in Bisbee for years—some for as long as fifteen years and have their wives and families there now—are very anxious to return.
>
> Among the men deported are property owners, Bisbee business men, Liberty Bond subscribers between the ages of 21 and 30, who have registered under the recent selective draft law, and others who are reservists under the military law passed in June, 1916.[40]**

On July 13, the *Bisbee Daily Review* greeted the deportation ecstatically on its front page:

> No longer does a blot remain on the escutcheon of Bisbee. "Wobblyism" has passed with the labyrinth of things discarded; as a coat is shaken from the back; as a boil is lanced and cleansed of its contents. . . . Without precedent in this or any other country, or any other age, was the occurrence of yesterday. It marked a golden date on the calender; a date when the law-abiding people of the community . . . drove from their midst the "Wobbly."[41]

In general, the press throughout the country either echoed this editorial's sentiments or chided the vigilantes for having gone a bit too far. The *New York Times*, in an editorial oddly entitled "Diversions of the

*In March 1917 copper sold for 36.3 cents per pound.

**A U.S. Army survey showed that of the 1,836 deported men, 520 owned property in Bisbee; 427 had registered for the draft; 433 were married with families; 205 had purchased Liberty Bonds; 62 had served in the armed forces; 426 had been members of the IWW. (*New York Times*, July 15, 1917.)

I.W.W.," as if the event had been staged by the Wobblies for the amuse-
ment of the American people, observed that "a Sheriff who makes his own
law is on dangerous and indefensible ground." and in this case, displayed
an "inhumanity which is worse than the I.W.W." However, Sheriff
Wheeler was "on the right track when he instructed his deputies to arrest
the I.W.W. men on 'charges of vagrancy.'" Imprisonment was the answer,
not deportation![42]

When the *Bisbee Daily Review* boasted that the event in its city was "without precedent," it certainly must have known that only a few days earlier,
sixty-seven strikers had been deported from Jerome, Arizona to Needles,
California. But these men had been allowed to return to Jerome. What made
the Bisbee deportation a unique "golden date on the calender" was that the
copper companies had decided that the deportees would not be allowed to
return to their homes. On July 14, the mouthpiece for these companies, the
*Bisbee Daily Review*, reported that when the men were released from the
boxcars at Hermanas, New Mexico, they were threatened with death or
bodily harm should they ever return to Bisbee. It commented editorially:

> Any talk of their coming back is nonsense. They will not be allowed to come
> back. We have been slow to act but once started it is a finish fight. The serious
> business of this district is the mining of copper ore, not the building of night
> schools of anarchism or idling on the streets or picketing public places and
> private works.[43]

When the men were abandoned at Hermanas, the local sheriff wired
Governor E. E. Lindsey of New Mexico warning that "serious trouble is
threatened" and asking for instructions. Governor Lindsey declared that
the IWWs should be treated humanely but not allowed to create disturbances. He directed the sheriff to feed the men who, as he had learned,
faced the "danger of starvation," and to provide them "with rations . . .
to prevent great suffering." At the same time he wired Washington,
expressing the opinion that the matter was a federal affair and asking President Wilson to take charge.[44]

Fred Brown, a volunteer organizer for the AFL, one of five AFL leaders
who were deported (as were thirty of thirty-nine members of the local
AFL Painters' Union), wired Gompers asking him to intercede with President Wilson. In fact, Gompers was getting so many letters complaining of
government inaction that he felt it necessary to call President Wilson's
attention to the fact that "some of the departments and other agencies of
the government are either ignoring the situation or in some instances are
positively hostile."[45]

## INTERVENTION BY PRESIDENT WILSON

Wilson directed Secretary of War Newton D. Baker to investigate, and in a letter to Governor Thomas Campbell of Arizona informing him of this action, he added:

> May I not respectfully urge the great danger of citizens taking the law into their own hands. . . . I look upon such actions with great apprehension. A very serious responsibility is assumed when such precedents are set.

Governor Campbell merely asked Sheriff Wheeler for an explanation for the deportations. He was satisfied when he received the following reply: "I can protect law abiding and peaceful citizens, but I cannot guarantee the technical rights of lawbreakers and criminals. I would not endanger the lives of loyal American citizens in attempting to protect the IWWs."[46]

Acting on President Wilson's orders, United States troops escorted the deportees from Hermanas to Columbus, New Mexico and lodged them in a tent colony erected for Mexican refugees during the border raids.[47] A reporter who accompanied the deportees to their new home, described their arrival:

> When the unshaved and unwashed crowd marched up to the refugee camp this afternoon they presented the strangest sight. . . . Many were without hats and wore soiled handkerchiefs on their heads to keep off the hot sun. Others limped from blistered feet, while old men and the physically unfit had difficulty in marching the mile to the camp from the railroad. One man fainted after reaching the camp and the hospital tent was crowded with minor cases during the afternoon, though no serious illness has been discovered.
>
> After the exiles had completed establishing camp they went to the big water tank in the camp and bathed their blistered feet, washed their clothes, and then slept in the shade of the wedge tents. They obey orders without comment, and seem to have accepted their fate for the present.[48]

At President Wilson's order, ex-Governor Hunt conducted an investigation of the refugee camp at Columbus. He spent five days at the camp, and in a report to Secretary of Labor William B. Wilson he noted that the deportees had organized their own police force and elected an executive committee to represent them. He added:

> The situation to them (the deportees) seems very simple and practical, and they are wholly unable to comprehend why their strike should be associated with the war, or held by anyone to be an act of unfaithfulness to the government in its emergency. The fact that the war is the direct cause of the enormous

profits being realized by copper producers they understand, but the point they hold to is that these tremendous additional profits are being realized, and that they are entitled to a share. . . . Whether or not there are individuals among them who are underserving; whether or not there are some without whom any community would be better off, collectively they have suffered a great wrong . . . the most sacred principles of human liberty upon which our government is founded . . . have been shockingly violated.[49]

On September 17, 1917, after the government had cut their rations to one-half, the last of the deportees left the New Mexico camp, and a month later, it was closed. But only a handful were allowed to return to Bisbee, and solely because their mining skills were badly needed.[50] A U.S. marshal in Bisbee wrote to Hunt:

The companies have put into effect a passport system between Bisbee and neighboring towns. . . . They hold "court" in the Copper Queen Dispensary where men are examined as to their right to stay in town, and all the crossroads are lined with "Cossacks" who examine everyone going or coming from town.[51]

The marshal was referring to the organization of a "kangaroo court." Anyone seeking to enter Bisbee was stopped outside the city limits, brought before the "court," which then decided whether he would remain in Bisbee, be allowed to leave "voluntarily," or go to jail. Passports were issued by the Douglas Chamber of Commerce and Mines and those who came into the Warren district had to have them in order to remain unmolested.[52] Hundreds were hauled before this "court" by Sheriff Wheeler and his deputies:

Trials were secret and a verdict of deportation was promptly and forcibly executed by deputy sheriffs. At the same time the Sheriff established "guards" at all entrances to the district who examined every person attempting to enter the camp. The reported object of these "guards" was to exclude from the camp any stray "wobbly" that might drift in and endanger the peace and safety of the community. The definition of this term "wobbly" was apparently left to the discretion of the individual guards and all "wobblies" were promptly and forcibly denied the right to enter the camp. . . .[53]

When the deportees first arrived in the camp set up for them by the federal government in Columbus, they told the reporter for the *New York Times* that they were hopeful they would not remain long. "The men believe that the President will order them sent back to their homes," he wrote. But he added: "There is no information in camp upon which to base this supposition."[54] He was correct. Those who left Columbus and returned to Bisbee, no matter how many years they had lived in that city or whether or not their families were still there, were not allowed to enter. Instead, they were promptly arrested for vagrancy, brought before the kangaroo court and "encouraged to leave town," or else face conviction and imprisonment. When A. S. Embree refused to leave Bisbee after returning from the Columbus camp, he was jailed for three months and then threatened with lynching if he did not leave permanently—and this after he had been tried in Tucson following a change of *venue* and freed by a jury minutes after testimony was completed.[55]

## THE FEDERAL GOVERNMENT INVESTIGATES

In vain, the deportees pleaded with President Wilson to provide them with federal protection so they could return to their homes in Bisbee.[56] The President confined himself to appointing a five-man commission to investigate the labor turmoil in Arizona. The commission, with Secretary of Labor William B. Wilson as chairperson and Assistant Secretary of Labor Felix Frankfurter as secretary, heard testimony in Bisbee from November 1 to November 5. In its report, the commission severely criticized those responsible for the Bisbee deportation. The deportation, the commission noted, had been decided upon at a meeting on July 11, participated in by managers and other officials of the Phelps-Dodge Corporation and the Calumet and Arizona Mining Company. There was no justification, the commission found, for the belief that the deportation was necessary to prevent violence or to safeguard life and property. "The deportation was wholly illegal and without authority in law, either State or Federal," the commission declared. It concluded its report with the demand that "all illegal practices and the denial of rights safeguarded by the Constitution and statutes must at once cease" and that those who took part in the unlawful deportations and the events that followed be prosecuted under the laws of Arizona. It called the attention of the United States Attorney General and the Interstate Commerce Commission to the possible violations of Federal law, and it urged President Wilson to recommend to Congress "that such occurrences hereafter be made criminal under the Federal law to the full extent of the constitutional authority of the Federal government. . . ."[57]

Acting on the Commission's report, the United States Department of Justice started an investigation of the Bisbee deportations. On May 15, 1918, twenty-one of Bisbee's leading mining officials were arrested on charges of "conspiracy to injure, oppress, threaten, and intimidate United States citizens" under Section 19 of the United States Penal Code.

Included were Phelps-Dodge officials Walter Douglas, Gerald Sherman, and Grant H. Dowell. (Sheriff Wheeler was in France at the time, serving with the American Expeditionary Forces.) The defense filed for a demurrer, on the ground that no federal laws had been violated. The court upheld the defense counsel's request. The Justice Department then appealed the lower court decision to the United States Supreme Court. Late in 1920, the high court ruled in favor of the defendants, saying the case was a matter for the state courts.[58]

In the meantime, civil suits for damages exceeding $6 million had been brought in the Arizona courts. But nothing came of these either. When Harry E. Wooton, a Phelps-Dodge employee, Loyalty Leaguer, and Bisbee vigilante, was tried as a representative case, he was acquitted on the first ballot, all the jurors agreeing that the deportation "had been a good thing."[59] The other civil suit plaintiffs then dropped their suits. In the end, a few settlements were reached out of court. In these few cases, each married man with a child was awarded $1,250; married men without children, $1,000, and single men, $500.[60]

## IMPACT OF THE BISBEE DEPORTATIONS

The outcome of the Bisbee deportations established a tragic precedent for U.S. democracy,* and none were to feel this more than the Mexican workers in the United States. Students of the subject have pointed out that once deportation was accepted as "necessary" to get rid of an unwanted population, "the rationalization for removal was facilitated." "In short," writes one student, "deportation became a tool used by management (and, more recently, by agricultural concerns) against a sector of labor with whom owners were at odds. It is this mentality that condoned mass deportations of Mexicans during the 1930s".[61]**

In his first message to the Arizona legislature after he was restored to office by the state Supreme Court, Governor Hunt denounced the Bisbee deportation as an act of "supreme lawlessness." In a letter to a member of

*The tactic of deportation reached its apex on December 21, 1919. Under authority of the Alien Act of October 6, 1918, which authorized the government to deport any alien who at any time after entering the United States was found to have been at the time of entry, or to have become thereafter, a member of an anarchist organization, 249 radicals were deported on the *Buford*, a vessel which the press dubbed "Soviet Ark," from Ellis Island in New York to Finland in order to preserve "America and the human race." (*New York Times*, Dec. 22, 1919.) This shameful episode in American history will be discussed in the next volume.

**Japanese-Americans felt the impact of the deportation hysteria during World War II when they were removed from their homes on the West Coast and forced to live in government camps.

the IWW in Columbus, New Mexico, Hunt wrote: "A ruthless Vested Interest under the guise of patriotism is going to crush all organized labor. The I.W.W.'s are the means to that end."[62]

The process had already started when the President's commission visited Arizona to investigate labor turmoil in that state. The commission spent the first two weeks in Globe and Miami, Arizona. There, it obtained an agreement in which management and the International Union of Mine, Mill and Smelter Workers promised not to interfere with the war effort by interrupting copper production. The agreement, to last for the duration of the war, made no provision for wage increases or other improvements in working conditions, merely providing for the appointment of a grievance committee made up of workers selected from the men actually employed in the mines. It then guaranteed that no one serving on the grievance committee would take a militant stand, by including the provision that "no employment should be made available for IWW members or for other persons who had been guilty of disloyal utterances against the United States." A similar agreement was then put into effect in the Warren district, which included Bisbee, and the Clifton-Morenci-Metcalf district. President Moyer of the IUMMSW not only hailed the agreement, but threatened to cancel the charter of any local that turned down the agreement.[63]

After the strikes ended, the mining companies recalled for employment all who had gone on strike except those "who have been guilty of utterances disloyal to the United States or who are members of any organization that refuses to recognize the obligation of contracts, or who have heretofore demonstrated their unfitness to work in the mine, *or whose employment for any reason is contrary to the best interests of the operations. . . .*" On this basis, they simply refused to employ any man who belonged to a union—IWW Or IUMMSW—and operated their mines as open shops.[64]

Meeting in Miami, Arizona in September 1918, the Arizona State Federation of Labor spoke in alarmed tones of the labor situation in the state. "The present weakened condition of the unions in the mining district is a cause for concern and regret on the part of all the elements of our population," it declared. Noting that "the continued weakness of several of the locals that were formerly the backbone of the labor movements in those localities and throughout the state" was threatening the future of organized labor in Arizona, the federation called for unified action to "enter upon a program of organization."[65]

It was a vain hope. The decline of organized labor in Arizona would not be stemmed until the advent of the New Deal, when the major copper companies were at last organized.[66]

# TRAGEDY AND CONFLICT IN BUTTE, MONTANA

While the Bisbee deportees were languishing in the Columbus, New Mexico camp, sharp struggles and tragedy took place during a copper strike in Montana.

Frank Little had joined the IWW in 1906. He was active in the Missoula, Fresno, and Spokane free-speech fights and in the organization of lumberjacks, metal miners, oil field workers, harvest bindle stiffs, and other migratory workers in the West and Southwest. By 1916 he was a member of the General Executive Board of the IWW and one of its strongest advocates of militant action. Little had sponsored the formation of the Agricultural Workers Organization and helped in its growth.

His opposition to World War I was well known in IWW circles. He did not share the "fatalistic, inevitable" stance of many Wobblies that opposition to the war was useless since war was inevitable under monopoly capitalism. Rather, Little argued: "The I.W.W. is opposed to all wars (except of course the class war), and we must use all our power to prevent the workers from joining the army." Ralph Chaplin warned Little against this position, arguing that opposition to the draft and the organization of resistance to military conscription would bring about the end of the IWW. But Little was adamant: "Better to go out in a blaze of glory than to give in. Either we're for this capitalistic slaughterfest, or we're against it. I'm ready to face a firing squad rather than compromise."[67] Little's uncompromising antiwar attitude made him one of the most unpopular of the generally disliked Wobblies.

But more than any patriotic reaction to Little's antiwar principles, his unpopularity was based on the danger he posed to the "copper trust" as a militant IWW organizer, and this, in the end, was why he was put to death. Frank Little was known in the metal mines of Arizona and Montana; during 1916 and 1917, he had been a "tireless organizer" in these states. He repeatedly urged the miners to protest wartime wage cuts that were imposed despite the rising price of copper. He had come to the aid of the Bisbee deportees, sending a stinging letter to Governor Campbell of Arizona demanding justice for the exiled men. In July 1917, Little came to Butte, Montana to help in another strike of metal miners—this one against the Anaconda Copper Company, at that time the largest copper producing company in the world, supplying over ten percent of the world's annual copper production. Economically and politically, "the Company," as Anaconda was called, dominated the entire state of Montana, including the great mining city of Butte.[68]

Organized labor had a rather unique history in Butte. From 1889 to 1903, the trade unions were extremely powerful, and Butte became known as the "Gilbraltar of Unionism."[69] During this "Golden Era," labor was able to gain most of its demands: the closed shop, collective bargaining, trade agreements, and recognition of the Butte Miners' Union. Affiliated with the Western Federation of Miners and representing 17,500 workers, it was one of the most powerful unions in the country.

But after 1903, the situation changed. The giant Anaconda company gained control of management and began using its vast power to destroy local labor unions. In 1912 Anaconda introduced the "rustling card," a permit to work which one had to have to be employed in the Butte mines:

> A miner applied at the company's central employment department, gave his personal and job history, and a list of references. He waited for several weeks until his references were checked out. If he was cleared he was given a "rustling card" which gave him access to "rustle the hill," that is to apply directly for work at any of the Anaconda mines and mines of other companies which required the "rustling card" as a minimum job requirement.[70]

With the spread of the "rustling card," Anaconda, rather than the unions, decided who was to be employed.

In 1914, IWW members opened an assault on the Butte Miners' Union, accusing it of having become conservative. Bitter battles, often fatal, broke out between the BMU and the IWW. On June 23, 1914 the union hall was dynamited and completely demolished. The Company of course took full advantage of the factional rivalry in the once powerful BMU to reduce it to a nonentity. By 1917 the decline of labor in Butte was complete. As Arnon Gutfield puts it:

> Butte turned from "closed shop" to "open shop"; the "rustling card" replaced the union card; collective bargaining was changed to individual bargaining; trade agreements were not replaced; mutual need and good will turned into riots and militia-patrolled streets; and 17,500 union miners became 16,000 unorganized miners.[71]*

On June 8, 1917 a fire broke out in the Speculator Shaft of the North Butte Mining Company, and 164 miners were burned to death. Solid cement bulkheads had prevented their escape. These were in direct

---

*Whether or not there was collusion between the Company and the IWW, as some historians claim, Vernon H. Jensen states that no labor situation was ever "more confused than the one in Butte. Almost everything was cockeyed." (*Heritage of Conflict: Labor Relations in the Nonferrous Industry up to 1930* [Ithaca, N.Y., 1950], p. 289.) The zigzagging vicissitudes of Butte unionism are traced in Jensen's work.

violation of the state law that specified that all bulkheads had to be easily accessible with openable doors.[72]

The disaster at the Speculator Shaft aroused deep bitterness among the workers in Butte. On June 11 and 12, a mimeographed sheet declared that "conditions in Butte are intolerable," and continued: "This is the cause of the death of nearly TWO HUNDRED MEN at the Speculator . . . and causes thousands of unmentioned deaths every year. . . . Any man or woman who has ordinary intelligence must realize whither we are drifting; must know that unless some action is taken at once we will be forced down lower in social scale than the Russian peasants ever were. ... ."[73]

On June 12, 300 angry men gathered in front of Carpenters' Union Hall in response to a circular calling for a new miners' union—a militant union that would make another Speculator tragedy an impossibility. Denied admission to the AFL union hall, they marched to Finlander Hall, home of the Butte IWW. There the new union was organized and named the Metal Mine Workers Union (Independent). At its formation the union claimed 1,000 members, many of whom were former members of the Butte Miners' Union. Among its leaders were the chairman, Tom Campbell, long-time dissident labor leader and former official of the Western Federation of Miners, and the secretary Joe Shannon, long associated with the Wobblies.[74]

The new union was denounced almost immediately by the mine operators, the local press (controlled by Anaconda), and traditional union leaders who jointly claimed that the so-called independent union was IWW-directed. This attack continued, despite repeated and earnest disavowals. M. M. Donoghue, president of the AFL Montana State Federation of Labor, issued a sharp statement charging that "labor unions are not in sympathy with any movement which has as its purpose merely the causing of trouble or which seeks to disrupt the production of copper at a time when the American government was so sorely in need of this metal." Donoghue promptly set about organizing a competing miners' union. The Silver Bow Trade and Labor Alliance, which was the AFL central labor organization for all unions in Silver Bow County (comprising Butte and its immediate environs) announced it would not recognize the new union. Mine operators issued a terse statement:

> The Butte mines will continue to operate. The miners of Butte will not permit a comparatively small band of cowardly agitators and non-workers to deprive them of their livelihood and drive them from their homes, but such protection as they require will be furnished them.[75]

But threats were of no avail. The new union, its numbers growing daily, presented a list of demands for higher wages and better working conditions to the copper companies and threatened to strike if they were not met. The MMWU demanded recognition of the new union as the bargaining agent for the miners; abolition of the "rustling card"; discard of the blacklist by the companies; state observance of the state mining laws; discharge of the state mining inspector; six dollars for an eight-hour day, the right of free speech and assembly, and greater union control over hiring. Demands for safety instruction for new miners and for the construction of manholes through the bulkheads were presented later.[76]

Led by Anaconda Copper, the mine operators summarily rejected these demands in a statement published on the front page of the *Butte Daily Post*. "The wages in Butte," they claimed, on the average were "the highest paid anywhere in the world." The working conditions were "better than the average and conditions were very much superior to those of many other camps." On the same page was a column entitled "Ghastly Story at Morgue," which described the day-long procession "of grieving relatives who attempted to find their loved ones among the dead [victims of the Speculator disaster]."[77]

The mine officials made it clear that no matter how justified the miners' demands, they would refuse to deal with the new union. "It is well known," one official declared, "that recently there has been a large influx into Butte of I.W.W.s and other unpatriotic and seditious persons, whose one aim is to paralyze our industries, and particularly those upon which the government is depending for its arms and ammunition." Under no circumstances would the mine operators recognize this element or any organization "made or controlled by it," or deal with "the seditious, treacherous IWWs."[78]

In demanding $6.00 per day for all men working underground, and a proportionate increase for those employed on the surface, the new union made it clear that the wage was to be an absolute wage, independent of the market price of copper. The previous scale of $4.75 per day was dependent on a 27-cent market price per pound of copper. If copper fell below this figure, wages decreased at a rate of 25 cents per day for each 2-cent drop. The companies had promised that the basic wage of $4.75 would be raised if copper rose above 31 cents per pound, but since February 1917, copper had been above 31 cents per pound—reaching a peak of 36.3 cents in March—and there had been no wage increase.[79]

As Arnon Gutfield has demonstrated, "after a two-year period of national prosperity, the Butte miner still remained below the basic comfort level of income. . . .' Eighty percent of the wage earner families in Butte were in debt, and the cost of living was much higher than elsewhere in the nation. At the same time, wages were not as good as in other sections of the country. Thus, contrary to the mining company claims, wages in Butte were not 'the highest paid anywhere in the world.' nor were living conditions 'superior to those in many other camps.'"[80]

On June 14, 1917 the mine managers refused to meet with a committee of union representatives. The Metal Mine Workers Union called a strike the following day. Within four days 3,000 men were on strike. Then, on June 18, the striking miners were joined by Butte Local 65 of the International Union of Electrical Workers, an AFL body, which declared a strike against the Montana Power Company. The union committee, headed by William F. Dunne, the local's secretary, had presented demands to the company for a 50-cent a day wage increase and urged that the miners' demands be granted. When these were rejected, the electricians went out.[81] One after another, the trade unions of Butte joined the miners and electricians—including the metal trades, machinists, boilermakers and blacksmiths. By June 29, 15,000 men were on strike.[82]

Headlines in the *Butte Daily Post* proclaimed: "IWW Agitators in West Are Working in Cause of Germany." The strikers were said to be "led by German sympathizers within the treacherous IWW." The cure proposed by the *Butte Miner*, a leading corporation organ, was "to round up all the ringleaders, who preached treason and hatred of the flag, and incarcerate them in places where they can be provided with work, which they should be made to perform if they desire to eat." In addition it called for direct action: "The time for half measures with these people has gone by, and the government must deal with them in the future with a firm instead of a weak hand, otherwise they may impair the successful outcome of the present war." The reason for the strike was clear—it was a "Plain Case of Conspiracy," and the intention was "to aid Germany and this was treason."[83]

On the other hand, William F. Dunne, editor of the *Miners and Electrical Workers Joint Strike Bulletin*, called the mine owners "unpatriotic and

---

*Gutfield points out that between 1914 and 1917, wages in Butte rose by thirty-six percent—from a range of $894 to $1,050 in 1914 in 1917 to the range of $1,215 to $1,400. The minimum subsistence level for a family of four in 1914 required annual income of $828, while the minimum comfort level required $1,108. "Thus the average miner at Butte earned barely enough to remain above subsistence level, and was certainly below the minimum comfort level." In June, 1917 the minimum subsistence level required an annual income of $1,106, while the basic comfort level was $1,413. (Arnon Gutfield, "The Spectacular Disaster in 1917: Labor Resurgence at Butte, Montana," *Arizona and the West* 11 [Spring 1969]: 33.)

hostile to the best interest of the nation in their rotten administration of the mines and their refusal to come to terms with the miners."[84]

Representative Jeannette Rankin, a Montana Republican and the first woman to sit in the United States Congress, aroused fury in the state's business circles when she wired her support of the miners' demands, adding to the animosity toward her caused by her vote against U.S. entry into World War I.[85] Another public official who was unpopular in those circles was District Attorney Burton K. Wheeler. Wheeler was the one public official who saw the strike for what it was. "Butte, for some time," he reported to the Department of Justice, "had been a volcano on the point of eruption, and the heavy toll of life in the Spectacular Mine catastrophe proved to be a flaming torch." The strikers, Wheeler emphasized, were motivated by a wish to improve their working conditions, and were not bent on sabotage and treason. Working conditions were poor; the miners needed higher wages for the maintenance of a reasonable standard of living, and they wanted the abolition of the obnoxious rustling card system. The 500 to 700 Wobblies in Butte persuaded the miners to strike because of these conditions. In regard to the newspaper claims of strikers' violence, Wheeler informed Attorney General Thomas W. Gregory that the strike in Butte was being conducted "in a manner heretofore unheard of in mining regions," with no violence or disorder being reported.[86]

By mid-July 1917, the companies had succeeded in breaking the strike front by offering better contracts to all but the miners. The contracts were accepted, and the miners were isolated. The companies appeared to be on the verge of success.[87]

## THE LYNCHING OF FRANK LITTLE

Into this situation came Frank Little, agitator, labor organizer, and a national officer of the Industrial Workers of the World. During the week of July 15, Little made several speeches in which he bitterly criticized the use of American troops to quell strikes, calling them "Uncle Sam's scabs in uniform." He minimized the importance of U.S. involvement in the overseas war, even as he urged a sustained strike against the mining companies. The local newspapers had a field day reporting Little's speeches and remarks under headlines like "SOLDIERS CALLED ARMED THUGS." The *Butte Miner* reported:

> Frank Little, Arizona strike leader, practically threatened the United States Government with revolution. Six thousand men filled the bleachers to overflowing and listened to Little's remarks. A frail man supporting the weight of

his body with the aid of crutches,* his face contorted with physical pain and the passion which rocked his body, the speaker worked himself into a maniacal fury as he denounced the capitalist of every class and nationality. . . . Little intimated a world-wide revolution of the working classes. . . . He boasted of the fact that the present-day world-wide conflict meant nothing to him. . . .[88]

Direct calls for action against Little were made in several papers:

The federal authorities not only in Montana but throughout the West, seem to be very lax in their duty when they allow such treasonable and incendiary agitators to travel at will around the country spreading the doctrine of hatred of this ·nation and its institutions. The longer the government postpones handling disloyal movements without gloves, the more difficult it will become to suppress it when it makes up its mind that it must be stopped.[89]

Little made a few additional speeches at closed meetings. Exactly what he said cannot be determined; the only reports are those of company detectives within the Metal Mine Workers' Union and the IWW local where he spoke.** However, it is clear that company officials feared he would succeed in keeping the mines paralyzed for an extended period. In an effort to break his influence, the mine operators offered the miners— not the MMWU—an increase in wages, a weekly payday, and a slight modification of the rustling card system. Nothing was said about union recognition, improvement of working conditions, or an absolute increase in wages. Few miners, however, returned to work on these terms.[90]

Through their private detectives, the companies heard that at a meeting of the MMWU, Little explained that the leaders of the union had failed to win their demands because they were not militant enough: "You fellows are conducting a peaceful strike! Great God! What would Uncle Sam say

*Little had suffered a broken leg in an automobile accident in Jerome, Arizona, where he had been directing the IWW organizing drive in the copper mines. Ralph Chaplin, who met Little in Chicago just before he departed for Butte, wrote later:

"I marveled at his courage in taking on a difficult and dangerous assignment like that in his present condition. 'It's a fine specimen the I.W.W. is sending into that tough town,' I chided him. 'One leg, one eye, two crutches—and no brains!'

"Frank laughed. He lifted a crutch as though to crown me with it. 'Don't worry, fellow-worker, all we're going to need from now on is guts.'" (From Ralph Chaplin, see n.67, p.281.)

The remark "no brains" referred to the fact that Little had vigorously opposed the position of Haywood, Richard Brazier, and others on the IWW General Executive Board who refused to take a stand against conscription, fearing that this would lead to the destruction of the IWW.

**The fact that Little was the only outsider allowed to address the MMWU was cited in the local press as proof that it was an IWW organization even though it called itself "independent."

to the soldiers he is sending to meet the German Army if they *laid down their arms* and said we are conducting a peaceful war."[91]

On July 27, Little delivered a public speech at Butte. The Butte *Daily Post* labeled it "a treasonable tirade," and in the same issue the paper inquired editorially of Butte citizens: "How long Is It [Butte] Going to Stand For the Seditious Talk of the I.W.W. Agitator?"[92]

At approximately 3 a.m. on August 1, 1917, six masked men drove up in an automobile to the front of 316 North Wyoming Street in Butte. One stood in front of the boarding house while the others entered, kicked in the door to Frank Little's room, and pulled and carried him to the car—as reported by Mrs. Nora Byrne, owner of the house.

The car moved a short distance. Then Little was removed and tied to the bumper. He was dragged to the Milwaukee Bridge, outside the city limits, was severely beaten, and hanged from a railroad testle. A small placard was pinned to his underwear with the inscription: "Others take notice, first and last warning, 3-7-77"—the old sign of a vigilante execution. At the bottom of the note the letters "L-D-C-S-S-W-T" were printed; the "L" was circled. Frank Little of the General Executive Board of the IWW was dead, lynched by persons unknown.[93]

The other capital letters apparently stood for other militant labor leaders. Shortly after Little's lynching, the "D" and "C", Wm. F. Dunne of the electrical union and Tom Campbell of the new mine union, received cards with the vigilante warning—"3-7-77"—by special delivery mail. So did other strike leaders. The warning was clear. Unless the strike was terminated, there would be further hangings.[94]

Butte workers responded in anger. Little's body was taken to a funeral parlor for public repose, and thousands walked by to pay homage to the militant labor leader, victim of the anti-labor vigilantes. On August 5, ten thousand people lined the streets of Butte for the funeral procession. At the head of the cortege marched a flag bearer and the two strike leaders who had been warned that they would be next to be lynched—Dunne and Campbell.* Behind them marched a band, members of the Pearce-Connolly Irish Independence Club, and 3,000 members of various unions. An on-the-spot observer noted that as the marchers filed past the

---

*Although Dunne paid tribute to Frank Little, he did not sympathize with his Wobbly views. Dunne believed that the Butte IWW was "composed in equal parts, of laborers and Anaconda detectives," and while he did not believe that Little was a company detective, he was "convinced that Little's presence in Butte had been arranged by those in the I.W.W. who were agents of the companies." (Arnon Gutfield, "The Murder of Frank Little; Radical Labor Agitation in Butte, Montana, 1917," *Labor History* 10 [January 1969]: 187.) There is no known evidence, however, for Dunne's belief.

building that housed the offices of the Anaconda Copper Company, they pointedly glanced up at the company offices, and then looked straight ahead again. "There was no word of complaint uttered," he wrote, "but tragedy was written upon each face, and I said to myself as I stood there, 'And some wonder why there is class hatred.'"[95]

The casket was covered with a red silk banner inscribed "A martyr to solidarity." The burial was without religious ceremony, and as the body was lowered into the grave, "La Marseillaise" was sung.[96]

## MINERS' UNIONIZATION DEFEATED

"The men who perpetrated the affair should be brought to justice," said Burton K. Wheeler in denouncing the murder of Frank Little. County Attorney Jackson at Butte, asked by Montana's Attorney General Sam C. Ford to investigate the lynching, said: "It is a cold-blooded murder and every effort will be used to apprehend the men who did it. If they are caught they will be prosecuted to the full extent of the law."[97] But nobody was ever caught and nobody was ever prosecuted. Will Campbell, editor of the *Helena Independent* and a member of the Montana Council of Defense, explained why nothing was done when he said that those in the state who decided everything, namely the heads of the corporations, were heard to comment publicly, "Good work: Let them continue to hang every I.W.W. in the state."[98]

The immediate effect of the lynching of Frank Little was the spread of the miners' strike. The union claimed it had proof that the Anaconda Copper Company had perpetrated the crime, and the workers' anger enabled the MMWU to close most mines, and because of the lack of ore, major smelters closed all over the state.[99]

But on August 10, Federal troops were ordered to Butte to patrol the streets leading to the mines. And as the strike spread, Senator Myers of Montana introduced into the U.S. Senate an anti-sedition bill that could have been used to guarantee the strike's defeat. When this failed to pass, a special session of the Montana legislature passed what have been called "incredible laws curbing the freedom of speech."[100] One such law was the Montana Sedition Act which provided that

> Any persons who shall utter, print, write or publish any disloyal, profane, violent, scurrilous, contemptuous, slurring or abusive language about the form of government of the United States, or the Constitution of the United States, or the soldiers or sailors . . . or the flag . . . shall be punished for each offense by a fine not less than $200.00 nor more than $20,000.00, or by imprisonment in the State Prison for not less than one year nor more than twenty years, or by both fine and imprisonment.[101]

The Montana Sedition Act was later incorporated into the Federal Sedition Act of 1918, introduced by Senator Thomas J. Walsh of Montana.[102] This was soon followed by the impeachment of Judge Charles L. Crum of Rosebud County because he had tried to act fairly and impartially in trials involving strikers. Then came the investigation of Burton K. Wheeler by the Montana Council of Defense and his resignation as district attorney. When Jeanette Rankin lost her bid for a Senate seat in 1918, she attributed her defeat to a campaign waged against her by the Anaconda Copper Company because of her support of the Metal Mine Workers Union and her denunciation on the floor of Congress of the lynching of Frank Little.[103]

The strike by the Metal Mine Workers Union, which had begun in June 1917, gradually died out as individual miners reluctantly returned to work, hard pressed for money to feed their families, and with little prospect of settlement by the adamant mine owners, who were fully supported by federal troops that remained in Butte long after the war had ended.* The strike was officially called off on December 18, 1917.[104]

According to one scholar, "the spontaneous eruption of an embittered Butte labor force following the tragic fire at the Spectacular Mine had come to naught."

But one new element emerged from the strike that did help labor in Montana to regain its strength. This was the launching of the Butte *Daily Bulletin*, a militant labor paper founded and edited by William F. Dunne, which lasted from 1917 to 1924. The *Bulletin* helped elect an entire slate of political candidates friendly to labor, almost elected as mayor of Butte its own editor, fought corruption in the local police department, and was instrumental in the removal of that department's key officers. It also fought the economic and political dominance of the area's only major employer—Anaconda Copper—and most of all, actively supported and publicized many of the progressive ideas, from the levying of state taxes on mine companies to industrial unionism, that swept Montana between 1917 and 1924.[105]

---

*Federal troops stayed on in Butte until 1921. "The troops," William Preston, Jr. points out, ". . . were quartered in barracks erected and owned by the mining companies, a practice that gave workers the idea that federal troops were guests of the management . . . (One can imagine the government housing troops in I.W.W. halls.)" (*Aliens and Dissenters: Federal Suppression of Radicals, 1903-1933* [Cambridge, Mass. 1963], p. 109.)

William F. Dunne,* was a militant Socialist, and he went on to become an editor of the Communist *Daily Worker* and one of the early leaders of the Communist Party of the United States.

*Dunne pointed out the need for such a daily labor paper during the 1917 strike, noting that the press of Montana was by and large controlled by the Anaconda Company. Anaconda owned the major papers in the following cities: Butte, Missoula, Helena, Miles City, Great Falls, and Billings. "The Company" also controlled the dispatches sent out of the state over the Associated Press wire. Thus, not only were the unions "effectively prevented from airing their viewpoints within Montana, but they were also hampered in presenting their arguments outside of Montana." By midsummer of 1917, strike leaders were convinced of the need for a daily newspaper to counter the incessant anti-union bias of the local press. Aid was sought from the Socialists of Butte and from a group of liberal young attorneys aligned politically against the Anaconda Company. Especially did they look for aid from Burton K. Wheeler. Both Wheeler and the Socialists responded affirmatively. Funds were raised by Wheeler and his friends and by Butte Socialists. The press of the old *Butte Socialist* was given to the new paper for its initial publication. On September 27, 1917, the new paper announced it would take its name from the *Strike Bulletin* and would be called the Butte *Daily Bulletin*. (Guy Halverson and William E. Ames, "The Butte *Bulletin*: Beginning of a Labor Daily," *Journalism Quarterly*,[Summer, 1969], pp. 260-66.)

# CHAPTER 14

# Wartime Repression: The IWW

## THE NATURE OF THE REPRESSION

Although America's participation in World War I was relatively short-lived, the war did in fact bring about massive repression against large numbers of people. Under the banner of "patriotism, heroism, and sacrifice," the Wilson Administration arrested and imprisoned dissenters and scattered and silenced all who opposed either its war propaganda or the corporate forces that were growing fat on war contracts. Those who were deemed insufficiently pro-war faced severe suppression.[1] The Administration pursued the dissenter, the critic, and the protester with a fury that had no precedent in American history since the Alien and Sedition Acts of 1798. From 1917 to 1919 the anti-radical hysteria and persecution increased steadily. Mob rule triumphed over reason; agents of the employers terrorized labor organizers, preachers, teachers, and editors—indeed, anyone "infected" with radicalism. Laws against espionage, sedition, and criminal syndicalism served as tools for widespread and simultaneous arrests. It was a time when violence and violations of civil liberty were judged to be national virtues.[2]

The Wilson Administration was not unaware of the lack of popular support for the war. However, it sought to combat opposition by using the twin devices of propaganda and repression. On the one hand there was the work of the Committee of Public Information in issuing large numbers of pamphlets, posters, little histories—written to order—patriotic literature, and other material justifying intervention, extolling the virtue of the "war to make the world safe for democracy," urging conformity, and shaping the news. On the other hand there was the openly vicious treatment of organized labor's more militant forces, the suppression of minorities, the harassment and imprisonment of dissenters, the blatant indifference to the lynching of Black people and the violence against them, and an unremitting national chauvinism.*

Although Wilson prided himself as an American historian, it remained for Victor Berger to remind the President of many instances in U.S. history when people had opposed a war without governmental persecution. Berger pointed out that Henry Clay, Daniel Webster, Charles Sumner, and Abraham Lincoln had used language similar to the St. Louis Proclamation in denouncing the Mexican War, and that during the Civil War, Lincoln had permitted much harsher criticism to pass unnoticed.[3] But Wilson paid no attention to these lessons from history.

## IWW—THE CHIEF TARGET

Although German immigrants, exiled Mexican revolutionaries, Socialists, and anarchists were subjected to repression once the U.S. entered the war, the IWW was the main target, singled out for destruction as a subversive organization. In its final report, signed by Secretary of Labor William B. Wilson, President Wilson's Labor Commission found that

> repressive dealings with manifestations of labor unrest is the cause of much bitterness, turns radical leaders into martyrs, and thus increases their following, and, worst of all, in the minds of the workers tends to implicate the Government as a partisan in an economic conflict. There is no doubt, however, that the Bisbee and Jerome deportations, the Everett incident,** the Little hanging, and similar acts of violence against workers have had a very harmful effect upon labor both in the United States and in some of the allied countries. Such incidents are attempts to deal with symptoms rather than causes. The I.W.W. has exercised its strongest hold in those industries and those communities where employers have most resisted the trade union movement, and where some form of protest against unjust treatment was inevitable. . . . Sinister influences and extremist doctrines may have availed themselves of these conditions; they certainly have not created them.[4]

Here was a condemnation of the policy the Wilson Administration itself was pursuing by instituting a wholesale assault on the IWW as an

---

*The Women's Peace Party noted with anger President Wilson's silence after the East St. Louis riots. "Six weeks have passed since the East St. Louis riots and no public word of rebuke, no demand for the punishment of the offenders, has come from our Chief Executive. These American Negroes have died under more horrible conditions than any noncombatants who were sunk by German submarines. But to our President their death does not merit consideration." (*Four Lights* 16 [August 25, 1917]: 32-33, in Papers of Women's Peace Party of New York, Swarthmore College Peace Collection.)

**The reference is to the Everett free speech fight and "massacre" of 1916. *See* Foner, *op. cit.*, 4: pp. 518-48.

organization, while failing to lift a finger to punish the agents of the giant corporations for their outrages against U.S. workers. Using federal troops under wartime emergency power, the War Department, by Wilson's orders, conducted raids on Wobblies and labor radicals throughout the country. The army raided IWW halls, broke up meetings, searched boxcars for migrant workers, arrested organizers, and jailed and illegally detained hundreds of "Wobblies." Military detachments, disguised as local police units, joined forces with the National Guard and company officials to break strikes and round up workers. Military intelligence officers engaged in counter-espionage activities in order to place suspected Wobblies under surveillance. Operatives were used to censor mail, spy on the IWW, and gather confidential data on thousands of citizens and aliens.[5]

Not long after the U.S. entry into World War I, the national and state governments developed an elaborate procedure for dealing with the "IWW menace." It included sudden and simultaneous dragnet raids; secret testimony from undercover agents and informants; seizure of correspondence, mailing lists, and membership cards; cross-examination of Wobblies without the presence of defense lawyers, and detention of IWW members *incommunicado*, or with excessive or no bail.[6]

Denunciations of the IWW and demands for its suppression encouraged mob assault against its members. Beatings, tarring and featherings and deportations were risked by Wobblies on entering many towns. A particularly shocking incident, of course, was the Bisbee deportation. But another occurred in Tulsa, Oklahoma on November 8, 1917. The Oil Workers Union No. 450 (OWU) was established by the IWW on January 1, 1917. Its affairs were to be handled by the AWO 400 in Minneapolis until such time as it became large enough to become independent. Locals of AWO 400 and OWU 450 were established in the oil producing region of Tulsa. As the union drive progressed, the Tulsa *World*, an organ of the oil companies, editorialized:

> The first step in the whipping of Germany is to strangle the IWW's. Kill them, just as you would kill any other kind of snake. Don't scotch 'em, kill 'em dead. It is no time to waste money on trials and continuance and things like that. All that is necessary is the evidence and a firing squad.[7]

On November 5, 1917, eleven Wobblies who were actively organizing the oil industry were arrested, tried in police court, and convicted on vagrancy charges. They were fined $100 each. Around 10 o'clock that night, the men were taken from their cells, supposedly to be returned to IWW headquarters, where they were to be released upon promising to leave Tulsa. However, the touring cars in which they were being transported were stopped by "black shrouded [and] hooded" members of the "Knights of Liberty," armed with rifles and pistols. The police escorting the men allowed themselves to be disarmed by the Knights without firing a shot, and the Wobblies were searched and bound. Six more automobiles carrying Knights, similarly clad and armed, arrived, and the entire procession moved to a "wild ravine" in the Osage Hills beyond the city limits.

The automobiles formed a circle with their headlights shining on an oak tree. The Wobblies were unbound and ordered to disrobe to the waist as the hooded figures kept their guns trained on them. One by one the IWWs were tied to the tree and "lashed on the back until the blood ran," with a double piece of new rope made of ⅝- or ¾-inch hemp. A brush was used to apply hot tar to the bleeding backs as the black-robed men in charge of the "ceremony" uttered the words: "In the name of the outraged women and children of Belgium." After the application of the tar, handfuls of feathers were rubbed into the men's backs.

Several of the victims boldly proclaimed their allegiance to the IWW and the working class, even as the tarring and feathering was proceeding. One of the older men pleaded for mercy. "I have lived here for 18 years," he said, "and have raised a large family. I am not an Industrial Worker of the World. I am as patriotic as any man here." But he was shown no mercy. The defenseless victims were then lined up facing west. "Let this be a warning to all Industrial Workers of the World to never come to Tulsa, Oklahoma, again," said the ringleader. "Now get!" With these words, gasoline was poured on the men's clothing and matches applied. As the Wobblies fled down the road, a fusillade of shots was fired after them.

Later that night, large printed signs appeared throughout Tulsa bearing these words: "Warning Posted. Notice to the IWW's: Don't let the sun set on you in Tulsa!—Vigilance Committee."

Police officers were interviewed afterward about the outrageous incident. Nothing could be done, reporters were told, since none of the Knights could be identified, inasmuch as the black robes, hoods, and masks hid all distinguishing features. But Thorstein Veblen, the distinguished economist and sociologist who investigated the incident, charged that the oil companies had organized the vigilantes. Since they controlled Tulsa, he declared, it was not surprising that the police concluded that there was nothing to be done. It was widely known that vigilante groups in the Midwest, especially in Oklahoma and Kansas, were spurred on against the Wobblies by the oil companies.[8]

# ANTI-IWW LAWS

From early 1917 and continuing into the 1920s, the federal and state governments, uniting with industrial interests, moved against the IWW, using the Selective Service, Espionage and Sedition Acts, and state laws that defined criminal syndicalism so as to curtail the activities of the Wobblies. Thus, added to the beatings, jailings, tarring and feathering, was the use of federal troops under the wartime emergency, along with federal and state judicial prosecutions.

Section 3 of the Espionage Act of June 15, 1917, provided that:

> Whoever, when the United States is at war, shall wilfully make or convey false reports or false statements, with intent to interfere with the operation or success of the military or naval forces of the United States or to promote the success of its enemies and whoever, when the United States is at war, shall wilfully obstruct the recruiting or enlistment service of the United States, shall be punished by a fine of not more than $10,000 or imprisonment for not more than twenty years or both.[9]

Yet even the Espionage Act was deemed insufficient. Attorney General Thomas Watt Gregory claimed that it "did not reach the individual casual or impulsive disloyal utterances."[10] However, government attorneys found that so-called traitorous motives were not provable, so the Department of Justice called for an amendment to the act.[11] The amendment of May 16, 1918—the Sedition Act—extended the penalties of the Espionage Act to cover obstruction of the sale of United States bonds and securities; the use of seditious language about the form of government, the Constitution, or the military uniform; oral or written attempts to encourage resistance to the United States; attempts to encourage its enemies; and advocacy of the curtailment of essential war production.[12]

From 1917 to 1920, twenty states enacted criminal syndicalism legislation designed primarily to suppress the IWW.[13] These laws were placed on the statute books at the request of employers, and their representatives were most vocal in calling for the enforcement of the laws. As Eldridge Foster Dowell points out in his comprehensive study of this legislation:

> In practically every state where a criminal syndicalist bill was passed, there is evidence of a bill having been sought by those interests and industries who were having trouble with the IWW, feared trouble with them, or were apprehensive concerning the effect of the IWW and radical doctrines on the more conservative unions in a period of labor unrest.[14]

The Idaho law, passed in March 1917, was among the first of the criminal syndicalist laws adopted in the World War I period. Based in part on a Wisconsin anti-anarchy statute and an earlier New York law, it was the prototype for the legislation passed in other states from 1917 to 1920. As enacted by the Idaho Legislature, the criminal syndicalism act included the following language:

> Section 2. Any person who: (1) by word of mouth or writing, advocates or teaches the duty, necessity or propriety of crime, sabotage, violence or other unlawful methods of terrorism as a means of accomplishing industrial or political reform, or (2) prints, publishes, edits, issues or knowingly circulates, sells, distributes or publicly displays any book, paper, document, or written matter in any form, containing or advocating, advising or teaching the doctrine that industrial or political reform should be brought about by crime, sabotage, violence, or other unlawful methods of terrorism with intent to exemplify, spread or advocate the propriety of the doctrines of criminal syndicalism; or (3) organizes or helps to organize or becomes a member of, or voluntarily assembles with any society, group or assemblage of persons formed to teach or advocate the doctrines of criminal syndicalism;
>
> Is guilty of a felony punishable by imprisonment in the State Prison for not more than ten years or by a fine of not more than five thousand dollars, or both.[15]

The criminal syndicalism acts were specifically drawn to cover the advocacy of doctrines as well as the commission of acts. It was not necessary to establish that members knew each other or the details of the plan or organization, provided only that the accused knew the purpose of the organization and agreed to participate in a plan to achieve that purpose.[16]

## THE GOVERNMENT RAIDS

July and August 1917 saw federal troops and vigilantes (though the two were often indistinguishable) raid IWW offices throughout the country. However, the Justice Department itself seemed to be doing little to move against the Wobblies. Toward the end of July, the *Wall Street Journal* called upon the Department to act at once to achieve the immediate suppression of the IWW. "Why wait?" it asked. "The nation is at war, and treason must be met with preventive as well as punitive measures. . . . Instead of waiting to see if their bite is poisonous, the heel of the Government should stamp them out at once."[17]

Vigilante tactics had been and were being tried and federal troops were joining in with raids and arrests. But these did not stop the IWW organizing drives. Haywood, General Secretary of the IWW, boasted:

They can't stop us. No matter what they do we will go on and on—until we—the roughnecks of the world—will take control of all production and work when we please and how much we please. The man who makes the wagon will ride in it himself. . . ."[18]

There was only one solution. The New York *Globe* put it succinctly: "The Bisbee plan does not work. Only the Government of the United States can destroy the troublesome I.W.W."[19] In response, President Wilson appointed Judge J. Harry Covington of the District of Columbia Supreme Court to investigate the IWW. Upon announcement of his appointment, Haywood invited him to visit IWW headquarters, where he would "be given access to books and papers and also given all the assistance possible in the inquiry."

Judge Covington ignored the invitation.[20] The reason soon became clear. In the morning hours of September 5, 1917, Justice Department agents and local police officers invaded Wobbly headquarters and the homes of IWW officials in Chicago, Fresno, New York City, Seattle, Spokane, Pittsburgh, Lincoln (Nebraska), Detroit, Salt Lake City, Superior (Wisconsin), Minneapolis, Duluth, Milwaukee, Portland (Oregon), Los Angeles, Omaha, Philadelphia, Miami, and every other city where the IWW had an office—sixty-four IWW headquarters in all. In addition, in many areas, Wobblies were rounded up "on the job".

Operating under what one historian has described as "perhaps the broadest search warrant ever issued by the American judiciary," federal agents seized everything they could lay their hands on: correspondence, minute books, typewriters, desks, even rubber bands and paper clips. From the Chicago headquarters alone the agents confiscated over five tons of material—"wagon loads of paper to examine for evidence of treason," as one contemporary journal put it.[21] But what is treason? "The IWW members are demanding and getting the right to organize, better working conditions, a shorter workday, and higher wages. That is what their treason consists of," said the state secretary of the Socialist Party of Washington.[22]

There was little outcry over the raid from newspapers, and the *Literary Digest*, in its summary of the reaction, concluded that "the press of free America . . . do not appear to regard the raids as one of those tyrannical persecutions of the downtrodden, such as our Republic was founded to prevent."[23] Even *The Public*, the progressive weekly published in Chicago, took the position that the Wobblies "should be the last to feel surprise. They have been uncompromising enemies of the State, and this is a time when the State must be equally uncompromising. . . . The IWW cannot expect to stay out of jail in war time."[24]

But *The Public* did note that a protest against the raids had been sent to President Wilson and Attorney General Gregory by the Boston League for Democratic Control, whose free speech committee, made up of Robert W. Dunn, Margaret Hatfield Chase, and Rev. George Grover Mills, declared: "The recent action by the authorities has not been duplicated in any country since the revolution set Russia free from such practices. Therefore, we regard these raids as a repetition of acts which we had hoped were anachronistic except in autocracies."[25]

## THE INDICTMENTS

The purpose of the raids, the United States attorney for Philadelphia acknowledged, was "very largely to put the IWW out of business."[26] During the next several weeks, in pursuit of this goal, Federal investigators went through the confiscated IWW material, and they selected from the tremendous mass of correspondence, pamphlets, newspapers, and other Wobbly literature, those items that would be used to bring 184 members to trial* on the charge of interfering with the war effort and encouraging resistance to the Selective Service Act. The defendants were tried in three separate groups, the first in Chicago, and later in Sacramento, California and Wichita, Kansas.

The indictments were virtually the same in all three cases. The Chicago federal grand jury indicted 165 IWW members on five counts. The first charged the defendants with conspiring with the deceased Frank Little and "diverse other persons," (who, being unknown, were unnamed) to violate federal law, to obstruct the war effort by means of sabotage and the

---

*These were not, however, the only IWW members brought to trial on charges growing out of the Espionage Act. In Portland, Oregon, Marie Equi, a local IWW activist and birth control advocate, was accused of having slandered the army by saying that the soldiers were "forced into the trenches" because they were conscripted and that they were "dirty, corruptible scum." Dr. Equi, defending herself without counsel, denied the charge, pointing out to the jury that since the army drew its members from all walks of life, "and includes the class in whose welfare I have always been interested—the working class—I could not possibly bring myself to call them 'dirty, corruptible scum.'" She claimed that the only reason for her indictment was the fact that she had supported the IWW's organizing drive in the lumber camps, and that her arrest had been instigated by "the Loyal Legion of Loggers and Lumbermen," the open-shop company union that was using the issue of patriotism to destroy the one union that threatened their income. Dr. Equi produced evidence that her phone had been tampered with after she had been indicted and that a dictaphone had been installed to monitor her conversations with patients. Nevertheless, the jury convicted her of "sedition," and she was sentenced to three years' imprisonment and a $500 fine. (*Seattle Union Record*, Nov. 9, 1918; *Portland Oregonian*, Nov. 8-12, 1918.)

destruction of property, and also by speaking and writing against the war and the draft. The second count, that they had conspired to threaten to interfere with workers' contracts with their employers. The third, that they had conspired to aid in the evasion of the draft. The fourth, that they had conspired to promote military insubordination. The fifth and last count charged that they had conspired to defraud certain employers through the mails.[27] The last count was thrown out even before the Chicago trial began.*

As William Preston, Jr. points out, the indictment pictured the IWW as "a vicious, treasonable conspiracy to oppose by force the execution of the laws of the United States and to obstruct the prosection of the war."[28] But a reading of the 32-page indictment clearly indicates that the "overt acts" to prove this "treasonable conspiracy consisted entirely of official statements, policy declarations, newspaper articles, and personal expressions of opinion in private and in organization correspondence. Not a single act was cited to justify the charges in the indictment." Correspondence was quoted, for example, indicating that Haywood directed an IWW organizer to visit a particular factory, mill, or mine. The purpose of the visit was not made clear in the correspondence, but this did not prevent the grand jury from concluding that the objective was either to sabotage plant operations or to interfere in some way with its production.

Another example: Emil Pouget's book, *Sabotage*, which had been published and distributed by the IWW in 1915, and which was quoted at length in the indictment, had, in fact, been withdrawn from circulation by the IWW's General Executive Board in 1917 and no new edition had been published. But no mention was made of its withdrawal in the indictment. Similarly, most of the quotations from *Solidarity* and many of the letters of Wobblies quoted in the indictment were written before the period covered by it.[29]

On the day following the raids of IWW headquarters, the *New York Times* announced:

*In the Wichita, Kansas trial, a new charge was added to the indictment—conspiracy to violate the Lever Act. It was applied in Kansas because of IWW activity in the wheat harvest and the oil fields, and it charged conspiracy to limit the production and transportation of farm products and petroleum. (Clayton R. Kopper, "The Kansas Trial of the IWW, 1917-1919," *Labor History* 16 [Summer 1975]: 343-44.)

**Even on the eve of the trial of the Wobblies in March 1918, the prosecution had yet to procure evidence to prove specific crimes. In a twenty-three page summary of the IWW's "criminal record," prepared by the prosecution and submitted to the Attorney General, there was not a single instance cited "of a specific crime committed by a Wobbly." (Melvyn Dubofsky, *We Shall Be all: A History of the Industrial Workers of the World*, [Chicago, 1969], p. 522.)

From a source of undoubted authority, a *Times* reporter learned here last night that the rounding up of the Industrial Workers of the World in various parts of the United States follows the revelation of a countrywide plot, the purpose of which included not only the destruction, as far as possible, of the wheat and corn crops in the West, and the disorganization of the mining industry, especially the copper industry, but the commission of a multitude of crimes, all intended to hamper the successful prosecution of the war against Germany.[30]

Shortly after Haywood was arrested and imprisoned with 165 other Wobblies in Chicago's antiquated Cook County jail, he told Carl Sandburg: "[We have] done nothing on the war one way or another. It is true we have called strikes, but they were not aimed at stopping the war." He was equally emphatic in denying that the IWW had accepted German money—an allegation which, though not contained in the indictment, he knew to be particularly damaging to the union's public image. "Not a dirty German dollar has ever come into our hands that we know of. . . . Every dollar we've got now and every dollar the organization will get comes from workingmen."[31]

In this disclaimer, the IWW's secretary-treasurer was supported by many radicals who, like the editors of the *Milwaukee Leader*, believed that "it is evident that the war is being made an excuse to put them [the IWW] out of business with an iron hand."[32] "Whether one relishes it or not," maintained the young Socialist Louis Fraina, "the fact is that the IWW has not acted against the war . . . and is chiefly if not exclusively at the moment interested in questions of wages and the regulation of industrial conditions."[33]

## THE IWW AND THE DRAFT

The charge that the IWW interfered with conscription, one of the five counts in the indictment, was in fact ironic because the IWW had actually refused to take a stand on the draft. As we have seen, shortly before the declaration of war, the IWW national office held up production of adhesive stickers it had planned to distribute. These said "Why Be a Soldier? " with the last word printed in dripping red letters. As June 15, 1917,—the day set aside for the registration of all draft age males—approached, the IWW made no recommendation to its members. On registration day there was a mass refusal to register in two localities, and in both instances, IWW members were involved. In the Mesabi range of northern Minnesota, over two hundred miners, veterans of the previous year's IWW-led strike,* were arrested for refusing to register. But IWW leaders had

*For a discussion of the Mesabi Range strike of 1916, *see* Philip S. Foner, *History of the Labor Movement in the United States* (New York, 1965) 4: 486-517.

warned them against giving the government any excuse to arrest them. The other incident took place in Rockford, Illinois, when Clyde Hough, an IWW member, and two other workers, were arrested for nonregistration. About six hundred men, mainly Wobblies and Socialists, then marched to the county jail and demanded either the release of the imprisoned men or the arrest of all the men in the crowd, since they too were unwilling to register. The sheriff arrested 138 men—all that the jail could hold—and ordered the crowd to disperse, which it did. Within a month, 117 of the men had been sentenced to a year at hard labor by District Judge Kenesaw M. Landis (whom we shall soon meet again) who called them "belly-aching, whining puppies." Although *Solidarity* carried reports of the Rockford affair, the IWW neither publicized the case nor rendered aid to the defendants.[34]

Some individual IWW members did advocate and practice dodging the draft, and a resolution adopted by the Augusta, Kansas local in May 1917, urged that "all members of the IWW resist conscription by refusing to join any band of potential murderers or by any other effective methods deemed advisable."[35] But from the time of the entry of the United States into the war until the indictments were handed down, the IWW as an organization had taken no stand on whether or not members should comply with the draft law. To the numerous members who wrote in inquiring about the IWW's position on the draft, the national office replied that there was no position. In late June 1917, a special session of the General Executive Board was convened in Chicago, but instead of resolving the issue, it became hopelessly deadlocked. Haywood and several other members maintained that the IWW should stick to industrial activities and that to challenge the draft would only invite repression without really making a dent in the war effort.

The only position which the Board could agree on was that Ralph Chaplin should be given the authority to print a statement over his own signature. Appearing in the July 20, 1917 issue of *Solidarity*, Chaplin's statement said that members who joined military forces had always been expelled from the IWW and that "the principle of the International solidarity of labor to which we have always adhered makes it impossible for us to participate in any and all of the plunder-squabbles of the Parasite class." It urged that members register for the draft, but that they also claim exemption from military service by writing on the registration form, "IWW, opposed to war."[36]

The one IWW leader who was most willing to engage in direct conflict with the selective service system was, as we have seen, Frank Little. At the General Executive Board meeting he argued vehemently but unsuccessfully for an outright anti-draft position.[37]

In short, the IWW limited its opposition to the war to rhetoric and took no specific antiwar action. The regional leaders of the IWW made conscription a matter of individual conscience. Roughly 95 percent of the eligible Wobblies registered with their draft boards, and most served when called. Victimized by patriotic vigilantes, the Wobblies protested that they were more interested in organizing workers to increase their wages and improve their working conditions than in opposing the war, much as they hated every war but the class war.[38]

But while the IWW did not advocate "draft-dodging," the Wobblies were not pacifists. They believed deeply that all wars except the class war benefitted only the capitalists while the workingmen bore the cost. Through its general anti-war, anti-imperialist stance, the IWW was identified with militant opposition to the war in its every phase, so that the editors of the *Michigan Socialist* insisted that the arrest and jailing of Wobbly leaders was "but a blind to conceal the government's real aim to crush organizations who insist upon telling the truth about the war and peace."[39]

But it also seems clear that the authorities were more concerned over the IWW's effectiveness in organizing labor's discontent and leading workers in strikes than over their lack of patriotism. As we have seen in a previous volume, from the very inception of the IWW, officials of the Department of Justice had sought to establish a basis for federal action against the Wobblies.* As early as 1912, President Taft had said he believed that firm repression "would carry California for the Republican ticket and return him to the presidency." In 1915, Woodrow Wilson, Taft's successor, ordered an investigation of the Wobblies, and even when the agent he dispatched to study the problem came back with a negative report, he was still determined to act against the Wobblies. Before 1917, however, federal investigations had failed to uncover evidence of a kind sufficient to justify criminal prosecution of the Wobblies. But with the passage of the Espionage Act of June 15, 1917, a federal means of indictment was established.

No less a person than Attorney General Henry M. Daugherty gave the real reason for the federal and state trials of the IWW when he said in 1922 that "in a great industrial nation such as ours, labor organizations are necessary, but they must be the right kind of unions under the right kind of leadership."[40]

*See Foner, *op. cit.*, 4: pp. 295, 482-86.

The "right kind of unions under the right kind of leadership" were, of course, the affiliates of the American Federation of Labor and the Gompers leadership. Haywood claimed that he was told by the writer Robert Bruere that Gompers was responsible for interesting the Department of Justice in the campaign to annihilate the IWW. One does not necessarily have to believe that were it not for Gompers' intervention the Wobblies would not have been prosecuted. But there is much evidence to show that when the IWW began to make inroads into AFL membership, especially in the West, the federal government worked with the Federation leadership to destroy the Wobblies. The *Coast Seamen's Journal* declared that the prosecution of the IWW was intended "to drive large numbers of men who . . . had a casual acquaintance with . . . [the IWW] to form labor unions under the AFL." IWW papers and documents seized by the Justice Department were turned over to Gompers by Attorney General Thomas W. Gregory "to help the Federation in its struggle with the radical Wobblies." Not only did Gompers fully support all legislation rushed through Congress dealing with espionage and sedition, he also worked closely with the Justice Department in ferreting out "subversives" in the labor movement, going so far as to place labor men on the payroll of the Department of Justice as agents and informers. Ralph Easley of the National Civic Federation was usually his intermediary in such matters.[41]

Gompers never once protested against the suppression of the IWW. On the contrary, he added to the hysteria against the Wobblies by denying that the IWW served any labor function and by labeling the organization as "an agent of the Kaiser." Similarly, Socialists such as Adolf Germer, Victor Berger, and Morris Hillquit were branded by Gompers as German sympathizers, not only because of their views, but also because their ethnic background was German.[42]

## THE GOVERNMENT SABOTAGES THE DEFENSE

Following the September 5, 1917 raids, Haywood requested that Herbert Mahler and C. E. Payne come to Chicago to organize the national defense work for the soon-to-be arrested and jailed Wobblies. Mahler was arrested later that month, but Payne was not. The General Executive Board split on the strategy to be taken for the trial. Some said that the IWW leaders should avoid the arrests and go underground. But Haywood and IWW attorney George F. Vanderveer convinced them to use the trial as propaganda for the cause. Haywood ordered those under indictment to submit to arrest, which they did.

Vanderveer made a motion to quash the indictment on the ground that it was based on hearsay and supported by evidence gathered in an unconstitutional manner. The bulk of the material taken from the general headquarters in Chicago, for example, was seized on the basis of search warrants issued on affidavits that failed either to specify the property to be taken or to establish facts from which magistrates could determine probable cause. But these objections were dismissed. There was some talk to the effect that the government had offered to dismiss the indictment if the IWW agreed not to use the arrests as propaganda, and that the Wobblies had refused to do so, but this was only conjecture.

After the IWW leaders had been imprisoned in the Cook County jail, the hard-pressed IWW tried to bail them out and plan a legal defense. To inhibit the Wobblies' defense efforts, the government maintained a rigid censorship policy under which the Post Office was instructed to withhold mailing privileges from defense committees, and to intercept, delay, and seize outright the IWW defense mail. The IWW's General Defense Committee, formed to coordinate defense activities, found its mail delayed by postal authorities for periods ranging up to eight and twelve months. Numerous categories of IWW material were barred from the mails altogether. The censorship became so tight that a copy of an IWW resolution *against* sabotage was declared to be unmailable—on the ground that it contained the word "sabotage"! When a small group of prominent liberals placed a fund-raising appeal in the *New Republic*, asking only that readers contribute to the defense fund in order to assure the IWW defendants of a fair hearing, the Post Office Department pressured the magazine into refusing to run the appeal in any subsequent issues.[43] Other government agencies pitched in too—alien Wobblies who handled defense literature were detained by immigration officials.

Under these circumstances, it took real courage to speak out in support of the IWW and urge funds for their defense. One who did was Helen Keller, the deaf mute and blind Socialist. Keller published "In Behalf of the I.W.W." in the *Liberator*, in which she asked: "Who is truly indicted, they or the social system that produced them? . . . Surely," she added, "the demands of the I.W.W. are just," and urging immediate assistance in their trial, she concluded:

> Despite their errors, their blunders and the ignominy heaped upon them, I sympathize with the IWW's. Their cause is my cause. While they are threatened and imprisoned, I am manacled.[44]

Through such appeals, sufficient funds were raised to release on bail the Wobblies who were in prison.

# THE CHICAGO TRIAL

On April 1, 1918, the longest criminal trial in United States legal history up to that time began in Chicago. Of the 113 IWW officials and members brought to trial, 101 remained to be tried. The others were either allowed a severance or had the indictments against them dropped.* Each of the remaining 101 was charged with more than one hundred separate crimes.[45]

Defense counsel Vanderveer and prosecuting attorney Frank K. Nebeker spent 29 days selecting the jury. Among the questions asked of prospective jurymen by Vendeveer were:

> You told Mr. Nebeker that you had never read any revolutionary literature. Have you never read in school, about American Revolution of 1776? Or the French Revolution which deposed the king and made France a republic? Or the Russian Revolution that overthrew the autocracy and the tsar?
>
> In our own Civil War, do you think it was right for Congress to pass a law which took away from the people of the South several million dollars worth of property in the form of chattel slaves—without compensation?[46]

The trial took place before Judge Kenesaw Mountain Landis, soon to become famous, in the aftermath of the 1919 Chicago Black Sox scandal, as baseballs first commissioner. Described by John Reed, who covered the trial for the *Liberator*, as possessing "the face of Andrew Jackson three years dead," Landis had earlier presided over the trial of the Wobblies and Socialists from Rockford, Illinois accused of evading the Registration Act, and had handed down harsh sentences after they were found guilty. Despite the fact that he had a son in the army, strongly supported the war, and vehemently disliked radicalism, Landis tried to convey an attitude of courtesy and fairness to the defendants. John Reed reported that it was

> . . . in many ways a most unusual trial. When the judge enters the courtroom after recess no one rises—he himself has abolished the pompous formality. He sits without robes, in an ordinary business suit, and often leaves the bench to come down and perch on the step of the jury box. By his personal order, spitoons are placed beside the prisoners' seats, so they can while away the long day with a chaw; and as for the prisoners themselves, they are permitted to take off their coats, move around, read newspapers. . . .[47]

Writing of the prisoners, Reed noted that he doubted if ever before in history had there "been a sight just like them. One hundred and one men— lumberjacks, harvest-hands, miners, editors; one hundred and one who

---

*Elizabeth Gurley Flynn and Carlo Tresca were allowed a severance from the other defendants, and were never brought to trial. The indictment against Arturo Giovannitti was dropped, much to his annoyance, since he wanted to be with his comrades.

believe that the wealth of the world belongs to him who creates it, and that the workers of the world should take their own. . . ."[48]

There were limits to Landis's air of fairness when it came to Benjamin Harrison Fletcher, the only black defendant in all the IWW trials. For example, Landis was angered because Fletcher's illness had forced the court to cancel the July 10 session. He revoked Fletcher's bail, and the black Wobbly had to spend two weeks in Cook County jail.[49*]

Judge Landis allowed the prosecution to present evidence in order to demonstrate the defendants' "frame of mind." Nebeker tried to prejudice the jury further than it already had been by the current hysteria against the IWW, by asking the defendants during cross-examination if they believed in marriage or free love. Vanderveer of course objected, but Landis allowed the questions. He also permitted the prosecution wide leeway in introducing IWW materials that were written and distributed before the declaration of war or, in other words, outside the period of the indictment.

On the other hand, when Vanderveer tried to show that the IWW had arisen out of "contemporary economic conditions," Landis stopped him. He ruled out any attempt to insert into the record the report of the Commission on Industrial Relations aimed at enabling the jury to understand the economic conditions in the United States that had given birth to the IWW and had led to its growth. He insisted that the defendants were on trial, not the country.

But Vanderveer was able to get around Landis's ruling that evidence relating to exploitative working conditions was not relevant and thus could not be introduced. He did this by having defendants testify about their own personal experiences in which "capitalist exploitation" was an overriding theme. Indeed, it is doubtful if any radical group had ever before made such use of the courtroom to set forth its philosophy and experience as did the IWW in 1918. Here is John Reed's description of a typical testimony by the defendants:

> I heard Frank Rogers, a youth grown black and bitter, with eyes full of vengeance, tell briefly and drily of the Speculator mine fire, and how hundreds of men burned to death because the company would not put doors in the bulk-heads. He spoke of the assassination of Frank Little,. who was hung by "vigilantes" in Montana, and how the miners of Butte swore to remember . . . and of Oklahoma, the tar-and-feathering of the workers at Tulsa. . . .

*Fletcher was the leader of the Marine Transport Workers' Union, which was especially strong in Philadelphia. For his activity in MTWU, see Foner, op. cit., 4: pp 125-27, 245; Philip S. Foner, Organized Labor and the Black Worker, 1619-1981, (New York,1982), pp. 112-14, 159-60.

All this has come out day by day, shocking story on story. I sat for the better part of two days listening to A. S. Embree tell again the astounding narrative of the Arizona deportations. . . . Many of the deportees had wives, families and property in Bisbee, some were not IWW's at all, and others that had no connection with the labor movement in any way. . . .

Listen to the scriptural simplicity of this: "Well, they grabbed us. And the deputy says, "Are you a member of the IWW?" I says, "yes," so he asked for my card, and I gave it to him, and he tore it up. He tore the other cards up that the fellow members along with me had, so this fellow member says, "There is no use tearing that card up, we can get duplicates." "Well," the deputy says, "we can tear the duplicates up, too."

And this fellow worker says, he says, "Yes, but you can't tear it out of my heart."[50]

The IWW defense consisted mainly of documentary evidence and testimony to demonstrate that the organization was engaged not in the alleged conspiracies against the selective service act, the Espionage Act, and other war statutes, but rather in the amelioration of labor conditions.[51] The defendants took pains to explain, and some felt they exaggerated, the extent to which the IWW had avoided outright opposition to the war effort. Haywood, who was on the stand for three days and was the star witness, testified that the IWW had never taken any action on conscription, and that he himself had never aided anyone in impeding the war effort. In fact, he cited an example in which the IWW was instrumental in the prosecution of the war, namely, the Philadelphia local of the Marine Transport Workers Union, led by Ben Fletcher, whose members had spent the duration of the war loading munitions, oil, and other supplies for shipment to the allies. Haywood denied that men had been expelled from the organization for joining the armed forces; two soldiers, testifying for the defense, said they had been IWW members before the war, planned to rejoin, and had encountered no hostility from other Wobblies on account of their service in the army.\* Another defense witness testified that the local IWW branch in Augusta, Kansas had chased one of its former leaders out of town because of his talk against the draft, even though originally it had endorsed his resolution against conscription.[52]

Ben Fletcher did not testify, but Walter T. Nef, John J. Walsh, and Edward F. Doree, Philadelphia Wobblies, told about the war activities of the marine transport workers. All three testified that the Wobblies controlled the Philadelphia docks, that relations between Black and white longshoremen were friendly and harmonious, and that although about

\*When A. C. Christ, one of the original 113 defendants, appeared in court in military uniform on April 1, the government quickly dismissed Christ's case. (*New York Times*, April 2, 3, 1918.)

eighty percent of their cargos consisted of powder, munitions, steel rails, and other war materials, no explosion or accident had occurred. Walsh indicated that only two or three detectives watched the docks in Philadelphia and they were looking for German, not IWW, saboteurs. On New York docks, which were not under Wobbly control, there were as many detectives as there were longshoremen. If the IWW had wanted to undermine the war effort, Walsh stated, sabotage would have been easy: "There is not a ship on the Atlantic coast that hasn't got IWW men in the fire room or on deck or in the galley as a cook even."

As an organizer, Walsh commented, he would have been among the first to know if the IWW wanted its members to refrain from registering. He told the court, "I know there were over two hundred members [from Philadelphia] volunteered and were drafted before I surrendered myself on December 5, 1917."[53]

Vanderveer hammered away at the prosecutor's inability to come up with any evidence specifically showing a conspiracy to obstruct the war. He protested vehemently that all of the government's evidence referred to letters, newspaper articles, union bulletins, and the like, which pertained to events prior to America's declaration of war on April 6, 1917, and was therefore inadmissable. He insisted that the government was trying to prove that anti-capitalism was the same as pro-Germanism and therefore constituted disloyalty to the United States.[54]

In the case of each strike that Nebeker had alleged had "deliberately interfered with the war effort," Vanderveer successfully demonstrated, through federal publications and reports, that the objectives were not political, but rather based on economic factors.[55]

In the face of the prosecution's obvious lack of evidence to support its case, Vanderveer was naïvely optimistic:

> Our record on the strike issue presented in the first and second counts, and on the issue of violence and destruction of property, is absolutely clean, and I have not the slightest doubt about our ability to make the position which the government has outlined in the indictment look ridiculous.[56]

He continued:

> Every day now furnishes some new reason for believing that the Chicago case will shortly be disposed of, probably on our motion to quash the indictment. . . . In large part, no doubt, this is because the Government . . . is afraid to take chances on the outcome of so public a trial.[57]

At the end of the trial, Vanderveer did not even present a closing argument to the jury. It appears that he believed his effective examination and cross-examination of witnesses, added to the ineffectiveness of the prosecution's case, left nothing upon which the jury could convict any one of the defendants.[58]

But it seems that the defendants did not share their counsel's optimism. Writing from his jail cell, A. S. Embree cautioned that regardless of the prosecution's lack of evidence and notwithstanding Vanderveer's effectiveness, "our men can be killed or jailed." James Rowan, another defendant, stated: "Of course we can expect nothing else than to be jailed for taking part in a strike . . . for we know that a rebellious slave is the worst criminal in the eyes of the master." Yet John Reed believed that these men "still have faith in the goodness of mankind, and the possibility of justice for the righteous." They had not given up on the working class, Reed wrote. After all, had not Rowan remarked: "What they can do in Russia, we can do in this 'Land of the Free'"?[59]

## THE VERDICT AND THE SENTENCES

Vanderveer's optimism soon proved to be unjustified. After the five-month trial, it took the jury just an hour to find all of the defendants guilty as charged—each and every defendant on each and every one of the four counts. The Wobblies were shocked by "the speed and the substance" of the verdict. Vincent St. John wrote: "I did not think that mob justice would prevail in a U.S. court."[60]

But the Wobblies should not have been surprised. For all the brilliance of their defense, they and their attorney might just as well have been talking to themselves. The trial took place in an atmosphere of hysteria that increased when the Bolshevik Revolution triumphed in Russia on November 7, 1917. The universal acclaim that had greeted the March revolution was gone. It was one thing for the Tsar to be overthrown; it was quite another to have the economic and political rule of the workers and peasants triumphant. A wholesale propaganda attack on the new Soviet government immediately began, with misinformation and misrepresentation as the main weapons of this propaganda.*

---

*How thoroughgoing this misinformation was, became a matter of public and scandalous record when Walter Lippmann and Charles Merz made a study of the way in which the *New York Times* had reported the *news* about the Bolshevik government in the first hundred days after November 7, 1917. Published as a special supplement of the *New Republic* on August 4, 1920, "A Test of the News" concluded that Americans who relied upon the *Times* for their source of information, had been totally misinformed about the *facts* of Soviet life for the one hundred days. When the IWW defendants were asked by the prosecution about their views of marriage and family life, they were expected to confirm the jury's view, gained from newspaper reports about the Soviet Union, that the Bolsheviks had abolished marriage and family life, and that all Wobblies had similar attitudes toward marriage and the family.

The trials of the Wobblies took place in an atmosphere of just such misinformation and misrepresentation. When the jury left the courtroom for lunch, they passed a movie theater whose marquee read, "The Menace of the IWW" and "The Red Viper." When they returned to the courtroom, they heard the prosecution inveigh against "The Menace of the IWW" and "The Red Viper." It was the "Menace," the "Red Viper" that stood in the dock, not the defendants. In words that were reminiscent of the Haymarket trial, the prosecution openly stated: "It is the IWW which is on trial here."[61] During the trial, John J. Walsh predicted the final verdict when he said: "We know it is a very easy matter any time for a long distance patriot like [Frank K.] Nebeker . . . to get up here and wave the flag in front of a jury. That is the whole trouble!"[62]

Apart from the coverage of the trial by John Reed in the *Liberator* and David Karsner in the New York *Evening Call*, both Socialist papers and both with meager circulations, coverage of the trial in most newspapers consisted of sensational charges against the IWW. Many of the charges were made in the form of out-of-court "disclosures" by the prosecution, of material that they could not introduce as evidence even with Landis's lenient standards. No publicity was given to the IWW's repudiation of the charges in the indictment, nor to the defendants' efforts to explain that the IWW's radical unionism was necessary in an era of high profits, low wages, and poor working conditions. Most shocking of all was the fact that the press completely ignored or played down the fact that F. M. Bailey, a government accountant who examined the organization's finances for the Department of Justice, specifically refuted the charge that the IWW's organizing drives were financed by German gold.[63]

What difference, after all, did that make? The *Outlook* told its readers before the jury announced its verdict:

> Regardless of their verdict it has been made clear during the course of this trial that we have in the United States a full-fledged revolutionary organization under a leadership as radical as any that existed in Russia prior to the overthrow of the autocracy.[64]

On August 31, 1918, Judge Landis, dropping his amiability, handed down the sentences. Seventeen defendants, whose connection with the IWW was tenuous (one was a nineteen-year-old Harvard sophomore who was not even an IWW member) got off lightly. They were either released on their own recognizance or received sentences of ten days in the county jail or one year and one day in federal prison. But eighty-three Wobblies were treated harshly. Thirty-five were sentenced to five years each in prison; thirty-three to ten years, and fifteen to twenty years. Total fines in the cases exceeded two million dollars.[65]

Haywood, Chaplin, James P. Thompson, "Red" Doran, James Rowan, and other veterans of IWW struggles received sentences of $30,000 fines and twenty years in prison each. Although no witness testified to Ben Fletcher's disloyalty during the trial, he was convicted on four counts. Prior to being sentenced, Fletcher told the court, "I have not engaged in any disloyal propaganda against the United States government. . . . My activities . . . have always been within the law. . . ." Referring to his voluminous correspondence introduced during the trial, Fletcher remarked, "I do not think you will find a scintilla bit of evidence therein to substantiate any claims that my efforts were disloyal." No matter. The only black defendant was fined $30,000 and sentenced to ten years in prison. Haywood later recalled that Fletcher "sidled over to me and said: 'The Judge has been using very ungrammatical language.' I looked at his smiling black face and asked: 'How's that, Ben?' He said: 'His sentences are much too long.'"[66*]

Not a single Wobbly fled the country or went underground between the time of conviction and sentencing. Richard Brazier, a defendant, maintained in 1966 that Landis's "generosity" in releasing them from a Cook County jail prior to sentencing was suspected. They believed that the judge expected them to run away so that he could label them cowards and fugitives.[67]

After being sentenced, the prisoners were sent by train to the federal penitentiary in Leavenworth to await release on bail while the appeal of their conviction went to the higher courts. We will deal in our next volume with the defense movement and the appeals, but here we note that in October 1920 the United States Circuit Court of Appeals reversed the convictions on the first two counts, but upheld them on counts three and four. Thus, the Wobblies were acquitted of conspiracy to prevent and hinder the government from executing numerous statutes for the prosecution of the war, and of conspiring to interfere with the production and transportation of food, clothing, and munitions essential to the carrying on of the war. They were found guilty of conspiracy to interfere with the enforcement of the Selective Draft Law and to violate the Federal Espionage Law and to

---

*Haywood added that at another time during the trial, Fletcher remarked "in a spirit of humor: 'If it wasn't for me, there'd be no color in this trial at all.' I might explain that he was the only Negro in the group." (*Bill Haywood's Book: The Autobiography of William D. Haywood* [New York, 1929], p. 325.)

obstruct Army and Navy recruiting. The Court of Appeals not only concurred in the guilty verdict but held that the admission of illegally seized evidence had not violated the defendants' constitutional rights because the defendants had been indicted as individuals, not as members of the IWW. The documents and records were considered tools of the crime and therefore were not protected by the Fourth Amendment against seizure.[68]

On April 11, 1921 the Supreme Court declined to review the trial!

After the Chicago co-defendants were found guilty, the government's battle to destroy the IWW shifted to Sacramento, California and Wichita, Kansas. But since both of these trials began in December 1918, one month after World War I ended, and took place under somewhat different circumstances, we shall study them in our next volume.

## WHAT HAPPENED TO THE IWW ARCHIVES?

"Wagon-loads of paper" had been confiscated from IWW headquarters by the federal authorities. Before the trials commenced, defense attorney Vanderveer submitted a petition for the return of "a large volume of papers, letters, books, documents, records and other property . . . unlawfully seized and taken from the possession of the defendants by officers of the United States Government in violation of the Fourth Amendment of the Constitution of the United States and the rights of said defendants thereunder. . . ."[69] But the petition was rejected by Judge Landis. Some of the IWW correspondence found its way into the transcript of the trial and the brief of the appeals to the U.S. Circuit Court of Appeals.[70] (But while seventy-five of Benjamin Harrison Fletcher's letters were read at the trial, only a few were printed as part of the official transcript.) These and others were also deposited in the Justice Department files and were later housed in the National Archives in Washington, D.C. They have been examined by a number of scholars, including this writer, but after William Preston, Jr. completed his research for *Aliens and Dissenters: Federal Suppression of Radicals, 1903-1933* (originally a doctoral dissertation at the University of Wisconsin), J. Edgar Hoover restricted and removed from the open archives those items that were deemed "sensitive." Among the collections still open after that order, which included portions of IWW correspondence, the most important were the pardon petitions of IWW prisoners— RG 240 Justice Department Record Groups in the National Archives.

In 1976, the National Archives decertified the investigative files of the Bureau of Investigation, the precursor of the FBI. Although the Bureau of Investigation files are no substitute for the original IWW records, they do throw new light on IWW activities, especially for the period 1918 to 1920.

But even this contains only a minute portion of the confiscated IWW correspondence.

It would be pleasant to report that the tons of material confiscated from the IWW have been located in some warehouse or cellar and will shortly be made available to students of the U.S. labor movement. Unfortunately, this is not the case. The answer to the question of what happened to the vast collection of IWW material confiscated by the federal authorities is that the bulk of it was destroyed by court order. On May 8, 1922, Judge George T. Page of the District Court of the United States, Northern District of Illinois, Eastern Division, issued an order "to destroy all correspondence, literature, pamphlets, and other books now located in rooms 858 and 959 of the Federal Building in the City of Chicago, State of Illinois, and in the warehouse of the Federal Fireproof Storage Company, in the City of Chicago, County of Cook, and State of Illinois." This material consisted of the property "seized from the defendants and from the headquarters of the Industrial Workers of the World, located at 1001 West Madison Street, Chicago, Illinois, and from various subordinate branches of said Industrial Workers of the World throughout the country on September 5, 1917. . . ."[71]

On July 13, 1925, U.S. Marshal Palmer E. Anderson and Deputy U.S. Marshal Leon H. Taskylan certified that "on July 10th & 11th 1925 [we] went to the Federal Storage at 871 No. State St., with 3 Laborers & Truck, took all of I.W.W. Paraphenilla [sic] . . . to the City Dump at 35th and Kidgie, destroyed and burned, using Gasoline etc., as said court orders for same."[72*]

---

*There was another fire, at the IWW headquarters, which destroyed all of the records from 1919 to 1923.

## CHAPTER 15

# Wartime Repression: The Socialists

On September 5, 1917, the day on which every IWW hall in the country was raided, the Socialist Party's national office in Chicago suffered a similar fate, and was occupied for three days by government agencies. At the same time, a party convention in Mitchell, South Dakota was dispersed by force.[1]

## SOCIALISTS TURN TOWARD SUPPORT OF THE WAR

Just as there is irony in the repression of the IWW on the ground that it opposed and interfered with the war whereas its activities in that direction were hardly extensive, so there is similar irony in the Wilson Administration's determined pursuit of the Socialists. Although they had voted for the St. Louis anti-war Majority Resolution, groups within the Socialist leadership soon began to abandon it and to drift slowly into the pro-war camp. It is true that Eugene V. Debs, Charles E. Ruthenberg, Edward Wagenknecht, Kate Richards O'Hare, and other Socialist leaders did conduct active anti-war campaigns, but, as Michael Bassett points out, this was not typical of the party as a whole, and at the very time that the Administration's persecution of the Socialists "had reached its height, much of the 'danger' of Socialist opposition to the war had passed."[2]

While giving lip service to the anti-war resolution, for example, Morris Hillquit worked actively to undermine it. During his mayoralty campaign in New York City in the fall of 1917, he insisted that the Socialists did not stand for an immediate withdrawal from the war.

> The Socialists would be the last class of people to advise our government to withdraw from the war, now that it is in it, and to leave all the nations of Europe to their own destinies.[3]

By way of emphasizing how far he had drifted from the St. Louis platform, Hillquit added that Socialists did not advocate violation of laws, although many believed that was the meaning of the Majority Report.[4]

The consequences of U.S. entry into the war seemed to many previously anti-war Socialists to hold out the prospect that Socialism would emerge from the conflict, so the war might be worthy of support. As we have seen, wartime agencies of control and planning proliferated. "The war had given to the government vast and unheard of powers," one Socialist observer recalled, "and one seemed to see under his eyes, the collectivist state in the making—a state without the democratic safeguards which Socialists demanded, but far removed from the ideal of the worshipper of *laissez-faire*."[5]

The Bolshevik Revolution provided another justification to Socialists who were drifting away from the St. Louis Majority Report. With but few exceptions, almost all Socialist Party members, officials, and journals praised the Russians for what they had achieved, and expressed support for the Bolsheviks. Both moderate and left members of the Socialist Party hailed the October revolution with enthusiasm.[6]* In addition, the assumption of many Socialists who had opposed the war—that there was no difference between the Allies and the Central Powers—was shaken by the harsh terms Germany imposed upon Bolshevik Russia in the Treaty of Brest-Litovsk. These Socialists naïvely believed that the Allies would come to the aid of the Bolsheviks and prevent Germany from crushing the "first Socialist republic in the world." Many, moreover, were enthusiastic about the Bolshevik peace proposals—"no indemnities, no annexations, free development of all nationalities"—and believed, again naïvely, that the Allies would help make them a reality. Lloyd George's speech of January 4, and especially Wilson's Fourteen Points speech four days later, gave rise to a much friendlier sentiment in Socialist circles toward the Allies. Led by Hillquit, these Socialists now proclaimed that it was no longer necessary to oppose the war, and they called for a new convention to scrap the St. Louis Proclamation.[7]

This trend to climb onto the pro-war band-wagon became even more pronounced around the time of the Third Liberty Loan drive of April 1, 1918. The seven Socialist aldermen in New York City, elected less than a half year earlier because the voters had thought they were strongly opposed to the war, suddenly announced support for the loan. Local

*However, left-wing Socialists were angered by the fact that the reformist-dominated National Executive Committee, at its meeting in December 1917, issued no endorsement of the Bolshevik regime. (*Class Struggle* 2 [Jan.-Feb., 1918]: 126-28.) As we shall see in our next volume, this issue was to cause a sharpening conflict between the left and right wings of the Party and hasten the split in 1919.

leaders of the Bronx and Brooklyn sections of the party immediately condemned this unauthorized reversal of Socialist policy, but then Congressman Meyer London published his endorsement of the Loan on April 17, and two days later the executive committee of the Jewish Socialist Federation appealed to the National Executive Committee to reverse the St. Louis resolution.[8]

In a speech in Congress on May 1, 1918, London not only affirmed his support of the war, but rationalized his position by asserting that Wilson had "adopted the substance of the international socialist movement for his presentation of the aims and objects of the United States in the war." So dazzled were Socialists like Hillquit and London by the glitter of Wilson's Fourteen Points that they forgot the basic point that the Bolsheviks had made and were still making—that the war was an imperialist war which no worker should support.[9]

## THE ATTACK ON SOCIALISTS BEGINS

It is ironic that at the very time that a large number of Socialists were openly asserting that the Socialist Party should publicly renounce the St. Louis Majority Report and support the President's war measures, the administration's campaign against the Socialist Party was reaching its peak, and federal authorities were busy arresting and proceeding against Socialist leaders. As Arturo Giovannitti put it in "Socialists and Suppression," published in the August 1918 issue of *Liberator*:

> The Socialist Party stands now convicted without trial of un-Americanism (whatever that may be) and is condemned to remain under a cloud of opprobrium until such time as it shall please the powers that be, to take the muzzle off its mouth. As there is hardly any sign that this will be done before the Kaiser is beaten . . . the Socialist Party will have to stand the jibes, the innuendoes and the insults of everybody that wants to take a fling at it. It can and will have to bleed on the battlefield for the cause of democracy.[10]

And "bleed" it certainly did. In its report to the 1919 Socialist Party convention, the National Executive Committee told a terrifying story:

> Within a year after adopting the St. Louis Program, hundreds of comrades were arrested and an era of persecution set in, "Patriotic" societies organized a White Terror in many parts of the country. Locals and branches were destroyed, party members were boycotted, and in some states, they were the victims of mobs. Our press was largely destroyed and the few publications that survived were deprived of their mailing privileges. Government spies dogged the heels of party members and in some of the larger cities our headquarters

were raided by government officials. Some were sacked by mobs. . . . In many parts of the country the only sources of information the party members had was the capitalist press. All the resources of the party had to be mobilized for the defense of our victimized members. . . .[11]

"Every time the government moves against the Socialists, the press applauds," the *Nation* remarked sadly, and went on:

In the almost unparalleled intolerance of other people's opinions if they differ from the prevailing one, Socialists are treated as if they are enemies of society, a direful brood hatching something so new and so dreadful no one can quite define it. "Society" shudders, our politicians rage, and our leaders of industry declare that, like the IWW, the Socialists ought to be hanged.

The one man whom the *Nation* singled out for most of the blame was Postmaster-General Albert Burleson. It charged that he was "largely responsible for handling the vendetta against the Socialists." Burleson, said the *Nation*, had "the breadth of view of a small Texan town."[12]

## SUPPRESSION OF THE SOCIALIST PRESS

"Unable to restrain himself," notes James Weinstein, "Burleson began seizing Socialist newspapers even before Wilson signed the Espionage Act."[13] His first move was against the Halletsville *Rebel* in Texas, champion of Black and white sharecroppers; he removed it from the mails with the issue of June 9, 1917. (This was six days before the Espionage Act was signed and became law.) Mailing privileges were soon also withdrawn from the *Masses*, the *Jewish Daily Forward*, and from several daily newspapers printed in German, Russian, and Hungarian. The New York *Call*, the only Socialist daily newspaper printed in English in the city, had its second-class mailing privileges revoked in the midst of Morris Hillquit's campaign for mayor on the Socialist ticket.[14]

The *Socialist News* of Cleveland was banned from the mails on June 25, 1917. The *Michigan Socialist* of Detroit received the same treatment the next day, and on June 30, the *International Socialist Review* and the *American Socialist* were declared unmailable.[15]

The *Milwaukee Leader* not only was denied its second-class mailing privileges but lost 15,000 subscribers outside of Milwaukee, as well as a large amount of advertising—all told, an estimated $500,000 during the first year.[16]

When the *American Socialist's* suppression became known, the following telegram was sent to a number of Congressmen:

The *American Socialist*, official publication of the Socialist party, refused admission to mails. We vigorously protest against this violation of federal constitution. Impossible for this government to convince the world we are engaged in war for democracy when constitutional guarantees at home are swept aside in such autocratic manner. In the interests of free press we appeal to you to immediately take this matter up with Solicitor Lamar of postal departments who seems to be executive censor of press of United States.[17]

A telegram was also sent to President Wilson:

Liberty edition of the *American Socialist*, containing an appeal to you, has been held up by the post office censor. Such action gives the lie to your proclamation that this is a war for democracy. Even Germany allows *Vorwaerts* and *Zukunft* to appeal to the Kaiser. We appeal to you to strike the muzzle from the American press and to reprimand those who would reduce this country below the level of the Czar's old reign.[18]

Both the Congress and the White House ignored the appeals. Wilson also ignored an appeal from Herbert Croly, the influential editor of the *New Republic*, urging him to use persuasion rather than suppression in dealing with the problem. Upton Sinclair, who had left the Socialist Party to support the war, wrote to Wilson from California urging him to stop the suppression of the Socialist press. None of these pleas were of any avail. Nor were Victor Berger's appeals on behalf of his paper, the *Milwaukee Leader*. Berger warned Burleson and others in the Wilson Administration that "suppression would hurt the moderate evolutionary socialists and aid those who believed in bloody revolution," and that it would "produce the same results as it did in Russia."[19] But Wilson and those around him were deaf to all appeals.

Faced with stern suppression, the *Appeal to Reason* deserted the cause and supported the war. Abraham Cahan, editor of the *Jewish Daily Forward*, also began to vacillate. When the Trading With the Enemy Act of October 1917 required foreign language newspapers to file translations of all material dealing with the war or foreign affairs, Cahan gave that as an excuse for abandoning the St. Louis resolution as a guide and began to agitate for a convention to revise the Majority Resolution.[20]

But the *American Socialist* appeared, reduced to two pages. It had to be changed twice to suit the censorship so that it could be transmitted through the mails. It was compelled to remove, among other things, a statement saying that it felt itself within the law in doing everything legally within its power to maintain its constitutional rights.[21]

On November 5, 1917, Victor Berger appealed to the Supreme Court of the District of Columbia—the only court with the right to call a cabinet officer before it—for a writ of *mandamus* to compel Burleson to restore the *Milwaukee Leader's* mailing rights. He contended that the Milwaukee Social-Democratic Publishing Company, which owned the *Leader*, had been deprived of its property without due process of law, and that the Espionage Act was unconstitutional.[22] In his answer, Burleson cited fifty-two items from twenty-five issues of the *Leader*, from June 18 to September 13, 1917, arguing that these and the remainder of the paper exhibited a willful intent to harm the war effort. In this "test case" for all the suppressed papers, the court agreed with the postmaster general, and on January 15, 1918, it rejected the appeal.[23]*

Another test case was that of the *Masses*. After Burleson had ordered the postmaster in New York City not to accept the August 1917 issue of the magazine for mailing, the publishers went into court and asked for a restraining order. The plea was argued before Judge Learned Hand. The government justified its action by citing four articles and four cartoons in the issue as violating the Espionage Act. "Liberty Bell," one of the cartoons, was considered offensive because it showed the bell completely broken. Solicitor Cannon, speaking for Burleson, admitted that Congress could not constitutionally restrict the freedom of speech, but he held that it could prevent the use of the mails for propagating opinions contrary to the interests of the country. This evoked the comment from Judge Hand:

> You cannot expound the meaning of the statute to apply to mailability and contrast it as applied to indictability. You cannot play fast and loose with it. That violates all ideas of law and its intent.[24]

Although he did not agree with the views expressed in the *Masses*, Hand issued a temporary restraining order. But Burleson still kept the *Masses* out of the mails. The magazine fought back, announcing in its October issue: "We have no intention of letting up in this fight." But in November, the temporary restraining order was reversed by the Circuit Court of Appeals. That court held that "liberty of circulating may be essential to freedom of press, but liberty of circulating through the mails is not, so long as its transportation in any other way as merchandise is not

*Appealed finally to the Supreme Court of the United States, the case was decided on March 7, 1921 against the *Leader*, with Justices Holmes and Brandeis dissenting. In his book, *Free Speech in the United States* (Cambridge, Mass., 1941), Zachariah Chafee, Jr. states that "No decision of the United States Supreme Court has gone so far in sustaining government powers. . . ." (pp. 298-99). Brandeis, in his dissent, attacked, among other things, Burleson's contention that the banning of one issue brought a periodical under the ban of complete restriction because it was not "regularly issued."

forbidden." The decision in *Masses Pub. Co. v. Patten* is generally regarded as "a major victory for repression."[25]

Arrests of Socialists were postponed until the Espionage Act was passed on June 15, 1917. But, as in the case of the IWW, pro-war mobs did not wait for government prosecution to silence Socialist anti-war spokespersons. Margaret Prevy, who had already made many enemies through her work for the Akron rubber workers during their 1913 strike, added to that number by distributing the anti-war resolution of the Socialist Party, of which she was a leading member in Ohio. When news reached Akron of the lynching of Frank Little, a pro-war mob attacked Prevy's home, shouting for her to get "the Little treatment." A local paper reported what happened next: "With a heavy loaded revolver in each hand, Margaret Prevy stood in her open front door facing the mob without fear, assuring them that she would kill the first half-dozen who dared to place their feet upon her veranda. The mob dissolved."[26]

## IMPRISONMENT OF KATE RICHARDS O'HARE

The first important figure indicted under the Espionage Act was Kate Richards O'Hare, the outstanding woman in the Socialist Party. O'Hare's anti-war position had become clear at the party's Emergency Convention in St. Louis, and after St. Louis she crisscrossed the country, condemning the conscription of the nation's youth. In a leaflet "Good Morning! Mr. American Citizen," she informed him that Uncle Sam demanded his son, as well as indirect taxes on food and other necessities. In July 1917 she was invited to speak to a small Socialist group in Bowman, North Dakota. The speech she gave was, in the main, the same one that she had already given seventy-five times, "always in the presence of a representative of the U.S. Department of Justice."[27] In Bowman, however, no Justice Department representative was in the audience as Kate O'Hare insisted that wars benefited capitalists; that neither the workers in unions nor the farmers had much to gain from the war that made millionaires of munitions manufacturers and other capitalists; and that regardless of who won the war, the problems facing the poor people—workers and farmers—would remain unsolved. Referring specifically to the justification for American entrance given by pro-war labor and government leaders, that the American people were now engaged in a war "for humanity and democracy," she replied that the war was fundamentally one for markets and trade, and that "ego-mad kings and profit-hungry traders" had "joined in an unholy league and the world war was the result. . . . The whole war itself is the supreme struggle of the capitalist class to decide which group of capitalists shall rule the world markets," she insisted, and she asked the women of

America, especially the women of the working class, "to weigh and consider, discuss and understand" the essential truth, and then decide if it was worth making "the supreme sacrifice of seeing their husbands and sons killed in such a cause." If they decided it was not, they should follow the example of those Socialists in Europe, like Jean Jaurès of France and Karl Liebknecht and Rosa Luxembourg of Germany, who had had the courage to denounce the war and their government's participation in the wholesale slaughter.*

Although O'Hare said nothing to urge resistance to conscription or even to voluntary enlistment in the army, an unidentified person wrote to Senator Porter Hames McCumber of North Dakota, claiming that he had heard O'Hare say that "American women who did not oppose the war and resist the government in the taking of the young men for the purposes of war were no better than brood sows as they willingly raised sons for the purpose of being murdered in the defense of the four million that J. P. Morgan owned." On July 23, 1917, Senator McCumber read the letter into the *Congressional Record*, and on the basis of this anonymous missive, Kate O'Hare was arrested, indicted, and tried und   the Espionage Act.[28]

Kate O'Hare's trial was highly publicized because of her stature and also because a mother of four young children might be sentenced to prison. The judge, however, was not in the least concerned. After he disallowed one-third of her witnesses, despite the efforts of her able attorneys, the verdict of guilty was a foregone conclusion. She was convicted on December 14, 1917 and sentenced to five years in the state penitentiary at Jefferson City, Missouri. In sentencing her, Judge Martin J. Wade declared: "Every day she is at liberty she is a menace to the government."[29]

During the nearly one and one-half years of legal proceedings following her conviction, O'Hare was free on bail supplied by millionaire Socialist William Bross Lloyd.** While her conviction was on appeal, Kate O'Hare continued to write articles against the war. When her paper, the *National Rip-Saw*, was suppressed, she changed its name to *Social Revolution* in order to present her radical stand against the war effort more effectively.[30]

---

*Jean L. Jaurès (1859-1914), French Socialist leader and founder of the famous newspaper *L'Humanité*, was active in the Dreyfus case and was the most prominent leader of the French Socialists, active as a speaker, writer, organizer, and legislator. His opposition to war led to his assassination on the eve of World War I.

Rosa Luxembourg (1870-1919), Polish-born German Socialist and theoretician, was imprisoned during World War I from 1915 to 1918 for her antimilitaristic stand. She joined with Karl Liebknecht in forming the Spartacus Party to emulate the Bolsheviks in Russia. She and Liebknecht were assassinated.

**Lloyd also provided bail for Haywood, Berger, and other Wobblies and Socialists.

She also supported the Green Corn Rebellion, which was organized in eastern Oklahoma. The tenant farmers in this cotton-producing area had long been ripe for radicalism, and Socialist and IWW organizers had criss-crossed the region for several years, resulting in the formation of a "Working Class Union," which admitted members regardless of race or sex. The Black and white sharecroppers had voted for Wilson in 1916 in the belief that he would keep the country out of war, and they now felt betrayed by his declaration of hostilities and imposition of the draft. They turned to violence, and in early August 1917 as many as 2,000 men assembled, cut telegraph lines, attempted to burn railroad bridges, and hoped to march to Washington to seize the government and stop the war, planning to subsist along the way on green corn and barbecued beef. Whites, Blacks, and a sprinkling of Indians made up the rebel force. The movement was suppressed by the militia; 450 rebels and hundreds of Socialists were arrested, along with scores of Wobblies. Eighty-eight were convicted in the federal courts of draft resistance and seditious conspiracy.[31] Thirty who had been sentenced to Leavenworth were released after Kate O'Hare marched their wives and children to Washington to picket the White House.[32]

In October, 1918, the Circuit Court of Appeals affirmed O'Hare's conviction, and the Supreme Court denied a petition the next March. In early April 1919 she traveled to Bowman to surrender to the federal marshal there, delivering a farewell address to sympathizers along the way. On April 15, 1919, during Easter week, the doors of the Missouri State Penitentiary, the largest state prison in the country, closed behind her.[33]

In her speech to the court before sentence was pronounced, O'Hare declared that she was a victim of a manufactured attempt to silence anti-war activists. "This case is one of those weary, grotesque things that have been growing out of war hysteria," she declared.[34] Other such "things" soon followed. In the year after O'Hare's trial, hundreds of anti-war Socialists (and a number of anarchists) were indicted on the charge of violating the Espionage Act. Leaders of the Socialist Party, as well as isolated individuals, were rounded up, brought to trial, found guilty, and sentenced to long prison terms.

## IMPRISONMENT OF ANARCHISTS

Louise Olivereau, a philosophical anarchist, was working in the IWW office in Seattle when the United States entered the war. She used almost her entire meager salary to put out appeals to young men not to register for the draft. She mimeographed leaflets and with the aid of young Socialists distributed them to draftees. In one of her circulars she reminded the soon-to-be soldiers that their government was organized for the protection of property, and that to the worker, it was

> . . . only a method of oppression by which he is made to work for the benefit of another class, from which he receives nothing, not even an adequate living. It is this thing which you are asked to protect with your life, for which you are ordered to go into the worst hell imaginable. . . . If you want to die to perpetuate this monster, for continuation of the power that oppresses you, and makes you slave your life away so others may live in luxury, why go ahead. Make yourself into fertilizer for the sunny fields of France. But if you are opposed, then resist, refuse to go, stay away. They can't do more than kill you—and it is better to die for truth and your ideals than for ideals you hate.[35]

Olivereau also mimeographed statements against war by Tolstoy, Lincoln, and Thoreau and sent them to lists of drafted soldiers. On September 5, 1917, when federal authorities raided the Wobbly hall in Seattle, they found copies of her mimeographed circulars and leaflets. Two days later she was indicted for violating the Espionage Act, and for lack of bail spent two months in jail awaiting trial. At her trial, she conducted her own defense, even questioning prospective jurors herself. After her limited peremptory challenges had been exhausted and the jury selection was completed, she opened her defense by saying in part:

> My purpose in these circulars was to call attention of drafted men to the fact that they are ordered to resign the right to think for themselves what was the best good of the country . . . on a question upon which they were given no opportunity to vote; the right to dispose of their own lives. . . . A large part of the material in my circulars was copied from books in the Public Library. . . . If the material was so seditious, why did the government continue to permit it to circulate? . . .
>
> The real issue in the case is, have citizens the right to think of their relation to war and government in any terms except compliant acceptance? Are we an autocracy like Czarist Russia or like the Germany we hate so much we entered the war to destroy it?[36]

In her address to the jury at the close of the trial, Olivereau delivered a lecture on the history and theory of anarchism, but devoted most of her speech to a defense of freedom of speech. "No country," she said, "with the possible exception of Russia under the old regime, has so sternly silenced minorities and otherwise denied its people these fundamental rights, as the United States. Especially since the declaration of war, the suppression has been so complete, so tyrannical, that thousands of people who are most conservative, who would be horrified at being called 'radicals' of any kind, are protesting against the undue severity visited upon those who exercise their supposed constitutional rights." She continued:

> Consider the labor situation in these United States during the past year. Forty corporations have made a net profit of $677,298,729 out of the war during the year 1916. That is not their total net profit; that is merely the amount by which their profit during the year 1916 is greater than the average profit during the three preceding years. Place opposite this fact the other fact that there have been serious strikes and other labor troubles in practically every great industry in the United States during the last year. . . . All attempts on the part of the workers themselves to obtain advances in wages, have been met with most bitter opposition on the part of employers. All attempts to secure better working conditions or shorter hours have also been bitterly opposed. The workers have been told that it was unpatriotic for them to desire more money or more leisure during war time.
>
> The life of citizens in these States today is at the mercy of war-mad fanatics. We, who have boasted of being the land of the free and the home of the brave, must, if we would preserve our lives and remain out of jail, seal our lips and lay our pens aside and submit to seeing our dearest and most cherished ideals of freedom and human dignity dragged through the blood and dust of war for the financial profit of those who keep us economically, mentally and spiritually enslaved.[37]

The jury was out less than thirty minutes, and brought in a verdict of guilty on six counts. Louise Olivereau was sentenced to ten years in prison.[38]

Olivereau believed in the anarchist philosophy but was not a member of any anarchist organization. The two leading anarchists in the United States, Emma Goldman and Alexander Berkman, joined her in prison. They had organized the No-Conscription League to fight the military draft, and they spoke out against the war and conscription at meetings sponsored by the League. Both were warned by Federal Marshal Thomas McCarthy, who made it clear that he was acting on orders from Washington, that he would arrest them if they organized another meeting against the draft. McCarthy was as good as his word. On June 15, 1917, four days after they had organized a protest rally in New York City, Goldman and Berkman were arrested and arraigned before the U.S. Commissioner on the charge of "conspiracy to induce persons not to register under the Conscription Law." The jury deliberated for only 39 minutes before finding both defendants guilty. Judge Mayer sentenced each of the defendants to the maximum—two years in prison, imposed on them the maximum

$10,000 fines, and recommended that they be deported after their sentences had been served.[39]

## IMPRISONMENT OF RUTHENBERG, WAGENKNECHT, AND BAKER

Twenty-seven Socialists were prosecuted under the Espionage Act during the summer of 1917. These included a Socialist candidate for governor of Minnesota, who was sentenced to five years in prison for anti-war campaign speeches. In Cleveland, Socialist candidate for mayor Charles E. Ruthenberg, state party secretary Alfred Wagenknecht, and state organizer Charles Baker were each sentenced to serve one year in the workhouse for making anti-conscription speeches.

Ruthenberg, who had emerged as the national leader of the left in the Socialist Party at the St. Louis Emergency Convention, addressed numerous meetings to rally support for the convention's anti-war resolution, along with Wagenknecht and Baker. At his trial in federal court in July 1917, Ruthenberg repeated the words he had delivered several times in Cleveland's public square, saying: "I am speaking to you as Karl Liebknecht spoke to the German nation, as he spoke in the Parliament of that country, when he denounced the war as a war of the ruling class and stated his unalterable opposition to the war." At the same trial, Wagenknecht declared after sentencing: "We know that capitalism is fashioning the hempen rope, will act as its own hangman, its own embalmer, its own grave digger."[40] Ruthenberg became the first general secretary of the Communist Party and served until his death on March 2, 1927. Wagenknecht became one of the charter members and early leaders of the party.

The summer of 1918 witnessed the trial and conviction of Eugene V. Debs, and of Victor Berger and four staff members of the Socialist National Executive Committee. It also saw the arrest in Cleveland of the black Socialists A. Philip Randolph and Chandler Owen, for speaking on street corners against the war.*

---

*Randolph and Owen were not the only Black Socialists to oppose the war. In Brooklyn, New York, the Rev. George Frazier Miller spoke against the war from his pulpit and refused to fly the nation's colors outside his church. (William M. Welty, "Black Shepherds: A Study of the Leading Negro Clergymen in New York City, 1900-1940," unpublished Ph.D. dissertation, New York University, 1969, pp. 151-53; Theodore Kornweibel, Jr., "Apathy and Dissent: Black America's Negative Responses to World War I," *South Atlantic Quarterly* 80 [Summer 1981]: 332).

# BLACK ANTI-WAR SOCIALISTS: RANDOLPH AND OWEN

In 1916, through the Independent Political Council, which they had founded in Harlem, Randolph and Owen led a campaign against the enlistment of Blacks in the national guard, distributing leaflets outlining reasons why they should not join. One of the reasons given was that they would be called upon "to fight for 'their country,' not a foot of whose land is theirs." Once the United States formally entered the war, the two black Socialists used their weekly, the *Messenger*, to urge blacks not to fight for a country that lynched, Jim Crowed, and disfranchised them.

The *Messenger* was militantly anti-war, agreeing with the St. Louis resolution that it was basically an imperialist war being fought by the many for the benefit of a few war profiteers. It went even further by emphasizing that colonial rivalries and the exploitation of black people and people of color generally were the real issues of the war.* The basic conflict and cause of the war, it insisted, was big-power competition for control of the cheap labor and rich resources of the nonwhite world. The *Messenger* favored the peace proposals the Bolsheviks had advanced as early as April 1917, which called for no annexations, no indemnities, and the self-determination of all peoples. It hailed the Bolshevik Revolution, calling it "the greatest achievement of the twentieth century," and announced that such a revolutionary upheaval might be good for the United States.[41]*

Many of these views were set forth not only in the *Messenger* but in the pamphlet *Terms of Peace and the Darker Races*, published in 1917 by Randolph and Owen, in which they called for a peace treaty that would be based on the principle that "government by the consent of the governed must be accorded for all peoples, whether white or black or brown," a right that had to be given to "Africa, China, and the Islands held by Great Britain, by the United States, and by other nations." Such a treaty, in addition to embodying freedom and independence for Africa and other colonies, should also guarantee an end to lynching, Jim Crowism, segregation, discrimination, and disfranchisement in the southern states. The pamphlet concluded:

*Another Black radical who saw the conflict as an imperialist-colonialist war was Cyril Briggs, the West Indian-born editor of the New York *Amsterdam News* who quit rather than agree to government censorship of his editorials, and founded the African Blood Brotherhood in late 1917 as a "revolutionary secret order." By mid-1918, the ABB was publishing its own organ, the *Crusader,* which argued that the struggle for black rights in the United States was linked to the need to liberate Africa from white imperialism. (Philip S. Foner, *American Socialism and Black Americans: From the Age of Jackson to World War II* [Westport, Conn., 1977], pp. 309-11.)

In the words of the Petrograd Council of Workers and Soldiers' Deputies: Workers of all countries—black and white! In extending to you our fraternal hand over mountains of corpses of our brothers, across rivers of innocent blood and tears, over smoldering ruins of cities and villages, over destroyed treasures of civilization, we beseech you to re-establish and strengthen international unity without regard to race or color.[42]

Early in the spring of 1918, federal agents raided the offices of the *Messenger*, ransacked the files and took all its back issues with them. Undaunted, Randolph and Owen not only continued to publish the Socialist weekly, but decided to bring their anti-war and anti-imperialist views to a wider public audience. They left New York late in the spring of 1918 to tour the Midwest. In addition to rallying the anti-war movements, their intention was to help build the Socialist Party by trying "to get colored people interested in Socialism." Bundles of the *Messenger* were shipped ahead to be sold at various points on the tour.

Randolph and Owen were under no illusions as to what might happen to them on their anti-war lecture tour. Nevertheless, the two young black Socialists did not mince any words in their speeches. While one inveighed against the war, the other sold copies of the *Messenger* with its anti-war message. Justice Department agents were usually in the crowd, taking notes of the speeches and purchasing copies of the *Messenger*.

In Cleveland, the Justice Department did more than take notes. During the first meeting, a Justice Department agent approached the podium while Randolph was speaking and placed him under arrest. Owen was similarly apprehended while selling the *Messenger* in the audience. The charge was violating the Espionage Act. The two spent three days in jail; bail offered by a wealthy Black woman was refused. Finally, Seymour Stedman, a leading Socialist Party lawyer, arrived to handle the defense, and two were released on bail. They were also freed because the judge refused to believe that two young black men could write the inflammatory articles in the July issue of the *Messenger*, and was convinced that they were being used by white Socialists. He threw out the charges, and told Randolph and Owen to leave town immediately.

After their release, they proceeded to Chicago to fulfill a prearranged engagement. They found that news of their arrest had preceded them and the minister of the church in which they were to have spoken had locked the doors and left town. "He wanted no part of us," Randolph later recalled, "so we just got ourselves a soap-box, set it up on the steps of the church, and went right on blasting the war. We couldn't sell any *Messengers* because they had been confiscated in Cleveland." He also pointed out that "the Negro community basically was friendly to our anti-war position, but the leadership was not. . . . The masses of the Negro community . . . were against the war, but they had no way of demonstrating it except attending meetings that were anti-war. We held meetings all over New York, and Philadelphia, and around the country, and the masses of people came out; but the leaders were afraid."[43]

Invariably, federal agents were in the crowds as Randolph and Owen continued to hold street meetings everywhere, and delivered orders to them to tone down their rhetoric and stop their attacks on President Wilson. They were also forbidden to set foot in Washington, D.C., but they took this ban as an invitation, hastened to the capital, and proceeded to lambaste the president in his own backyard. Their tour was cut short when Owen received notice from his draft board; he reluctantly went into the army. Randolph, who was classified 4-A, was able to keep the *Messenger* going, although rather irregularly, until Owen returned early in 1919.[44]

In his biography of A. Philip Randolph, Jervis Anderson tries to explain how (except for the brief incident in Cleveland) the two black Socialists were able to stay out of jail, despite the vigorous anti-war tone of their speeches and editorials in the *Messenger*. Anderson's theory is that the Justice Department may have felt that it had a weak case against them, and that Wilson did not want to act against black anti-war dissenters.[45] Since the government had an even weaker case against Ben Fletcher, the black Wobbly who was sentenced to ten years in Leavenworth and fined $30,000 and Wilson showed no sensitivity to black opinion in his case, it is hardly likely that this was the reason. It is more likely that the president shared the reaction of the Cleveland judge, namely, that they could not themselves have thought up the ideas contained in their speeches and articles in the *Messenger*. In fact, the high literary quality of the *Messenger*, in general, caused considerable comment among a wide circle of critics.[46]

The anti-war black Socialists, however, did not get off without some punishment. They had barely returned to New York when they learned that Postmaster General Burleson had denied second-class mailing privileges to the *Messenger*.[47]

## PERSECUTION OF VICTOR BERGER

In the midst of his campaign for United States Senator from Wisconsin, Victor Berger, the first Socialist Congressman, was indicted for violating the Espionage Act. Berger was seeking the seat vacated as a result of the death of Senator Paul O. Hasting, a pro-war and anti-Socialist fanatic, and he made the issue of peace the central theme of his campaign. "I want you to vote for me," he told his audiences, "because, if elected, I shall work for an immediate, general and lasting peace. . . . Those who do not agree with me . . . those who want to continue this war for another year, for two years or five years—need not vote for me, I don't want their votes."[48] Berger advocated the confiscation of all war profits, denouncing "as abhorrent to every decent American the coining of the blood of American boys into swollen profits for the American plutocrats who dragged us into the European war and who now demand its indefinite continuance for their further enrichment."

Berger also called for the withdrawal of American troops from Europe for defensive use at home, a proposal that caused Senators William E. Borah and Henry Cabot Lodge to denounce him; even Morris Hillquit voiced his disagreement. (Lodge called it "an absolutely disloyal proposition."[49]) Berger also promised to work, if elected, for legislation to combat unemployment and prevent an economic depression after the war, and to provide for the nationalization of trusts and transportation and communications facilities. His posters proclaimed:

> The issue is clear—heaven or hell—peace or war—Socialists or profiteers and their following.[50]

On March 9, 1918, while he was campaigning, Berger was indicted, charged with conspiracy to violate the Espionage Act. The attacks upon him immediately mounted in severity. His posters were smeared with paints of assorted hues, his picture was defaced, and he was burned in effigy. "Businessmen refused to display his window cards," writes his biographer, "distributors of his literature were arrested in small towns 'simply to intimidate others,' newspapers refused to print his advertisements, and his posters could not be erected in many areas. Even his life was threatened."[51] Berger told what it was like years later in a speech on the floor of Congress:

> Imagine the capitalist papers . . . every day asking for a mob to lynch you, in more or less veiled language, under the pretext that you are a disgrace to the city and State. Imagine, further, getting letters—anonymous letters, of course—every day, while mail was delivered to you, threatening you with death. Also imagine patriotic students in the university town hanging you in effigy on lampposts and burning you at the stake after solemn processions. . . . And what was worse than all of these things, imagine the Secret Service man going to advertisers, especially department stores, and also reaching by some mysterious influence all of your out-of-town advertisers, and getting them to cut out their advertisements at once [in the *Milwaukee Leader*]. . . .[52]

When the votes were counted, however, Berger ran second, gaining the amazing vote of 110,487 of a total of 423,393 cast. He carried the city of Milwaukee by a plurality of 2,500. It is the opinion of a number of scholars that in keeping with the ugly temper of the campaign, many of his votes were simply thrown out and that he actually won the election.[53] It is significant that, while awaiting trial under his indictment, Berger was reelected to Congress by a 5,500 plurality. The victory, in Berger's view, was a "vote for an early and lasting peace."[54] But this did not stop the government from proceeding with his trial, nor did the fact that the war had already been over for a month when the trial got under way cause any change in the plans of the Wilson Administration.

We will deal with this trial, in which Berger faced a twenty year prison term, in our next volume. But here we should note that this right-wing Socialist's bitter experience—he called himself "the most indicted man in the history of the country," having been indicted five times[55]—caused Berger to change his attitudes toward the AFL and the IWW. He still disapproved of the IWW's tactics, but now, for the first time, he voiced the opinion that the organization represented a valid expression of industrial unionism. On May 6, 1918, during the trial of the IWW leaders on the charge of violating the Espionage Act, Berger donated ten dollars to a defense fund, writing to IWW Secretary A. Wouri that the industrial union had "stood the test of being a class organization infinitely better than the trade unions. Gompers' cohorts have in the main proved to be the tail end of capitalism." He anticipated "that the IWW (or some labor organization that will succeed it but that will inherit its matchless spirit) is destined to take the place of the American Federation of Labor."[56]

## IMPRISONMENT OF EUGENE V. DEBS

When Kate Richards O'Hare was convicted for violating the Espionage Act, Debs was so incredulous that he wrote to her that if she actually did serve time in prison, "I shall feel guilty to be at large."[57] He was soon to find himself in the dock and sharing prison life with O'Hare and other Socialist comrades.

Debs accepted an invitation to speak at the Ohio convention of the Socialist Party in Canton, on June 16, 1918. Thus far, the federal government had chosen to ignore him, perhaps because he had been relatively passive in the months following U.S. entrance into the war. Moreover, Debs had lent his support to the movement for a special convention to revise the St. Louis Majority Report.[58]

But this reluctance ended during the spring of 1918, and Debs became a major target of the federal government. When it was reported in the press that Debs was now a pro-war advocate, as witness his support for a special convention to revise the St. Louis Majority Report, he reacted vehemently. Ordinarily, he wrote in May 1918, it had been a rule of his to ignore false charges and misstatements concerning him in capitalist publications. But "an exception appears in the report now being circulated . . . that I have changed my front and am now . . . appealing for the support of the administration in the prosecution of the war to the bitter end." Claiming he had "not changed in the slightest," Debs stressed that there was nothing in the St. Louis Proclamation "to apologize for or retract." He explained that in calling for a special convention he was looking toward the adoption of a "more complete and comprehensive restatement" of the Socialist Party's opposition to the war. The party, he concluded, should make its stand "so clear that there could be no doubt in regard to it either on the part of our enemies or our friends. . . . I have condemned the German majority Socialists and I am not going to imitate their perfidy, much as the capitalist press may abuse me for not doing so."[59]

This was the Debs who spoke at Canton, Ohio on June 16, 1918. Introduced by Margaret Prevy of Akron as the best loved and most hated of all men in the United States," Debs spoke for two hours. He reaffirmed his support of the St. Louis Proclamation, defended the IWW and condemned the violence against them, denounced the persecution of his Socialist comrades, denounced the evils of capitalism, and praised the Bolshevik Revolution, saying:

> Our hearts are with the Bolsheviki of Russia. Those Russian Comrades of ours . . . have laid the foundation of the first real democracy that ever drew the breath of life in this world. And the very first act of the triumphant Russian revolution was to proclaim a state of peace with all mankind, coupled with a fervent appeal not to kings, not to emperors, rulers or diplomats, but to the PEOPLE of all nations.

In his speech, Debs' references to the war were limited, and not nearly as vigorous as his previously stated opposition to U.S. entry into the conflict.* But in speaking to American youth, he said: "You are fit for something better than slavery and cannon fodder." E. S. Weitz, the United

---

*David Shannon observes that "when read today," Debs' Canton speech "does not seem to be a strong criticism of America's role in World War I." (David A. Shannon, *The Socialist Party of America: A History* (Chicago, 1955): 114.)

States attorney for the Northern District of Ohio, had appointed a stenographer to record Debs' speech. (The government also had agents at the meeting circulating among the 1,200 people present to check on draft cards.) That stenographic transcript was used as evidence against Debs when he stood trial in September in a federal court in Cleveland, charged with having violated the Espionage Act by obstructing the war effort and encouraging resistance to the draft, a charge Debs did not deny.[60]

"No man in the United States is too big to be prosecuted under the Espionage Act," Weitz told a reporter for the *Cleveland Plain Dealer*, and he indicated that if, on examining the transcript, he found that the Socialist leader had made statements that violated the Espionage Act, he would act at once "to have him prosecuted." Editorially, the *Cleveland Press* hailed this statement, insisting that in his Canton speech, "Debs had done more to aid the Hun Kaiser than all the pro-German Germans in America." There were only two places where "war obstructionists . . . rightly belong," the paper went on—Germany or the penitentiary.[61]

Despite his boasting, Weitz could not by himself decide to prosecute Debs. He sent a copy of the Debs speech to the Attorney General in Washington, pointing to passages he thought to be in violation of the law and asking for advice about possible prosecution. It is interesting, as an indication of how broadly the Espionage Act was interpreted, that Weitz wrote: "You will note the sentence on page 16, to the effect that the IWW in its career has never committed as much violence against the ruling class as the ruling class has committed against the people. This, of course, is the kind of criticism of the government of the United States which I believe Congress intended to forbid by its enactment of the amended Espionage Act."[62] Although the Justice Department did not think prosecution would be successful in this case, it did not forbid Weitz to proceed with it. The latter immediately got a grand jury to indict Debs.[63]

During the trial, Debs presented no defense, believing that "it would be useless to make a defense."[64] He told the jury that he "would not retract a word" of all that he had uttered, to save himself from the penitentiary:

I have been accused of having obstructed the war. I admit it. Gentlemen, I abhor war. I would oppose the war if I stood alone. . . . I wish to admit everything that has been said respecting me from this witness chair. I wish to admit everything that has been charged against me except what is embraced in the indictment. . . . I cannot take back a word. I cannot repudiate a sentence. I stand before you guilty of having made this speech . . . prepared to take the consequences of what there is embraced."[65]

Debs was quickly found guilty, and on September 14, 1918, Judge David C. Westenhaver sentenced him to ten years in prison. Prior to the sentencing, the court clerk asked Debs if he would like to make a final statement. The resulting speech to the court has been called "a masterpiece of American oratory."[66] Most well known is the concluding section, in which Debs employed the metaphor of a storm-tossed sailor to describe the people's struggle:

I can see the dawn of the better day for humanity. The people are awakening and in due time they will come to their own.

When the mariner, sailing over tropic seas, looks for relief from his weary watch, he turns his eyes toward the southern cross, burning luridly above the tempest-vexed ocean. As the midnight approaches, the southern cross begins to bend, and the whirling worlds change their places, and with starry fingerpoints, the Almighty marks the passage of time on the dial of the universe, and though no bell may beat the glad tidings, the lookout knows that the midnight is passing—the relief and rest are close at hand.

Let the people take heart and hope everywhere, for the cross is bending, the midnight is passing, and joy cometh with the morning. . . .

I am now prepared to receive your sentence.[67]

## A HUNG JURY

One of the few hung juries during the war involved Anna Louise Strong. The Seattle Socialist had been arrested under the Espionage Act for distributing an anti-conscription pamphlet that she had authorized while she was an officer of the American Union Against Militarism and which had been endorsed by the Seattle Central Labor Union. Brought to trial, she reminded the jury in her testimony: "What's unlawful about that dodger?* Printed before the Conscription Law was passed, wasn't it, when ninetenths of this country thought Conscription un-American? Even if it hadn't been, who prevents free-born Americans from attacking an oppressive law?" She quoted from the leaflet headed "No Conscription! No Involuntary Servitude!" the following words from Daniel Webster: "Where is it written in the Constitution . . . that you may take children from their parents . . . and compel them to fight the battles of any war in which the folly and wickedness of the government may engage?"

*Another expression for a pamphlet or handbill.

Her testimony helped bring on the hung jury.[68]* But Strong was not tried again. Hulet Wells, former president of the Seattle Central Labor Council, Sam Sadler, an editor of the Seattle *Daily Call* and the *Union Record*, two outstanding Pacific Coast labor papers, and Joe and Morris Pass were not so fortunate. They were indicted for circulating a leaflet against conscription, and their first trial, in which they received wide labor support, resulted in a hung jury. A second trial, however, resulted in convictions and the four were each sentenced to two years in prison. Before he left for prison, Hulet Wells told the Seattle Labor Council that "someone who thought he was a friend of mine recently stated that he would like to see me freed, but that he wanted to see the IWW's kept in jail. I don't want my liberty on any such terms as that." The delegates cheered the statement for ten minutes.[69]

## WITH NEITHER LOGIC NOR REASON

Logic and reason both flew out of the window as the so-called violations of the Espionage Act were prosecuted. Some defendants received sentences of one or two years, while others were sentenced to ten or twenty years for precisely the same kinds of speeches or writings. The Washington state secretary of the Socialist Party was convicted for having displayed an anti-war circular on a bookcase in his office at a time when the office was being visited by men between the ages of 18 and 45 and thus subject to duty in the armed forces.[70] A. Hitchcock, a Cleveland Socialist, was arrested on the complaint of a person who was not present at the time for a remark he was alleged to have made while visiting a sick friend in his home.[71] Scott Nearing and the American Socialist Society were indicted for distributing the anti-war pamphlet, *The Great Madness*, authored by Nearing, which charged financial interests with fomenting the war in order to distract the American people from the country's social ills. The district court trial resulted in Nearing's acquittal, but in the conviction of his co-defendant, the American Socialist Society. Morris Hillquit, who served as defense counsel in the case, contended that the "peculiar verdict left the American Socialist Society convicted of conspiracy with itself."

*It also helped bring about her removal from the school board of Seattle, a post to which she had been elected with trade union support in 1916. A petition was drafted calling for her removal on the ground that she had distributed literature opposing conscription. The fact that the anticonscription circular was distributed a week before the passage of the Selective Service Act did not matter. Although Anna Louise Strong received the support of organized labor in Seattle, the power of the commercial press and of middle-class forces and wartime hysteria was too strong, and she was recalled from her position on the school board—but only by a margin of 2,000 votes out of 85,000. (Anna Louise Strong, *I Change Worlds: The Remaking of an American* [New York, 1935]:55-66; *Seattle Union Record*, Oct. 27, 1917 and Nov. 9, 1918.)

The circuit court of appeals decided that the verdict was not inconsistent, since the jury might have believed that Nearing "did not write these harmful views with the idea of obstructing the recruiting and enlistment service of the United States," but may have been convinced that the Society had printed and distributed them with a criminal intent.[72*]

Perhaps the low point of logic and reason in the suppression of anti-war dissidents was reached in the case of Rose Pastor Stokes, the "Cinderella Socialist" who had married millionaire Socialist J. Graham Phelps Stokes. She was arrested and tried, not for anything she had said or written against the war, but for having sent a letter to the *Kansas City Times* containing the sentence: "No government which is for the profiteers can be for the people, and I am for the people, while the government is for the profiteers." At her trial under the Espionage Act, Judge Van Valkenburgh instructed the jury that the right to criticize the government was restricted to those who supported the war, and he directed its attention to Stokes' declared sympathy for the Bolshevik Revolution, an offense which, while not punishable under the Espionage Act, demonstrated the danger of her attack on profiteers. The court found that her statement tended to interfere with the operation and success of the armed forces because of its possible influence on the parents, wives, sisters, brothers, sweethearts, and friends of the men in service and of those registered for the draft. Rose Pastor Stokes was sentenced to ten years in prison. The circuit court of appeals sustained the lower court in finding that the "profiteers" sentence in Stokes' letter violated the Espionage Act, but reversed the earlier judgement because of Van Valkenburgh's improper instructions to the jury.[73**]

*Scott Nearing did not go to prison because of his opposition to the war, but he did lose his position as a professor and dean of the arts college at the University of Toledo. This was the second time he had been fired from a university. From about 1908 on, Nearing was deeply involved in the fight against child labor. This proved to be an intolerable irritant to the trustees of the University of Pennsylvania where he was a young economics professor at the U. of P.'s Wharton School. As secretary of the Pennsylvania Child Labor Committee, Nearing had lectured widely on the evils of child exploitation, and he was dismissed by the University.

**Even more inane, perhaps, was the action of the government in seizing the film of a movie entitled *The Spirit of '76* because the portrayal of British soldiers bayoneting women and children and carrying away young women during the Wyoming massacre in the course of the American Revolution would have the effect of arousing antagonism between the American and British peoples, thereby weakening U. S. loyalty toward an ally. Judge Bledsoe conceded that everything depicted in the film was historically accurate, "is written upon the page of history and will have to stand, whomsoever may be injured or hurt by the recital or recollection of it," but maintained that this was no time for it to be presented. By his order, the film was seized, the business was bankrupted after a loss of more than one hundred thousand dollars, and Robert Goldstein, its producer, was convicted of attempting to cause insubordination in the armed forces. (*New York Times*, Feb. 3, 1918.)

# THE ST. LOUIS MAJORITY REMAINS INTACT

The very severe repression suffered by the Socialist Party and its members undoubtedly weakened many sections and locals and even led more timid members to withdraw from the party, but it did not force it to either abandon or revise the St. Louis manifesto. When the joint meeting of the National Executive Committee and the state societies met in Chicago in the summer of 1918, it was in the very midst of the Wilson Administration's vendetta against the Socialist Party, and there were those present who urged a revision of the St. Louis manifesto in the hope of appeasing the federal government. But during the later stages of the meeting, Eugene V. Debs, who was out on bail while his ten-year sentence was being appealed, arrived and pleaded with the delegates not to consider weakening the party's opposition to the war. He told the applauding delegates:

> I earnestly hope that there be no thought on the part of any of the comrades here to change the party's attitude towards the war. . . . The master class of our own country, pretending to be waging a war for democracy, have done everything in their power to destroy democracy. . . . We propose in the face of all opposition, all of the hatred and all of the persecution, to bear aloft our banner and to wage increasingly the war for the emancipation of the workers of the world.[74]

Following this, the joint meeting disbanded with the St. Louis Majority Report still intact.

# CHAPTER 16

## Labor at the War's End

Despite the long-time striving of the labor movement to improve working conditions, on the eve of World War I the twelve hour day and seven day week were still in effect in a substantial number of workplaces, and the average wage of an industrial worker stood at about fifteen dollars a week.[1] For a brief period the war changed much of this, giving rise to a number of favorable labor conditions. Unemployment, in some cities as high as 30 percent in 1914, virtually disappeared. The wartime labor shortage opened up new job opportunities to black and women workers at higher wages than they had been earning before the war.

## INCREASE IN UNION MEMBERSHIP

The government's war labor policies greatly benefitted both the American Federation of Labor and the Railroad Brotherhoods. Between January 1917 and January 1919, AFL membership rose by almost a million—from 2,371,434 to 3,260,168. In 1918 alone, the Federation increased in size by 19.6 percent, and by November of that year, AFL membership had surpassed three million.[2]

Membership in the machinists' union rose from 112,500 in 1917 to 330,600 in 1920; the boilermakers' union, from 31,200 in 1917 to 103,000 in 1920; the carpenters, from 231,700 in 1917 to 331,500 in 1920; and the meatcutters, from 7,300 in 1916 to 65,208 in 1920.[3]*

In transportation, the total union membership rose from 623,300 in 1916 to 1,256,100 in 1920. The Brotherhood of Railroad Trainmen had 133,000 members in 1913; by 1919 its membership had increased 47 percent to 196,000. The Locomotive Engineers had 73,000 members in 1913,

*This great increase in unionized meatcutters was partly the result of the packinghouse strike struggle under the leadership of William Z. Foster.

and by 1920 it had grown to 96,000, an increase of 31.5 percent. The Brotherhood of Locomotive Firemen grew 38 percent, from 91,000 in 1913 to 125,900 in 1920.[4]

Between 1914 and 1920, total trade union membership increased from 2,687,100 to 5,047,800. Whereas in 1910, organized workers represented only 8.6 percent of all wage earners, by 1920 the percentage had more than doubled to 17.5.[5]

The wartime expansion of unionism, however, was confined mainly to workers in the building, transportation, metal, machinery, shipbuilding and clothing industries. Workers in these industries accounted for about three-fourths of the total increase in union membership between 1915 and 1920.[6] In most of these cases, moreover, unionism was expanding where it had already made inroads before the war; in few industries did increases take place where there had been no prior organization before the war.[7]

A major reason for this situation was that very little progress was made in industrial unionism during the war. The AFL success in the meatpacking industry, under the leadership of William Z. Foster, had held out hopes for the future of industrial unionism, but the Federation's leaders refused to learn any lessons from the victory in packinghouse.[8]

While the AFL and Railroad Brotherhoods were flourishing, the radical forces in the labor movement were suffering setbacks. As we have seen, federal and state governments joined employers in attacking the Industrial Workers of the World. With their leaders arrested and jailed and their members harassed and intimidated, the Wobblies were effectively eliminated as a force for the industrial organization of workers. In the process, a long-standing threat to Gompers' leadership of the AFL was also eliminated. The legitimate demands of workers who had rallied to the IWW were no longer seen as expressions of the striving to end widespread exploitation and profiteering, but instead were stigmatized as products of German espionage and intrigue.

The mass migration of black workers to the industrial centers of the North during the war provided rich opportunities for their unionization. Pressure for such organization came from local unions within and from Negro leaders outside the AFL, but the entrenched Federation old guard pursued its traditional policy of outright exclusion in most cases or segregation into separate unions.

Women workers fared somewhat better. By 1920, 8 percent of all trade union members were women, and 6.6 percent of all working women were organized—a fivefold increase in a decade.[9]

# WARTIME WAGES

Both organized and unorganized workers saw their wages increase during the war. As we noted earlier, in 1917 some 1,227,000 workers were involved in strikes, and in 1918 this rose to 1,240,000. Despite the increases in the costs of living, real wages advanced, increasing 19 percent for all industrial workers between 1915 and 1919. Both the skilled and unskilled workers won gains, although the unskilled workers' gains were mainly from more regular employment and overtime work. Eli Ginzburg and Hyman Berman estimate that during the years 1914 to 1919, "the gains of the laboring man in real wages and leisure combined were approximately 25 percent. . . ."[10] The average annual wage paid on the nation's railroads increased from $828 in 1915 to $1,820 in 1920.[11]

Nevertheless, millions of workers were unable to keep up with the rise of prices of commodities, both wholesale and retail, which, by 1918 had "assumed almost incredible proportions."[12] On January 9, 1918, Secretary of Labor William B. Wilson conceded that reports that all workers had benefitted economically from the war were far from the truth:

> With the exception of the sacrifices of the men in the armed service, the greatest sacrifices have come from those at the lower rung of the industrial ladder. Wage increases respond last to the needs of this class of labor and their meager returns are hardly adequate, in view of the increased cost of living. It is upon them that the war pressure has borne most severely. Too often there is the glaring inconsistency between our democratic purposes on this war abroad, and the autocratic conduct of those controlling industry at home.[13]

# RECORD OF THE WAR LABOR BOARD

The most important single agency of the war period in the field of industrial relations was the War Labor Board, established in April 1918. During its life of sixteen months, eight were months when the nation was at war. The Board issued awards, findings, recommendations, and orders in 490 cases. Despite the great praise heaped upon it, its record was mixed. It is true that the Board adhered to the principle that workers had the right to bargain collectively through representatives of their own choosing, and that they were not to be discharged for membership in trade unions, or in any way to be subjected to discrimination because of such membership. On the other hand, the Board also followed the precept that labor must not exercise "coercion" in attempting to induce nonunion workers to affiliate or employers to accept agreements. In establishments where both union and nonunion workers were employed, this situation was to be maintained for the duration of the war.[14]

Where no unions existed, the War Labor Board sponsored employee representation schemes. The first was instituted at the Pittsfield, Massachusetts plant of the General Electric Company. There, elected department committees dealt with department management, and the chairmen of such committees comprised the general plant committee, which dealt with general management. A representative of the War Labor Board supervised the elections.

All told, 125 representation plans were introduced by the Board. Although at first employers were reluctant to cooperate with the employee representation plans, they "soon recognized their usefulness as a substitute for unionism, amenable to their control," and many of the larger corporations, such as Youngstown Sheet and Tube Company, International Harvester Company, and Goodyear Tire and Rubber Company, took the initiative in installing employee representation plans, which resulted in the establishment of company unionism in those plants.[15]

The War Labor Board's policy on the hours of labor was that the "basic eight-hour day is recognized as applying in all cases in which existing law requires it. In all other cases, the question . . . shall be settled with due regard to governmental necessities and the welfare, health and proper comfort of the workers."[16] But the eight-hour day was almost never mandated. Longshoremen in South Atlantic ports continued to work ten-hour shifts, and night workers at American Locomotive in Richmond, Virginia toiled 57½ hours per week. Even after the adoption by the War Labor Board in June 1918 of a clause providing pay at time-and-a-half for overtime after eight hours, no clear eight-hour precedent was set. A Bureau of Labor Statistics report in 1921 summarized the War Labor Board's decisions on hours in the phrase, "NO GENERAL RULE ESTABLISHED."[18]

The steel industry was the best example of the unevenness of wartime control of hours of labor. It was not until October 1918 that the steel industry adopted the "basic eight-hour day" as a war measure. But the war was to last just six more weeks. After it ended, much of the steel industry returned to extremely long hours. In fact, the twelve-hour day was more widespread in the steel industry in 1919 than it was in 1911. Despite high, and what one historian calls "naïve" hopes among reformers, no lasting precedents were established by the war policies.

Nevertheless, although the long sought eight-hour day was still not the national standard, working hours did decrease during the war. In 1914, only 11.8 percent of the wage earners in manufacturing worked 48 hours or less per week. By 1919, this percentage had more than quadrupled to 48.7 percent.[19]

While in theory the War Labor Board advocated "equal pay for equal work" for both sexes, in practice this principle was accepted in only a limited number of cases. In most occupations where women had taken men's places, they generally worked at lower time rates, and not infrequently at lower piece rates.[20]

A principal weakness of the War Labor Board was its inability to reach decisions promptly in a number of important cases. Its first award was not rendered until June 12, 1918, two and a half months after the Board had been established.

Of the 490 cases involving the War Labor Board, three are especially significant. In the case of *Employees v. Western Union Telegraph Co.*, the question to be determined was whether an employer could "insist upon his right to decide that his employees should or should not enjoy the privilege of membership in trade unions of their choice."[21] The workers charged that the company had denied them the right to organize and that their membership in the Commercial Telegraphers' Union, an AFL affiliate, had led to the discharge of about three hundred workers from Western Union's Seattle plant. These actions, they argued, constituted a violation of one of the cardinal principles of the War Labor Board, which guaranteed "the equal right of workers and employers to form their own organizations and deal collectively through such organizations."[22]

On June 1, 1918, the War Labor Board handed down a compromise proposal. The Western Union Telegraph Company was to reinstate those employees who had been discharged for having joined the Commercial Telegraphers' Union and was to cease and desist from future discrimination against employees who chose to join the union. However, the company was not required to recognize the CTU nor to deal with it. Instead, it had to recognize and deal with committees of workers. The workers, for their part, had to agree not to initiate any work stoppages and to submit all grievances to the War Labor Board.[23]

The employees of the Western Union Company and the representatives of the Commercial Telegraphers' Union accepted the compromise proposal, but Western Union refused. It would neither reinstate those workers it had discharged for joining the CTU, nor recognize the union.[24]

The dispute was finally turned over to President Wilson who directed that letters be sent to the Western Union Telegraph Company and the

Postal Telegraph Commercial Company, a firm that had been charged with similar violations. In these communications Wilson publicly requested compliance with the War Labor Board's recommendations.[25]

Clarence H. Mackay, president of Postal Telegraph, capitulated and agreed that for the duration of the war his company would waive its right to discharge those workers who chose to become union members. But President Newcomb Carlton of Western Union refused to accede to President Wilson's request. "If I have to choose between allowing the unionization of the essential employees of the Western Union Telegraph Company and government control," Carlton insisted, "I would choose the latter."[26]

At President Wilson's request, Congress passed a resolution authorizing the president to take over possession and control of the nation's telegraph and telephone systems. On July 31, 1918, control of the nation's telegraph and telephone lines passed over to the national government.[27]

This outcome was promptly hailed as evidence that the government would not hesitate to support the War Labor Board and would take all necessary actions to bring any employer into line who refused to go along with a Board decision.[28] But in the end, the workers gained little. The telegraph and telephone lines were placed under the control of Postmaster General Albert S. Burleson, and, as we have seen, he was even more opposed to union recognition than some of the companies had been before the government takeover. Opposition to the unionization of telegraph and telephone workers actually increased under government control.[29]

The War Labor Board also dealt with two strikes of the Machinists' Union. On July 12, 1918, about half of the workers employed by the Smith and Wesson Arms Company of Springfield, Massachusetts went on strike. The company maintained a nonunion shop and required its employees to sign "yellow dog" contracts pledging not to join a union. It had not only refused to confer with an employees' committee appointed to meet with management for the purpose of negotiating a general wage increase, but it had discharged all of the committee members. Following this action, a large number of employees joined the Machinists' Union. They, too, were discharged. This was the spark that ignited the strike.[30]

On August 21, 1918, the War Labor Board ordered the company to desist from using the "yellow dog" contracts and to re-employ all workers who had been dismissed as a result of union affiliation, with compensation "for all time lost by them on account of their discharge." The company was also directed to provide a means for collective bargaining.[31]

When the company indicated that it would disregard the Board's orders concerning discrimination against union members,* President Wilson directed Secretary of War Baker to "commandeer the Smith and Wesson Arms plant in Springfield."[32]

In September 1918, members of the Machinists' Union employed at the Remington Arms Company in Bridgeport, Connecticut went on strike in protest against an award handed down by the War Labor Board. Although the Board had granted the workers wage increases and the basic eight-hour day, it had reversed an earlier decision of the Ordinance Department with respect to job classifications—a major source of grievance for the workers.[33]

In spite of the opposition of the Machinists' Union leaders, who wanted no part of a strike that would halt war production, the Remington workers in Bridgeport remained solidly behind the strike. On September 13, 1918, President Wilson took steps to break it. In a message to the strikers, Wilson threatened that unless they returned to work and abided by the War Labor Board's decision, the government would withdraw draft exemptions from those men who were within the draft age and who had been granted such exemptions on occupational grounds. He also threatened to bar the strikers from future "employment in any war industry in the community in which the strike occurs for a period of one year." Moreover, during this one-year period, "the United States Employment Service will decline to obtain employment for you in any war industry elsewhere in the United States, as well as under the War and Navy Departments, the Shipping Board, the Railroad Administration, and all other Government agencies."[34]

Faced with such an unprecedented threat and the determination of President Wilson to use full dictatorial powers to break the strike, the strikers voted on September 17 to end their walkout and returned to work. However, they expressed their dissatisfaction with the president's strikebreaking role by forming a labor party in Bridgeport.[35]

The Bridgeport munitions strike was only one of many indications that labor struggles did not cease after the United States entered the war and after the pledges of the unions' leaders not to strike. In the first eight

---

*Smith and Wesson argued that the terms of the award by the War Labor Board contradicted the precedent established by the U. S. Supreme Court's decision in the case of *Hitchman Coal and Coke Company v. Mitchell et al* (December 1917), in which a union was enjoined from organizing workers who had signed "yellow dog" contracts. The Board rejected this view, insisting that "when representatives of the leading employers of the country agreed to the principles of the Board, they waived their legal rights under the Hitchman decision, just as in substance the trade union leaders had waived their right to conduct strikes." (*Monthly Labor Review*, January 1918, pp. 146-72; Charles O. Gregory, *Labor and the Law* [New York, 1958]: 178-81.)

months of the War Labor Board's existence, over two thousand work stoppages were recorded by the Bureau of Labor Statistics. Pressures generated by the rapid rise in living costs and by rampant profiteering on the part of employers moved workers into struggle from coast to coast. Labor's militancy was met by repressive measures, mostly directed against the IWW and the Socialists, but it also forced the government to afford workers a new degree of recognition in the War Labor Board's endorsement of collective bargaining. In its summary of the Board's work, the *American Labor Year Book* noted: "On the whole . . . the Board firmly established the principle for the period of the war, that union affiliations were not to be subject to discriminatory action on the part of employers. It is unquestionable that this action by the Board protected effectually the growth of the unions and was a direct means of increasing their membership in very large numbers."[36]

As events were to prove, the qualification "for the period of the war" was prophetic.

In a number of respects, the first World War marked a new era in U. S. labor history, but in none was that more evident than in the relationship between the government and the American Federation of Labor. "No important measure vitally affecting labor is now taken," declared the *New Republic*, "without consultation with the leaders of the American Federation of Labor, and in the most important government boards the wage earners are represented." When the *Nation* criticized the government's choice of Samuel Gompers to travel throughout Europe to assess labor conditions there, Postmaster General Burleson banned the issue from the mails. Solicitor General Howard Lamar informed Oswald Garrison Villard, the *Nation's* editor, that Gompers "has rendered inestimable service to this government during the war in holding labor in line," and that "while this war is on we are not going to allow any newspapers in this country to attack him."[37] The AFL leadership had been fully absorbed into the war apparatus.

## THE AFL AND POSTWAR RECONSTRUCTION

Before leaving the impact of the first World War on the U.S. labor movement, we should examine the role labor planned to play when the war ended. Having assumed the mantle of "Labor's Spokesman," the AFL made it clear that its pronouncements on the subject represented labor's program for postwar reconstruction.

In November 1917, the first AFL convention held in wartime took place in Buffalo, New York. On the opening day, the Executive Council presented a report on "Reconstruction Proposals," but it focused attention only on the problem of potential unemployment of veterans following demobilization. The Council urged that the convention present a plan for remuneration to sustain veterans until they were able to get jobs, and advocated the creation of employment agencies to assist in finding the jobs. The convention adopted these proposals and thereby took the first step toward a reconstruction policy, but it was so general and broad as to be almost meaningless.

Of the 165 resolutions presented to the convention, only one concerned itself with postwar reconstruction. It asked for the protection of skilled workers from unemployment due to the importation of foreign products and was adopted with only a slight amendment.[38]

By the time the next AFL convention met, in June 1918 in St. Paul, Minnesota, much attention was being paid in labor circles to the British plans for reconstruction. One was outlined by the Whitley Commission, a subcommittee of the British Reconstruction Commission. It recommended the introduction of mixed industrial councils "to secure for the workpeople a greater share in and responsibility for the determination and observance of the conditions under which their work is carried out." Although this did not go far enough to satisfy the militants in the British labor movement represented by the shop stewards movement,* it was criticized by Gompers as not applicable to American labor and its traditional political policies. Gompers was also critical of *Labour and the New Social Order*, the manifesto of the British Labor Party for the reconstruction of English society after the war, which he characterized as the "clap-trap and demagoguery of the political socialists." The manifesto envisioned the creation of a socialist commonwealth and urged specifically that the state recognize its responsibility to prevent unemployment and to provide maintenance for those out of work. It also called for "common ownership of the means of production," the complete overhauling of the taxation system so that the main burden would fall on private business and those with substantial incomes, and appropriation by the state of all the "surplus wealth" of the nation.

Although *Labour and the New Social Order* was widely hailed in many labor circles in the United States, Gompers dismissed it as offering labor

---

*The shop stewards movement was greatly influenced by "events in Russia," and made the shop the unit of industrial representation. Under this plan, each workshop set up a committee whose function was to confer with the employer about production and the conditions of labor. Decisions were to be arrived at in a "democratic" manner. (Leland Olds, "The Temper of British Labor," *Nation* 108 [April 19, 1919]: 603.)

"little practical help for real achievements." "In the future, as in the past," he insisted, "we must trust to the economic organization of the workers."[39]

At the 1918 AFL convention, three resolutions were introduced that dealt with postwar reconstruction. The first called for concerted action by the national AFL and its affiliates for the establishment of the eight-hour day. Gompers supported it as a practical proposal, devoid of the aforementioned "clap-trap and demagoguery," so it was unanimously adopted.[40]

The second resolution asked for convention approval of the postwar program adopted by the Inter-Allied Labour Conference held in Nottingham, England, which consisted of representatives of organized labor from England, France, Belgium and Italy. This proposal was opposed by Gompers and went down to defeat.[41]

The convention then placed the matter of postwar reconstruction in the hands of the Executive Council, which was to conduct an investigation of the problem and offer the fruits of its investigation to Congress.[42] Gompers thereupon set up a Committee on Reconstruction and a Committee on Social Insurance. In December 1918 he convened an executive meeting of these committees and proceeded to caution them to go slow on reconstruction because "it has been given to no one to be able to solve this great problem in its entirety."[43]

The report of the Committee on Reconstruction, unveiled in late December 1918, reflected Gompers "go slow" advice. It demanded the right to organize; an American standard of living with reasonable hours of labor; equal pay for women; the abolition of child labor; the right of public employees to organize; government ownership of public and semi-public utilities; a graduated tax on usable land in excess of the acreage cultivated by the owner; a guarantee of free speech; the development of state colleges and universities; the establishment of municipal, state, and federal employment agencies under the joint control of employers and trade unions; improved housing; and generous treatment of returning servicemen.[44]

Nothing was said about black workers and the problems they would face after the war. The only concern expressed about postwar employment of any particular group related to the returning servicemen, who, it was said, should be aided by the government in finding work, provided with sustenance while unemployed, and given the opportunity for easy and ready access to land.[45] The committee report also failed to deal with other important concerns of workers.

The AFL's vision of the "new era" that was to follow the war reaffirmed its traditional nonpartisan political policy. There was to be no labor party. The "program" was to be realized by winning over the major parties and by carrying on the trade union policies of the past. "It is not good now to rock the industrial boat," Gompers insisted.[46]

## "LABOR'S FOURTEEN POINTS"

But many AFL members, especially those who had come into the movement during the war, looked forward to considerably more in the future. Angered by the bloated profits of both the old and new millionaires, while their own wages were shrinking under the impact of the ever rising cost of living, and stimulated by the events in Russia, they wanted more than the traditional AFL policies. On October 6, 1918, the Chicago Federation of Labor requested that the Illinois State Federation of Labor "call a convention in the future for the purpose of considering the advisability of forming in Illinois an independent labor party along the lines of the British Labor Party but adapted to American conditions."[47]

Some time later, the Chicago Federation made public a platform entitled "Labor's Fourteen Points" (possibly intended to supplement Wilson's "Fourteen Points"), which was to be submitted to the Illinois State Federation convention and the AFL convention. It asked for support for "the formation of an Independent Labor Party nationally, by State and by City," with "Labor's Fourteen Points" as its program. The latter included demands for "democratic control" of industry; the nationalization of natural resources, railways, telegraph, ships, coal mines and grain elevators; worker representation in all departments of government and at international conferences; disarmament; "open diplomacy;" and struggle against "economic imperialism."

"Labor's Fourteen Points" also included a number of the demands in the AFL's reconstruction program, such as "the unqualified right of workers to organize and to deal collectively with employers through such representatives of their unions as they choose," and an eight-hour day and a 44-hour week in all branches of industry, with minimum rates of pay sufficient to maintain a decent standard of health and comfort. It went beyond the AFL program, however, in calling not only for equal pay for equal work, but also for "complete equality of men and women in government and industry, with the fullest enfranchisement of women." Unfortunately, nothing specific about black workers was included.

It called for free speech, as did the AFL, but it also demanded the "complete restoration at the earliest possible moment of all fundamental political rights—free speech, free press, and free assemblage; the removal

of all war-time restraints upon the interchange of ideas . . . and the liberation of all persons held in prison or indicted under charges due to their
championship of the rights of Labor of their patriotic insistence upon the
right guaranteed to them by the constitution."

Finally, "to carry out this work to expose the trust press and the vested
interests they represent and to keep Labor informed as to its welfare, etc.,
a daily newspaper to be published in the interests of all the workers."[48]

On December 5, 1918, the Illinois State Federation of Labor endorsed
"Labor's Fourteen Points" and joined the Chicago Federation of Labor in
calling for an independent labor party.[49] The program later became the
basis for the platform of the Chicago-centered labor party that was established in the fall of 1919, which will be discussed in our next volume.

Thus, as World War I came to an end, there was clear evidence of
mounting opposition in the ranks of labor to the course followed by the
Gompers leadership of the AFL. Even in those unions whose leaders
emphasized their loyalty to everything that Gompers stood for, dissatisfaction with the Gompers outlook was mounting. The mood among rank-and-
file unionists was summed up in the phrase: "Wait Till The War Is
Over!"[50]*

## THE AFL CONFRONTS THE PEACE

As early as March 1916, Gompers had sent to the labor movements of
Europe his proposal for a world labor congress to be held at the same time
and place as the peace conference at the end of the war. He was disappointed when the British Trade Union Congress rejected his proposal
because it refused to meet with German unionists while the war was on.
He wrote to Will Thorne, a Labor Member of Parliament, warning him
against allowing feelings engendered by the war to destroy the ideals of
fraternity and internationalism. Instead, advised Gompers, the bitterness
and vengeance resulting from war should be directed against the causes of
war in order to help building a better world. The old nationalistic ideals
must be abandoned in favor of internationalism, since the wellbeing of the
workers of one nation was closely interwoven with the wellbeing of the
workers of all nations. "Unless we are big enough and broad enough to
subordinate less important matters to the broad general purposes of the
promotion of labor's ideals in the affairs of the world," wrote Gompers,
"the ideal of internationalism must be declared impracticable. . . . Fighting for the right is one thing and declaring that after the fight is over there

*In our next volumes, we will discuss how the labor movement, especially the rank-and-file,
reacted to the ending of the war.

shall not be a common ground upon which international fraternity should be resumed upon a better and firmer fundamental basis is quite another."[51]

## THE AFL AND EUROPEAN PEACE FORCES

Once the United States entered the war, Gompers forgot all about international ideals, and he and the other top leaders of the AFL began to oppose the movement for an international labor peace conference before the Central Powers were completely destroyed. Gompers argued that the war had wiped out the international bonds of the working class and had proved that nationalism was and should be a stronger force; therefore, he asserted, allegiance to one's government took precedence over all other relationships. In his view, President Wilson's Fourteen Points constituted the only possible basis for peace talks, and to discuss any other possible terms with representatives of the "enemy" labor movement would be to engage in treason. Only after the workers of Germany and Austria had settled the issue of peace with their own governments could they earn the right to participate in labor peace discussions.[52]

When revolution broke out in Russia in March 1917 , the Tsar was overthrown, a republic was established, and soviets of workers' and soldiers' deputies were created in all the large cities. On May 5, 1917, the Petrograd Soviet issued a call for an international conference of Socialist Party members from all the warring countries to be held in neutral Stockholm to discuss "peace without annexations or indemnities on the basis of the self-determination of peoples."[53] As the cry "On to Stockholm" spread throughout the belligerent countries, governments on both sides of the war became alarmed at the tremendous scope of the anti-war movement. In the United States, President Wilson launched a massive propaganda campaign condemning the Stockholm peace conference. Although Gompers had nothing to do with the socialist movement, with the approval of the United States government he joined the campaign to discredit the Stockholm meeting. He sent cablegrams to the Petrograd Soviet, the French federation of labor, the French Socialist Party, and the British Labor Party. He informed the Russian workers that they could count on the wholehearted support of the American people in the war against Germany, but warned them against playing into the hands of the "pro-Kaiser socialists." To the British and French labor movements he argued that the Stockholm conference was the product of insidious influences at work to create pro-Kaiser propaganda and to divide the Allies. Ignoring the fact that the call for the conference had come from the Petrograd Bolsheviks, Gompers insisted that it had originated with German and pro-German socialists, whose aims were to bring about a Kaiser-dictated peace or to deceive the Russian socialists into betraying the Allies by consenting to a separate peace.[54]

During the war, the headquarters of the International Federation of Trade Unions were shifted to Amsterdam and operated under a new acting president, the Dutch labor leader Jan Oudegeest.* Karl Legien the original IFTU president, now decided that the Federation should present labor's proposals for the peace treaty to the Stockholm socialist conference. At his request, Oudegeest called a meeting of the IFTU to be held at the same time and place as the socialist gathering. Gompers and the AFL Executive Council rejected an invitation to send American representatives to the IFTU conference. With the help of the AFL, the Allied governments refused to give passports to delegates for either the socialist or the trade union conference. The former was therefore postponed and the latter was held with delegates from the Central Powers and the neutral countries. But in view of the limited nature of the meeting, the delegates decided to call another conference in Bern on September 17 to discuss labor's demands in connection with the peace terms. The Executive Council of the AFL rejected an invitation to attend the Bern conference on the grounds that the proposed meeting was premature, would lead to no good end, and would be injurious to the Allied war effort.[55]

The AFL policy provoked a bitter conflict with the British and French labor movements. The strife was intensified when the AFL refused to allow its delegation to go to England and France in the spring of 1918 to sit with representatives of German and Austrian labor.[56] This AFL delegation had been given the task of attempting to stiffen the morale of Allied labor and counter the pro-peace sentiment among European workers.[57]

Gompers and the AFL Executive Council was very receptive when the Wilson Administration agreed to subsidize the travel of an AFL delegation to Europe in the summer of 1918. The purpose of this mission, too, was to diminish the desire for peace of European labor, and to head off the efforts of Arthur Henderson, the British labor leader, to bring about a conference of labor delegates from all of the belligerent nations.** Gompers cabled Henderson that if an inter-Allied labor conference were arranged at the

---

*The International Federation of Trade Unions was established before World War I, but its activities were disrupted by the outbreak of the war. The Allied labor movements discontinued their dues payments, as did the AFL, in 1914. The IFTU was reorganized after the war at a meeting in Amsterdam in 1919.

**Although Henderson was a member of the British cabinet, the State Department refused him a visa in April 1918 "lest he infect American labor with the socialist peace virus." (David M. Kennedy, *Over Here: The First World War and American Society* [New York, 1980], p. 355).

time he would be in England, he would be glad to participate. Such a conference was promptly arranged, and the AFL Executive Council appointed Gompers' lieutenant John Frey of the molders' union, Charles Baine of the boot and shoe workers, William J. Bowen of the bricklayers, and Edgar Wallace of the United Mine Workers to serve on the mission with Gompers.[58]

## THE INTER-ALLIED SOCIALIST CONFERENCE

The developing clash between European labor advocates of peace and the AFL advocates of military victory came to a head at the Inter-Allied Socialist Conference held in London in September 1918 to consider the question of peace negotiations. On the opening day, the AFL delegates refused to sign credentials as representatives to a socialist conference. After considerable debate, it was agreed that the meeting was a socialist and labor conference; the AFL credentials were accepted, and the Federation delegates were seated.

Gompers was appointed to the drafting committee and Frey to the war aims committee, of which he was secretary. Gompers told Frey how to act: "Fight for the AFL program, and start fighting from the minute you go in. Give them hell!"[59]*

On the second day, Gompers read an AFL resolution on war aims, based primarily on declarations of the two previous Federation conventions. The resolution declared the war to be a contest between democracy and autocracy, called on Allied workers to support the military effort of their governments until the enemy had been defeated and the autocratic governments of the Central Powers destroyed, endorsed President Wilson's Fourteen Points as the only basis for peace, recommended representation of workers on the official peace conference delegations of each country, and called for a world labor conference at the same time and place as the peace conference.

On the third day, the committee on international relations discussed, among other questions, that of Russia. The majority report of the committee expressed sympathy with organizations in Russia that were for continuing the struggle against Germany. It warned the workers of the Allied countries against the dangers of Allied intervention in Russia, which would only strengthen reactionary efforts to restore tsarism, and under the pretext of fighting Bolshevism, serve reaction against socialism and

*Frey later recalled that Gompers also told him: "Don't call a spade a spade, call it a son-of-a-bitch. F--- them." (John Frey Memoir, Columbia University Oral History Collection, Butler Library, Columbia University.)

democracy: ". . . To such a policy the working classes of the Western democracies would have the elementary duty of offering opposition without stint."

The two AFL delegates on the committee presented a minority report. They favored intervention for the purpose of "counteracting the sinister influence of the Central Powers upon the so-called Bolshevik Government, which has suppressed the utterances and aspirations of the great majority of the Russian working classes." After a long discussion, a compromise formula was adopted on the question of intervention, which actually justified it under certain circumstances. The conference would not oppose intervention influenced "only by a genuine desire to preserve liberty and democracy in an ordered and durable world peace in which the beneficent fruits of the Revolution shall be made permanently secure."

At the insistence of Gompers, Frey wrote the report of the important Committee on War Aims. In all important aspects, the report followed closely along the lines of the AFL resolution on war aims. The report was adopted by an overwhelming majority, and Gompers was thus successful in his mission of defeating the movement for peace by negotiation and for an immediate international labor conference.[60]* Three days after the conference, Ambassador to Britain Walter Hines Page told Gompers that the proceedings of the conference had been sent to Germany and Austria, that they proved that the AFL had broken down the peace movement, and that this would have a considerable effect in convincing the German government and people that there was no longer any hope for either a negotiated peace or a breakdown in the morale of Allied workers.[61]

Gompers' "steamrolling tactics" at the conference, and his insistence that no concession be made to the agitation for a conference among labor and socialist groups for an end to the war, angered European labor. In France, he attended a meeting of representatives of the French labor movement where he listened to talk of the need to end the war "as long as I could endure them and then I tersely told them they were traitors to the cause of the French people."[62] In Italy, the popular acclaim that greeted rumors of an armistice led Gompers to warn the Italian people against showing either weakness or an undue longing for peace.[63]

Ray Stannard Baker, who was on a special reconnaissance mission to Europe for President Wilson in 1918, reported that to bring "a message of interminable war, and for no clear or democratic or socially constructive

---

*In response to pressure from the AFL delegation, the conference ultimately decided to postpone the convening of an international labor and socialist peace conference until the time of the general peace conference.

purpose" as Gompers was doing, "was not very promising." Baker caustically described Gompers' actions:

> He strode full fronted throughout Europe, so sure of himself and his entire
> equipment of ideas, so conscious of the immense power of American labor
> behind him, that he scattered to the right and left all peoples of all nations. He
> told British, French, and Italian labor leaders, quite positively, what they must
> do to be saved.[64]

The fact that the government of the United States had subsidized the AFL delegation to Europe in the summer of 1918, and that Gompers and his associates had demonstrated absolutely no sympathy for the war-weariness of European workers or for their desire to end the fighting, left these workers with the distinct feeling that the leading representatives of organized labor in the United States were far removed from the needs of the working class.[65]

## GOMPERS BOYCOTTS BERN MEETING

Following his return from Europe, Gompers became determined to reconstruct the old IFTU along the lines of the "pure-and-simple unionism" of the AFL rather than in the socialist pattern of most European labor movements. He felt it was necessary to purge the international organization of the influence of the socialists. This attitude brought him into even greater conflict with European labor leaders, who wished to continue the IFTU along traditional socialist lines.[66]

Before Gompers could act to put his plan into effect, Jan Oudegeest, the acting president of the IFTU, writing from its new headquarters in Amsterdam, requested the national trade union centers to appoint delegates to an international trade union conference to be held at the same time and place as the peace conference. This labor conference would consider both the future of the IFTU and the peace programs recommended by recent labor-socialist conferences.[67]

Gompers, however, was unwilling to cooperate, insisting that the AFL must take the initiative in calling for an international conference that would be committed to Wilson's Fourteen Points as the only basis for peace.[68] Accordingly, the Executive Council declined the invitation, and Gompers informed Oudegeest that the AFL would issue its own call for a conference. Oudegeest eventually decided to postpone the proposed general meeting of the IFTU until after the peace conference and then to hold the meeting in Amsterdam.[69] It met in July, 1919 (see p.364).

The AFL now proposed the holding of an international labor congress at the same time that the Paris Peace Conference met, bringing together labor representatives of the Central Powers and the Allies in Paris.[70] However, the Allies refused to permit German or Austrian labor delegates on French soil. Gompers appealed to Wilson: "Persistence in this course by Allied governments may make impossible American labor coming to Paris and there rendering assistance. Indeed the American Federation of Labor will be humiliated and made the laughing stock of the world. If objection is removed American labor delegates myself included can leave the United States soon and remain in Paris until Peace Conference convenes and be of some service and thereafter meet with labor conference and help guide the conference aright."[71]

When Gompers' appeal failed to persuade the Allied governments to permit "Labor's Peace Congress" to meet in Paris, labor and Socialist groups in the Allied, Central, and neutral nations decided to convene in Bern, Switzerland. Gompers, however, refused to go along. He was opposed to any conference in which political parties participated or that took place in a neutral country, such as Switzerland, at which representatives of the enemy nations would be present. In those circumstances, the delegates of the Central Powers would come as equals and not as representatives of defeated nations. Gompers was determined that they must admit their guilt for inaugurating the war, "and thus destroy their dominant influence in the international movement."[72]

While all the other labor groups were preparing to meet in Bern, the AFL decided to meet in Paris. The Executive Council designated Gompers and four vice-presidents—James Duncan, William Green, John Alpine of the Plumbers, and Frank Duffy of the Carpenters—as delegates to the Paris labor conference. On January 20, 1919, the AFL delegates met in London with the Parliamentary Committee of the British Trade Union Congress. They failed, however, to dissuade the Parliamentary Committee from attending the Bern Conference, but they did receive a promise that the group would cooperate later with the AFL in forming a new trade union international.[73]

From London, the AFL delegates went to Paris, but once again they failed to dissuade the labor representatives—in this case, the Confédération Général de Travail (CGT)—from attending the Bern Conference. Thus, when that assemblage met in the first week of February, the AFL delegates remained in Paris conferring with President Wilson and the American Commission to Negotiate the Peace.[74]

To Gompers' consternation, the delegates at the labor and socialist conference in Bern, representing seventeen Allied, Central Power, and neutral nations, refused to condemn the Bolsheviks and to fix the war guilt on Germany. Instead, the Conference issued a proclamation to the workers of the world, calling for the abolition of wage labor and for workers' control of industry in order to avoid exploitation. Until these goals were achieved, the workers should secure protection against the influences of capitalist competition through labor legislation enacted by an international labor parliament that would be part of a league of nations.[75]

Gompers called this last-named body an "impossible super-parliament." He also expressed his resentment against European labor leaders who rejected his leadership, and he attacked French Socialist sympathy for "Bolsheviki" as constituting "treason to democracy and labor internationalism."[76]

## THE COMMISSION ON INTERNATIONAL LABOR LEGISLATION

Despite temporary setbacks, Gompers was soon able to regain a dominant position in the international labor movement. For one thing, under strong pressure from the AFL, President Wilson appointed him as the labor representative of the American Commission to Negotiate the Peace. Then the Paris Peace Conference decided to incorporate special labor clauses into the peace treaty "in the hope of dampening the flames of communist revolution." For this purpose it established an advisory Commission on International Labor Legislation. President Wilson appointed Gompers as the American labor representative to this body; the four other members of the AFL delegation still in Paris were named to act as advisers to the AFL president. While these appointments helped increase Gompers' prestige, they did the opposite for Wilson. As David M. Kennedy points out, by associating himself with Gompers and by adopting his approach to the European left, Wilson helped to insure his "political impotence when he finally sat down to the Peace Conference table in Paris on January 12, 1919."[77]

At its first meeting on February 1, 1919, the Commission on International Labor Legislation elected Gompers chairman. That body met to formulate a program for postwar employment and to advise the Paris Peace Conference delegates on labor issues. Its work included the specific tasks of investigating and compiling statistics on international labor standards, presenting legislative proposals to the plenary session of the Peace Conference, and constructing the League of Nations machinery for adjusting international labor problems.

Despite the pleas of the Women's Trade Union League, working women were not represented at the Commission meetings, and only Gompers represented the views of U.S. labor. The WTUL got Wilson's belated agreement that women should have a voice, and sent Rose Schneiderman and Mary Anderson to Paris, at WTUL expense, as spokespersons for "100,000 organized women, members of the Women's Trade Union League in the United States."[78]

The Commission divided its work into two categories: (1) the drawing up of a draft convention for a League organization of international labor, and (2) the submission of recommendations for a declaration of labor principles to be incorporated into the final peace treaty. On the first item, the group accepted, as a basis for discussion, a British proposal to establish an international labor organization consisting of annual international labor conferences and an international labor office. The labor conferences were to enact labor laws that the member nations would be required to ratify and put into operation. The labor office was to be an administrative agency that would collect and distribute information on labor matters and enforce international labor legislation. Each national delegation to the labor conferences was to be composed of one representative of the government with two votes and one representative each for the employers and organized labor, each possessing one vote.[79]

Gompers led the opposition to this British plan and proposed a number of amendments. He objected to the requirement that draft conventions of the international labor conference be enacted into legislation by the member nations. He pointed out that in the United States many matters of labor legislation were within the sole jurisdiction of the various states, and, unlike the situation in Europe, the central government did not have total jurisdiction over labor matters.

The British plan was incompatible with the AFL philosophy, for the Federation had traditionally opposed such legislation as a socialistic enhancement of government power. Gompers argued further that the proposed authority might allow the international labor organization to force the United States to lower some of its already established labor standards in order to equalize international standards. Gompers also objected to the proposed method of representation and voting for the labor conferences. In the belief that government was always on the side of the employers, he was convinced that conference votes of national delegations would almost invariably be three to one against labor.

The protest of the U.S. delegation, which threatened to submit a minority report, was effective. Despite the vigorous objections of the British representatives, the Commission decided that draft conventions of the international labor conferences should be in the form of recommendations rather than laws. The national delegations were to be required merely to submit these recommendations to their respective governments for consideration. The requirement would apply only if the recommendations did not call for lower standards than those already in existence in a country. The system of penalties for non-compliance with conference conventions was deleted, and its application left to the League of Nations. No change, however, was made in the representation and voting procedure for the international conferences.[80]

The AFL submitted a list of ten clauses to be adopted by the Commission as part of a labor charter and a declaration of labor principles to be incorporated into the peace treaty. Three of the clauses were adopted without modification by the Commission. They declared that the labor of a human being should not be treated as a commodity or an article of commerce; that all workers had the right to a wage sufficient to maintain a reasonable standard of life; and that women should receive equal wages for equal work. The right of free association was recognized, but the AFL declaration for freedom of speech, press, and assembly was dropped. It was agreed that no commodity should be shipped in international commerce if children under the age of fourteen had been employed in its production. (The AFL had proposed sixteen as the minimum). The AFL further proposed that the workday in industry and commerce should not exceed eight hours except in the case of extraordinary emergency; the Commission amended this to read eight hours a day or forty-eight hours a week, and excepted countries in which the workers' industrial efficiency was relatively low.

Four of the AFL's recommendations for labor clauses were rejected and three were added to the Labor Charter by the Commission. These provided for a weekly rest, equality of treatment for foreign workmen, and a system of factory inspection for each country.[81]

The WTUL women brought with them a list of proposals that would have assured recognition of the rights of working women for inclusion in the declaration of labor principles of the Peace Treaty—demands for compulsory education of children up to the age of sixteen and part-time education up to eighteen years; abolition of child labor; an eight-hour day and a 44-hour week; no night work for women; one day's rest in seven; equal pay for equal work; equal opportunities for men and women in trade and technical training; social insurance against sickness, accidents, industrial disease, and unemployment; provisions for old age; pensions and maternity benefits; the full enfranchisement of women so that they might have "political, legal and industrial equality," as well as "the protection of motherhood and the guarantee to every child of the highest possible development."[82]

Arriving too late to present their program, Schneiderman and Anderson met with Colonel E. M. House and Professor James T. Shotwell of the American peace delegation. However, the only specific concession made to women workers was the inclusion in the declaration of labor principles of a provision calling for "equal pay for men and women." Mary Anderson came home from Paris disappointed by the lack of sincerity of male political and labor leaders, but convinced that the time had come "for labor women everywhere to get together and work together."[83]

The Commission concluded its work on March 4 and submitted its final report containing the draft constitution for the international labor organization and the declaration of labor principles to the Peace Conference. The report was adopted by the Conference on April 11 and became Part XIII of the Treaty of Versailles, generally referred to as the Labor Convention or Labor Charter.

## THE AFL AND THE VERSAILLES TREATY

After the Paris Peace Conference adjourned, the AFL delegation returned home and immediately launched a campaign for support of the Versailles Treaty, and especially for the League of Nations as the new approach to world peace. The first task was to win approval by the 1919 AFL convention. This had to be accomplished against the opposition of Irish nationalists within the AFL who resented the fact that the Peace Treaty did not guarantee independence for Ireland, as well as others who viewed the Versailles Treaty as an imperialist pact. The provisions for heavy reparations from the defeated enemy, for the French occupation of Germany's coal-rich Saar Basin, for Japan's continued occupation of German holdings and trading rights in China, and others of this type, revealed that the war had really been a struggle of the imperialists to carve up the world.[84]

When the AFL convention met in Atlantic City in June 1919, it was presented with a report by the Executive Council which, while conceding that the peace treaty was not perfect, still hailed it as the "nearest approach to perfection that ever has been reached in the international affairs of mankind," and as an affirmation of the principles for which the Federation stood and fought. In fact, the 1916 AFL convention had endorsed the concept of a league of nations to maintain peace. Therefore, the Council concluded, the treaty provided the best machinery yet devised for the prevention of war by upholding the principles of justice in place of strength as the guiding spirit in international relations. As for the labor clauses, they were praised for recognizing that the well-being of the wage earners was of supreme international importance.

The main opposition to the treaty was voiced by Andrew Furuseth, president of the Sailors' Union of the Pacific, who expressed the fear that the League would become a super-parliament that would be able to fix labor laws and labor standards in every country of the world. Furuseth argued that under the covenant,

> . . . the League of Nations takes jurisdiction over the daily life of the working people throughout the entire world. It says that it deems it its duty and will endeavor to make labor conditions humane and just in nations, members of the League, and in the nations with which the League has commercial and industrial relations. That embraces every working man and woman throughout the entire world. If the League has the authority to say the conditions of labor shall be humane and just, there is no possibility to deny that it has the sole right to prescribe what is humane and just. There can be no higher authority anywhere, so that whatever is adopted as humane and just by the League will necessarily have to stand as humane and just, regardless of any protest that the working men of any part of the world may feel inclined to lodge against such finding.

Furuseth also criticized the labor charter for failing to guarantee free speech and press, prohibit involuntary servitude, and assert the seamen's right to leave their ships. "There isn't a solid thing here," he declared, "that leaves any of the American ideals in the document, and then legislation under it is to be enacted by men from all these places who could not understand even the question of involuntary servitude."

Gompers replied that "some people are so constituted that if you were to give them Paradise they would find some fault with it," and he intimated that Furuseth was disloyal to the AFL. But Furuseth insisted that he opposed the grant of power to the League of Nations which, he charged, created in fact a "super-legislature." He objected to the handling of labor issues through the treaty power, and it was his view that it could be used to lower labor standards at home. Gompers asked what barrier there would be against future wars if the League of Nations were defeated. The treaty was not perfect, he admitted, but perfection was not to be expected when peoples with different histories, traditions, and interests were involved, especially in a first attempt. He denied that there was anything in the covenant to prevent American labor from pressing for better conditions; it aimed only at bringing up the standards of the workers of the backward nations.

A good deal of the opposition to endorsement of the treaty at the convention came from Irish nationalists. When it became clear that their objection would get nowhere, Frank McNulty of the International Brotherhood of Electrical Workers introduced an amendment "that nothing in the League of Nations as endorsed by this convention can be construed as denying the right of self-determination and freedom in Ireland." The proposal was ignored, and Gompers appealed to the delegates to endorse the Versailles Treaty and the League of Nations without any qualifications. His proposal was approved by a vote of 29,909 to 420, with 1,830 not voting.[85]

However, at just about the same time, the Versailles Treaty and the League of Nations were coming under sharp attack both in Congress and in the country as a whole. The *New Republic* spoke for many Americans when it urged the Senate to repudiate the Versailles Treaty, calling it an "inhuman monster" hatched by the political servants of an "inhumane and complacent capitalist society." The Socialists condemned the treaty because it had been "formulated behind closed doors by predatory elder statesmen of European and Asiatic imperialism," it had transferred territories against the will of their populations, and it had been used as a device to blockade and brutally suppress peoples seeking the freedom implied in the right of self-determination. In addition, it had given birth to the reactionary League of Nations, "the Capitalist Black International."[86]

In the Senate, the attacks against the treaty and the League of Nations came from Republicans, led by Henry Cabot Lodge, and from progressives, led by Robert M. LaFollette. Lodge, speaking for sections of American monopoly capitalism, wanted the United States to have a free hand in world affairs. LaFollette objected to the injustices of the treaty and its tendency to continue imperialist domination and perpetuate existing wrongs.

By September 1919 it was clear even to President Wilson that the treaty's ratification by the Senate was in real danger. The ailing president decided to take his case directly to the people; on September 3 he set out by train for a barnstorming trip of the western states, to rouse public opinion against the failure of the Senate to ratify the treaty. But on October 4, 1919, Wilson suffered a paralytic stroke, and his activity for the treaty and the League of Nations ceased.

Gompers tried to rally support for the stricken president. He lauded the peace treaty and the League of Nations, calling the latter "the only safety we know of for the future and the only spiritual recompense we have found for the anguish of the past." He pointed to the labor measures incorporated into the treaty on the recommendation of the Commission on

International Labor Legislation, and warned that if this approach was not approved it would open the way for Bolshevism: ". . . This world is now seething . . . and if we do not give labor and the masses of the people the full right and opportunity of expression, they will find another way of expressing themselves."[87]

During this period, Gompers spent much of his time attempting to rally support for ratification. He wrote articles and editorials, prepared a pamphlet for general distribution, and, along with some 250 leaders in American life, signed an appeal designed to apply pressure on the Senate to ratify the Treaty of Versailles without "delaying" reservations. In the entire campaign, Gompers and the AFL Executive Council worked closely with the League to Enforce Peace.

In the final weeks of the Senate debate over ratification, the labor provisions of the treaty came under increasing attack. On November 18, the Senate adopted an amendment withholding assent to the labor provisions. This amendment became number thirteen of the fourteen "Lodge Reservations" that circumscribed America's obligations under the League Covenant.[88*]

# CONFERENCE OF THE INTERNATIONAL LABOR ORGANIZATION

Meanwhile, beginning on October 29, 1919 and lasting until November 29, the first Conference of the International Labor Organization (ILO) was taking place in Washington. On June 24 the AFL Executive Council voted to send a committee to wait upon President Wilson and urge him to convoke the International Labor Conference. In response, on August 11, 1919 the U.S. Secretary of State sent telegrams to all the nations of the world, except Russia, Mexico, and the Dominican Republic, inviting "each national which is or prior to the said meeting shall become a member of the International Labor Organization . . . to send its delegates and other representatives to Washington for the purpose of attending said Conference." It is significant that although no obstacles were put in the way of German and Austrian delegates, neither the Soviet Union nor the two Latin American countries with which the United States was having difficulties at the time, were invited.

Gompers had urged Secretary of Labor William B. Wilson to persuade

---

*The most important of the reservations concerned Article X in which Lodge proposed to limit the U.S. pledge to defend other nations against aggression, and to make that pledge in any case contingent on Congressional approval. (*New York Times,* Nov. 7, 1919.)

President Wilson, the State Department, and other authorities that unless labor representatives of Germany and Austria, as nonmembers of the League and the ILO, were allowed to attend the conference, many trade union centers, including the British Trade Union Congress, would refuse to send representatives. However, he had no objection to excluding labor representatives from the Soviet Union.[89]

The United States government decided not to participate officially in the conference. Instead, the AFL and the U. S. Chamber of Commerce were designated to represent the United States. The AFL promptly named Gompers, but the Chamber of Commerce declined the invitation.[90]

While the conference was in session, it was subjected to bitter attacks in the Senate from conservative Republicans. Pointing to the presence of British and French Socialists as delegates, Republican Senator Lawerence Y. Sherman of Illinois called the conference "a menace to the continued domestic peace and good order of our country." "The radicals are here," he thundered. "They are here for no good purpose." He urged that the "alien conspirators sojourning in our midst" be deported.[91] Some of the conference delegates were so angered by the attack that they "privately favored adjourning then and there."[92]

But the conference continued in session, and by the time it adjourned on November 29, 1919, it had adopted six labor conventions, including the eight-hour day convention, which was later ratified. Germany and Austria were admitted as equal members, the first such action after the war. The Governing Body of the International Labor Organization was constituted, and when the conference closed, the ILO was already a functioning organization.[93] Praising the action taken at the Washington conference, R. J. Caldwill of the American Association for Labor Legislation (AALL) declared that its work had done much "to counteract the spread of Bolshevism."[94]

Ten days before the Washington conference adjourned, on November 19, the Senate rejected the Versailles Treaty. An incensed Samuel Gompers vehemently attacked the Senate, suggesting that the ILO was the principal reason for the rejection:

> I believe that the Senate did not ratify the treaty for two reasons: first, hope for partisan political advantage; second, because that treaty provides for an international minimum standard for the working people of all countries.[95]

Following the rejection by the Senate of the Treaty of Versailles in its original form, Gompers and the AFL, along with many other pro-League individuals and organizations, indicated a readiness to compromise and achieve a modified version of the League. Gompers made his position clear in the following message to the League to Enforce Peace:

> Importance of establishing League so great that reservations not depriving League of essential effectiveness okay rather than lose opportunity to create institutions which will mark beginning of a new era in international relations. But no reservations ought to be accepted under which our government would shirk responsibility of membership. Would be repugnant to American ideals and character.[96]

Gompers and the Executive Council continued their support of Senate ratification on that basis, but in March 1920, the second attempt at ratification ended unsuccessfully.

The AFL's 1920 convention in Montreal again endorsed the Versailles Peace Treaty. This time, the convention resolution opposed delaying reservations but admitted that needed corrections could be made in the future. However, the defeat of the Democrats in the 1920 election doomed American participation in the League of Nations.[97]

## THE AFL AND THE IFTU

The Senate's refusal to ratify the Versailles Treaty limited the effectiveness of the International Labor Organization. It was not until 1934, when the United States accepted membership, that U.S. labor was represented in the ILO, although the AFL did attempt to maintain cooperative relations with the international organization in Geneva.[98] On the other hand, the AFL did not reaffiliate with the International Federation of Trade Unions until 1935.

In late July 1919, the IFTU met in Amsterdam to consider international labor's policy toward the peace treaty and to decide on the permanent form of the IFTU. Gompers headed an AFL delegation to the Amsterdam meeting consisting of himself, Daniel Tobin, and John J. Hynes.[99]

At this conference, the lines were clearly drawn between the European labor movement and the AFL. Hardly a session passed without "stormy discussions" and "collisions." Gompers found himself in the minority and was forced to give way on almost all the important issues.[100] One of the sharpest points of controversy between the American delegates and several European delegates arose over the labor clauses of the Versailles Treaty. The conference criticized the entire program as an inadequate expression of the demands of the international working classes. Only the British and American delegations supported a substitute resolution offered by Gompers. On the issue of the League of Nations, Gompers sponsored a resolution of endorsement, but another resolution that withheld endorsement while criticizing the League's capitalist and anti-socialist bias was passed in its place, with the American delegates abstaining. The AFL delegates also voted against resolutions supported by European delegates condemning the blockade of Russia, endorsing socialism and general strikes in support of political objectives, and on other ideologically oriented issues.[101]

After the old IFTU had been dissolved, the conference adopted a constitution and by-laws for a new organization with the same name. W. A. Appleton of Great Britain was elected president of the new organization, and the headquarters of the IFTU were established in Amsterdam. The AFL delegates refused to commit the Federation to joining the new international organization, leaving the decision up to the next AFL convention. With Gompers bitterly denouncing the "outrageous high-handed" manner in which the European delegates had acted in Amsterdam, the prospects for affiliation were slim. Therefore, it was not surprising that the AFL's 1920 Montreal convention endorsed the hostile attitude displayed by Gompers toward the IFTU and referred the question of affiliation back to the Executive Council for further investigation. As a result, it was more than fifteen years before the AFL affiliated with the new IFTU.[102]

While U.S. labor was not represented in either the ILO or the IFTU, representatives of women workers were helping to fill the gap. When they were in Paris for the Peace Conference as representatives of the WTUL, Rose Schneiderman and Mary Anderson explored with other women the possibility of an International Working Women's Conference, and the League issued a call to women labor leaders in European countries to meet in Washington for such a conference on October 28, 1919.

## INTERNATIONAL CONGRESS OF WORKING WOMEN

With expenses underwritten by the National Women's Trade Union League, whose president was Margaret Dreier Robins, the first International Congress of Working Women attracted fifty delegates from eighteen countries, and visitors from seven others.* The league not only sponsored and underwrote the Congress, it also prepared a "Union Women's Labor Program" for consideration by the delegates. This was a comprehensive "Program of Social and Industrial Reconstruction" and called for many of the special legislative measures for women workers that had been brought to Paris by Schneiderman and Anderson, including an eight-hour day, a

*Delegates attended from the USA, Great Britain, Poland, France, Sweden, Belgium, Norway, Argentina, Canada, Czechoslovakia, India, Cuba, Denmark, Japan, The Netherlands, Serbia, Spain, and Switzerland.

40-hour work week, equal pay for equal work, equal opportunities for trade and technical training, social insurance with maternity benefits, compulsory insurance against unemployment for men and women alike, and consideration of the payment of unemployment benefits to workers on strike. The program also called for freedom of speech, the press, and assembly, and for public ownership of natural resources.[103]

Although it was called the "Union Women's Labor Program," few provisions in the league's reconstruction program dealt with either unionization or the labor movement. Almost every measure was either political or legislative in nature. The same could be said of the First International Congress of Working Women that met in Washington, D.C., in late October and early November 1919. In opening the Congress, Margaret Dreier Robins made a telling point when she noted:

> Women had no direct share in the terms of the Peace Treaty. It's a man-made peace. Women have had no direct share in the labor platform, with its emphasis on the protection of women in industry rather than its emphasis on the participation of women in plans to protect themselves which is significant of the attitude of men, even in the labor movement, toward women.

The "labor platform" stressed at the Congress was geared entirely to legislation. Several days were consumed in discussing laws establishing a universal eight-hour day for working women. This was followed by a discussion of the need for laws providing maternity benefits for working women—before, during, and after the birth of a child.

In none of these discussions was there any mention of either a role for the trade unions or the need for organizing working women into unions. In fact, the only reference to this aspect of the situation came in a message to the Congress from "Representative Negro Women of the United States in behalf of Negro Women Laborers of the United States."' Noting that two million black women engaged in such pursuits warranted "representation in the Council," the message pointed out that they had "very limited

---

*The "Memorial" was signed by Elizabeth C. Carter, Executive Worker, War Work Council, YWCA, and Honorary President, National Association of Colored Women's Clubs; Mamie R. Rosse, President, Conference Branch M, Missionary Society, Liberia, West Coast of Africa; Leilia Pendleton, Folder and Compositor, Washington, D. C.; A. G. Green, Community Secretary, Public Schools of D. C.; Mary Church Terrell, Honorary President, National Association of Colored Women's Clubs, Washington, D. C.; Eva A. Wright, Milliner, Ohio and Washington, D. C.; Nannie H. Burroughs, President, National Training School for Women and Girls, Washington, D. C. ("Typed Proceedings of the First International Congress of Working Women, October 28 to November 5, 1919," NWTUL Papers, Library of Congress).

means of making their wishes known, and of having their interests advanced through their own representatives":

> Therefore, we, a group of Negro women, representing those two million of Negro women wage-earners, respectfully ask for your active cooperation in organizing the Negro women workers of the United States into unions, that they may have a share in bringing about industrial democracy and social order in the world.

Apart from applauding the appeal, however, the Congress did nothing about it.[104]

## INTERNATIONAL FEDERATION OF WORKING WOMEN

In Geneva, in October 1921, delegates from twelve nations met and changed the name of the Congress to the International Federation of Working Women. They then adopted a constitution and elected Margaret Dreier Robins of the National Women's Trade Union League as president.

The declared objective of the Federation was "to unite organized women in order that they may resolve upon the means by which the standard of the life of the workers throughout the world may best be rasied." This time, however, priority was given to trade unionism.

The organization's declared goals were: first, to "promote trade union organization among women," and to develop an international policy that gave special consideration to the needs of women and children; second, to examine all projects for legislation proposed by the International Labor Conference of the League of Nations; and third, to advocate the appointment of working women to organizations affecting the welfare of workers.

As far as membership was concerned, the Federation was to consist of "national trade union organizations containing women members and affiliated to the International Federation of Trade Unions," but it would also admit working women's organizations that accepted its aims and agreed "to work in the spirit and follow the principles of the International Federation of Trade Unions." In emphasizing that the Federation would "promote trade union organization among women," its Constitutional Committee noted: "That means that it shall in every way possible help get women into the trade unions, not to form new trade unions apart from those already in existence, but to help strengthen those unions that there are."[105]

Upon assuming the presidency, Robins declared that the first task of working women of the world was "to make war against war." "The first battle in that war," she continued, "is to stop increasing armaments.

Armaments breed war." She then cited winning "the right to our daily bread" as the first domestic task of women workers, and, after pointing out that unemployment cast its shadow over workers' homes everywhere, she declared vigorously that "either unemployment or capitalism must go. If competitive private industry cannot employ the able and willing workers, then is competitive private industry doomed." Robins then urged working women to try direct political action as a means of achieving their goals. "When we are hungry and homeless and idle or slaughtering our brothers or killing our sons, let us vote against the government without regard to party."[106]

## CHAPTER 1

1. Barbara Tuchman, *The Guns of August*, New York, 1962, p. 325.
2. Woodrow Wilson, *The Hope of the World*, New York and London, 1920, pp. 101-03.
3. *American Socialist*, Aug. 15, 1914.
4. See Merele Farsod, *International Socialism and the World War*, Cambridge, Mass., 1935.
5. *Milwaukee Leader*, Sept. 23, 1914; *American Socialist*, Oct. 24, Nov. 21, 1914.
6. New York *Call*, Aug. 29, 1914.
7. Philip S. Foner, *Karl Liebknecht and the United States*, Chicago, 1978, pp. 3-25.
8. *Masses*, Feb. 1915, p. 14; *American Socialist*, Jan. 4, 1915; James Weinstein, *The Decline of Socialism in America, 1912-1925*, New York, 1967, pp. 120-21.
9. Ray Ginger, *The Bending Cross: A Biography of Eugene Victor Debs*, New Brunswick, N.J., 1949, p. 328; *American Socialist*, Sept. 5, 12, 1914; *Masses*, Sept. 1914, p. 16; Norman Bindler, "American Socialism and the First World War," unpublished Ph.D. thesis, New York University, 1940, pp. 28-30.
10. William English Walling, ed., *The Socialists and the War*, New York, 1915, p. 23; H. Gorter, "Imperialism, the World War and Social Democracy," *International Socialist Review* 15 (May 1915): 646.
11. New York *Call*, Aug. 12, 1914; *The Socialist and Labor Star* (Huntington, W. Va.), Aug. 1914; Huntington *Argus Star*, Aug. 28, 1914; *American Socialist*, Aug. 22, 1914.
12. New York *Call*, Aug. 9, 1914.
13. American Socialist, Sept. 19, 1915.
14. New York *Call*, Feb. 28, March 13, 1915.
15. *American Socialist*, Dec. 26, 1914; Jan. 9, 1915.
16. Michael E. R. Bassett, "The Socialist Party of America, 1912-1919: Years of Decline," unpublished Ph.D. thesis, Duke University, 1963, pp. 89-90.
17. New York *Call*, Aug. 22, Sept 2, Oct. 4, 1914.
18. Max Bertch, "Unemployment, 1914-1915," unpublished M.A. thesis, Columbia University, Economics Division, 1928, p. 12.
19. New York *Call*, Jan. 15-17, 1915.
20. Ray Stannard Baker, *Woodrow Wilson*, (Garden City, 1933) 5: 179-84, 189.
21. Ibid., pp. 175-78; *New York Times*, Jan. 8, 1936.
22. Allan L. Benson, *A Way to Prevent War*, Girard, Kan., 1915, p. 175; Harold W. Currie, "Allan L. Benson, Salesman of Socialism, 1902-1916," *Labor History* 11 (Summer 1970): 300-02.
23. New York *Call*, Jan. 24, 1915; Morris Hillquit to Carl D. Thompson, Jan. 20, 1915, Socialist Party of America Papers, Duke University Library.
24. New York *Call*, Aug. 13, 1914.
25. Ibid., Sept. 10, 1914; *International Socialist Review* 15 (June 1915): 753.
26. *War Memoirs of Robert Lansing*, Indianapolis, 1935, p. 128.
27. *American Socialist*, May 15, 1915.
28. Ibid.
29. Ibid.; Alexander Trachtenberg, ed., *The American Socialists and the War*, New York, 1917, pp. 11-19; *Socialist News*, Cleveland, May 22, 1915.
30. *New York Times*, Dec. 7, 1914.
31. Robert D. Ward, "The Origin and Activities of the National Security League, 1914-1919," *Mississippi Valley Historical Review* 47 (June 1960): 51; *New York Times*, July 2, 1915.
32. *New York Times*, Nov. 5, 7, 1915.
33. Reprinted in *International Socialist Review* 16 (Nov. 8, 1915): 267.
34. *Masses*, July 1916, p. 13.
35. *Appeal to Reason*, Feb. 19, 1916; New York *Call*, Dec. 29, 1915; Philip S. Foner, *Helen Keller: Her Socialist Years*, New York, 1967, pp. 73-81.
36. *Must We Arm?* A Debate between Augustus P. Gardner and Morris Hillquit, April 2, 1915, Stenographic Report, New York, 1916, pp. 29-31.
37. *American Socialist*, Feb. 12, 1916; New York *Call*, March 15, 1915.
38. *American Socialist*, Nov. 6, 1915.
39. Rochester (N.Y.) *Herald*, Nov. 28, 1915. See also *American Socialist*, Dec. 19, 1914.
40. New York *Call*, Jan. 8, 1916; "The Socialist Referendum, 1915," William J. Ghent Papers, Wisconsin State Historical Society; W. J. Ghent to Algernon Lee, April 30, 1916, Algernon Lee Papers, Tamiment Institute Library, New York University; Harold Sheburn Smith, "William James Ghent: Historian and Reformer," unpublished Ph.D. thesis, University of Wisconsin, Madison, 1957, pp. 365-66.
41. *American Socialist*, August 28, 1915, Feb. 5, April 22, June 12, 1916; New York *Call*, Feb. 14, 1916; Trachtenberg,

pp. 27-30.

42. *American Socialist*, Jan. 17, 1916; New York *Call*, Jan. 8, 1916.

43. *American Socialist*, May 15, 1915.

44. Ibid., May 22, 1915.

45. Ibid., Nov. 27, 1915.

46. New York *Call*, reprinted in *Literary Digest*, March 26, 1916.

47. Amos R. E. Pinchot, *History of the Progressive Party, 1912-1916*, ed. Helene M. Hooker, New York, 1958, pp. 213-25.

48. Joseph E. Cohen in *American Socialist*, March 25, 1916.

49. "War and Militarism versus Labor and Progress," undated leaflet issued by Local New York, Socialist Party, Local New York Papers, Tamiment Institute Library, New York University.

50. *American Socialist*, Oct. 28, 1916.

51. New York *Call*, Oct. 4, 1916.

52. Ibid., Oct. 16, 1916.

53. New York *World*, Oct. 20, 1916.

54. John Reed to the National Executive Committee, Oct. 13, 1916, Socialist Party of America Papers, Duke University Library.

55. *International Socialist Review* 16 (Oct. 1916): 243-44.

56. *New Republic* 8 (Oct. 7, 1916): 243-45.

57. New York *Call*, Nov. 9, 1916; *Survey* 37 (Nov. 18, 1916): 172.

58. *American Socialist*, Nov. 18, 1916; James Weinstein, p. 27.

59. *American Socialist*, Jan. 20, 1917.

60. Henry L. Slobodin, "The State of the Socialist Party," *International Socialist Review* 17 (March 1917): 539-41.

61. *International Socialist Review* 17 (Dec. 1916): 365-66.

62. Robert Lansing to Gerard, April 18, 1916, and Gerard to Lansing, May 4, 1916, in Department of State, *Papers Relating to the Foreign Relations of the United States, 1916, Supplement*, Washington, 1929, pp. 232-36., 257-60.

63. Ray Stannard Baker and William E. Dodd, eds., *The Public Papers of Woodrow Wilson* (New York, 1925-26): 422-26.

64. Charles Seymour, *American Diplomacy during the World War*, Baltimore, 1934, p. 210.

65. The standard works on the Wilson administration's policy toward the Allies being so one-sided as to make war inevitable are Clinton Hartley Grattan, *Why We Fought*, New York, 1929; Walter Millis, *Road to War: America, 1914-1917*, New York 1935; Charles C. Tansill,

*America Goes to War*, Boston, 1938; and Alice M. Morrissey, *The American Defense of Neutral Rights, 1914-1917*, Cambridge, Mass., 1939. A more recent study emphasizing the same theme is John W. Coogan, *The End of Neutrality: The United States, Britain, and Maritime Rights, 1899-1915*, Ithaca, N.Y., 1981. For Peterson, *see* H. C. Peterson, *Propaganda for War*, New York, 1956, p. 122.

66. *Hearings before the Special Senate Committee on the Investigation of the Munitions Industry*, United States Senate, 74th Cong., 2nd sess., Washington, 1937. Many of the same documents were published in the *New York Times* of Jan. 8-12, 1936, and are also to be found in Ray Stannard Baker, *Woodrow Wilson*, Garden City, 1935, vol. V.

67. *New York Times*, Jan. 8, 10, 1936.

68. Ibid., Jan. 10, 1936.

69. Ibid.

70. Ibid.; Paul Birdsall, "Neutrality and Economic Pressures, 1914-1917," *Science & Society*, Spring 1939, p. 222.

71. "Down With War," 2-page leaflet issued by the National Office, Socialist Party, Chicago, copy in Socialist Party of America Papers, Duke University Library; *American Socialist*, February 17, 1917.

72. *Ohio Socialist*, Feb. 1917, p. 1.

73. *American Socialist*, March 24, 1917; *Socialist Party Bulletin* 1 (March 1917): 1.

74. *New York Times*, Feb. 6, 1917.

75. Ibid., March 8, 1917; New York *Call*, March 18, 1917.

76. *National Rip-Saw*, Jan. 1917, pp. 25-27; Philip S. Foner, *Karl Liebknecht and the United States*, Chicago, 1978, pp. 31-32.

77. *New York Times*, March 5, 1917.

78. New York *Tribune*, March 10, 1917; *Independent* 89 (March 26, 1917): 532.

79. *International Socialist Review* 17 (March 1917): 155-57; *New York Times*, Feb. 11, 1917; *Ohio Socialist*, Feb. 1917, p. 1.

80. Philip S. Foner, *The Bolshevik Revolution: Its Impact on American Radicals, Liberals, and Labor*, New York, 1967, pp. 15-16.

81. Morris U. Schappes, "World War I and the Jewish Masses (1914-1917)," *Jewish Life*, Feb. 1955, p. 19.

82. Foner, *Bolshevik Revolution*, p. 16; New York *Call*, April 1, 1917; *Cleveland Citizen*, April 28, 1917.

83. János Jemnitz, "Between Revolution and Reformism: The European Working

Class Movement in 1917," *Studia Historica*, Budapest 118 (1975): 118-19.

84. *Socialist Party Bulletin* 1 (March 1917): 14.
85. New York *Call*, March 24, 1917.
86. Ibid., March 26, 1917.
87. Ibid., March 31, 1917.
88. *Socialist Party Bulletin* 1 (March 1917): 15.
89. New York *Call*, March 13, 1917; *American Socialist*, March 17, 1917.
90. Memorandum of March 20, 1917, Confidential Memoranda, *Papers Relating to the Foreign Relations of the United States: The Lansing Papers, 1915-1920*, 1 (Washington, D.C., 1940): 628-29.
91. Memorandum of March 20, 1917, Ibid., (my emphasis—P.S.F.).
92. *Cleveland Citizen*, March 31, 1917; *Socialist News*, Cleveland, April 7, 1917.
93. *New York Times*, April 3, 7, 1917.
94. *Socialist News*, Cleveland, April 7, 1917; Oakley C. Johnson, *The Day is Coming: Life and Work of Charles E. Ruthenberg*, New York, 1957, pp. 109-10.
95. *American Socialist*, March 31, 1917; *New York Times*, April 4, 1917; *Benson's Magazine*, April 1917, p. 14.
96. Ray Ginger, *The Bending Cross: A Biography of Eugene Victor Debs*, New Brunswick, N.J., 1949, p. 342.
97. "Stenographic Report of the Emergency National Convention, Socialist Party, 1917," p. 18; *American Socialist*, April 14, 1917; *Socialist News*, Cleveland, April 14, 1917.
98. David Shannon, *The Socialist Party of America*, Chicago, 1967, p. 94.
99. *American Socialist*, April 21, 1917; *Socialist News*, Cleveland, April 21, 1917.
100. *New York Times*, April 4, 1917.
101. *Milwaukee Leader*, April 3, 1917. See also New York *Call*, April 7, 1917.
102. Louis Waldman, *Labor Lawyer*, New York, 1945, p. 46.
103. *American Socialist*, April 14, 21, 1917.
104. *American Labor Yearbook*, New York, 1917-18, pp. 313-16; *American Socialist*, April 21, 1917; *Class Struggle*, May-June 1917, p. 41.
105. John Spargo, *Americanism and Social Democracy*, New York, 1918, pp. 287-92.
106. *American Socialist*, April 21, 1917.
107. *Socialist News*, Cleveland, April 21, 1917.
108. New York *Call*, April 14, 1917.

109. Charles Edward Russell to J. Phelps Stokes, April 8, 1917, J. Phelps Stokes Papers, Butler Library, Columbia University.
110. Shannon, pp. 213-15.
111. Allan Benson to Charles Edward Russell, May 14, 1917, Charles Edward Russell Papers, Library of Congress. Chester M. Wright to J. Phelps Stokes, May 26, 1917; A. M. Simons to Stokes, May 7, 24, 1917; Stokes to Chester M. Wright, May 9, 1917; Stokes to Simons, May 9, 1917; Stokes to Randolph Bourne, May 7, 1917; Upton Sinclair to Stokes, May 4, 1917; all J. Phelps Stokes Papers, Butler Library, Columbia University.
112. *International Socialist Review* 17 (May 1917): 654-55; *American Socialist*, May 17, 1917.
113. John Spargo to A. M. Simons, April 12, 1917, Algie M. Simons Papers, State Historical Society of Wisconsin.
114. *Independent* 91 (July 14, 1917): 43; *Current Opinion* 68 (Aug. 1917): 73-75.
115. New York *Call*, June 6, 1915.
116. *Intercollegiate Socialist*, March 1915, p. 16.
117. "Circular," September 1914, Letter Books, Local New York; Minute Book, Executive Committee, Aug. 14, 1914, Local New York, Socialist Party Papers, Tamiment Institute Library, New York University.
118. American Socialist, Sept. 19, Oct. 3, 10; Dec. 26, 1914.
119. Ibid., Jan. 16, Sept. 11, 1915.
120. New York *Call*, June 23, 1915.
121. *American Labor Year Book*, 1917-18, p. 336.
122. New York *Call*, Sept. 11, 1915; American Socialist, March 6, 1915.
123. Milwaukee Leader, Aug. 14, 1916.
124. New York *Call*, April 22, 1916.
125. *American Socialist*, April 14, 1917.
126. New York *Call*, April 20, 1916.
127. *Socialist News*, Cleveland, April 7, 1917; Johnson, pp. 100-110.
128. Charles Leinenweber, "Socialist Opposition to World War I," *Radical America* 2 (March-April, 1968): 32.

## CHAPTER 2

1. *Solidarity*, Aug. 8, 1914; Coast Seamen's Journal 28 (Sept 23, 1914): 8; *Locomotive Firemen's and Enginemen's Magazine* 57 (Oct. 1914): 473; *Journal of the Knights of Labor* 34 (Sept. 1914): 3; *Railway Conductor* 31 (Oct. 1914): 729; *Miners' Magazine* 15 (Sept. 1914):

2; David Levin, "Organized Labor and the Military, 1897-1917," unpublished M.A. thesis, University of Wisconsin, Madison, 1950, pp. 134-35.

2. Quoted in Gary M. Fink, *Labor's Search for Political Order: The Political Behavior of the Missouri Labor Movement, 1890-1940*, Columbia, Mo., 1973, p. 62.

3. *Cigar Makers' Journal* 38 (Sept. 1914): 2; *Carpenter* 34 (Sept. 1914): 13; *Shoe Workers' Journal* 15 (Sept. 1914): 13; *International Molders' Journal* 50 (Oct. 1914): 50; Levin, p. 135.

4. Melvyn Dubofsky, "Organized Labor in New York City and the First World War, 1914-1918," *New York History* 42 (Oct. 1961): 16.

5. *United Mine Workers' Journal* 25 (Sept. 10, 1914): 2; *Locomotive Firemen's and Enginemen's Magazine* 57 (Oct. 1914): 475; *Miners' Magazine* 15 (September 1914): 3; Levin, p. 136.

6. *Stove Mounters' and Range Workers' Journal* 19 (Nov. 1914): 330; *United Mine Workers' Journal* 25 (Aug. 13, 1914): 6; *Solidarity*, Oct. 30, 1914; Levin, p. 137.

7. *Miners' Magazine* 15 (Dec. 1914): 3. See also *International Musician* 14 (Sept. 1914): 10; *Coast Seamen's Journal* 28 (Oct. 17, 1914): 17; *Journal of the Electrical Workers* 14 (Nov. 1914): 450; Levin, pp. 137-38.

8. *New York Call*, Aug. 7, 1914.

9. *Coast Seamen's Journal* 27 (Aug. 19, 1914); 27; Simeon Larson, *Labor and Foreign Policy: Gompers, the AFL, and the First World War, 1914-1918*, Rutherford, N.J., 1975, pp. 17-18; Samuel Gompers, *American Labor and the War*, New York, 1919, pp. 219-20.

10. Samuel Gompers to Ed Nolte, Aug. 6, 1914, AFL Archives, State Historical Society of Wisconsin.

11. *Proceedings of the Sixteenth Session of the International Typographical Union*, 1914, pp. 93-94; Levin, p. 139.

12. *Proceedings of the National Arbitration and Peace Congress*, New York, 1907, pp. 250-51, 290-91; *American Federationist* 13 (June 1907): 417-18; *Advocate of Peace* 49 (May 1907): 97-120.

13. Gompers, *American Labor and the War*, pp. 142-46.

14. *American Federationist* 21 (Sept. 1914): 726-29; Larson, p. 24; Bernard Mandel, *Samuel Gompers: A Biography*, Yellow Springs, Ohio, 1963, p. 350.

15. Gompers, *American Labor and the War*,

pp. 20-21; Larson, p. 24; *American Federationist* 31 (Oct. 1914): 867; *Proceedings*, AFL Convention, 1914, p. 489.

16. Florence Calvert Thorne, *Samuel Gompers, Statesman*, New York, 1957, p. 146; Samuel Gompers, *Seventy Years of Life and Labor* 2 (New York, 1925): 354.

17. Ralph M. Easley to Samuel Gompers, Oct. 13, 1914, Gompers Papers, AFL Archives, State Historical Society of Wisconsin.

18. Samuel Gompers to Ralph M. Easley, Oct. 20, 1914, ibid.

19. *Proceedings*, AFL Convention, 1914, pp. 467-68; *New York Times*, Nov. 13, 1914; New York *Call*, Nov. 14, 1914; *American Federationist* 22 (Jan. 1915): 17, 40-41.

20. *Proceedings*, AFL Convention, 1914, pp. 473-74; Larson, p. 27.

21. Quoted in *AFL Weekly News Letter*, Nov. 28, 1914, and in Larson, pp. 23-24.

22. Philip S. Foner, *History of the Labor Movement in the United States* 4 (New York, 1965): 554-55.

23. *Solidarity*, Oct. 3, 1914; Frederick C. Giffin, *Six Who Protested: Radical Opposition to the First World War*, Port Washington, N.Y., 1977, p. 121; *American Federationist* 31 (Oct. 1914): 868-69.

24. *Plumbers', Gas and Steamfitters' Journal* 19 (Feb. 1915): 30; *Locomotive Firemen's and Enginemen's Magazine* 58 (April 1915): 455; Levin, p. 141.

25. New York *Call*, Feb. 27, 1915.

26. Ibid., April 16, 1915.

27. Ibid., April 18, 1915.

28. *Coast Seamen's Journal*, May 9, 1915; Larson, p. 52.

29. New York *Call*, May 19, 1915.

30. Ibid.

31. Lewis Lorwin, *The American Federation of Labor*, Washington, D.C., 1933, p. 140; *The Outlook* 110 (June 30, 1915): 48-50.

32. Larson, p. 52.

33. Lorwin, p. 140.

34. Ernest Bohm to Samuel Gompers, June 15, 1915, AFL Archives, State Historical Society of Wisconsin; New York *Call*, June 12, 1915.

35. New York *Call*, June 10, 12, 1915.

36. Samuel Gompers to Ernest Bohm, June 18, 1915, Gompers Papers, AFL Archives, State Historical Society of Wisconsin.

37. Samuel Gompers to Woodrow Wilson, enclosing copy of Gompers to Ernest

Bohm, June 28, 1915, Woodrow Wilson Papers, Library of Congress; *New York Times*, June 20, 1915; Larson, p. 53; M. Twining to Samuel Gompers, June 23, 1915, Gompers Papers, AFL Archives, State Historical Society of Wisconsin.

38. "Bryan and Labor," *The Outlook* 110 (June 30, 1915): 481-83; New York *Call*, June 20, 1915.

39. *New York Times*, June 20, 1915; New York *Call*, June 20, 1915.

40. Ibid.

41. New York *Call*, Aug. 26, 1915; *Biographical Directory of the American Congress*, 1774-1971, Washington, D.C., 1971, pp. 658-59.

42. H. B. Perham to Samuel Gompers, May 29, 1915, Gompers Papers, AFL Archives, State Historical Society of Wisconsin.

43. Copy of call in AFL Archives, ibid.

44. "Telephone conversation between Mr. Gompers and Congressman Frank Buchanan, June 21, 1915, and memorandum dictated by President Gompers after the phone conversation," Gompers Papers, AFL Archives, ibid.

45. Typewritten report of Labor's Peace Congress, Washington, D.C., June 22, 1915, AFL Archives, Washington, D.C.

46. Ibid.; *New York Times*, May 22, 1917.

47. Frank Buchanan, President, Labor's National Peace Council, to "My dear Sir and Brother," June 30, 1915, AFL Archives, Washington, D.C.

48. Frank Buchanan to W. F. Kremer, July 13, 1915, records of *U.S. v. Rintelen, Buchanan, et al* (Criminal Case, U.S. District Court for the Southern District of New York), in National Archives.

49. Gompers to Frank Morrison, June 12, 1915; Gompers to David Kreyling, July 30, 1915; Gompers to John M. Bogart, August 7, 1915, Gompers Papers, AFL Archives, State Historical Society of Wisconsin.

50. Philip S. Foner, *Women and the American Labor Movement: From Colonial Times to the Eve of World War I*, New York, 1979, pp. 491-96; Amy Newes, "Women as Munition Makers," *Survey* 37 (January 6, 1917): 381-83; Florence Peterson, "Strikes in the United States, 1880-1936," U.S. Department of Labor, *Bulletin No. 651*, Washington, D.C., 1938, p. 21.

51. Bridgeport *Post*, July 21-24, 1915; *New York Times*, July 23-24, 1915.

52. *New York Times*, July 17, 1915.

53. Ibid., July 18, 1915; New York *Call*, July 18, 1915.

54. *New York Times*, July 18, 1915.

55. Ibid.

56. Ibid., July 20, 24, 1915.

57. New York *Call*, July 24, 1915; *New York Times*, July 31, 1915.

58. Draft memorandum by Ralph M. Easley, "German Sabotage in the U.S., 1915-1916," n.d., National Civic Federation Papers, New York Public Library; Larson, p.44.

59. Mandel, p. 356. *See also* Gompers, *Seventy Years of Life and Labor* 2: 336-49.

60. *New York Times*, July 19, 1915; Frank McDonald to Thomas S. Farrell, Aug. 20, 1915, AFL Archives, State Historical Society of Wisconsin.

61. New York *Call*, Aug. 26, 1915; Larson, p. 55.

62. Cecil Spring-Rice to Edward Grey, June 10, 1915, in Stephen Gwynn, ed., *The Letters and Friendships of Sir Cecil Spring-Rice* 2 (Boston and New York, 1929): 272-73.

63. Larson, p. 55.

64. Gompers, *Seventy Years of Life and Labor* 2: 341-42; *New York Times*, Sept. 3, 1915.

65. Gompers to John Brisbe Walker, September 2, 1915, Gompers Papers, AFL Archives, State Historical Society of Wisconsin.

66. John Golden to John H. Bogart, Aug. 13, 1915, copy in AFL Archives, State Historical Society of Wisconsin.

67. Homer D. Call to John H. Bogart, Aug. 16, 1915, copy in AFL Archives, State Historical Society of Wisconsin.

68. Clifton James Child, *German-Americans in Politics 1914-1917*, Madison, Wisc., 1939, pp. 130, 142; Levin, pp. 143-44.

69. Testimony before the grand jury as well as correspondence of Labor's National Peace Council are in *U.S. v. Rintelen, Buchanan, et al.*, National Archives. Other information relating to Labor's National Peace Council may be found in Franz von Rintelen von Kleist, *The Dark Invaders: Wartime Reminiscences of a German Naval Officer*, New York, 1933, pp. 83-133, 166-81; George S. Viereck, *Spreading the Germs of Hate*, New York, 1930, pp. 99-101; *Hearings, Brewing and Liquor Interests and Bolshevik Propaganda*, Subcommittee of the U.S. Judiciary, U.S. Senate, 65th Congress, 1st Session, x-xv.

70. *U.S. v. Rintelen, Buchanan, et al.*

71. Ibid.

72. Ibid.

73. *New York Times*, Dec. 29, 1915.
74. Ibid., May 21, 1917.
75. Testimony of Ernest Bohm before grand jury, in *U.S. v. Rintelen, Buchanan, et. al.*
76. *New York Times*, Sept. 22, 1917.
77. *New York Tribune*, Nov. 14, 1915; *New York Times*, Nov. 17, 1915.
78. New York *Call*, Nov. 23, 1915.
79. Proceedings, AFL Convention, 1915, pp. 131-38.
80. New York *Call*, Nov. 23, 1915; *Proceedings*, AFL Convention, 1915, pp. 216, 230-32.

## CHAPTER 3

1. *Background of Selective Service*, Washington, D.C., 1949, Appendix, pp. 204-65.
2. *The Public Papers of Woodrow Wilson* (New York, 1925-27) 2: 1-121.
3. Samuel Gompers, "Preparedness for National Defense," *Senate Document 311*, 64th Congress, 1st Session; *American Federationist* 23 (Jan. 1916): 48; (March 1916): 175.
4. William Menkel, "The Plattsburg Response: A Citizens' Movement Toward Military Preparedness," *American Review of Reviews* 52 (July-December 1915): 301-08.
5. James R. Sperry, "Organized Labor and Its Fight Against Military and Industrial Conscription," unpublished study in possession of present writer, pp. 8-10.
6. Gompers to General Leonard Wood, Sept. 15, 1915, Woodrow Wilson Papers, Library of Congress; also published in Robert Cuff, ed., "Samuel Gompers, Leonard Wood and Military Preparedness," *Labor History* 12 (Summer 1971): 280-88.
7. Gompers to Kate Barnard, Feb. 25, 1916, Gompers Papers, AFL Archives, State Historical Society of Wisconsin. *See also* Samuel Gompers, *American Labor and the War*, New York, 1919, p. 63.
8. San Francisco *Labor Clarion*, March 7, 1916.
9. *Metal Polishers', Buffers', and Platters' Journal* 34 (Jan. 1915): 34; *Plumbers', Gas and Steamfitters' Journal* 19 (March 1915): 31; *Shoe Workers' Journal* 17 (April 1916): 18; David Levin, "Organized Labor and the Military, 1897-1917," unpublished M.A. thesis, University of Wisconsin, Madison, 1950, p. 154.
10. *Metal Polishers', Buffers', and Platters' Journal* 34 (March 1915): 38; *International Molders' Journal* 51 (August 1915): 580; Levin, op. cit., pp. 155-57.
11. *Metal Polishers', Buffers', Platters and Brass Workers' Journal* 34 (Dec. 1915): 13; *Railway Conductor* 32 (Dec. 1915): 925; Levin, pp. 156-57.
12. *National Guard Magazine* 12 (May 1915): 94; *Army and Navy Journal* 53 (April 22, 1916): 1063.
13. *Literary Digest*, April 6, 1916, pp. 957-58.
14. *New Republic*, June 10, 1916, pp. 137-39.
15. Ibid.
16. St. Louis *Post-Dispatch*, March 11, 1916, quoted in *National Rip-Saw*, May 1916, p. 11.
17. *United Mine Workers' Journal* 77 (Jan. 20, 1916): 37-38.
18. *Machinists' Monthly Journal* 27 (Nov. 1915): 1095; 28 (February 1916): 171.
19. *International Musician* 15 (Sept. 1915): 9; Levin, pp. 159-60.
20. *Teamsters' Magazine* 12 (July 1915): 77; Levin, p. 161.
21. *American Pressman* 26 (Jan. 1916): 269; Levin, p. 162.
22. *Advance Advocate* 25 (March 1916): 7; Levin, p. 162.
23. *Locomotive Firemen's and Enginemen's Magazine* 60 (Feb. 1916): 1189; (March 1916): 324.
24. *Fur Worker*, Dec. 15, 1916, p. 4; *Journal of the Switchmen's Union* 18 (Feb. 1916): 77; *Proceedings of the Thirty-Third Annual Convention of the Illinois State Federation of Labor, 1915*, pp. 279, 291-93.
25. *American Pressman* 25 (August 1915): 331; *Advance Advocate* 25 (Sept. 1916): 14; Levin, p. 165; *Railway Carmen's Journal* 21 (April 1916): 200-01.
26. Simeon Larson, "The American Federation of Labor and the Preparedness Campaign," *Historian* 37 (Nov. 1974): 72; San Francisco *Labor Clarion*, May 26, 1916; Richard H. Frost, *The Mooney Case*, Stanford, Cal., 1968, p. 63.
27. *United Mine Workers' Journal* 27 (March 1916): 4; *Locomotive Firemen's and Enginemen's Magazine* 60 (March 1916): 324; *American Pressman* 25 (Aug. 1915): 331; Levin, pp. 162-63.
28. *Proceedings*, California State Federation of Labor Convention, 1916, p. 40.
29. New York *Call*, Jan. 22, 1916.
30. Ibid., July 11, 1916.
31. *Proceedings of the Ninth Convention of the Industrial Workers of the World*,

1916, p. 138.
32. "Preparedness," *Industrial Worker*, Dec. 8, 1915.
33. *Masses*, March 1916, p. 12.
34. *Industrial Union News* 4 (Dec. 1915): 1.
35. David Montgomery, "Labor and the Republic in Industrial America, 1860-1920," *Mouvement Social* (France) 111 (1980): 210-11.
36. *International Socialist Review* 16 (July 1916): 7.
37. *The Public*, May 26, 1916, pp. 482-83; *Labor Herald*, June 2, 1916.
38. *The Public*, June 2, 1916, p. 514.
39. Ibid., May 26, 1916, p. 482.
40. Ibid.
41. *International Socialist Review* 16 (July 1916): 9.
42. Chicago *Tribune*, May 20, June 4, 1916.
43. *Labor Review*, April 7, 1916, quoted in *New York Times*, June 3, 1916.
44. Gary M. Fink, *Labor's Search for Political Order: The Political Behavior of the Missouri Labor Movement 1890-1940*, Columbus, Mo., 1973, pp. 61-62.
45. *New York Times*, July 16, 1896; *Army and Navy Journal*, Sept. 9, 1916, p. 36.
46. *The Public*, June 2, 1916, p. 514.
47. *Coast Seamen's Journal*, June 28, 1916; Robert Wright, *Industrial Relations in the San Francisco Bay Area, 1900-1918*, Berkeley and Los Angeles, 1960, pp. 309-10; Frost, pp. 65-66.
48. San Francisco *Labor Clarion*, May 26, 1916; Frost, p. 65.
49. San Francisco Chamber of Commerce, *Law and Order in San Francisco: A Beginning*, San Francisco, 1916, p. 19.
50. San Francisco *Examiner*, July 11, 1916.
51. Ibid.; San Francisco *Bulletin*, July 11, 1916.
52. Robert Knight, *Industrial Relations in the San Francisco Bay Area, 1900-1918*, Berkeley and Los Angeles, 1960, p. 305.
53. San Francisco *Bulletin*, July 21, 1916.
54. Ibid.
55. Ibid.
56. Ibid.
57. San Francisco *Examiner*, July 20-21, 1916; *Coast Seamen's Journal*, June 16, 1916; San Francisco *Labor Clarion*, July 14, 1916; Knight, p. 310.
58. San Francisco *Bulletin*, July 23, 1916; San Francisco *Examiner*, July 23, 1916.

**CHAPTER 4**

1. San Francisco *Examiner*, July 23, 1916.
2. Richard H. Frost, *The Mooney Case*, Stanford, Cal., 1968, pp. 90-91.
3. Curt Gentry, *Frame-Up: The Incredible Case of Tom Mooney and Warren Billings*, New York, 1967, pp. 84-85.
4. San Francisco *Examiner*, July 23, 1916.
5. Ibid., July 27, 1916.
6. Gentry, pp. 36-37.
7. William Z. Foster, "The Molders' Convention," *International Socialist Review* 12 (December 1912): 486-87.
8. F. Monaco, "San Francisco Shoe Workers' Strike," Ibid., 13 (May 1913), pp. 818-19.
9. Gentry, p. 50.
10. Robert Knight, *Industrial Relations in the San Francisco Bay Area, 1900-1918*, Berkeley and Los Angeles, 1960, pp. 307-08.
11. Frost, pp. 22-23.
12. Philip S. Foner, *History of the Labor Movement in the United States* 4 (New York, 1965): 276; Frost, pp. 37-43.
13. "Chronology of Events in the Mooney Case," n.p., Frank P. Walsh Papers, New York Public Library.
14. Elizabeth Gurley Flynn in *Daily Worker*, July 26, 1956, based on a statement to her by a San Francisco motorman present at the council meeting.
15. Philip Taft, *Organized Labor in American History*, New York 1964, pp. 328-29.
16. *New York Times*, Sept. 5, 1917.
17. Gentry, p. 683; *New York Times*, Sept. 5, 1972.
18. *Blast*, April 1, 1916.
19. United States Committee on Public Information, *Report on the Mooney Dynamite Case in San Francisco*, Washington, D.C., 1918, p. 16.
20. Ibid., pp. 24-32; American Civil Liberties Union, *The Story of Mooney and Billings at a Glance*, New York, 1930, p. 14.
21. San Francisco Grand Jury, *Testimony and Proceedings, Documents*, Aug. 2-3, 1916.
22. Richard Drinnon, introduction to *Blast*, Westport, Conn., 1977, n.p.
23. Robert Minor, *The Frame-Up System: Story of the San Francisco Bomb*, San Francisco, 1916, p. 2; Robert Minor to Frank P. Walsh, Aug. 19, 1916, Frank P. Walsh Papers, New York Public Library.
24. "A Protest and Appeal," *The Public*, Sept. 8, 1916, p. 852.
25. *Documents Relating to the Trial of Warren K. Billings in the Superior Court and the District Court of Appeals* (San Francisco, 1916-18) 3: 162-35; 4: 224-65.
26. Philip Taft, *Organized Labor in American History*, New York 1964, p. 330.

27. San Francisco *Examiner*, Oct. 2, 1916.
28. *Proceedings of the Seventeenth Annual Convention of the California State Federation of Labor, 1916*, pp. 34-36.
29. Ibid., pp. 37-44.
30. Tom Mooney to Dear Sirs and Brothers, Oct. 23, 1916, Mother Mary Harris Jones Papers, Department of Archives and Manuscripts, Catholic University of American Library.
31. San Francisco *Labor Clarion*, Oct. 29, 1916.
32. *Fur Worker*, Dec. 5, 1916, p. 4.
33. Tom Mooney to Locals UMWA, San Francisco, Oct. 23, 1916, Mother Mary Harris Jones Papers, ibid.
34. Chicago *Tribune*, Nov. 29, 1916; Gentry, pp. 173-74.
35. New York *Call*, Dec. 3, 1916; *Masses*, Dec. 12, 1916, p. 14.
36. Gentry, p. 176.
37. Tom Mooney to Mother Jones, San Francisco, Dec. 28, 1916, Mother Mary Harris Jones Papers, ibid.
38. Ibid.
39. Frank P. Walsh to Robert Minor, Aug. 30, 1916, Frank P. Walsh Papers, New York Public Library; Tom Mooney to Local No. 1, IMU of N.A., San Francisco, Oct. 13, 1916, Mother Mary Harris Jones Papers, ibid.
40. Gentry, pp. 194-95.
41. George P. West, "Prejudice Speaks from the Bench," *New Republic* 68 (July 25, 1930): 282.
42. Bourke Cochran, *To the Commissioners Appointed by the President to Investigate the Conditions Under Which Thomas J. Mooney Was Convicted of Murder*, New York, 1917, pp. 12-20.
43. New York *Call*, Feb. 5, 1917.
44. *The Public*, March 2, 1917, p. 32.
45. Ibid., p. 34.
46. Ibid.
47. "Industrial Relations Committee on Mooney Case," *Oakland World*, Feb. 23, 1917.
48. Ernest Jerome Hopkins, *What Happened in the Mooney Case*, New York, 1932, pp. 112-34.
49. Seattle *Union Record*, April 20, 1917; Philip S. Foner, *Women and the American Labor Movement: From World War One to the Present*, New York, 1980, p. 32.
50. Bernard Mandel, *Samuel Gompers: A Biography*, Yellow Springs, Ohio, 1963, pp. 370-80.
51. Ibid., p. 381.
52. Woodrow Wilson to William D. Stephens, May 11, 1917; William D. Stephens to Woodrow Wilson, May 11, 1917, Woodrow Wilson Papers, Library of Congress.
53. Fremont Older, *My Own Story*, New York, 1926, pp. 234-46; Evelyn Wells, *Fremont Older*, New York, 1936, pp. 184-90.
54. San Francisco *Bulletin*, Sept. 20, 21, 22, 1917.
55. United States Committee on Public Information, *Report of the Mooney Dynamite Case in San Francisco*. Submitted by President Wilson's Mediation Commission, Official Bulletin, Washington, D.C., 1918, p. 36.
56. Woodrow Wilson to William D. Stephens, Jan. 22, 1918, Woodrow Wilson Papers, Library of Congress.
57. Gentry, pp. 234-36.
58. San Francisco *Bulletin*, Nov. 29, 1918.
59. Gentry, pp. 260-61.
60. United States National Commission on Law, Observance and Enforcement. Section on Lawless Enforcement of Law. *Mooney-Billings Report: Suppressed by the Wickersham Commission*, New York, 1932.

## CHAPTER 5

1. Simeon Larson, *Labor and Foreign Policy: Gompers, the AFL, and the First World War, 1914-1918*, Rutherford, N.J., p. 79.
2. *United Mine Workers' Journal* 28 (Feb. 1, 1917): 4.
3. *Cigar Makers' Journal* 41 (Feb. 1917): 2.
4. *Pattern Makers' Journal* 28 (Feb. 1917): 16.
5. *Carpenter* 37 (March 1917): 39.
6. David Levin, "Organized Labor and the Military, 1897-1917," unpublished M.A. thesis, University of Wisconsin, Madison, 1950, p. 170.
7. Ibid.; *Journal of the Switchmen's Union* 19 (March 1917): 57.
8. *See*, for example, *Machinists' Monthly Journal* 29 (Feb. 1917); *Coast Seamen's Journal* 30 (Feb. 14, 1917): 6; *Journal of the Electrical Workers* 16 (Jan. 1917): 365; *Miners' Magazine* 15 (March 1917): 4; *Advanced Advocate* 26 (March 1917): 4; *International Molders' Journal* 53 (March 1917): 183; *Shoe Workers' Journal* 18 (April 1917): 15; Levin, p. 171.
9. *Locomotive Firemen's and Enginemen's Magazine* 62 (April 1, 1917): 11; *Miners' Magazine* 15 (March 1917): 1;

Levin, pp. 171-72.

10. *New York Times*, Feb. 5, 1917.

11. Larson, p. 80; Fargo Trades and Labor Assembly to Gompers, Feb. 10, 1917, AFL Archives, State Historical Society of Wisconsin.

12. *Coast Seamen's Journal*, March 28, 1917.

13. *New York Times*, Feb. 5, 1917.

14. *Minneapolis Tribune*, Feb. 11, 1917.

15. Gompers to Karl Legien, Feb. 4, 1917; Karl Legien to Gompers, Feb. 11, 1917, State Historical Society of Wisconsin.

16. Gompers to Count Johann von Bernstoff, Feb. 10, 1917, ibid.

17. Letters and telegrams to Gompers, Feb. 6-15, 1917, AFL Archives, State Historical Society of Wisconsin.

18. "Labor and the War," *New Republic*, Feb. 10, 1917, pp. 37-38.

19. Gompers to Champ Clark, Feb. 10, 1917, Gompers Papers, State Historical Society of Wisconsin.

20. *New York Times*, Feb. 20, 1917.

21. Rowland H. Harvey, *Samuel Gompers: Champion of the Toiling Masses*, Stanford, Cal., 1935, p. 211; Marc Karson, *American Labor Unions and Politics, 1900-1918*, Carbondale, Ill., 1958, p. 161.

22. Gompers to AFL Executive Council, Feb. 28, 1917, AFL Archives, State Historical Society of Wisconsin.

23. Franklin H. Martin, *Digest of the Proceedings of the Council of National Defense During the World War*, Washington, D.C., 1934, pp. 97-98. (Sen. Doc. No. 193, 72C 2S).

24. Gompers to AFL Executive Council, Feb. 28, 1917, AFL Archives, State Historical Society of Wisconsin.

25. Ibid.; Bernard M. Baruch, *American Industry in the War Industries Board*, New York, 1941, p. 87; Bernard Mandel, *Samuel Gompers: A Biography*, Yellow Springs, Ohio, 1963, pp. 360-61.

26. Samuel Gompers, "American Labor's Position in Peace or in War," *American Federationist* 24 (April 1917): 272; Gompers to Presidents of the National and International Unions, March 2, 1917 (emphasis in original); Gompers to AFL Executive Council, Feb. 28, 1917, AFL Archives, State Historical Society of Wisconsin.

27. *Amalgamated Journal* 18 (March 22, 1917): 2.

28. American Federation of Labor, *Labor and the War*, Washington, D.C., 1918, pp. 62-64.

29. *American Federationist* 24 (April 1917): 227-30.

30. Louis L. Lorwin, *The American Federation of Labor: History, Policies, and Prospects*, Washington, D.C., 1933, p. 195.

31. Ibid., p. 143; Karson, p. 95.

32. Selig Perlman and Philip Taft, *History of Labor in the United States, 1896-1932* (New York, 1935) 4: 408.

33. *New York Times*, March 13, 1917.

34. Martin, pp. 100-02.

35. Larson, pp. 83-84.

36. *See* Gompers to Woodrow Wilson, March 6, 1917, Gompers Papers, AFL Archives, State Historical Society of Wisconsin.

37. *New York Times*, March 13, 1917; Harvey, p. 217.

38. M. G. Scott to Gompers, March 28, 1917, AFL Archives, State Historical Society of Wisconsin.

39. John P. White to Gompers, March 3, 1917, ibid.

40. "Labor's Position in the Present Crisis," *Advance* 1 (April 13, 1917): 4.

41. Daniel J. Tobin to Gompers, March 30, 1917, AFL Archives, State Historical Society of Wisconsin.

42. *International Teamster* 14 (April 1917): 9-11.

43. *New York Times*, Sept. 13, 1917; *Fur Worker*, April 3, 1917.

44. Larson, p. 86.

45. Philip S. Foner, *The Fur and Leather Workers Union*, Newark, N.J., 1950, pp. 40-48.

46. *The Tailor* 27 (May 27, 1917): 3.

47. Lodge 368, I.A.M., G. Schleinkofer, Pres., Aug. Marobin, Rec. Secy., to Gompers, March 19, 1917, AFL Archives, State Historical Society of Wisconsin.

48. Lorwin, pp. 145-48.

49. *New York Times*, March 14, 1917.

50. Mandel, p. 362; Gompers, Labor and the War, pp. 240-41.

51. Mandel, p. 362.

52. Larson, pp. 89-90; Dallas C. Jones, "The Wilson Administration and Organized Labor, 1912-1919," unpublished Ph.D. dissertation, Cornell University, 1959, pp. 318-22; Leonard Philip Krivy, "American Organized Labor and the First World War, 1917-1918," unpublished Ph.D. dissertation, New York University, 1965, pp. 17-18, 25-27.

53. H. M. Merrill, chairman Legislative Committee, Schenectady Trades Assembly, to Gompers, March 29, 1917, AFL

Archives, State Historical Society of Wisconsin.

54. *Ladies' Garment Cutter* 5 (April 7, 1917): 2.

55. *Fur Workers* 1 (April 3, 1917): 4.

56. *Seattle Union Record*, April 9, 1917.

57. Krivy, p. 32.

58. Gary M. Fink, *Labor's Search for Political Order: The Political Behavior of the Missouri Labor Movement 1890-1940*, Columbus, Mo., 1973, pp. 61, 68; Krivy, p. 33.

59. Paul S. Taylor, *The Sailors' Union of the Pacific*, New York, 1923, pp. 134-35; "Our Country At War," *Coast Seamen's Journal* 30 (April 4, 1917): 6.

60. *International Teamster* 15 (April 1918): 8.

61. Matthew Josephson, *Sidney Hillman: Statesman of American Labor*, Garden City, New York, 1952, p. 161.

62. J. C. Wines to Gompers, November 6, 1917, AFL Archives, State Historical Society of Wisconsin; Fink, p. 68.

63. William D. Haywood, *Bill Haywood's Book: The Autobiography of William D. Haywood*, New York, 1929, pp. 300-01; *Industrial Worker*, April 14, 1917; "Wobblies and Draftees: The I.W.W.'s Wartime Dilemma, 1917-1918," *Radical America* 1 (Sept.- Oct. 1967): 10-11.

64. *See* James Weinstein, *The Decline of Socialism in America, 1912-1925*, New York, 1967, pp. 48-53.

65. *Advance* 1 (April 6, 1917): 4.

66. Ibid., p. 1.

67. Ibid., 1 (April 20, 1917): 4; Weinstein, p. 49.

68. U.S. Department of Labor, U.S. Employment Service, *U.S. Employment Service Bulletin*, July 31, 1918, p. 6.

## CHAPTER 6

1. Frank L. Grubbs, Jr., *The Struggle for Labor Loyalty: Gompers, the A.F. of L., and the Pacifists, 1917-1920*, Durham, N. Car., 1968, pp. 21-23.

2. Ibid., p. 26.

3. Emily Balch, Joseph Cannon, Morris Hillquit, Judah Magnes, Louis Lochner to Gompers, May 10, 1917; Gompers to Louis Lochner, May 10, 1917, Gompers Papers, AFL Archives, State Historical Society of Wisconsin.

4. Grubbs, Jr., pp. 28-30; *Advance* 1 (May 25, 1917): 2.

5. People's Council of America, *Report of the First American Conference for Democracy and Terms of Peace*, May 1917, New York Public Library, and Swarthmore Peace Library, Swarthmore College.

6. Frank L. Grubbs, Jr., "The Struggle for the Mind of American Labor, 1917-1919," unpublished Ph.D. dissertation, University of Virginia, 1963, p. 56.

7. Survey, Aug. 4, 1917, p. 441.

8. *New York Times*, August 20, 1917; *The Fur Worker*, Aug. 6, 1917.

9. *Political Committee, People's Council of America, June 3, 1917*, Swarthmore Peace Library, Swarthmore College; *New York Times*, June 24, 1917.

10. Scott Nearing, *The People's Council of America, What It Is, What It Stands For*, New York, 1917, Copy in New York Public Library.

11. New York Call, August 14, 1917; *New York Times*, Aug. 16, 1917; *Advance* 1 (July 20, 1917): 2.

12. Samuel Gompers, *Seventy Years of Life and Labor* (New York, 1925) 2: 382.

13. Grubbs, Jr., *The Struggle for Labor Loyalty*, pp. 59-60.

14. Robert Maisel to Gompers, June 9, 26, 1917; Gompers Papers, AFL Archives, State Historical Society of Wisconsin.

15. Gompers, Seventy Years of Life and Labor, vol. 2, pp. 380-81.

16. *New York Times*, June 24, 1917; New York Call, June 30, 1917.

17. Grubbs, Jr., The Struggle for Labor Loyalty, pp. 60-65.

18. John Spargo to Gompers, July 30, 1917, AFL Corr., State Historical Society of Wisconsin; John Spargo, Columbia Oral History Collections, Special Collections, Columbia University.

19. J. Phelps Stokes to Chester M. Wright, July 12, 1917, J. Phelps Stokes Papers, Butler Library, Columbia University.

20. George Creel to Gompers, July 28, 1917, AFL Corr., State Historical Society of Wisconsin; Frank L. Grubbs, Jr., "Council and Alliance Labor Propaganda, 1917-1919," *Labor History* 7 (Spring 1966): 156-57.

21. New York Call, October 7, 1917; Larson, p. 144.

22. J. Phelps Stokes to John Spargo, July 25, 1917, J. Phelps Stokes Papers, Butler Library, Columbia University.

23. Gompers to AFL locals, Aug. 15, 1917, Gompers Papers, State Historical Society of Wisconsin.

24. *Proceedings*, AFL Convention, 1917, p. 291.

25. Larson, p. 143; Grubbs, Jr., *The Struggle for Labor Loyalty*, pp. 58-60.

26. *New York Times*, Aug. 5, 1917.

27. *Locomotive Firemen's and Enginemen's Magazine* 63 (Aug. 15, 1917): 13. *See also Coast Seamen's Journal* 30 (Aug. 8, 1917): 6; *Journal of the Switchmen's Union* 19 (Sept. 1917): 501; *Machinists' Monthly Journal* 29 (Oct. 1917): 847.

28. Grubbs, Jr., *The Struggle for Labor Loyalty*, pp. 58-60.

29. *New York Times*, Aug. 29, 1917; Charles Merz, "West with the People's Council," *New Republic* 12 (Sept. 8, 1917): 157-59.

30. Grubbs, Jr., *The Struggle for Labor Loyalty*, pp. 61-62.

31. Ibid., pp. 63-64.

32. New York Times, Sept. 18, 1917.

33. "Where Loyal Labor Stands," *Literary Digest* 55 (Sept. 15, 1917): 15.

34. Frank P. Walsh to George Creel, Aug. 30, 1917; George Creel to Frank P. Walsh, Sept. 1, 1917, Frank P. Walsh Papers, New York Public Library; Ronald Radosh, American Labor and United States Foreign Policy, New York, 1969, pp. 59-60.

35. *New York Times*, Sept. 6, 1917.

36. Woodrow Wilson to Samuel Gompers, Aug. 31, 1917, Wilson Papers, Library of Congress; *New York Times*, Sept. 8, 1917.

37. *New York Times*, Sept. 1917.

38. Grubbs, Jr., *The Struggle for Labor Loyalty*, pp. 67-68.

39. *New York Times*, Sept. 8, 1917.

40. *Coast Seamen's Journal*, Sept. 26, 1917; *Fur Worker*, Oct. 6, 1917; Larson, p. 144.

41. *Proceedings*, AFL Convention, 1917, pp. 20-24.

42. Grubbs, Jr., *The Struggle for Labor Loyalty*, p. 91.

43. *Proceedings*, AFL Convention, 1917, pp. 282-84.

44. Ibid., pp. 286-87.

45. Ibid., p. 283.

46. Ibid., pp. 290-93.

47. Ibid., pp. 307-08.

48. Grubbs, Jr., *The Struggle for Labor Loyalty*, p. 105; Harry W. Laidler, *Socialism in Thought and Action*, New York, 1925, pp. 428-29.

49. Larson, p. 145.

50. Ibid.; Grubbs, Jr., The Struggle for Labor Loyalty, pp. 107-08.

51. Grubbs, Jr., "The Struggle for the Mind of American Labor," pp. 162-65; Robert Maisel to Gompers, Oct. 5, 10, 1917, AFL Archives, State Historical Society of Wisconsin.

52. *New York Times*, Nov. 7, 1917; J. Phelps Stokes in New York *World*, Oct. 7, 1917

53. Grubbs, Jr., "The Struggle for the Mind of American Labor," p. 114.

54. Grubbs, Jr., *The Struggle for Labor Loyalty*, p. 87.

55. New York *Call*, Nov. 14, 1917.

56. Grubbs, Jr., *The Struggle for Labor Loyalty*, p. 89.

57. Ibid., p. 91.

58. "Why the War Must Be Won," American Alliance publications, AFL Archives, State Historical Society of Wisconsin.

59. Grubbs, Jr., "The Struggle for the Mind of American Labor," pp. 150-61.

60. Ibid., pp. 162-63.

61. Ibid., pp. 164-66.

62. Ibid., pp. 167-69.

63. Report, AALD, Feb. 20, 1918, AFL Archives, State Historical Society of Wisconsin.

64. Radosh, pp. 67-68.

65. Grubbs, Jr., "The Struggle for the Mind of American Labor," p. 273.

66. Larson, p. 147.

## CHAPTER 7

1. Margaret A. Hobbes, "Wartime Employment of Women," *American Labor Legislation Review* 8 (1918): 332.

2. Philip S. Foner, *Women and the American Labor Movement: From World War I to the Present*, New York, 1980, pp. 21-22; *Living Age* 285 (July 1917): 3; *Industrial Management* 55 (1917): 351.

3. *New York Times*, July 20, 1918.

4. Mary Van Kleeck and Mary McDowell, "The New Position of Women in American Industry," U.S. Department of Labor, Women's Bureau, Bulletin No. 12, Washington, D.C., 1920, p. 17.

5. *41st Annual Report of the Young Women's Christian Association*, Chicago, 1917, p. 21.

6. *Seattle Union Record*, Jan. 12, Aug. 10, 24, Nov. 2, 1918.

7. W. T. Gilman, "Women and Heavy War Work," *Scribner's Monthly* 65 (1918): 113-16; Hobbes, "Wartime Employment of Women," pp. 33-38; Dudley Harmon, "What Are These War Jobs for Women?" *Ladies' Home Journal* 31 (Nov. 1917): 91-92; *New York Times*, Jan. 12, 17, 1918; Esther Norton, "Women in War Industries," *New Republic* 13 (Dec. 15, 1917): 179-81; Florence Kelley, "The War and Women Workers," *Survey* 39 (March 9, 1918): 628-31; Benedict Crowell and R. F. Wilson, *How America Went to War: The*

*Armies of Industry,* (New Haven, 1921) I: 188, 259; II: 530-31; Van Kleeck and McDowell, "New Position of Women in American Industry," pp. 11-93.

8. H. F. Porter, "Detroit Plans Recruitment of Women for War Work," *Industrial Management* 35 (Aug. 1917): 659.

9. Alfred L. Smith, ed., "Increased Employment of Women in Industry During Wartime," *Annual Report of the New York Merchants' Association, 1917,* p. 10.

10. Van Kleeck and McDowell, *New Position of Women in American Industry,* pp. 94, 97, 100.

11. "Women in Machine Shops," *American Machinist* 68 (May 2, 1918): 768; J. V. Hunter, "The Training of Women as Machine Operators," *American Machinist* 68 (Sept. 26, 1918): 565.

12. "Women in Industry," *Survey* 38 (April 19, 1918): 112.

13. U.S Department of Commerce, Bureau of the Census, *Twelfth Census of the United States, 1900, Occupation,* IX, 8-10; U.S. Department of Labor, Women's Bureau, *What Industry Means to Women Workers,* Washington, D.C., 1925, pp. 5-6.

14. Maurine Weiner Greenwald, "Women Workers and World War I: The American Railroad Industry, A Case Study," *Journal of Social History* 9 (Winter 1975): 154. *See also* Maurine Weiner Greenwald, *Women, War, and Work: The Impact of World War I on Women Workers in the United States,* Westport, Conn., 1980, pp. 93-96.

15. Pauline Goodmark, "The Facts of Women in War Industries," *New Republic,* Dec. 29, 1917, p. 251; Sister M. Laurite Kroger, "Women in Industry During World War I," unpublished M.A. thesis, University of Cincinnati, 1950, pp. 23-26; Anna Center Schneiderman, "The Influence of the World War on Women in Industry," unpublished M.A. thesis, Columbia University, 1929, pp. 44-46; Tamah Veronica Jenkins, "Some Aspects of the Labor Movement with Special Emphasis on Women and Children, 1915-1919," unpublished M.A. thesis, Atlanta University, 1968, pp. 16-18; Florence Kelley, *Wage Earning Women in War Time,* New York, 1920, pp. 264-69.

16. "World War and Defense, 1910-1919—Survey of Certain Plants," typewritten report, Women's Bureau, War Department, Box 20, U.S. Department of Labor, National Archives.

17. Barbara Klaczynska, "Working Women in Philadelphia, 1900-1930," unpublished Ph.D. dissertation, Temple University, 1975, p. 104.

18. *Seattle Union Record,* Aug. 18, Oct. 27, 1917.

19. Foner, *Women and the American Labor Movement,* pp. 21-22.

20. Van Kleeck and McDowell, p. 761.

21. Ibid., pp. 135-36.

22. *Ladies Home Journal* 34 (Sept. 1917): 32.

23. Memo 26, April 1919, from Women-in-Industry Service to Secretary of Navy, Re: Philadelphia Naval Aircraft Factory, Women's Bureau, War Department, Box 20, U.S. Department of Labor, National Archives.

24. To Mary Van Kleeck, Director, Woman-in-Industry Service, from Helen Byrnes, Industrial Agent, Woman-in-Industry Service, Women's Bureau, War Department, Box 20, Folder 263, April 25, 1918, U.S. Department of Labor, Women's Bureau, War Department, "Wages of Work of Women in the United States Arsenal and Ordinance Plants Working for Government," typewritten report, Box 29, Folder 383, National Archives; Minutes of the Conference between United States Government, Cloth Manufacturers and Cloth Weavers Union 72, typewritten report, pp. 41-42, U.S. Department of Labor, National Archives.

25. U.S. Railroad Administration, "Complaint 73, Pennsylvania Railroad—Assistant Locomotive-Dispatcher," typewritten report, Box E-101, National Archives; U.S. Railroad Administration, "Discrimination in Rates of Pay; Women Coach Cleaners—West Philadelphia Yard," Box E-98, Folder 19V, National Archives.

26. U.S. Bureau of Labor Statistics, "Wartime Employment of Women," *Monthly Labor Review* 7 (Oct. 1918): 193-218; Gordon Watkins, *Labor Problems and Labor Administration in the United States During the World War,* Urbana, Ill., 1919, pp. 72-75; "Where War Wages Do Not Reach," *Survey* 40 (June 22, 1918): 351-52.

27. Signe K. Toksvig, "Houses for Women War Workers," *New Republic,* Jan. 19, 1918, p. 344.

28. Benedict Crowell, *Report of America's Munitions, 1917-1918,* Washington, D.C., 1919, p. 125; Crowell and Wilson,

I: 187; Amy Hewes, "Women as Muni-tion Makers," *Survey* 37 (Jan. 6, 1917): 381-85.

29. *Ladies' Home Journal* 34 (Nov. 1917): 83.

30. *Atlantic Monthly* 127 (Oct. 1920): 250; Theresa Wolfson, *The Woman Worker and the Trade Unions*, New York, 1926, p. 29.

31. *New York Times*, May 1, 2, 1917; *Seattle Union Record*, Jan. 12, 1918.

32. *Butcher Workman*, July 1917, p. 15.

33. *Annual Report of Walter B. Hines, Director-General of Railroads, 1919*, Washington, D.C., 1920, p. 61.

34. Elizabeth Kemper Adams, *Women Professional Workers*, Chatauqua, N.Y., 1921, pp. 233-35; Grace Coyle, *Present Trends in Clerical Occupations*, New York, 1928, p. 11.

35. Greenwald, "Women Workers and World War I, p. 156. *See also* Greenwald, *Women, War and Work*, pp. 93-96.

36. *Annual Report of W. G. McAdoo, Director General of Railroads*, 1918, Washington, D.C., 1919, p. 18.

37. Ibid., p. 73.

38. Ibid., p. 17.

39. Greenwald, "Women Workers and World War I," p. 157; Greenwald, *Women, War and Work*, p. 98.

40. *New York Times*, Jan. 15, July 24, 1918; "Women in Munitions Work," *Outlook* 118 (April 24, 1918): 682.

41. Greenwald, "Women Workers and World War I," p. 154.

42. W. S. Woytinsky, et al., *Employment and Wages in the United States*, New York, 1953, pp. 179-82.

43. U.S. Employment Service, *Bulletin*, August 6, 1918, p. 3; Chicago *Tribune*, Aug. 1, 1918; *New York Times*, December 16, 1917, March 6, 1918.

44. John Maurice Clark, *The Costs of the World War to the American People*, New Haven, Conn., 1931, p. 45.

45. Clarence D. Long, *The Labor Force in Wartime America*, Occasional Paper 14, National Bureau of Economic Research, New York, March 1944, p. 46.

46. C. E. Persons, "Women's Wages in the United States," *Quarterly Journal of Economics* 29 (Feb. 1915): 201-34.

47. *Seattle Union Record*, Jan. 12, 1918.

48. George E. Haynes, *Negro Newcomers in Detroit*, New York, 1918, p. 14.

49. Allan Spear, *Black Chicago*, Chicago, 1967, pp. 141, 152; Sadie Tanner Mossell, "The Standard of Living Among One Hundred Negro Migrant Families in Philadelphia," *Annals of the American Academy of Political and Social Science*, November 1921, p. 175.

50. Lorenzo J. Greene and Carter J. Woodson, *The Negro Wage Earner*, New York, 1930, pp. 342, 344.

51. Greenwald, *Women, War, and Work*, pp. 23-24.

52. Emmett J. Scott, collector, "Letters from Negro Migrants, 1916-1918," *Journal of Negro History* 4 (July 1919): 299-300, and reprinted in Rosalyn Baxandall, Linda Gordon, and Susan Reverby, editors, *America's Working Women*, New York, 1976, p. 133.

53. Scott, *Negro Migration During the War*, p. 55; *Textile World Journal* 53 (Nov. 24, 1917): 13.

54. Quoted in Nancy J. Weiss, *The National Urban League, 1910-1940*, New York, 1973, p. 98.

55. Chicago Commission on Race Relations, *The Negro in Chicago*, Chicago, 1922, pp. 385-87, 419-20, reprinted in Jerold S. Auerbach, *American Labor: The Twentieth Century*, Indianapolis, 1969, pp. 146-48.

56. Greenwald, *Women, War, and Work*, p. 23.

57. "The Armstrong Association," *Opportunity*, August 1923, p. 25; "Annual Reports of the Armstrong Association" (Philadelphia, 1917), pp. 12-13; 1918, pp. 6-7; Klaczynska, "Working Women in Philadelphia," pp. 53-55.

58. Greenwald, *Women, War, and Work*, p. 26.

59. U.S. Department of Labor, Women's Bureau, *The Negro Woman Worker*, Bulletin No. 165 (Washington, D.C., 1958), p. 8.

60. Ibid., pp. 8-11. *See also* Alice S. Cheyney, "Negro Women in Industry," *Survey* 46 (April 23, 1921): 119.

61. U.S. Department of Labor, Women's Bureau, Bulletin No. 100, Box 40, National Archives; Barbara Klaczynska, "Why Women Work: A Comparison of Various Groups—Philadelphia, 1910-1930," *Labor History* 17 (Winter 1970): 85-86; Memo to Agnes Paterson from Mrs. Helen B. Irwin, March 3, 1919, Box 40, Women's Bureau, Department of Labor, National Archives.

62. Klaczynska, "Why Women Work," p. 85; Greenwald, *Women, War, and Work*, p. 26.

63. Cheney, "Negro Women in Industry," p. 119; U.S. Bureau of Labor Statistics,

*Wages and Hours in Slaughtering and Meat Packing, 1917*, Washington, D.C., 1918, p. 1083.

64. Jenkins, "Some Aspects of the Labor Movement," p. 30.
65. Philip S. Foner, *Organized Labor and the Black Worker, 1619-1981*, New York, 1982, pp. 121-22.
66. U.S. Railroad Administration, "Unsanitary Conditions of Cleaning Yards Due to Use of Toilets by Cleaners," Complaint No. 81, typewritten report, Box E-101, Folder 260, National Archives; Klaczynska, "Working Women in Philadelphia," pp. 56-57.
67. U.S. Railroad Administration, "Women's Service Section, Department of Labor Series 14, Folder 194— "Discrimination in Rates of Pay," Complaint Nos. 83, 81; U.S. Railroad Administration, "Unsanitary Conditions of Cleaning Yards,"; Greenwald, "Women Workers and World War I," p. 168.
68. Charles Wesley, *Negro Labor in the United States, 1980-1925*, New York, 1927, p. 262.
69. "Colored Women in Industry in Philadelphia," *Monthly Labor Review* 12 (May 1921): 1047.
70. Minutes of Meetings of the Board of Managers and the Executive Committee of the Young Women's Christian Association, Dec. 13, 1917, cited in Abbey Joan Parises, "A History of the Early Years of the Chicago YWCA: 1876-1918," unpublished M.A. thesis, Roosevelt University, 1975, p. 71.
71. Roger Baldwin quoted in Herbert J. Seligman, "The Negro in Industry," *Socialist Review* 8 (Feb. 1920): 170.
72. Sterling D. Spero and Abram L. Harris, *The Black Worker: The Negro and the Labor Movement*, New York, 1931, p. 169.
73. Horace R. Cayton and George S. Mitchell, *Black Workers and the New Unions*, Chapel Hill, 1939, p. 31; Foner, *Organized Labor and the Black Worker*, p. 133.
74. Joyce Shaw Peterson, "Black Automobile Workers in Detroit, 1910-1930," *Journal of Negro History* 54 (Summer 1979): 179.
75. Ibid.
76. George Carmody to Charles Schwab, September 18, 1918, Records of U.S. Shipping Board, Record Group 32, National Archives.
77. S. L. Mash to L. C. Marshall, Aug. 30, 1918, Records of U.S. Shipping Board, Record Group 32, National Archives.
78. New York *Call*, Aug. 9, 1917.
79. Foner, *Organized Labor and the Black Worker*, p. 134.
80. John D. Finney, Jr., "A Study of Negro Labor During and After World War I," unpublished Ph.D. dissertation, Georgetown University, 1957, p. 178.

**CHAPTER 8**

1. Grosvenor B. Clarkson, *Industrial America in the Work War*, New York, 1923, pp. 49-50. Robert D. Cuff, *The War Industries Board: Business-Government Relations during World War I*, Baltimore, 1973, pp. 32-35.
2. Alexander M. Bing, *War-Time Strikes and Their Adjustment*, New York, 1921, p. 273.
3. Cutrice N. Hitchcock, "The War Housing Program and Its Future," *Journal of Political Economy* 27 (April 1919): 242-44.
4. Lawrence Veiller, "The Housing of the Mobilized Population," *Annals of the American Academy of Political and Social Science* 58 (July 1918): 21-25.
5. Lewis H. Allen, *Industrial Housing Problems*, Boston, 1917, pp. 5-6.
6. Bing, pp. 4, 259-60.
7. Frank Duffy, "The Shipbuilding Controversy," *Amalgamated Journal* 19 (March 21, 1918): 1; "War Profiteering," ibid. 19 (Feb. 21, 1918); War Labor Policies Board, *Report of Committee on Conditions of Living*, August 20, 1918, p. 2, National Archives; Leonard Philip Krivy, "American Organized Labor and the World War, 1917-1918: A History of Labor Problems and the Development of a Government War Labor Program," unpublished Ph.D. dissertation, New York University, 1965, p. 54.
8. Matthew Josephson, *Sidney Hillman: Statesman of American Labor*, Garden City, N.Y., 1952, p. 163; *Advance*, July 13, 1917, p. 1; Philip S. Foner, *Women and the American Labor Movement: From World War I to the Present*, New York, 1980, p. 48.
9. *Fur Worker*, Sept. 1917, p. 3; Krivy, p. 56.
10. Ray Stannard Baker, *Woodrow Wilson: Life and Letters* 7 (New York, 1938): 100, 247-48, 422.
11. George L. Barnett, "American Trade Unionism and the Standardization of

Wages During the War," *Journal of Political Economy* 27 (Oct. 19, 1919): 672.

12. *Monthly Labor Review* 7 (Dec. 1918): 268-70; Joseph Andrew Lieberman, "Their Sisters Keepers: The Womens' Hours and Wages Movement in the United States, 1890-1925," unpublished Ph.D. dissertation, Columbia University, 1971, pp. 352-53.

13. John Lombardi, Mobilizing Labor in 1917 and 1918, Los Angeles, 1942, p. 7.

14. John D. Finney, Jr., "A Study of Negro Labor During and After World War I," unpublished Ph.D. dissertation, Georgetown University, 1957, p. 206.

15. Bing, p. 12; Harold U. Faulkner, *Labor in America*, New York, 1957, p. 133.

16. John Steuben, *Labor in Wartime*, New York, 1940, p. 35.

17. Bureau of Labor Statistics, *Monthly Review*, June 1920, p. 79.

18. David Brody, *Steelworkers in America: The Nonunion Era*, Cambridge, Mass., 1960, p. 132.

19. Selig Perlman and Philip Taft, *History of Labor in the United States*, vol. 3 of John R. Commons and Associates, p. 74.

20. *New York Times*, Nov. 12, 1916.

21. Edward C. Kirkland, *A History of American Economic Life*, New York, 1969, p. 475.

22. *Advance* 1 (May 11, 1917): 1.

23. Krivy, p. 76.

24. Ibid., p. 77.

25. L. C. Marshall, "The War Labor Program and Its Administration," *Journal of Political Economy* 26 (May 1918): 427.

26. *Advance* 1 (July 13, 1917): 1.

27. Josephson, p. 162; Krivy, p. 82.

28. Bernard M. Baruch, *American Industry in the War: A Report of the War Industries Board, March, 1921*, edited by Richard H. Hippelheuser, New York, 1941, pp. 73-85; Grosvenor B. Clarkson, *Industrial America in the World War: The Strategy Behind the Line, 1917-1918*, Boston and New York, 1923, p. 23.

29. Samuel Gompers, *Seventy Years of Life and Labor* (New York, 1925) 2: 366; *First Annual Report of the Council of National Defense, 1917*, Washington, D.C., 1918, p. 75.

30. *First Annual Report*, pp. 79-87; Council of National Defense, Committee on Labor, *Organization of the Committee: Scope and Objects: Preliminary Activities, Outline of Plans of Subcommittees; Membership List*, Washington, D.C., 1917.

31. Marc Karson, *American Labor Unions and Politics, 1900-1918*, Carbondale, Ill., 1958, pp. 145-56; Foner, *Women and the American Labor Movement*, p. 62; Krivy, pp. 118-22; Gompers to Woodrow Wilson, May 10, 1917, GLB.

32. *New Republic*, July 7, 1917, p. 264.

33. *American Labor Year Book, 1917-18*, New York, 1918, p. 12; Simeon Larson, *Labor and Foreign Policy*, Rutherford, N.J., 1972, pp. 108-09.

34. *Monthly Labor Review* 5 (Oct. 1917): 30-33; *Advance*, August 31, 1917, p. 1.

35. K. Austin Kerr, "Decision for Federal Control: Wilson, McAdoo, and the Railroads, 1917," *Journal of American History* 54 (December 1967): 550-60; Leo Troy, "Labor Representation on American Railways," *Labor History* 2 (Fall 1961): 296; Allen LaVerne Shephard, "Federal Railway Labor Policy," unpublished Ph.D. dissertation, University of Nebraska, 1971, pp. 121-23.

36. *Coast Seamen's Journal*, Aug. 29, 1917.

37. Louis S. Reed, *The Labor Philosophy of Samuel Gompers*, New York, 1930, p. 155; Dallas L. Jones, "The Wilson Administration and Organized Labor, 1912-1919," unpublished Ph.D. dissertation, Cornell University, 1955, p. 332; Krivy, pp. 109-10; Philip Taft, *The A.F. of L. in the Time of Gompers*, New York, 1957, p. 347; *Proceedings*, AFL Convention, 1917, p. 3; Krivy, pp. 11-12.

38. Gompers to Thomas R. Marshall, April 27, 1917, Gompers Papers, AFL Archives, State Historical Society of Wisconsin.

39. Seattle *Union Record*, March 3, 1917.

40. *United Mine Workers' Journal*, March 22, 1917.

41. Gompers to James Duncan, March 23, 1917, Gompers Papers, AFL Archives, State Historical Society of Wisconsin.

42. Quoted in Gompers to Miss Marguerite Browder, April 17, 1917, Gompers Papers, ibid.

43. Franklin H. Martin, *Digest of the Proceedings of the Council of National Defense During the War*, Washington, D.C., 1934, p. 12; Grosvenor B. Clarkson, *Industrial America in the World War*, Boston and New York, 1924, p. 32; Larson, p. 130.

44. John T. Smith, Secretary, Kansas City Labor Council, to Gompers, April 22-17, Gompers Papers, ibid.

45. John W. Rogers to Gompers, April 11, 1917, Gompers Papers, ibid

46. Marguerite Browder, Secretary, Stenographers, Typewriters, Bookkeepers &

Assistants' Union .14268, to Gompers, reprinted in Gompers to Marguerite Browder, April 17, 1917, Gompers Papers, ibid.

47. Gompers to Marguerite Browder, April 17, ibid.

48. Hugh Frayner, "Organized Labor and the War," *Proceedings of the American Academy of Political Science* 7 (February 1918): 136; H. C. Peterson and Gilbert C. Fite, *Opponents of War, 1917-1918*, Madison, Wisc. 1957, p. 136; Karson, p. 96; American Federation of Labor, *Labor and the War*, Washington, D.C., 1918, p. 71.

49. Krivy, pp. 63-64.

50. U.S. Council of National Defense, *First Annual Report of the Council of National Defense, 1917*, Washington, D.C., p. 76.

51. *Chicago Tribune*, April 9, 1917.

52. Ibid.

53. George Kalon, chairman, Federal Labor Union No. 146539, Fitchburg, Mass., to Gompers, April 16, 1917, Gompers Papers, ibid.

54. Chas. MacGowan to Gompers, May 4, 1917, ibid.

55. Watson Malone & Sons to Gompers, April 13, 1917, ibid.

56. Daniel J. Tobin to Gompers, April 12, 1917, ibid.

57. W. W. Stone to Gompers, Cleveland, May 3, 1917, ibid.

58. *The Carpenter* 37 (May 1917): 4; Robert A. Christie, *Empire in Wood: A History of the Carpenters' Union*, Ithaca, N.Y., 1954, p. 219; *Cleveland Citizen*, April 28, 1917.

59. C. O. Young to Gompers, April 15, 1917, Gompers Papers, ibid.

60. Gompers to Daniel Tobin, April 17, 1917; Gompers to Edward Anderson, April 10, 1917; Gompers to Newton D. Baker, June 28, 1917, all in Gompers Papers, ibid.; Samuel Gompers, "To Steady, Not to Hinder," *Machinists' Monthly Journal* 29 (April 1917): 456.

61. "Amplification of Declaration Adopted by the Executive Committee," April 16, 1917, *First Annual Report of the Council of National Defense, 1917*, pp. 76-77.

62. Krivy, p. 62.

63. Larson, pp. 100-01; Bernard Mandel, *Samuel Gompers, A Biography*, Yellow Springs, Ohio, 1963, pp. 372-77; Robert A. Christie, *Empire in Wood*, Ithaca, N.Y. 1956, pp. 219-21; Louis B. Wehle, "The Adjustment of Labor Disputes Incident to Production for War in the United States," *Quarterly Journal of Economics*, 32 (Nov. 1917): 133-36; Louis B. Wehle, *Hidden Threads of History*, New York, 1953, pp. 17-23.

64. Dallas L. Jones, p. 226.

65. Mandel, p. 375.

66. Larson, p. 101.

67. Christie, pp. 219-21.

68. Gompers to All Trade Union Officers, April 8, 1918, Gompers Papers, AFL Archives, State Historical Society of Wisconsin.

69. Gompers to Henry Cabot Lodge, June 24, 1917, GLB.

70. *United Mine Workers' Journal*, June 20, 1918, p. 15.

71. *First Annual Report of the Council of National Defense, 1917*, pp. 79-81; Krivy, p. 117.

72. Bureau of Labor Statistics, *Monthly Review*, June 1919, pp. 303-28.

73. Ibid., pp. 327-28.

74. San Francisco *Examiner*, July 22-24, 1917; Elizabeth Reis, "Cannery Row: The AFL, the IWW, and the Italian Cannery Workers," *California History* LXIV(Summer, 1985): 175.

75. Reis, pp. 177-84.

76. *Ibid.*, p. 184.

77. *Ibid.*

78. *Ibid.*, pp. 189-91.

79. Alexander M. Bing, *War-Time Strikes and Their Adjustment*, New York, 1921, p. 30n.

80. *New York Times*, Sept. 4, 1917.

81. Bing, p. 30n.

82. *Ibid.*

83. *Ibid.*; Montana Department of Labor and Industry, *Third Biennial Report*, p. 39.

84. Maurine Weiner Greenwald, *Women, War, and Work: The Impact of World War I on Women Workers in the United States*, Westport, Conn., 1980, pp. 173-74.

85. *Ibid.*, p. 174.

86. *Ibid.*

87. *Ibid.*

88. *New York Times*, March 31, 1918.

89. Greenwald, p. 175.

90. Bing, p. 30n.

91. Krivy, p. 278.

92. Samuel Gompers, *Organized Labor and the War of 1917: Lecture Delivered at the Army War College, Washington Barracks, D.C., March 7, 1922*, p. 29, AFL Archives, State Historical Society of Wisconsin; Krivy, p. 253.

93. Watkins, vol. II, p. 79.

94. U.S. Department of Labor, "Report of the President's Mediation Commission," *Sixth Annual Report of the Department of*

*Labor,* Washington, D.C., 1918, pp. 16-26.
95. Ibid., pp. 18-20.
96. Shepherd, pp. 151-52.
97. National War Labor Board, *Proclamation of the President of the United States Creating the National War Labor Board,* Washington, D.C., 1918, pp. 1-6.
98. Ibid., pp. 15-20.
99. Bureau of Labor Statistics, *Monthly Review,* Aug. 1918, pp. 70-71; Krivy, pp. 315-16.
100. Krivy, p. 317.
101. Ibid., p. 318.
102. *Literary Digest* 57 (April 13, 1918): 16.
103. Reprinted in ibid.
104. Krivy, pp. 318-20.

**CHAPTER 9**

1. Darrel H. Smith, *The United States Employment Service: Its History, Activities, and Organization,* Baltimore, 1923, pp. 60-62.
2. *Seattle Union Record,* Oct. 29, 1918.
3. Mary Chamberlain, "Women and War Work," *Survey* 38 (May 19, 1917): 153-54; Esther Norton, "Women in War Industries," *New Republic,* Dec. 15. 1917, pp. 179-81.
4. Don D. Lescohier, *The Labor Market,* New York, 1919, p. 182.
5. Sophonisba P. Breckenridge, "Investigation of Frankford Arsenal," Nov. 1917; Grace Abbott, "Report on Brooklyn Navy Yard," Dec. 1917, copy in Grace Abbott to Sophonisba P. Breckenridge, Dec. 8, 1917, both in Sophonisba Breckenridge Papers, Library of Congress.
6. *New York Times,* March 1, 1918.
7. Joseph Andrew Lieberman, "Their Sisters' Keepers: The Women's Hours and Wages Movement in the United States, 1890-1925," unpublished Ph.D. dissertation, Columbia University, 1971, pp. 352-54.
8. "Attack on Labor Laws Is Begun in Rush for Profits," *Advance,* April 27, 1917, p. 1.
9. Ibid., July 13, 1917, p. 1.
10. *Monthly Labor Review* 5 (Oct. 1917): 30-33; *Advance,* Aug. 31, 1917, p. 1.
11. Matthew Josephson, *Sidney Hillman, Statesman of American Labor,* Garden City, N.Y., 1952, pp. 186-87; Leonard Philip Krivy, "American Organized Labor and the First World War, 1917-1918: A History of Labor Problems and the Development of a Government War Labor Program," unpublished Ph.D. dissertation, New York University, 1965,

pp. 234-38.
12. Allen LaVerne Shepherd, "Federal Railway Labor Policy, 1913-1926," unpublished Ph.D. dissertation, University of Nebraska, 1971, p. 71.
13. Ibid., pp. 120-30.
14. Ibid., pp. 131-32.
15. Ibid., p. 72.
16. Report of the Railroad Wage Commission, United States Railroad Administration, National Archives; Shepherd, pp. 139-40.
17. Shepherd, pp. 140-41.
18. W. S. Carter, "Effect of Federal Control on Railway Labor," *Proceedings of the Academy of Political Science* 8 (1918-1920): 198-210; Maurine Weiner Greenwald, "Women Workers and World War I: The American Railroad Industry, A Case Study," *Journal of Social History* 9 (Winter 1975): 157.
19. U.S. Congress, Senate Committee on Education and Labor, 64th Cong., 2d Sess., 1917, Report No. 897, *Women's Division of the Department of Labor.*
20. Alexander M. Bing, *War-Time Strikes and Their Adjustment,* New York, 1921, pp. 156, 293; *Literary Digest,* Nov. 24, 1917, pp. 14-15.
21. Walter Willoughby, *Government Organization in Wartime and After,* New York, 1919, pp. 221-58.
22. Waldo G. Leland and Newton D. Mereness, *Introduction to the American Official Sources for the Economic and Social History of the World War,* New Haven, 1926, pp. 253-55.
23. "Press release on the function of the 'Women-in-Industry Service,'" July 12, 1918, National Women Trade Union League Papers, Box 27, Library of Congress (hereinafter cited as NWTUL Papers); *New York Times,* July 23, 1918; Lieberman, p. 363; Marc Karson, *American Labor Unions and Politics, 1900-1918,* Carbondale, Ill., 1958, pp. 124-25.
24. Mary Van Kleeck, "For Women in Industry," *Survey* 37 (December 23, 1916): 327-29; "Women-in-Industry Service," *Monthly Labor Review* 7 (August 1918): 67.
25. Helen Ross, "Report on Inspection of Freight House, Santa Fe Railroad, Topeka, Kansas, Oct. 28, 1918," RG14 WSS File 55, National Archives, also quoted in Greenwald, p. 166.
26. U.S. Department of Labor, *First Annual Report of the "Women-in-Industry Service,"* Washington, D.C., 1919, pp. 7-8,

27-29. There is also material relating to the early actions of the Service in Record Group 86, National Archives, which contains the records of the "Women-in-Industry Service," including Mary Van Kleeck, "Outline of Proposed Labor Standards for Women War Workers," July 1918.

27. This is based on the material in Record Group 86, National Archives, and the *First Annual Report of the "Women-in-Industry Service*, pp. 8-10.

28. "Minimum Wage Rates," *Monthly Labor Review* 7 (Nov. 1918):188; National War Labor Board, *Principles and Rules of Procedure*, Washington, 1919, pp. 4-5.

29. Lieberman, p. 366.

30. A. R. Reid to Louis F. Post, April 25, 1918, quoted in John D. Finney, Jr., "A Study of Negro Labor During and After World War I," unpublished Ph.D. dissertation, Georgetown University, 1957, p. 159.

31. Ibid., p. 165.

32. Ibid., pp. 176-77.

33. Ibid., pp. 179-82.

34. Philip S. Foner, *Organized Labor and the Black Worker, 1619-1981*, pp. 103-07

35. *Chicago Defender*, April 12, 1918.

36. United States Railroad Administration Memorandum, Nov. 7, 1918, *Records of the United States Railroad Administration*, Record Group 14, National Archives.

37. NAACP telegram to William G. McAdoo, Nov. 29, 1918, USRA Files, Record Group 14, NA.; *Crisis*, February, 119, pp. 189-90.

38. Letter signed by William C. Graves, Director, Chicago Urban League; T. Arnold Hill, Executive Secretary, Chicago Urban League; L. Hollingsworth Wood, President, National Urban League; E. K. Jones, Executive Secretary, National Urban League; John T. Emlen, Secretary and Treasurer, Armstrong Association of Philadelphia, to George Foster Peabody, Nov. 25, 1918, USRA Files, Record Group 14, NA.

39. J. R. Shillady, Executive Secretary, NAACP, to William G. McAdoo, Nov. 29, 1918, USRA Files, Record Group 14, NA.

40. J. R. Shillady to President Woodrow Wilson, Nov. 19, 1918, National Association for the Advancement of Colored People Papers, NAACP Labor Files, Library of Congress.

41. Armstrong Association to W. G. McAdoo, Dec. 12, 1918; American Railroad Employees Association to W. G. McAdoo, Dec. 14, 1918, USRA Files, Record Group 14, NA.

42. W. G. McAdoo to J. R. Shillady, Dec. 1, 1918, USRA files, Record Group 14, NA.; J. R. Shillady to W. G. McAdoo, Dec. 11, 1918, ibid.

43. Finney, Jr., pp. 189-90.

44. W. D. Hines to W. G. McAdoo, Dec. 6, 1918, USRA Files, Record Group 14, NA.

45. "Administrative Order of C. R. Gray, Director of Operations USRA," Dec. 9, 1918," USRA Files, Record Group 14, NA.

46. W. D. Hines to W. G. McAdoo, Dec. 6, 1918; W. G. McAdoo to G. F. Peabody, Dec. 4, 1918, USRA Files, Record Group 14, NA.

47. Finney, p. 192.

48. Shepherd, p. 132; Harry D. Wolf, *The Railroad Labor Board*, Chicago, 1917, p. 59; Leo Troy, "Labor Representation on American Railways," *Labor History* 2 (Fall 1961): 297.

49. War Labor Policies Board to G. E. Haynes, Aug. 19, 1918, Records of the War Labor Policies Board, Record Group 117, NA.; L. A. Gabriel to R. R. Lewis, July 21, 1918, ibid.

50. G. E. Haynes to War Labor Policies Board, Aug. 14, 1918, WLPB Files, Record Group 117, NA.

51. G. E. Haynes to J. R. Shillady, Aug. 19, 1918, NAACP Labor Files; J. R. Shillady to Frank Morrison, Oct. 14, 1918; Frank Morrison to J. R. Shillady, Sept. 22, 1918, ibid.

52. T. C. Erwin to H. W. Bunker, Oct. 30, 1918, NAACP Labor Files; J. R. Shillady to G. E. Haynes, Oct. 31, 1918; G. E. Haynes to J. R. Shillady, Oct. 26, 1918, ibid.

53. J. H. Collins Jr., to Charles Schwab, Aug. 17, 1918; R. G. Jennings, Chairman of the Colored Committee of Drillers, to United States Shipping Board, July 9, 1918, Records of the United States Shipping Board, Record Group 32, NA.

54. J. H. Collins to C. Schwab, Aug. 17, 1918, USSB Files, Record Group 32, NA.

55. George Carmody to C. Schwab, Sept. 18, 1919, USSB Files, Record Group 32, NA.

56. J. H. Collins to Charles Schwab, Aug. 17, 1918, USSB Files, Record Group 32, NA.

57. George Carmody to C. Schwab, Sept. 18, 1918, USSB Files, Record Group, 32, NA.
58. S. L. Mash to L. C. Marshall, Aug. 30, 1918, USSB Files, Record Group 32, NA.
59. *New York Times*, May 24, 1918.
60. Walter F. White, "'Work or Fight' in the South," *New Republic* 18 (March 1, 1919): 144-46.
61. Finney, Jr., p. 203.
62. Ibid., pp. 203-05; L. F. Post to W. B. Wilson, October 5, 1918, Files of the Secretary of Labor, National Archives; New Orleans *Daily Picayune*, Sept. 22, 1918.
63. Ibid.
64. Ibid.
65. White, pp. 144-46; J. R. Shillady to President Woodrow Wilson, Sept. 15, 1918, Files of Secretary of Labor, NA.
66. J. R. Shillady to G. E. Haynes, Sept. 17, 1918; J. R. Shillady to President Woodrow Wilson, Sept. 25, 1918, Files of Secretary of Labor, NA.
67. J. R. Shillady to G. E. Haynes, Sept. 17, 1918; G. E. Haynes to J. R. Shillady, Sept. 18, 1918; Memorandum on Compulsory Work Laws, G. E. Haynes to W. E. Wilson, March 20, 1919, Records of Department of Negro Economics, Department of Labor Files, NA.
68. Finney, Jr., pp. 207-08.

## CHAPTER 10

1. *Butcher Workman*, May 1917.
2. *New Republic*, June 4, 1919, pp. 202-03.
3. *Proceedings*, AFL Convention, 1918, p. 38.
4. Samuel Gompers, "Don't Sacrifice Womanhood," *American Federationist* 24 (Aug. 1917): 747-49; *Seattle Union Record*, August 18, 1917. *See also* Samuel Gompers, "Women Workers In War Time," *American Federationist* 24 (Sept. 1917): 812-14.
5. Samuel Gompers to Andrew Wenneis, Secretary-Treasurer, International Fur Workers' Union, May 22, 1917, International Fur and Leather Workers' Union Archives.
6. "There Is No Shortage of Labor," *American Federationist* 24 (October 1917): 22-25.
7. Samuel Gompers to Andrew Wenneis, Secretary-Treasurer, International Fur Workers' Union, Oct. 12, 1917, International Fur and Leather Workers' Union Archives; *Seattle Union Record*, August 18, 1917; *Advance*, April 27, 1917, p. 6;

Marc Karson, *American Labor Unions and Politics, 1900-1918*, Carbondale, Ill., 1958, pp. 145-56.
8. "Female Labor Arouses Hostility and Apprehension in Union Ranks," *Current Opinion*, April 1918, pp. 292-93. *See also* report of "Workingwomen in Wartime Conference," *New York Times*, Dec. 16, 1917.
9. *New York Times*, June 9, 1917; *Proceedings*, AFL Convention, 1918, pp. 202, 219.
10. "Controversies Regarding the Right of Women to Work as Conductors," *Women Street Car Conductors and Ticket Agents*, Washington, D.C., 1921, pp. 2, 3.
11. U.S. Department of Commerce and Labor, Bureau of the Census, *Special Reports, Street and Electric Railways, 1902*, Washington, D.C., 1902, p. 79; U.S. Department of Commerce and Labor, Bureau of the Census, *Special Reports, Street and Electric Railways*, 1907, Washington, D.C., 1910, pp. 193, 201.
12. *Motorman and Conductor*, Nov. 1917, p. 21; Leo Wolman, *The Growth of American Trade Unions, 1880-1923*, New York, 1924, p. 135.
13. *Monthly Labor Review* 7 (April 1918) 1030-32; Gary M. Fink, editor, *Biographical Dictionary of American Labor Leaders*, Westport, Conn., 1974, p. 227; *Trade Union Leader*, May 25, Dec. 21, 1918.
14. *Motorman and Conductor*, Sept. 1918, p. 31.
15. Benjamin M. Squires, "Women Street Railway Employees," *Monthly Labor Review* 6 (May 1918): 1049-50; *Trade Union Leader*, Nov. 30, 1918.
16. Reprinted in Maurine Weiner Greenwald, *Women, War and Work: The Impact of World War I on Women Workers in the United States*, Westport, Conn., 1980, p. 151.
17. *Trade Union Leader*, April 27, 1918.
18. *New York Times*, May 5, 1918.
19. Ibid., May 10, 1918; Squires, pp. 1049-50.
20. *New York Times*, May 11, 1918.
21. Greenwald, p. 155.
22. *New York Times*, May 20, 1918; *Seattle Union Record*, September 7, 1918.
23. *New York Times*, May 21, 1918.
24. Greenwald, p. 155.
25. Life and Labor, Jan. 1919, p. 15; *Report of the Cleveland Railway Company for the Fiscal Year Ended December 31*,

*1918*, Cleveland, Ohio, Jan. 29, 1919.

26. Entry 4, National War Labor Board Docket .491, *Employees v. Cleveland Street Railway of Cleveland, Ohio*, March 17, 1919, National Archives.

27. Ibid.

28. Ronald M. Benson, "Searching for the Antecedents of Affirmative Action: The Case of the Cleveland Conductorettes in World War I," 1975 paper in possession of present writer, p. 5.

29. *New York Times*, Sept. 24, 1918; Entry 4, National War Labor Board Docket .481, National Archives; *Cleveland Plain Dealer*, Dec. 7, 8, 12, 14, 1918; *Monthly Labor Review* 6 (June 1918): 55-57.

30. Cleveland Plain Dealer, Dec. 14, 1918; *Women Street Car Conductors and Ticket Agents*, p. 8.

31. *Life and Labor*, Jan. 1919, p. 14; Benson, pp. 8-9.

32. Benson, p. 9.

33. *Trade Union Leader*, Dec. 21, 1918.

34. *Cleveland Plain Dealer*, Dec. 3, 1918; *New York Times*, December 4, 1918.

35. *Cleveland Plain Dealer*, Dec. 4, 1918; *New York Times*, Dec. 4, 1918.

36. *Women Street Car Conductors and Ticket Agents*, p. 9.

37. Ibid.; Benson, p. 11.

38. Frank P. Walsh to Ethel Smith, Dec. 2, 1918, Frank P. Walsh Papers, New York Public Library.

39. Rose Moriarty to Frank P. Walsh, Dec. 13, 1918, ibid.; *Life and Labor*, March 1919, p. 52.

40. *Life and Labor*, April 1919, p. 98; Benson, pp. 13-14.

41. *New York Times*, March 17, 1919; *Life and Labor*, April 1919, p. 98.

42. Rose Moriarty to Frank P. Walsh, March 20, 1919, Frank P. Walsh Papers, New York Public Library; *New York Times*, March 19, 1919; *Cleveland Plain Dealer*, March 19, 1919.

43. *New York Times*, March 19, 1919.

44. *Women Street Car Conductors and Ticket Agents*, pp. 11-12.

45. Greenwald, p. 172.

46. Ibid., pp. 172-74.

47. Ibid., pp. 176-77.

48. *Women Street Car Conductors and Ticket Agents*, p. 15; *New York Times*, April 27, 1919; Valerie J. Conner, "'The Mothers of the Race' in World War I: The National War Labor Board and Women in Industry," *Labor History* 21 (Winter 1979-80): 43-44; Greenwald, pp. 176-78.

49. *Seattle Union Record*, Dec. 1, 1917, June 8, 1918.

50. Greenwald, *Women, War and Work*, pp. 122-23.

51. Harry Honig, *Brotherhood of Railway Clerks*, New York, 1937, pp. 164, 281-84; *Seattle Union Record*, Nov. 2, 1918.

52. Maurine Weiner Greenwald, "Women Workers and World War I: The American Railroad Industry: A Case Study," *Journal of Social History* 9 (Winter 1975): 169.

53. *Seattle Union Record*, Sept. 22, 1917.

54. Ibid., Nov. 30, Dec. 15, 1918.

55. George Foster, *International Brotherhood of Electrical Workers*, New York, 1926, pp. 34-35; Electrical Worker, Sept. 1917, p. 80.

56. Foster, p. 110; Greenwald, *Women, War, and Work*, p. 203.

57. *Seattle Union Record*, Aug. 18, 1917.

58. Jack Barbash, *Unions and Telephones: The Story of the Communications Workers of America*, New York, 1953, pp. 5-6; Thomas R. Brooks, *Communications Workers of America: The Story of a Union*, New York, 1977, pp. 12-13; *Seattle Union Record*, Aug. 4, 1917.

59. *Seattle Union Record*, Oct. 6, 13, 20, 1917.

60. Ibid., Oct. 20, 1917.

61. Ibid., Nov. 3, 1917.

62. Ibid., Nov. 24, 1917.

63. Ibid., Dec. 8, 15, 1917.

64. Ibid., Dec. 29, 1917.

65. Ibid., Nov. 30, 1918.

66. Julia O'Connor, "History of the Organized Telephone Operators' Movement," *The Union Telephone Operator*, Jan.-Feb. 1921, clippings in National Women's Trade Union League Papers, Arthur and Elizabeth Schlessinger Library on the History of Women in America, Radcliffe College.

67. Seattle Union Record, Aug. 3, Nov. 24, 1918.

68. Ibid., Aug. 31, 1918.

69. Ibid., Aug. 31, 1918; O'Connor, "History of the Organized Telephone Operators' Movement," *The Union Telephone Operator*, January, February, March, May, 1921.

70. *Seattle Union Record*, Oct. 5, 1918.

71. Ibid., Nov. 9, 16, 23, 1918.

72. Ibid., Nov. 30, 1918.

73. Ibid.

74. O'Connor, "History of the Organized Telephone Operators' Movement," *The Union Telephone Operator*, May 1921.

75. Leo Wolman, *The Growth of American*

*Trade Unions, 1880-1923*, New York, 1924, p. 162.

**CHAPTER 11**

1. *International Molders' Journal*, reprinted in New York *Call*, July 1, 1919.
2. Quoted in Charles H. Wesley, *Negro Labor in the United States: A Study in American Economic History*, New York, 1927, pp. 65- 66.
3. *Proceedings*, AFL Convention, 1916, p. 148.
4. Sterling D. Spero and Abram L. Harris, *The Black Worker*, New York, 1931, p. 102; Philip S. Foner, *Organized Labor and the Black Worker, 1619-1981*, New York, 1982, p. 137.
5. Allen D. Grimshaw, editor, *Racial Violence in the United States*, Chicago, 1969, pp. 58-59.
6. "Report of the Special Committee Authorized by Congress to Investigate the East St. Louis Riots," *House Documents*, CXIV, Sixty-fifth Congress, 1918, pp. 2-4; Elliott M. Rudwick, *Race Riot at East St. Louis, July 2, 1917*, Carbondale, Ill., 1964, pp. 166, 217; U.S. Department of Labor, *Negro Migration, 1916-1917*, Washington, D.C., 1919, p. 131.
7. Rudwick, pp. 35-68.
8. "Documents of the Race Riot at East St. Louis," introduction and notes by Robert Asher, *Journal of the Illinois State Historical Society* 65 (Autumn 1972): 328.
9. *New York Times*, July 12, 1917.
10. J. H. Walker to William B. Wilson, July 5, 1917; William B. Wilson to Commissioner of Labor Statistics, July 16, 1917, Files of the Secretary of Labor, National Archives.
11. John D. Finney, Jr., "A Study of Negro Labor During and After World War I," unpublished Ph.D. dissertation, Georgetown University, 1957, p. 120.
12. For the entire report, *see* Philip S. Foner and Ronald Lewis, editors, *The Black Worker: A Documentary History from Colonial Times to the Present* (Philadelphia, 1980) 5: 318-32.
13. *Intercollegiate Socialist* 6 (Dec. 1916-Jan. 1918): 25; Foner, *Organized Labor and the Black Worker*, p. 138.
14. Elliott M. Rudwick, *Race Riot at East St. Louis, July 2, 1917*, Carbondale, Ill., 1964, p. 146.
15. New York *Call*, July 22, 1917.
16. Philip S. Foner, editor, *The Voice of Black America: Major Speeches of Negroes in the United States, 1797-1972*, New York, 1972, p. 624.
17. *Proceedings*, AFL Convention, 1917, p. 182.
18. Ibid., pp. 279-80.
19. Ibid., pp. 349-50.
20. Ibid.
21. Foner, *Organized Labor and the Black Worker*, p. 140.
22. New York *Age*, Nov. 22, 1917.
23. Ibid., Feb. 16, 1918.
24. *The Crisis* 18 (March 1918): 417.
25. J. R. Shillady to Rev. W. C. Gannett, March 1, 1918, National Association for the Advancement of Colored People Labor File, National Association for the Advancement of Colored People Papers, Library of Congress.
26. *The Crisis* 18 (March 1918): 417.
27. New York *Age*, April 17 and May 4, 1918.
28. Finney, Jr., pp. 287-88.
29. Foner, *Organized Labor and the Black Worker*, p. 140.
30. Finney, Jr., pp. 289-91.
31. Ibid., p. 291.
32. Ibid., pp. 292-93.
33. *Proceedings*, AFL Convention, 1918, pp. 130-33.
34. Ibid., pp. 198-99.
35. Finney, pp. 294-96.
36. Ibid., pp. 297-99.
37. Foner, *Organized Labor and the Black Worker*, p. 141.
38. *New Appeal*, April 20, 1918.
39. Dennis Clark Dickerson, "Black Steelworkers in Western Pennsylvania, 1915-1950," unpublished Ph.D. dissertation, Washington University, St. Louis, 1978, pp. 54-55.
40. Richard R. Wright, Jr., *The Negro in Pennsylvania*, Philadelphia, 1911, p. 108.
41. David Brody, *The Butcher Workmen: A Study of Unionization*, Cambridge, Mass., 1964, pp. 1-13, 85-86.
42. William Z. Foster, *From Bryan to Stalin*, New York, 1937, p. 91.
43. Ibid., pp. 91-96; Brody, p. 76; William Z. Foster, *American Trade Unionism*, New York, 1946, p. 25.
44. Brody, pp. 76-78; Foster, *Bryan to Stalin*, pp. 94-96.
45. Brody, pp. 79-80.
46. Ibid., pp. 80-82; Foster, *Bryan to Stalin*, p. 99.
47. John Howard Kaiser, "John Fitzpatrick and Progressive Unionism, 1915-1925," unpublished Ph.D. dissertation, Northwestern University, 1965, p. 41.

48. Ibid., pp. 93-94.
49. Alma Herbst, *The Negro in the Slaughtering and Meatpacking Industry in Chicago*, Boston and New York, 1932, pp. 129-43.
50. Ibid., pp. 145-48.
51. Earl Browder, "Some Experiences in Organizing Negro Workers," *Communist* 9 (1930): 38; William J. Tuttle, Jr., "Labor Conflict and Racial Violence—The Black Worker in Chicago, 1894-1919," *Labor History* 10 (Summer 1969): 425; Carl Sandburg, *The Chicago Race Riots*, New York, 1919, p. 48; James W. Ford, "Foster and Negro-Labor Unity," *Masses & Mainstream*, March 1951, p. 23.
52. William M. Tuttle, Jr., *Race Riot: Chicago in the Summer of 1919*, New York, 1970, p. 180.
53. Philip S. Foner, *Women and the American Labor Movement: From World War I to the Present*, New York, 1980, pp. 64, 67.
54. Chicago Commission on Race Relations, *The Negro in Chicago*, Chicago, 1922, p. 89, and reprinted in Jerold S. Auerbach, *American Labor: The Twentieth Century*, Indpls., 1969, p. 151.
55. Ibid.
56. *Life and Labor*, May, June-July, Aug. 1918; *Proceedings of the Biennial Convention of the National Women's Trade Union League*, 1919, pp. 14-17.
57. Mildred Rankin to Margaret Dreier Robins, Aug. 10, 1918, Margaret Dreier Robins Papers, University of Florida Library, Gainesville, Florida.
58. *Norfolk Journal and Guide*, March 3, May 12, 1917.
59. *Norfolk Ledger-Dispatch*, Sept. 3, 1917.
60. Ibid., Sept. 8, 1917.
61. *Norfolk Journal and Guide*, Sept. 29, 1917.
62. Norfolk *Ledger-Dispatch*, Oct. 3, 1917; *Virginian-Pilot*, reprinted in *Norfolk Journal and Guide*, Oct. 5, 1917.
63. *Norfolk Journal and Guide*, Oct. 5, 1917.
64. *Norfolk Ledger-Dispatch*, Nov. 12-14, 1917; Foner, *Women and the American Labor Movement*, p. 67.
65. Spero and Harris, p. 116; R. R. Wright, Jr., "The Negro Skilled Mechanic in the North," *Southern Workman* 38 (March 1909): 165-66.
66. Foner, *Organized Labor and the Black Worker*, p. 147; Allen La Verne Shepherd, "Federal Railway Labor Policy, 1913-1926," unpublished Ph.D. dissertation, University of Nebraska, 1971, p. 155.
67. Spero and Harris, p. 124; *Chicago Defender*, May 21, 1921; Finney, Jr., pp. 345-46.
68. Foner, *Organized Labor and the Black Worker*, p. 148.
69. Philip S. Foner, *American Socialism and Black Americans: From the Age of Jackson to World War I*, Westport, Conn., 1977, pp. 274-78.
70. *The Messenger*, Nov. 1917, p. 3; June 1918, p. 8.
71. Foner, *American Socialism and Black Americans*, pp. 278-79; *The Messenger*, Nov. 1917, p. 3.
72. Foner, *American Socialism and Black Americans*, p. 279.
73. *The Messenger*, July 1918, pp. 7-8.
74. Foner, *Organized Labor and the Black Worker*, p. 150.
75. "The Negro Worker," by Anise, Seattle Union Record, reprinted in *The Messenger*, July 1919, p. 8.

## CHAPTER 12

1. Melvyn Dubofsky, *We Shall Be All: A History of the Industrial Workers of the World*, Chicago, 1969, p. 345.
2. Philip Taft, "The Federal Trials of the I.W.W.," *Labor History* 3 (Winter 1962): 58.
3. John Reed, "The Fighting I.W.W. in America," *Communist International*, No. 13, 1920, p. 90.
4. *Industrial Worker*, April 12, 1917.
5. Portland *Oregonian*, Aug. 18, 1917.
6. Robert L. Tyler, *Rebels of the Woods: The I.W.W. in the Pacific Northwest*, Eugene, Oregon, 1962, p. 90.
7. *Industrial Worker*, April 5, 1917.
8. Ralph Winstead, "Evolution of Logging Conditions in the Northwest Coast Battle," *One Big Monthly*, May 1920, p. 26; E. Bigelow Thompson, "The Case of the Lumber Jack, *World Outlook*, June 1920, p. 18.
9. Quoted from United States Circuit Court of Appeals for the Ninth Circuit, *Anderson et al v. United States of America in error Transcript of Record Upon Writ of Error to the United States District Court of Northern California, Northern District, 1919*, pp. 69-70.
10. *Aberdeen World*, July 10, 1917.
11. Portland *Oregonian*, Aug. 2, 1917; *Industrial Worker*, July 14, 1917.
12. *Solidarity*, June 30, 1917.
13. Robert C. Sims, "Idaho's Criminal Syndicalism Act: One State's Response to

Radical Labor," *Labor History* 15 (Fall 1974): 511-15; Tyler, p 126; *Aberdeen World*, July 17-22, 1917.

14. Tyler, p. 128.
15. Portland *Oregonian*, July 21, 1917.
16. Ibid., July 12-Aug. 2, 1917.
17. Tyler, p. 24; Portland Oregonian, Aug. 2, 3, 1917.
18. Portland *Oregonian*, Aug. 3, 1917.
19. Alexander M. Bing, *War-Time Strikes and Their Adjustment*, New York, 1921, pp. 260-63.
20. Seattle *Post-Intelligencer*, July 31, Aug. 1, 1917; Dubofsky, p. 360-65; Tyler, p. 121.
21. *Industrial Worker*, July 27, 1917.
22. *Portland Oregonian*, Aug. 12, 1917.
23. *The Truth About the I.W.W.*, New York, April 1918, p. 12.
24. Dubofsky, p. 368.
25. *Portland Oregonian*, Aug. 17, 1917.
26. Ibid., Aug. 16, 1917.
27. Ibid., Aug. 18, 1917.
28. *Industrial Worker*, Aug. 2, 1917.
29. Tyler, p. 114; Sims, p. 518.
30. Seattle *Post-Intelligencer*, Aug. 21, 23, 1917.
31. *Portland Evening Telegram*, Aug. 28, 1917.
32. *Portland Oregonian*, Sept. 17, 1917.
33. A. H. Prince, "How the I.W.W. Brought About the 8-Hour Day in the Lumber Industry," *One Big Union Monthly*, March 1, 1919, pp. 22-24.
34. James Rowan, *The I.W.W. In the Lumber Industry*, Seattle, n.d., p. 51.
35. Robert Bruere, "The Industrial Workers of the World," *Harpers Monthly*, July 1918, pp. 122-23.
36. Portland *Oregonian*, Sept. 12-Oct. 14, 1917.
37. Bruere, pp. 124-25.
38. Ibid., p. 126.
39. Rowan, p. 51.
40. Bruce P. Disque, "How We Found a Cure for Strikes," *System*, Sept. 1919, pp. 132-33.
41. Jensen, p. 128.
42. Ibid., p. 127.
43. Ibid., p. 129; "President's Mediation Commission Report," *Reports of the Department of Labor*, 1918, Washington, D.C., 1918, pp. 21-22.
44. *Portland Oregonian*, Nov. 13, 1917.
45. *Industrial Worker*, Sept. 26, October 13, 1917.
46. Ibid., Dec. 5, 1917.
47. *The Lumber Industry and Its Workers*, Chicago, nd, p. 82.
48. Harold Hyman, *Soldiers in Spruce*, Los Angeles, 1963, pp. 19-20.
49. Cf. *Portland Oregonian*, March 2-3, 1918.
50. Robert C. Tyler, "The United States Government as Union Organizer: The Loyal Legion of Loggers and Lumbermen," *Mississippi Valley Historical Review* 47 (Dec. 1960): 434-51; Hyman, pp. 18-22; Dubofsky, pp. 370-74.

**CHAPTER 13**

1. Charles H. Watson to Bernard Baruch, April 11, 1917; Samuel Gompers to Charles H. Moyer, April 20, 1917; Gompers to Bernard Baruch, April 20, 1917, Gompers Papers, AFL Archives, State Historical Society of Wisconsin.
2. *Industrial Worker*, Jan. 15, 22, 29, 1917; James Byrkit, "The Bisbee Deportation," in James C. Foster, editor, *American Labor in the Southwest; The First One Hundred Years*, Tucscon, 1982, p. 87.
3. "The Strike at Ajo," *Miners' Magazine*, Jan.-Feb. 1917.
4. Philip S. Foner, *History of the Labor Movement in the United States* 6 (New York, 1982): 22; *The Public*, July 20, 1917.
5. *Bill Haywood's Book: The Autobiography of William D. Haywood*, New York, 1929, p. 277.
6. Byrkit, p. 87.
7. Ibid.
8. Michael E. Casillas, "Mexican Labor and Strife in Arizona, 1896-1917," unpublished M.A. thesis, University of New Mexico, 1979, p. 117; Philip Taft, "The Bisbee Deportation," *Labor History* 5 (Spring 1972): 8.
9. James W. Byrkit, "Life and Labor in Arizona, 1901-1921," unpublished Ph.D. dissertation, Claremont Graduate School, 1972, pp. 288-94.
10. Taft, p. 9.
11. Ibid., p. 4.
12. Robert Glass Cleland, *A History of Phelps-Dodge*, New York, 1952, p. 111.
13. Byrkit, "The Bisbee Deportation," p. 87.
14. *Bisbee Daily Review*, June 26, 27, 1917.
15. Taft, p. 8.
16. *Report of the Bisbee Deportation Made by the President's Mediation Commission to the President of the United States*, Bisbee, Arizona, Nov. 6, 1917, pp. 7-8; Meyer H. Fishbein, "The President's Mediation Commission and the Arizona Copper Strike, 1917," *Southwestern Social Science Quarterly* 30 (Dec.

1949): 176-77.

17. *Bisbee Daily Review*, July 28-Aug. 1, 1917.

18. Alan V. Johnson, "Governor G. W. P. Hunt and Organized Labor," unpublished M.A. thesis, University of Arizona, 1964, pp. 77-78.

19. *Bisbee Daily Review*, July 11, 1917; Taft, p. 12.

20. Foner, vol. 6, pp. 16, 20n; Byrkit, "The Bisbee Deportation," p. 86.

21. John A. Lindquist, "The Jerome Deportation of 1917," *Arizona and the West* 11 (Feb. 1969): 233-40; *Jerome News*, July 18-23, 1917.

22. *Arizona Republican*, July 20, 1917; Casillas, p. 113.

23. Taft, p. 13; *Bisbee Daily Review*, July 10-12, 1917.

24. *Bisbee Daily Review*, July 12, 1917; *New York Times*, July 13, 1917.

25. Byrkit, "The Bisbee Deportation," p. 90; *Bisbee Daily Review*, July 13, 1917.

26. *New York Times*, July 13, 1917; Byrkit, "The Bisbee Deportation," p. 90.

27. Byrkit, "The Bisbee Deportation," p. 91.

28. J. F. McDonald to G. W. P. Hunt, July 24, 1917, in Johnson, p. 82.

29. Taft, p. 15.

30. *New York Times*, July 13, 1917.

31. Taft, p. 15.

32. Byrkit, "The Bisbee Deportation," p. 93.

33. Leslie Marcy, "The Eleven Hundred Exiled Copper Miners," *International Socialist Review* 17 (Sept. 1917): 160-62; *Bisbee Daily Review*, July 13, 1917; Byrkit, "Life and Labor in Arizona," p. 302.

34. *Bisbee Daily Review*, July 13, 14, 1917.

35. *Bisbee Daily Review*, July 13, 1917.

36. *New York Times*, July 14, 1917.

37. Ibid.; Byrkit, "The Bisbee Deportation," p. 93.

38. *New York Times*, July 13, 14, 1917.

39. Ibid., July 13, 1917.

40. Ibid., July 14, 1917.

41. Reprinted in Taft, p. 14.

42. *New York Times*, July 14, 1917.

43. Reprinted in Taft, p. 14.

44. *New York Times*, July 14, 1917.

45. Fred Brown to Gompers, July 13, 1917; Gompers to Woodrow Wilson, August 10, 1917, Gompers Papers, State Historical Society of Wisconsin; Dallas L. Jones, "The Wilson Administration and Organized Labor, 1912-1919," unpublished Ph.D. dissertation, Cornell University, 1956, pp. 223-24.

46. *New York Times*, July 14, 15, 1917.

47. Byrkit, "The Bisbee Deportation," p. 94.

48. *New York Times*, July 15, 1917.

49. Johnson, p. 84.

50. Byrkit, "Life and Labor in Arizona," p. 304.

51. J. F. McDonald to G. W. P. Hunt, July 24, 1917, in Johnson, p. 82.

52. *Bisbee Daily Review*, July 19, 1917.

53. Taft, p. 23.

54. *New York Times*, July 15, 1917.

55. Taft, p. 24.

56. Ibid., p. 23.

57. *Report on the Bisbee Deportations. Made by the President's Mediation Commission to the President of the United States*, Bisbee, Arizona, Nov. 6, 1917.

58. Byrkit, "Life and Labor in Arizona," pp. 440-45.

59. Ibid., pp. 445-50; Byrkit, "The Bisbee Deportations," pp. 98-99.

60. Byrkit, "Life and Labor in Arizona," pp. 445-50; *Survey*, June 21, 1919, pp. 121-22.

61. Casillas, pp. 122-13. *See also* Abraham Hoffman, *Unwanted Mexican Americans in the Great Depression: Repatriation Pressures, 1929-1939*, Tucson, 1974; Ronald E. Hester, "The Bisbee Deportation," MS Chicano Studies, Hayden Library, Arizona State University; David Wright, "The Bisbee Deportation," MS Chicano Studies, Hayden Library, Arizona State University; John H. Lindquist and James Fraser, "A Sociological Interpretation of the Bisbee Deportation," *Pacific Historical Review* 36 (July 1968): 404-32.

62. Johnson, p. 85; Taft, p. 29.

63. Arizona Republican, Oct. 27, Nov. 6, 1917.

64. Taft, pp. 26-27.

65. *Arizona Labor Journal*, Sept. 13, 1918; Johnson, p. 85.

66. Byrkit, "The Bisbee Deportations," p. 99.

67. Patrick Renshaw, *The Wobblies: The Story of Syndicalism in the United States*, Garden City, N.Y., 1967, pp. 206-07; Ralph Chaplin, *Wobbly: The Rough-and-Tumble Story of an American Radical*, Chicago, 1948, p. 209.

68. Gutfield, "The Murder of Frank Little: Radical Labor Agitator in Butte, Montana, 1917," *Labor History* 10 (Spring 1969): 178

69. Vernon H. Jensen, *Heritage of Conflict: Labor Relations in the Nonferrous Metals Industry up to 1930*, Ithaca, N.Y.,

1950, p. 289-353.

70. Paul F. Brissenden, "The Butte Miners and the 'Rustling Card,'" *American Economic Review*, Dec. 1920, p. 765.

71. Gutfield, p. 179.

72. *Third Biennial Report of the Department of Labor and Industry, 1917-1918*, Helena, Montana, 1918, pp. 21-22. Hereinafter cited as *Third Biennial Report*.

73. Guy Halverson and William E. Ames, "The Butte *Bulletin*: Beginnings of a Labor Daily," *Journalism Quarterly*, Summer, 1969, p. 262.

74. *Third Biennial Report*, p. 18; Arnon Gutfield, "The Speculator Disaster in 1917: Labor Resurgence at Butte, Montana," *Arizona and the West* 11 (Spring 1969): 32.

75. *Third Biennial Report*, p. 19; Halverson and Ames, p. 265.

76. *Third Biennial Report*, pp. 18-9; Gutfield, "Speculator Disaster," p. 32.

77. *Butte Daily Post*, June 13, 1917, cited in Gutfield, "Speculator Disaster," p. 32.

78. Ibid.

79. Gutfield, "Speculator Disaster," p. 33.

80. Ibid.

81. Halverson and Ames, p. 83.

82. *Third Biennial Report*, pp. 19-20.

83. Gutfield, "Speculator Disaster," pp. 33-34.

84. Ibid., p. 36.

85. Ibid.

86. Burton K. Wheeler to Attorney General Thomas W. Gregory, August 21, 1917, Department of Justice File 186701-27-25, National Archives, and cited in Gutfield, "Speculator Disaster," p. 36.

87. Gutfield, "Murder of Frank Little," p. 183.

88. "Soldiers Called Armed Thugs," reprinted in ibid., p. 183.

89. *Butte Miner*, July 12, 1917, reprinted in ibid., p. 184.

90. Ibid., pp. 185-86.

91. Ibid., p. 186.

92. "Seditious Talk of the I.W.W. Agitator," Butte *Daily Post*, July 28, 1917, cited in Gutfield, "Murder of Frank Little," p. 186.

93. Gutfield, "The Murder of Frank Little," pp. 177-78; *New York Times*, August 2, 1917.

94. Halverson and Ames, p. 264.

95. George W. Davis, *Sketches of Butte*, Boston, 1921, pp. 138-39; Halverson and Ames, p. 264.

96. Gutfield, "Murder of Frank Little," pp. 185-86.

97. *New York Times*, Aug. 2, 1917.

98. Gutfield, "Murder of Frank Little," p. 186.

99. *Third Biennial Report*, p. 20.

100. Gutfield, "Speculator Disaster," p. 38.

101. *Laws Passed by the Extra-ordinary Session of the Legislative Assembly (Feb. 14-15, 1918)*, Helena, Montana, nd, pp. 28-29; Gutfield, "Speculator Disaster," p. 38.

102. Arnon Gutfield, "The Ves Hall Case, Judge Bourquin and the Sedition Act of 1918," *Pacific Historical Review* 37 (May 1968): 163-78.

103. Gutfield, "Speculator Disaster," p. 38.

104. *Third Biennial Report*, p. 21.

105. Halverson and Ames, pp. 260, 264-66.

## CHAPTER 14

1. A full story of the suppression of radicals during World War I is Gilbert C. Fite and H. C. Peterson, *Opponents of War, 1917-1918*, Madison, Wisc., 1957, and William Preston, Jr., *Aliens and Dissenters: Federal Suppression of Radicals, 1903-1933*, Cambridge, Mass., 1963. A recent study that shows the degree of wartime repression is David M. Kennedy, *The First World War and American Society*, New York, 1981.

2. Preston, Jr., pp. 103-08.

3. Stephen Vaugh, *Holding Fast the Inner Lines: Democracy, Nationalism, and the Committee on Public Information*, Chapel Hill, N. Car., 1980, p. 122; Edward J. Muzik, "Victor L. Berger, A Biography," unpublished Ph.D. dissertation, Northwestern University, 1960, p. 309.

4. "The Labor Report," *The Public*, Feb. 10, 1918, p. 197.

5. Preston, Jr., pp. 110-14.

6. Ibid., pp. 116-18.

7. Tulsa *World* quoted in National Civil Liberties Bureau, *The "Knights of Liberty" Nob, and the I.W.W. Prisoners at Tulsa, Oklahoma*, New York, 1918, p. 13.

8. Ibid., pp. 3-13; *Solidarity*, Nov. 18, 1917; Earl Bruce White, "The IWW and the Mid-Continent Oil Field," in James C. Foster, editor, *American Labor in the Southwest: The First One Hundred Years*, Tucson, 1982, pp. 65-76; David G. Wagaman, "The Industrial Workers of the World in Nebraska, 1914-1920," *Nebraska History* 10 (Fall 1975): 311-14; Joyce Kornbluh, editor, Rebel Voices: An I.W.W. Anthology, Ann Arbor, Mich., 1964, pp. 332-34; Thorstein Veblen, "Using the I.W.W. to Harvest Grain," *Journal of Political*

*Economy* 40 (December 1932): 797-807; Preston, Jr., p. 131.

9. Quoted in Leslie Fishbein, "Federal Suppression of Leftwing Dissidence in World War I," *Potomac Review* 6 (Summer 1974): 48-49.

10. Ibid., p. 49.

11. Ibid.

12. Ibid.

13. Eldridge Foster Dowell, *A History of Criminal Syndicalism in the United States*, Baltimore, 1939, pp. 45-47.

14. Ibid., p. 51.

15. Robert C. Sims, "Idaho's Criminal Syndicalism Act: One State's Response to Radical Labor," *Labor History* 15 (Fall 1974): 513.

16. Fishbein, p. 53.

17. Reprinted in *Literary Digest*, July 28, 1917, p. 20.

18. Ibid., p. 21.

19. Reprinted in ibid., p. 20.

20. *Solidarity*, Oct. 20, 1917.

21. Melvyn Dubofsky, *We Shall Be All: A History of the Industrial Workers of the World*, Chicago, 1969, p. 406; *Literary Digest*, September 22, 1917, p. 17.

22. *Literary Digest*, July 28, 1917, p. 20.

23. Ibid., Sept. 22, 1917, p. 17.

24. Reprinted in ibid., July 28, 1917, p. 20; *The Public*, September 14, 1917.

25. *The Public*, Sept. 14, 1917.

26. Frank K. Kane to Thomas W. Gregory, Sept. 7, 1917, File 186701-39-4, D/J 60, National Archives.

27. Philip S. Foner, editor, "United States of America vs. Wm. D. Haywood, et al.; The I.W.W. Indictment," *Labor History* 11 (Fall 1970): 500-06; Philip Taft, "The Federal Trials of the IWW," *Labor History* 3 (Winter 1962): 60-62.

28. Preston, Jr., p. 132.

29. Foner, "The I.W.W. Indictment," pp. 501-02.

30. *New York Times*, Sept. 7, 1917.

31. Frederick C. Griffin, *Six Who Protested: Radical Opposition to the First World War*, Port Washington, N.Y., 1977, p. 127.

32. Reprinted in *Literary Digest*, Sept. 22, 1917, p. 17.

33. Griffin, p. 127.

34. "Wobblies and Draftees: The IWW's Wartime Dilemma, 1917-1918," *Radical America* 1 (Sept.-Oct. 1967): 8-10.

35. Dubofsky, pp. 353-60, 374-75; Clayton R. Koppes, "The Kansas Trial of the IWW, 1917-1919," *Labor History* 16 (Summer 1975): 352.

36. "Wobblies and Draftees," pp. 12-13.

37. Ralph Chaplin, *Wobbly: The Rough-and-Tumble Story of an American Radical*, Chicago, 1948, pp. 208-09.

38. Dubofsky, pp. 334-44, 357, 383-84; Fishbein, p. 48.

39. Griffin, p. 127.

40. *Address by the Attorney General of the United States Hon. Henry M. Daughterty at Canton, Ohio, October 21, 1922*, n.p., n.d., p. 8. *My emphasis. P.S.F.*

41. William D. Haywood, *Bill Haywood's Book*, New York, 1929, p. 299.

42. *Coast Seamen's Journal*, May 8, 1918; Thomas W. Gregory to Gompers, Dec. 7, 1917, Department of Justice Files, Gregory Papers, National Archives; Thomas W. Gregory to Ralph M. Easley, April 1, 1918; Easley to Joseph P. Tumulty, May 5, 1917, National Civic Federation Papers, New York Public Library; Gompers, *American Labor and the War*, pp. 262-63; Simeon Larson, *Labor and Foreign Policy: Gompers, the AFL, and the First World War, 1914-1918*, Rutherford, N.J., 1975, pp. 148-49.

43. *New York Times*, Sept. 29, 1917; Patrick Renshaw, *The Wobblies: The Story of Syndicalism in the United States*, New York, 1968, p. 223; Fishbein, pp. 54-55; Philip Taft, "The Federal Trials of the IWW," *Labor History* 3 (Winter 1962): 65-66; "Wobblies and Draftees," pp. 14-15.

44. Helen Keller, "In Behalf of the I.W.W.," *Liberator*, March 1918, p. 13.

45. *New York Times*, April 2, 1918.

46. *Liberator*, Sept. 1918, p. 22; reprinted in John Stuart, editor, *The Education of John Reed: Selected Writings*, New York, 1955, p. 88.

47. Ibid., p. 87.

48. Ibid., p. 88.

49. New York *Call*, Sept. 5, 1920.

50. *Liberator*, Sept. 1918, pp. 23-24; reprinted in Stuart, p. 89.

51. U.S. Department of Justice, *Annual Report of the Attorney General for the United States for the year 1918*, p. 53.

52. William D. Haywood, *Evidence and Cross Examination of William D. Haywood in the case of the U.S.A. v. Wm. D. Haywood, et al.*, Chicago, n.d., pp. 69-87, 103-04, 265-66; U.S. v. Haywood, et al., pp. 5935-8325, 8334, Boxes 110-5, IWW Collection, Wayne State University Library.

53. Ibid., pp. 5976, 5978, 5982, Box 110-4; pp. 134-35, Box 118-6, IWW Collection, Wayne State University Library.

54. Ibid., p. 5935, Box 110-4; pp. 9325, 9334, Box 114-5, IWW Collection, Wayne State University Library.
55. Dubofsky, pp. 434-35.
56. George F. Vanderveer to Frank P. Walsh, Dec. 31, 1917, Frank P. Walsh Papers, New York Public Library.
57. George F. Vanderveer to Frank P. Walsh, March 19, 1918, Frank P. Walsh Papers, New York Public Library.
58. Dubofsky, p. 436.
59. A. S. Embree to Editor, *Solidarity*, September 29, 1917; James Rowan to John Graves, Jan. 10, 1918, in *U.S. v. William Dudley Haywood, et al.*, File 186701-57, Section 2, DIJ 60, National Archives; Dubofsky, p. 430.
60. Dubofsky, p. 433.
61. Renshaw, p. 262.
62. *U.S. v. Haywood, et al.*, p. 351, Box 118-6, IWW Collection, Wayne State University Library.
63. "Wobblies and Draftees," pp. 113-14.
64. L. H., "The IWW on Trial," *Outlook* 119 (July 1917): 448.
65. Taft, "The Federal Trials," pp. 74-75; Dubofsky, pp. 436-37.
66. *U.S. v. Haywood, et al.*, p. 25, Box 118-6, Wayne State University Library; *Bill Haywood's Book*, pp. 324-25.
67. Richard Brazier, "The Mass I.W.W. Trial of 1918: A Retrospect," *Labor History* 7 (Spring 1966): 191-92.
68. Taft, pp. 80-91.
69. *Petition for Return of Papers Filed by Attorney George F. Vanderveer In the District Court of United States of America for the Northern District, The United States of America v. Haywood, et al., March 18, 1918*.
70. *See In the Supreme Court of the United States v. U.S. A Transcript of Record and United States Circuit Court of Appeals for the Seventh Circuit, October Term, 1920. Haywood, et al., v. United States of America Brief and Argument for Defendant in Error*. Several of the letters are quoted in Taft, pp. 61-71; *U.S. v. Haywood, et al.*, p. 25, Box 118-6, IWW Papers, Wayne State University Library.
71. *Files of Criminal Case 6125, United States v. William Dudley Haywood, et al.*, Federal Records Center, Chicago, Illinois. I wish to thank Mr. Bruce C. Harding, Chief, Regional Archives Branch, Federal Records Center, Chicago, for his kind assistance in the use of the files.
72. Ibid.

## CHAPTER 15

1. *New York Times*, Sept. 6, 1917.
2. Michael Bassett, "The American Socialist Party and the War, 1917-1918," *Australian Journal of Politics and History* 20 (Spring 1970): 279-80.
3. Morris Hillquit, "Freedom of the Press," broadside, October 2, 1917, Morris Hillquit Papers, Tamiment Institute Library.
4. Ibid.
5. Harry W. Laidler, in *Intercollegiate Socialist Review* 7 (Dec.-Jan., 1918-1919): 8.
6. Philip S. Foner, *The Bolshevik Revolution: Its Impact on American Radicals, Liberals, and Labor*, New York, 1967, pp. 15-18; V. Malkov, "The Great October Revolution and the US Working-Class Movement," *Social Sciences*, USSR Academy of Sciences, 8 (1977): 20-23.
7. Bassett, "American Socialist Party," p. 285; New York *Evening Call*, Jan. 19, 1918; *Literary Digest* 56 (Jan. 1918): 11.
8. *New York Times*, April 18, 20, 1918.
9. Ibid., May 2, 1918; Morris U. Schappes, "The Attitude of Jewish Labor in World War I, 1917-1918," *Jewish Life* March 1955, p. 22.
10. Arturo Giovannitti, "Socialists and Suppression," *Liberator*, Aug. 1918, p. 22.
11. *Proceedings*, Socialist Party National Convention, Aug. 30-Sept. 5, 1919, Chicago, 1919, p. 12.
12. "The Proper Attitude toward Socialism," *Nation* 105 (November 27, 1917): 711-12.
13. James Weinstein, *The Decline of Socialism in America, 1912-1925*, New York, 1969, p. 144.
14. *New York Times*, July 17, Aug. 12, Oct. 12, 1917.
15. *The Public*, Sept. 23, 1917, p. 113.
16. Edward J. Muzik, "Victor L. Berger, Biography," unpublished Ph.D. dissertation, Northwestern University, 1960, p. 280.
17. *The Public*, July 6, 1917, p. 651.
18. Ibid., p. 652.
19. Herbert Croly to Woodrow Wilson, Oct. 19, 1917; Upton Sinclair to Woodrow Wilson, Oct. 22, 1917, Woodrow Wilson Papers, Library of Congress; Muzik, p. 280.
20. Schappes, p. 22.
21. *The Public*, July 20, 1917, p. 699.
22. Muzik, p. 283.
23. Ibid.

24. *The Public*, July 27, 1917, p. 724.
25. H. C. Peterson and Gilbert C. Fite, *Opponents of War, 1917-1918*, Madison, Wisc., 1957, p. 97.
26. *Cleveland Socialist*, July 12, 1917; *New Leader*, April 25, 1925.
27. Philip S. Foner and Sally Miller, editors, *Kate Richards O'Hare: Selected Writings and Speeches*, Baton Rouge, La., 1982, pp. 19-21, 121-42.
28 Ibid., pp. 23-24.
29. Bernard S. Brommel, "Kate Richards O'Hare: A Midwestern Pacific Fighter for Free Speech," *North Dakota Quarterly* 55 (Winter 1976): 9-19. The article contains a detailed discussion of the trial.
30. Foner and Miller, pp. 23-23; David Shannon, "Kate Richards O'Hare Cunningham," in Edward T. James, ed., *Notable American Women, 1607-1950*, Cambridge, Mass., 1970, pp. 118-19.
31. Weinstein, pp. 139-40, 161; *New York Times*, Aug. 4-6, 1917; Charles C. Bush, "The Green Corn Rebellion," unpublished M.A. thesis, University of Oklahoma, 1932, pp. 1-22; Works Progress Administration, Federal Writers' Project, of Oklahoma, *Labor History of Oklahoma*, Oklahoma City, 1939, pp. 40-42; Garin Burbank, *When Farmers Voted Red: The Gospel of Socialism in the Oklahoma Countryside, 1910-1924*, Westport, Conn., 1976, pp. 133, 135, 144-48; Theodore Kornweibel, Jr., "Apathy and Dissent: Black Americans Negative Responses to World War I," *South Atlantic Quarterly* 80 (Summer 1981): 331-32.
32. For a novel on the Green Corn Rebellion that mentions the work of Kate Richards O'Hare, *see* William Cunningham, *The Green Corn Rebellion*, New York, 1935.
33. Foner and Miller, p. 21; Neil K. Basen, "Kate Richards O'Hare: The 'First Lady' of American Socialism, 1901-1917," *Labor History* 21 (Spring 1980): 176-77.
34. Brommel, p. 17.
35. Jessie Lloyd, "One Woman's Resistance," appendix 2 in Harvey O'Connor, *Revolution in Seattle: A Memoir*, New York, 1964, pp. 248-61.
36. *The Louise Olivereau Case*, preface by Minnie Parkhurst, Seattle, 1918, pp. 20-38; Seattle *Daily Call*, Sept. 8, Dec. 1, 4, 1917.
37. *The Louise Olivereau Case*, pp. 39-40.
38. Ibid., p. 5.
39. Frederick C. Griffin, *Six Who Protested: Radical Opposition to the First World War*, Port Washington, N.Y., 1977, pp. 106-13.
40. *Voices of Revolt: Speeches and Writings of Charles E. Ruthenberg*, New York, 1928, p. 12; Phil Bart, "The S.P.'s St. Louis Convention of 1917," *Daily World*, April 23, 1977.
41. Philip S. Foner, *American Socialism and Black Americans: From the Age of Jackson to World War II*, Westport, Conn., 1977, pp. 269, 273-76; Theodore Kornweibel, Jr., *No Crystal Stair: Black Life and the MESSENGER, 1917-1928*, Westport, Conn., 1975, Chapter 1.
42. A Philip Randolph and Chandler Own, *Terms of Peace and the Darker Races*, New York, 1917, pp. 30-32.
43. Foner, *American Socialism and Black Americans*, pp. 262-63; *New York Post*, Dec. 30, 1959; *Messenger*, April 1922, p. 310; Jervis Anderson, *A. Philip Randolph: A Biographical Portrait*, New York, 1972, pp. 106-08; Kornweibel, Jr., "Apathy and Dissent," p. 336.
44. Foner, *American Socialism and Black Americans*, p. 283.
45. Anderson, pp. 108-09.
46. Foner, *American Socialism and Black Americans*, p. 283.
47. Ibid., p. 284.
48. *Milwaukee Leader*, March 9, 16, 18, 28, 1918; Muzik, p. 288.
49. *Milwaukee Leader*, March 30, 1918; *Congressional Record*, 65th Congress, 2nd Session, p. 4634; Muzik, pp. 292-93.
50. *Milwaukee Leader*, April 1, 1918; Muzik, p. 289.
51. Muzik, pp. 288-89.
52. *Congressional Record*, 69th Congress, 1st Session, p. 6404.
53. Muzik, p. 290.
54. *Milwaukee Leader*, Nov. 6, 1918; Muzik, p. 293.
55. Muzik, p. 294.
56. Weinstein, p. 178; Muzik, p. 310.
57. Eugene V. Debs, "Conviction of Kate O'Hare," *Social Revolution* 1 (Jan. 1918): 5.
58. Griffin, p. 32.
59. "A Personal Statement," unidentified newspaper clipping, dated May 1918, in *Eugene V. Debs Scrapbooks* 10 (1915-20), Tamiment Institute Library, NYU; Griffin, pp. 32-33.
60. Debs' Canton speech is printed in full in *The Debs White Book* Girard, Kansas, n.d., pp. 3-36.
61. Griffin, pp. 34-35.
62. David A. Shannon, *The Socialist Party in*

*America: A History*, Chicago, 1955, p. 114.

63. Ibid., p. 115.

64. David Karsner, *Debs*, New York, 1919, pp. 18-19. The trial is covered at length in Ray Ginger, *The Bending Cross: A Biography of Eugene V. Debs*, New Brunswick, 1949, Chapter 18.

65. Karsner, pp. 23-24.

66. Richard Oestreicher, "A Note on the Origins of Eugene V. Debs' 'Bending Cross' Speech," *Indiana Magazine of History* 76 (March 1980): 55.

67. Oestreicher, p. 55; *Debs' Address to the Jury and Statement to the Court*, Chicago, n.d., pp. 19-20.

68. Anna Louise Strong, *I Change Worlds: The Remaking of an American*, New York, 1935, pp. 56-66; *Seattle Union Record*, October 27, 1917.

69. Harvey O'Connor, *Revolution in Seattle: A Memoir*, New York, 1964, pp. 105, 115-18, 161.

70. Leslie Fishbein, "Federal Suppression of Leftwing Dissidence in World War I," *Potomac Review* 6 (Summer 1974): 51.

71. Weinstein, p. 161.

72. Fishbein, p. 56.

73. *New York Times*, March 24, 1918; *Stokes v. United States* 64 Fed. 22 (Circuit Court of Appeals, Eighth Circuit, March 9, 1920).

74. "Minutes of the Joint Conference of the National Executive Committee and State Secretariat, August 10, 11, 12, 1918, unpublished stenographic report, Socialist Party of American Papers, Duke University Library; Ginger, pp. 372-78.

## CHAPTER 16

1. Paul H. Douglas, *Real Wages in the United States, 1890-1926*, Boston, 1930, p. 208.

2. *Proceedings*, AFL Convention, 1919, p. 105.

3. Selig Perlman and Philip Taft, *History of Labor in the United States, 1896-1932*, New York, 1935, p. 410, (Volume 4 of Commons and Associates).

4. Leo Wolman, *The Growth of American Trade Unions, 1880-1923*, New York, 1924, p. 117.

5. Ibid., p. 116.

6. Harry A. Millis and Royal E. Montgomery, *Organized Labor*, New York and London, 1945, p. 133.

7. Ibid., p. 134.

8. David Brody, *Steelworkers in America: The Non-Union Era*, Cambridge, Mass., 1960, p. 214.

9. Philip S. Foner, *Organized Labor and the Black Worker, 1916-1981*, New York, 1982, pp. 142-43; Philip S. Foner, *Women and the American Labor Movement: From World War I to the Present*, New York, 1980, p. 92.

10. Eli Ginzberg and Hyman Berman, *The American Worker in the Twentieth Century: A History Through Autobiographies*, New York, 1963, p. 150; Douglas, p. 219.

11. *Railroad Trainman* 37 (April 1920): 200; *Railroad Worker* 17 (Oct. 1919): 12-13.

12. Alexander Trachtenberg, editor, *American Labor Year Book 1919-1920*, New York, 1920, p. 50.

13. *Sixth Annual Report of the Secretary of Labor*, 1918, p. 87.

14. Millis and Montgomery, pp. 138-39.

15. Perlman and Taft, p. 409; National Industrial Conference Board, *Collective Bargaining Through Employee Representation*, New York, 1933, pp. 7-15.

16. "Principles and Policies to Govern Relations Between Workers and Employers in War Industries for the Duration of the War," appended to Alexander M. Bing, *War-Time Strikes and Their Adjustment*, New York, 1921, p. 310.

17. Trachtenberg, editor, *American Labor Year Book, 1919-1920*, 42-57, 168-69.

18. National Bureau of Labor Statistics, *Bulletin No. 287*, Washington, D.C., 1921, pp. 71-72.

19. Gerald G. Eggert, "Fight for the Eight-Hour Day," *American History Illustrated*, May 1972, p. 43; Millis and Montgomery, p. 469.

20. A. B. Wolfe and Helen Olson, "War-Time Industrial Employment of Women in the United States," *Journal of Political Economy* 27 (October 1919): 660.

21. *Sixth Annual Report of the Secretary of Labor*, 1918, p. 105; Leonard Philip Krivy, "American Organized Labor and the First World War, 1917-1918: A History of Labor Problems and the Development of a Government War Labor Program," unpublished Ph.D. dissertation, New York University, 1965, pp. 321-22.

22. Vidkunn Ulriksson, *The Telegraphers: Their Craft and Their Unions*, Washington, D.C., 1953, p. 9.

23. Richard B. Gregg, "The National War Labor Board," *Harvard Law Review* 33 (Nov. 1919): 52; Krivy, p. 322.

24. Ulriksson, p. 9; The Western Union Telegraph Company, *The Western Union and the War Labor Board: The Compa*

*ny's Position*, New York, 1918, pp. 11, 17.

25. Krivy, p. 323.

26. *Nation* 106 (June 8, 1918): 667; *Sixth Annual Report of the Secretary of Labor*, 1918, p. 106; Krivy, p. 324.

27. *New York Times*, July 31, Aug. 1, 1918.

28. *New Republic* 15 (June 8, 1918): 163-64; Bing, pp. 75-76.

29. Julio O'Connor, "History of the Organized Telephone Operators' Movement," *Union Telephone Operator* 1 (June 1921): 14-20.

30. Krivy, pp. 327-28.

31. Bureau of Labor Statistics, *Bulletin No. 287*, p. 260.

32. *Sixth Annual Report of the Secretary of Labor*, 1918, p. 106.

33. Gregg, pp. 54-55.

34. *Ray S. Baker, Woodrow Wilson: Life and Letters* (New York, 1927-39) 8: 400, 402-10.

35. Krivy, p. 326; New York *Call*, Oct. 2, 1918.

36. Bureau of Labor Statistics, *Monthly Review*, June 1919, pp. 303-25; *American Labor Year Book*, 1919-20, p. 49.

37. Dallas Jones, "The Wilson Administration and Organized Labor, 1912-1919," unpublished Ph.D. dissertation, Cornell University, 1954, pp. 322-24; *New Republic* 16 (Sept. 7, 1918): 157; Oscar Garrison Villard, *Fighting Years: The Memoirs of a Liberal Editor*, New York, 1939, p. 355; Stanley Shapiro, "The Great War and Reform: Liberals and Labor, 1917-19," *Labor History* 12 (Summer 1971): 333.

38. *Proceedings*, AFL Convention, 1917, pp. 136-41, 312-13.

39. *New Republic*, Jan. 19, 1918, pp. 331-32; Jan. 26, 1918, p. 381; *American Federationist* 25 (April 1918): 304-05; Shapiro, p. 328.

40. *Proceedings*, AFL Convention, 1918, pp. 158, 221.

41. Ibid., pp. 158-59.

42. Ibid., pp. 236-37.

43. *American Federationist* 26 (Jan. 1919): 34.

44. Ibid., Feb. 1919, pp. 129-41.

45. Ibid.; *Proceedings*, AFL Convention, 1919, pp. 70-80.

46. *American Federationist* 26 (Jan. 1919): 35.

47. Truman C. Bigham, "The Chicago Federation of Labor," unpublished M.A. thesis, University of Chicago, 1924, pp. 108-09.

48. Los Angeles *Citizen*, Dec. 6, 1918.

49. Ibid.

50. Jay Lovestone, *The Government-Strikebreaker*, New York, 1923, p. 11.

51. Gompers to Will Thorne, Oct. 21, 1916, Gompers Letterbooks, Library of Congress.

52. Gompers to John Golden and Joseph Lord, Aug. 7, 1917, Gompers Papers, AFL Archives, State Historical Society of Wisconsin; Gompers to W. A. Appleton, Jan. 19, 1918, Gompers Letterbooks, Library of Congress; *New York Times*, Feb. 23, 1918; Gompers, *Seventy Years* 2: 405-06.

53. Arno J. Mayer, *Political Origins of the New Diplomacy 1917-1918*, New York, 1970, pp. 194-95.

54. Gompers to Allied Trade Union Officials, May 8, 1917; Gompers to Jouhaux and Lindquist, June 27, 1917, Gompers Letterbooks, Library of Congress.

55. New York Times, Feb. 18, 1918; Samuel Gompers, "Labor Internationally," *American Federationist* 25 (Aug. 1918): 690-92.

56. Gompers to Arthur Henderson, July 26, 1917; Gompers to Robert Lansing, March 18, 1918, Gompers Letterbooks; *New York Times*, February 20, 1918.

57. "The War Diplomacy of American Labor," *New Republic* 14 (March 2, 1918): 126-27.

58. Gerald Russell Gorden, "The AFL, the CIO, and the Quest for a Peaceful World Order, 1914-1946," Ph.D. thesis, University of Maine, Orono, 1967, pp. 30-31.

59. Bernard Mandel, *Samuel Gompers, A Biography*, Yellow Springs, Ohio, 1963, p. 408.

60. Gompers to John Alpine, September 4, 1918, Gompers Papers, AFL Archives, State Historical Society of Wisconsin; Gompers, *Seventy Years* 2: 428-35.

61. Mandel, p. 410.

62. Gompers, *Seventy Years* 2: 440-41; Mandel, pp. 409-10.

63. Gordon, p. 33.

64. Arno J. Mayer, *Politics and Diplomacy of Peacemaking: Containment and Counterrevolution at Versailles, 1918-1919*, New York, 1969, p. 44; Mandel, p. 407.

65. *Literary Digest*, June 22, 1918.

66. Gordon, pp. 34-35.

67. Gompers to Oudegeest, Nov. 12, 1918; Oudegeest to Gompers, Dec. 2, 1918, Gompers Papers, AFL Archives, State Historical Society of Wisconsin; Lewis R. Lorwin, *Labor and Internationalism*, New York, 1929, pp. 186-87.

68. Mandel, p. 418.
69. Oudegeest to Gompers, Dec. 2, 1918, Gompers Papers, AFL Archives, State Historical Society of Wisconsin.
70. Lorwin, p. 166.
71. Samuel Gompers to Woodrow Wilson, Dec. 21, 1918, Woodrow Wilson Papers, Library of Congress.
72. Bernard Mandel, pp. 420-21.
73. Report of AFL Delegation to the Peace Conference, *Proceedings*, AFL Convention, 1919, pp. 13-31.
74. Ibid.
75. *Report of International Conference of Trade Unions, Bern, February 5-10, 1919.*
76. Samuel Gompers, "The French Socialists and the Bolsheviki," *American Federationist* 26 (Jan. 1919): 61-65.
77. David M. Kennedy, *Over Here: The First World War and American Society*, New York, 1980, p. 357.
78. Ibid., pp. 78-81, 132; James T. Shotwell, *At the Paris Peace Conference*, (New York, 1937) 1: Chapters XI-XII.
79. *Literary Digest*, Feb. 8, 1919; Mandel, p. 423.
80. Proceedings of the Commission on International Labor Legislation, *Official Bulletin*, vol. 1 (1919-1920), Geneva, 1923, pp. 1-49.
81. Ibid., pp. 167-183.
82. *New York Times*, March 7, 1919.
83. Ibid., March 30, 1919; Samuel Gompers, *Seventy Years of Life and Labor* (New York, 1925) 2: 483-84, 494, 510; Philip S. Foner, *Women and the American Labor Movement: From World War I to the Present*, (New York, 1980) pp. 131-32.
84. *Proceedings*, AFL Convention, 1919, pp. 85-86.
85. Ibid., pp. 399-426.
86. Kennedy, p. 359; New York *Call*, Nov. 29, Dec. 2, 7, 1918; *Eye-Opener*, Sept. 19, 1919.
87. Mandel, p. 423.
88. *New York Times*, Nov. 19, 1919.
89. Daniel P. Moynihan, "The Washington Conference of the International Labor Organization," *Labor History* 3 (Fall 1962): 315-16.
90. Ibid., pp. 329-30.
91. *Congressional Record*, 66th Cong., 1st Sess., pp. 7916-18.
92. Moynihan, p. 332.
93. Ibid.
94. *New York Times*, Dec. 9, 1919.
95. Ibid.
96. Frank L. Grubb, Jr., "Organized Labor and the League to Enforce Peace," *Labor History* 14 (Spring 1973): 256.
97. Philip Taft, *The A. F. of L. in the Time of Gompers*, New York, 1957, p. 439.
98. Gordon, pp. 52-53.
99. Lorwin, op. cit., p. 191; Gompers to J. Oudegeest, May 22, 1919, Gompers Letterbooks, Library of Congress.
100. Gordon, p. 49.
101. "Report of the A.F.L. Delegation to the I.F.T.U. Congress at Amsterdam," *American Federationist* 26 (Oct. 1919): 929-33; Mandel, pp. 447-48; *New York Times*, June 29, 1919.
102. Gompers to AFL Executive Council, Nov. 19, 1919, Gompers Papers, AFL Archives, State Historical Society of Wisconsin; Samuel Gompers and Matthew Woll, "The European Brainstorm," *American Federationist* 27 (Oct. 1920): 919; Lorwin, op. cit., pp. 259-60.
103. *New York Times*, Oct. 12, 1919.
104. This discussion is based on the typed "Proceedings of the First International Congress of Working Women, Oct. 28-Nov. 5, 1919," in the National Women's Trade Union League Papers, Library of Congress.
105. *Proceedings of the First Biennial Congress, International Federation of Working Women*, Geneva, Switzerland, Oct. 22-24, 1921, copy in NWTUL Papers; *Labor*, Nov. 19, 1921; Alice Henry, *Women and the Labor Movement*, New York, 1923, pp. 212-15.
106. *New York Times*, Oct. 18, 1921; *Labor*, Oct. 22, Nov. 19, 1921.

# Index